THIS CERTIFICATE FOR
TWENTY-FIVE CEN
Will be redeemed with curre
on Sections 333 and 334, De
Canal, near Old Town, Al
August 1, 1837.
E. Morris, Pr. Philadelphia.
V
5
FIVE
5
6712
THE
CITIZENS B
OF BALTIMORE
FIVE
BALTIMORE
American Bank Note Company.
TEN DOLL
MARYLAND.
186
SNOW HILL
ON DEMAND
DUE THE BEARER
TWENTY FIVE CENTS
in Merchandise.
25
CENTS
O PAY THE
ARTER CE
my Store, in Warfieldsburg, Ca
John Nicol
30, 1841.
Five Dollars
Cash.
20
50
ORT DEPOSI
THE COMMISSION
to bearer
MARYLAND
Will pay
FIFTY CENTS
CENTS
Port Deposit, Nov. 5. 1862.
Treas.
American Bank Note Co. Philad.
BALTIMORE
TEN DOLLARS
SAVINGS INST

MONEY AND BANKING IN MARYLAND

Money & Banking in Maryland

PART ONE

A Brief History of Commercial Banking in the Old Line State

STUART R. BRUCHEY AND ELEANOR S. BRUCHEY

PART TWO

A Catalogue of Maryland's Paper Money, 1790–1865

DENWOOD N. KELLY, ARMAND M. SHANK JR.,
AND THOMAS S. GORDON

WITH A FOREWORD TO THE CATALOGUE BY RICHARD G. DOTY

MARYLAND HISTORICAL SOCIETY
BALTIMORE

Maryland Historical Society
201 West Monument Street
Baltimore, MD 21201

Founded 1844

First Edition

Designed by Martha Farlow
Manufactured in the United States of America

LIBRARY OF CONGRESS CATALOGING-IN-PUBLICATION DATA
Money and banking in Maryland / Stuart R. Bruchey . . . [et al.]. — 1st ed.
p. cm.
ISBN 0-938420-52-6
1. Banks and banking—Maryland—History—18th century. 2. Banks and banking—Maryland—History—19th century. 3. Money—Maryland—History—18th century. 4. Money—Maryland—History—19th century. 5. Paper money—Maryland—Catalogs. 6. Maryland—History.
I. Bruchey, Stuart, 1917–
HG2611.M3M66 1996
332.1'09752—dc20 96-558
CIP

Contents

Acknowledgments

Without the cooperation of numerous institutions, organizations, and individuals this book would never have appeared. Likewise, many collectors and dealers have been more than generous in loaning notes for photographing or in furnishing needed historical or geographical information.

The Maryland Historical Society and Museum and Library of Maryland History has provided working and storage space during the preparation of this book and has arranged for most of the needed financing for its publication. The members of the society's staff, particularly those in the library and the Prints and Photographs Division, have been unfailingly helpful in answering our many requests for the location of needed reference material on the subject of the issuers of currency. Francis O'Neill, Joseph Maguire, Paula Velthuys, Marcy Silver, Laura Rice, Angela Anthony, and Jeff Goldman have been particularly patient and helpful in this respect.

The Johns Hopkins University made available for our inspection its sizable collection of Maryland (and other states) obsolete currency, through the courtesy of Susan G. Tripp, the former Director of University Collections.

The Smithsonian Institution's Museum of American History, in which the National Numismatic and Philatelic Collections are maintained, has also been very cooperative, permitting the inspection of their Maryland obsolete notes. Of even more importance was the willingness of Dr. Richard G. Doty, Curator of the National Numismatic Collection, to write the foreword to the catalogue.

The Enoch Pratt Free Library of Baltimore has kindly made available its newspaper microfilm files and collateral materials housed in the Maryland Room at the Library.

Several of the county or local historical societies in Maryland, Pennsylvania, and Delaware have also been very helpful in providing photocopies of items in their collections.

Prior to the auction sale of the proofs of obsolete currency from the Archives of The American Bank Note Company the numismatic staff at Christie's, New York, arranged for our inspection of all Maryland items in the sale and furnished us with many excellent photocopies. To them we are most grateful, particularly to James Lamb and Christine Deussen.

Similarly, the officers and staff of R. M. Smythe & Co., Inc., New York, have very willingly permitted the photography of numerous notes for our use.

Finally, the collectors, historians, and professional numismatists whose names appear on the following list have all helped in many ways and are due our hearty thanks. One collector in particular deserves special mention: Leonard M. Rothstein, M.D. Over the years he has formed an outstanding collection of Maryland obsolete paper money and has kindly made it totally available to the authors for study and photography. Additionally, Dr. Rothstein, despite a very busy medical practice, has consistently made himself available for advice and counsel whenever requested.

James A. Haxby, author of the four-volume *Standard Catalogue of United States Obsolete Bank Notes, 1782–1866,* has been particularly helpful and cooperative. He furnished for our use excellent photographs of Maryland bank notes illustrated in his magnum opus and freely gave permission to use his descriptions of notes for which photographs were not available. Most of these were abstracted from contemporary counterfeit detectors, thus saving us the time and effort of going to these original sources. To Jim we are very grateful.

Samuel Adkins
Douglas B. Ball
Donald Lee Benson
Christian Blom
Frank L. Blumberg
Robert Lee Burton
Dr. J. W. Carberry
Gloria Jean Cox
Grover Criswell
Thomas M. Denly
Roger Durand
Leo J. Eckert, Curator, The Boys Town Collection
Jeffrey Ferrand
C. John Ferreri
Paul Finck
Dennis Forgue
Martin Gengerke
Stephen Goldsmith
Phil Greenslet
Bruce Hagen
James B. Haxby
John Henry (deceased)
James Hirtle
Ron Horstman
Winton F. Hurley
Richard Jones
Willis Karner
Don Kelly
Ed Kuszmar
Coleman Leifer
Art Leister
Keith Littlefield
Milton Lynn
John W. McGrain
Lawrence Marsh
Harvey Eugene Meeks (deceased)
Levin P. Messick
Paul Mied
Al Mincho
Claude Murphy Jr.
Eric P. Newman
Leonard M. Rothstein, M.D.
Herb and Martha Schingoethe
Austin Sheheen Jr.
Hugh Shull
Arleigh Slabaugh
Mrs. Charles C. Stieff II
James Thompson
Robert A. Vlack
George Wait
Joseph Warehime
Byrne Waterman
Barry Wexler
H. Graham Wood

PART ONE

A Brief History of Commercial Banking in the Old Line State

A Brief History of Commercial Banking in the Old Line State

STUART R. BRUCHEY
ELEANOR S. BRUCHEY

"Neither a borrower nor a lender be," Shakespeare's Polonius advises his son Laertes in *Hamlet,* for "loan oft loses both itself and friend." Polonius's advice remains sound where one person lends to another—especially in the absence of collateral. Even in the sixteenth century, however, loans were essential for business purposes.

Credit was then and always will be the lifeblood of economic life. Without it, production, employment, sales, and consumption extend only as far as an individual's or a firm's purchasing power—represented by the current supply of money and exchangeable goods and services. Credit permits economic activities to outgrow cash purchases and mere bartering and thus to increase in both volume and scope. Enabling entrepreneurs to outbid less efficient users of resources, credit paves the way to economic growth. Credit is oriented toward the future, and through its extension commercial banks improve the quality of life for shareholders, employees, and the communities they serve.

For much of early American history, banks performed another service: They provided the great bulk of the colonial and then national money supply. They did so by making loans in the form of banknotes or by creating deposits on which the borrower might draw by check.

Both as to banking and currency, the experience of Maryland offers a rich and telling tale.[1]

Colonial Money

For nearly two centuries after European settlers arrived in America, the colonists conducted—or attempted to conduct—business without banks and without their own currency. In that "age of mercantilism," men of affairs believed that a nation's true treasure lay in its stock of gold and silver. Adhering to this logic, the British banned the export of precious metals, even to the colonies. They, after all, had been acquired in the first place to serve as markets for English manufactured goods and as sources of raw materials; if the colonies were encouraged to develop economically, they would soon become less dependent on the Mother Country, which would lose in the bargain. British policy therefore called for strict limitations on colonial manufacturing, incorporation, and any attempt to increase the money supply.

Money in colonial America therefore became a jumble of foreign coin, governmental and private paper, and monetized commodities—all of it, for most of the time, inadequate for the needs of business. The principal gold coins circulating in the colonies were the Portuguese Johannes, or Joe; the moidore; and the Spanish and French pistole. The most important silver coin was the Spanish piece of eight (eight reals), superseded in 1728 by the Spanish milled dollar. The Spanish silver dollar was the chief element in the colonial specie supply, and so it was that Congress in 1786 adopted it as the monetary standard for the United States. Circulating currency also included Dutch, German, and English coins. Most of the coin probably came from the West Indies. Whatever its source, it tended to be reexported to Britain to help balance the perennially unfavorable balance of trade (the colonial appetite for English goods and services far exceeded the value of colonial exports).

Although we do not know how many of these coins circulated at any given time, we can suppose that—because of the sparseness of the population—they did not change hands very rapidly. They thus had only limited effect as economic multipliers. Even more surely, the use of the coins was attended by some risk and inconvenience. Coins were clipped, sweated, and otherwise made to yield some of their metallic content. These practices became so common that before closing a deal the wise merchant weighed coins to determine their real worth.

The mint value of gold and silver coins depended on the pure metal they contained. For more than two centuries after 1600, the pound sterling contained 1,718.7 grains of fine silver, so that a shilling had 83.94 grains of pure metal. Since Sir Isaac Newton's official assay at the English mint in 1704 gave the dollar a rating of 386.8 grains of fine metal, it followed that the Spanish dollar was worth 4 shillings, 6 pence (4s 6d) of English money. Hoping to lure precious metals into their respective jurisdictions, colonial assemblies competed with one another in enacting legislation raising the legal value of the Spanish piece of eight and other coins proportionally. The prescribed value of the dollar climbed to 5s and 6s, even to 7s and 8s. Legislators in effect decreased the silver content of the shilling, since it would thereafter take fewer dollars to pay off a debt in shillings. They overvalued colonial money and devalued English money.

The device worked, but only briefly and not well. Some of the colonies enjoyed a small measure of success in attracting specie (pirates tended to bring their stolen gold and silver to ports where its legal value was highest). But because the rates differed from one colony to the next, it was manifestly impossible for all to benefit at the same time. Furthermore, the inflow increased the money supply and tended to raise the general price level in direct proportion to the overvaluation. There was a second consequence: English merchants trading with the colonies complained that the increased shilling value of Spanish money permitted the colonists to pay off their debts with fewer Spanish coins. In 1704 the Board of Trade obtained a royal proclamation, followed by an act of Parliament in 1708, which forbade the colonies to rate Spanish pieces of eight at more than 6 shillings, an overvaluation of 33.3 percent. The act was widely ignored, however, and many of the colonies pushed the legal value of foreign coins to even higher levels.

In their continuing effort to cope with the problems of an inadequate and insufficient money supply, colonists adopted substitutes, one of them monetized staples. By this device, an act of assembly stated the value in pounds, shillings, and pence at which the articles would be received in public and private payments. In the case of Maryland and Virginia, taxes and other debts were sometimes payable in tobacco.

In terms of international trade, Maryland—like other slave-labor colonies to the south—carried on a rather direct system of exchange with England and Scotland, one that also depended on tobacco. Planters bartered tobacco (or rice, or indigo) for English or Scottish merchandise. Both parties to a transaction had to keep bookkeeping records of the values involved in the exchange, the unit of account serving in late seventeenth-century Maryland as a standard of deferred payment or credit. Thus "bookkeeping barter" facilitated trade even when money was unavailable. Note, however, that the unit of account was usually pounds sterling, shillings, and pence—or the pounds, shillings, and pence as defined by law in a given colony (i.e., as the "lawful money" of the province)—whereas the actual means of payment were Spanish coin, tobacco, or other commodities. Thus in practice the two essential functions of money—a means of payment and a unit of account—were divided in colonial America, as in so many other times and places in history.

In addition to specie and designated commodities, the colonists also used various kinds of paper as means of payment. Among these were warehouse receipts or notes for tobacco inspected and stored in public warehouses in accordance with Virginia (1714, 1730) and Maryland (1747) legislation designed to elevate the quality of the tobacco citizens used in payment of taxes.

Intended for local circulation, the notes were made legal tender in all tobacco payments. Because taxes, duties, court fees, and even the salaries of the established-church clergy were all paid in tobacco, the holder of a note had only to present it at the warehouse to have it redeemed by the inspectors in tobacco of the kind the note called for.

Such tobacco was called "transfer tobacco" as distinct from "crop tobacco" deposited in a warehouse to await exportation. Since the value of these notes fluctuated with the price of tobacco, they failed to provide a stable currency.

Stability was a prime concern in developing colonial commercial centers, including Baltimore after about 1750. Paper substitutes for hard money were familiar in Baltimore and in other port cities, where business transactions generated promissory notes and bills of exchange. When endorsed, such notes passed from hand to hand in payment of debt. While the circle this paper moved in was small, so too were the business communities that generated it. Their very intimacy made it possible for businessmen to know one another's general affairs and reputations well and thus to accept each other's promises and orders to pay. In truth, only part of the business community benefited from these bills, namely, merchants who engaged in foreign trade and who sold primarily at wholesale. Retail storekeepers, whether urban or rural, rarely required a formal IOU from those making purchases on credit; the storekeeper's ledgers recorded debt and its repayment. Commercial paper was circulating debt, and since no commercial banks existed, merchants made loans by discounting the paper, that is, by deducting an interest charge from the face value of the note or bill. Thus private paper served as a vehicle for loans as well as a means of payment.

The colonists also discovered the usefulness of public "bills of credit." Colonial assemblies authorized the issuance of bills of credit on the basis of two types of security, one land and the other the credit of the colony supported by tax funds. In the first case, the legislature established a loan office, struck off a sum in bills, and declared them to be legal tender. Commissioners of the loan office proceeded to lend the bills in limited sums, the loans usually being secured by a mortgage on landed property double the value of the sum loaned. Borrowers were required to pay interest each year but were given a period of eight to ten years to repay the principal. During that time the bills became a part of the circulating currency as borrowers spent them to buy and improve land or to pay off debt.

These so-called land banks—not banks at all in the sense in which we understand the term, but rather batches of paper money resting on the security of land—provided individuals with the long-term credit needed to expand their agricultural activities, gave government a source of revenue in the form of interest payments, and supplied the public at large with more circulating money.

In the eighteenth century the colonies began to use land banks to combat depressions. New York did so in 1715 and 1737, Pennsylvania and Delaware in 1723 and 1729, New Jersey in 1723, and Maryland in 1733. Although modern analysts do not agree on the price effects of such issues, it is noteworthy that few contemporaries doubted that land banks stimulated the economic growth of the country.

These land banks were most successful in the middle colonies, where interest the government collected was sufficient to pay most of the ordinary cost of administration and served as a substitute for taxes. In 1782 a contemporary historian, George Chalmers, attributed the "singular prosperity" of Pennsylvania in part to the "prudent policy of promoting enterprise by feeding circulation with loans of paper money, gradual yet moderate."[2] That province managed a land bank so well for more than fifty years before the Revolution that the price level during that time exhibited more stability than the American price level has during any succeeding fifty-year period in U.S. history.

Experience in the South and in New England was different. Virginia never adopted a land bank, but in both Carolinas and in New England land-bank loans played a part in the decline of the currency's value. Excessive issues of currency in Rhode Island in particular helped bring on the first statutory regulation of paper money by Parliament in 1751.

Bills issued on the credit of the colony came into being initially because of the need to finance the costs of war. Maryland's bills were used chiefly in war finance. Their success then led legislatures to turn to the same means of meeting financial emergencies in peacetime. Given the relatively small tax base, scarcity of specie, lack of liquidity, and urgency of need, especially in wartime, the colonies found themselves unable to depend on taxation or borrowing. Once authorized by the assembly, an issue was turned over to officials to pay out to the public creditors. Usually the authorizing act provided for calling in and retiring the bills by earmarking the proceeds of specific taxes for the purpose. For example, a tax would be levied for a five-year period and its proceeds used to redeem one-fifth of the bills annually. Essentially the system, aptly termed one of "currency finance," provided a way to anticipate tax revenues.[3] It therefore partook of the character of a forced loan.

What sustained the value of these bills? They were not convertible into specie, nor as a rule did they earn interest. Usually, however, they were made a legal tender in both public and private transactions, a feature that at least promoted their utility. Unquestionably, their value was also sustained in part by the tax fund earmarked for their redemption. And since the money was created and upheld solely by political acts, confidence in the government was also essential to its value. Additional props to confidence were legal-tender provisions and redemption funds. Probably the most important prop was the knowledge that the quantity issued did not overly exceed the amount of business transacted—the requirements of trade at existing levels.

When excessive issues were authorized, depreciation followed. In

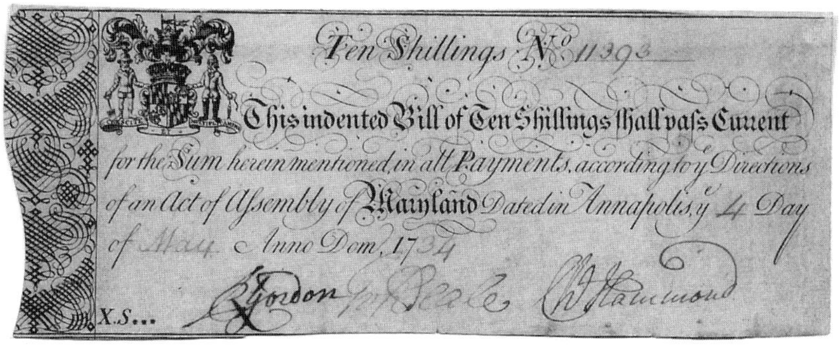

Indented legal tender bill for 10 shillings, 1734. To prevent poor tobacco from depressing the market, the Maryland assembly in 1733 created a loan office that was to pay 30 shillings to each taxable person for the destruction of 150 pounds of trash tobacco in 1734 and 1735. Printed in England from engraved copper plates on fine laid paper watermarked "MARYLAND." (Maryland Historical Society)

New England and the Carolinas, paper currency depreciated considerably, but in the middle colonies it worked quite well. In fact, wholesale prices in New York and Philadelphia, and in New Jersey and Delaware, were more stable in the colonial period than from the adoption of the Constitution to the Civil War.

Maryland's experiment with paper money did not prove altogether successful. The colony went to special pains in 1733 to sustain the value of its paper. A substantial part of the authorized issue of £90,000 currency had been loaned to individuals—at 4 percent interest—not only on the security of land but of silver plate and leaseholds as well. In addition, the colony established a sinking fund to inspire confidence in the ultimate redeemability of the paper.[4] Yet the bills depreciated rapidly. By 1739 exchange had risen as high as £200 paper to £133 gold and silver, or £100 sterling. A reason assigned at the time for the depreciation was that paper was not made legal tender for officers' fees or parish levies. In part, however, the depreciation owed to the fact that the issue was excessive—the extra money was not yet needed. Even after that first emission of 1733, tobacco remained the primary medium of exchange.

But by 1764 Maryland's bills of credit were much in demand, and large emissions thereafter held their value. They did so because Baltimore's growth increased the volume of business transactions beyond the ability of tobacco and tobacco notes to mediate.

Tobacco notes continued to serve Virginia's currency needs as well until the colony's participation in the French and Indian War forced it to resort to a paper emission in 1755—the last colony to do so. Had the war not occurred, Virginia might have continued indefinitely to meet its currency needs with tobacco notes. For although that province, like Maryland, was shifting some of its resources out of tobacco and into wheat, urban growth did not accompany that development.

Although the costs of war accounted for a general pattern of "currency finance" in the colonies, urban and business growth in the leading port cities generated a daily need for larger amounts of money. Circulating money made business dealings far easier to transact.

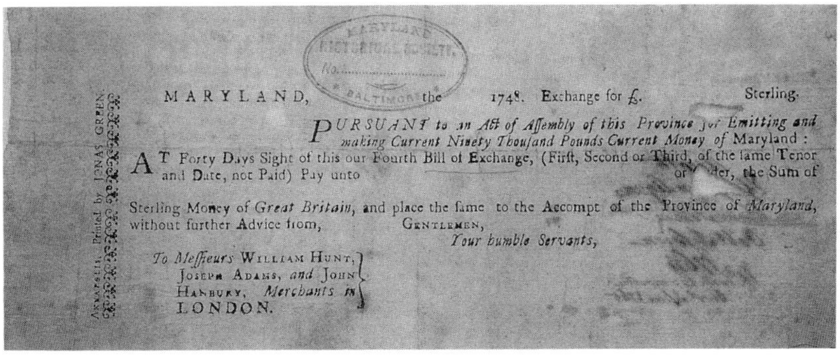

MARYLAND, the 174 . Exchange for £. Sterling.

PURSUANT to an Act of Aſſembly of this Province for Emitting and making Current Ninety Thouſand Pounds Current Money of Maryland:

AT Forty Days Sight of this our Fourth Bill of Exchange, (Firſt, Second or Third, of the ſame Tenor and Date, not Paid) Pay unto or Order, the Sum of

Sterling Money of Great Britain, and place the ſame to the Accompt of the Province of Maryland, without further Advice from, Gentlemen,

Your humble Servants,

To Meſſieurs William Hunt, Joseph Adams, and John Hanbury, Merchants in London.

Annapolis: Printed by Jonas Green.

Blank bill of exchange, Annapolis, 1748. This note, printed by the capital city's first newspaperman, Jonas Green, was payable "on sight" forty days after being issued. (Maryland Historical Society)

Colonial Economic Development

Maryland's economic growth in the seventeenth and eighteenth centuries depended directly on population, export crops, and the meteoric rise of Baltimore. Not until the early eighteenth century did native-born Marylanders, black and white, develop resistance to indigenous diseases like malaria and live long enough to have large families. From then on, population figures turned sharply upward. The number of people in Maryland grew from an estimated 6,000 in 1640 to more than 34,000 in 1700. By 1770 some 200,000 people lived in the colony, and ten years later about 248,000. The population was widely dispersed, scattered along the watercourses of the tidewater Chesapeake, and at first almost universally devoted to the cultivation of tobacco. In 1730 Maryland sent 40,606,000 pounds of tobacco to Great Britain (35,080,000 to England and 5,526,000 to Scotland). By 1742, that total had risen to 53,206,000; in 1770 Maryland exported 100 million pounds of the weed to the Mother County, almost half to Glasgow, whose merchant houses—by means of representatives or "factors"—opened stores in the Chesapeake, sold British goods, and accepted tobacco in exchange.[5]

Despite this growth in cultivation and exports, the tobacco trade failed to generate urban development. Tobacco had no need for cities. The ability of seagoing vessels to call for their cargoes at the planter's dock or at riverine stores encouraged the direct exchange of tobacco for goods. Although a few plantation landings grew into small villages—Upper Marlboro on the Anacostia and Georgetown on the Potomac, for example—towns gained little ground as long as tobacco was king. Maryland's principal city through most of the colonial period, Annapolis, illustrated the point. As the meeting place of the General Assembly, its function was perhaps more political than economic.[6]

This situation changed dramatically under the impact of basic economic changes that called for the services of resident wholesale merchants. Foreign demand for wheat, especially in the West Indies, and its high price in relation to tobacco led to an increased cultivation of grain on the upper Eastern Shore, in the Patapsco region, in western Maryland, and the Pennsylvania piedmont. German immigrants flocked to the Monocacy and Antietam valleys. There they raised cattle and other provisions as well as wheat. Fredericktown and Hager's Town were soon laid out as "wilderness" market towns where producers and consumers of grain and cattle could meet and conduct business.

The export demand for wheat had the farthest-reaching consequences. In 1762 the governor of Maryland complained of "there being no town or port in Maryland where any considerable quantity of country produce can be purchased at once or altogether"; much of the colony's wheat and flour was going to Philadelphia.[7] Marylanders and southern Pennsylvanians who saw the natural advantages of nearby Baltimore Town soon cut roads through the woods and fields to connect the rich granary of the hinterland to the village on the Patapsco. By 1770 eight roads crossed the Pennsylvania-Maryland border southwest of the Susquehanna and led to Baltimore. Over these roads heavy wagons brought loads of wheat, Indian corn, and smaller quantities of flax, hemp, and tobacco to Baltimore for export.

Thus the export trade in wheat and flour lay behind the rise of Baltimore. Since backcountry wheat, unlike tidewater tobacco, had to be delivered to dockside, the older system of direct exchange was no longer possible. Furthermore, farmers could not undertake long trips over country roads on the chance that a vessel would be lying in wait for their crops. Nor could they postpone their homeward trips to wait for goods they wanted in return. Baltimore wholesalers had to build warehouses to store crops until ready for shipment, and retail stores had to keep a constant stock of goods on hand. In this more complex system of exchange the wholesale merchant was the key figure, for it was he who purchased backcountry produce for export and imported goods for the shelves of retailers. In a fairly short time, the inflow of wheat from the backcountry created the role of wholesale middleman and around him gathered a supporting cast of retailers, clerks, suppliers, bookkeepers, housebuilders, and others who performed the services a growing community required. Milling flour, baking bread for export, distilling spirits, and shipbuilding became the town's most important industries. In the immediate neighborhood an iron industry also developed, one that brought about more attendant industries.

As late as 1750 resident John Moale's sketch of Baltimore showed it to be a straggling village, with about 200 occupants and twenty-five houses. By 1774 there were 564 houses and 5,924 people. Five years earlier the young English visitor William Eddis had described with enthusiasm some of the effects of the town's increasing trade:

> Persons of a commercial and enterprising spirit, emigrated from all quarters to this new and promising scene of industry. Wharfs were constructed; elegant and convenient habitations were rapidly erected; marshes were drained; spacious fields were occupied for the purposes of general

utility; and within forty years, from its first commencement [in 1729], Baltimore became not only the most wealthy and populous town in the province, but inferior to few on this continent, either in size, number of inhabitants, or the advantages arising from a well-conducted and universal commercial connection.[8]

Banking in the Early Republic

Baltimore's growth continued at an accelerating pace during the Revolution. Its setting at the head of the Patapsco River—13 miles from the Chesapeake Bay and 205 miles from the Atlantic Ocean—protected it from British sea raids. Thus favored, Baltimore developed into a leading port for the West India trade. Freed from mercantilist British policies that controlled shipping and manufacturing and freed also from Annapolis's colonial monopoly as a customs collector, the town quickly shed its provincial character. New merchants crowded into the town. They came from foreign countries—six French commercial houses were founded in Baltimore during or soon after the war—and from other parts of America, principally Pennsylvania.

Indeed, new merchants largely controlled the city's wartime and postwar trade. Some of the new men, Jeremiah Yellott among them,

Face and back of a rare "propaganda" four-dollar note, July 26, 1775. The busy face (top), impressed from a woodcut by Thomas Sparrow of Annapolis, depicts Britannia receiving a congressional petition, while on the right America tramples a scroll marked "slavery" in front of Continental troops; the left has George III dancing on the Magna Carta and applying a firebrand to a besieged American city. The back shows Britannia and America—alternatively, and much to be desired—clinging to the olive branch of peace. Frederick Green of Annapolis printed the note. (Maryland Historical Society)

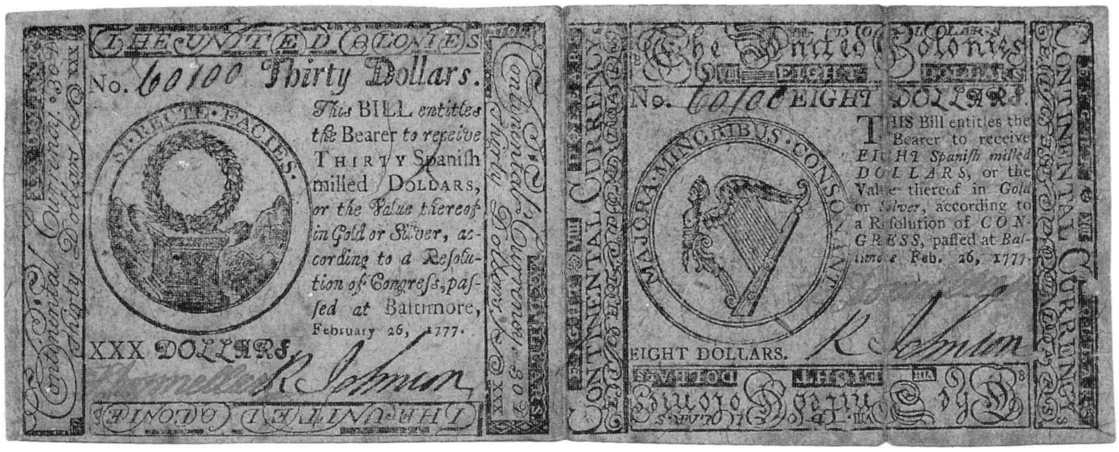

"Baltimore Issue" Revolutionary paper currency, redeemable in Spanish milled dollars "or the value thereof in Gold or Silver, according to a resolution of Congress passed at Baltimore Feb. 26, 1777." (Maryland Historical Society)

also prospered as privateer captains. Yellott, William Patterson, Robert Gilmor, and other wartime arrivals soon played leading roles as projectors of Baltimore's first banks. In 1782 the city was said to have a population of 8,000. Viewing Baltimore in 1783, George Washington expressed his "earnest Wish, that the Commerce, the Improvements and universal Prosperity of this flourishing Town, may, if possible, increase with even more Rapidity than they have hitherto done."[9] Gen. Nathaniel Greene also paid a visit to the town that year, noting in his diary that it was "a most thriving place. Trade flourishes and the spirit of building exceeds belief. Not less than 300 houses are put up in a year. Ground rents are little short of what they are in London. The inhabitants are men of business."[10]

Despite the optimistic projections of Washington and other visitors in the early postwar period, Baltimore and its trade languished during most of the years between 1783 and 1789. In August 1785, for example, the *Maryland Journal* complained that "Commercial Opposition of Great Britain, against the United States of America still continues; the various accounts from the West-India Islands can leave no Doubt of their Determination rigorously to abide by their Navigation System. Our Trade feels the Effects of these illiberal Measures."[11] Prices of American exports fell in relation to those of imported goods, the terms of trade declining each year between 1784 and 1789 from an index of 112 to 88.

Not surprisingly, Baltimore merchants and seamen led the fight in Maryland to ratify the new federal Constitution, which offered promises of stronger U.S. diplomacy, naval power, and currency. World events helped the new government deliver on some of its promises. In 1793 western Europe went to war over republican French expansionism, and the needs of the belligerents were considerable.

Foreign conflict opened a new era for American trade. The war made such demands on British shipping that British prohibitions against American vessels entering its West India ports were simply un-

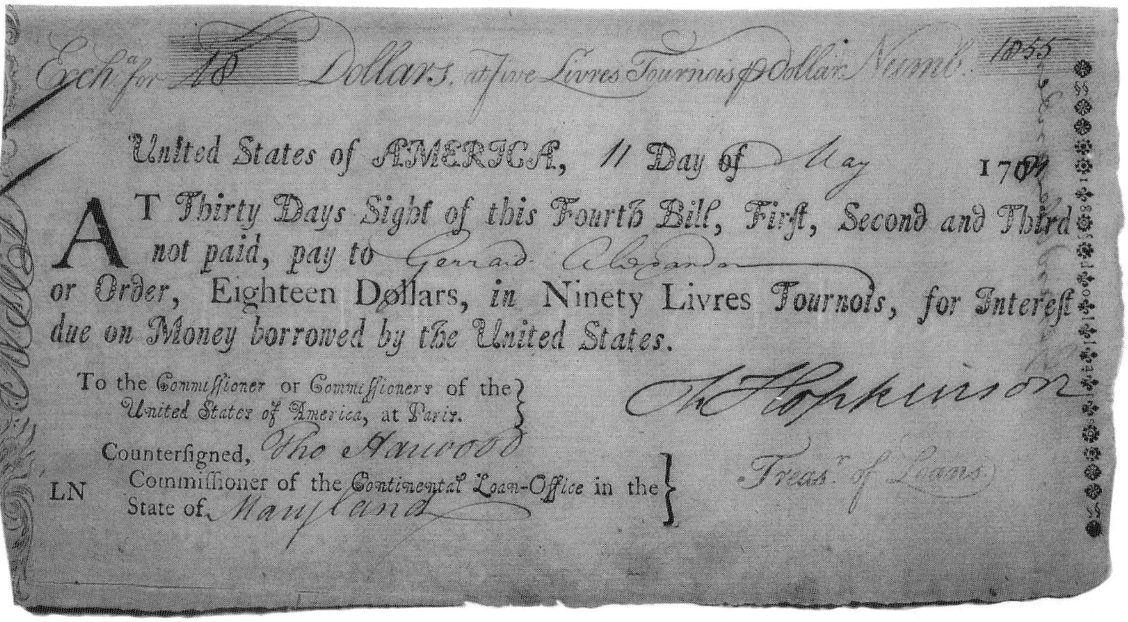

Exch.a for 18 Dollars, at five Livres Tournois p Dollar. Numb. 1855

United States of AMERICA, 11 Day of May 1781

AT Thirty Days Sight of this Fourth Bill, First, Second and Third not paid, pay to Gerrard Alexander or Order, Eighteen Dollars, in Ninety Livres Tournois, for Interest due on Money borrowed by the United States.

To the Commissioner or Commissioners of the United States of America, at Paris.

Th Hopkinson

Countersigned, Tho Harwood

Treas.r of Loans

LN Commissioner of the Continental Loan-Office in the State of Maryland

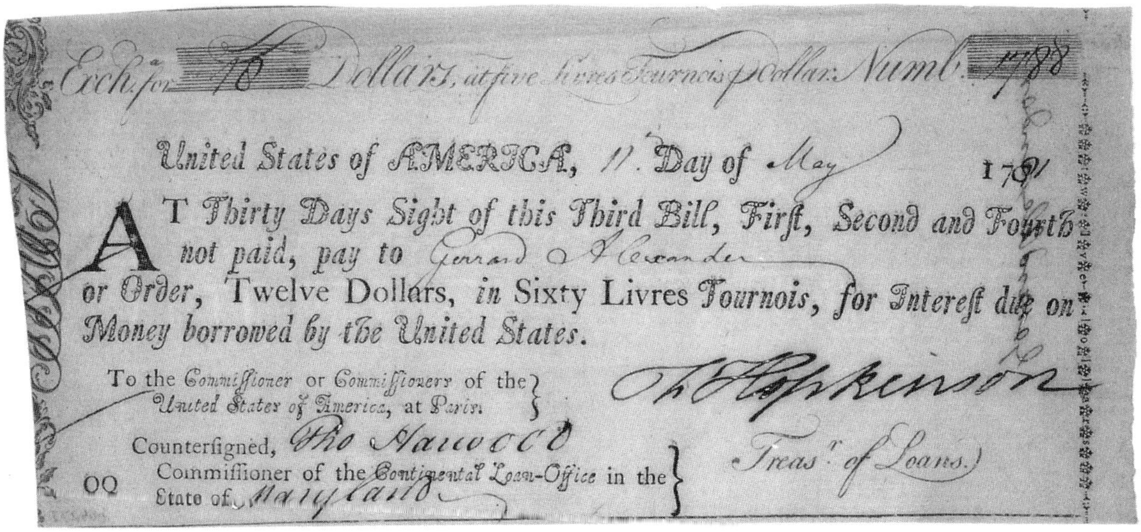

Exch.a for 18 Dollars, at five Livres Tournois p Dollar. Numb. 1788

United States of AMERICA, 11 Day of May 1781

AT Thirty Days Sight of this Third Bill, First, Second and Fourth not paid, pay to Gerrard Alexander or Order, Twelve Dollars, in Sixty Livres Tournois, for Interest due on Money borrowed by the United States.

To the Commissioner or Commissioners of the United States of America, at Paris.

Th Hopkinson

Countersigned, Tho Harwood

Treas.r of Loans

OO Commissioner of the Continental Loan-Office in the State of Maryland

Bills of exchange, 1781, drawn on the commissioner of the United States in Paris for $18 and payable to Gerrard Alexander for interest due on money borrowed by the United States. Bills of this type were prepared in quadruplicate and sent abroad via different vessels to ensure their safe arrival. (Maryland Historical Society)

enforceable. Aware that enemy naval superiority would put an end to its own colonial shipping, France threw open all its ports in the West Indies, East Indies, the Isle of France, and Bourbon to the neutral Americans. To the extent that the French decrees gave privileges not enjoyed before the war, they conflicted with the British "Rule of 1756," which held that a neutral might not in wartime engage in a trade closed to it in time of peace.

At first the British interpreted this principle generously, seizing only those neutral vessels that sailed directly to Europe with French West Indian produce. Indirect voyages were allowed, laying the basis for a richly profitable American carrying trade. Baltimore merchants brought French-colonial products home, landed, and then reexported them—to great advantage (see Table 1). The combined value of domestic and foreign goods in Maryland's (largely Baltimore's) ship-

Table 1. Value of Exports from Maryland, 1791–1815 (in thousands)

Year	*Domestic*	*Foreign*	*Total*
1791	$2,239		
1792	2,623		
1793	3,665		
1794	5,686		
1795	5,811		
1796	9,201		
1797	9,811		
1798	12,746		
1799	16,299		
1800	12,264		
1801	12,767		
1802	7,914		
1803	3,707	1,371	5,078
1804	3,938	5,213	9,151
1805	3,408	7,450	10,859
1806	3,661	10,919	14,580
1807	4,016	10,282	14,298
1808	764	1,956	2,721
1809	2,570	4,056	6,627
1810	3,275	3,213	6,489
1811	4,553	2,280	6,833
1812	3,956	1,929	5,885
1813	2,782	1,005	3,787
1814	238	10	248
1815	4,086	950	5,036

Source: Timothy Pitkin, *A Statistical View of the Commerce of the United States of America* (New Haven, 1835), 50–56.

ments increased steadily before the Peace of Amiens in 1803, then resumed its upward swing until the Jefferson administration's policy of halting or embargoing American shipping in 1807. While figures for foreign goods are unavailable before 1803, the role of the carrying trade appears clearly both in the increased value of exports in 1794 and in the decline of 1802–3, when peace sent commerce into its prewar channels.

Silt from tobacco fields filled the Little Gunpowder River and doomed the town of Joppa, once the seat of Baltimore County. Annapolis continued its decline as a seaport; visiting the capital shortly after the Revolution, the traveler Dr. John D. Schoepf simply stated, "There is little or no trade." Baltimore's population boomed by comparison—13,500 in 1790; 46,555 in 1810; 80,625 in 1835. At the onset of the reexport trade, the Irish traveler Isaac Weld noted that "with a few exceptions" all the inhabitants of Baltimore were "engaged in trade, which is closely attended to."[12]

Population and business growth called for an increased volume of currency and credit. Should the currency take the form of public paper or private paper, bills of credit issued by state governments or banknotes issued by private corporations? Debtors in particular always favored public paper because the quantity issued would cheapen its value and enable them cheaply to pay off debts incurred in currency of higher value like gold or silver. Creditors, of course, had opposing interests. During the 1780s seven states authorized the issuance of bills of credit, with four of the seven—including Maryland—declaring the bills to be legal tender in private payments. Seeking to protect their interests, alarmed merchants and storekeepers refused to accept the cheap money. Armed attacks on creditors and tax collectors took place in Maryland in 1786. That year unrest in Massachusetts culminated in Shay's Rebellion, in which a Revolutionary War captain led a group of farmers into revolt against the state government.

Written in such unsettled circumstances (aggravated by state laws postponing the collection of debts or providing for their payment in installments or in commodities rather than in money), the Constitution forbade the states to coin money, make anything but gold or silver a tender in payment of debt, or pass any law impairing the obligation of contract.

Suspicion of public paper and its administrators among the founders kept the new federal government out of the business of issuing currency. Less dangerous to the public interest, private paper in the form of banknotes was, at least in theory, subject only to the restraint of economic self-interest. As Secretary of the Treasury Alexander Hamilton noted in his report calling for a congressionally chartered (but not directed) national bank in 1790, "the prosperity of the institution, is the only Security, that can always be relied upon for a careful and prudent administration."[13] Congress responded to Hamilton's report by granting a twenty-year charter to the Bank of the United States, and in 1792 Baltimore became the site of one of the bank's eight branches. Its capital, apportioned by the parent bank in Philadelphia, rose from $200,000 in March 1793, to $400,000 in August 1795, and to $600,000 in April of 1800.

The Bank of the United States became an important issuer of notes, which were an institutional promise to pay its bearer the sum specified on the face of the note, to pay it on demand, and do so in specie. Banks issued notes to successful applicants for loans, or, alternatively, opened up a line of credit in their ledger on which a borrower might draw by check—such credits being readily convertible into banknotes when cashed by a payee. A well-run bank would therefore seek to protect its specie reserves from the excessive demands brought on by too large a volume of loans.

The policy of the Baltimore branch reflected that of the parent bank in Philadelphia, whose highly conservative philosophy shone through in its balance sheets for the years 1792–1800. For most of that period the relationship between notes in circulation and specie reserves was close, ranging from a high of 4.93 to 1 in 1794 to a low of 0.96 in 1800. The average for the nine years was merely 1.95 to 1, less than two dollars in banknotes for every dollar in specie. Fragmentary minutes of the board of directors' meetings leave no doubt of the parent bank's awareness of its power and duty to keep the supply of bank credit within careful limits. In an important policy statement of October 1795, the board made it clear that it regarded itself as guardian of the nation's "System of Bank Credit." That month it made two significant recommendations to the branches: first, that each branch accept only the notes of banks located in the same city as itself and, second, that the branches expand their discounts with great caution.[14]

Even before establishment of Hamilton's congressionally chartered bank, in 1790 the Maryland General Assembly by a wide margin granted a state charter to the Bank of Maryland. Subscriptions to its authorized capital stock of $300,000 were opened in Baltimore, and within fourteen days the bank had raised $200,000. Because Baltimore's trade required ever-more credit and credit-granting institutions, the assembly in 1795 issued a charter to the Bank of Baltimore, fixing its capital at $1.2 million. The combined capital of Baltimore banks remained less than $2 million until 1804, when lawmakers chartered the Farmers & Merchants Bank (authorized capital at $1.2 million) and the Union Bank ($3 million). The Union Bank opened as a limited partnership, residents of each Maryland county being allotted 500 shares at $100 per share (1,000 shares to Anne Arundel County) of its authorized capital.

Baltimore would have benefited from a still larger pool of credit, but unfavorable balances of foreign trade curtailed the supply of specie upon which capital and credit depended. Too, it was the policy of the Baltimore branch of the Bank of the United States to restrict the paper-money issues of state-chartered banks by returning the notes to their parent institutions at the end of each day. Insufficient capital and lodged deposits, together with the restraining influence of the Bank of the United States, curbed Baltimore's flow of credit and also made it impossible to accommodate every merchant who presented a promissory note or bill of exchange for discount. In 1804 a local newspaper estimated that Baltimore banks rejected $120,000 in good paper every week. An early student of banking in Maryland believed that Baltimore banks "confined their discounts largely to a small number of friends, and did not grant accommodations to all simply on the merit of the paper offered."[15]

On the other hand, the Baltimore branch of the Bank of the United States discounted paper with such liberality (or partiality) that

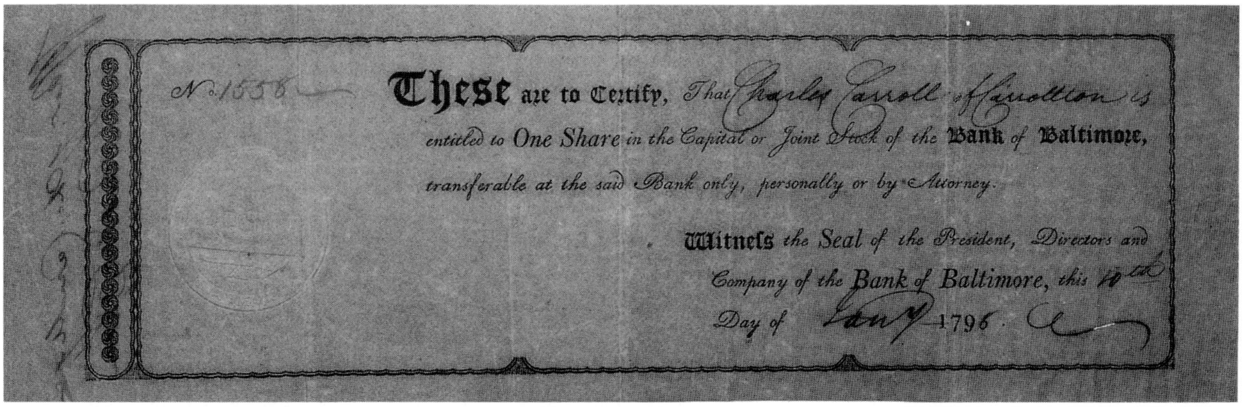
N° 1558

These are to Certify, That Charles Carroll of Carrollton is entitled to One Share in the Capital or Joint Stock of the Bank of Baltimore, transferable at the said Bank only, personally or by Attorney.

Witness the Seal of the President, Directors and Company of the Bank of Baltimore, this 10th Day of Jany 1796.

Charles Carroll of Carrollton, signer of the Declaration of Independence, purchased this share of stock in the Bank of Baltimore in January 1796. (Maryland Historical Society)

by November 1804 it had accumulated some $83,000 in bad debts. While it later managed in the main to avoid additional losses, in March of 1811 only one-fourth of its outstanding loans of nearly $900,000 represented discounts of real business paper. The remainder arose from accommodation lending, that is, the discounting of promissory notes whose existence reflected the fact that two merchants had agreed to accommodate each other by drawing up and exchanging promises to pay. This paper clearly originated not in actual business transactions but in the mutual need for currency or credit.

Neither the Bank of the United States nor its successor, the Second Bank of the United States (chartered for twenty years in 1816), were central banks in the modern sense of "banks of last resort." Yet both institutions came as close as they could at the time to exercising powers like those of modern central banks. As in the case of the Federal Reserve Board in the late twentieth century, the policies of these two nineteenth-century institutions bespoke, above all, a determination to keep inflation at bay.

At least in the nineteenth century, this determination grew out of the underlying concept that the amount of wealth in a country was fixed. The proper function of bank credit, accordingly, was not to increase wealth but to ease its transfer. We may describe this view as quaint, but the same cannot be said of the bank's advice on how to determine the proper volume of credit it should offer its branches. "Experience will soon convince you," William Bingham of Philadelphia—the most influential member of the board of the first Bank of the United States—wrote the branch at Norfolk in April of 1800, "that the average amount of your Deposits, forms the essential Basis of Bank Operations, enabling you to extend, or compelling you to contract, the Sphere of your operations."[16] What is striking about this advice is the modernity of its substitution of deposits for capital as the basis for figuring the proper volume of loans and discounts.

The "deposits" Bingham referred to were undoubtedly *lodged* deposits—those placed in a bank for safekeeping; he could not have meant *created* deposits, because they were a form of credit itself rather than the basis for it. In fact, the practice of extending a loan by opening an account for the borrower—crediting that account the sum loaned (minus interest), and giving the borrower a supply of checks with which to draw upon the account—was much more prevalent early in our history than is commonly supposed (some students of banking argue that they became important only around the time of the Civil War, when the first clearing houses appeared). In the relatively small cities of the late eighteenth and early nineteenth centuries, most merchants probably maintained accounts in the same banks in their respective cities. The bank itself served as a clearing house, charging the account of the drawer of the check and crediting the account of the drawee. The Baltimore trading firm of Robert Oliver & Brothers, established in 1796, drew checks on the Bank of Maryland and other Baltimore banks nearly two out of every three times in which it made payments of any kind in the 1790s.

The supply of currency, credit, and the means of payment all expanded and thus helped support the volume of transactions that accompanied Baltimore's trade increase. A newspaper report in 1804 that currency had remained almost stationary for ten years was surely much exaggerated.[17] At the same time, the flow of bank credit was uneven and inadequate. Contractions of credit helped dry up the money supply, making it difficult for merchants either to buy more goods or to pay for past purchases.

Baltimore's commercial banks concentrated their resources in foreign trade. As banks of issue, they had to maintain specie reserves that would enable them to redeem banknotes on demand. They generally made loans for the purchase of outward- or inward-bound cargoes. These notes were short-term (less than one year) and self-liquidating (i.e., repayable from the proceeds of selling the cargo). But farmers and manufacturers needed loans for longer periods, and the need led to the savings bank. This institution did not issue notes and, while no less concerned with the security of its loans, stood in a better position than commercial banks to make long-term loans.

Undeterred by bank-doctrine warnings (despite the risks inherent in long-term loans), Maryland lawmakers soon addressed the need for long-term credit. In 1805, chartering the Farmers Bank of Maryland (the first in the United States to pay interest on deposits), the assembly established a bank to make loans "on more extended principles than have heretofore been adopted by similar institutions." Directors received authority to lend money to such people as farmers, mechanics, and manufacturers at 6 percent interest if the borrower offered adequate security.[18] The Savings Bank of Baltimore, chartered in 1819, contributed further to the industrialization of Baltimore City by means of long-term loans. In the same period members of the assem-

Table 2. Country Banks in Maryland, 1810–1818

Title	*Location*	*Year Chartered*	*Capital*
Elkton Bank of Maryland	Elkton	1810	$300,000
Farmers Bank of Somerset and Worcester	Snowhill	1812	200,000
Branch at Salisbury	Salisbury	1814	—
Cumberland Bank of Allegany	Cumberland	1812	200,000
Bank of Somerset	Princess Anne	1814	200,000
Conococheague Bank	Williamsport	1814	250,000
Bank of Caroline	Denton	1814	200,000
Susquehanna Bridge and Bank Company	Port Deposit	1815	250,000
Havre de Grace Bank	Havre de Grace	1815	300,000
Bank of Westminster	Westminster	1816	300,000
Branch at Fredericktown	Fredericktown	1821	—
Planters Bank of Prince George's County	Upper Marlboro	1818	200,000
Centreville Bank of Maryland[a]	Centreville	1818	200,000
Farmers Bank of Leonardtown	Leonardtown	1818	100,000
Frederick County Bank	Frederick	1818	500,000
North and South Branch Bank of Potomac	Old Town	1819	250,000
Total			$3,450,000

[a]Did not open for business

Source: Adapted from Alfred C. Bryan, *History of State Banking in Maryland* (Baltimore: Johns Hopkins Press, 1899), 43, and Harvey Eugene Meeks, comp., *Maryland Bank Register, 1790–1964, Updated to December 31, 1979: A Record of the Chartered Banks of Maryland during the Past One Hundred and Ninety Years* (Baltimore: Bank Commissioner, State of Maryland, 1982).

bly, responding as well to the appeals of agricultural, milling, mining, lumbering, and other interests in the state, granted savings-bank charters to country banks in twelve Maryland counties (see Table 2).

By December 1820, eight of the thirteen country banks had failed, probably victims of weak organization and bad real estate loans. In most cases the management structure seems to have meant the cashier; presidents exercised nominal authority, served part-time, and claimed no compensation. Unprotected from the pressures and/or blandishments of the bank's directors and officers, cashiers too often succumbed to temptation. Unsecured loans and sweetheart discounts were transacted in extraordinary amounts. City banks suffered from the same faulty management scheme as the country banks until 1821, when the Union Bank of Baltimore took the lead by deciding to pay the president for full-time services.

In any event, long-term loans secured only by land accounted for most of the country-bank failures of the period—and the pattern recurred again and again in American history. When the prices of agricultural commodities went up, as for example wheat prices did in 1816, farmers who were able to bought more land and put it under the plow. But when commodity prices fell, as did wheat in 1817, farmers were unable to meet their obligations. Banks foreclosed and then found themselves in possession of real estate whose value had fallen along with the decline in commodity prices. With their resources locked up in unmarketable real estate, the banks were unable to redeem their notes in hard cash and thus suspended such payments almost continually from 1817 to 1820.

City banks by no means escaped the perils of unsound practice. They, too, made long-term loans. Baltimore banks typically required two endorsements on a promissory note, but—despite changing circumstances of the endorsers, changes that naturally occurred over time—it was common for paper to run four or five years without any change in the endorsement. Frequent renewals thus could convert short-term loans into long-term loans and long-term loans into very long-term loans. Partly as a result, Baltimore banks between 1816 and 1821 lost huge amounts on bad paper. By the early 1820s almost half (9 of 21) of Maryland banks had collapsed. These failures carried a high price tag—$1.8 million, or more than 22 percent of all active capital.

We cannot easily sort out the roles insider lending and lengthy loans played in the large number of Maryland bank failures, but clearly the bank capital available in the early 1820s was insufficient for the needs of Maryland business, whether rural or urban. Any explanation for that shortfall must include the problem of investments mandated by the state. The General Assembly granted and renewed bank charters with an expiration date included as part of the enabling legislation. Most charter periods were fairly brief, and when questions of rechartering arose, Maryland, along with other states, decided to use its power to make banks financial partners in various "internal improvement" plans, meaning the construction of roads, canals, and bridges. In 1813 the assembly extended the charters of all state banks to January 1835, on two conditions. First, the banks of Baltimore, Hagerstown, Conococheague, and Cumberland had to subscribe to as much stock as would raise the funds necessary to complete a modern road between Baltimore and Cumberland, where it would meet the new National Road to the West. Second, all banks in the state had to pay an annual tax of $20,000—later changed to a tax of twenty cents on every $100 of capital—to be used as a fund to support a general system of tuition-free public schools. The state in effect rechartered banks only after extorting their cooperation on various projects. The road-financing subscriptions, totaling an estimated $1.5 million, turned out to provide but a small portion of the total costs, and the investment proved poor for the banks. The best of the stocks paid no dividends at all for a number of years, and then seldom more than 2 or 3 percent a year.

No account of early banking in Maryland would be complete without the story the state played, if inadvertently, in the development of American constitutional law. In an effort to protect local banks from the restraints upon business the Baltimore branch of the Bank of the United States imposed, the General Assembly in 1818 made it unlawful for any bank that had established an office or branch in Maryland without a state charter to issue notes except on stamped paper purchased from a state office. Banks could elect to purchase the paper, issued in ascending denominations, or pay a flat fee of $15,000 a year. State law thus imposed a tax on a congressionally chartered institution. Officers of the Baltimore branch ignored the law, and the state soon sued one of the bank's cashiers, James W. M'Culloch. While Maryland won state-tribunal judgments, the bank appealed to the U.S. Supreme Court.

Maryland lawmakers thereby fell afoul of John Marshall, a Virginian who had fought in the Revolution, grown disgusted at the weakness of the Confederation Congress, and since 1801 had served as Supreme Court Chief Justice. Marshall was eager to rule on the constitutionality of the Maryland measure, and he did so in 1819, in the case of *M'Culloch v. Maryland.* Speaking for a unanimous court (and turning aside every argument of old Luther Martin, the bank's attorney and a leader of the Maryland bar), the chief justice made one of his most forceful statements on the powers and implied powers of the federal government. The Constitution, he said, explicitly granted the general government not only authority to tax and borrow money, but also such powers as might be "necessary and proper" to exercise those and other responsibilities. Congress had acted within its bounds when it established the Bank of the United States, and since the power to tax involved the power to destroy, Maryland's law was, he declared, unconstitutional and void.[19]

There were two Maryland twists to this story. First, the M'Culloch whom Marshall immortalized turned out to be at the center of a ring of crooks who embezzled more than $1 million from the bank before being exposed. Second, despite Marshall's doctrine of overarching federal powers, Americans who stood with Andrew Jackson considered the national bank a "monster" intent on devouring weaker institutions chartered by the states and a chief cause of the long economic depression that began in 1819. Cleverly linking the Bank of the United States to monopoly and special privilege, Jackson as president in 1832 vetoed a bill to recharter the bank and then, in the fall of the following year, ordered a Marylander, treasury secretary (later John Marshall's successor as chief justice) Roger Brooke Taney, to remove federal deposits from the expiring "monster." Deprived of these large sums, the institution lost much of its power to influence the volume of discounts and deposits that state-chartered institutions offered. So, in a sense, Maryland won its war against the bank after all.

Riding the Roller Coaster Economy

Removal of that rival from the field coincided with extraordinary economic development in Maryland, especially in Baltimore, and a new round of legislative bank chartering. During these years Baltimore manufacturing continued to grow and diversify; it included sugar refining, flour milling, glass cutting, plaster making, and spice grinding. Steamboat lines, canals like the Chesapeake & Ohio and the Chesapeake & Delaware, and railroads, most notably the Baltimore & Ohio, changed transportation patterns dramatically and promised still more opportunity. All such growth raised the cry for more banking capital.

In 1830 Maryland depended on twelve state banks, eight of them in Baltimore. Their total capital stood at $5.4 million, exclusive of

Vignettes from Chesapeake & Ohio Canal (top) and Baltimore & Ohio Railroad stock certificates, vividly demonstrating the promise Maryland internal-improvements projects carried with them in the early nineteenth century. (Maryland Historical Society)

$1.5 to $2 million employed by the Baltimore branch of the Bank of the United States. The shortage of banks stemmed from another "monopoly"—the special arrangements dating from 1813 between the assembly and those rechartered banks that agreed to finance building of the Baltimore-to-Cumberland road: Part of the deal had been a legislative moratorium on further bank chartering. Expansion took the form both of new banks (the assembly chartered seventeen between 1829 and 1836; five never opened) and increases in the capital several of the old banks employed. Ten of the newly chartered banks were to open outside of Baltimore, in seven counties. Five were in the city, whose bankers in 1835 received a ten-year moratorium on new charters there in exchange for their support of another western Maryland road-building venture. With more than $3.7 million subscribed to these new institutions, banking capital in Baltimore increased by $4.8 million, or half again as much as it had been. The state's banking capital rose from $7.4 million in 1829 to slightly more than $19 million in 1836.

Banking in Maryland during these years well demonstrated the volatility of the American economy. Banks continued to come and go. In the aftermath of Jackson's dismantling of the Bank of the United States, its director in the years 1833–34 (the weakened bank remained in business under a Pennsylvania state charter) placed such restrictions on credit as to force interest rates to highs of 18 to 36 percent. The country plunged into deep recession. The Susquehanna Bank of Port Deposit failed in 1834; the Commercial Bank of Millington in eastern Kent County closed in 1836.

Neither of those firms fell with as much noise as did the Bank of Maryland in 1834. Here was not just bad luck. Published audits disclosed mismanagement bordering on fraud. Circulating notes exceeded specie reserves by a ratio of 50 to 1. The main culprits appear to have been Evan Poultney, former president of the bank, and three directors—Reverdy Johnson (later U.S. senator and minister to the Court of St. James), John Glenn, and Evan T. Ellicott. Poultney and two of the directors had joined in partnership with two other parties

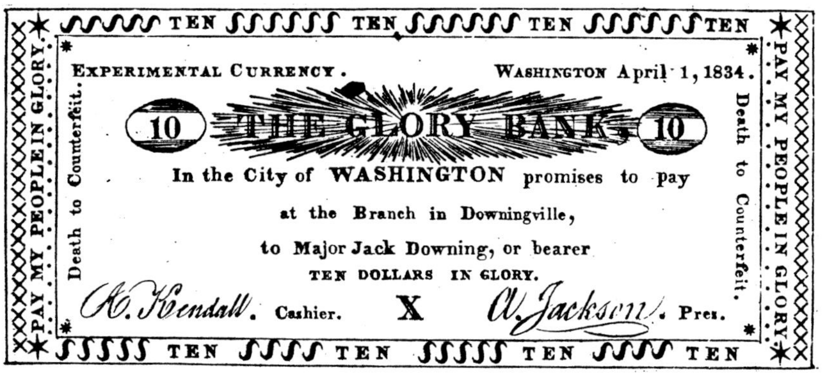

Satirical $10 note from the pen of Jack Downing (the humorist's real name was Seba Smith), supposedly issued in Washington, April 1, 1834. It poked fun at the Bank of the United States, but by extension banks generally. (Maryland Historical Society)

to deal in the stock of the bank, using its funds to make purchases. They also had used nearly a million dollars in bank funds to purchase a majority share of the General Insurance Company, and chosen the partners, president, and managers of the company. Small depositors in the bank lost $2 million in savings while bank officers escaped by declaring themselves insolvent. Fueling the flames of public resentment was the practice of imprisoning debtors unable to pay their obligations (in 1831 about 1,000 Baltimoreans had been jailed for owing $10 or less). In the summer of 1835 irate depositors saw no justice and turned to vengeance. A mob stoned the windows of Reverdy Johnson's house, pillaging, shooting, and setting bonfires elsewhere in the city. Antagonism between rich and poor was inflamed the more when Johnson and other victims of the bank riot managed to win indemnities from the Whig-controlled legislature for their losses during the riot.

The Panic of 1837 produced equally distressing outcomes. It originated in heavy British investments in American internal improvement projects and lively interest in purchases of American cotton for British textile mills. Late in 1836 the Bank of England, convinced it was losing specie to the United States, curtailed the outflow of capital. British demand for cotton declined, the price of cotton fell, and the credit structure, keyed to the use of cotton as security, collapsed. When in 1839 the Bank of England further tightened credit and then ceased to export gold and silver altogether, American banks suspended specie payments. The resulting contraction of the money supply brought on a severe deflation, the price level between 1830 and 1843 falling more than 40 percent. The venerable Bank of the United States had heavily committed its money to cotton, which planters had overproduced. The bank stopped paying specie for paper in 1839, and suspension fell very heavily upon Baltimore, where investments of some $4 million disappeared. Just before suspension, the discounts of Maryland banks had stood at $16.4 million, with issues amounting to $3.4 million. By the beginning of 1840 discounts were down to $2.5 million and issues to $500,000.

Aggravating the situation were the heavy investments of Maryland's banks in the stocks of various state-sponsored canal, turnpike, and other "improvement" companies. The state itself had incurred large debts in the course of its own investments in these companies and lacked the resources even to pay interest on its debt. To assist the firms the state granted a number of them specific powers of issuing paper currency. The Baltimore & Ohio and Annapolis & Elkridge railroad companies, just as the Chesapeake & Ohio Canal Company, were empowered to issue $4 million in variously denominated stock orders, certificates of debt, or toll notes—all secured by bonds of the state or city of Baltimore or by mortgaged property. City of Baltimore

Cartoonist's view of the malfeasance that brought down the Bank of Maryland and caused riots in 1835. On the left a well-dressed bank director gestures reassuringly to a woman and her child; monkeys acting as puppeteers for other monkeys abound in the center of the cartoon, which focuses righteous attention on an act of pure pillage—a wheelbarrow of cash pushed by a scoundrel and pulled by a hog. (Maryland Historical Society)

and B&O Railroad paper circulated generally and, after the disappearance of specie, supplied the most reliable fractional money. Meanwhile, all Maryland banks violated the law by receiving and passing notes of $5 or less denomination. Three banks confessed to issuing small notes, although two of the three claimed that the power to do so had been given by their charters. Some of the notes in circulation at the time bore denominations as small as one and a half cents. Not until March of 1842, after Pennsylvania banks resumed specie payments, did their Maryland counterparts follow suit.

Hard times in the late 1830s and early 1840s seriously reduced the banking capital of the state—both by bank failure and investor skittishness. The Franklin and Citizens Banks of Baltimore folded, as did the Planter's Bank of St. Mary's County. The drop in banking capital amounted to $2.3 million, with at least $715,000 due to outright loss.

Industrial expansion led the way to recovery in Maryland. In 1844 the assembly allowed state banks to make loans upon promissory notes or obligations under seal (secured by mortgage) for any period up to five years at 6 percent interest. The availability of long-term loans encouraged industrial expansion. More important, Maryland's investments in internal improvements began to bear heavy fruit. By mid-century the B&O had made Baltimore the commercial hub and shipping center for much of the coal, lumber, and farm products that flowed from western Maryland, Virginia, and Pennsylvania and the eastern Ohio River Valley.

In this brighter climate, lawmakers allowed old banks to enlarge their capital, incorporated new ones, and converted seven savings institutions to regular banks of discount and issue. In all, seventeen new banks appeared in the state between 1843 and 1862, raising a total of $3 million in new capital. Four of the seven refitted savings banks were located in Baltimore, bringing an increase of $1.4 million to the city's available capital. In March 1854, the assembly made possible even larger increases, permitting Baltimore banks to increase their capital at will and, when suitable, simply reporting the increase to the state treasurer and paying what they owed into the school fund (not less than $100,000 could be added at any one time). Over the next four years new capital from all sources exceeded $2.8 million. In 1843 twenty Maryland banks claimed capital of slightly more than $9.7 million; in 1858 thirty-one banks held $12.5 million. In the economic downturn that came in 1857, only two Maryland banks failed, both in Allegany County and apparently because of overeager investment in the Georges Creek coal fields.

Almost immediately after the general resumption of specie payments in 1858, the banks of Baltimore agreed to follow the example of New York and Boston and organize a clearing house. Before its organization, a commercial bank during the course of the business day would accept for deposit checks drawn on accounts at other banks (as well as drafts, notes, and bills of exchange). After crediting the account of the depositor, it would recover the sums involved by employing one or more runners to return the checks and other items to the banks on which they had been drawn. The system was cumbersome, time-consuming, and not altogether safe. The association of banks in a clearing house made it possible to effect at one place at a fixed time the daily exchanges between members and to settle the balances resulting from such exchanges.

The total number of banks clearing at the time in Baltimore was thirty-one. Fourteen of them formed the Baltimore Clearing House Association: the Union Bank of Maryland, Commercial and Farmers Bank, Franklin Bank, Western Bank, Mechanics Bank, Farmers and Merchants Bank, Marine Bank of Baltimore, Farmers and Planters Bank, Citizens Bank, Fells Point Savings Institution, Chesapeake Bank, Bank of Commerce, the Merchants Bank, and the Bank of Baltimore. The Union Bank of Maryland became the depository bank that managed the system (its cashier serving as ex-officio manager until 1928, when the group established quarters in the Baltimore branch of the Federal Reserve Bank at 114 East Lexington Street). Besides handling the transactions of the Clearing House in its banking

Enoch Pratt as a young man, at about the time he played a part in founding the Baltimore Clearing House. (Maryland Historical Society)

rooms, the Union Bank also served as a depository for any monies any member bank might care to leave on special deposit for safekeeping purposes. The depository issued certificates for the amount involved; they were receivable in payment of clearing-house balances.

The Civil War provided a defining moment in terms of the meaning Americans would attach to "liberty," "freedom," and "nation," but with the outbreak of war in 1861 the federal government's fiscal needs were uppermost in the minds of most worldly Unionists. The war exerted powerful influences on state banking. In the fall of that year, President Lincoln's secretary of the treasury borrowed (inferentially by force) $100 million in gold from Northern banks. Drained of their specie reserves, the banks drifted toward suspension. The premium on gold began a rise that by 1863 had reached a level of 220 percent.

With gold out of circulation, the federal government broke precedent and in early 1862 began to handle its increasing debt by issuing paper money as legal tender. Printed in green ink on their reverse sides, these noninterest-bearing U.S. notes soon became popularly known as "greenbacks." Then, since U.S. bonds could not be sold abroad, Congress created a domestic market for them by passing the National Bank Act in February 1863, and a stronger measure in June 1864. These measures invited state-chartered banks to reorganize under national charters and to invest heavily (at least one-third of a bank's total capital and not less than $30,000) in federal war bonds.

Besides helping to pay for the war, the legislation created a new system of nationally chartered banks and furnished the country with a uniform paper currency. Upon receipt of a bank's purchase of bonds, a newly created comptroller of the currency in the Treasury Department turned over to the bank the same amount (less 10 percent) in national banknotes. Uniform in design, backed by federal bonds, and supervised by the federal government, these notes replaced the 7,000 variations of bills that more than 1,600 state banks issued at the time. In the event the bank failed, the bonds were to be liquidated and the noteholders compensated without loss.

For those Maryland bankers who did not enlist, the war probably was most memorable for its uncertainties and inconveniences. In Frederick, the war had a more painful effect, for in the summer of 1864, attempting to lift some of the pressure from Lee's besieged army at Petersburg, Virginia, Gen. Jubal A. Early led a large force of Southern troops on a raid through western Maryland. His troops ransacked Hagerstown. When in July they reached Frederick, home of a high-ranking Confederate officer, Bradley T. Johnson, the rebels called on the mayor and town authorities to come up with $200,000 "current money" in exchange for sparing the city. After a hastily called town meeting, Frederick's five banks and savings institutions (on promise of

Face and back of a $10 bank-note, this one from the National Farmers and Planters Bank of Baltimore dated 1865 and signed by its president, Enoch Pratt. (Armand Shank Collection)

reimbursement) agreed to supply the amount according to their assets. The money, in greenbacks, went out to the waiting Confederates in a wagon loaded with stuffed baskets.

Meanwhile, some Maryland banks lost little time obtaining national charters. The Farmers Bank of Maryland, chartered in 1805, became the Farmers' National Bank of Annapolis; the Mechanics Bank of Baltimore, founded in 1806, converted to the National Mechanics' Bank of Baltimore. The most important and long-lived of the new banks, First National Bank of Baltimore, emerged with a federal charter in 1864. But prominent Baltimore institutions—those not deeply involved in note issues—were in no hurry to exchange their state status for national charters. In early March 1865, with the Confederacy on the brink of defeat, Congress overcame their reluctance by passing a bill assessing a 10 percent tax on state-bank notes. Fence-sitting Maryland bankers prepared to join the national system; why pay 10 percent for the privilege of making a loan at 6 percent? In 1865 twenty-four Maryland banks took out national charters. By the end of

Check drawn on the Hagerstown Bank, 1871. The bank pictured Columbia on the left and its own offices in the upper right. (Maryland Historical Society)

1867 only six state-chartered banks remained—small-town banks that could not meet the national bank's minimum bond purchase. In 1871 two of them were left.

Maryland Banking in the Gilded Age

Painfully divided during the war, Marylanders afterward picked up old economic threads and forged ahead in new directions. Baltimore resumed its position as an important and competitive port in foreign trade. Industry there flourished: Especially strong before the war in sugar refining and shoemaking, Baltimore after the war became important for its men's clothing, canning, fertilizer, and iron and steel industries. Although of declining industrial importance in the nation as a whole during the period, Maryland in 1910 ranked first among the South Atlantic states (Delaware, Maryland, Virginia, West Virginia, North Carolina, South Carolina, Georgia and Florida) in the value of products and in the value added by manufactures. Agriculture, much disrupted by the war, entered a period of decline, especially in terms of the emerging national economy.

By far most of the state's industry took place in Baltimore, but in 1890 official observers believed that the trend toward manufacturing had begun to reach all corners of Maryland.

> Many of the manufacturers of Maryland have during the past years, sought more advantageous locations in the rural districts for the conduct of their business, notably, in the towns of Laurel, Frederick, Hagerstown and Cumberland in the west, and Havre de Grace, Cambridge, Easton and Salisbury in the east. In many of these towns new factories have been erected and many hands have been given employment to the great advantage of the rural population.[20]

If the example of Baltimore proved reliable, this dispersal of industry would carry with it a demand for more credit-granting institutions in the counties.

The Taylor Bank in Berlin, Worcester County, grew up because of light industries—lumbering, milling, brickmaking—but mainly on the basis of strawberries. The town lay at the intersection of two rail

The Doubtful Bank Note, *Harper's Weekly*, March 15, 1873. Counterfeiting—being cheated by bad money—continued to worry Americans in the Gilded Age. Here a worrisome mother awaits the merchant's assessment. (Armand Shank Collection)

lines, one connecting Chesapeake Bay, Salisbury, and Ocean City, the other leading north to Philadelphia and farther down the Delmarva peninsula. Berlin's success in marketing strawberries—millions each year—and fruit trees called for a reliable local bank, and in 1890 a native-born school teacher and lawyer, Calvin B. Taylor, opened one (by no means the town's first) on the south side of the Odd Fellows Hall. Despite a devastating fire in 1901, Taylor's small firm flourished —perhaps in part because of his own activities as a church, lodge, and political leader in the community. In 1907, deciding to incorporate, Taylor obtained a state charter that established the bank's capital at $50,000 (500 shares at $100 par value). Taylor retained a controlling influence, and the bank became a chief source of credit for small businesses and homeowners in the region. By 1915 Taylor's bank reported assets of nearly $262,000.[21]

By 1897 Baltimore was home to a total of thirty commercial banks, whose combined capital amounted to almost $14 million. Along with

Beyond counterfeiting was the problem of paper as paper (inadequately backed notes), which many late-nineteenth-century Americans viewed with stubborn suspicion. This supposed $1,000 bill declared in fine print that it was "Redeemable nowhere, in nothing, and by nobody"; nonetheless, by law, "this money shall circulate freely." (Maryland Historical Society)

the rest of the country, Baltimore also experienced a marked acceleration in the formation of trust companies in the 1890s. In the early 1880s there had been only one; thirteen sprang up between 1895 and 1900, with an aggregate capital and surplus of $40 million. Two of them led the way. The first, Safe Deposit and Trust Company, formed in March 1864 under the directorship of a Massachusetts-born Unionist and hardware merchant, Enoch Pratt, whose interests before and during the profitable war had extended to shipping, railroads, and insurance. Pratt believed that Baltimoreans, besides a fresh source of capital, needed a safe place to keep their valuables.

At first the Safe Deposit made its home in the basement of the Farmers and Planters National Bank, where Pratt served as president, but in the mid-1870s work began on a truly secure building on South Street. The noted architect Frank P. Baldwin designed this structure, which employed the latest in construction technology and went up with such immensity as to win acclaim as a marvel of its age. A storage or silver vault had a four-foot-deep foundation and even thicker walls, with portholes so that guards could peer inside on their rounds. A fire- and burglar-proof safe was built on top of the silver vault. At 31 × 36 × 15 feet in dimension and with walls that alternated concrete with welded three-inch iron and steel plates, the company's safe was "probably the largest, strongest, and most scientifically built one in the world," the *Baltimore Sun* reported. Baldwin crafted the exterior with massive walls and heavy stonework, he said, "to show clearly the object for which it was built." Opened in November 1876, the building "impresses the eye with a sense of security and solidity that is still further carried out in all the details of the work." That same year the assembly granted Safe Deposit authority to exercise fiduciary powers, that is, to oversee the financial management of estates. Safe Deposit became the first corporation in Maryland, and one of the first in the country, with such power.[22]

Not long after, in 1884, Pratt also became one of the founders of another principal Baltimore trust bank, Mercantile Trust and Deposit Company. With its own fiduciary, checking, savings, loans, safekeeping, and foreign-bank departments, the Mercantile pioneered in multiple customer services. It built another monument to probity and security—this one in heavy Romanesque style, in 1886. The Mercantile's Great Vault almost made that of the Safe Deposit and Trust seem porous by comparison (it boasted five doors—three outer ones fireproof, two more burglar-proof). "So strong as to resist the invasion of armed force," the company later claimed; into it, in addition to items of gold and silver and precious stones, went things as varied as treasured papers, dueling pistols, and funerary ashes. The first president of the Mercantile, John Gill, had grown up in Annapolis, attended the University of Virginia, and during the war attained the rank of general in the Confederate army. Placing this veteran in a working relationship with Pratt, the Mercantile through the turn of the century vividly illustrated Maryland's blending of contesting cultures.[23]

But there were many such illustrations. While financing industrial development in Maryland, Baltimore capital also supported the rebuilding of railroads, street railways, utilities, cotton mills, coal companies, iron works, phosphate mines, and lumber operations throughout the old Confederacy. Much of the invested money belonged to the Safe Deposit and Mercantile Trust companies, and among the most active investors was Henry Walters, whose father, William T. Walters, had helped to found Safe Deposit and Trust. At the turn of the century the *Manufacturers Record* of Baltimore, part journal and part advertising agent for the city, set the figure for such investment at $100 million.[24]

Although twenty-one of the city's commercial banks remained nationally chartered in 1897, nine operated under state charters. Those

The impressive Safe Deposit and Trust Company building, fire- and burglar-proof, at the time of its opening in 1876 (*above*); a later photograph of its skylighted interior (*below*). (Courtesy of Mercantile–Safe Deposit & Trust Company)

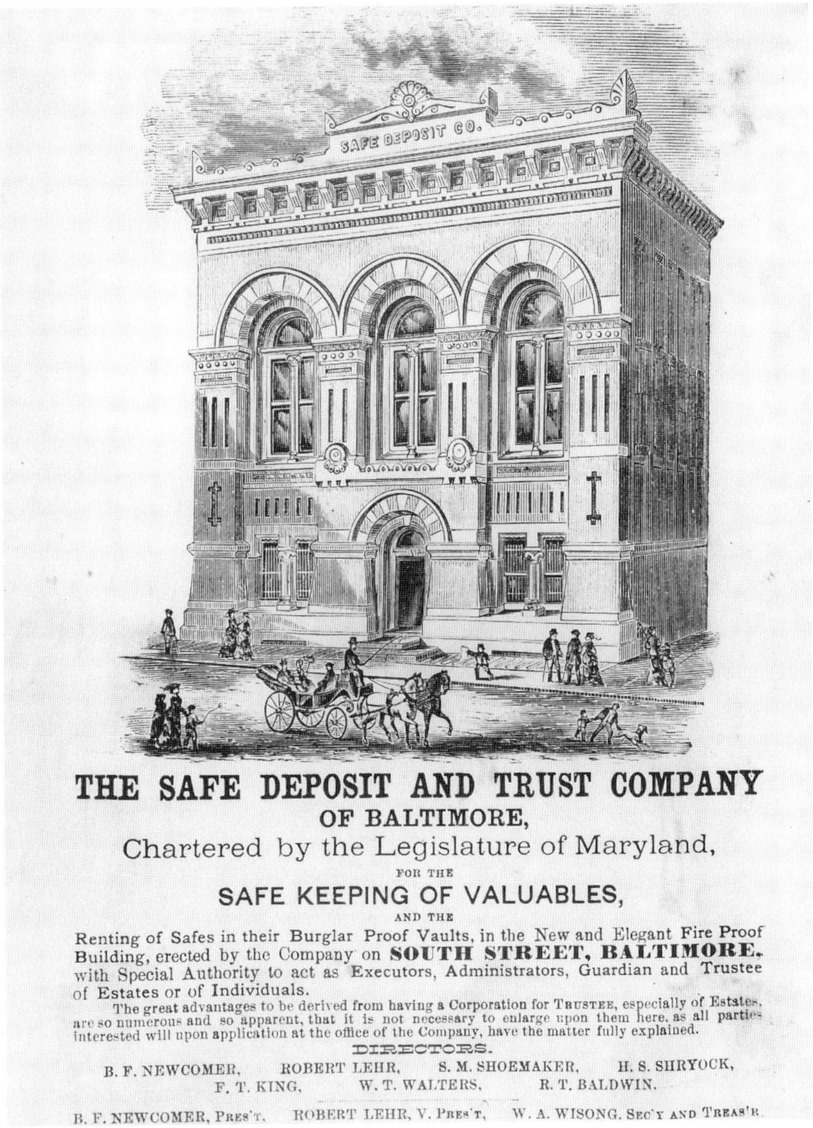

A conference of Mercantile Trust and Deposit's leadership in about 1900. President John Gill sits at the desk, a spittoon on the floor to his right. (Courtesy of Mercantile–Safe Deposit & Trust Company)

Posting ledgers at Safe Deposit and Trust in the 1890s. (Courtesy of Mercantile–Safe Deposit & Trust Company)

nine represented a pattern at the time—even more noticeable in the country as a whole—away from national and back to state charters. In 1870 about 17 percent of American banks were in business by state authority alone; by 1910 nearly 40 percent of all banks were state-chartered, completely reversing the late–Civil War trend. Bankers had rediscovered the advantages of state charters while noting shortcomings in the national bank system. National bank minimum-capital requirements remained high by comparison to those of most states.

National banks could not make loans on the security of real estate—an obvious disadvantage for rural banks. (Congress eased this restriction as part of the act establishing the Federal Reserve System.)

More seriously, the national system had failed to dampen fluctuations in the business cycle. National banks could keep three-fifths of their required reserves as deposits in other national banks located in seventeen regional financial centers. Banks in these reserve cities could, in turn, keep half of their reserves in national banks in New York, which served as the system's central reserve city. Because of their ties to Wall Street, the New York City banks could afford to pay relatively high interest rates, investing the excess reserves that were strongly attracted by these rates in call loans to dealers in securities.

A pinch came whenever the stock market weakened. Country banks and reserve city banks outside New York tended to call back their deposits in New York, and in turn the New York banks were forced to call in their securities loans, thus increasing the downward pressure on the stock market. In addition, the seasonal demand for cash in the hinterlands produced an annual crisis in the spring, followed by a recovery in the summer. The recurrent need to liquidate stocks to meet the demands of the lenders of call funds created waves of selling and persistent market collapses. In the post–Civil War period the market panicked in 1873, 1884, 1903, and 1907, with the demand for cash frequently becoming too great for New York banks to meet. The results were familiar—bank failures and worsening financial crisis.

In Baltimore the Clearing House adopted special measures to meet these emergencies when, understandably, depositors tended to withdraw their funds for safekeeping. They did so to such an extent that, even though the banks contracted their loans, some were unable to meet the adverse balances created against them at the Clearing House. To meet these demands and thereby discourage a contraction of loans, the clearing house banks lent mutual aid to one another. They authorized the issue of special loan certificates, secured by depositing securities with a committee, which member banks could use in settling balances at the clearing house. The arrangement protected banks against loss of their cash reserves and made the settlement of exchanges between member banks much simpler and easier. Banks of the Clearing House thus could assure the business community of some additional security in hard times.

State Reform and the Federal Reserve

In the spring of 1896 Baltimore bankers further strengthened their means of mutual aid by forming the Maryland Bankers Association, a move that was part of a national trend. Faced with the certainty of federal and state regulation, bankers (like other trade and professional groups in the period) realized that they should speak with a strong

When in the spring of 1896 the Maryland Bankers Association first convened, the arrangements committee proudly showed that members came from towns and cities all over Maryland, from Berlin to Oakland, Emmitsburg to Crisfield. (Courtesy of the Maryland Bankers Association)

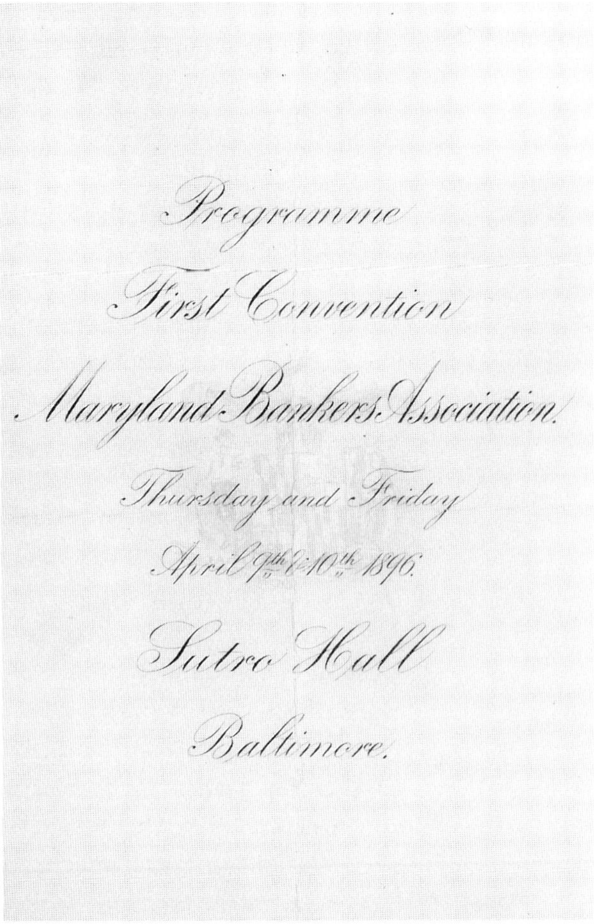
Programme

First Convention

Maryland Bankers Association.

Thursday and Friday

April 9th & 10th 1896.

Sutro Hall

Baltimore.

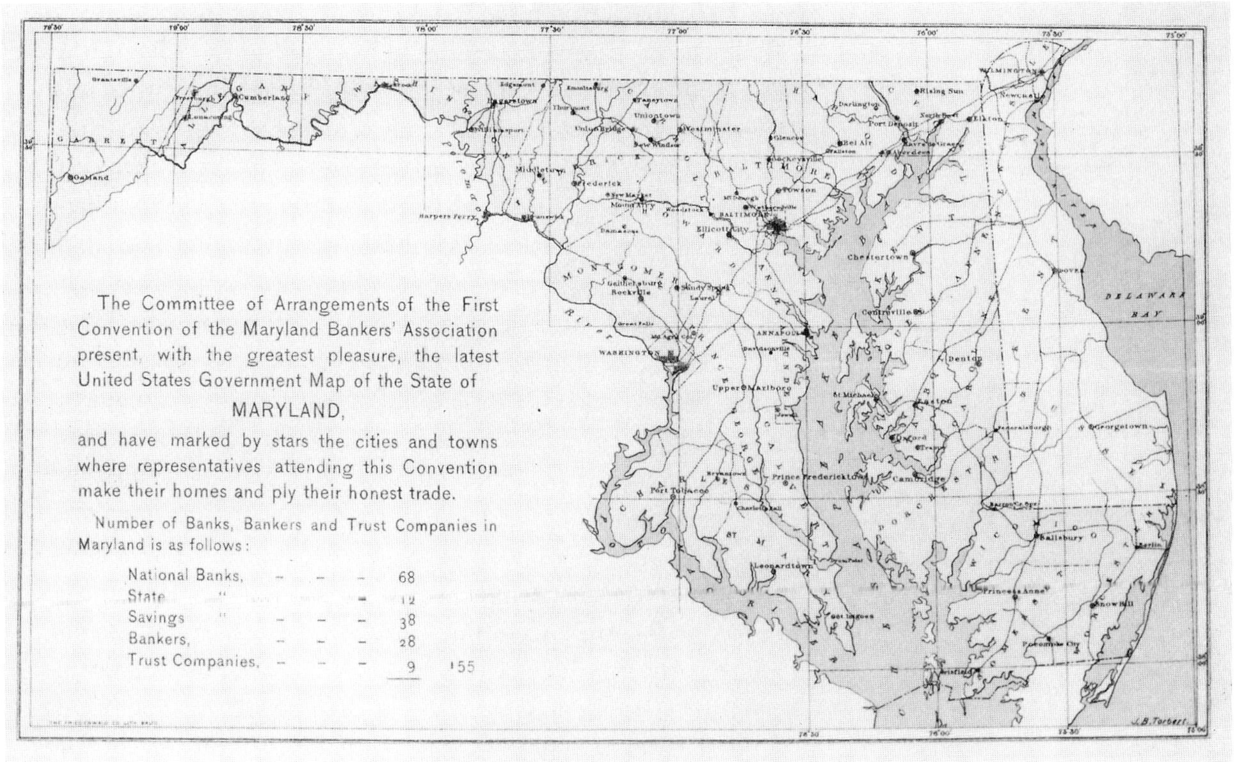

and reasonably clear voice in legislative halls. A national bankers group had formed twenty years earlier.

Ninety-three of the state's financial institutions—fifty from Baltimore and forty-three from the counties—responded to the association's call for an April meeting in Baltimore. Members then elected as president Enoch Pratt, the Safe Deposit and Trust founder and philanthropist who also served as head of the Baltimore Clearing House. By June 1910 the association's membership committee was able to report that "awakened interest . . . in our annual gatherings" had produced the largest increase in any one year. Twenty-one institutions joined the association in 1910, bringing its total membership to 191—or nearly 80 percent of the state's 247 banks.[25]

The association soon became a powerful force in Annapolis. In 1907, at its twelfth annual convention, it established a special committee to study Maryland banking law. The following year H. B. Wilcox, association president, urged his colleagues to establish a standing legislative committee that would "investigate the many proposed laws and take steps to defeat the undesirable ones." The association sought to establish some governance of state banking. Bankers believed that the interests of prudent management and the protection of depositors alike required serious legal reform. State banks and trust companies, Wilcox said in 1908, "should certainly be required by law to keep as cash reserve a specified proportion of their deposits."[26]

In an address before the association in 1909, J. Dukes Downes, Maryland's state bank examiner, argued forcefully and similarly. In seven years in that role, he had seen only five bank failures in Maryland, all of them "the result of gross mismanagement." Laws on the books set no limit to the amount of loans that a bank could make to any one person, firm, or enterprise and did not reach "those parties who, individually, or as a partnership, advertise and assume to conduct a bank, having neither a charter from the Legislature nor being incorporated under general laws." These "no capital banks" should come under the same supervision as other Maryland banks, which themselves should reveal more of their workings; while some of them, according to Downes, conducted business without sufficient or proper security for the deposits they held, others accumulated "too much surplus and undivided profits." Why not, he asked, issue a periodic "frank statement" of each bank's actual resources and liabilities?[27]

Downes and the association kept the big banks, meaning Baltimore banks, uppermost in view, but he and his friends also wanted to shepherd rural Maryland institutions. The "country bank man"—although by no means he alone—needed to be kept abreast of changing currents of thought affecting banking, Downes said in 1909, and small banks were "constantly springing up in the towns and villages of our State." Downes believed one could find more money in the counties than earlier; he also observed that "these small local banks reach the people of the communities as the larger and more distant banks cannot." Surround rural bankers with "good, sound, conservative laws," Downes declared; "do not handicap them, but be liberal and at the same time safe—and I predict that they will continue to develop and add materially to the banking interests of Maryland." Downes called for "a banking law that would be fair to the banks and at the same time give satisfactory service and security to the people."[28]

In 1910 lawmakers obliged by adopting the Uniform Banking Bill, which the bankers association both prepared and presented to the assembly. This measure created a state Banking Department and banking commissioner under the state's Board of Public Works. The commissioner would review and pass upon all applications to establish new banks or increase a bank's capital stock (the assembly established minimum-capital and other conditions). He also was to examine and approve the articles of association, and, at least once a year, visit each of the nonnational banks in the state to inspect and examine their affairs.

To ensure that the commissioner could conduct those inspections with all necessary authority, the assembly required banks to give him free access to all their vaults, books, and papers. In addition, he could require bank officers, trustees, employees, and agents—any material witnesses—to answer questions about the bank's affairs. If, after completing his examination, the commissioner found a bank to be insolvent or its continuance hazardous to the public, he was to report those findings to the governor, who through the attorney general might bring proceedings against the bank. In the event of insolvency, the commissioner assumed control of the bank's affairs.[29] To this new post Gov. Austin Lane Crothers appointed Mr. Downes.

During his first six months in office, Downes called upon the state's roughly 100 banks and trust companies for a total of four reports of condition, afterward reporting that the new law was "well received by the banking interests of the state" and that he had received "hearty cooperation and assistance." Maryland's commercial banks and trust companies disclosed assets (or "aggregate resources") ranging between $89.7 million and $97.8 million. At the end of 1910, the state's twenty-three savings banks showed additional resources of more than $97.7 million. Downes had authorized the establishment of three new banks and one trust company. On the other side of the ledger, he had seized control of the affairs and assets of two savings banks. One of them, the Savings Bank of Brunswick, he said had been guilty of "the most inexcusable carelessness and negligence" in keeping its books and accounts; when he examined the bank, "it was found impossible to ascertain its actual condition." Still, "considering the fact that for years, during the rapid growth and expansion of the State

After the great fire of early February 1904, Mercantile Trust and Deposit had lost some of its windows, but the vault and its contents had escaped damage. (Courtesy of Mercantile–Safe Deposit & Trust Company)

banking business in Maryland, and in a period when much laxity and looseness prevailed in legislation affecting banking corporations," Downes noted "the generally excellent condition and conscientious methods of institutions coming within the scope and authority of the Bank Commissioner."[30]

The state's bankers also came together as a group to improve the practice of their profession much in the way of the American Institute of Banking, organized in 1900 (the next year Baltimore established one of its forty chapters). At the Maryland bankers' meeting in 1908, the president of the Baltimore chapter, James D. Garrett, explained that banking "was becoming more and more a science," so that a "bank man cannot know too much to equip him for the duties of his profession." The institute thus sought to train its members in those branches of "practical education" that directly bear on the business of banking; to "originate and circulate literature relating to the art and science of banking and business administration"; and, by means of arrangements with colleges, universities, and correspondence schools (the last of special assistance to "the country bank man"), to teach members the "principles of banking, the science of finance, applied economics, commerce, accounts and other subjects of practical value to them." The Baltimore chapter claimed to be recognized "as one of the leading chapters" in the nation—fourth in membership (more than 600 individual members in 1908) "and first in educational work and progressiveness."[31]

On the national scene, banking and the public continued to suffer the consequences of inadequate policy. The problem was that during financial panics the supply of currency—coin and paper money—was inelastic. Panics occurred when a large number of depositors doubted that their bank deposits could be converted into currency. Testing their doubts, they tended to confirm them. Had there been some way to expand the volume of currency early in a panic situation, the doubts of deposit holders could be allayed and depression possibly avoided. The panic of 1893 sparked action on the part of bankers. Following it, A. Barton Hepburn, president of the Third National Bank of New York and later chairman of Chase National Bank, called the

Lobby of the Hagerstown Bank at about the turn of the century. (Courtesy of Hagerstown Trust Company)

currency system "ill-conceived, unresponsive to the various interests of our great nation, and prejudicial to renewed and stable prosperity."[32] At the American Bankers Association convention the next year in Baltimore, Hepburn and Charles Christopher Homer, president of the Second National Bank of Baltimore, put into motion a plan—labeled the "Baltimore Plan"—which ultimately served as the basis for the Federal Reserve Act of 1913. The Baltimore Plan advocated a guaranty fund supplied by the federal government; it provided an emergency-note-issue capacity that bore direct relation to a bank's total capital. It continued to serve as a basis for discussion of reform at the Indianapolis Monetary Convention in 1897 and in a study by the Currency Commission of the American Bankers Association, which Hepburn chaired.

The Maryland Bankers Association vigorously supported monetary and banking reform along the lines of the Baltimore Plan. At its annual convention in November 1901, the association unanimously adopted resolutions lamenting the "inevitable check upon trade and the oft ruinous unsettling of values" that accompanied periods of financial stringency and calling for an "elastic asset currency." The association appointed three of its members to urge key members of Congress to adopt such a measure. Order in the money markets demanded a bank that could act as a lender of last resort, one that had the ability to create reserves through its credit-granting power and thus support banks that were in danger of failing during a panic.[33]

The Panic of 1907 helped to galvanize support for the Aldrich-Vreeland Act, which provided both a temporary solution and further impetus to long-term reform. This temporary solution authorized groups of banks threatened by depositor panic to issue an emergency currency backed by specified types of their loan and investment assets—with a progressively rising tax on such emergency issues to ensure that they would be retired after the end of the emergency. The Aldrich-Vreeland measure promoted long-term reform by establishing a national monetary commission that would make extensive studies of monetary and banking systems and propose changes. Under the chairmanship of Senator Aldrich of Rhode Island, the commission held hearings and made recommendations that led directly to passage of the Federal Reserve Act in 1913 and, the next year, establishment of the Federal Reserve System.

The Federal Reserve reflected deep historic fears of concentrated financial power. Rather than a single central bank, the new law created twelve Federal Reserve districts and designated a central bank for each. All national banks were required to join the system; state banks were permitted to do so provided they met federal standards. To enable the district central banks to create reserves in times of financial stringency, they received the power to issue a new currency—Federal Reserve notes—with which they could purchase securities in the open market. Such purchases, when deposited in member banks and credited to the account of the depositing Federal Reserve bank, automatically increased the reserves of member banks and permitted them to expand their loans and discounts. Even more important in the eyes of the creators of the system was the ability of the district central banks to use Federal Reserve notes to buy up, at a discount, commercial paper previously discounted and held by the member banks.

At first, observers believed that this process of rediscounting commercial paper—including manipulation of the rediscount rate around the market rate of interest—would be the primary means for controlling credit and promoting financial stability. In 1916 an amendment further expanded the money-creating powers of the Federal Reserve by allowing district central banks to make direct loans or advances, secured by eligible commercial or governmental paper, to member banks at the rediscount rate.

In theory, the central banks discounted paper in accordance with the "real bills" doctrine; in practice, lending officers at the Reserve banks determined the "eligibility" of bills offered for discount, thus effectively separating money from any rigid standard. The authors of the Federal Reserve Act so thoroughly expected the gold standard to continue to operate that they built into the law few links between the Reserve System and gold.

Marylanders might have viewed that omission with interest, because Charles C. Homer, cocreator of the Baltimore Plan that served as the basis for the Federal Reserve Act, had taken the lead in the state

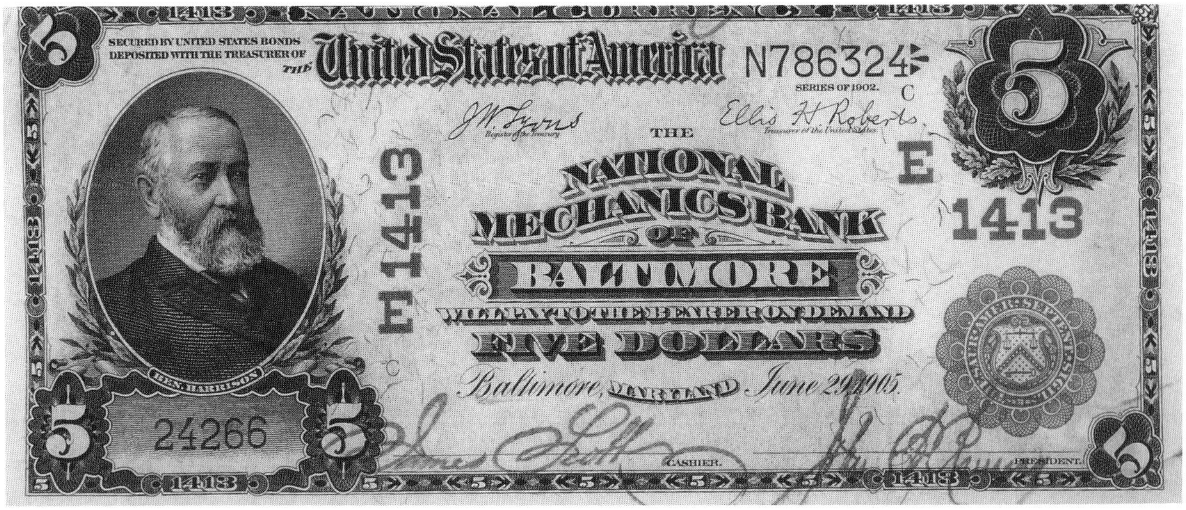

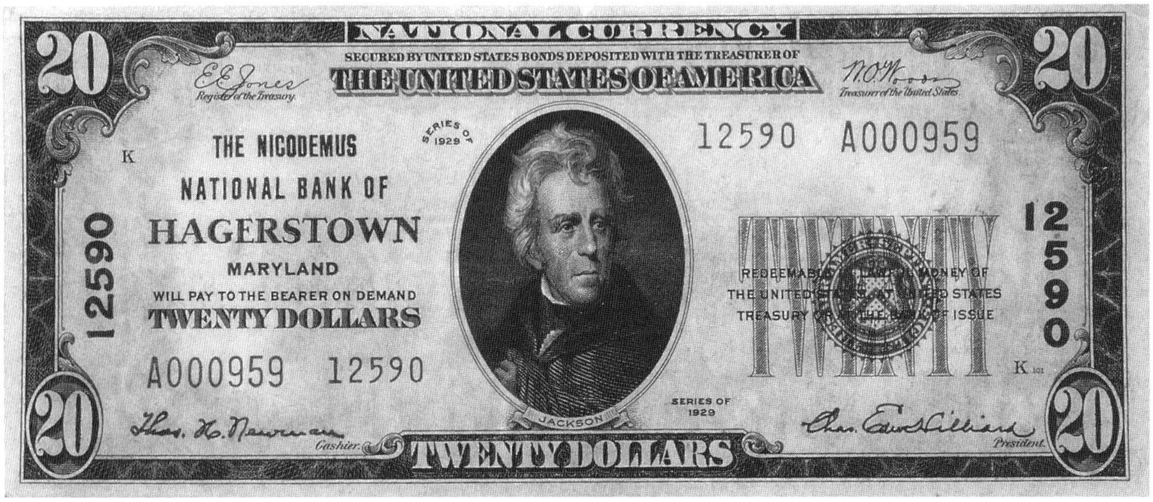

National currency notes of Maryland institutions—one from the National Mechanics Bank of Baltimore in 1905 and another, more like the currency in use today, issued by the Nicodemus National Bank of Hagerstown, series of 1929. (Maryland Historical Society)

in countering populist proposals for "free silver." He, in fact, had sponsored the first resolution the Maryland Bankers Association passed in 1896. "We are unalterably opposed to the Free Coinage of Silver and to every debasement of our currency, in whatsoever form it may be presented," the bankers had declared.

> We firmly and honestly believe that the true interests of our country will be best served by its rigid adherence to the gold standard of value, the continuance of which will not only preserve its financial integrity and the future welfare of its citizens, from the wage-earner to the capitalist, but will insure, through the prompt restoration of confidence, that rapid development of its resources which will eventually place it first among the commercial nations of the earth.[34]

Founding Fathers of the Federalist persuasion must have smiled in satisfaction.

Much to the regret (and the lasting regret) of Baltimoreans, the Federal Reserve organization committee declared Richmond, Virginia, the seat of the central bank for the Fifth Federal Reserve District. But not without protest. The Maryland Bankers Association, Baltimore Clearing House, Baltimore Stock Exchange, and principal trade organizations of the city banded together to stage a mass rally at the Lyric Theater in Baltimore to protest the slight. More than 3,000 people attended; they heard the Republican governor, Phillips Lee Goldsborough, Baltimore's Democratic mayor James Harry Preston, and a full dress parade of prominent bankers, merchants, and manufacturers make impassioned pleas for the committee to change its collective mind. In letters and other written complaints, Baltimoreans offered statistics that compared the rival cities in terms of population, bank deposits, bank clearings, foreign shipments, assessed valuation of property, manufacturing establishments, wage earners, and value of products. The ratios were 5 to 1 in favor of the Queen City of the Patapsco, which, the committee heard, ranked seventh among American cities in total population. Richmond stood thirty-ninth.[35]

Disappointing as was the failure of Baltimore's appeal, legal counsel for the Baltimore group assured the organization committee of the city's determination to give its hearty cooperation to the new law. Eventually the Fed awarded the city a consolation prize in the form of a Baltimore branch of the Richmond bank. Meanwhile, Maryland's banks continued to perform successfully. In 1914 the bank commissioner remarked that, despite the "general depression" that had afflicted the business and financial world "for some time past," Maryland banks had enjoyed a prosperous year. They were in "sound condition," and there was "every reason to believe that they will experience no difficulty in looking after the needs of their customers and meeting every reasonable demand that may be made upon them."[36]

When the bank commissioner law passed, Maryland's state banks, trust companies, and savings institutions claimed total assets of $186.4 million. By the end of 1920, Maryland banks almost had doubled, numbering 193 financial institutions. Their total assets had reached $403.8 million.

World War I and Its Aftermath

The outbreak of the Great War in Europe in 1914 and U.S. involvement three years later did nothing to slow development or impair the prosperity of Maryland's banks and trust companies—war, in fact, encouraged them (see Table 3). Changes in business conditions in 1917, the commissioner reported afterward,

> do not appear to have affected our state banking institutions unfavorably nor retarded their growth and development. Our state system readily met all demands made upon it, and gave hearty co-operation to the Federal Reserve Bank in placing the Liberty Loan Bonds. The call of the Government was met by a patriotic response from all our institutions, which did everything in their power, both by individual effort and by liberal subscriptions, to make the loans a success.

Maryland's savings banks subscribed generously to the bonds and at first sold other securities in a depressed market to pay for them. In 1917 savings banks' resources dropped nearly $1.4 million while those of state banks and trust companies increased by nearly $22 million. By the end of the war the mutual savings institutions which, said the commissioner, "experienced a loss in resources in the previous year, have kept pace with the state banks and trust companies . . . notwithstanding heavy withdrawals due to the purchase of Liberty Bonds by their depositors." At the close of 1918, the savings banks showed an increase of no less than $7.8 million.[37]

From about the turn of the century, through the world war and into the 1920s, Maryland farmers enjoyed general prosperity. Strong markets accounted for the good times, but ready credit did as well, and thus the attention of bankers to farms and farming. After 1927, when it set up an agricultural committee, the Maryland Bankers Association invested particularly in the state's future farmers. The association organized Boys Clubs throughout the state, aiming thereby both to encourage the best practices in farming and animal husbandry and to keep young men on the farm. The committee chair said in 1928,

> Our work has been to encourage and assist the farmer boys in their club work and the farmers' daughters in their domestic science activities and

Table 3. Total Resources of Maryland Banks and Trust Companies, 1911–1949

Year	*Number of Institutions*	*Resources*
1911	114	$103,474,064
1915	141	157,655,892
1920	176	267,648,738
1925	144	425,030,149
1930	134	529,015,467
1931	119	459,911,836
1932[a]	—	—
1933	125	294,002,985
1934	128	298,158,725
1935	126	284,676,851
1936	124	335,234,005
1937	121	324,200,522
1938	118	350,677,008
1939	114	393,474,444
1940	113	427,503,348
1945	106	1,001,276,192
1949	103	935,508,503

[a]No data

Source: Annual Reports of the Bank Commissioner of the State of Maryland.

> endeavor to show them that by scientific methods, up-to-date machinery, well-bred cattle and poultry the farm can be made as attractive and as remunerative as any other calling. Our efforts have been along inspirational lines, to take their eyes out of the furrows and give them a clearer, broader vision.

The boys did not receive the usual inducements of prize money or medals; they attended special week-long sessions at the University of Maryland in College Park, national dairy and poultry shows, and international cattle-judging contests. The association worked through the county extension agents who served on the public payroll. The Boys Clubs enrolled about 2,200 in 1928; nine years later the number had risen fivefold.[38]

The Maryland economy as a whole suffered slight downturns in the early and late twenties, and some banks, as always, retired from business. The bank commissioner's annual reports regularly described "the progress made in the liquidation of institutions in receivership." Reasons for a closing often carried a story of human interest (or of human folly). The Stevensville Bank of Maryland had closed in 1918, for example, when the commissioner discovered that the cashier had deducted $71,000 from depositors' accounts, transferring balances to new sheets and removing the old ones. The cashier was arrested; the bank reopened for business after restoring the missing funds—thanks in large part to the cashier's family (banking in Maryland could still be old-fashioned). The Lafayette Bank in Baltimore, opened in 1920, adopted the "very bad policy of borrowing money in order to make loans," the directors hoping thereby to increase their deposits. When they failed to make arrangements to protect depositors and creditors, the commissioner quickly closed the bank.[39]

The large patterns were of consolidation and profits. Maryland banks performed handsomely in the 1920s. Annual reports of the bank commissioner show that total loans and discounts rose from some $125 million in 1920 to $256 million in 1930 (see Table 4). Undivided profits and surplus accounts revealed impressive outcomes, loans rising from more than $6 million in 1920 to nearly $9 million in 1930 and deposits climbing from about $18 million to $38 million. At the end of 1923, reported the bank commissioner, Maryland's banks had "experienced another year of continued growth and prosperity." When in the spring of 1930 the Maryland Bankers Association convened in Atlantic City, its president, Alexander Armstrong of Hagerstown's First National Bank, pointed out that during the 1920s the combined capital stock of Maryland institutions increased by about $12 million. In that time surplus and undivided profits had doubled, reaching about $33 million.[40]

Meanwhile, liquidations by consolidations and mergers continued, mirroring the merger wave that swept over the nation's corpora-

Table 4. Maryland Banks and Trust Companies: Loans and Discounts, Undivided Profits and Surplus, 1918–1940

Year	*Loans & Discounts*	*Undivided Profits*	*Surplus*
1918	$ 91,645,955	$3,964,000	$15,476,367
1920	125,662,138	6,154,670	18,245,611
1925	208,858,506	5,918,594	28,024,026
1930	256,142,885	8,854,650	38,459,900
1931	204,485,980	5,767,491	34,737,571
1932[a]	—	—	—
1933	103,008,132	2,900,263	19,717,803
1934	64,702,261	2,270,219	25,252,885
1935	64,564,780	4,553,210	14,646,735
1940	123,285,333	6,141,881	16,261,786

[a]No data

Source: Annual Reports of the Bank Commissioner of the State of Maryland.

tions in the 1920s. Larger state banks or trust companies (if never as many as a half dozen in any year of the 1920s) steadily acquired smaller institutions and operated them as branches—branching being permitted under Maryland law. Savings banks, and especially trust companies, appear to have been more active in this process than state-chartered commercial banks. Nevertheless, in the ten years ending December 31, 1929, while the total assets of the state's financial institutions increased from $398 million to $713 million, the number of institutions fell from 184 to 150. Armstrong of the Maryland Bankers Association noticed a "trend of banking consolidation throughout the State."[41]

As an example, Armstrong might have pointed to the Baltimore Trust Company, which recently had opened a striking thirty-four-story office building at Light, Baltimore, and Redwood Streets in downtown Baltimore and boasted of nineteen branch offices throughout the city. Baltimore Trust had formed in 1910 by consolidating two late-nineteenth-century trust companies. In 1925 Baltimore Trust merged with the Atlantic Exchange Bank and Trust Company, which itself had come into being only three years earlier when the National Exchange Bank, dating from 1906, merged with the young Atlantic Trust Company, organized in 1921. Then in January 1929, Baltimore Trust merged again, this time with the National Union Bank of Maryland, an ancient institution the assembly had chartered in 1804 (its president, former governor and incumbent U.S. senator Phillips Lee Goldsborough, assumed the presidency of Baltimore Trust). Half a year later, in November, Baltimore Trust merged with the Century

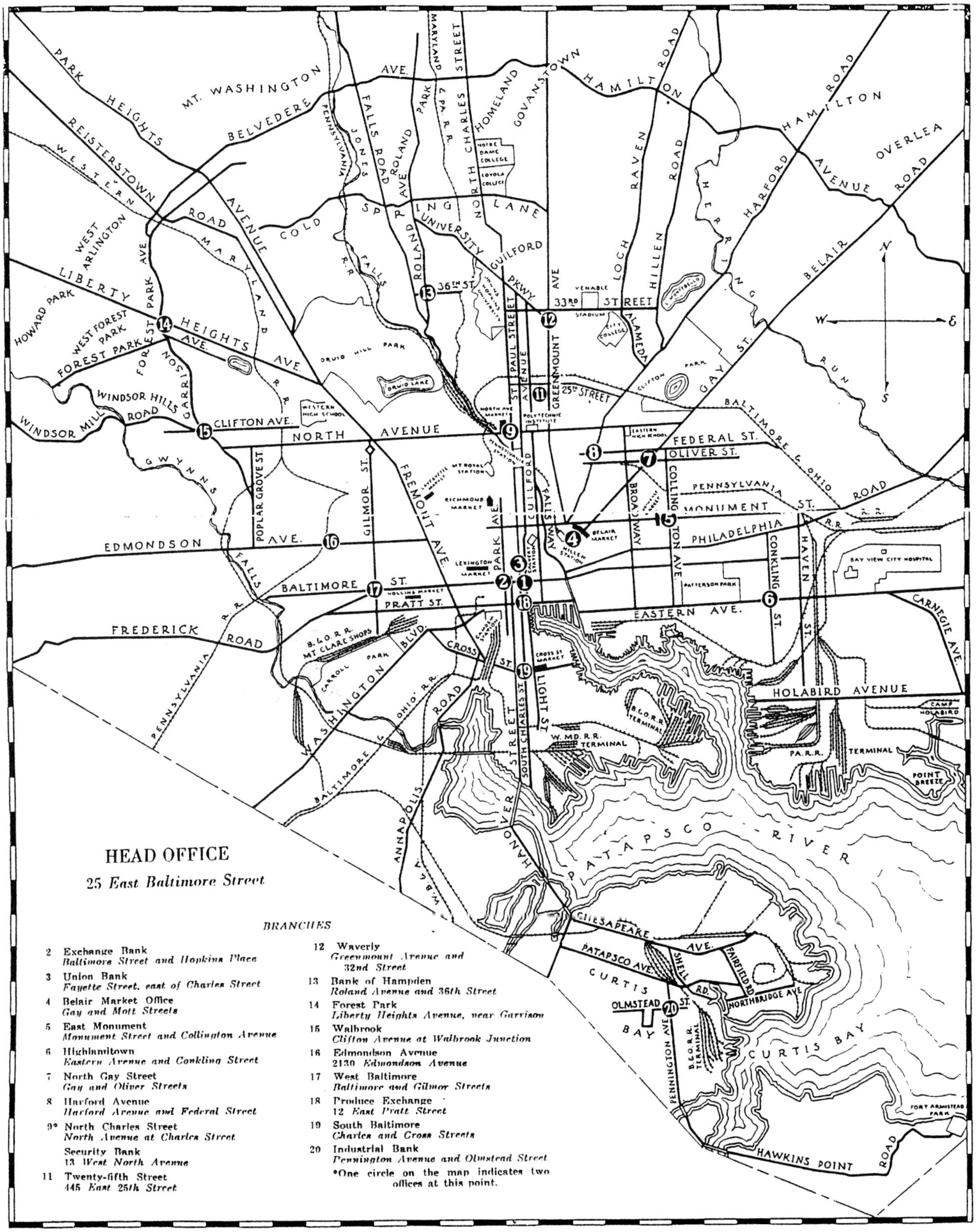

In 1929, not long before the October stock-market crash, Baltimore Trust Company proudly noted how many parts of the city its various branches served. (Courtesy of NationsBank)

Trust Company, giving the company combined assets approaching $100 million.

Describing itself as "the largest financial institution in Maryland in point of resources," Baltimore Trust fittingly made its home in an Aztec Revival/Art Deco structure the public first visited with awe that December. It was the tallest building in the city, Baltimore's "sky-scraper." It was not merely a place of work, however; it was a work of art. Incredibly, it had gone up in eighteen months. Designed by the Baltimore firm of Taylor and Fisher, built of Indiana limestone and six million Baltimore bricks, it featured a five-story ornamented stone base, a fifteen-story brick body, and a tapered, rugged tower whose "rich capping of arches and winged buttress caps, topped by a steep, ribbed roof of copper and gold" gave the top a "soaring quality." The building's lavish exterior included corbeled cornices where stone base met brick tower and, on the Light Street front, carved figures representing those things that had contributed most to Baltimore's progress or marked its history—Medicine, Textiles, Shipping, Manufacturing, the Telegraph, the 1904 Fire, the Star Spangled Banner, Printing, and Railroading, Horseracing, Education, and Banking. Bronze sculpture work embellished the doorways and ground-floor windows. The bank's lobby simply dazzled—its mosaic floors, historic murals, mezzanines, imported marble columns, richly detailed ironwork, heavy chandeliers, and polychrome ceiling ("vaguely reminiscent of Italian ceilings of that type, but extremely modern in detail") beautiful enough to distract from business. The bank itself proudly and rightly declared that the third-mezzanine-floor boardroom "might have been lifted bodily from a Florentine palace."[42]

At their next spring meeting, members of the Maryland Bankers Association listened to assurances that they had "a most enviable record in the banking world," especially considering the frequency of bank failures in the United States during the last three years—more than in any similar period over the last sixty years. Maryland bankers could see in their profits a tribute to their management, the association president said; they had "every right to feel very proud of their record."[43]

The Great Depression

In the heady atmosphere of the 1920s, consumers purchased durable goods "on time" and took out mortgages to buy homes. In the first three quarters of 1929, household liabilities increased by 20 percent in contrast with a rise of only 12 percent in 1928. The stock-market crash of October 1929 led to a catastrophic $3 billion fall in the nation's consumer spending. It also reduced the value of financial paper like stocks, bonds, and life insurance policies—by 4 percent in 1929–30, 6 percent in 1930–31, and 8 percent in 1931–32. Price deflation increased

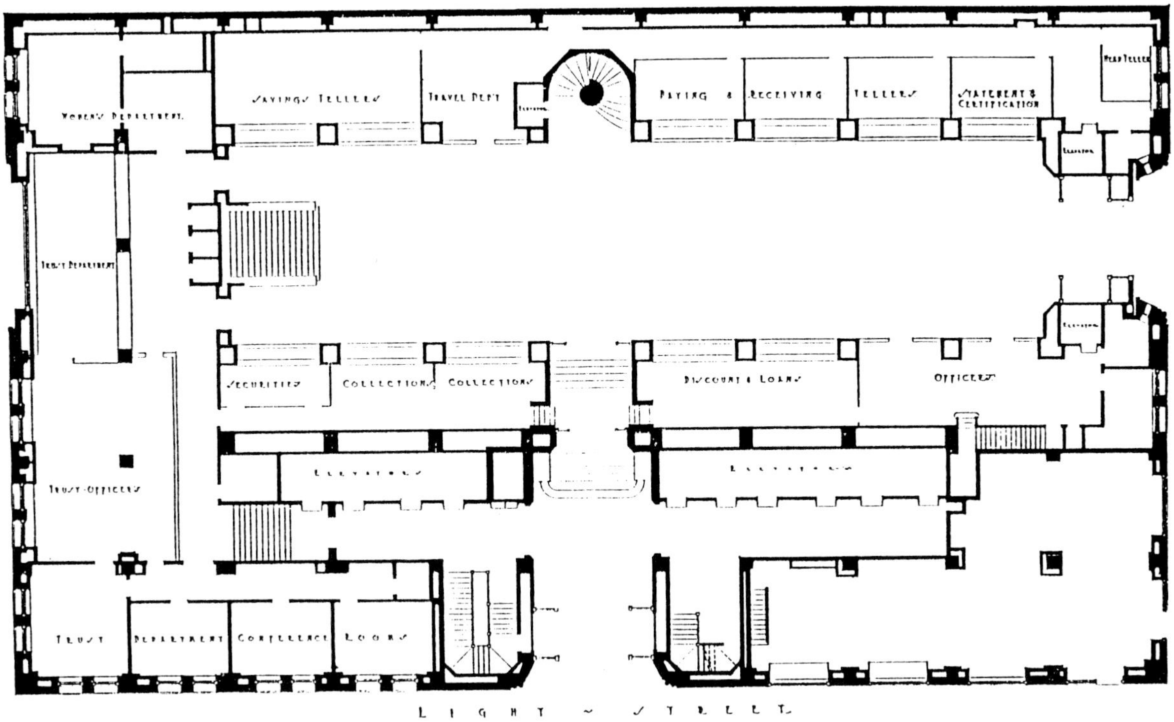

Ground-floor plan (*above*) and completed interior of the ornate Baltimore Trust skyscraper (*below left*); the building's exterior when it opened in 1929 (*below right*). (Courtesy of NationsBank)

the real burden of indebtedness. The sharp decline in aggregate spending, interacting with and reinforced by the continuing decline in residential housing, turned what might have been a relatively mild recession into the beginnings of a major depression. The fundamental cause of the Great Depression, then, was the fall in aggregate demand.

Demand collapsed in Maryland, too, as unemployment climbed throughout the state in 1931, reaching nearly 20 percent in Baltimore. Consolidation Coal Company in the Georges Creek region operated at half strength. By the middle of 1932, just four in ten Maryland plants stood at full production and employment. Declining purchasing power sapped the confidence of businessmen and made them reluctant to borrow. Despite low interest rates, the loans and discounts of Maryland's banks plunged from more than $256 million at the end of 1930 to $204.5 million a year later. By the end of 1933 they were down to $103 million; in the next two years the figure hovered in the neighborhood of $65 million.

Panicky depositors began early on to withdraw their funds from Maryland's banks, and some of them began to fail. One noteworthy victim of the early Depression in Baltimore was the Baltimore Trust Company, whose customers called en masse for their money in the fall of 1931. That year fifteen state banks—all of them country banks—went under in Maryland. Again and again George W. Page, bank commissioner until he resigned in February 1933, reported banks falling into receivership "on account of the abnormal withdrawal of funds from the bank and the shrinkage of assets." Most troubled banks had exhausted their reserves. In the case of the Peoples Bank of Somerset County in Princess Anne, "many irregularities on the part of some of the officers and employees of the bank," including "a vast number of overdrawn accounts," resulted in heavy losses and forced Page to close the bank in November 1931.

Even so, of fifteen banking institutions closed during the year ending February 1, 1932, "no less than seven have effected a reorganization," Page reported at the time, "and are now reopened and again doing business." He was far from pessimistic, perhaps in part because that month President Hoover signed a bill creating the Reconstruction Finance Corporation. Hoping to halt deflation and restore employment, the RFC assisted beleaguered banks and railroads with extensions of credit in the form of tax-free bonds.

In Annapolis, Gov. Albert C. Ritchie, a conservative Democrat who generally hoped to avoid federal intervention, asked Page to review Maryland's banking laws and recommend changes. Just before Franklin D. Roosevelt's inauguration as president in early 1933, the commissioner suggested that the state place a limit on the amount that a commercial bank could lend to any one person, firm, or corporation (earlier one of Bank Examiner Downes's recommendations) and raise the minimum capital requirements for incorporated banks and trust companies. Page pointed out that, of the nation's failed banks in the 1920s, three out of five had been small banks in small towns and banks whose capital ranged between $25,000 and $50,000.

> Changes in our economic and social life such as the advent of the automobile, with the passing of the country store and the practice of paying high interest on deposits made it impossible for small banks in small communities to survive. They had not sufficient capital to support a reasonable amount of fixed expenses, and were dropping off before the depression came.[44]

Maryland, he added, had not been free from trouble in this respect. He recommended raising the minimum capital from $25,000 to $50,000.

Page believed the system basically sound: Between 1921 and 1927, he pointed out, just one Maryland bank had closed, and it shortly reopened, while in the same period 4,509 had closed nationwide. Between 1921 and late 1932, 28 banks closed in Maryland compared to a total of 10,484 throughout the country.[45] Yet in early 1933 pressure on cash reserves was enormous. At the Mercantile Trust Company worries grew that they might not prove sufficient; more and more companies were withdrawing their money. Vice-president Fred G. Boyce asked the head teller, Paul Price, how much cash was on hand. One hundred thousand dollars in the vault, Price replied, and about $75,000 in the teller's cash drawers. "Well, you call up Brinks when you get back to your desk," Boyce ordered. "I want it to be a hundred thousand dollars a trip and I want it to be four trips a day."[46] Boyce could place $4 million in the vault and maintain that reserve level.

Of course, not all banks had the Mercantile's liquidity. Convinced that economic recovery depended on restoring public confidence in the nation's financial system, President Roosevelt in March 1933 issued an executive order suspending banking activities throughout the country and forbidding dealings in gold (the British had complicated recovery by departing from the gold standard in 1931). The presidential order made national a bank holiday that thirty-four individual states, Maryland among them, already had declared. By the president's order, no bank could reopen for business until its condition had been examined either by the treasury secretary (in the case of member banks of the Federal Reserve System, five in Maryland) or by state banking authorities. Banks found to be safe and liquid would reopen immediately (the Merc's head teller later said that his firm "never closed").[47] Those in doubtful condition would await corrective measures. Unsound institutions would be closed and liquidated.

Fifty-two Maryland banks did not immediately reopen. The overwhelming majority of these institutions, forty-three, were country banks, that is, located in small towns. Two others, a trust company and a savings bank, had done business in Annapolis. Only seven were Baltimore banks. Most, thirty-two, were commercial banks; twelve were savings banks; eight were trust companies. Following reorganization, all except two reopened in 1933 or early 1934 (Baltimore Trust liquidated itself voluntarily in 1933 and went into receivership in 1935). A dozen other institutions operated under restrictions and the direct control of the bank commissioner, then John J. Ghingher, pending reorganization or liquidation. One of these, a savings bank, was located in Baltimore. Between 1929 and 1939, when the total number of the state's commercial banks, savings banks, and trust companies averaged 155 per year, a remarkably small number of Maryland banks (33) closed (see Table 5). Only a single bank failed in each of the years 1929, 1930, 1935, and 1937; astonishingly, only two of the failures were Baltimore banks. Additional bank examinations probably worked to the industry's advantage; a major New Deal measure, the Glass-Steagall Banking Act of June 1933, included a provision establishing the Federal Bank Deposit Insurance Corporation (later simply FDIC), which aimed to safeguard the long-range interests of bankers and depositors alike. In time all state banks in Maryland—even some that did not join the Federal Reserve System—became members of the FDIC, thus subjecting themselves to annual examinations by federal authorities.

The records of undivided profits achieved by Maryland's banks and trust companies during the Depression decade underlined Commissioner Page's view of basic soundness. After declines in 1933 and 1934, profits rose nearly threefold between 1934 and 1939. The figures for another component of capital, the surplus account, were also strong.

These successes owed much to the ability of Maryland banks to adjust their investment strategies to fundamental changes affecting the supply of money in the 1930s. In an effort to bring an end to the severe deflation and unemployment, Congress cooperated with an executive policy designed to raise the price level by devaluing the dollar. In early 1934, after passage of the Gold Reserve Act, President Roosevelt issued a proclamation which, by reducing the gold content of the dollar by about 40 percent, raised the price of an ounce of gold from its old official level of $20.67 to $35 an ounce, an increase of nearly 70 percent. The U.S. Treasury stood ready to buy any quantity of gold offered at the fixed price. A heavy increase in the world's physical output of gold followed, and a golden avalanche struck the United States. From the end of 1933 to the end of 1937 the nation's monetary gold stock rose from $4,036 million to $12,760 million, with more than 63 percent of the increase coming from imports—Australian, South

Table 5. Maryland Banks in Final Liquidation and Receivership, 1929–1939

Year	*Commercial Banks* Baltimore	*Commercial Banks* Country	*Trust Companies* Baltimore	*Trust Companies* Country	*Savings Banks* Baltimore	*Savings Banks* Country	*Totals*
1929[a]	0	0	0	1	0	0	1
1930	1	0	0	0	0	0	1
1931	0	11	0	1	0	3	15
1932[b]	[1]	[1]	0	0	[1]	0	[3]
1933	0	1	2	1	0	0	4
1934	0	4	0	1	1	1	7
1935	0	1	0	0	0	0	1
1936	0	0	0	0	0	0	0
1937	0	1	0	0	0	0	1
1938	0	0	0	0	0	0	0
1939	0	0	0	0	0	0	0

[a]Year ending February 1930, for 1929 and so forth for each succeeding year.
[b]No data (estimates)

Source: Annual Reports of the Bank Commissioner of the State of Maryland.

African, Russian, and British Columbian. After the outbreak of European war in the late 1930s, the inflow was supplemented by large imports of foreign capital—both long-term and short—seeking asylum from the conflict.

These massive imports of gold brought exactly the monetary effects that Congress and the administration had expected. Congress had taken pains to discourage the Federal Reserve Board from neutralizing the imports—as it had done between 1929 and 1933—by raising the reserve requirements of member banks (the Banking Act of 1933 not only centralized control of the system in the board of governors; it moved the board from New York to Washington, where it would be more responsive to the policy goals of the administration). The reserves of the banking system swelled, and the golden flood had a decisive effect on the stock of money, which rose at an annual average rate of nearly 11 percent—one of the largest rises on record—between April 1933 and March 1937. Gold policies achieved their monetary objectives but failed to end the Depression. Even at the peak of the business cycle in 1937, unemployment continued to loom large and per capita output was lower than it had been in 1929.

These monetary policies did, however, impact upon the investment portfolios of the nation's banks, including those of Maryland. The rising river of gold created huge quantities of excess bank reserves which, in turn, lowered interest rates and yields on bonds. Money was easy, but business was "very disappointing," observed J. Roland Chaffinch of Denton, president of the Maryland Bankers Association in 1940. "No one seems to know what to buy for an investment, and to lend money in any volume has been impossible."[48]

As the nation geared up its national defense program, the state bank commissioner reported total deposits of $604,668,000 in Maryland's banks—a record high. More than two-thirds of bank deposits consisted of cash and U.S. securities. The commissioner attributed the forms of the increased deposits to "the lack of operations through normal business channels for suitable commercial loans." While expressing concern for the adequacy of capital funds to protect the deposits, he also believed that what mattered was the nature of the assets and their risk factors rather than some such artificial formula as the "ten to one rule"—that is, one dollar of capital for every $10 of deposits. At any rate, he didn't expect this high degree of liquidity to persist. Maryland banks had increased their total loan portfolios by some $16.3 million; they had begun to finance the National Defense program, and its volume of industrial activity made further increases highly likely.[49]

World War II and the Cold War Peace

The Japanese attack on Pearl Harbor focused the "banking business" on the largest concern imaginable—survival of the nation's highest values and way of life. War loans to the government in 1941 were substantial. In February 1942 Maryland banks, "as evidenced by their liquid position and capital structures," remained "in a splendid position to assist our country in the necessary war program," declared banking commissioner John W. Downing. The state's banks had been "among the first institutions to qualify as agents for the U.S. Treasury Department in the sale of Defense Savings Bonds," he reported, "and at the present time every bank, trust company and mutual savings institution is actively engaged in this work, giving willingly of their time and personnel." Marylanders were using their excess earnings as well as their present deposits to buy Defense Savings Bonds.[50]

Leading bankers had predicted no further rise in total deposits during the war, but rise they did—reaching a succession of all-time peaks during the war years. At the end of 1943 they exceeded $900 million, in 1945 $938 million. Treasury borrowing accounted for this "remarkable rise," Downing noted in 1944; he credited Maryland banks for having faced heavy responsibilities in helping to finance the war, handling Ration Banking, and collecting federal withholding taxes. Despite these "extra burdens," the state's banks showed reasonable earnings. By the beginning of 1945, the commissioner expressed diminishing concern with the ratio of capital to total deposits; fully 84 percent of deposits in Maryland institutions were invested in assets based on government credit. Between Pearl Harbor and early 1945 total deposits in Maryland's banking institutions increased by 76 percent—from $503.7 million to $1.1 billion.[51]

Even before V-E day, bankers began to turn their attention to the problems that peace would bring—the financing of private enterprises, large and small, and governmental refunding of the federal debt. The cessation of hostilities in the late summer of 1945 brought the country face to face with the problems of peacetime reconversion. Maryland's banks considered themselves quite well situated. Industry in Maryland "long since" had started in the direction of retrofitting; it was "reasonably well abreast of the Country generally in this respect," Downing believed. There was evidence for—bankers hoped for—a revival of private borrowing. Maryland nonetheless experienced in 1946 "a most vicious spiral of real estate prices" in the wake of wartime restrictions and accumulated savings among those who could enter the new-home market. Unable to check this cycle of rising prices, bankers did worry about establishing "sound loaning policies" in the superheated environment. All in all, the tremendous growth in bank resources during the war, a change in their quality of assets, and an increase in liquidity encouraged the view that Maryland banks were then "better equipped than at any time in the past to perform their proper banking functions, namely, safeguarding of their depositor's funds and accommodation of the Country's credit needs."[52]

By early 1947 private loans were once again rising in demand. Expansion was then under way in commercial loans, mortgage loans, and loans to finance the purchase of consumer goods. Total demand and time deposits of individuals and corporations in Maryland's banks had risen by nearly 9 percent between 1945 and 1946—indicative of the progress being made toward normal peacetime operations. Of the nearly 12 percent increase in the total loans of the state's banks, particular interest attached to the growing volume of loans to World War II veterans. The state's Banking Department set about to eliminate the old Reconstruction Finance Corporation's investment in certain Maryland state banks and trust companies—replacing, if successful, federal funds with local stock ownership. Revising and strengthening capital, said Commissioner Downing, had been the state's policy. Maryland's banking institutions had shown an increase of more than $8 million in capital during the year—a substantial part of the increase being derived from retained net profits. Many banks, however, were undertaking recapitalization programs, raising additional funds from the sale of stock in order to be "better capitalized for peacetime operations." The loan portfolios of Maryland's banks and trust companies continued to show marked increases in 1947—rising by $37 million, or nearly 18 percent. Downing was confident that the bankers

Customers patiently wait for service at the Nicodemus National Bank in Hagerstown, 1949 (*above*); the impressive door to the bank's main vault (*below*). (Courtesy of First National Bank of Maryland)

were "alert to the dangers to themselves and to borrowers of an over-expansion of credit."[53]

Whether the nation's banks or federal fiscal and monetary policies were to blame, the annual rate of increase in the wholesale price level between June 1946 and August 1948 rose to 16.4 percent—more than five times that registered during the period of wartime price controls. Inflation at such a rate was bound to have political consequences, and from the end of 1948 to at least the early 1960s, the politically powerful fear of inflation in large measure shaped public policies that contributed to a long period of stable prices. Government policies may have helped to stabilize price levels, but they could not prevent downturns in the business cycle. The fifteen years after the end of World War II were pockmarked by a series of recessions, one in 1949, followed by three others during the Eisenhower administration—in 1953–54 (after the Korean War), in 1957–58, and in 1960–61.

Recession had few serious effects on the loan portfolios of Maryland's commercial banks, however. The Citizens Bank of Riverdale in Prince George's County, which had opened in 1928, offered a vivid example of how many Maryland banks grew in the postwar years. In early 1952, with population in the county booming, it changed its name to the Citizens Bank of Maryland, Riverdale, merged with the National Bank of Maryland, Silver Spring, in 1964, and, four years later, after combining with a Riverdale trust company, became one the state's largest banks. Along with Suburban Trust Company in Hyattsville, which formed of a number of smaller Montgomery

Behind the teller's cage at the Hancock Bank in 1952. Mary Ellen Bohrer (left), teller, and Dan Heller (right), assistant cashier, doubtless knew every customer personally. (Courtesy of First National Bank of Maryland)

County and Prince George's banks in 1951, Citizens Bank illustrated the financial gains to be made in suburban Washington, D.C., housing, commercial development, and transportation.

Buoyed by heavy federal presence and Cold War spending in the state, and driven by the credit needs of businesses to build up inventories or plant capacity and by consumers to finance purchases of goods or real estate, the loan totals of Maryland's state banks and trust companies rose year after year, from approximately $200 million at the end of 1945 to more than $4 billion in 1977. The commercial banks enjoyed an increasing share of Maryland's consumer credit industry. In 1956, they held $11.7 billion of the total of $42.3 billion in total consumer credit. By 1969 the share of the commercial banks in a total of $102.1 billion had risen to $32.7 billion. The biggest single item financed was the automobile, the financing of which constituted a third of the total in almost any given year.[54]

The capital accounts of Maryland banks, fed by retained earnings and by sales of stock or stock notes, exhibited similar increases during these years, keeping pace with the security requirements of rising deposits. Somewhat surprisingly, certainly at first glance, were the declines registered in the number of state banks and trust companies. Numbering 97 at the end of 1952, those institutions fell to 73 by June 1973. One subtraction reflected a unanimous decision shareholders of both firms made in 1953: to merge the venerable Safe Deposit and Trust Company with the nearly as old Mercantile Trust and Deposit

Table 6. Financial Condition of Maryland State-Chartered Banks, Trust Companies, and Mutual Savings Institutions, 1949–1989

Year[a]	*Total Loans*	*Total Assets, Liabilities*	*Total Deposits*	*Surplus, Undivided Profits, Reserves*
1949	$306,967,505	$1,383,344,017	$1,257,323,998	$98,195,797
1954	558,342,448	1,710,094,877	1,559,159,626	111,642,413
1959	987,742,353	2,135,295,328	1,931,190,011	141,789,637
1964	1,443,765,231	2,658,006,011	2,402,996,845	176,898,138
1969	2,382,547,654	3,839,232,716	3,360,171,433	265,810,020
1974	3,963,120,400	6,158,207,600	5,345,975,800	390,841,700
1980	6,903,053,000	10,712,979,000	9,247,195,000	712,889,000
1984	8,138,224,000	13,381,921,000	10,856,188,000	893,993,000
1989	17,398,409,000	26,008,850,000	20,730,713,000	—[b]

[a]As of December 31.

[b]No data.

Source: Annual Reports of the State Bank Commissioner.

Employees hard at work in the Safe Deposit and Trust Company office about the time the firm merged with Mercantile Trust and Deposit. (Courtesy of Mercantile–Safe Deposit & Trust Company)

Company, thus forming the prestigious Mercantile–Safe Deposit & Trust Company. Meanwhile, the number of branch outlets rose almost continuously—to 318 in the summer of 1973. In-state branching responded to what William H. Kirkwood Jr., bank commissioner in 1954, referred to as "the continued decentralization of the City through the establishment of the large urban shopping centers."[55] Suburbanization required banks to cater to the service needs of people spread over distances—and quite far from the bank's principal offices.

Maryland bankers, along with most citizens of the state, black and white alike, watched with mounting concern as the quest for racial justice in the country turned violent in the late 1960s. Marylanders experienced some of the confrontation and destruction first-hand—in Cambridge in 1963, 1964, and 1967, and in Baltimore after the assassination of Dr. Martin Luther King in April 1968. As members of the community, often serving voluntarily to further charitable and like causes, bankers could support the principles of equal opportunity, equal justice, and the fulfillment of personal hopes; as professionals entrusted with other people's money, they had no choice but to call for the protection of lives and property and the safeguarding of a bank's resources. They faced decisions—particularly in considering loan applications—in which a customer's hopes and the institution's responsibility to depositors could force difficult choices. Bankers could not be revolutionaries, but bankers also tended to be persons of education and community spirit. Since the 1890s, at least, a growing

The role of women bank employees expanded greatly during World War II. Here, probably in the postwar period, a secretary types while listening to taped dictation. (Courtesy of Mercantile–Safe Deposit & Trust Company)

number of them had been women, who typically worked as clerks but even before the changes brought on by two world wars did sometimes attain higher position. Apparently one of the first woman to break into the industry had been Fanny Wilen, who in 1884 joined the staff at the old Safe Deposit and Trust Company. Her male colleagues quickly accepted her; in fact, just before her first Christmas with the firm they sent her a long (actually typed) mock-poetic message praising her, among other things, because in her presence "Our young men have been converted from braying Donkeys."[56] (Fanny later married another young employee, who himself went on to become a director of the bank.)

In the early 1970s Maryland bankers enlisted in a number of programs to avoid thwarted hopes and encourage wider participation in the industry. Maryland National Bank (formed in 1961 out of Baltimore National and soon strengthened itself by acquiring or merging with banks in Easton, Montgomery County, and Hagerstown) had been the first bank in the state to integrate its staff. Maryland National eventually created a Community Development Group that aimed "to provide creative and flexible mortgage financing solutions, especially for low- and moderate-income first-time home buyers."[57] Baltimore commercial banks underwrote the city's Council for Equal Business Opportunity, an attempt dating from 1967, to identify and capitalize promising African-American entrepreneurs. Baltimore's commercial and savings banks in 1975 committed $1 million to a loan program designed to prevent the decline of the neighborhood surrounding Patterson Park in East Baltimore.

Maryland National Bank's lobby (in the old Baltimore Trust building) as it appeared in about 1970. (Courtesy of NationsBank)

With increasing success, Maryland bankers opened their doors to African-American (and female) recruits for management positions. The Maryland Bankers Association encouraged the wide distribution and viewing of an American Bankers Association film devoted to the problem of opportunity and its achievement regardless of race. In the spring of 1977 the *Maryland Banking Quarterly* further explored that issue; a transcribed exchange with Robert L. Douglass, chair of the General Assembly's Black Caucus, purposefully sought to deepen awareness of the special needs of minorities—both in obtaining financial services and in finding a way to enter the industry (Harbor Bank of Maryland, the state's first African American–owned banking firm, opened in the fall of 1982). The association later expanded these efforts, sponsoring lectures, seminars, and classes for young people of all backgrounds, striving to make them aware of the opportunities banking offered them.[58]

The Challenges of the Late Twentieth Century

By the late 1970s bankers, along with other professional Americans, could feel the ground shifting beneath them. For one thing—as the rise in consumer credit already had demonstrated—the children and grandchildren of those Americans who had endured the Great Depression seemed far less fearful of personal debt; Americans as never before were willing to live on credit. Second, the pace of technological innovation in the industry perhaps never had been faster, or its social-economic implications heavier. Federal investment in research and development—especially military and space-related—produced a revolution in computer and communications technology. Computers led to vastly more efficient recordkeeping in the banking industry; computer networking and microchip electronics generally led to the appearance, and triumph, of automated teller machines that permitted customer service at every hour of every day, at countless "convenient locations."

Finally, and with palpable effect, the growing sophistication of worldwide telecommunications increasingly placed banking in a global web of financial markets. Suddenly competitive market forces were international as well as national. Capital now could move noiselessly and instantaneously in response to market opportunities and interest rates practically everywhere in the world. International means of movement meant that, potentially, there was more capital to be had, and increased supplies gave rise to new and expanded credit outlets. Banks thus became part of a much larger financial-services industry whose advertising campaigns routinely tried to persuade consumers to borrow and buy goods on credit. Maryland's commercial banks, like those nationwide, found themselves competing with such traditional loan providers as credit unions, thrifts or savings and loan institutions, investment banks, insurance companies, and even a firm that called itself "The Money Store."

Banks found themselves hobbled by antiquated regulations that severely limited the scope—financial and geographical—of their operations, and if they were to compete in the new market they would have to break those bonds. In seeking fewer restrictions and more freedom to maneuver, they reflected increasing public impatience with government regulations. Such "red tape" too often added to production costs and made it difficult for American industry to compete with foreign competitors. In the late 1970s the Carter administration sponsored deregulation of the airline and trucking industries; pressure to do more increased during the presidencies of Ronald Reagan and George Bush.

In Maryland the state's bank commissioners and the Maryland Bankers Association played leading roles in efforts to unfetter banks and promote flexibility. Since 1958 the association's salaried executive manager—first William B. Elliott—had traveled to Annapolis when necessary during legislative sessions (the group occupied space in the Maryland National Bank Building); in order to keep abreast of accelerating changes in the late 1970s, Elliott's successor, William K. Weaver, laid plans to move the association's office to Annapolis. In 1981 the bank commissioner, Joseph R. Crouse, undertook a program to reevaluate those bank-related statutes and regulations that had become "archaic and, in this highly competitive era of rapidly changing banking needs, an impediment to the provision of banking services." The commissioner and bankers who reported to him suggested reforms that included subjecting commercial banks to a single inspection per year (state and FDIC examiners might conduct joint examinations). Maryland that year liberalized restrictions on the borrowing limits of state banks and increased the lending limits of state banks to individual borrowers.[59]

In other respects, state policy displeased commercial bankers. Since the 1960s, following the example of the Bank of America's Bank Americard, banks in the state had issued credit cards to customers who enlisted in a credit-purchase and monthly payment plan. Maryland "usury" laws limited the interest rates banks could charge for this service. As a result, several important Maryland banks—Maryland National Bank, First National Bank of Maryland, Equitable Bank, N.A. (controlled by Cleveland interests after April 1981), and Suburban Trust among them—moved their credit-card operations to neighboring and corporate-friendly Delaware.[60]

Maryland bankers naturally wanted their home state to be every bit as hospitable to the industry as Delaware; they also sought release from restrictions on where and with whom they could do business. Historically, banks (whether state or national in terms of charter) operated within their states' boundaries. In the deregulatory climate of the mid-1980s, with multistate and multibank holding companies forming, bank mergers proceeding at a quick pace, banks buying up savings and loan associations (which could cross state lines), and electronic fund-transfer systems growing in importance, "the once clear and absolute regulatory prohibition against interstate banking" began to blur noticeably. Some industry observers believed that de facto interstate banking already had arrived. Beginning with states eager to attract outside investment (Alaska, Maine, South Dakota), the movement to lower bars against "foreign" banks (and to branch abroad) steadily gained ground—generally on a reciprocal basis. The New England states adopted regional reciprocal legislation in the early 1980s; the southeastern states, Maryland not included, did so as well. "On both the federal and state levels," Commissioner Crouse declared in 1982, "the tide of deregulation relentlessly rises." The federal agency

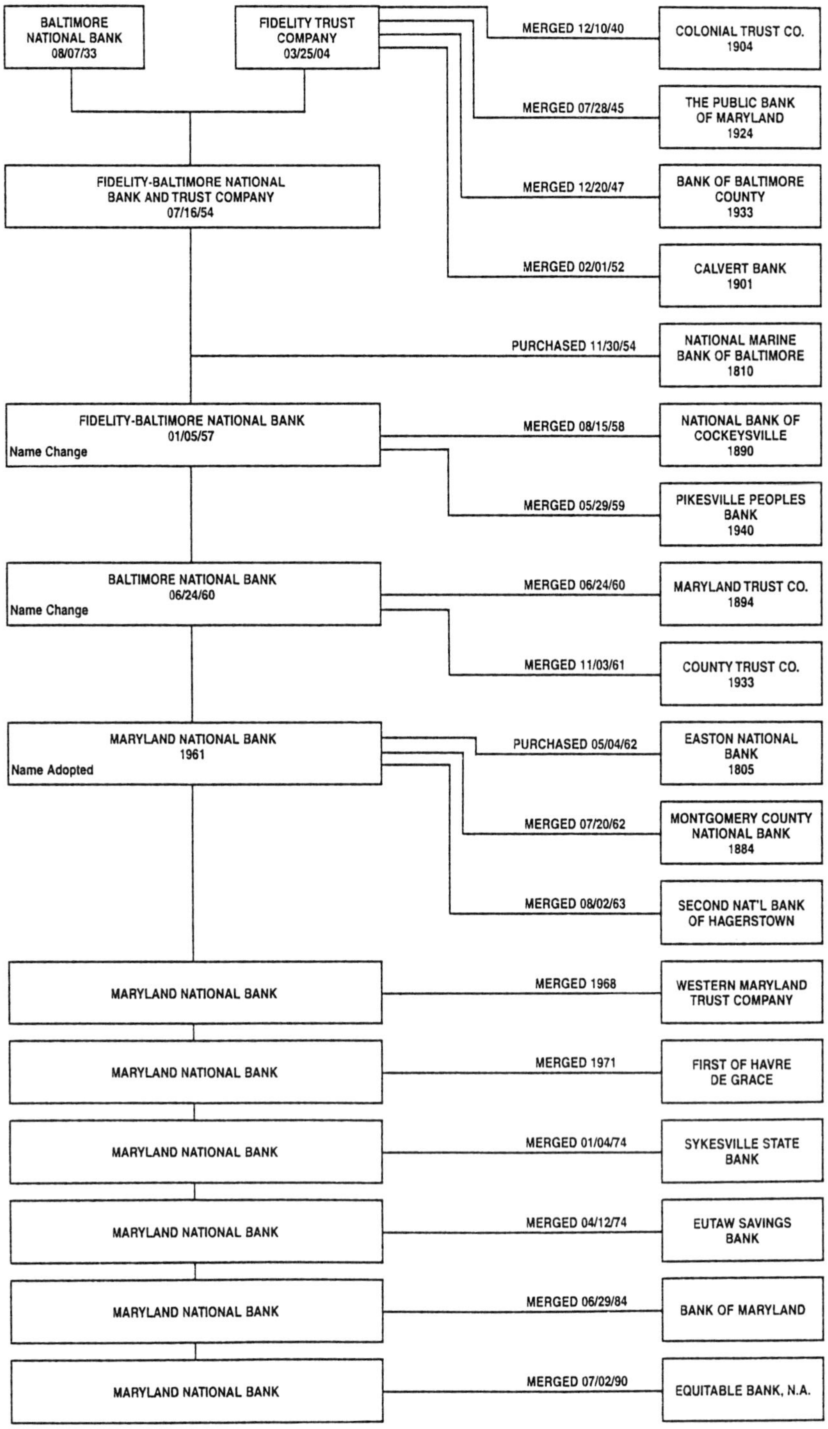

Maryland National Bank's "family tree," from the chartering of Fidelity Trust Company in 1904 to the merging of MNB with Equitable Bank in 1990. (Courtesy of NationsBank; redrawing by Maryland Bankers Association)

heads comprising the Depository Institutions Deregulation Committee continued efforts the following year to reduce or eliminate interest-rate, balance, and maturity restrictions on deposits.[61]

Maryland's bankers went to the legislature in 1982–83 seeking comprehensive reform that would stimulate commercial banking. Working in cooperation with sympathetic senators—Jerome F. Connell Sr. of Glen Burnie, finance committee chair Melvin A. Steinberg of Baltimore, and Laurence Levitan of Potomac—the bankers introduced a measure known in the legislative process as Senate Bill 591. Passed with broad support, the act relaxed interest-rate restrictions on credit-granting institutions, permitted annual fees on credit-card users, and expanded access to loans secured by second mortgages. The new law also allowed out-of-state bank holding companies to acquire stock in newly chartered Maryland banks, thus providing services to customers outside the state while limiting efforts to attract customers away from existing Maryland institutions. H. Grant Hathaway, Maryland Bankers Association president, described the law as "a significant development in the legislative philosophy in our state. The Legislature has basically reached the conclusion that the best protection the consumer can have is open market competition as opposed to arbitrary regulatory restrictions."[62]

The themes of electronic automation, deregulation, and mergers amplified and supported one another. In the summer of 1983 the number of state-chartered depository institutions numbered four fewer (96) than a year before, and the state's new bank commissioner, Margie Muller (formerly of Maryland National Bank and the Union Trust Company), viewed the trend as national in scope and on the increase. Deregulation, she said, "generates efforts to expand markets and to achieve economies of size." Charles W. Cole Jr., president of First National Bank of Maryland (an Irish bank holding company recently had bought a controlling interest in the bank), spoke out in favor of full interstate banking—with no limitations—when he addressed a gubernatorial committee on the subject in the fall of 1984. "The commercial banking industry is in a period of change unlike any in its history," Cole said, "and few precedents have been set to effectively guide it in adapting to change." How Maryland responded to those changes in the industry, he emphasized, would necessarily affect not only the growth and strength of the state's banks, but "the capacity of the state itself to ensure its future growth." By the middle of the following year, after a legislative session in which the assembly took such advice and effectively removed all restrictions on "foreign" acquisitions, the number of Maryland banks had dropped to 66.[63]

Out-of-state purchases continued; in early 1986 Sovran Financial Corporation of Norfolk purchased Suburban Trust. Chase Manhattan of New York (through a Baltimore affiliate) and Mellon Bank of Pitts-

The new competition from "money center" or large New York City banks, as portrayed in the pages of the *Baltimore Sun,* April 3, 1985. (Courtesy of Thomas Flannery)

"Mind If I Squeeze in Here?"

burgh (operating in Bethesda with a Maryland charter) purchased a total of four troubled savings and loans—whose pattern of failures nationwide caused a scandal at the time. The merger movement extended to rural banks. In the fall of 1986 the Sudlersville Bank of Maryland joined the Chestertown Bank of Maryland; the Bank of Damascus became part of Citizens Bank and Trust Company in early 1987.[64]

In a merger that attracted great attention, Commissioner Muller on the last day of 1985 approved a bid by the Bank of Virginia Company, Richmond, to purchase Union Trust Bancorp of Baltimore. Thus the old Union Trust Company—among whose ancestors was the Bank of Baltimore that had formed in 1795—became Signet Bank/Maryland. This momentous change in the Maryland banking community roughly coincided with completion of the Signet Tower, begun as the Union Trust Tower—a twenty-four-story pink granite structure that featured tiered upper floors and tinted windows in the contemporary office-building mode. Designed by the Baltimore architectural firm RTKL, the tower went up at the northeast corner of Baltimore and St. Paul Streets—on the site of the original and every succeeding Union Trust Company headquarters. Although artistically not as remarkable (or as high) as the old Baltimore Trust skyscraper down the street (then the home of Maryland National) or designs for the adjacent Merritt Tower (which finally topped Maryland National by a few feet), the Signet Tower was important for representing the com-

The Signet Tower in the mid-1990s. (Courtesy of Signet Bank)

mitment of commercial bankers to downtown Baltimore. Mercantile–Safe Deposit & Trust had built a tall structure as part of the earlier Charles Center redevelopment plan; Union Trust had invested heavily in Harborplace, which had opened in the summer of 1980. But Union Trust could claim faith with a high profile: groundbreaking ceremonies for the new tower in 1984 had taken place the same day as the infamous predawn departure of the Baltimore Colts.[65]

Maryland bankers joked among themselves about the distinction between being the state's *bank of choice* and the *largest bank* in the state. They may thus have whistled in the dark, because Maryland institutions did little buying of other state's banks (though they did branch out in the mid-'80s, Maryland National and Equitable to Washington, D.C. and Northern Virginia; First National to those places but also to Florida and Pennsylvania).[66] On the other hand, in 1993 Sovran—by then NationsBank, the largest bank in the southeastern United States—bought Maryland National. If Baltimoreans were sorry to see MNB disappear beneath the "rising tide" of deregulation and mergers, they were pleased when the new owners of the old Baltimore Trust Building freshly painted and gilded its venerable roof.

In these uncertain circumstances, Maryland bankers largely succeeded in holding onto their share of the market and in providing their customers with the services they needed in a free economy. Commissioner Crouse earlier had referred correctly to a "coalescence of banking and investment industries" as Maryland financial institutions diversified their services and otherwise responded to the new environment. Maryland's financial industry, he said, "is part of a national market and is being swept into the international stream of financial services." The relaxation of interest-rate regulation on both sides of the balance sheet—besides rewarding the industry with a strong income mix—brought about a proliferation of deposit and loan packages, giving consumers, as Muller wrote in 1984, "a sometimes bewildering array of offerings and challenging them to 'shop' for financial services for the first time." To permit better-informed choices, depository institutions for their part now had to disclose rates, fees, and conditions more fully than ever before and publish their funds-availability policies for deposited checks.[67]

Deregulation often inspired the "rising tide" figure of speech, and Maryland bankers perhaps thought of another watery metaphor—sailing in poorly charted seas—as they dealt with legislators. John B. Bowers Jr., since 1986 chief executive officer of the association, encouraged members to work hard at both the state and federal levels. The association's committee on government relations annually reviewed thousands of state bills, targeting some of them for "close review" and lobbying either for their defeat or passage. The association won on some issues and lost on others. One significant victory in Washington was enactment of the Riegle-Neal Interstate Banking and Branching Efficiency Act, which Pres. Bill Clinton signed in September 1994. This milestone banking law permitted an adequately capitalized, adequately managed bank holding company freely to acquire banks in other states. Largely preempting state interstate banking statutes, Riegle-Neal (fully effective in June 1997) authorized interstate branching with minimal restrictions. The states were to decide at what level they wished to participate.[68]

Maryland bankers, true to the entrepreneurial spirit of Enoch Pratt and Henry Walters, obtained an enabling act in the spring of 1995. In the future, out-of-state banks or banking institutions could establish a branch in Maryland by opening one "de novo," purchasing an existing branch from a bank or an insured depository institution, or either purchasing or merging with a Maryland bank. "We wanted to provide Maryland banks with maximum flexibility and freedom of choice on a reciprocal basis," Bowers explained. "By opting early, Maryland banks can begin to expand their franchises to serve their natural markets, irrespective of geopolitical boundaries, a full two years before the federal law takes effect. This gives our institutions a valuable competitive advantage over banks based in states waiting until 1997 to allow interstate branching."[69]

"There is something special about being a banker," Charles W. Hoff III of Frederick declared at the 1995 annual meeting of the Maryland Bankers Association. Hoff then served as president, an office his father had held some thirty years before. "We contribute our time, our talent, and our dollars in service to our communities," not only because it's good business, said Hoff, but because "inherently the business of bankers is to serve" their customers and communities. He knew of few industries in which "this trait is as inbred."[70]

The large pattern of commercial banking in Maryland supported his view. One of the truly diversified states in the nation in terms of industry, commerce, and social and cultural traditions, Maryland for almost all its history had benefited from wide investments and an ability, to paraphrase the designer/developer James W. Rouse, to employ capital to "haul dreams into focus."[71]

If they remained watchful of trends and adaptive as they always had been, and if they found new ways to balance growth with environmental needs and limits, Maryland bankers and their customers could expect continued good fortune.

Acknowledgments

The authors acknowledge large debts to Professor John Higham of Johns Hopkins University, who recommended that we be asked to undertake this study, and to Robert J. Brugger, chair, publications committee, Maryland Historical Society. William T. Murray III, E. Mason Hendrickson, and John B. Bowers Jr. first brought together the idea of publishing a book on money and banking in Maryland to help mark the centennial of the Maryland Bankers Association. We also wish to express our warm appreciation for the helpful contributions—not to mention hospitality in Annapolis!—of John B. Bowers Jr., T. Wayne Kirwan, and Kenneth R. Smith, Maryland Bankers Association. We also are indebted to Armand Shank and Denwood Kelly for useful suggestions and for the loan of some older books that would have been unavailable elsewhere. For help with illustrative materials and research details, warm thanks also go to John Riggin, NationsBank; Suzanne Wolff, Mercantile–Safe Deposit & Trust Company; Celine M. Toth, Signet Bank/Maryland; E. Mason Hendrickson, formerly of First National Bank of Maryland; William J. Burke, Taylor Bank; Don Corbett, First National Bank; and Don Harsh, Hagerstown Trust Company. Last, but not least, we would like to express our appreciation to the staffs of the Maryland Historical Society, the Johns Hopkins University Library, the Hall of Records in Annapolis and the Enoch Pratt Free Library in Baltimore for the kinds of aids with which scholars are everywhere familiar—and without which research and writing would not be possible.

Notes

1. Principal sources in the story of Maryland banking include Alfred C. Bryan, *History of State Banking in Maryland* (Baltimore: Johns Hopkins Press, 1899), which covers the 1790s to 1864 and remains indispensable. Two primary sources provide rich detail for the later period: the annual reports of the Maryland bank commissioner and the proceedings of the annual conventions of the Maryland Bankers Association. We have supplemented those leading sources with our own work: See Stuart Bruchey, *Robert Oliver: Merchant of Baltimore, 1783–1819* (Baltimore: Johns Hopkins Press, 1955); Eleanor Bruchey, *The Business Elite of Baltimore, 1880–1914* (New York: Arno Press, 1976); and Eleanor Bruchey, "The Industrialization of Maryland, 1860–1914," in *Maryland: A History, 1632–1974,* ed. Richard Walsh and William Lloyd Fox (Baltimore: Maryland Historical Society, 1974). For background see also Robert J. Brugger, *Maryland: A Middle Temperament, 1634–1980* (Baltimore: Johns Hopkins University Press, 1988); Aubrey C. Land, *Colonial Maryland: A History* (Millwood, N.Y.: KTO Press, 1981); Gloria L. Main, *Tobacco Colony: Life in Early Maryland* (Princeton: Princeton University Press, 1982); Katherine L. Behrens, *Paper Money in Maryland, 1727–1789,* Johns Hopkins University Studies in Historical and Political Science, ser. 41 (Baltimore: Johns Hopkins Press, 1923); Clarence P. Gould, *Money and Transportation in Maryland, 1720–1765,* Johns Hopkins University Studies in Historical and Political Science, ser. 33 (Baltimore: Johns Hopkins Press, 1915); Harvey Eugene Meeks, comp., *Maryland Bank Register, 1790–1964, Updated to December 31, 1979: A Record of the Chartered Banks of Maryland during the Past One Hundred and Ninety Years* (Baltimore: Bank Commissioner, State of Maryland, 1982), copy available at Maryland Historical Society; John J. McCusker and Russel R. Menard, *The Economy of British America* (Chapel Hill: University of North Carolina Press and the Institute of Early American History and Culture, 1985); Elliot Buse, *150 Years of Banking on the Eastern Shore: A History of the Easton Bank of Maryland* (Baltimore: Schneidereith and Sons, 1955), and Suzanne Wolff, *Mercantile-Safe Deposit & Trust Company: A Brief History* (Baltimore: Mercantile-Safe Deposit & Trust, n.d.). On national and international economic developments see W. Elliot Brownlee, *Dynamics of Ascent: A History of the American Economy,* 2nd ed. (New York: Knopf, 1979); Stuart Bruchey, *Enterprise: The Dynamic Economy of a Free People* (Cambridge: Harvard University Press, 1990); Sidney Ratner, James H. Soltow, and Richard Sylla, *The Evolution of the American Economy* (New York: Basic Books, 1979); and Richard H. Sylla, "Small Business Banking in the United States, 1780–1920," in *Small Business in American Life,* ed. Stuart Bruchey (New York: Columbia University Press, 1980).

2. Quoted in Richard A. Lester, "Currency Issues to Overcome Depression in Pennsylvania, 1723–1729," *Journal of Political Economy* 46 (1928): 325.

3. See E. James Ferguson, *The Power of the Purse* (Chapel Hill: University of North Carolina Press, 1961).

4. Ibid., 8, and Behrens, *Paper Money in Maryland.* See also Richard A. Lester, *Monetary Experiments: Early American and Recent Scandanavian* (New York: Augustus Kelley, 1939), 27–28, 31, and Curtis P. Nettels, *The Money Supply of the Colonies before 1720* (Madison: University of Wisconsin Press, 1934), 180.

5. See Carville Earle and Ronald Hoffman, "Staple Crops and Urban Development in the Eighteenth-Century South," *Perspectives in American History* 10 (1976), and Alan Karras, *Sojourners in the Sun: Scottish Migrants in Jamaica and the Chesapeake, 1740–1800* (Ithaca, N.Y.: Cornell University Press, 1992).

6. But see Edward C. Papenfuse, *In Pursuit of Profit: The Annapolis Merchants in the Era of the American Revolution, 1763–1805* (Baltimore: Johns Hopkins University Press, 1975).

7. Horatio Sharpe, quoted in Richard Pares, *Yankees and Creoles* (Cambridge, Mass.: Harvard University Press, 1956), 41.

8. Eddis, quoted in Gould, *Money and Transportation in Maryland,* 238–39.

9. Washington, quoted in *Maryland Journal,* December 23, 1783.

10. Greene, quoted in Edward Spencer, ed., *An Account of the Municipal Celebration of the 150th Anniversary of the Settlement of Baltimore . . . With a Sketch of the History . . . of the City* (Baltimore, 1881), 12.

11. *Maryland Journal,* August 2, 1785.

12. John D. Schoepf, *Travels in the Confederation,* transl. and ed. A. J. Morison, 2 vols. (Philadelphia, 1911), 1:366; Isaac Weld, *Travels through the States of North America . . . During the Years 1795, 1796, and 1797,* 2 vols. (London, 1800), 1:4, 5.

13. "Report on a National Bank," December 13, 1790, *Papers of Alexander Hamilton,* ed. Harold C. Syrett, 26 vols. (New York: Columbia University Press, 1961–73), 7:325, 331.

14. Minutes, board of the Bank of the United States, October 27, 1795, Box 18, fol. 347, Papers of James O. Wettereau, Special Collections, Columbia University, New York.

15. Bryan, *State Banking in Maryland,* 36.

16. Minutes, board of the Bank of the United States, April 22, 1800, Box 18, fol. 347, Wettereau Papers.

17. *Federal Gazette and Baltimore Daily Advertiser,* February 23, 1804.

18. *Laws of Maryland* (1804), chap. 61; see also Bryan, *State Banking in Maryland,* 23–24, 37–38.

19. See Paul S. Clark and R. Samuel Jett, *Luther Martin of Maryland* (Baltimore: Johns Hopkins University Press, 1970).

20. Maryland Bureau of Industrial Statistics and Information, Fourth Biennial Report, 1890–91 (Baltimore, 1892), 6.

21. George and Suzanne Hurley et al., *Calvin B. Taylor, Banker: The First One Hundred Years* (Privately published, 1990), 30–34.

22. See exhibit copy, Mercantile-Safe Deposit & Trust Company, Baltimore.

23. Ibid.

24. *Manufacturers Record,* September 3, 1914, pt. 2, pp. 33–34.

25. Maryland Bankers Association (MBA) Proceedings (1910), 23–24; (1896), 29.

26. Ibid. (1908), 15.

27. Ibid. (1909), 29.

28. Ibid., 28–29.

29. *Laws of Maryland* (1910), chap. 219.

30. Annual Report, Bank Commissioner of the State of Maryland (hereafter ARBC) (1911), 4, 6–9.

31. MBA Proceedings (1908), 86–87.

32. Quoted in Larry Sweikart, Introduction, *Encyclopedia of American Business* (New Haven: Yale University Press, forthcoming), xi.

33. MBA Proceedings (1901, 1902)

34. Ibid. (1896), 20–21.

35. "An Appeal to Justice: Presenting Baltimore's Claims to a Regional Bank" (Baltimore, 1913), Maryland Historical Society, Pamphlet 719, Baltimore.

36. ARBC (1915), 10.

37. ARBC (1918), 10–11; (1919), 10.

38. MBA Proceedings (1928), 25–33.

39. ARBC (1920), 8–9; (1922), 5–6.

40. MBA Proceedings (1930), 15.

41. Ibid.

42. Baltimore Trust Company newsletter, December 6, 1929, NationsBank archives, Baltimore.

43. MBA Proceedings (1930), 13.

44. This quotation and the one in the paragraph above are from ARBC (1932), 6–13.

45. Ibid. (1933), 1–7.

46. See exhibit copy, Mercantile-Safe Deposit & Trust Company, Baltimore.

47. Ibid.

48. MBA Proceedings (1940), 12–13.

49. Ibid. (1941), 3–4.

50. Ibid. (1942), 3–4.

51. ARBC (1944), 3; (1945), 3–4.

52. ARBC (1946), 3–4.

53. ARBC (1947), 3–4; (1948), 3–4.

54. See ARBC for total-loan figures; on the place of the automobile in consumer debt see MBA, *Banking News,* February 1970, 5.

55. ARBC (1954), 3.

56. See exhibit copy, Mercantile–Safe Deposit & Trust Company, Baltimore.

57. Maryland National Bank Community Development Group Fact Sheet, 27 October 1992, "Banks and Banking" Vertical File, Enoch Pratt Free Library, Baltimore (the group organized in 1987); William F. Hallstead, "New Prospects for Black Business," *Maryland Magazine* 5 (Winter 1972): 16–20.

58. "Banking Talks with Robert L. Douglass, Chairman, Maryland Legislature Black Caucus," *Maryland Banking Quarterly* 6 (Spring 1977): 2.

59. ARBC (1981).

60. William K. Weaver to Del. John W. Douglass, September 8, 1983, and Weaver to Del. Frederick C. Rummage, September 24, 1985, Maryland Bankers Association files, Annapolis.

61. Rich Jones, Lucinda Simon, and Beverlee Guild, "Regulating Financial Institutions: Interstate Banking," *State Legislative Report,* Legislative Management ser. 9:1 (Denver: National Conference of State Legislatures, 1984), 2–13.

62. H. Grant Hathaway to membership, Annual Legislative Report, MBA, April 1983; ARBC (1983).

63. ARBC (1983); Charles W. Cole Jr., Statement Delivered in Response to an Invitation to Appear before the Governor's Committee on Interstate Banking, September 20, 1984, Maryland Bankers Association files, Annapolis.

64. *Signet Bank: 200 Years Proudly Serving Maryland's Communities* (Baltimore: Signet Bank/Maryland, 1995); Edward Lyell Gunts, "A Babel of Towers," *Baltimore Magazine* (June 1984).

65. ARBC (1983, 1985, 1986, 1987); G. J. Manderfield to membership, Annual Legislative Report, Maryland Bankers Association, April 1985. See also Jesse Glasgow, "City Banks: A History of Change," *Baltimore Sun,* March 13, 1983, and Daniel Berger, "Banking on Growth," March 21, 1983, both in "Banks and Banking" Vertical File, Enoch Pratt Free Library, Baltimore.

66. Business section, *Annapolis Capital,* November 20, 1984.

67. ARBC (1982, 1984).

68. See MBA annual meeting minutes, especially those for 1989, 1990, 1992, MBA files, Annapolis; on Riegle-Neal see *Congressional Quarterly Almanac* (Washington, D.C.: Congressional Quarterly, 1994), 99.

69. Kenneth R. Smith, "General Assembly Passes MBA-Supported Tax, Branching Acts," *Maryland Banker* 9 (October–November 1995): 1.

70. Charles W. Hoff III, Maryland Bankers Association annual meeting minutes, 1995, Maryland Bankers Association files, Annapolis.

71. Rouse in *Time* magazine quoted in Brugger, *Maryland,* 674.

PART TWO

A Catalogue of Maryland's Paper Money, 1790–1865

Foreword to the Catalogue

RICHARD G. DOTY
Curator, Numismatic Collection
Smithsonian Institution

Maryland was a full participant in the rise and fall of obsolete currency, and the state's experience places it well within the fiscal mainstream of nineteenth-century America. Yet there was much that was unusual, even unique, about the Maryland story. Maryland's middle position between North and South gave its pre-greenback banking and monetary affairs a peculiar quality, as did the dominant position of one place, Baltimore, in the state's financial history. Maryland controlled its banks and their currency to a remarkable degree, which set Maryland apart, as did a persistent reliance on private, low-denomination notes, or scrip, for many of its daily transactions. Scrip, in fact, was one of the most important components of Maryland's money, of incalculable importance for the local historian.

The system of private note-issuing banks, the force behind the "obsolete" note, was a reaction to the War of American Independence, which was largely financed by the issue and circulation of promissory state and national currency. Supported by good intentions and patriotic zeal, the paper depreciated as insurgent fortunes declined. By the end of the 1770s, the best of it was traded at one-fortieth of its nominal value. Public paper had been so thoroughly discredited that in 1787 the framers of the new federal government had no trouble seeing to it that public power was kept out of the currency business: the Constitution said nothing about whether federal authorities might have the right to issue and circulate paper, and it prohibited the state governments from doing so in explicit terms. That left a difficulty. Alexander Hamilton and the hard-money congeries of lawyers and merchants who wrote the Constitution would have preferred a nation whose money was composed entirely of cold cash or specie. This would be impossible, for at least two reasons. The first was that very little gold and silver was currently available as the raw materials of coining (the mining wealth of California and Virginia City, Nevada, lay far in the future), and, while other people's coins could be recycled to create new American ones, the amount of specie coming into the country was directly tied to international trade, much of it flowing out as rapidly as it had flowed in, regardless of whose name appeared on it. Still, our first coins were, in fact, created from foreign metallic sources—Cornish copper for cents and half cents, Mexican silver and Peruvian gold for more imposing denominations—and the public might in time have secured an adequate monetary supply were it not for the activity of the American economy, which grew with such rapidity that, even with occasional slumps, a federal supply of coinage would likely have remained several steps behind the needs of the people. The classical monetary theories of an Alexander Hamilton soon proved unrealistic in a dynamic American setting. We needed more money, and quickly; we got it through the private, note-issuing bank.

Marylanders began circulating private, low-value notes during and after the War of 1812. A number of businesses were represented in this early series, centering on Baltimore. Turnpikes issued notes. So did a Baltimore grocer named David Stirratt (whose 6 1/4-cent note bore a date of October 1827); a butcher; and the Indian Queen Hotel (its note for 12 1/2 cents represents one of the earliest products ever circulated by an establishment of this type). So did the Baltimore Post Office, whose 20-cent note was thoughtfully postmarked with the date of issue, May 25, 1815.

Counterfeiting was a perpetual problem for these early issuers. Much security printing was now going on in New York and Philadelphia, but the printers there, and their customers in Maryland and elsewhere, encountered two problems basic to the craft at this time. If they employed the easiest printing method, creating notes from movable type, their products would be easy to counterfeit. If they employed the other available method, intaglio printing from engraved plates, their wares would be much more difficult to counterfeit, but also much more difficult to create in the quantities necessary for the new American economy, based increasingly upon the private bank note.

The only practicable medium for creating engraved plates at the time was copper. A fairly soft metal, copper was reasonably easy to roll out flat with the technology of the day and easy to engrave. But it also wore out quite quickly. Copper plates needed constant retouching, which inevitably allowed slight variations to creep into the final product, variations that threatened the absolute consistency, which was and is at the heart of any security printing.

Fortunately, by 1800 a new material, steel, began to appear in sufficient quantity and quality so as to be useful in security printing. Steel greatly outlasted copper, meaning that a much larger number of "pulls" could be taken from an unretouched steel plate than from a copper one. Security would be enhanced. Monetary production would be increased.

The fact that more steel was now available meant nothing without a battery of technological improvements to take advantage of it. These came along apace, some from Britain, others conceived in the United States. New rolling methods were devised, allowing the harder metal to be rolled out flat enough for printing. A genius from Newburyport, Massachusetts, named Jacob Perkins invented a way to engrave a design on soft steel, then harden it for use on a steel plate—or on a steel roller, which could then create a multiplicity of identical design elements on steel printing plates. Perkins invented the art of siderography, and he and fellow craftsmen like Asa Spencer did something even more important, something as crucial to our development as a nation as it has been overlooked. Working in a time when hard money was scarce or completely unavailable, they made possible the creation of mass paper money in its place. The early obsolete bank note, product of their craft and skill, has been condemned as a fake and a fraud; but without it, this would be a very different county, and a much smaller and weaker one.

Perkins's first improvements in bank-note printing were in place by around 1805. His early developments, predominantly employed in the New England states, included a series of individualized slugs with the name of the bank and the denomination of the note within a blocky, dark background. The slugs were created as needed, while the backgrounds were mass-produced by his new process of replication. The results were some of the most homely notes ever circulated in this country. But they were also nearly impossible to counterfeit, and that of course was what Perkins had intended. Unlike other printers' products of the day, his notes were also printed on both sides, employing the same processes for the backs as for the faces. These notes were printed in a single color, black, as was nearly all other currency through the first four decades of the nineteenth century. Armed with new processes, confronting the need for more currency, the number of American note-issuing banks increased with each new decade. To be sure, there were setbacks in the aftermath of the War of 1812, and again in the middle 1820s; but the general trend was an increase of banks and bank notes, a further complication and perfection of the printing processes employed in the trade.

The demise of the second Bank of the United States in 1836 opened the door to a wave of new, private banks in Maryland and elsewhere, some of which were worthy additions to their local fiscal communities, others which were instruments of speculation, even fraud. The states did little to supervise banking, and the federal government had signaled its abdication. Unless bankers and businessmen showed exemplary restraint in making loans and issuing currency, the American economy would be in major difficulty. Yet like all Americans, the note issuers were interested in making money, in getting ahead.

By the middle 1830s, the American bank note was assuming its typical form. The new production and security printing processes of Perkins, Spencer, and the other pioneers were now in universal employment. The results were varied. The creation of the transfer vignette (the term used to refer to the mass production of complex imagery, involving a master plate, a transfer roll, and a working plate) made possible near-perfect consistency in the placement of design elements between one bank note and another. Tiny variations existed, of course, as a close inspection of the notes on a sheet of the same denomination will attest; but to all intents and purposes, each note of a specific denomination from a given bank would, and must, look like every other note of the same denomination from the same institution. Since they were produced by mechanical rather than manual processes, those vignettes could be larger than ever before, bringing a new artistic quality to the average note.

The choice of subject matter was constantly expanding, subject only to the discretion or whim of the bank president. In earlier times, small oval portraits of the Marquis de Lafayette and DeWitt Clinton had appeared on notes with annoying regularity—not so much because these worthies occupied a particular place in the American pantheon but because the printers had created master vignettes of them fairly early, and, while the stock of imagery remained limited, the two heroes were in constant demand. But those times were rapidly coming to an end: the expansion of banking in the 1830s meant more business for the printers, who in turn had the financial resources to experiment, to hire gifted artists and engravers, to create entire libraries of images for the delectation of potential customers. Famous paintings were copied and placed on the notes, ensuring that the average American was familiar with the prize contents of many a museum, even if he or she had never been inside it. Famous heroes received their due, as did humbler benefactors of the Republic. Scenes from mythology and allegory were perennial favorites, the latter a reflection of the American predilection for the didactic, the uplifting. But one suspects that some of the treatments afforded to the former, with scantily clad goddesses and nymphs, was intended for another purpose altogether—the 1835 version of soft-core pornography.

The notes reflected more contemporary considerations as well. Ordinary people now began appearing on them—not to the degree they would in the last years of the medium, but with a sufficient frequency to make one wonder whether Andrew Jackson's apotheosis of the Common Man might not have hit home with those entrusted with the creation of our paper money. Two other elements, both manifestations of modernity and speed, made their appearance an the 1830s—the steamboat and the train. The earliest monetary image of a railway train appeared upon a Maryland note—as a small lower-center detail on an 1831 ten-dollar bill from a Port Deposit issuer, the Susquehanna Bridge & Bank Company. That bank—along with a good many others in Maryland—went under during the Panic of 1837, but the image remains.

The economic hard times of the late 1830s and early 1840s left indelible marks on Maryland's currency. With the disappearance of banks, a wide assortment of institutions began to circulate low-denomination scrip. Improvement companies received authority from the assembly to issue what were variously called stock orders, certificates of indebtedness, or toll notes. The Baltimore and Ohio Railroad and the Annapolis and Elkridge were empowered to float such currency, as were the Tidewater and Chesapeake & Ohio canal companies. The C&O was responsible for a large number of notes and scrip, either directly emitted by the company or by merchants doing business along the banks of the canal. Other expedients included the issues of the Baltimore Savings Institution, which failed ingloriously in the summer of 1840. One of its small-change notes has survived with a sour observation on its back—"Stopt pay Sept 9th/1840/Presdt ran away"—which might serve as an epitaph to the entire age.

The city of Baltimore did its bit by issuing small-change notes in denominations of five cents to two dollars, with issue-dates of May 16, 1837 (the two-dollar note depicted Battle Monument). Private citizens and organizations in Baltimore and elsewhere also provided substitutes for small change. Their intentions in many instances were fraudulent—issue enough scrip to make a modest living, then skip town or otherwise refuse payment. But many of the issuers were businessmen and others who had a sincere interest in promoting the public good (as well as their own). We have notes from a variety of professions and associations, including a distiller, a shoemaker, the proprietor of a public bathhouse, several hotels, and a group calling itself the Vauxhall Drinking Institution. These notes, most of them appearing in the years 1837 to 1840, make up some of the prominent features of Maryland currency and set it apart from the monies of other areas.

By the 1850s, when Maryland, with the rest of the country, had grown more prosperous and gradually expanded its supply of banks, the obsolete bill had assumed its final form. Still generally uniface, it was printed with a precision of execution, an absolute mastery of technique, and an artistry of design that still strike us today as remarkable. This currency was, quite simply, the most beautiful paper money ever created in this country.

There is a more-than-photographic immediacy about the images that adorned these notes. Their views show us not what America was like a century and a half ago, but what America thought it was like at the time. White men seem virile, confident; white women appear to be fragile, retiring. African Americans look happy with their lot.

Native Americans apparently were not; hundreds of images show a brave gazing disconsolately at the comings of civilization. The bills depict factories—those temples of the new industrial order—as modern and clean and farms as idyllic homesteads. Symbols of the modern era—train, steamboat, telegraph—abound on the notes. The images may have belied the reality, but they did so with artistry and class. And who is to say that federal paper currency today reflects any underlying reality at all? It has become a medium of commerce alone. This earlier paper money aspired to the ornamental.

It became truly colorful. Before about 1848 virtually all bank notes were printed in a single color, black, and most were uniface (a few institutions in the South, the region most dependent on paper currency and therefore most concerned about counterfeiting, circulated biface currency, the backs of which were printed in a second color). By the mid-1840s an additional color was making a cautious appearance on the faces of obsolete notes in the form of a bar or "protector," most commonly in red (considered the color most resistant to alteration), running across the portion of the note where the denomination was spelled out. This modest addition had become commonplace by midcentury, and the use of a second color, or even a third, became more the rule than the exception as the 1850s progressed. The second color could be applied to details of the dies containing the denominations (as with some issues of the Hagerstown Bank), or it could be added as a network over part or nearly all of the black first printing (as it was with several charming notes from the Alleghany Bank).

New printing methods had an effect that was by no means accidental: fancier, less forgeable notes cost far more to develop and print than did simpler, more vulnerable ones, and printing firms began to merge, creating larger organizations with more extensive capital and devouring smaller firms in the process. The climax came in 1858 with the organization of the American Bank Note Company, a consortium of virtually everyone who was anyone in the profession. The new firm was in fact an early example of a trust, and it was so successful that it soon monopolized federal as well as private printing contracts.

Of course, the new, more elaborate printing technology was primarily intended to deter counterfeiting and alteration of paper money and only secondarily to delight the public. Forging and alteration of private bank notes were constant problems from the beginning of the medium to its end. Penalties against such falsification were never severe enough to put an end to the problem, and profits to anybody with a press and a plate—or to anyone who was simply very gifted with a pencil—were too tempting to ignore. The determination of banks and printers to defeat tampering led to every improvement in technology and design, the legitimate issuers of paper managing to keep barely one step ahead of their competition. Hailed as a most effective antiforgery tool, legal bicolor printing had its illegal imitators within a few years of its introduction.

Later, during the Civil War, American currency underwent pressures so severe as to finally alter its very nature. After the firing on Fort Sumter, an emergency subsidiary monetary system rose up, based entirely on private and public scrip. For coinage substitutes of a dollar or more, North and South employed a medley of merchants' notes, paper from the central governments (and states, in the case of the Confederacy), and private bank notes of the traditional type. Both sections needed immense amounts of paper to continue the fighting as well as to supply their civilian economies, and the orthodox private bank note was simply inadequate to the demands imposed upon it. By the National Banking Act of February 25, 1863, the Lincoln administration obtained money to carry on the war, won some measure of control over the affairs of private banks, and also created the national bank note, our most interesting type of federal currency, a blend of old and new.

Under the banking act, private institutions in effect surrendered their assets to the U.S. government, receiving in return federal bonds against which they could issue national bank notes, backed by the full faith and credit of the Union. Maryland's banks began to join the new system in earnest after the General Assembly's somewhat tardy enabling act of March 1865. As they did, an era in the state's numismatic history came to an end.

We are reminded of the evolutionary nature of the change by a curious note now in the Armand Shank Collection, a twenty-dollar bill from the Howard Savings Bank of Baltimore, dated 1863, the year before the appearance of the last Maryland obsolete notes. It was not returned for payment until 1915, but it was then duly honored by the Howard Bank's successor, the National Exchange Bank. Transition from the old system to the new had been completed, a single note with ties to both eras representing the change.

Maryland's dependency on note-issuing private banks for the bulk of its circulating currency typified American experience before the federal greenback, but we should not overlook the wonderful variety and richness of Maryland's scrip. Other states saw merchants, firms, and towns circulating small-change notes during periods of economic stress, but more professions and types of groups were represented in Maryland than anywhere else.

We should remember that, while we have scrip from periods of economic stress, we also have it from more prosperous times: we tend to think of scrip as a phenomenon of economic contraction, of fear for the future that takes normal small change out of circulation. From the Maryland example we know that scrip can also reflect economic growth, during which the economy needs more small change than it can obtain from the usual sources. In this circumstance, Maryland merchants, such as the grocer David Stirratt, took matters into their own hands, circulating their own temporary bills until better communication or cash flow returned coinage to the locality.

Beyond its importance for local business history, scrip is interesting for two related reasons. For one, a very large percentage of it was tariffed at either 6 1/4 or 12 1/2 cents. Issues bearing these seemingly odd denominations make very good sense if we remember that they represented paper substitutes for the Spanish-American half real and real. This in turn suggests two things about our national and local economies of the period. It informs us that the United States was still heavily dependent on countries to its south, especially Mexico, for much of its circulating silver coin. It also indicates that Maryland was still closely connected with the economy of the American South throughout these years, because Northern scrip largely had abandoned 6 1/4 and 12 1/2 cent issues for those of five or ten cents.

A further point to note is that a large percentage of these small-change issues bore the images of the coins they were meant to represent or replace. This practice began as early as 1816—when a half real made its appearance on a Bank of Baltimore issue for 6 1/4 cents—and it remained common procedure for the next quarter of a century. As one might expect, the great majority of the coins depicted bear Mexican, Peruvian, or Bolivian mint marks (an *M* with a small *o* above, or LIMAE or PTS monograms, respectively). We are not surprised, because these mints were the most active of the later Spanish Empire; their products found their way in commerce from Cape Cod to California. But occasional anomalies spring up: Boonsboro produced a fifty-cent note featuring a four-real piece (the equivalent of the American half dollar) from Guatemala City! The four-real coin was the least popular and least produced denomination in the Spanish Empire. Moreover, Guatemala City was one of the smallest mints in all Latin America. How did this particular coin turn up on the Boonsboro note? A closer examination of the use of Spanish-American colonial coins on Maryland scrip would be worthwhile.

The next and final major era of Maryland small-change notes occupied the early 1860s, a direct result of the hoarding phenomenon of the Civil War. Such scrip issuance extended through the middle of 1864, far longer than it did in most parts of the North. The usual runs of businesses and municipalities are seen on these issues, although the Civil War appears to have generated less scrip in Maryland than it did in several other places.

The obsolete note and its cousins were used early here, and they were a constant feature of Maryland life for three-quarters of a century. They were welcome visitors, by and large, to the people of that day. They made the buying and selling of goods and services possible. The showiest of them, the private bank notes, inspired, instructed, and amused the state's citizens and help to make possible Maryland's economic growth. Maryland's early paper merits the description from Ovid's *Ars Poetica,* part of which appeared on another bit of numismatic Americana, William Wood's coinage of the 1720s: *Omne tulit punctum qui miscuit utile dulci* ("He took all the applause, who combined the pleasant and the useful").

Pleasant to look upon, useful for business, Maryland's early paper money has another meaning for us, but one of an equal or greater importance: it presents an indelible image of ourselves when young.

Introduction to the Catalogue

DENWOOD N. KELLY
ARMAND M. SHANK JR.
THOMAS S. GORDON

The intent of this book is to provide a broad overview of the factors that led to the issuance of currency and scrip in Maryland between the years 1790 and 1865; and, most important, to provide a catalogue of such notes. In compiling the listings in the catalogue, every variety of such "obsolete" currency of which the authors have any knowledge has been included, together with illustrations and descriptions of the notes. Their issuers included banks, savings institutions, local governments, transportation companies, manufacturers, and merchants, to name a few categories.

Undoubtedly, additions to the listings will materialize once this book is published and collectors and others match their holdings against the catalogue listings. Those who have such unlisted notes are encouraged to report them so that their existence can be recorded in the numismatic press.

Rarity Schedule

Although most amateur and professional numismatists prefer that a catalogue listing include a dollar valuation for each note, fluctuations in observed auction realizations and over-the-counter asking prices make it nearly impossible to compile meaningful valuations of any lasting nature. For this reason the authors, like many others, decided to use rarity factors, as shown in the table below. They are familiar to most collectors and dealers; individual users may decide upon their own conversion factors. Users must also bear in mind that condition plays an important part in the value of any note irrespective of its rarity.

Rarity	*Number Known*	*Rarity*	*Number Known*
R-1	More than 200	R-5	11–25
R-2	101–200	R-6	6–10
R-3	51–100	R-7	1–5
R-4	26–50		

In those instances in which the survival of notes known to have been issued is still in doubt, the acronymn SENC (Surviving Examples Not Confirmed), as developed by James Haxby, has been used.

Using the Catalogue

The basic arrangement of the catalogue is alphabetic by place of issue as shown on the note, and then by the title or name of the issuer. Notes issued by municipalities appear first under each place of issue, followed by those of other issuers. Those issued by banks, savings institutions, municipalities, and various commercial enterprises generally have the corporate or business name of the issuer prominently displayed on the face of the note, along with the signatures of one or more principal officers, such as the president and cashier or secretary. So-called merchants' or tradesmen's scrip often identify the issuer solely by a handwritten signature, in varying degrees of legibility, and sometimes with an added street address in the redemption clause on the face of the note. A bank at which the notes may be redeemed is only occasionally shown on such scrip.

The format of the listings follows a standardized pattern. Immediately below the name of the place of issue there appears a brief summary of its salient historic and geographic features. Identification of each issuer and its type of business is given, when available, before the actual listing of its issued notes begins.

The notes of each issuer are arranged in ascending denominational order, each note being illustrated, when desirable, and described. The descriptions are in standardized format, giving a catalogue number, denomination, date of issue, method of printing (engraving, lithography, letterpress), printer's imprint, other needed descriptive data and, if a commercial bank, the Haxby number in parentheses. Whenever the design of a note includes a vignette of a Maryland subject (monument, view, structure, or portrait), its identification is included in the aforementioned descriptive data. Finally, a rarity factor is given following the typical pattern familiar to collectors, R-1 to R-7, explained in a foregoing section.

The catalogue numbers used are "constructed numbers," each group of one or three digits separated by decimal points having an assigned meaning. The first group identifies the *place* of issue, the next group identifies the *issuer,* and the final group the *actual note* under consideration. In each grouping, breaks between numbers have been made to accommodate new discoveries subsequent to publication. This will be particularly noticeable in the final grouping, which identifies individual notes, as additional denominations are certain to be reported.

Sample Number: 5.117.22

5	117	22
Place of Issue	Issuer	Individual
(Baltimore)	A Merchant of Baltimore	Bank Note

The following fictitious example of a typical description which would appear beneath an illustrated note should give the reader an idea of what to expect.

5.13.17
6 1/4c Printed date March 28, 1837. Lithography, imprint: Lith. by E. Weber, Balt. Brick red security overprint, 10 cents. Vignette of Battle Monument, Baltimore, in left panel. (MD5G20)

The Printers

Most Maryland banks utilized the services of the large banknote engraving and printing firms in New York and Philadelphia for the production of their dollar denomination notes. In the relatively few instances in which banks issued fractional currency (small change notes), local printers were most often used, because of the time and cost factors involved.

It was in the production of small change scrip that local printers were most extensively involved. Job printers in Baltimore were very active, particularly in the printing of merchants' scrip. Through the use of one or another of the several methods of letterpress printing such as typography, stereotype, or woodcuts, such notes could be printed quickly and inexpensively. A job printer with a good variety of type fonts was in an excellent position to furnish notes personalized to the desires of a potential issuer, particularly as a wide range of cuts for vignettes, counters, end plates, and other decorative devices was readily available from type foundries. Joseph Robinson, active in Baltimore from 1808 to 1860, and John Murphy, active in Baltimore as a job and book printer from 1833 to about 1865, were probably the most prolific producers of such notes, their customers having been spread across the state, and well into Delaware, Pennsylvania, New Jersey, and Virginia. Both printers, Murphy in particular, also printed "stock notes" of standardized designs and denominations which were sold to issuers either directly or by stationers who stocked supplies for their customers.

In addition to the numerous Baltimore printers who produced scrip notes, similar activities, although on a lesser scale, went on in the counties. Much of the county printing was done by local newspaper publishers, all of whom did job printing for their customers.

Stone lithography was another printing method used in Baltimore to print small change notes, although on a much smaller scale than typography. The process was brought to Baltimore in 1834 by Edward Weber, a German émigré. Weber's successor and nephew, August Hoen, and Hunckel & Son are the only other local lithographers whose imprints have been recorded on Maryland notes.

Copper, and later, steelplate engraving was relatively rarely used for the printing of scrip because of its higher cost.

In preparing the following listing of recorded printers of Maryland banknotes and municipal and merchants' scrip, separate sections for Maryland and non-Maryland printers have been provided for the convenience of those whose interests lie primarily in printing methodology and history, rather than in the notes themselves. The printers are listed alphabetically, basically as their imprints appear on the actual notes. In the Maryland section, brief biographical and business data has been included for the various printers.

Maryland

W. D. Bell. Bell was a job printer in Hagerstown in the 1837–40 period.

Bull & Tuttle. Edmund Bull and William Tuttle were book and job printers in Baltimore at the northwest corner of Baltimore and Gay streets between 1835 and about 1845. By 1842 they were also the publishers of the *Baltimore Clipper,* a daily newspaper.

The *Citizen*. This weekly newspaper was published in Frederick in the 1821–61 period.

Cone, Freeman & Co. Joseph Cone and William H. Freeman were engravers and copperplate printers in Baltimore in the early part of the nineteenth century. Freeman was listed in Baltimore city directories as an engraver, but not as a printer, from 1810 until 1816. Joseph Cone apparently affiliated with Freeman in 1817, as the 1817–18 directory lists the firm of Cone & Freeman as engravers and copperplate printers in East Street, next to the Mechanics Bank. This listing continued until the 1824 edition in which Cone appeared alone, "upstairs at the northeast corner of Baltimore and Calvert Streets," while Freeman was listed as a counselor-at-law on the east side of Monument Square. Cone disappeared from the listings in the 1829 directory, while Freeman continued until 1836 as a counselor-at-law. *The Dictionary of Artists in America, 1564–1860* lists Cone as an engraver in line and stipple who moved from Philadelphia to Baltimore.

The *Examiner*. This weekly newspaper was published in Frederick in the 1813–44 period. Initially called the *Political Examiner,* it underwent several minor variations in title until finally using the simplified title, the *Examiner,* in the late 1830s until 1844.

The *Herald*. This weekly newspaper was published in Hagerstown, 1839–1907.

A. Hoen & Co. August Hoen was the nephew of Edward Weber, who sent to Germany for him as Weber's lithographic business prospered. Prior to Weber's death in 1848, Hoen had been made a partner in the firm and ultimately became his uncle's successor; however, it was not until 1853 that the firm name was changed to A. Hoen & Co. Relatively few small-change notes are encountered which bear the Hoen imprint. By the time he took over the business it had grown materially and was concentrating more on fine lithographic printing of bonds, stock certificates, checks, promissory notes, and book illustrations, posters, charts, and other high quality color printing. Successive generations of the Hoen family continued the business until 1981 when it was finally closed.

Hunckel & Son. The first listing of this firm in Baltimore city directories was in the 1856–57 edition when it appeared simply as "lithographers" at 34 Second Street. In 1858, they appeared as "commission merchants and branch of lithographic establishment in Bremen." By 1859, their office had been moved to 124 W. Lombard Street and the senior Hunckel (George) had apparently returned to Germany as his directory listing merely showed "h[ome] in Bremen" after his name. Otto Hunckel, the son, continued to be listed as a commission merchant, with Pracht & Voneiff at the same Lombard Street address. The Hunckels were still doing lithographic printing in 1862, evidenced by the nicely designed and lithographed fractional currency for William Wilkens & Co. dated December 1, 1862. Apparently, the lithographic business terminated not long thereafter, as listings when directories resumed publication in 1864 after their Civil War hiatus merely showed residential entries for George and Otto.

Lucas & Deaver. Emanuel K. Deaver appeared as a "printer," as did James Lucas, in the 1822 Baltimore city directory. In the 1824 edition, they appeared as a partnership with an address at the corner of Calvert Street and Lovely Lane. This continued until the 1845 edition in which only Mrs. E. K. Deaver appeared, her husband apparently having died in late 1844. Lucas continued the business for some years. Lucas & Deaver were not active in the production of scrip, only one example of their imprint having been recorded, that on a note issued by Bryan & Nicholson in Annapolis.

Medairy. John Medairy was listed as an engraver at 24 N. Gay Street in Baltimore directories as early as 1817. He had learned his trade as an apprentice to William H. Freeman, and functioned primarily as an engraver rather than a printer for most of his career, which continued until 1857.

Medairy & Bannerman. John Medairy and William W. Bannerman were engravers and copperplate printers in Baltimore from about 1837 to 1841 "at the southeast corner of Baltimore and Calvert Streets, upstairs." Bannerman continued working on his own as a copperplate printer after the dissolution of the partnership, about 1841, until his death four years later.

Murphy & Spalding. R. B. Spalding and John Murphy were printers in Baltimore on Frederick Street near Gay Street from about 1837 to 1839. Spalding had been the proprietor of the Baltimore Type Foundry prior to his partnership with Murphy; in city directories from 1837 to 1847 he also appeared as a commission agent. His brief sojourn in the printing business was probably a secondary interest.

John Murphy. First appearing as a "general book and job printer" in the 1840–41 directory, Murphy quickly became the most active of the Baltimore printers who produced small change scrip during the "Hard Times" of 1837–41. His imprint appeared on such notes throughout Maryland and in several adjoining states until well into the 1860s. His business address was always on Market (Baltimore) Street, at several locations between South and Charles streets.

Joseph Robinson. A long-time book and job printer in Baltimore, Robinson was listed continuously in directories from 1808 to 1860, operating from various addresses on Baltimore Street between South and Charles streets. He was also listed as a bookseller, stationer, and the proprietor of a circulating library, frequently all of the foregoing. His imprint is found on small change notes until about 1845, particularly on those issued by Baltimore banks during the 1815–18 era.

John Sands. Listed in the Baltimore directories as an engraver and copperplate printer, his shop was located at the southeast corner of Baltimore and South streets from 1824 to 1827.

Samuel Sands. First listed in Baltimore directories in the 1829 edition as an engraver and copperplate printer at Baltimore and South streets, Samuel Sands must have had a relationship with John Sands who had preceded him in listings at a similar address and who had dropped from the listings the same year. Samuel continued to be listed until the 1853–54 edition.

John D. Toy. Appearing regularly in Baltimore directory listings from 1819 until well after the Civil War, Toy was a book and job printer. Based upon recorded notes bearing his imprint, Toy's volume of work in the field of scrip notes was small.

E. Weber & Co. Edward Weber and his wife emigrated from Germany and settled in Baltimore in 1834. Weber, who had received his training in stone lithography from Alois Senefelder, the originator of the process, began his commercial lithographic business in Baltimore in 1835 and enjoyed success from the beginning. Prior to his death in 1848, Weber sent to Germany for his nephew, August Hoen, who became his partner and successor. Hoen eventually married his uncle's widow, although it was not until 1853 that the firm name was changed to A. Hoen & Co. Weber printed many small-change notes for businessmen in Baltimore, particularly during the 1837–41 period.

John W. Woods. First appearing in Baltimore directories in the 1833 edition, Woods was listed simply as a "printer, opposite Peal's [*sic*] Museum, Calvert st." By 1835, he had moved to the corner of Baltimore and Light streets, and in 1840 he acquired a partner, Benjamin Crane, and moved to 1 N. Charles St. The partnership lasted until about 1844 when Crane left to become a dealer in millinery goods. Woods continued as a busy book and job printer for a number of years, publishing Baltimore city directories from 1858 to 1886. Based upon the appearance of his imprints on scrip notes, his volume of work in this field was small, only one issue with his imprint for the municipality of Emmitsburg in 1837 being on record.

Non-Maryland Engravers and Printers

Imprints of the following engravers and printers have been recorded on notes issued by Maryland banks, savings institutions, private banking houses, municipalities, transportation companies, and other business firms, both large and small. The year dates following the engravers' and printers' names are those during which they are known to have been in business under the specific names shown. It should also be remembered that as certain companies merged to form the American Bank Note Company, existing plates continued in use for some time and frequently the logo, "ABCo," was merely added to the original plates to reflect the transition.

The American Bank Note Company, New York and branches, 1858–end

Bald, Cousland & Co., New York and Philadelphia, 1854–58

Beaver & Dainty, Philadelphia, 1818–20

Burton & Gurley, New York, 1838–39

Burton, Gurley & Edmonds, New York, 1837–45

J. (John) Dainty, Philadelphia, 1815–17

Danforth, Bald & Co., New York and Philadelphia, 1850–52
Danforth & Hufty, New York and Philadelphia, 1847–49
Danforth, Spencer & Hufty, Philadelphia and New York, 1844–46
Danforth, Underwood & Co., New York/Underwood, Bald, Spencer & Hufty, Philadelphia, 1836–43
Danforth, Wright & Co., New York, 1856–58
Doty & McFarlane, New York, 1863
Draper & Co., Philadelphia, 1845–50
Draper, Fairman & Co., Philadelphia, 1823
Draper, Toppan & Co., Philadelphia and New York, 1840–44
Draper, Toppan, Longacre & Co., Philadelphia and New York, 1835–39
Draper, Underwood & Co., Philadelphia, 1828–31
Draper, Underwood, Bald & Spencer, Philadelphia, 1833
Draper, Welsh & Co., Philadelphia, 1851
Fairman, Draper, Underwood & Co., New York, 1825–32
Charles P. Harrison, Philadelphia, 1809
Hufty & Danforth, Philadelphia and New York, 1848–51
Manly & Orr, Philadelphia, 1837
E. Morris, Philadelphia, 1837
Murray & Draper, Philadelphia, 1810–12
Murray, Fairman & Co., Philadelphia, 1818–22
Murray, Draper, Fairman & Co., Philadelphia, 1812–13
National Bank Note Co., 1862
New England Bank Note Company, Boston, 1837–38
Rawdon, Wright & Co., New York, 1828–31
Rawdon, Wright & Hatch, New York, 1832–46
Rawdon, Wright, Hatch & Edson, New York, 1835–58
Charles Toppan & Co., Philadelphia, 1831–37
W. (William) Robinson, Philadelphia, 1815–18
Toppan, Carpenter & Co., Philadelphia, 1856–61
Toppan, Carpenter, Casilear & Co., Philadelphia, 1851–55
Underwood, Bald & Spencer, Philadelphia, 1835–36
Underwood, Bald, Spencer & Hufty, Philadelphia/Danforth, Underwood & Co., New York, 1836–43
Wellstood, Hanks & Co., New York, 1855
Wellstood, Hanks, Hay & Whiting, New York, 1852–55
E. P. Whaites, New York, ca. 1832

Imprints of non-Maryland printers are to be found on some altered banknotes that were originally printed for non-Maryland banks. Those that the authors have recorded are:

Baldwin, Adams & Co.
Durand & Company, New York
E. Barbour & Co. (1846)
Terry Pelton & Co.
Perkins

1 ANNAMESSEX, SOMERSET COUNTY

This small hamlet situated on the Little Annamessex River near its mouth on Tangier Sound was first settled by Quakers in 1662. Also known as Somers Cove, the name was finally changed in 1866 to Crisfield, in honor of John W. Crisfield, a prominent attorney in Princess Anne, who, as president of the Eastern Shore Rail Road Company, was instrumental in having a spur line constructed to the town. The name "Annamessex" (locally pronounced "Annamessick") apparently derives from the Algonquin language, its probable English equivalent being "it rushes beneath [the bank]."

1.1 Unidentified Issuer

1.1.2 R-7

10c Printed partial year date 186_. Letterpress, no imprint.

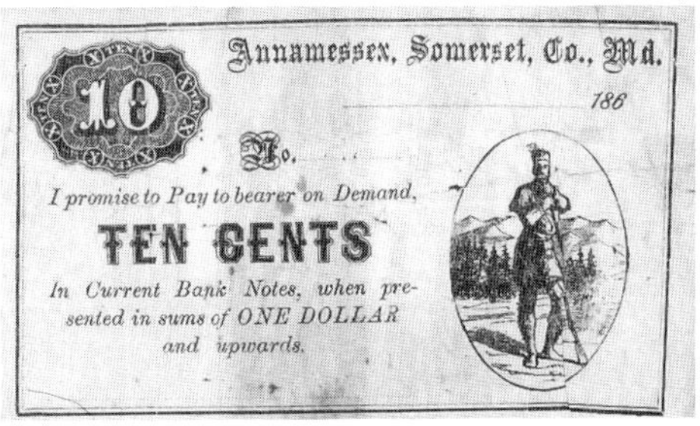

1.1.2

2 ANNAPOLIS, ANNE ARUNDEL COUNTY

Originally called Providence (1649), and Anne Arundel Town, the name became Annapolis in 1695, named for Anna Stuart, later (1702) Queen Anne of England.

2.1 Annapolis & Elkridge Rail Road Company

Chartered in 1837, this railroad ran between Annapolis and the Washington branch of the Baltimore & Ohio Railroad, a distance of about 20 miles. Construction was completed in late 1840, and the railroad opened for travel on December 26, 1840, carrying 949 passengers in its first month of operation. Scrip was issued in 1841, redeemable in amounts of $50 or more in 6% stock of the City of Annapolis. The company operated with financial difficulty until it consolidated with and became part of the newly incorporated Baltimore & Drum Point Rail Road Co. on April 10, 1880.

2.1.1 R-7

6 1/4c Printed year date 1841. Lithography, imprint: Lith. by E. Weber & Co., Baltimore. Similar to $1.00, No. 2.1.5, with variations in design of end panels.

2.1.2 R-7

12 1/2c Printed year date 1841. Lithography, imprint: Lith. by E. Weber & Co., Baltimore. Similar to $1.00, No. 2.1.5, with variations in design of end panels.

2.1.3 R-7

25c Printed year date 1841. Lithography, imprint: Lith. by E. Weber & Co., Baltimore. Similar to $1.00, No. 2.1.5, with variations in design of end panels.

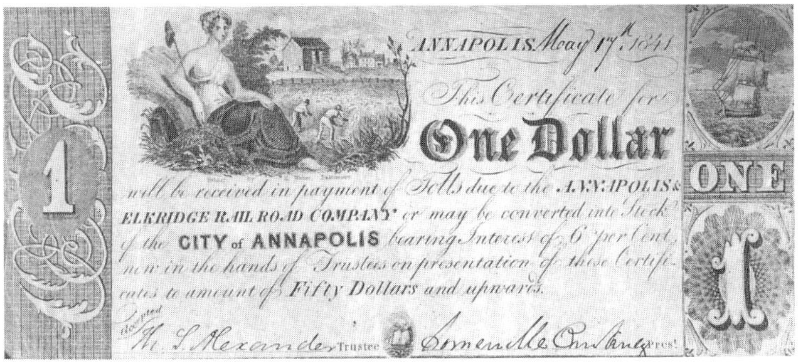

2.1.5

2.1.4 R-7

50c Printed year date 1841. Lithography, imprint: Lith. by E. Weber & Co., Baltimore. Similar to $1.00, No. 2.1.5, with variations in design of end panels.

2.1.5 R-7

$1.00 Printed year date 1841. Lithography, imprint: Lith. by E. Weber & Co., Baltimore.

2.2 Bryan & Nicholson

The issuers were the proprietors of a general store; they have been tentatively identified through census indexes as either Luther or William Bryan and Joseph S. Nicholson, respectively.

2.2.2 R-7
12 1/2c Ca. 1840–41. Letterpress, imprint: Lucas & Deaver, Printers, Baltimore.

2.2.4 R-7
50c Ca. 1840–41. Letterpress, imprint: Lucas & Deaver. Similar to 12 1/2c, No. 2.2.2.

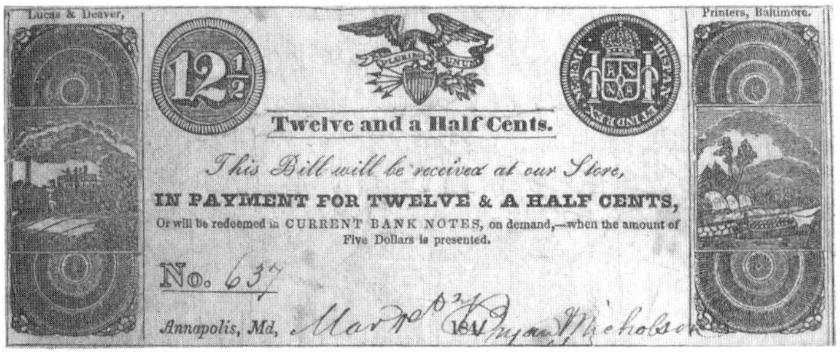

2.2.2

2.3 Farmers Bank of Maryland

Operated as an unchartered association until 1805. Charter approved January 12, 1805; converted to and became the Farmers National Bank of Annapolis in 1865. Branches in Easton, Elkton, and Frederick also issued notes.

2.3.1 R-7
6 1/4c Printed date June 10, 1815. Letterpress, no imprint. (MD5G20)

2.3.2 SENC
12 1/2c Printed date June 10, 1815. Lithography, no imprint. Similar to 6 1/4c, No. 2.3.1. (MD5G24)

2.3.3 SENC
25c Printed date June 10, 1815. Lithography, no imprint. Similar to 6 1/4c, No. 2.3.1. (MD5G25)

2.3.4 R-7
50c Printed date June 10, 1815. Letterpress, no imprint. (MD5G32)

2.3.5 SENC
$1.00 Ca. 1810–40s. Engraving, imprint: Harrison. Similar to counterfeit $1.00, No. 2.3.5 c. (MD5G36)

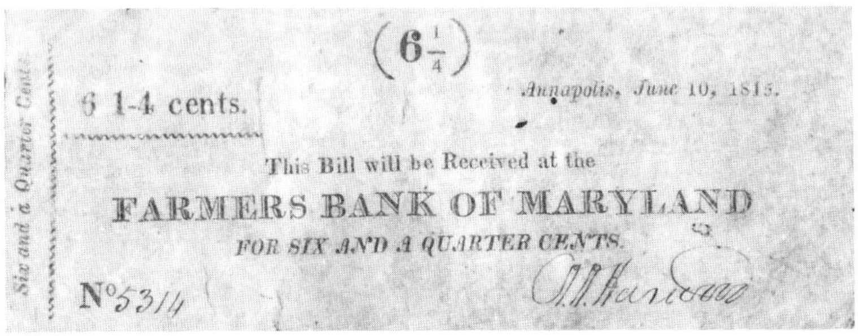

2.3.1

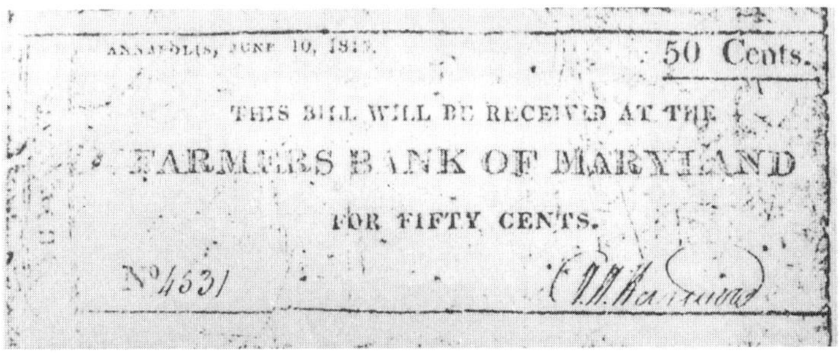

2.3.4

2.3.5 C R-5

$1.00 Ca. 1810s–40s. Engraving, no imprint. Counterfeit of $1.00, No. 2.3.5. (MD5C36)

2.3.7 P R-7

$1.00 Ca. 1845–50. Engraving, imprint: Draper & Co., Philada. Proof. (MD5G40)

2.3.9 R-7

$2.00 Ca. 1810s–40s. Engraving, imprint: Harrison. (MD5G44)

2.3.11 P R-7

$3.00 Ca. 1810s–40s. Engraving, imprint: Harrison, Sc. Proof. (MD5G48)

2.3.11 C R-6

$3.00 Ca. 1810s–40s. Engraving, imprint: Harrison. Sc. Counterfeit of $3.00, No. 2.3.11 P. (MD5C48)

2.3.13 SENC

$5.00 Prior to 1805. No information available. Issued by the association before being chartered in 1805. (MD5G8)

2.3.14 SENC

$5.00 Ca. 1810–40s. Engraving, imprint: Harrison. Similar to counterfeit $5.00, No. 2.3.14 C. (MD5G52)

2.3.5 C

2.3.7 P

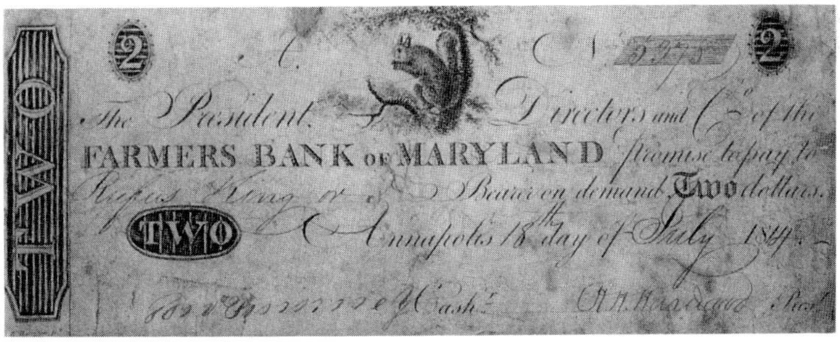

2.3.9

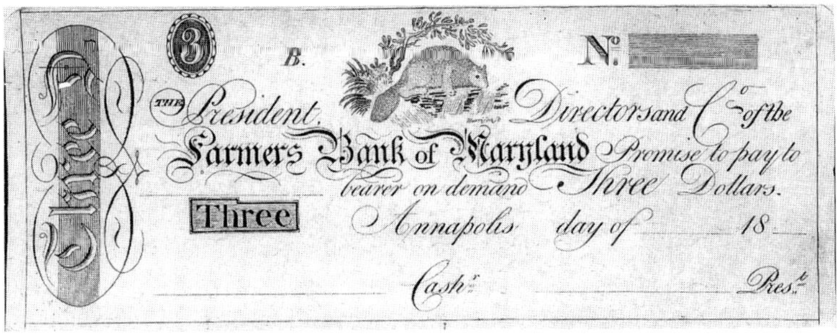

2.3.11 C

2.3.14 C R-6

$5.00 Ca. 1810–40s. Engraving, no imprint. Counterfeit of No. 2.3.14. (MD5C52)

2.3.15 P R-7

$5.00 Ca. 1825–30s. Engraving, imprint: Fairman, Draper, Underwood, N.Y. Proof.

2.3.16 A SENC

$5.00 Ca. 1830s. Engraving, imprint: Unknown. Altered from $5.00 Bank of Maryland. No other information available. (MD5A10)

2.13.17 SENC

$5.00 Ca. 1830s–40s. Engraving, imprint: Unknown. *Center:* Woman with sheaf. (MD5N5)

2.3.18 P R-7

$5.00 Ca. 1845–50. Engraving, imprint: Draper & Co. Philada. Proof. (MD5G56)

2.3.19 A R-7

$5.00 Ca. 1854–58. Engraving, imprint: Bald, Cousland & Co. *Left-left center:* Horses running to right / V. *Right center:* Liberty and Ceres flanking shield surmounted by horse's head. *Right:* 5 / oval portrait of girl shading eyes with left hand. *Between signatures:* Sleeping dog. Red FIVE overprint. Altered from $5.00 Bank of Morgan, Ga., 2GA235G8a. (MD5A5)

2.3.20 S SENC

$5.00 Ca. 1856–58. Engraving, imprint: Danforth, Wright & Co. *Left:* 5 / two Indian men, one standing and one kneeling, both facing right. *Right:* 5 / oval male portrait. *Between signatures:* Woman swimming. From a modified plate, originally for a counterfeit $10.00 on the Wyoming Bank of Wilkes Barre, Pa., PA715C20. (MD5S5)

2.3.21 A R-7

$5.00 Ca. 1857. Engraving, imprint: New England Bank Note Co. *Center:* Steamboat. *Left:* V / oval portrait of Clay. *Right:* 5 / oval portrait of Washington. Red ornate FIVE overprint. Altered from $5.00 Waubeek Bank, De Soto, Neb., NE30G8a. (MD5A15)

2.3.14 C

2.3.15 P

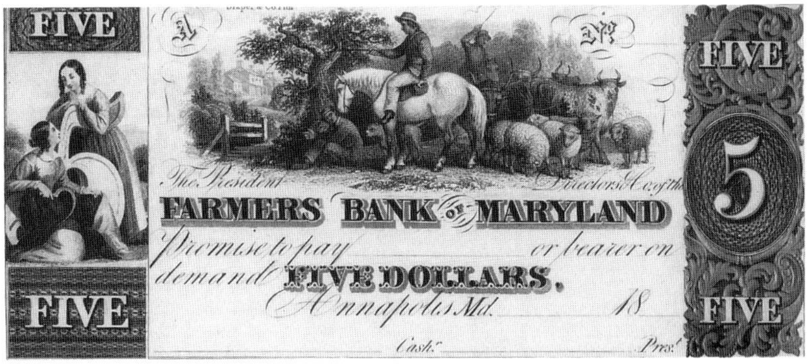

2.3.18 P

2.3.26 P

2.3.24 SENC

$10.00 Prior to 1805. No information available. Issued by the association before being chartered in 1805. (MD5G10)

2.3.25 SENC

$10.00 Ca. 1810s–40s. Engraving, imprint: Harrison. No information available. Similar to counterfeit $10.00, No. 2.3.25 C. (MD5G60)

2.3.25 C SENC

$10.00 Ca. late 1830s. Engraving, imprint: Harrison. Counterfeit of $10.00, No. 2.3.25. (MD5C60)

2.3.26 P R-7

$10.00 Ca. 1825–30s. Engraving, imprint: Fairman, Draper, Underwood, N.Y. Proof.

2.3.27 SENC

$10.00 Ca. 1830s. Engraving, imprint: Unknown. Altered from $10.00 Bank of Maryland, Baltimore. No other information available. (MD5A20)

2.3.28 P R-7

$10.00 Ca. 1845–50. Engraving, imprint: Draper & Co. Philada. Proof. (MD5G64)

2.3.29 S R-7

$10.00 Ca. 1856–58. Engraving, imprint: Danforth, Wright & Co. Phila. Spurious. (MD5S10)

2.3.32 SENC

$20.00 Prior to 1805. No information available. Issued by the association before being chartered in 1805. (MD5G12)

2.3.33 SENC

$20.00 Ca. 1810s–40s. Engraving, imprint: Harrison. No information available. (MD5G68)

2.3.33 C SENC

$20.00 Ca. late 1830s. Engraving, imprint: Harrison. Counterfeit of $20.00, No. 2.3.33. (MD5C68)

2.3.28 P

2.3.29 S

2.3.35 P

2.3.34 A SENC

$20.00 Ca. 1830s. Engraving, imprint: Unknown. Altered from $20.00, Bank of Maryland, Baltimore. No other information available. (MD5A25)

2.3.35 P R-7

$20.00 Ca. 1845–50. Engraving, imprint: Draper & Co., Phila. Proof. (MD5G70)

2.3.36 A R-7

$20.00 Ca. 1850s–60s. Engraving, no imprint. "State of Maryland" and "Annapolis" printed by letterpress, rest of note engraved. Red 20 overprint. Circulating counterfeit, altered from the $20.00 note of the Farmers Bank, Wickford, R.I., RI565G12a. (MD5A30)

2.3.38 SENC

$50.00 Prior to 1805. No information available. Issued by the association before being chartered in 1805. (MD5G14)

2.3.39 SENC

$50.00 Ca. 1810s–40s. Engraving, imprint: Harrison. No information available. (MDG72)

2.3.40 P R-7

$50.00 Ca. 1845–50s. Engraving, imprint: Draper & Co., Phila. Proof. (MD5G74)

2.3.42 P R-7

$100.00 Ca. 1845–50s. Engraving, imprint: Draper & Co., Phila. Proof. (MD5G76)

2.3.42 S SENC

$100.00 Ca. 1850–52. Engraving, imprint: Danforth, Bald & Co. Similar to No. 2.3.88 S listed under Frederick Branch. Spurious note. (MD5S15)

2.3.36 A

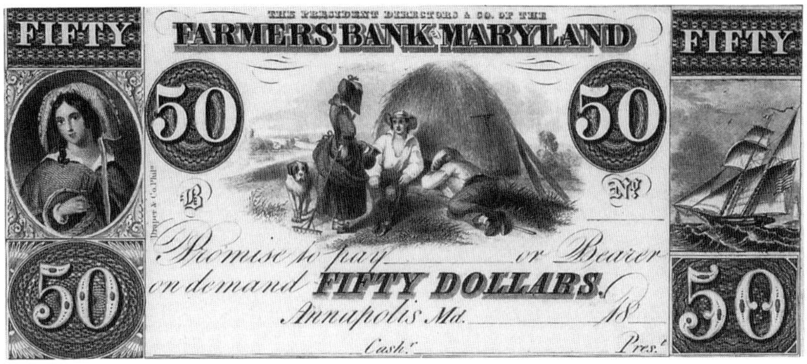

2.3.40 P

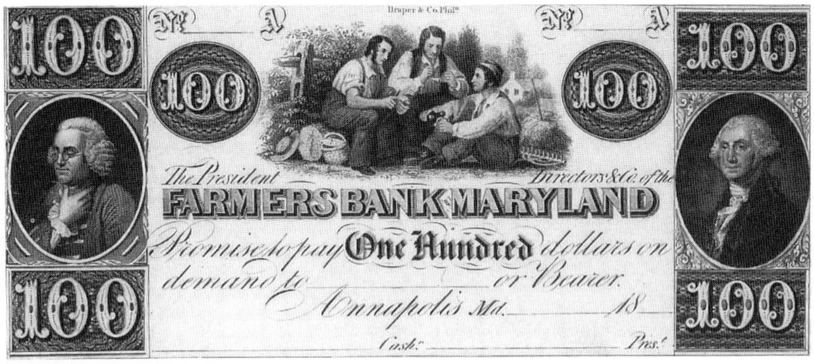

2.3.42 P

EASTON BRANCH

This branch operated from 1805 to 1853, when it became the Easton Bank of Maryland.

2.3.46 R-7

5c Printed date 6th March 1815. Engraving, imprint: Murray, Draper, Fairman & Co.

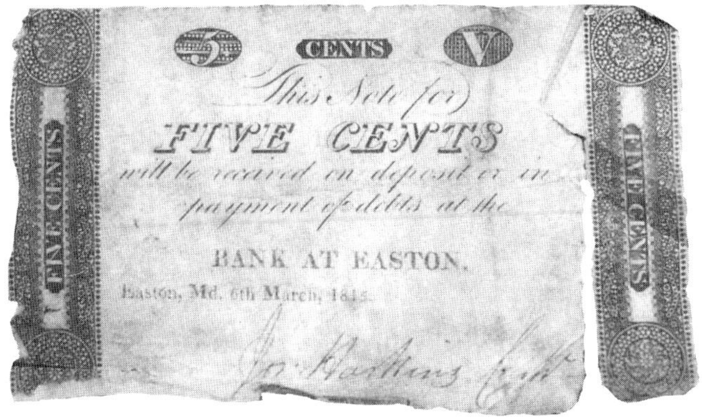

2.3.46

2.3.49 R-7

25c Printed date 6th March 1815. Engraving, imprint: Murray, Draper, Fairman & Co. (MD5G77)

2.3.50 R-7

50c Printed date Sept. 4th, 1815. Engraving, imprint: Murray, Draper, Fairman & Co. (MD5G78)

2.3.51 SENC

$1.00 Ca. 1810s–40s. Engraving, imprint: Harrison. Similar to counterfeit $1.00, No. 2.3.51 C. (MD5G80)

2.3.51 C R-6

$1.00 Ca. 1840s. Engraving, no imprint. Counterfeit of $1.00, No. 2.3.51. (MD5C80)

2.3.52 P R-7

$1.00 Ca. 1845–50. Engraving, imprint: Draper & Co. Philada. Proof.

2.3.54 SENC

$2.00 Ca. 1810–40s. Engraving, imprint: Harrison. Similar to counterfeit $2.00, No. 2.3.54 C. (MD5C84)

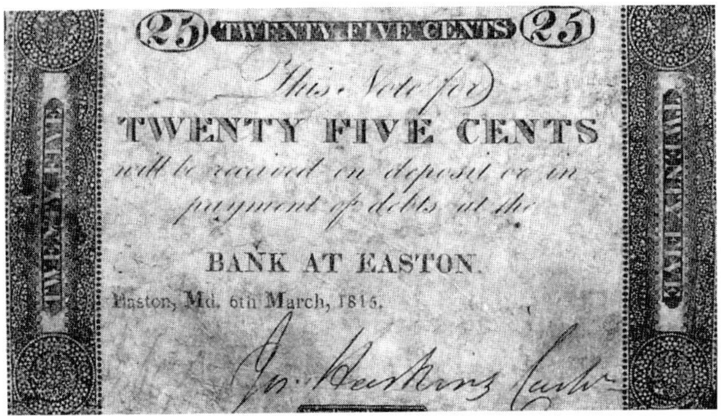

2.3.49

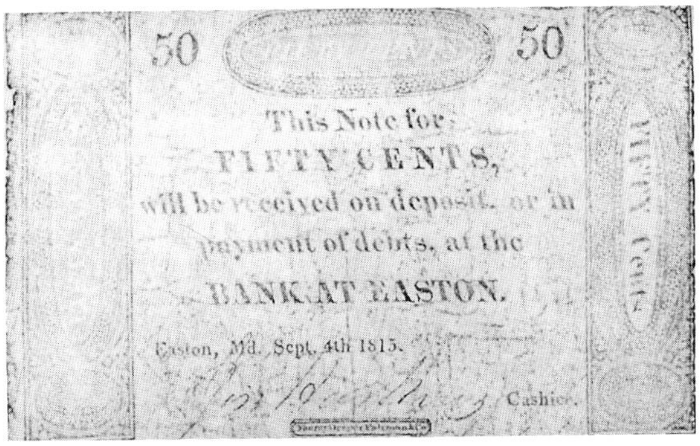

2.3.50

2.3.51 C

2.3.52 P

2.3.54 C R-5

$2.00 Ca. 1810s–40s. Engraving, imprint: Harrison. Counterfeit of $2.00, No. 2.3.54. (MD5C84)

2.3.56 SENC

$5.00 Ca. 1810s–40s. Engraving, imprint: Harrison. Similar to counterfeit $5.00, No. 2.3.56 C. (MD5G88)

2.3.56 C R-5

$5.00 Ca. 1825–30. Circulating counterfeit (see *Bicknell's Counterfeit Detector & Bank Note List,* June 1, 1835, Phila.). Engraving, imprint: Harrison Sc, under vignette. The illustrated note was apparently accepted and then detected, hence the endorsement on its face, "Charged to Profit & Loss, July 23, 1830." Counterfeit of $5.00, No. 2.3.56. (MD5C88)

2.3.58 SENC

$10.00 Ca. 1810s–40s. Engraving, imprint: Harrison. *Center:* Unknown; similar to $20.00, No. 2.3.59. *Left:* Panel with BRANCH across. (MDG92)

2.3.54 C

2.3.56 C

2.3.59 R-5

$20.00 Ca. 1810s–40s. Engraving, imprint: Harrison. Reprint. Similar to counterfeit $20.00, No. 2.3.59 C. (MD5G96)

2.3.59 C SENC

$20.00 Ca. 1810s–40s. Engraving, imprint: Harrison. Counterfeit of $20.00, No. 2.3.59. Photo of defaced plate. (MD5C96)

ELKTON BRANCH

Date of establishment is unknown. Closed in mid-1830s.

2.3.63 SENC

$1.00 Ca. 1810s–30s. Engraving, imprint: Harrison. No other information available. (MD5G104)

2.3.65 SENC

$2.00 Ca. 1810s–30s. Engraving, imprint: Harrison. No other information available. (MD5G108)

2.3.67 SENC

$5.00 Ca. 1810s–30s. Engraving, imprint: Harrison. No other information available. Similar to counterfeit $5.00, No. 2.3.67 C. (MD5G112)

2.3.67 C SENC

$5.00 Ca. 1810s–30s. Engraving, imprint: Harrison. No other information available. Counterfeit of $5.00, No. 2.3.67. (MD5C112)

2.3.69 SENC

$10.00 Ca. 1810s–30s. Engraving, imprint: Harrison. No other information available. (MD5G116)

2.3.71 SENC

$20.00 Ca. 1810s–30s. Engraving, imprint: Harrison. No other information available. (MD6G120)

FREDERICK BRANCH

This branch operated from 1807 to 1853, when it became the Central Bank of Frederick.

2.3.75 SENC

$1.00 Ca. 1809–40s. Engraving, imprint: Harrison. Similar to counterfeit No. 2.3.75 C. (MD5G130)

2.3.75 C R-6

$1.00 Ca. 1820–45. Engraving, imprint: Harrison fct. Counterfeit of No. 2.3.75. (MD5C130)

2.3.76 P R-7

$1.00 Ca. 1845–50. Engraving, imprint: Draper & Co., Philada. Proof.

2.3.78 SENC

$2.00 Ca. 1810s–40s. Engraving, imprint: Harrison. Similar to $1.00, No. 2.3.75. (MD5G134)

2.3.80 SENC

$5.00 Ca. 1810s–40s. Engraving, imprint: Harrison. Similar to $10.00, No. 2.3.83. (MD5G142)

2.3.82 R R-7

$10.00 Ca. 1809. Engraving, imprint: Harrison. Raised from $1.00, No. 2.3.75, MD5G130.

2.3.83 R-6

$10.00 Ca. 1810s–40s. Engraving, imprint: Harrison, fct. (MD5G146)

2.3.75 C

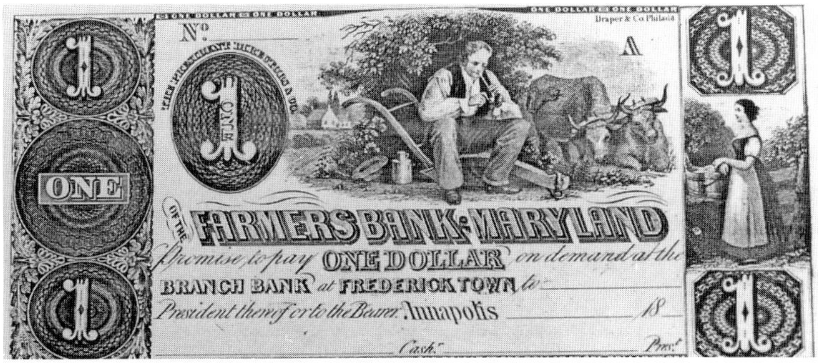

2.3.76 P

2.3.82 R

2.3.83

2.3.88 S R-7

$100.00 Ca. 1850–56. Engraving, imprint: Danforth, Bald & Co., New York & Phila. Spurious note. (MD5S20)

2.3.88 S

FOR BRANCH BANK USE

Town name to be inserted in manuscript at time of use.

2.3.92 P R-7

$5.00 Ca. 1845–50. Engraving, imprint: Draper & Co. Phila. Proof. (MD5G160)

2.3.93 P R-7

$10.00 Ca. 1845–50. Engraving, imprint: Draper & Co., Phila. Proof. (MD5G166)

2.3.94 P R-7

$20.00 Ca. 1845–50. Engraving, imprint: Draper & Co., Philada. Proof.

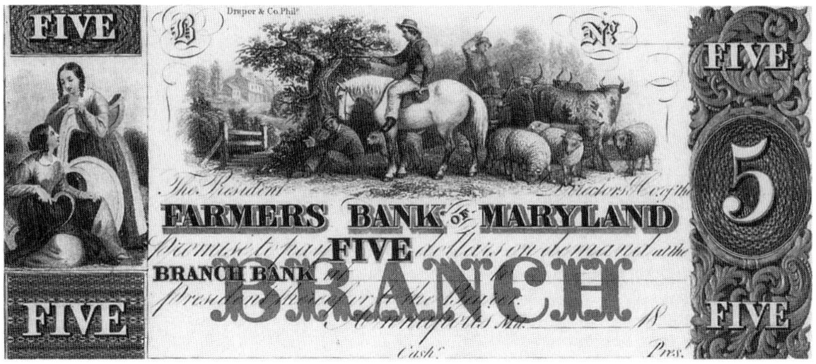

2.3.92 P

2.3.93 P

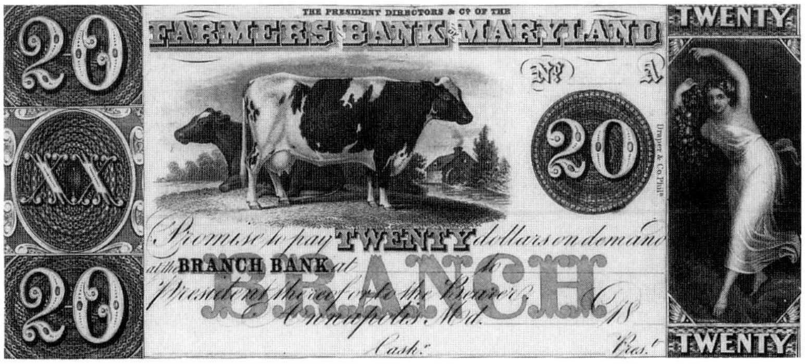

2.3.94 P

2.3.95 P R-7

$50.00 Ca. 1845–50. Engraving, imprint: Draper & Co., Philada. Proof.

2.3.96 P R-7

$100.00 Ca. 1845–50. Engraving, imprint: Draper & Co., Philada. Proof.

2.3.95 P

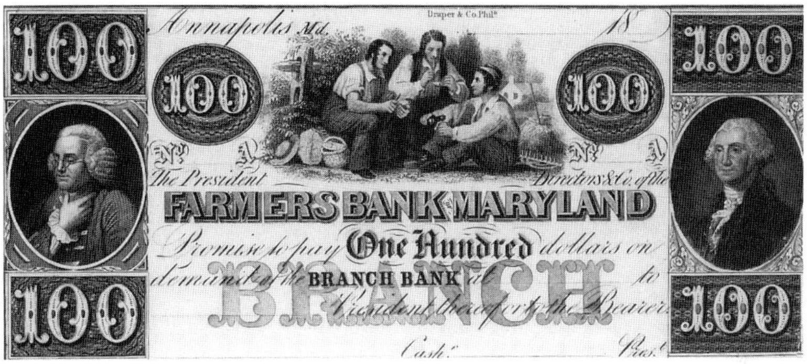

2.3.96 P

2.4 G. S. Grammer

The issuer was a storekeeper.

2.4.2 R-7

12 1/2c Printed partial date, Jan'y 1840. Letterpress, imprint: MURPHY, PRINT. BALT. Center vignette is Baltimore and harbor from Whetstone Point.

2.4.4 R-7

50c Printed partial date, October 1839. Letterpress, imprint: Robinson, PRINTER, Baltimore.

2.4.2

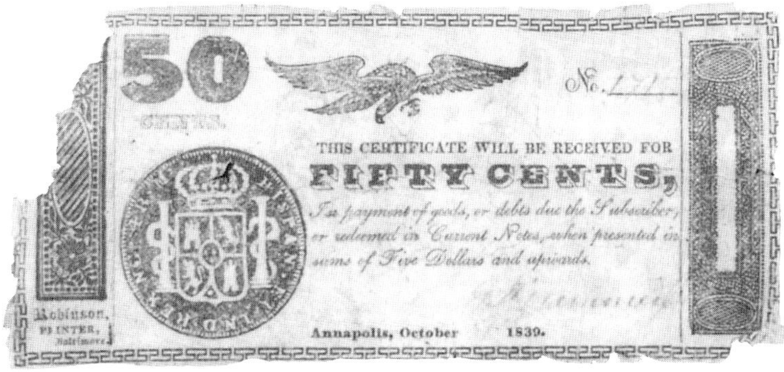

2.4.4

2.5 Ben H. Hall

The issuer was the agent for the sale of Brandreth's Pills, a popular patent medicine, in the Annapolis vicinity. He also maintained sales offices at three locations in Baltimore, as evidenced by the following advertisement in the December 21, 1839, edition of the Maryland Republican:

Ben H. Hall, Agent
For the City of Annapolis & Vicinity
BRANDRETH'S PILLS
Offices Corn. Light & Mercer St.
80 S. Charles St.
72 Saratoga St.
Exclusive Purpose of Selling
Brandreth's Pills

2.5.2 R-7
12 1/2c Printed date Dec. 16, 1839. Letterpress, imprint: MURPHY, PRINT. BALT.

2.5.4 R-7
50c Printed date Dec. 16, 1839. Letterpress, imprint: MURPHY, PRINT. BALT.

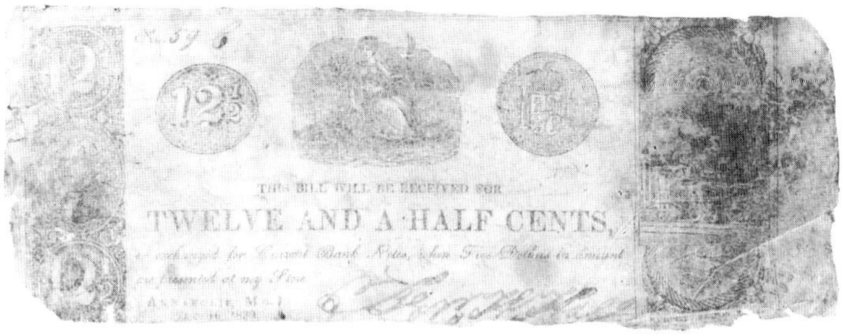

2.5.2

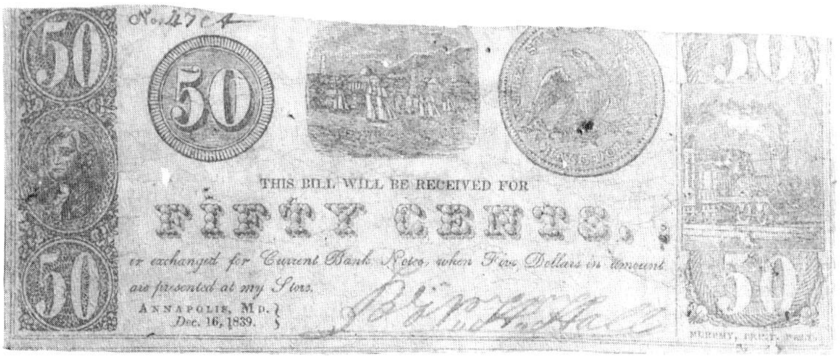

2.5.4

2.6 E. W. Hall

The issuer was the proprietor of a general store and probably was connected with Ben H. Hall, as exactly similar 12 1/2-cent notes, differing only in the signatures, are recorded for each issuer.

2.6.2 R-7
12 1/2c Printed date Dec. 16, 1839. Letterpress, imprint: MURPHY, PRINT. BALT. Similar to 12 1/2c, No. 2.5.2, of Ben H. Hall.

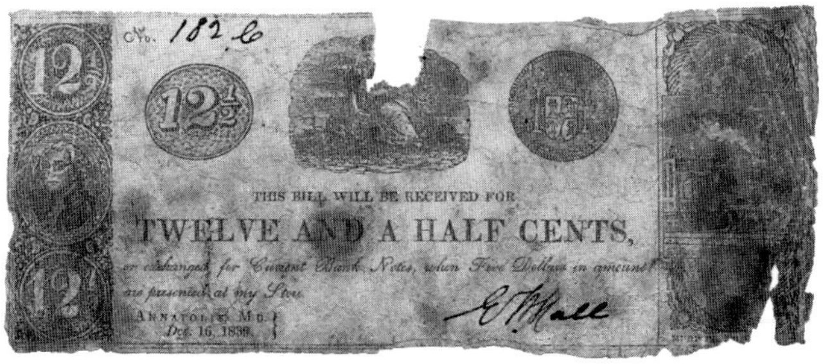

2.6.2

2.6.3 R-7

25c Ca. 1840. Lithography, no imprint (in all probability by E. Weber, Baltimore).

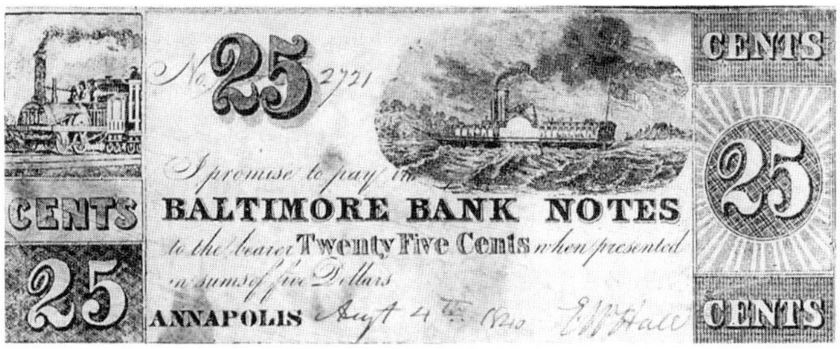

2.6.3

2.7 Old Dan Tucker

The note illustrated below is a joke prepared by an unknown humorist who had access to an unsigned remainder from an as-yet-unidentified issue printed in 1840. The manuscript "uncurrent" inserted in the beginning of the redemption promise quite accurately describes the validity of the issuer's commitment. The place of issue, Annapolis, was inserted by hand, too, and the original printed year date of 1840 was altered to 1849 by the addition of a tail to the zero. The crowning touch, of course, was the signature, "Old Dan Tucker," which was the title of a minstrel show favorite by Stephen Foster.

2.7.1 R-7

6 1/4c Printed year date 1840 altered to 1849. Letterpress, no imprint. Judging by the cuts used for the end plates and the general appearance of the note, it was probably the work of either Bull & Tuttle or Murphy & Spalding, both of Baltimore.

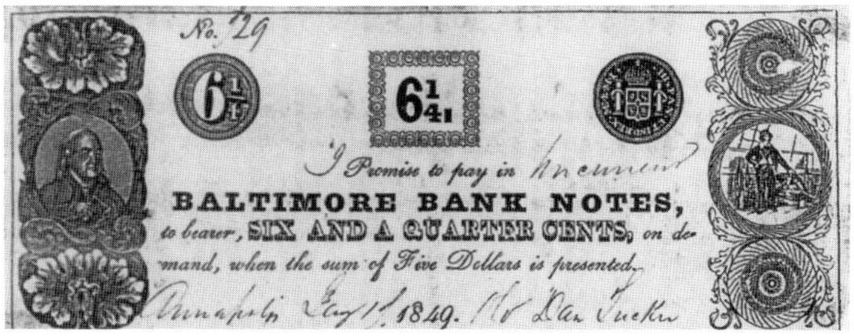

2.7.1

2.8 Issuer Unidentified (signature not deciphered)

2.8.4 R-5

$1.00 Printed partial year date 184_. Engraving, imprint: Horton, Balt. One-day sight draft, directing Joseph N. Fearson, Georgetown, D.C., to pay in current Virginia bank notes when presented in sums of five dollars.

2.8.4

2.8.5 R-5

$1.00 Printed year date 1843. Engraving, imprint: Horton, Balt. Similar to $1.00, No. 2.8.4, except that the year date is completely printed.

2.8.5

4 ANTIETAM, WASHINGTON COUNTY

Although not an incorporated town, Antietam was the name applied to the company town that grew up around the location of iron-smelting activity. The name Antietam has generally been used to describe the location of the bloody Civil War battle of Antietam Creek just to the north near Sharpsburg.

4.1 Anti-Eatam Iron Works

Iron smelting had been started at the mouth of Antietam Creek, a small tributary of the Potomac River, in 1763, the works passing into the hands of John Brien and John McPherson in 1806. By 1840, the foundry was operated by John McPherson Brien & Co. The hyphenated spelling, "Anti-Eatam," dates back to the mid-eighteenth century, being an Anglicized phonetic rendering of an Indian word said to mean "swift water."

4.1.2 P R-7
12 1/2c Ca. 1840. Engraving, imprint: Underwood, Bald, Spencer & Hufty, Philada. / Danforth, Underwood & Co., N.Y. Proof.

4.1.3 R-7
25c Ca. 1840. Engraving, imprint: Underwood, Bald, Spencer & Hufty, Philada. / Danforth, Underwood & Co., New York.

4.1.3 P R-7
25c Ca. 1840. Engraving, imprint: Underwood, Bald, Spencer & Hufty, Philada. / Danforth, Underwood & Co., New York. Proof.

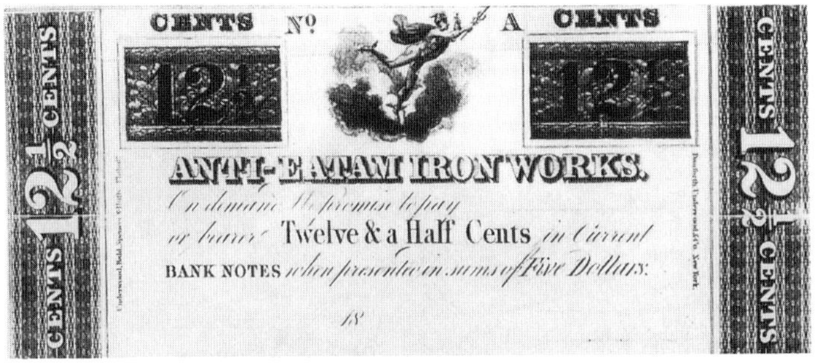

4.1.2 P

4.1.3

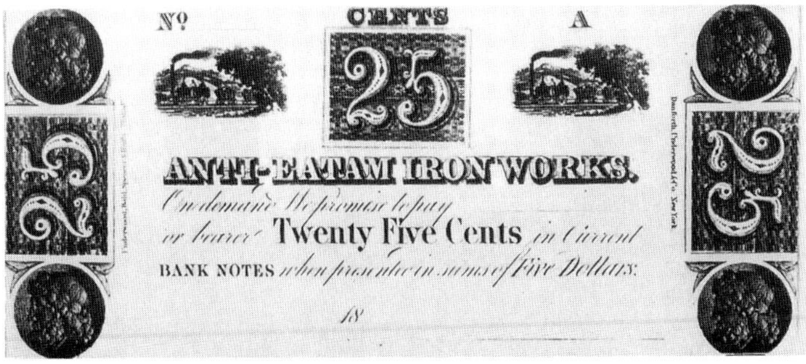

4.1.3 P

4.1.4 P R-7

50c Ca. 1840. Engraving, imprint: Underwood, Bald, Spencer & Hufty, Philada. / Danforth, Underwood & Co., New York. Proof.

4.1.5 R-7

$1.00 Ca. 1840. Engraving, imprint: Underwood, Bald, Spencer & Hufty, Philada. / Danforth, Underwood & Co., New York.

4.1.5 P R-7

$1.00 Ca. 1840. Engraving, imprint: Underwood, Bald, Spencer & Hufty, Philada. / Danforth, Underwood & Co., New York. Proof.

4.1.6 P R-7

$2.00 Ca. 1840. Engraving, imprint: Underwood, Bald, Spencer & Hufty, Philada. / Danforth, Underwood & Co., New York. Proof.

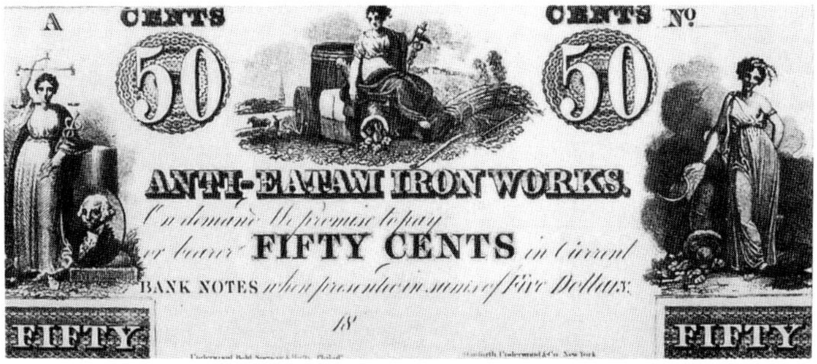

4.1.4 P

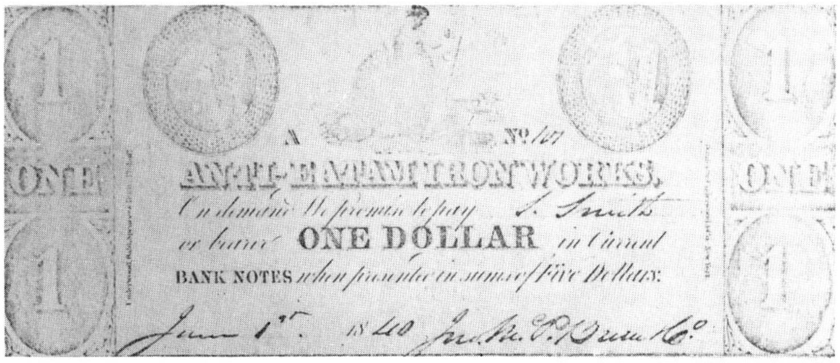

4.1.5

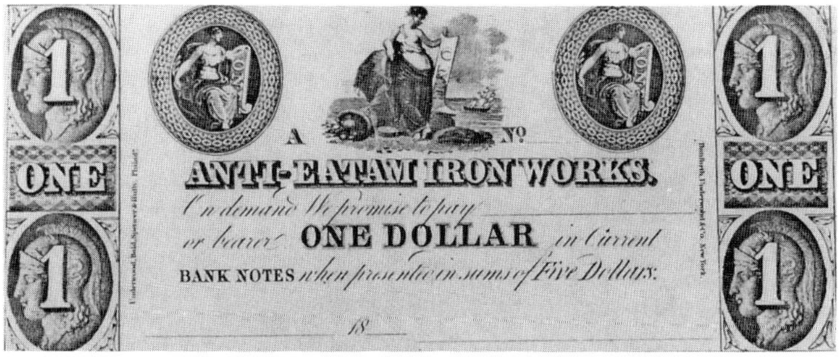

4.1.5 P

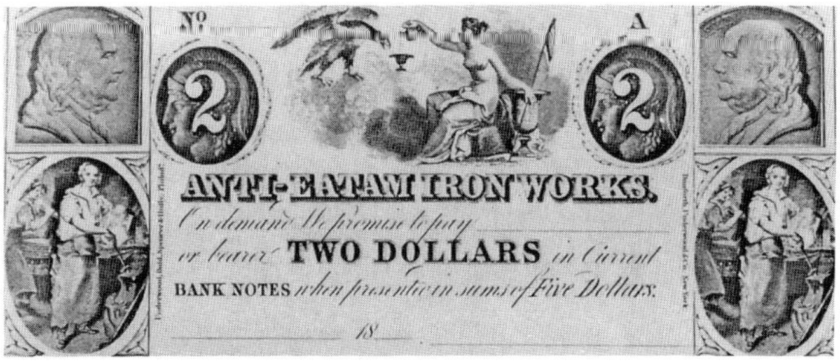

4.1.6 P

4.1.7 R-7

$3.00 Ca. 1840. Engraving, imprint: Underwood, Bald, Spencer & Hufty, Philada. / Danforth, Underwood & Co., New York.

4.1.7 P R-7

$3.00 Ca. 1840. Engraving, imprint: Underwood, Bald, Spencer & Hufty, Philada. / Danforth, Underwood & Co., New York. Proof.

4.1.7

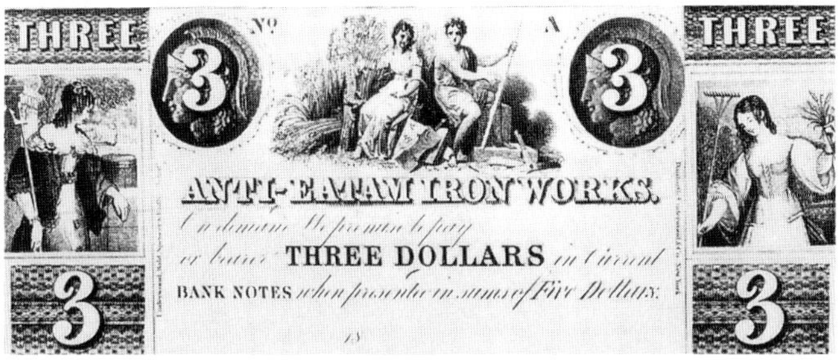

4.1.7 P

4.2 O. N. & T. O. Richmond

The issuers were proprietors of a general store, who utilized "stock notes" printed in New York.

4.2.4 R-6

50c Ca. 1864 or later. Lithography, imprint: Doty & McFarland 123 Wm. St. N.Y. Town, county, state, and issuer's names overprinted in light violet by letterpress.

4.2.7 R-6

$3.00 Ca. 1864 or later. Lithography, imprint: Doty & McFarlan 123 Wm. St. N.Y. Town, county, state, and issuer's name overprinted in light violet by letterpress.

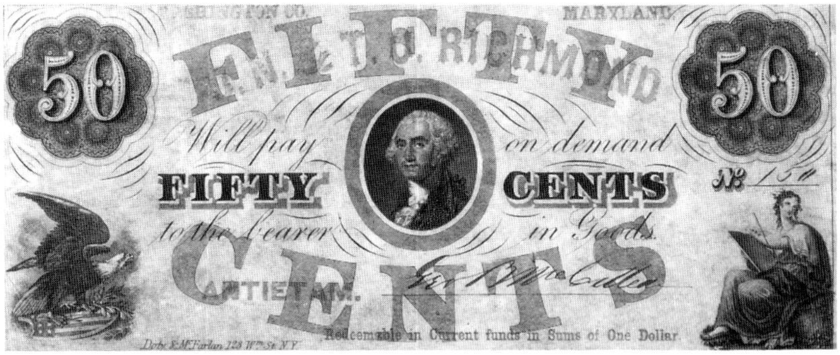

4.2.4

4.2.7

4.2.8 R-5

$5.00 Ca. 1864 or later. Lithography, imprint: Doty & McFarlan 123 Wm. St. N.Y. Town, county, state, and issuer's name overprinted in light violet by letterpress.

4.2.9 R-6

$5.00 Ca. 1864 or later. Lithography, imprint: Doty & McFarlan 123 Wm. St. N.Y. Similar to $5.00, 4.2.8, but without town, county, state, and issuer's name.

4.2.8

4.2.9

5.1 BALTIMORE

Laid out in 1729 on lands then owned by Thomas Carroll, Baltimore Town was consolidated in 1745 with Jones Town (Old Town), which had been established in 1730 and "erected" by a bill enacted by the General Assembly of Maryland in 1732. The bill described Jones Town as a "town on a Creek Divided from the Town lately laid out in Baltimore County called Baltimore Town." The place name, Baltimore, derived from the Calvert family; George Calvert, the father of Cecil Calvert, having become Lord Baltimore of the Barony of Baltimore in Ireland in 1625.

5.1 City of Baltimore

The suspension of payment in specie by the banks in Baltimore in May of 1837, as a consequence of similar action by the banks of Richmond, Philadelphia, and New York, precipitated a severe problem for the business community because of the resultant shortage of small change. As reported in the *Baltimore Sun* of May 17, 1837, the two boards of the city council met on Monday, May 15, in "extraordinary session at the insistence and call of the Mayor to consider the subject of issuing small paper notes or city certificates." An ordinance was passed "authorizing the issue of certificates for the purpose of supplying small change in the absence of specie." Six commissioners were appointed "to issue the certificates to an amount not exceeding $100,000 in the whole, in sums of 5 cents, 10 cents, 25 cents, 50 cents, $1.00 and $2.00." Apparently the demand for the certificates was considerable, as the Sun of Friday, June 30, 1837, published the following brief news item:

> More Shin Plasters.—At a meeting of both boards of the City Councils, last evening, an ordinance was passed authorising the issue of certificates to the amount of three hundred and fifty thousand dollars, in addition to the one hundred thousand already issued.

All the notes issued by authority of the mayor and city council bear the printed date of May 16, 1837, referring back to the passage of the original ordinance. Apparently the first notes to appear were those printed by letterpress, in black over a colored background bearing the imprint "Horton, Printer." John S. Horton was a local printer who worked in Baltimore from about 1833 to 1842; he was obviously able to produce these notes quickly to fill the need until the engraved notes produced by Rawdon, Wright & Hatch of New York were delivered. This well-established firm of banknote engravers produced handsome notes for the city in the denominations of 6 1/4c, 12 1/2c, 25c, 50c, 75c, and $1.00. Draper, Toppan, Longacre & Co., banknote engravers of Philadelphia and New York, also printed city notes in $1.00 and $2.00 denominations. Each note issued had to be signed by one of the six commissioners appointed in accordance with the ordinance of May 15, 1837. The authors have recorded the following signatures on notes:

A. G. Cole	S. Moore
F. Lucas Jr.	John B. Seidenstricker
R. J. Cross	

5.1.1 R-5

5c Printed date May 16, 1837. Letterpress, imprint: Horton, Printer. With red underprint. Reverse of U.S. half dime at left.

5.1.1

5.1.2 R-4

6 1/4c Printed date May 16, 1837. Engraving, imprint: Rawdon, Wright & Hatch, New York.

5.1.2

5.1.4 R-5

12 1/2c Printed date May 16, 1837. Engraving, imprint: Rawdon, Wright & Hatch, New York. Reverse of Spanish 1 real coin.

5.1.4

5.1.5 R-7

25c Printed date May 16, 1837. Letterpress, imprint: Horton, Printer. With green underprint. Reverse of U.S. quarter dollar.

5.1.6 R-5

25c Printed date May 16, 1837. Engraving, imprint: Rawdon, Wright & Hatch, New York.

5.1.7 R-7

50c Printed date May 16, 1837. Letterpress, imprint: Horton, Printer. With blue underprint. Reverse of U.S. half dollar.

5.1.8 R-5

50c Printed date May 16, 1837. Engraving, imprint: Rawdon, Wright & Hatch, New York. Reverse of Spanish 4 reales coin.

5.1.9 R-7

75c Printed date May 16, 1837. Engraving, imprint: Rawdon, Wright & Hatch, New York. Reverse of 3 Spanish 2 reales coins.

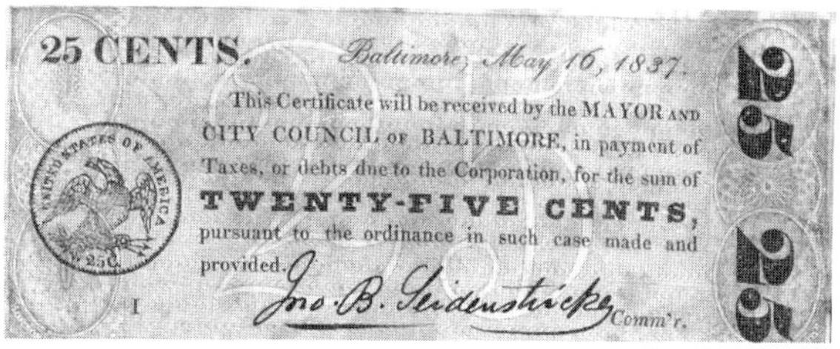

5.1.5

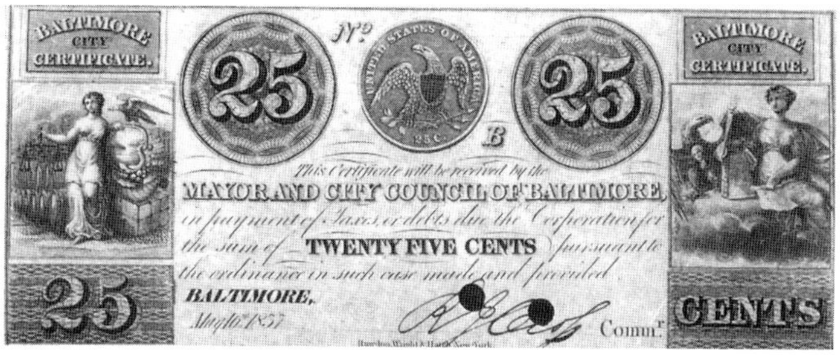

5.1.6

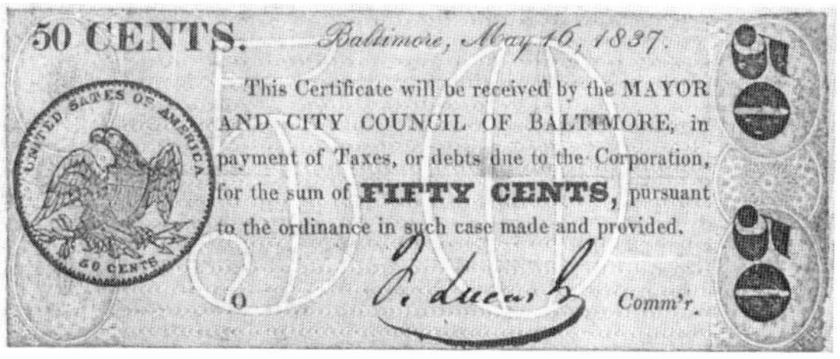

5.1.7

5.1.8

5.1.9

5.1.10 R-7

$1.00 Printed date May 16, 1837. Letterpress, imprint: Horton, Printer. With olive green underprint.

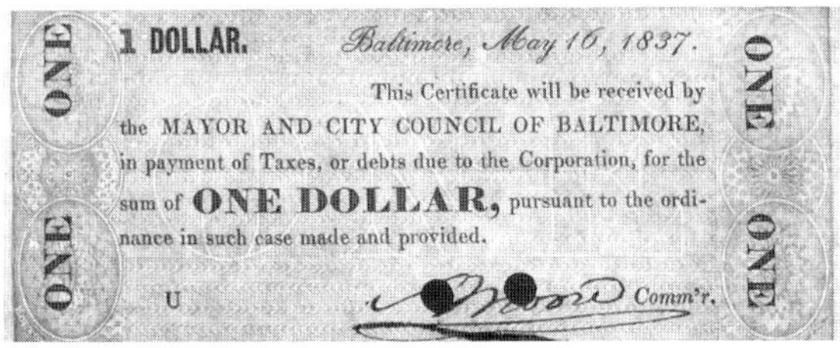

5.1.10

5.1.11 R-6

$1.00 Printed date May 16, 1837. Engraving, no imprint. Reverse of Spanish 8 reales coin.

5.1.11 P R-7

$1.00 Printed date May 16, 1837. Engraving, no imprint. Reverse of Spanish 8 reales coin. Proof.

5.1.11

5.1.12 R-4

$1.00 Printed date May 16, 1837. Engraving, imprint: Draper, Toppan, Longacre & Co., Phila. & N.Y.

A short news item in the *Baltimore Sun* of September 7, 1837, reported that a number of counterfeits of the $1.00 city note had been circulated in the Centre Market the previous day. The engraving was described as "indifferently executed" and the signature of "F. Lucas, jr." was not well done. Which of the $1.00 notes listed above was the subject is not known. The most likely candidate, in the authors' opinion, is No. 5.1.10.

5.1.12

5.1.13 R-6

$2.00 Printed date May 16, 1837. Engraving, imprint: Draper, Toppan, Longacre & Co., Phila. & N.Y. Vignette of Battle Monument, Baltimore, at right.

5.1.13

5.2 The American Bank

Charter approved March 10, 1856. Reportedly closed in 1858, the bank was revived in the early 1860s and circulated notes bearing dates as late as 1863 are often seen.

5.2.1 R-3

$1.00 Printed partial date 186_. Engraving, imprint: National Bank Note Co. Green security overprint at left end and ONE at center. Daniel Webster at lower right. (MD10G2a).

5.2.2 R-4

$2.00 Printed partial date 186_. Engraving, imprint: National Bank Note Co. Green security overprint at each end. Henry Clay at lower right. (MD10G4a)

5.2.3 R-4

$3.00 Printed partial date 186_. Engraving, imprint: National Bank Note Co. Green security overprint at border and large "3-3." Andrew Jackson at upper left. (MD10G6a)

5.2.4 R-2

$5.00 Ca. 1858. Engraving, imprint: Bald, Cousland & Co., Phila. & New York. Red FIVE security print. (MD10G2a) *Note:* Haxby catalog number also used on $1.00.

5.2.1

5.2.2

5.2.3

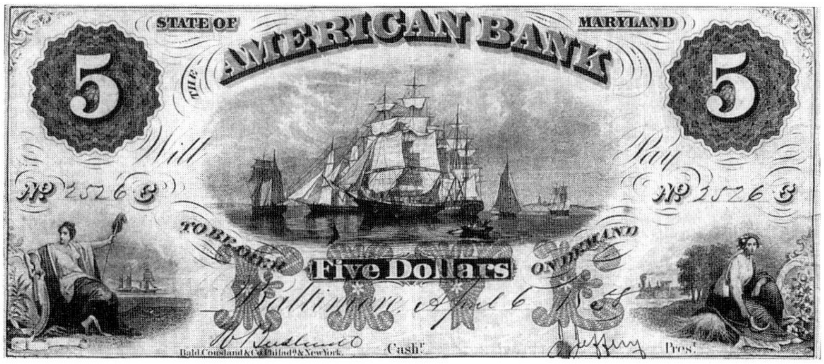

5.2.4

5.2.4 P R-4

$5.00 Ca. 1858. Engraving, imprint: Bald, Cousland & Co., Phila. & New York. Red FIVE security print. Proof of No. 5.2.4.

5.2.5 P R-4

$5.00 Ca. 1858. Engraving, imprint: Bald, Cousland & Co., Phila. & New York. Same as No. 5.2.4, except without red security overprint. Proof.

5.2.6 R-4

$5.00 Ca. 1858. Engraving, imprint: Bald, Cousland & Co., Phila. & New York. Security network and "V V" in green as well as red FIVE security print. (MD10G2b)

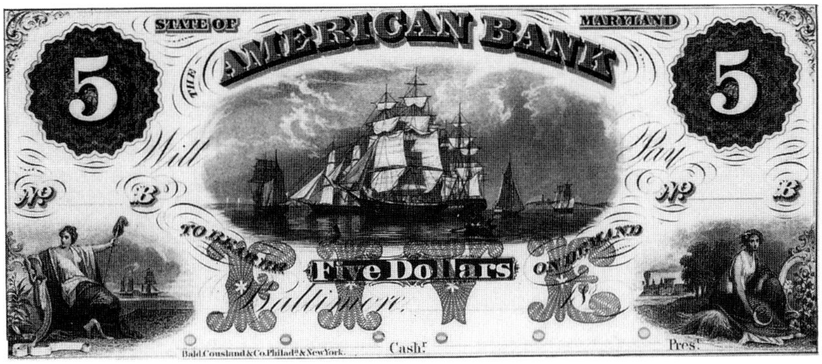

5.2.4 P

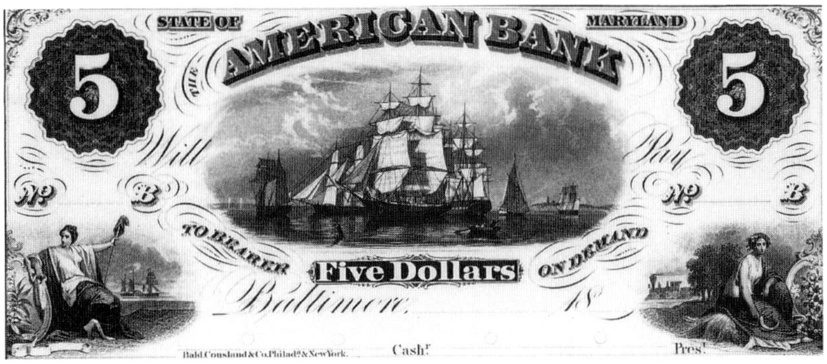

5.2.5 P

5.2.6

5.3 American Coffee House

J. D. Webster was the proprietor of this coffeehouse at 9 North Liberty St.

5.3.1 R-7

6 1/4c Printed date July 1, 1840. Letterpress, imprint: Murphy, Printer, 146 Market St.

5.3.1

5.3.3 R-7
25c Printed date July 1, 1840. Letterpress, imprint: Murphy, Printer, Baltimore. Vignette of Baltimore Harbor looking north from Federal Hill.

5.3.4 R-7
25c Printed date July 1, 1840. Letterpress, imprint: Manly & Orr, Printers, Philadelphia.

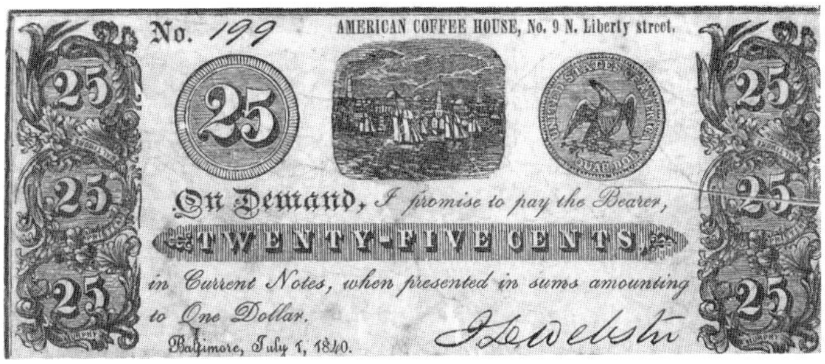

5.3.3

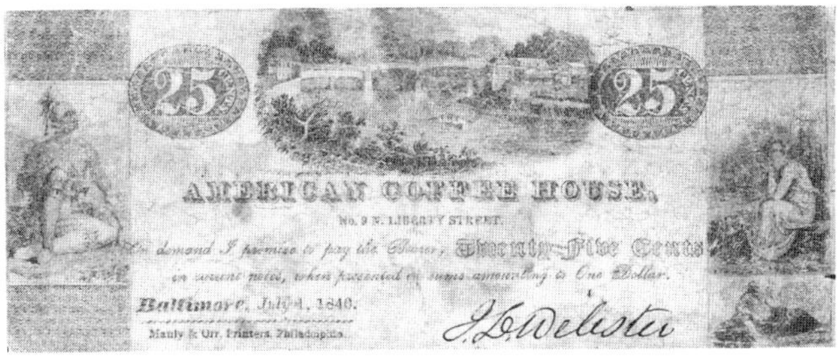

5.3.4

5.4 The Atlantic Company of Baltimore

The act to incorporate this company was passed by the General Assembly of Maryland on February 5, 1836. There were eight original stockholders and the purpose of the company was for "establishing a line or lines of steamships or other vessels, for the conveyance of passengers and property on the ocean to and from Baltimore, or elsewhere." Interestingly, the act specifically stated that "nothing herein contained shall be so construed as to confer banking privileges on said corporation, nor the right to issue any bill or note in the form or style of a bank note." Despite this restriction, the promissory notes issued by the company are very much in the format and design of bank notes and they apparently circulated in much the same fashion.

5.4.1 R-7
$1.00 Ca. 1836–40. Engraving, imprint: Rawdon, Wright, & Hatch, New York. Same design as $100.00, No. 5.4.8.

5.4.2 R-7
$2.00 Ca. 1836–40. Engraving, imprint: Rawdon, Wright & Hatch, New York. Same design as $100.00, No. 5.4.8.

5.4.1

5.4.3 R-7

$3.00 Ca. 1836–40. Engraving, imprint: Rawdon, Wright, & Hatch, New York. Same design as $100.00, No. 5.4.8.

5.4.8 R-7

$100.00 Ca. 1836–40. Engraving, imprint: Rawdon, Wright & Hatch, New York. The left and right vignettes show portraits of Charles Carroll of Carrollton and William Penn respectively. Reverse of $100.00 note.

5.4.9 R-7

$500.00 Ca. 1836–40. Engraving, imprint: Rawdon, Wright & Hatch, New York. Similar in design to $100.00, No. 5.4.8. Late reprint by the American Bank Note Company from the original plate.

5.4.3

5.4.8

5.5 The Bank of Baltimore

Charter approved December 24, 1795. Opened for business January 2, 1797. Converted to and became the National Bank of Baltimore in 1865. The bank was located at the northeast corner of Baltimore and St. Paul streets.

Post notes of unknown denominations and designs were issued before 1800 and during the 1830s.

5.5.1 R-7

6 1/4c Printed date 1815. Letterpress, imprint: J. Robinson, Printer. Similar to 12 1/2c, No. 5.5.5. (MD15G4)

5.5.2 SENC

6 1/4c Printed date 1816. Letterpress, imprint: J. Robinson, Printer. Similar to 12 1/2c, No. 5.5.5. (MD15G4a)

5.5.4 SENC

12 1/2c Printed date 1815. Letterpress, imprint: J. Robinson Printer. Similar to 12 1/2c, No. 5.5.5. (MD15G8)

5.5.5 R-4
12 1/2c Printed date 1816. Letterpress, imprint: J. Robinson Printer. (MD15G8a)

5.5.6 R-7
12 1/2c Printed date 1816. Letterpress, imprint: J. Robinson Printer. Similar to 12 1/2c, No. 5.5.5, except on pink paper.

5.5.8 R-7
25c Printed date 1815. Letterpress, imprint: J. Robinson, Printer. Similar to 12 1/2c, No. 5.5.5. (MD15G12)

5.5.9 SENC
25c Printed date 1816. Letterpress, imprint: J. Robinson, Printer. Similar to 12 1/2c, No. 5.5.5. (MD15G12a)

5.5.11 SENC
50c Printed date 1815. Letterpress, imprint: J. Robinson, Printer. Similar to 12 1/2c, No. 5.5.5. (MD15G16)

5.5.12 SENC
50c Printed date 1816. Letterpress, imprint: J. Robinson, Printer. Similar to 12 1/2c, No. 5.5.5. (MD15G16a)

5.5.14 R-7
$1.00 Ca. 1815–18. Letterpress, no imprint.

5.5.15 R-7
$1.00 Ca. 1815–18. Engraving, imprint: Murray, Draper, Fairman & Co. Same as No. 5.5.16, except for date. (MD15G20)

5.5.16 R-6
$1.00 Printed partial date 184_. Engraving, imprint: Murray, Draper, Fairman & Co. (MD15G20a)

5.5.17 R-7
$1.00 Printed partial date March 1st, 184_. Engraving, imprint: Danforth, Spencer & Hufty, New York / Spencer, Hufty & Danforth, Philada. Same as No. 5.5.18, except for date. (MD15G24)

5.5.18 R-6
$1.00 Printed partial date March 1, 18__ (ca. 1861). Engraving, imprint: Danforth, Spencer & Hufty, New York / Spencer, Hufty & Danforth, Philada. (MD15G24a)

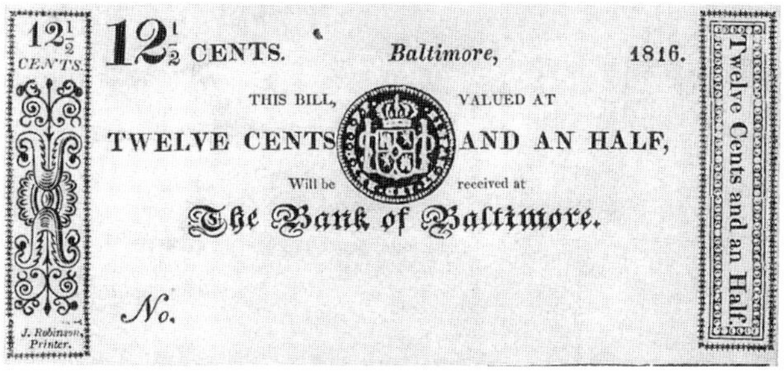

5.5.5

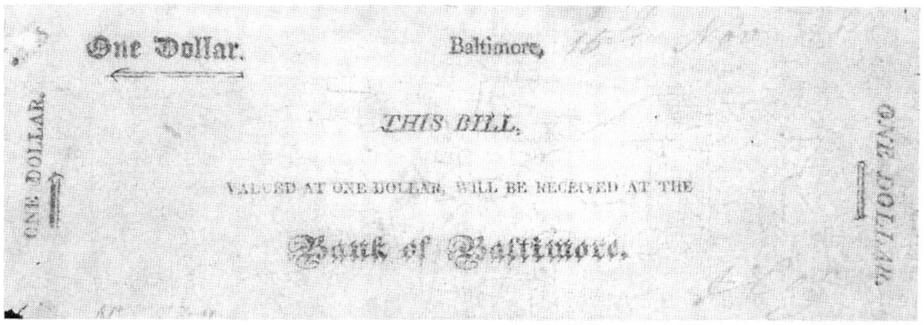

5.5.14

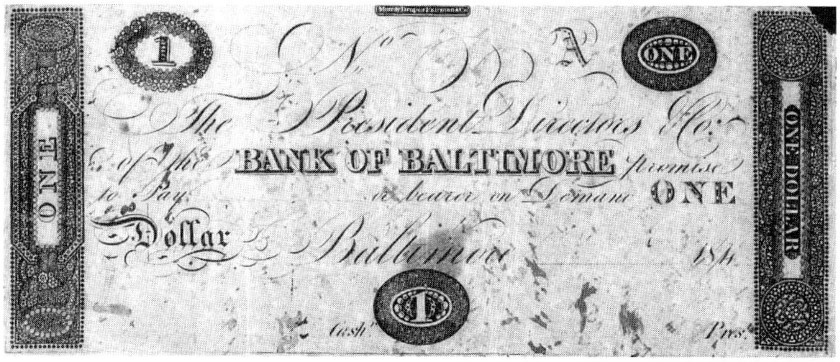

5.5.16

5.5.18

5.5.18 P R-6

$1.00 Printed partial date March 1, 18__ (ca. 1861). Engraving, imprint: Danforth, Spencer & Hufty, New York / Spencer, Hufty & Danforth, Philada. Proof of No. 5.5.18.

5.5.19 R-7

$1.00 Printed date March 1, 1862. Engraving, imprint: Danforth, Spencer & Hufty, New York / Spencer, Hufty, & Danforth, Philada. Similar to No. 5.5.17, but with THE PRESIDENT, DIRECTORS & CO. OF added in small letters above the beginning of the bank's name and date. (MD15G24b)

5.5.20 SENC

$2.00 Ca. 1810s. Engraving, imprint: Murray, Draper, Fairman & Co. Similar to No. 5.5.21. (MD15G28)

5.5.21 R-6

$2.00 Printed partial date 184_. Engraving, imprint: Murray, Draper, Fairman & Co. (MD15G28a)

5.5.21 C R-4

$2.00 Printed partial date 184_. Engraving, imprint: Murray, Draper, Fairman & Co. Counterfeit of No. 5.5.21. (MD15C28a)

5.5.23 SENC

$3.00 Printed partial date 181_. Engraving, imprint: Murray, Draper, Fairman & Co. Same as No. 5.5.24, except for date. (MD15G32)

5.5.24 R-7

$3.00 Printed partial date 184_. Engraving, imprint: Murray, Draper, Fairman & Co. Similar to No. 5.5.23, except for date. (MD15G32a)

5.5.24 C R-7

$3.00 Printed partial date 184_. Engraving, imprint: Murray, Draper, Fairman & Co. Counterfeit of No. 5.5.24. (MD15C32a)

5.5.18 P

5.5.19

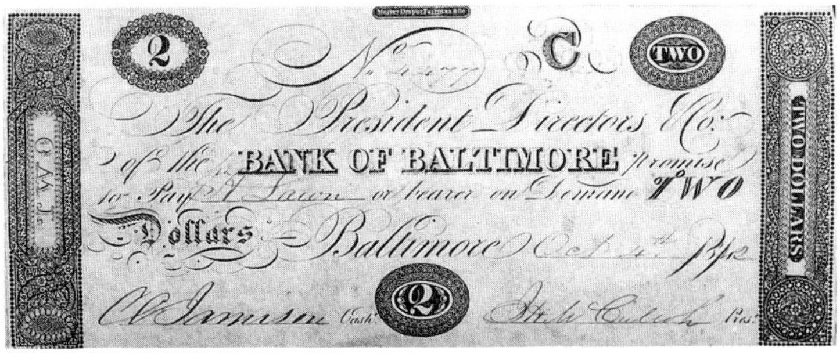

5.5.21 C

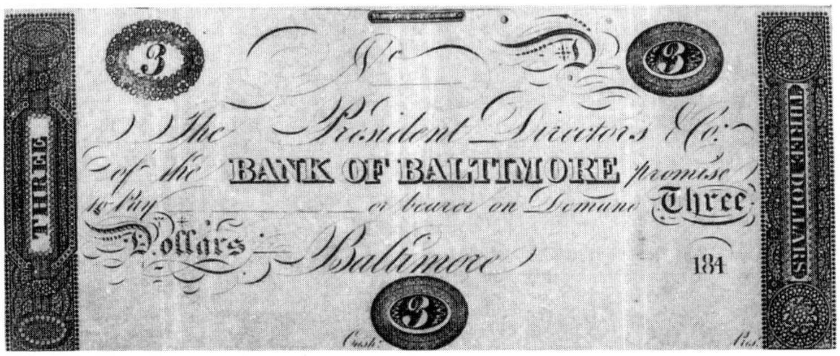

5.5.24

5.5.26 R-7

$5.00 Ca. 1790s. Engraving, no imprint. (MD15G36)

5.5.27 SENC

$5.00 Printed date 180_. No imprint (Perkins). Similar to counterfeit No. 5.5.27 C. (MD15G40)

5.5.27 C R-6

$5.00 Printed partial date 180_. Engraving, no imprint. Counterfeit of No. 5.5.27. (MD15C40)

5.5.29 R-7

$5.00 Ca. late 1800s–early 1810s. Engraving, no imprint. (MD15G42)

5.5.29 P R-7

$5.00 Ca. late 1800–early 1810s. Engraving, no imprint. Proof of No. 5.5.29.

5.5.29 C R-6

$5.00 Ca. 1810. Engraving, no imprint. Counterfeit of No. 5.5.29. (MD15C42)

5.5.31 R-7

$5.00 Ca. 1810s–30s. Engraving, imprint: Murray, Draper, Fairman & Co. Similar to counterfeit No. 5.5.31 C. (MD15G46)

5.5.31 C R-6

$5.00 Ca. 1820–30s. Engraving, imprint: Murray, Draper, Fairman & Co. Counterfeit of No. 5.5.31. (MD15C46)

5.5.33 P R-5

$5.00 Ca. 1830s. Engraving, imprint: Draper, Underwood, Bald & Spencer. Proof. (MD15G54)

5.5.34 R R-7

$5.00 Ca. 1840s. Engraving, imprint: Murray, Draper, Fairman & Co. Raised from $1.00, No. 5.5.15 or No. 5.5.16. (MD15R5)

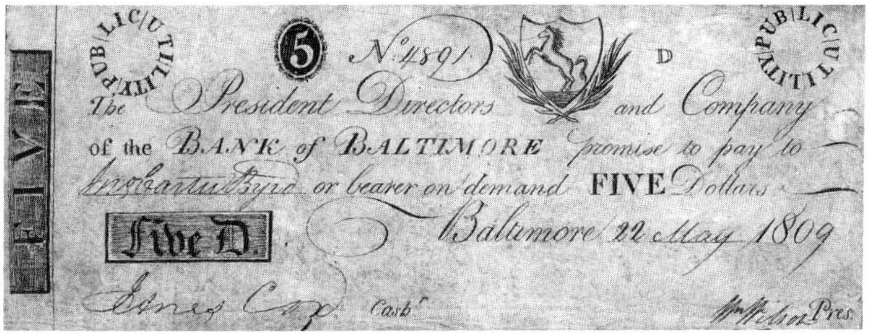

5.5.27 C

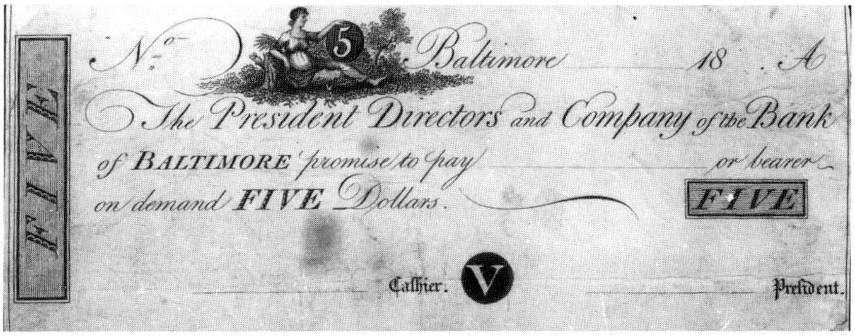

5.5.29 P

Detail of genuine vignette, 5.5.29

Detail of counterfeit vignette, 5.5.29 C

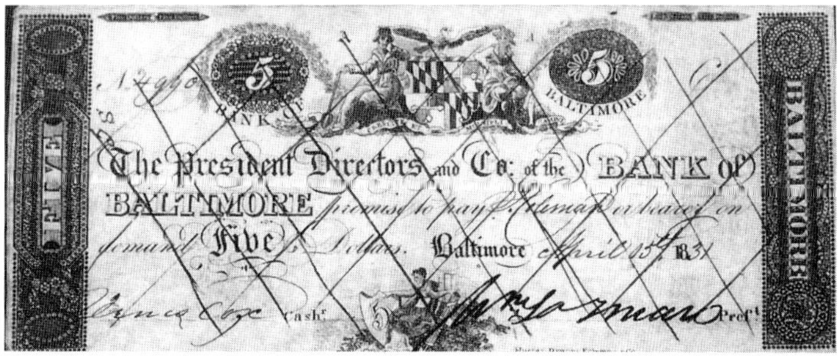

5.5.31 C

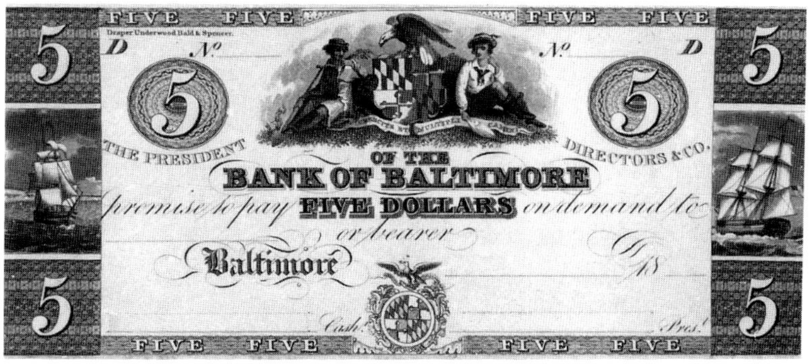

5.5.33 P

5.5.35 R-7

$5.00 Ca. 1850s. Engraving, imprint: Underwood, Bald, Spencer & Hufty; Danforth, Underwood & Co. (MD15G58)

5.5.36 P R-6

$5.00 Ca. 1840s–50s. Engraving, imprint: Underwood, Bald, Spencer & Hufty / Danforth, Underwood & Co. Similar to No. 5.5.35, without THE PRESIDENT, DIRECTORS & CO. on either side of the central vignette. Proof.

5.5.37 SENC

$10.00 Ca. 1790s. No information available. (MD15G62)

5.5.38 R-7

$10.00 Printed partial date 180_. Engraving, no imprint (Perkins). Similar to counterfeit No. 5.5.38 C. (MD15G64)

5.5.38 C R-7

$10.00 Printed partial date 180_. Engraving, no imprint (Perkins). Counterfeit of No. 5.5.38. (MD15C64)

5.5.39 SENC

$10.00 Ca. 1810s. Engraving, no imprint (Perkins). Similar to No. 5.5.38 except for date. (MD15G66)

5.5.39 C R-6

$10.00 Ca. 1810s. Engraving, no imprint (Perkins). Counterfeit of No. 5.5.39. (MD15C66)

5.5.41 SENC

$10.00 Ca. 1810s. Engraving, no imprint. Similar to counterfeit No. 5.5.41 C. (MD15G70)

5.5.41 C R-6

$10.00 Ca. 1810s. Engraving, no imprint. Counterfeit of No. 5.5.41. (MD15C70)

5.5.35

5.5.36 P

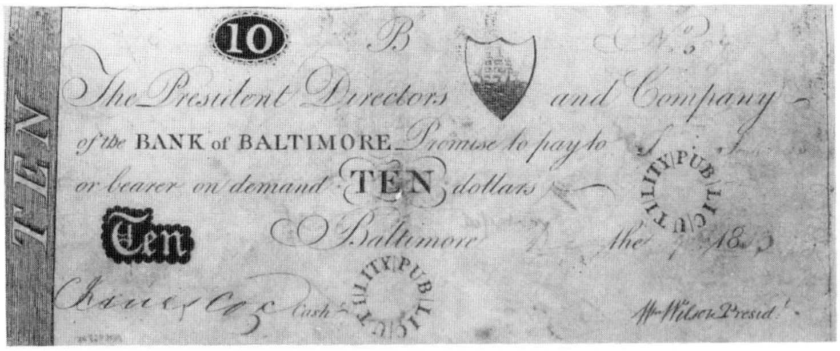

5.5.38

5.5.38 C

5.5.43 SENC

$10.00 Ca. 1810s–1830s. Engraving, imprint: Murray, Draper, Fairman & Co. Similar to counterfeit No. 5.5.43 C. (MD15G74)

5.5.43 C R-3

$10.00 Ca. 1820s–1830s. Engraving, imprint: Murray, Draper, Fairman & Co. Counterfeit of No. 5.5.43. This counterfeit was reported in the *Sun* of October 6, 1837, as having been detected at Robinson's Exchange Office. (MD15C74)

5.5.45 S R-7

$10.00 Ca. 1838. Engraving, imprint: New England Bank Note Co. Spurious. (MD15S5)

5.5.46 R SENC

$10.00 Ca. 1840s. Engraving, imprint: Murray, Draper, Fairman & Co. Raised from No. 5.5.21 or No. 5.5.21 C. (MD15R10)

5.5.47 P R-6

$10.00 Ca. 1850s. Engraving, imprint: Underwood, Bald, Spencer & Hufty, Philada. & N. York. Proof. (MD15G78)

5.5.48 SENC

$20.00 Ca. 1790s. No information available. (MD15G82)

5.5.49 SENC

$20.00 Printed year date 1800. Engraving, no imprint (Perkins). Similar to counterfeit No. 5.5.49 C. (MD15G86)

5.5.49 C R-7

$20.00 Printed year date 1800. Engraving, no imprint (Perkins). Similar to No. 5.5.51 except for date. (MD15C86)

5.5.50 SENC

$20.00 Printed year date 1809. Engraving, no imprint (Perkins). Similar to No. 5.5.51 except for date. (MD15G86b)

5.5.50 C R-7

$20.00 Printed year date 1809. Engraving, no imprint (Perkins). Counterfeit of No. 5.5.50. (MD15C86b)

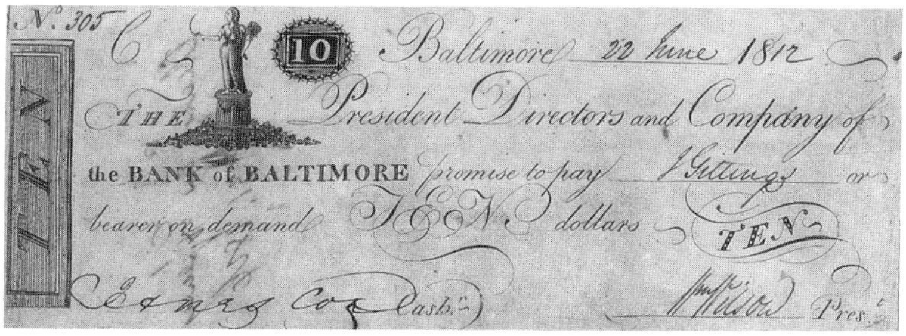

5.5.41 C

5.5.43 C

5.5.45 S

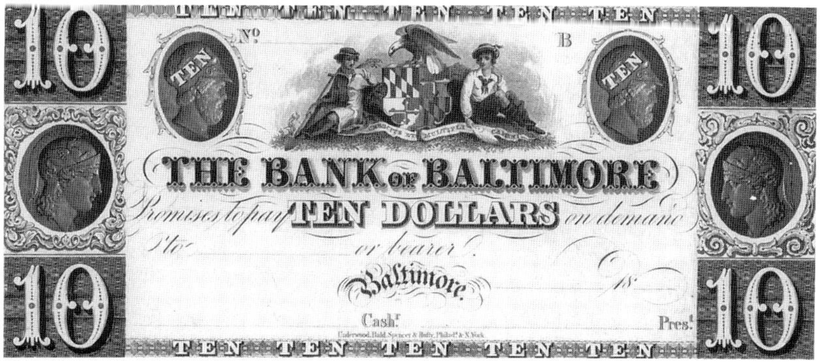

5.5.47 P

5.5.51 SENC
$20.00 Ca. 1810s. Engraving, no imprint (Perkins). Similar to counterfeit No. 5.5.51 C. (MD15G86c)

5.5.51 C R-6
$20.00 Ca. 1810s. Engraving, no imprint (Perkins). Counterfeit of No. 5.5.51. (MD15C86c)

5.5.53 R SENC
$20.00 Ca. 1840s. Engraving, imprint: Murray, Draper, Fairman & Co. Raised from $1.00, No. 5.5.15 or No. 5.5.16. (MD15R15)

5.5.54 P R-7
$20.00 Ca. 1850s. Engraving, imprint: Toppan, Carpenter, Casilear & Co. *Right:* Farmer and sailor flanking shield surmounted by eagle. 20 at lower right. *Left:* 20. Proof. (MD15G94)

5.5.56 P R-7
$50.00 Ca. 1810s–20s. Engraving, imprint: Murray, Draper, Fairman & Co. Proof.

5.5.57 R-7
$50.00 Ca. 1820s–30s. Engraving, imprint: Fairman, Draper, Underwood & Co. (MD15G100)

5.5.59 R SENC
$50.00 Ca. 1824. Engraving, imprint: Murray, Draper, Fairman & Co. Raised from $5.00, No. 5.5.29. (MD15R20)

5.5.60 P R-7
$50.00 Ca. 1850s. Engraving, imprint: Toppan, Carpenter & Casilear, Phila. Proof. (MD15G104)

5.5.61 SENC
$100.00 Ca. 1795–99. Engraving, no imprint. No additional information available.

5.5.62 SENC
$100.00 Ca. 1810s–1830s. Engraving, imprint: Murray, Draper, Fairman & Co. Similar to counterfeit No. 5.5.62 C. (MD15G110)

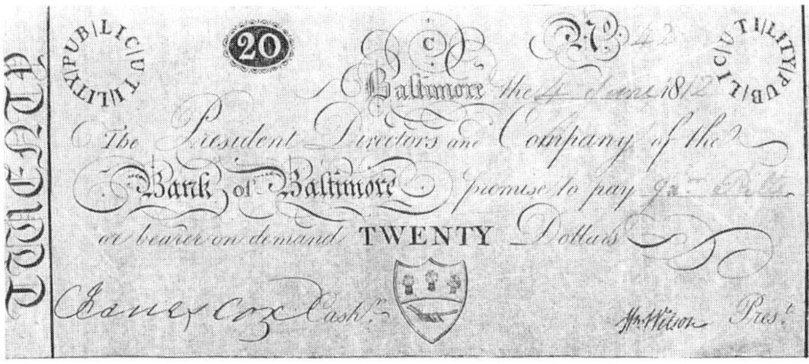

5.5.51 C

5.5.54 P

5.5.56 P

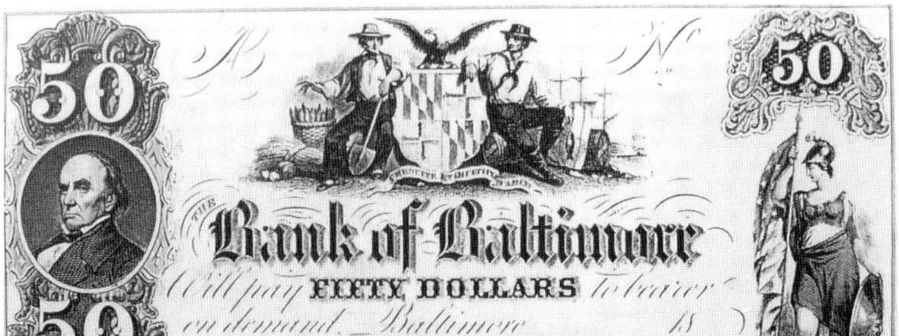

5.5.60 P

5.5.62 c R-7

$100.00 Ca. 1862. Engraving, imprint: Murray, Draper, Fairman & Co. Counterfeit of No. 5.5.62.

5.5.64 p R-7

$100.00 Ca. 1850s. Engraving, imprint: Toppan, Carpenter, Casilear & Co. Phila. Proof. (MD15G114)

5.5.64 c SENC

$100.00 Ca. 1850s. Engraving, imprint: Toppan, Carpenter, Casilear & Co., Philada. Counterfeit of same design as No. 5.5.64 p. (MD15C114)

5.5.66 r SENC

$100.00 Ca. 1850s. Engraving, imprint: Toppan, Carpenter, Casilear & Co. Raised from $20.00 of same design as No. 5.5.54 p. (MD15R25)

5.5.67 p R-7

$500.00 Ca. 1830s–1850s. Engraving, imprint: Underwood, Bald, Spencer & Hufty, Philada. / Danforth, Underwood & Co., New York. Proof. (MD15G118)

5.5.68 p R-7

$1000.00 Ca. 1830s–50s. Engraving, imprint: Underwood, Bald, Spencer & Hufty, Philada. / Danforth, Underwood & Co. New York. Proof. (MD15G122)

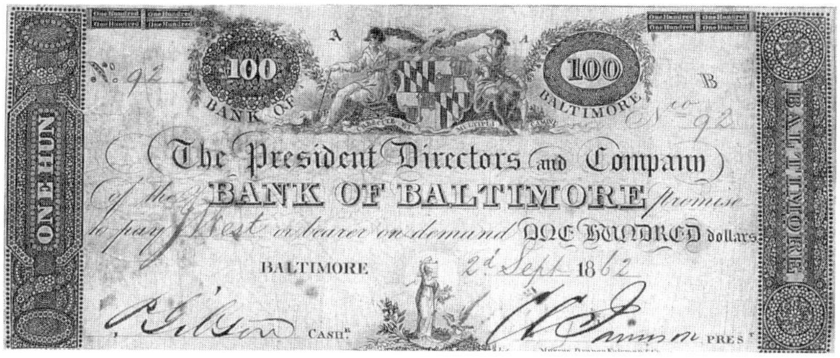

5.5.62 c

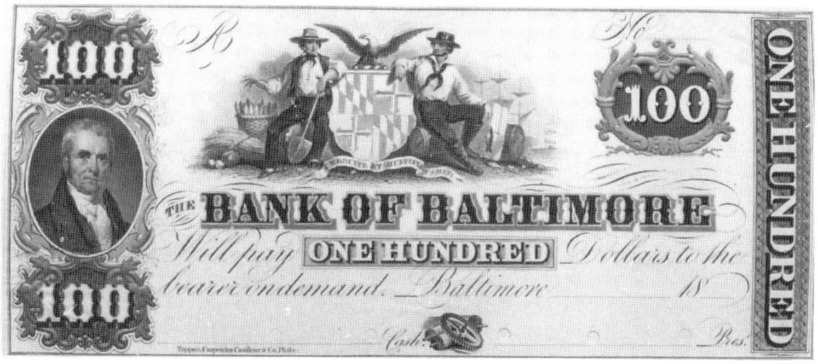

5.5.64 p

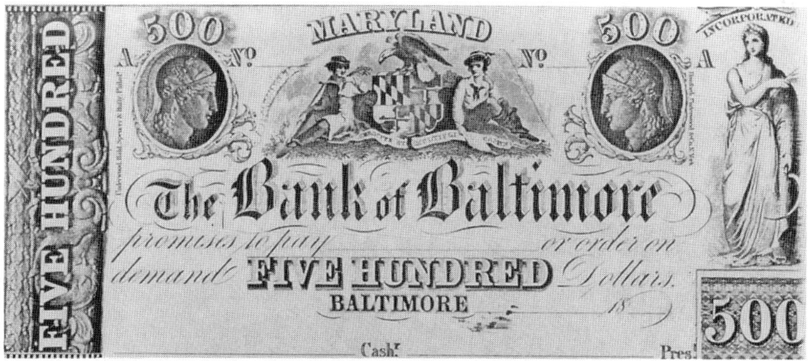

5.5.67 p

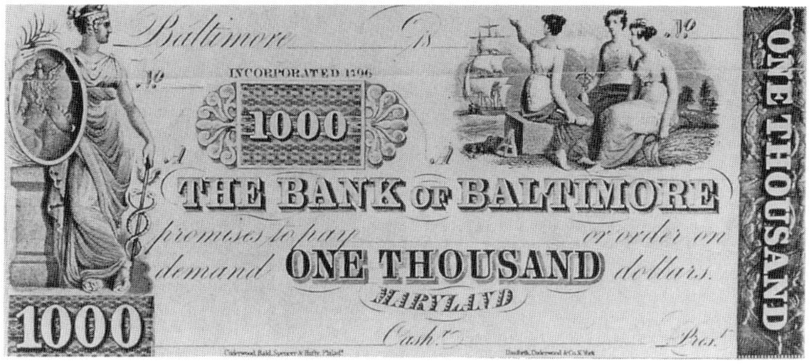

5.5.68 p

5.6 Baltimore Bank

A nonexistent bank, which is represented only by fraudulent notes that were intended to pass for those of the Bank of Baltimore.

5.6.6 S R-7

$20.00 Ca. 1807. Engraving, no imprint. Spurious. (M16S10)

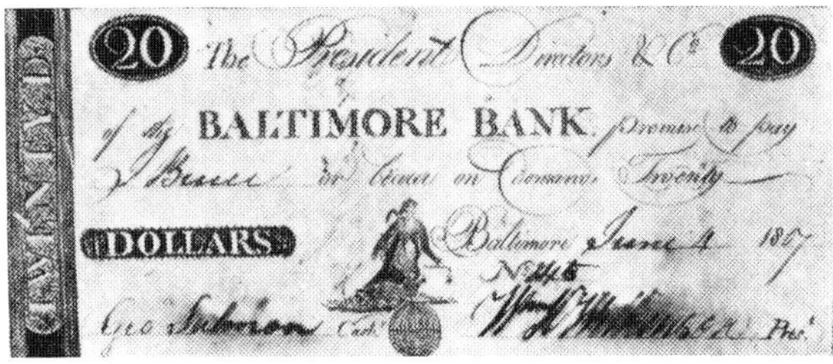

5.6.6 S

5.8 Baltimore City Hotel

The *Baltimore Sun* for a period of some months during the "hard times" of 1837–41 ran many editorials, news items, and letters from readers on the subject of "shinplasters" and the refusal of the various banks to redeem their currency issues in specie. An amusing series of "news items" concerning a fictitious "Tompkins" family and its problems with shinplasters appeared in July 1837. Following an editorial against the proliferation of scrip on July 13, 1837, there appeared the item illustrated herewith.

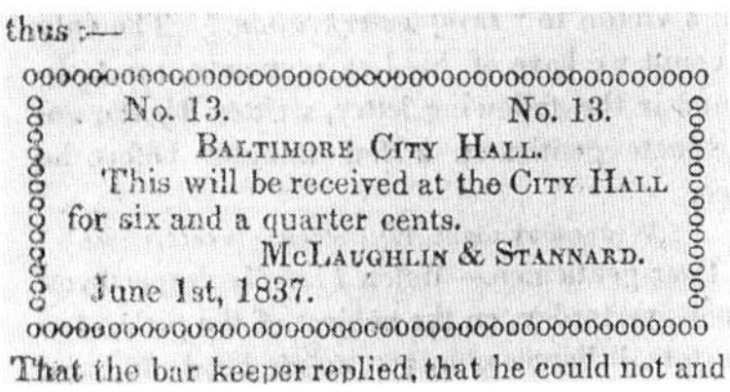

thus :—

No. 13. No. 13.
BALTIMORE CITY HALL.
This will be received at the CITY HALL for six and a quarter cents.
McLAUGHLIN & STANNARD.
June 1st, 1837.

That the bar keeper replied, that he could not and

The City Directory for 1837–38 has the following listing: "McLaughlin & Stannard, City Hotel (formerly Barnum's) cor Calvert and Fayette sts." The 1840–41 edition contains a similar listing which also included the additional information that the two men were the proprietors of the Hotel. In the 1842 edition, D. Barnum appears as the proprietor, the other two names having disappeared. The "note" shown in the *Sun* article, having been made up from printer's type, has never been recorded, of course. However, just prior to the completion of this book, the lovely little 6 1/4c note shown below came to light. The use of "City hall" in the newspaper "illustration" instead of the "City Hotel" on the actual note may have been simply a typesetter's error or, at least as likely, an editorial change designed to embarrass the City administration which had issued scrip on May 16, 1837.

5.8.1 R-7

6 1/4c Printed date June 1st, 1837. Engraving, imprint: Horton, Balto. Vignette of the City Hotel and, to its right across Fayette St., the Battle Monument at the intersection of Calvert and Fayette streets.

5.8.1

5.9 Baltimore & Frederick Turnpike Road

Incorporated in 1805, this company began work on the road the same year. By late 1807, the company had completed or had under construction 37 of its 62 miles of road from Baltimore to Boonsborough. The road followed a westward course from Baltimore and Eutaw streets in Baltimore to Boonsborough, via Ellicott's Mills, New Market, Frederick, and Middletown. In 1809, the Maryland General Assembly granted permission for the construction of a road from Frederick to Harper's Ferry. A third extension carried the road westward from Boonsborough to the beginning of the Cumberland

Turnpike Company's road which, in turn, connected with the National Road at Cumberland. Small-change scrip reportedly was issued between 1814 and 1816 in denominations up to 50 cents and withdrawn and destroyed in 1818.

5.9.2 R-7

2c Printed date 1st Jan. 1816. Letterpress, imprint: Jos. Robinson, Printer. Similar to 3c note, No. 5.9.3.

5.9.3 R-7

3c Printed date 1st Jan. 1816. Letterpress, imprint: Jos. Robinson, Printer.

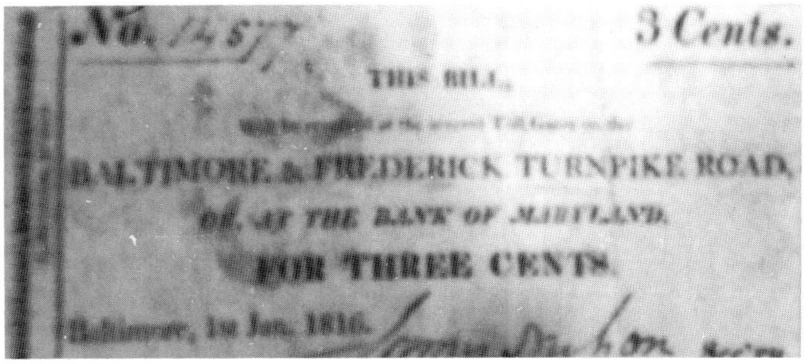

5.9.3

5.10 Baltimore & Ohio Railroad Company

First operating in 1830 with horsedrawn cars, the B&O ran as far as Ellicott's Mills, 13 miles west of Baltimore. One of Peter Cooper's steam locomotives was soon used experimentally, making the run to Ellicott's Mills in slightly over an hour. In 1835, a branch line linked Baltimore with Washington; and by 1842 the railroad ran as far west as Cumberland. During the years 1839 to 1841 the stock of the city of Baltimore, which had been received by the Baltimore & Ohio in payment of a subscription to the railroad company's stock by the city, had fallen so low in the market that the railroad company could not realize par for the city stock. The company, therefore, adopted the plan of issuing the certificates described below, which in turn were accepted at their face amount by contractors and others from whom the B&O purchased supplies. The certificates, which were widely accepted as media of exchange during the acute shortage of small change, entitled their holders to stock of the city of Baltimore when presented to the city in sums totaling not less than $100.

5.10.1 SENC

6 1/4c Dated May 18, 1840. Surviving example not confirmed but recorded by D. C. Wismer in the *Coin Collectors Journal,* December 1940. No other information available.

5.10.2 R-4

12 1/2c Printed date February 10, 1841. Engraving, imprint: Draper, Toppan & Co. Phila & New York.

5.10.3 R-5

25c Printed date February 10, 1841. Engraving, imprint: Draper, Toppan & Co. Phila. & New York.

5.10.2

5.10.3

5.10.4 R-5

50c Printed date February 10, 1841. Engraving, imprint: Draper, Toppan & Co., Phila. & New York.

5.10.5 P R-7

$1.00 Printed date January 1, 1840. Engraving, imprint: Draper, Toppan & Co. Phila. & New York. "Prest." located to the left of large numeral "1." Similar to No. 5.10.6. Proof.

5.10.6 R-7

$1.00 Printed date January 1, 1840. Engraving, imprint: Draper, Toppan & Co. Phila. & New York. "Prest." located to the right of large numeral "1" and signature lines prepared for a second signature of a person signing "for" the president.

5.10.7 P R-7

$1.00 Printed date January 1, 1840. Engraving, imprint: Underwood, Bald, Spencer & Hufty, Philada; Danforth, Underwood & Co., New York. "Pres't" located to right of large numeral "1" with single signature line. Proof.

5.10.8 P R-6

$1.00 Printed date January 1, 1840. Engraving, imprint: Underwood, Bald, Spencer & Hufty, Philada; Danforth, Underwood & Co. "Pres. t" located to right of large numeral "1" with second signature line above "For" and engraved signature of the president, Louis McLane. Similar to No. 5.10.7 P. Proof.

5.10.9 R-7

$2.00 Printed date January 1, 1840. Engraving, imprint: Draper, Toppan & Co., Phila. "Pres't" to the left of the large numeral "2."

5.10.10 R-7

$2.00 Printed date January 1, 1840. Engraving, imprint: Draper, Toppan & Co., Phila. With "For" preceding the signer's signature and the engraved signature of the president, Louis McLane. Similar to No. 5.10.9.

5.10.4

5.10.6

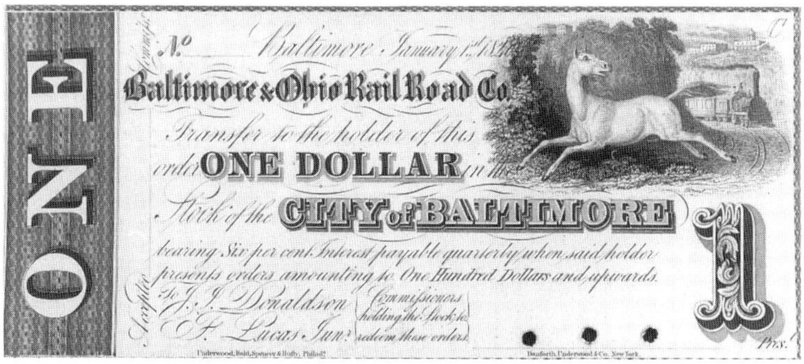

5.10.7 P

5.10.9

5.10.11 R-7

$3.00 Printed date January 1, 1840. Engraving, imprint: Draper, Toppan & Co. Phila. With "For" preceding the signer's signature and the engraved signature of the president, Louis McLane.

5.10.12 P R-7

$5.00 Printed date January 1, 1840. Engraving, imprint: Draper, Toppan & Co., Phila. & New York. Proof.

5.10.13 SENC

$5.00 Center vignette with 3 cherubs. Surviving example not confirmed but recorded by D. C. Wismer in the *Coin Collectors Journal,* December 1940. No other information available.

5.10.14 P R-7

$10.00 Printed partial date 1840. Engraving, imprint: Draper, Toppan & Co., Phila. Proof.

5.10.16 SENC

$50.00 Surviving example not confirmed but recorded by D. C. Wismer in the *Coin Collectors Journal,* December 1940. No other information available.

5.10.18 SENC

$100.00 Surviving example not confirmed but recorded by D. C. Wismer in the *Coin Collectors Journal,* December 1940.

5.10.11

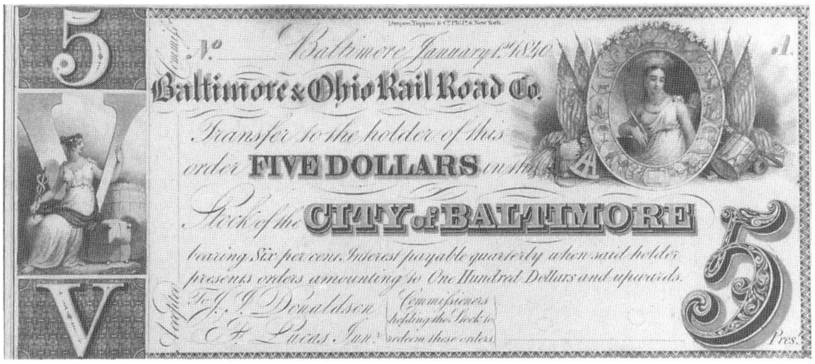

5.10.12 P

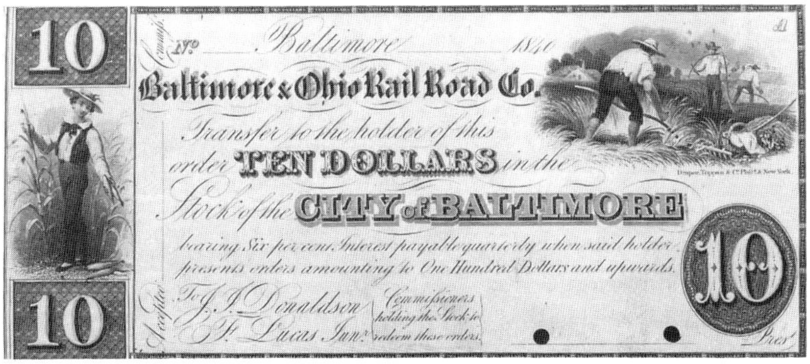

5.10.14 P

5.11 The Baltimore Real Estate Savings Institution

Established in January 1840 with a small office "on north Gay street," the principal officers being John W. Clark, president, and Henry Baker, treasurer. The office was moved to "No. 9 Lombard street, between South and Calvert streets," on March 2, 1840. On May 21, 1840, a notice in the *Sun* announced "the election of Joseph W. Stewart President, Vice John W. Clark, resigned." The following day a short notice appeared to the effect that the institution was permanently located at 6 Lombard St. and was open daily from 9 A.M. to 3 P.M. After the collapse of several other "shin-plaster establishments" on September 9, the office was moved back to "Gay street near Bel-Air market" on September 15. Finally, on October 28, 1840, the business was suspended after a mob wrecked the office and was never reopened.

5.11.1 R-6

6 1/4c Printed partial date 184_. Lithography, imprint: Lith. by Ed. Weber Baltimore.

5.11.3 R-4

12 1/2c Printed partial date 184_. Lithography, imprint: Lith. by Ed. Weber Baltimore.

5.11.5 R-4

25c Printed partial date 184_. Lithography, imprint: Lith. by Ed. Weber, Baltimore.

5.11.6 R-3

25c Ca. 1840. Engraving, imprint: Underwood, Bald, Spencer & Hufty, Philada. / Danforth, Underwood & Co., New York.

5.11.6 P R-7

25c Ca. 1840. Engraving, imprint: Underwood, Bald, Spencer & Hufty, Philada. / Danforth, Underwood & Co., New York. Proof.

5.11.8 R-3

50c Ca. 1840. Engraving, imprint: Underwood, Bald, Spencer & Hufty, Philada. / Danforth, Underwood & Co., New York.

5.11.8 P R-7

50c Ca. 1840. Engraving, imprint: Underwood, Bald, Spencer & Hufty, Philada. / Danforth, Underwood & Co., New York. Proof.

5.11.1

5.11.3

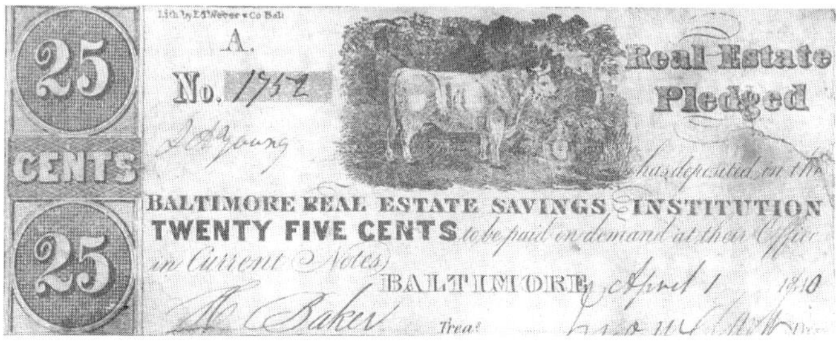

5.11.5

5.11.6

5.11.8

5.11.9 R-3

$1.00 Ca. 1840. Engraving, imprint: Underwood, Bald, Spencer & Hufty, Philada. / Danforth, Underwood & Co., New York.

5.11.9 P R-7

$1.00 Ca. 1840. Engraving, imprint: Underwood, Bald, Spencer & Hufty, Philada. / Danforth, Underwood & Co., New York. Proof.

5.11.10 R-4

$2.00 Ca. 1840. Engraving, imprint: Underwood, Bald, Spencer & Hufty, Philada. / Danforth, Underwood & Co., New York.

5.11.12 P R-7

$5.00 Ca. 1840. Engraving, imprint: Underwood, Bald, Spencer & Hufty, Philada / Danforth, Underwood & Co., New York. Proof.

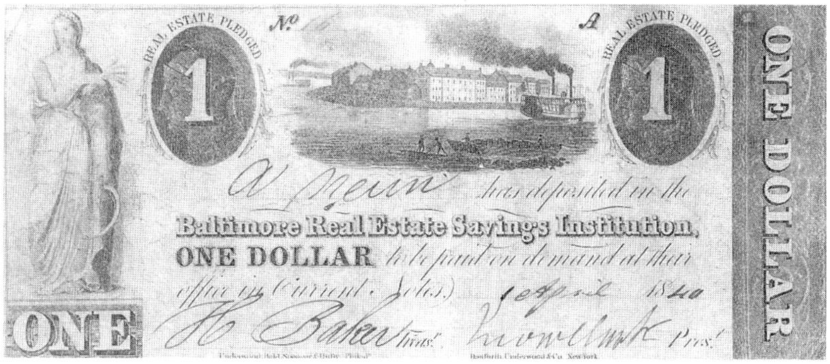

5.11.9

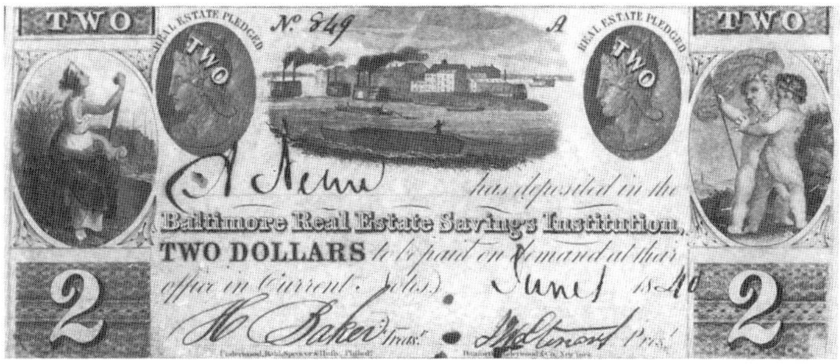

5.11.10

5.11.12 P

5.12 Baltimore and Reisterstown Turnpike Road Company

Incorporated in 1805, this company built a road 66 feet in width with 24 feet in stone or gravel, from Franklin Street in Baltimore to Reisterstown and thence in two directions toward the Pennsylvania line. It was completed in 1815. The first office in Baltimore was at the northeast corner of Liberty and German (now Redwood) streets; about 1813 the office was moved to Chatham Street near St. Paul's Lane. James Carroll was president and John F. Harris secretary of the company. It was discontinued as a toll road about 1915.

5.12.3 R-7

3c Printed date January 27, 1816. Letterpress, no imprint.

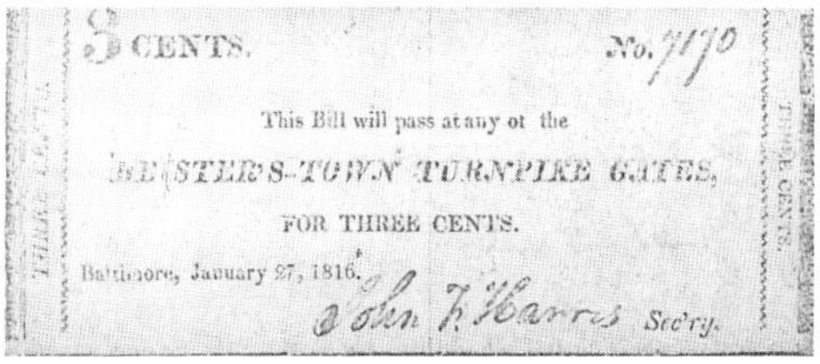

5.12.3

5.13 The Baltimore Savings Institution

A charter of a Baltimore Savings Institution was approved by the Maryland General Assembly on February 6, 1834, eighteen prominent Baltimore businessmen being the original incorporators. According to the charter, persons who made regular weekly deposits of at least one dollar and no more than five dollars for twelve consecutive months would have the privilege of becoming a member of the corporation. There was a provision for the issue of stock certificates with a par value of $26.00 each to such corporate members. All monies so received were to be invested in "public stocks or other securities" at the discretion of the directors. The corporation was specifically prohibited from issuing "any bill, note, or other device in the nature of a Bank Note." No evidence of the actual operation of this institution has been found.

An institution of the same name opened for business in the late spring of 1840, a newspaper advertisement of June 13 advising that it "is established upon a permanent basis" with an office "in North Charles Street one door from Baltimore Street." The public was informed that persons holding the notes of the institution could have them redeemed in Baltimore bank notes by presenting them at the office between 9 A.M. and 3 P.M. Three months later, on September 9, 1840, the institution failed to open for business, its president, Fred. H. Knapp, having disappeared. A few days later, he was reportedly seen in New York City. On September 17, 1840, he was arrested in Albany and returned to Baltimore, and three days later freed on bail of $1,000. No record of his ultimate fate has been found, nor that of his two associates, H. K. Murray and W. A. Benson, whose signatures also are to be found on the institution's notes.

A fitting denoument for this ill-fated endeavor is provided by an "endorsement" on the back of one of the institution's 25c notes, reading simply:

Stopt pay Sept. 9th
1840
Presdt. ran away

5.13.1 R-5
6 1/4c Printed date June 12, 1840. Letterpress, imprints: JOHN MURPHY PRINTER BALTO, on the vignette of the Battle Monument at left center, and MURPHY PRINTER on the vignette of the square-rigged ship at lower left. Text begins ON DEMAND THE.

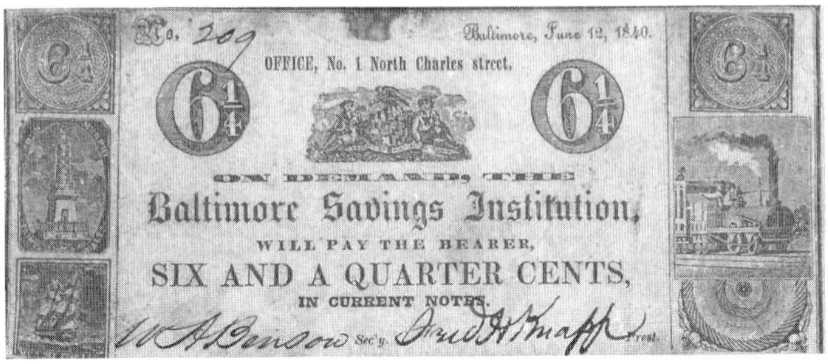

5.13.1

5.13.2 R-5
6 1/4c Printed date July 1, 1840. Letterpress, imprint: MURPHY, PRINTER. Similar to No. 5.13.1, but with changed printed date; first line of text reads TREASURER OF THE and third line PAY THE BEARER.

5.13.3 R-3

6 1/4c Printed date August 1, 1840. Letterpress, imprint: MURPHY, PRINTER 146 Market Street. Similar to No. 5.13.2. but left end features a vignette of George Washington, the date line relocated to lower left replacing the space for the secretary's signature, and the street address moved to the upper right. The text begins TREASURER OF THE and the third line reads PAY THE BEARER. The president's printed name is in relatively large type.

5.13.4 R-4

6 1/4c Printed date August 1, 1840. Similar to No. 5.13.1 but the president's printed name is in smaller type. Minor variations in the spacing of the letters in the third and fourth lines of the text and their relative alignments may be found.

5.13.5 R-4

12 1/2c Printed date June 12, 1840. Letterpress, imprint: MURPHY, PRINTER. Text begins ON DEMAND THE, and the third line reads WILL PAY THE BEARER. No printed name beneath the president's signature line. Street address above state arms vignette, upper center; date line upper right above coin.

5.13.6 R-4

12 1/2c Printed date July 1, 1840. Similar to No. 5.13.5, but with changed printed date; first line of text reads TREASURER OF THE, and third line, PAY THE BEARER.

5.13.7 R-3

12 1/2c Printed date August 1, 1840. Similar to No. 5.13.6 but with date line relocated to lower left replacing space for secretary's signature, and street address relocated to upper right. "For Fred. H. Knapp, Prest." inserted beneath signature line at lower right. Minor variations in the spacing of the letters in PAY THE BEARER and TWELVE AND A HALF CENTS and their relative alignments may be found.

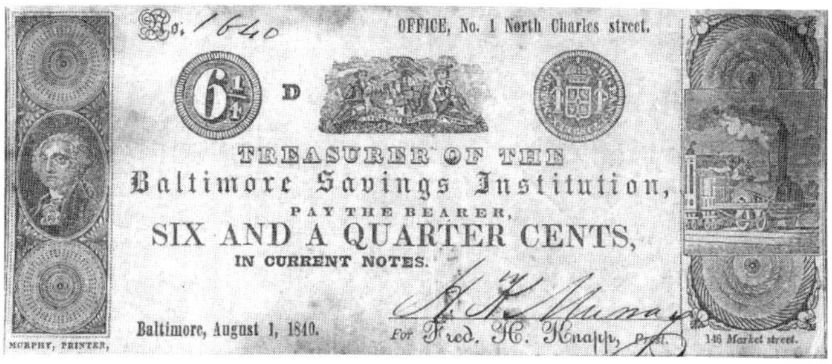

5.13.3

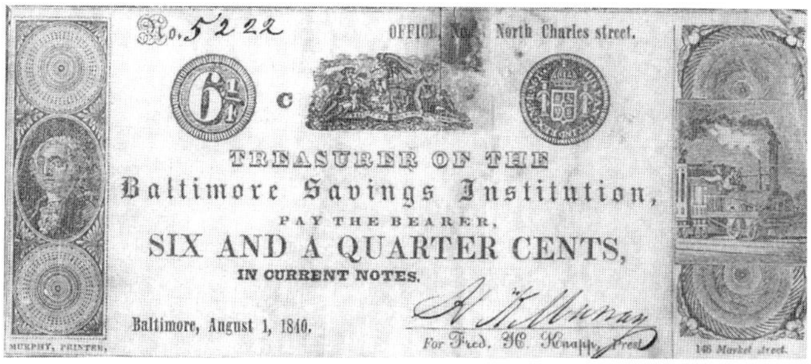

5.13.4

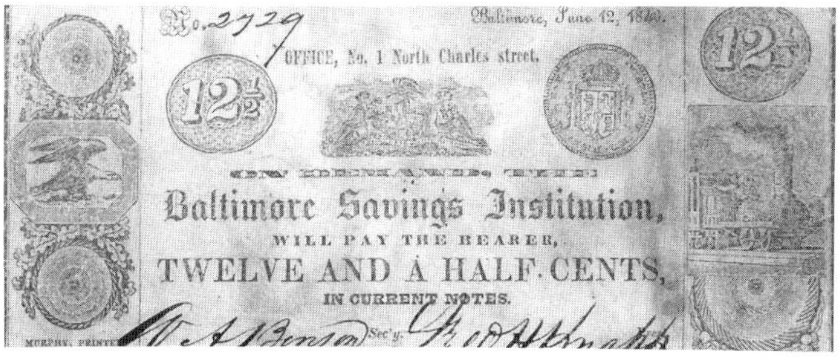

5.13.5

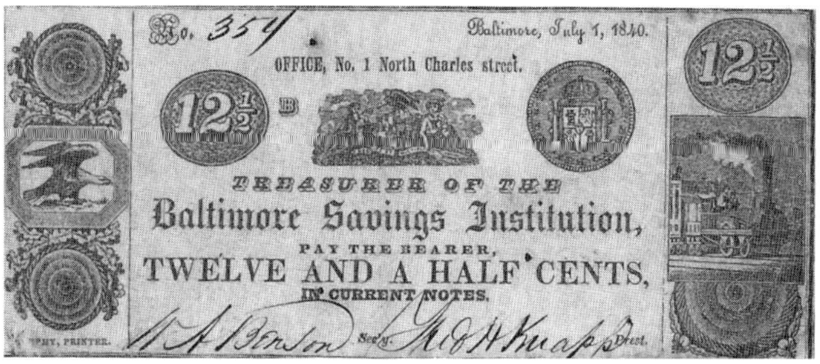

5.13.6

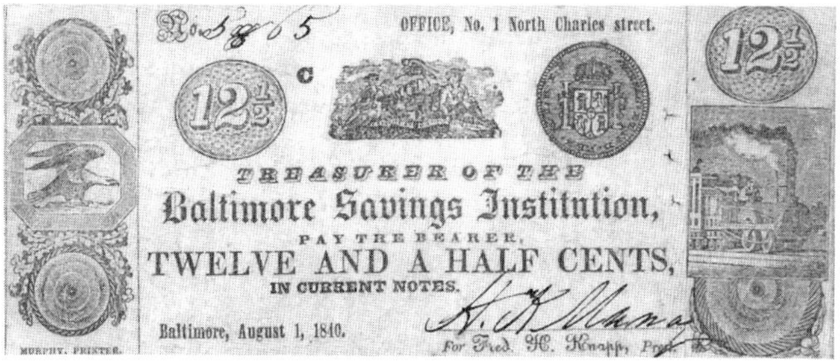

5.13.7

5.13.8 R-3

12 1/2c Printed date August 1, 1840. Similar to No. 5.13.7, but printed "Fred. H. Knapp" in taller letters.

5.13.9 R-3

25c Printed partial date 184_. Ca. 1840. Lithography, imprint: E. Weber & Co., Lith., Balto. The central vignette depicts a view of Baltimore, looking north from Federal Hill.

5.13.10 R-1

25c Ca. July 1840. Engraving, imprint: Underwood, Bald, Spencer & Hufty, Philada. / Danforth, Underwood & Co., New York.

5.13.10 P R-7

25c Ca. July 1840. Engraving, imprint: Underwood, Bald, Spencer & Hufty, Philada. / Danforth, Underwood & Co., New York. Proof.

5.13.11 R-2

25c Printed date August 6, 1840. Similar to No. 5.13.10 with full printed date and "Office, No. 1 Charles St." inserted at lower left in place of secretary's signature space, which has been moved to space above the president's signature and the word "for" added. The payment legend has also been changed by removing a space for the manuscript insertion of a payee's name.

5.13.12 SENC

25c Ca. 1840. Listed in "An Index of State Bank Notes that Illustrate Presidents" by John A. Muscalus as illustrating George Washington. No other information available.

5.13.13 R-1

50c Ca. July, 1840. Engraving, imprint: Underwood, Bald, Spencer & Hufty, Philada. / Danforth, Underwood & Co., New York.

5.13.13 P R-7

50c Ca. July 1840. Engraving, imprint: Underwood, Bald, Spencer & Hufty, Philada. / Danforth, Underwood & Co., New York. Proof.

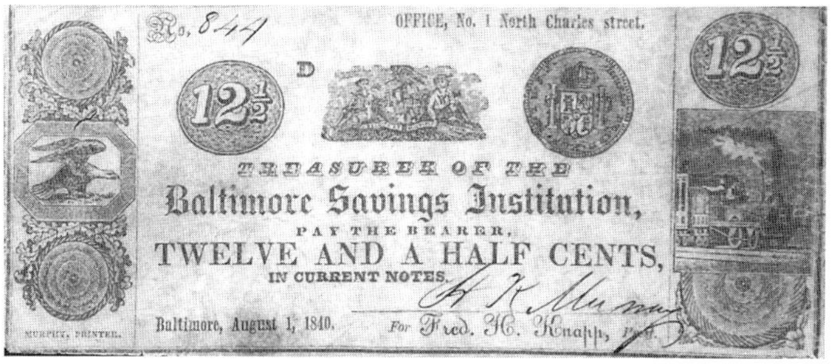

5.13.8

5.13.9

5.13.10

5.13.11

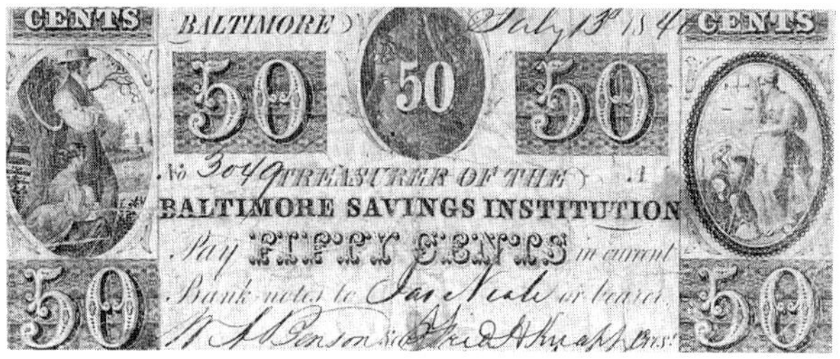

5.13.13

5.13.14 R-4

50c Printed date August 6, 1840. Similar to No. 5.13.13, with added street address, date, and other changes as in 25c, No. 5.13.11.

5.13.16 R-6

$1.00 Printed partial date 184_. Ca. 1840. Engraving, imprint: Underwood, Bald, Spencer & Hufty, Philada. / Danforth, Underwood & Co., N. York. Right-end vignette is Battle Monument, Baltimore.

5.13.17 R-1

$1.00 Ca. July–August 1840. Engraving, imprint: Underwood, Bald, Spencer & Hufty, Philada. / Danforth, Underwood & Co., New York.

5.13.17 P R-7

$1.00 Ca. July–August 1840. Engraving, imprint: Underwood, Bald, Spencer & Hufty, Philada. / Danforth, Underwood & Co., New York. Proof.

5.13.18 R-4

$1.00 Printed date August 6th 1840. Similar to $1.00, No. 5.13.17, but with the printed date and address, "Office, No. 1 Charles St." in lower left corner of center panel.

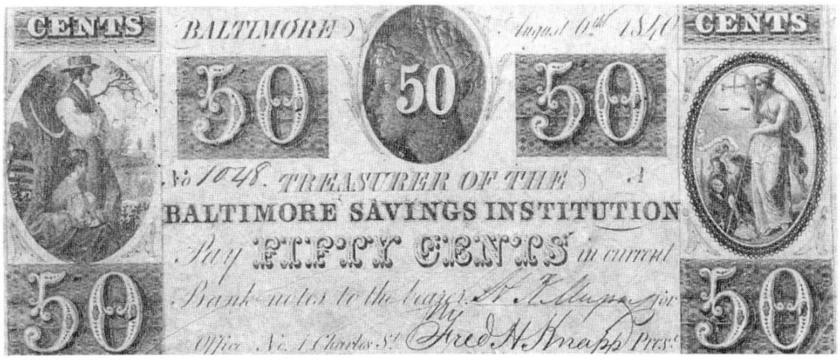

5.13.14

5.13.16

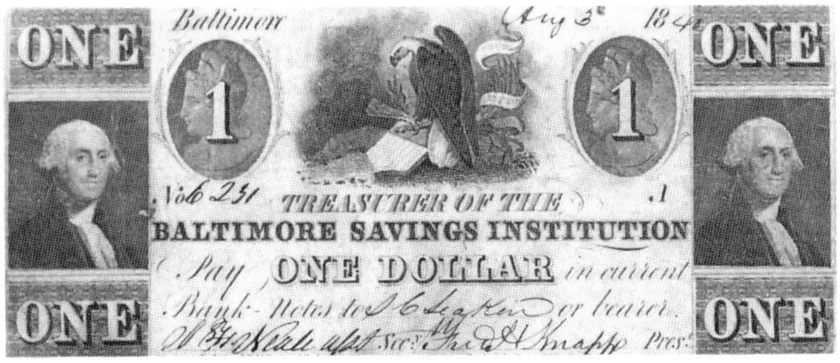

5.13.17

5.13.18

5.13.19 R-5

$1.00 Ca. August–September 1840. Engraving, imprint: Underwood, Bald, Spencer & Hufty, Philada. / Danforth, Underwood & Co., New York.

5.13.19 P R-7

$1.00 Ca. 1840. Engraving, imprint: Underwood, Bald, Spencer & Hufty, Philada. / Danforth, Underwood & Co., New York. Proof.

5.13.20 R-5

$2.00 Ca. August–September 1840. Engraving, imprint: Underwood, Bald, Spencer & Hufty, Philada. / Danforth, Underwood & Co., New York.

5.13.20 P R-7

$2.00 Ca. 1840. Engraving, imprint: Underwood, Bald, Spencer & Hufty, Philada. / Danforth, Underwood & Co., New York. Proof.

5.13.19

5.13.19 P

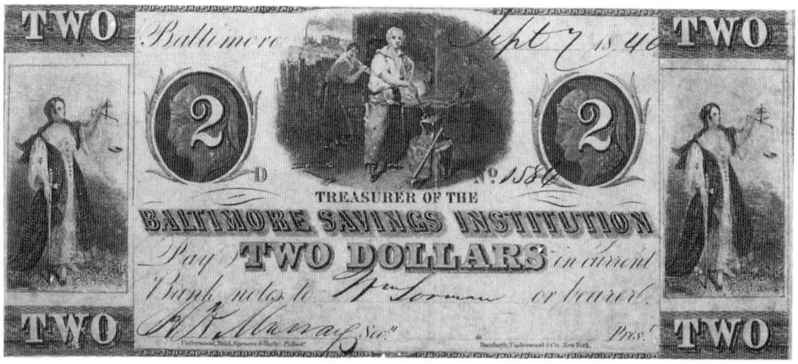

5.13.20

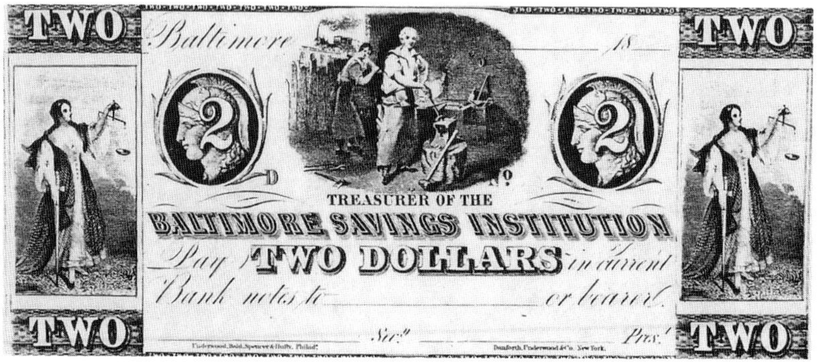

5.13.20 P

5.14 **The Baltimore & Susquehanna Railroad Company**

Incorporated under the laws of Maryland, February 13, 1828, the railroad was first opened for traffic in August 1838, and progress was reasonably steady for several years. By 1853, four main lines were in operation, the 1853 annual report listing them as Baltimore to York, Pa.; Wrightsville, York, and Gettysburg Railroad; York and Cumberland Railroad; and Hanover Branch Railroad. The main Baltimore office was at Calvert Station, Franklin and Calvert streets. In 1854, the road was merged with the York & Maryland Line Railroad Co., the York & Cumberland Railroad Co., and the Susquehanna Railroad Co. to form the Northern Central Railroad, which later was merged into the Pennsylvania Railroad system.

According to a review of the annual report of the company in the *Sun,* December 30, 1840, among the company's debts were $15,300 in $100.00 notes, $20 in fives and tens, and $509 in one- and two-dollar notes, although none of the lower denomination notes have been recorded.

5.14.7 R-1

$100.00 Ca. late 1830s. Engraving, imprint: Rawdon, Wright & Hatch, New York. These 6% interest bearing notes are often classified as bonds by some collectors, although they circulated freely as currency.

5.14.7

5.15 **Baltimore and York-Town Turnpike Road Company**

This company was incorporated in 1805 and work on the turnpike began in 1808, the necessary capital having been raised the previous year. Work was completed early in 1810, the road running from Baltimore to the Pennsylvania state line, following the route of the present Greenmount Avenue and York Road. From the state line, the York and Maryland Line Turnpike Road Company continued the road to York, Pennsylvania.

5.15.3 R-7

3c Printed date 3rd January 1815. Letterpress, no imprint.

5.15.3

5.16 John M. Barrett

The issuer was the proprietor of the New Theatre Tavern, adjoining "the Theatre, Holliday street," being so listed in the 1816 city directory. By 1819 John Barrett was the proprietor of a tavern at the corner of Chatham Street and St. Paul's Lane, while the New Theatre Tavern had been taken over by Thomas Barrett, obviously a relative. For other scrip issued at this tavern, see New-Theatre Tavern.

5.16.1 R-7
6 1/4c Printed date September 23, 1815. Letterpress, no imprint.

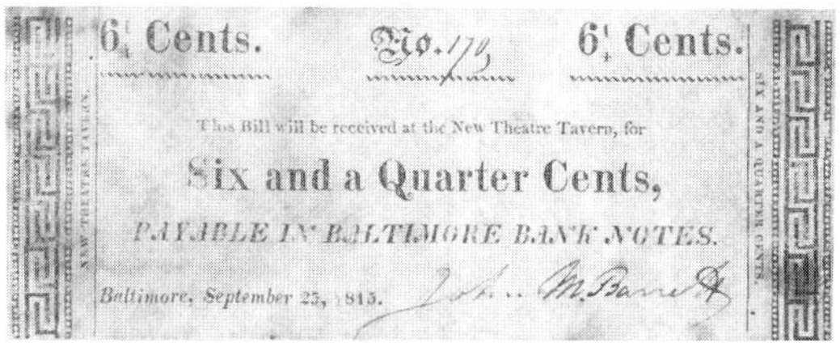

5.16.1

5.17 Berkeley Coal Mining and Railroad Company

The issuer, a Virginia company at the time of issue (1837) of the note illustrated below, was in Berkeley County (now a part of West Virginia). Its treasurer in 1837 was William W. Woodville, a resident and commission merchant in Baltimore, who as early as 1833 had been auditor of the Baltimore & Ohio Rail Road Company. He was listed for over 20 years in Baltimore city directories, variously as a merchant, stock and commission agent, and stockbroker. Woodville's location in Baltimore obviously explains his selection of the Union Bank of Maryland in that city for the redemption of the company's notes he had signed.

5.17.2 R-7
10c Printed year date 1837. Letterpress, no imprint. (Va.#PB15-04)

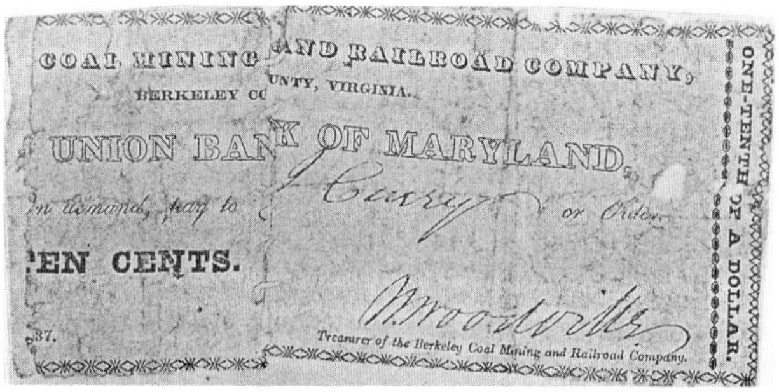

5.17.2

5.18 Black Horse Tavern

William O. C. Fritschler operated the Black Horse Tavern on "Pennsylvania Avenue, east of Biddle Street" according to the 1840–41 city directory. He also signed as "President" notes of the Western Savings Institution with an address of 60 Pennsylvania Avenue. Neither the tavern nor the savings institution was ever listed in directories of the period despite their appearance on the notes signed by Fritschler. For further information, refer to the issues of that institution.

5.18.2 R-7

12 1/2c Printed partial date May __ 18__ (ca. 1840). Letterpress, no imprint. This note was apparently issued by Fritschler shortly prior to his affiliation with the Western Savings Institution.

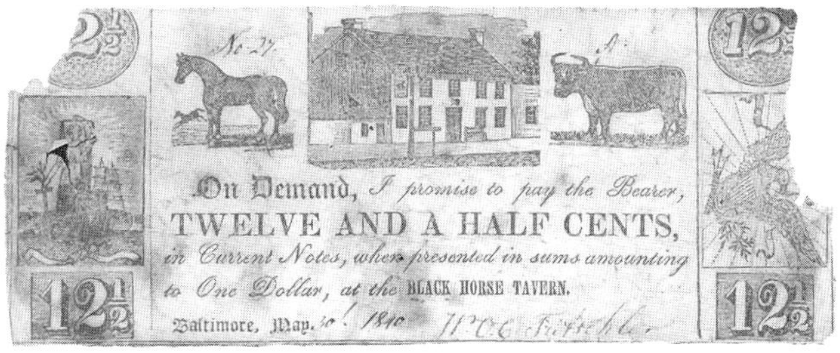

5.18.2

5.19 Phebus Botts

The identity of "Phebus Botts," the signer of this note, has not as yet been established.

5.19.3 R-7

25c Printed date May 1, 1840. Letterpress, imprint: Murphy, Printer, Baltimore.

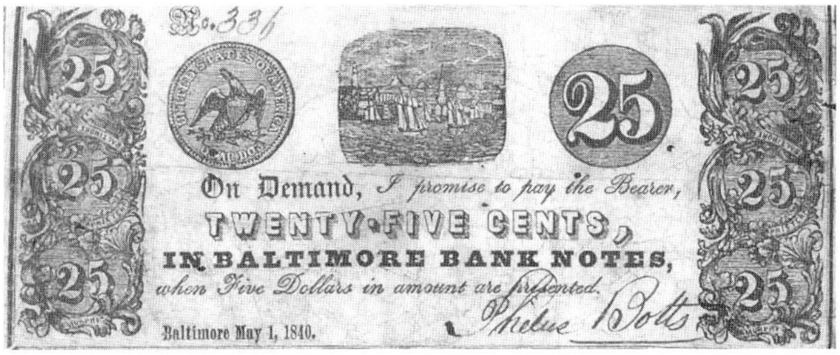

5.19.3

5.20 Cornelius Brown

The issuer was listed in the 1840 city directory as a huckster. Apparently, he issued small-change scrip in change to his customers, having arranged with stallholders in the various markets to accept them for him in redemption.

5.20.1 R-7

6 1/4c Printed date April 23, 1840. Letterpress, imprint: MURPHY & SPALDING PRINTER.

5.20.2 R-7

12 1/2c Printed date April 23, 1840. Letterpress, imprint: MURPHY, PRINT. BALT.

5.20.1

5.20.2

5.21 Brunswick & Florida Line

The principal route of this stagecoach line ran from Brunswick, Georgia, west and south to New Orleans via Tallahasee, St. Joseph, Mobile, and way points. Notes were prepared for use by the line's agent in Baltimore, a major port of departure for freight and passenger vessels bound for the South. Transferring to the overland route saved considerable time for travelers bound for New Orleans and way points by eliminating the lengthy sea voyage down the coast and around the southern tip of Florida. The Baltimore agent for the line was Jacob Brandt, the agent for the Powhatan Steam Packet Co., 73 Light Street Wharf. Although circulated notes of the line's Baltimore agent have not as yet been recorded, they were listed in the "List of Small Notes Circulating in Baltimore," published in the *Baltimore Clipper*, a daily newspaper, on September 11 and 12, 1840.

5.21.2 P R-7
12 1/2c Ca. 1840. Engraving, imprint: Underwood, Bald, Spencer & Hufty, Philada. / Danforth, Underwood & Co., New York. Proof.

5.21.3 P R-7
25c Ca. 1840. Engraving, imprint: Underwood, Bald, Spencer & Hufty, Philada. / Danforth, Underwood & Co., New York. Proof.

5.21.4 P R-7
50c Ca. 1840. Engraving, imprint: Underwood, Bald, Spencer & Hufty, Philada. / Danforth, Underwood & Co., New York. Proof.

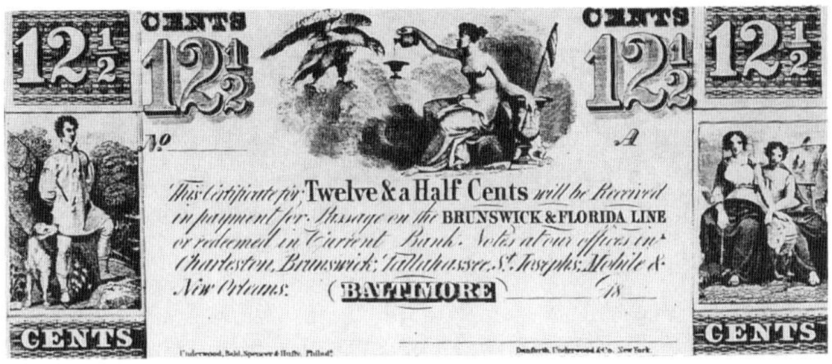

5.21.2 P

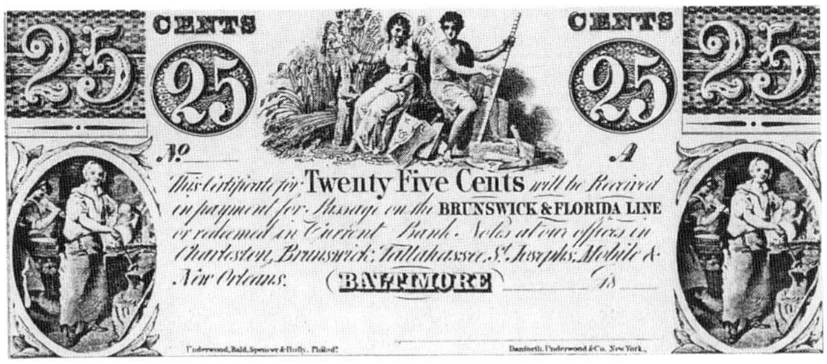

5.21.3 P

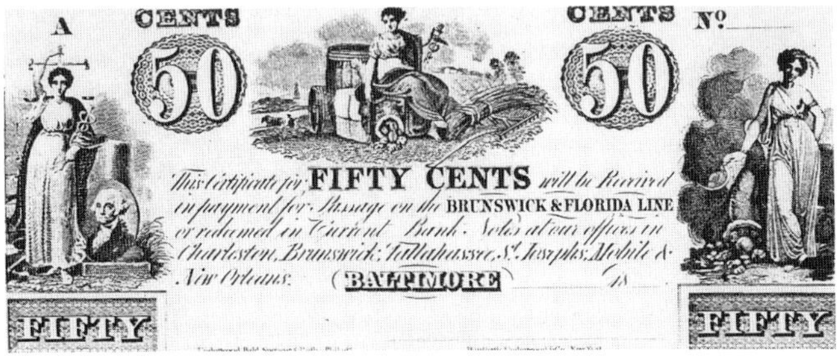

5.21.4 P

5.21.5 P R-7

$1.00 Ca. 1840. Engraving, imprint: Underwood, Bald, Spencer & Hufty, Philada. / Danforth, Underwood & Co., New York. Proof.

5.21.6 P R-7

$2.00 Ca. 1840. Engraving, imprint: Underwood, Bald, Spencer & Hufty, Philada. / Danforth, Underwood & Co., New York. Proof.

5.21.7 P R-7

$3.00 Ca. 1840. Engraving, imprint: Underwood, Bald, Spencer & Hufty, Philada. / Danforth, Underwood & Co., New York. Proof.

5.21.8 P R-7

$65.00 Ca. 1840. Engraving, imprint: Underwood, Bald, Spencer & Hufty, Philada. / Danforth, Underwood & Co., New York. Although actually a ticket for passage from Mobile to Charleston, this was redeemable for cash at any office of the company. Proof.

5.21.5 P

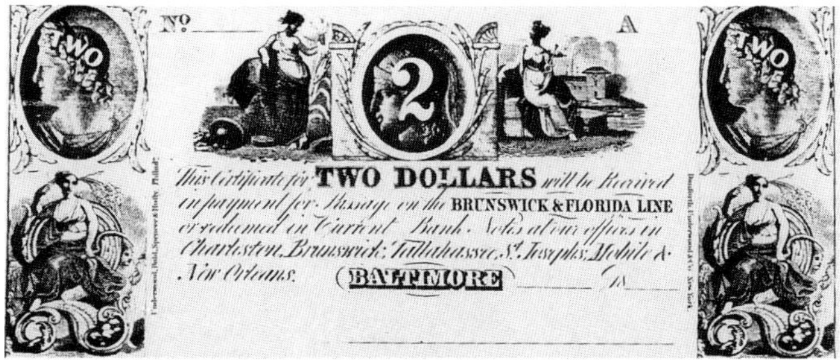

5.21.6 P

5.21.7 P

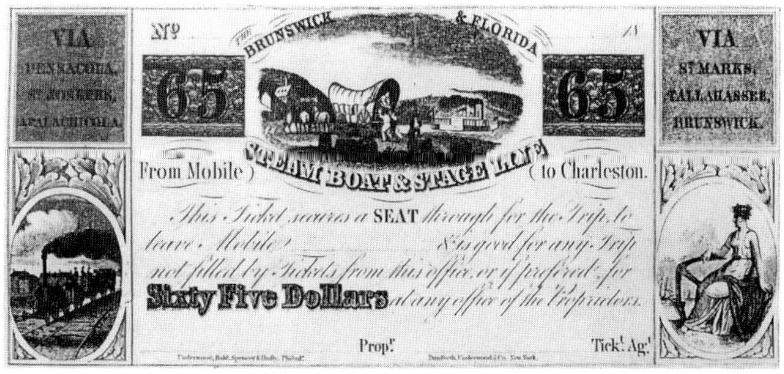

5.21.8 P

5.22 Geo. H. C. J. Bush

The issuer was a shoemaker whose shop was on Conway Street, west of Green Street, and whose residence was at 162 Hanover street where he agreed to redeem his scrip between 1 and 2 P.M. In the "List of Small Notes Circulating in Baltimore" published in the *Baltimore Clipper* of September 12, 1840, Bush's occupation was given as a huckster, indicating a second occupation.

5.22.1 R-7

6 1/4c Printed year date 1840. Letterpress, no imprint.

5.22.2 R-7

12 1/2c Printed year date 1840. Letterpress, no imprint.

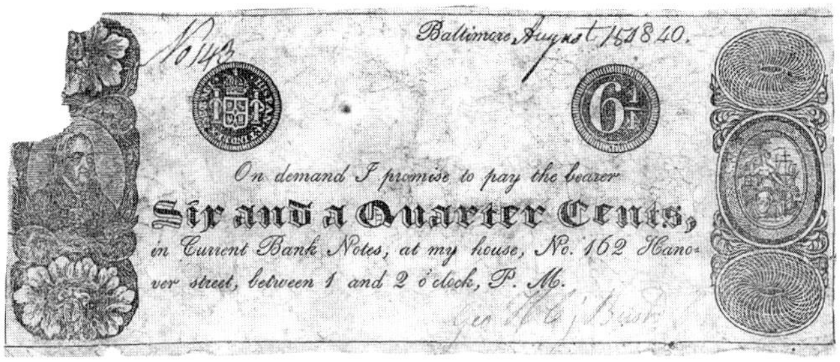

5.22.1

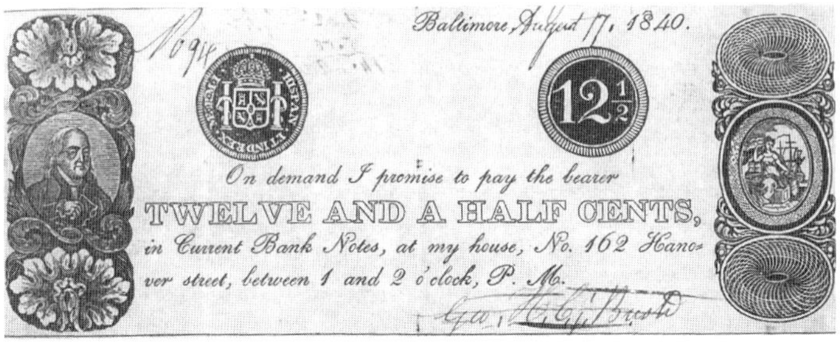

5.22.2

5.23 Central Savings Institution

Charter approved February 25, 1833; suspended operations in 1840. The charter expired in 1845 and was not renewed. The office was located at 8 Light St.

5.23.1 R-5

6 1/4c Printed year date 1840. Lithography, no imprint.

5.23.2 R-5

12 1/2c Printed year date 1840. Lithography, no imprint. Similar to 6 1/4c, No. 5.23.1.

5.23.3 R-6

25c Printed year date 1840. Similar to 6 1/4c, No. 5.23.1, with incorrect spelling, "Centeral."

5.23.1

5.23.3

5.23.4 R-3
25c Printed year date 1840. Similar to No. 5.23.3, with spelling corrected, although portions of the deleted E were incompletely erased. "When presented in sums of five dollars" added to the redemption sentence.

5.23.5 R-3
25c Printed year date 1840. Same as No. 5.23.3, with spelling completely corrected.

5.23.6 R-4
50c Printed year date 1840. Lithography, imprint: E. WEBER, Lith.

5.23.7 R-6
$1.00 Partial printed date 184_. Ca. 1840. Lithography, imprint: Lithogr. by Edw. Weber & Co. Baltimore.

5.23.4

5.23.5

5.23.6

5.24 N. U. Chafee

The issuer, Nicholas U. Chafee, was the proprietor of a distillery on the Hookstown Road, now Pennsylvania Avenue, from 1837 to 1840. He issued scrip in varying denominations according to contemporary newspaper reports, although only $1.00 and $3.00 notes have been seen by the authors. The recorded part of the Chafee story began with a news article in the *Sun* of October 29, 1840, to the effect that a $1.00 note signed by Chafee which "appeared to be from the same plate as those issued by Cohen [J. I. Cohen & Bros.], had been shown to a Philadelphia paper and would without close inspection be readily taken for one of Cohen's." It went on to say that similar notes had been passed in Baltimore with relatively little success. On November 24, 1840, the illustrated editorial appeared, following several civil suits brought against Chafee.

On November 30, it was reported that Justice Schaeffer had given judgment for the plaintiffs. Apparently Chafee failed to satisfy the judgments. On December 11, a lengthy article appeared in the *Sun* reporting on unsuccessful attempts by police officers to serve warrants on Chafee, both at his home and at his distillery, for non-satisfaction of legal judgments and, finally his barricading of himself and some supporting employees at his distillery. On December 14 there was a lengthy tongue-in-cheek report that Nicholas Chafee has been "captured at Fort Distillery" apparently without real opposition, by Constable A. J. Keller. He was bound over, under $200 bail, to appear at the February term of Baltimore City Court. Next, on January 26, 1841, the following notice appeared in the *Sun:*

> NOTICE. - All persons indebted to Nicholas U. Chafee are hereby notified to make payment to the subscribers who have been duly appointed his permanent Trustees.
>
> T. Yates Walsh, Court House Lane
> Wm. George Baker, 29 St. Paul St.
> 21eo-1t Permanent Trustees

On January 29, a lengthy news article reported on Chafee's trial the previous day. T. Yates Walsh, attorney for the defendant, based his defense on the Act of 1831, Chapter 317, on the basis that the notes were null and void. Neilson Poe, for the holders of the notes, said that Chafee did not fall under the definition of the act, and thus the notes were not voided by it. The case was continued until the following day. Finally, on February 20, 1841, Chafee was found guilty of resisting arrest and fined $10 and costs. No record of the ultimate outcome of the judgments for the plaintiffs in the civil suits, nor whether Chafee redeemed his notes, as he said he intended to do, has been found. Judging from the number of Chafee notes in existence, it is probable that he failed to make good on his promise to redeem.

5.24.5 R-4

$1.00 Ca. 1839–40. Lithography, imprint: Baltimore, Lithogr. by Ed. Weber & Co. Plate letter A. The central vignette and general design were copied by the lithographer from a similar engraved $1.00 note issued by J. I. Cohen & Brothers, reputable private bankers in Baltimore. The similarity was probably requested by Chafee.

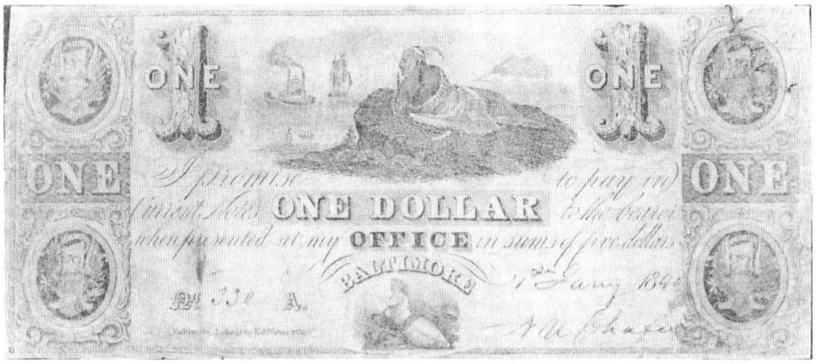

5.24.5

5.24.6 R-3

$1.00 Printed year date 1840. Lithography, imprint: Lith. of Ed. Weber & Co., Baltimore. Plate letter B.

The two notes differ in many ways. Both central vignettes differ in minor details; the corner counters are different; and the promissory legends differ, the plate letter A note specifying payment "at my office" while the B note is nonspecific. In the B note the year date is completely printed and the small human figure on the shore seems to have a dog on a leash. Also the prominent headband at the upper right corner of the vignette on A is barely visible.

5.24.6

5.24.8 R-7
$3.00 Printed partial date 184_. Lithography, imprint: lith of E. Weber & Co., Baltimore.

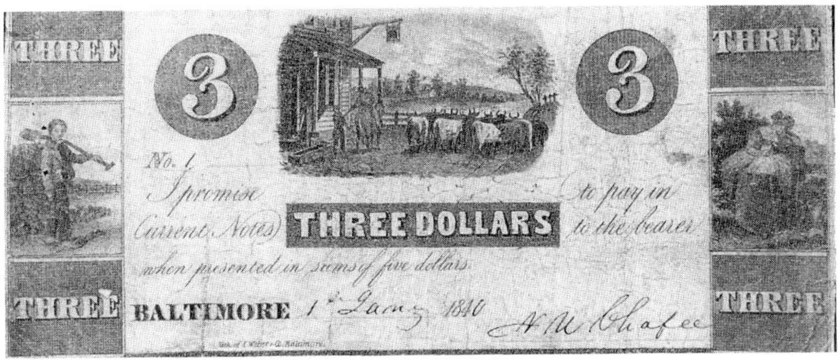

5.24.8

5.25 The Chesapeake Bank

Charter approved March 19, 1836; voluntary liquidation 1880. It was located at the corner of North Street (now Guilford Ave.) and Fayette Street.

5.25.1 A SENC
$1.00 Ca. 1810s–20s. Engraving, imprint: Maverick & Leney. *Center:* Liberty seated and Prosperity standing, flanking shield bearing three plows and surmounted by horse's head; 1. *Right:* 1; ONE DOLLAR; 1, across. Altered from $1.00 State Bank at Trenton, Trenton, N.J., NJ560-G4. (MD20A10)

5.25.2 P R-7
$1.00 Printed date May 2nd, 1842. Engraving, imprint: Underwood, Bald, Spencer & Hufty, Philada / Danforth, Underwood & Co., New York. Proof.

5.25.3 P R-7
$1.00 Printed date March 2nd, 1846. Engraving, imprint: Rawdon, Wright & Hatch, New York. Proof. (MD20G4)

5.25.4 A R-6
$1.00 Ca. 1849. Engraving, imprint: Boston Banknote Co., 59 State Street. Altered from $1.00. Bank of Owasso, Owasso, Mich., MI305G2. (MD21A5)

5.25.5 SENC
$1.00 Printed date March 2nd 1863. Engraving, imprint: Rawdon, Wright & Hatch, New York. Similar to No. 5.25.3 P, except for date and possible overprint. (MD20G4a)

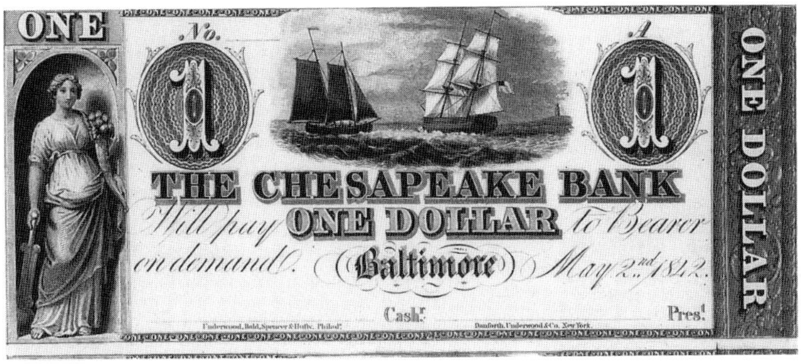

5.25.2 P

5.25.3 P

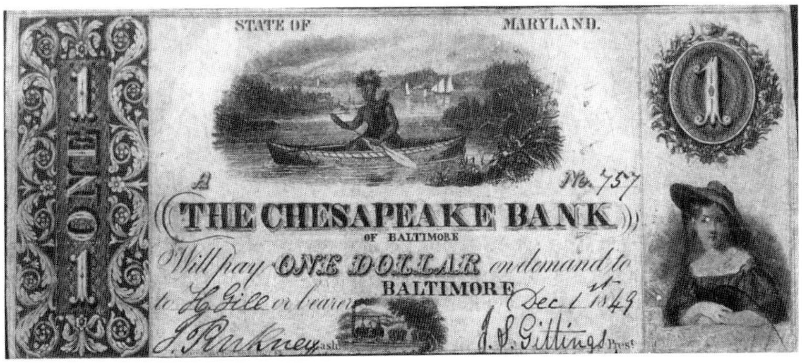

5.25.4 A

5.25.6 A R-7

$2.00 Ca. 1810s–20s (although bank did not open until 1836). Engraving, imprint: Maverick & Leney. *Center:* 2; on die, Liberty and Prosperity seated flanking shield bearing three plows and surmounted by horse's head; II on die. *Left and right:* TWO, across. *Between signatures:* 2. Altered from $2.00 State Bank at Trenton, Trenton, N.J., NJ560G10. (MD20A15)

5.25.6 A

5.25.7 SENC

$2.00 Printed date March 2nd 1846. Engraving, imprint: Rawdon, Wright & Hatch, New York. *Center:* 2; Ceres seated, train on bridge in background; 2. *Left:* 2 / woman seated with distaff and pail / TWO. *Right:* 2 / farmer seated holding rake, one hand on plow / TWO. (MD20G8)

5.25.10 A

5.25.8 SENC

$2.00 Printed date March 2nd, 1862. Engraving, imprint: Rawdon, Wright & Hatch, New York. Similar to No. 5.25.7, except for date and possible overprint. (MD20G8a)

5.25.12 A

5.25.9 A SENC

$3.00 Ca. 1820s. Engraving, imprint: Fairman, Draper, Underwood & Co. *Center:* 3; Liberty and Prosperity seated flanking shield bearing three plows and surmounted by horse's head; oval portrait of Washington. *Left:* THREE, across. *Right:* 3 / Justice standing, right arm with balance resting on column, left hand on hip. *Between signatures:* Two jockeys on racehorses. Altered from $3.00 State Bank at Trenton, Trenton, N.J., NJ560G16. (MD20A25)

5.25.14 A

5.25.10 A R-6

$3.00 Ca. 1837. Engraving, imprint: Chas. Toppan & Co., Phila. Altered from $3.00 Susquehanna Bank, Port Deposit, Md., No. 102.11.3. Note that the last *e* is missing from "Chesapeake." (MD20A20)

5.25.11 SENC

$5.00 Ca. 1830s–40s. Engraving, imprint: Draper, Toppan, Longacre & Co. Similar to No. 5.25.19, except for imprint. (MD20G12)

5.25.12 A R-7

$5.00 Ca. late 1830s–40s. Engraving, imprint: Rawdon, Wright & Hatch. Altered from $5.00 Chippeway County Bank, Sault De St. Mary, Mich., MI390G8. (MD20A35)

5.25.13 R SENC

$5.00 Ca. 1830s–50s. Engraving, imprint: Rawdon, Wright & Hatch. Raised from $1.00 of same design as No. 5.25.3 P. (MD20R5)

5.25.14 A R-6

$5.00 Ca. 1840. Imprint: Rawdon, Wright & Hatch, New York. Altered from $5.00 Commercial Bank of Millington, Millington, Md., No. 83.1.3. (MD20A30)

5.25.15 A SENC

$5.00 Ca. 1840s. Engraving, imprint: Boston Bank Note Co. *Center:* V on eight-pointed star; sloop, sailing ship and steamboat at sea. *Left:* 5 / V / 5. *Right:* 5 / FIVE / primitive train, in circle. *Between signatures:* Harbor scene, three men in boat. Altered from $5.00 Bank of Owasso, Owasso, Mich., MI305G8. (MD20A40)

5.25.16 A

5.25.19

5.25.16 A R-6

$5.00 Ca. 1840s. Engraving, imprint: Underwood, Bald, Spencer & Hufty, Phila.; Danforth, Underwood & Co., New York. Altered from $5.00 Tenth Ward Bank, New York City, NY1935G16. (MD20A45)

5.25.17 S SENC

$5.00 Ca. 1840s. Engraving, imprint: Rawdon, Wright & Hatch. *Center:* 5; eagle on shell in ocean facing left; 5. *Left:* 5 / locomotive at wharf / 5. *Right:* 5 / sailing ship / 5. *Between signatures:* Dog and strongbox. From a fraudulently modified plate, originally for a $5.00 note of the Geauga Insurance Co., Painesville, Ohio. Spurious. (MD20S10)

5.25.18 SENC

$5.00 Ca. 1840–50s. Engraving, imprint: Toppan, Carpenter & Co. (MD20G12a)

5.25.19 R-6

$5.00 Ca. 1861. Engraving, imprint: Toppan, Carpenter & Co. Philada. and ABN Co. monogram. (MD20G12b)

5.25.20 S SENC

$10.00 Ca. 1830–40s. Engraving, no imprint. *Center:* Sheaf and plow, reapers in background. *Right:* Eagle and shield. Spurious. (MD20N10)

5.25.21 R SENC

$10.00 Ca. 1830–50s. Engraving, imprint: Rawdon, Wright & Hatch. Raised from $1.00 of same design as No. 5.25.3 P. (MD20R10)

5.25.22 P R-7

$10.00 Ca. 1830s–50s. Engraving, imprint: Rawdon, Wright & Hatch. *Center:* Female seated, Mercury approaching with cornucopia, spread eagle with scroll. *Left:* Jackson. *Right:* Van Buren. Proof. (MD20G14)

5.25.23 A R-7

$10.00 Ca. 1840s. Engraving, imprint: Rawdon, Wright & Hatch, New York. Altered note.

5.25.24 A SENC

$10.00 Ca. 1840s. Engraving, imprint: Rawdon, Wright & Hatch. Altered from $10.00 Commercial Bank of Millington, Millington, Md., No. 83.1.7. (MD20A50)

5.25.25 A SENC

$10.00 Ca. 1840s. Engraving, imprint: Danforth, Underwood & Co.; Underwood, Bald, Spencer & Hufty. *Center:* Diagonal 10 on medallion head; presentation of the Declaration of Independence; diagonal 10 on medallion head. *Left:* 10 / sailor standing with U.S. flag in left hand, in oval / X. *Right:* X / Pat Lyon standing by forge. in oval / 10. *Between signatures:* Eagle. Altered from $10.00 Tenth Ward Bank, New York City, NY1935G18. (MD20A55)

5.25.26 S SENC

$20.00 Ca. 1830s–40s. Engraving, imprint: Draper, Toppan & Co. *Center:* Woman reclining with iron chest. *Left:* Portrait of Franklin. *Right:* Train. Spurious. (MD20N15)

5.25.27 A SENC

$20.00 Ca. 1830s–40s. Engraving, imprint: Rawdon, Wright & Hatch. *Center:* 20 on large die; farm produce and implements, train in left background. *Left:* XX / nude Hebe standing in clouds, feeding large eagle above left shoulder. *Right:* 20 on large die / small eagle with shield / XX. *Between signatures:* Pledge in circle. Altered from $20.00 Chippeway County Bank, Sault De St. Mary, Mich., MI390G12. (MD20A60)

5.25.28 SENC

$20.00 Ca. 1830s–50s. Engraving, imprint: Rawdon, Wright & Hatch. *Center:* 20; Indian man at left and sailor at right, both standing, flanking shield surmounted by eagle, schooner in right background; 20. *Left:* 20 / square portrait of Jackson / 20. *Right:* 20 / square portrait of Van Buren / 20. *Between signatures:* Ship. (MD20G16)

5.25.24 A

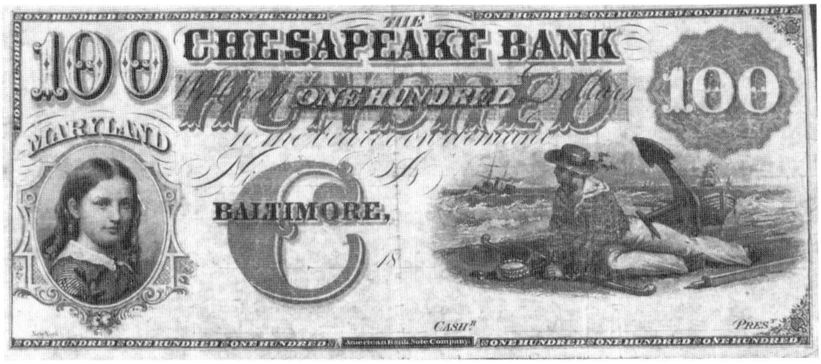

5.25.33

5.25.29 S SENC

$20.00 Ca. 1840–50s. Engraving, imprint: Unknown. *Center:* Indian woman on cliff overlooking river, train, and city. Spurious. (MD20N20)

5.25.30 SENC

$50.00 Ca. 1830–50s. Engraving, imprint: Rawdon, Wright & Hatch. *Center:* Portrait of Carroll; 50; portrait of Webster. *Left:* Hebe feeding eagle / 50. *Right:* Indian man with bow and arrow / 50. *Between signatures:* Ship. (MD20G20)

5.25.31 SENC

$50.00 Ca. 1860s. Engraving, imprint: American Bank Note Co. *Center:* 50; ship, other ships in background. *Left:* FIFTY / blacksmith. *Right:* 50 / female portrait. Green tint. (MD20G24a)

5.25.32 SENC

$100.00 Ca. 1830–50s. Engraving, imprint: Rawdon, Wright & Hatch. *Center:* 100; woman holding torch seated on globe, eagle with portrait of Washington on its breast at left; 100. *Left:* Portrait of Carroll / 100 / portrait of Webster. *Right:* Woman with seahorses at feet, cherub floating in clouds. *Between signatures:* Ship. (MD20G28)

5.25.33 R-7

$100.00 Ca. 1860s. Engraving, imprint: American Bank Note Company. Black on white with green "C," green die at upper right and green HUNDRED with green network behind. (MD20G32a)

5.26 The Chesapeake Savings Fund

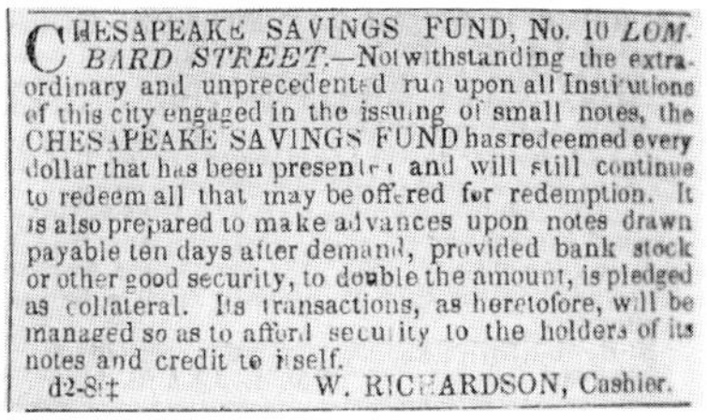

CHESAPEAKE SAVINGS FUND, No. 10 *LOMBARD STREET.*—Notwithstanding the extraordinary and unprecedented run upon all Institutions of this city engaged in the issuing of small notes, the CHESAPEAKE SAVINGS FUND has redeemed every dollar that has been presented and will still continue to redeem all that may be offered for redemption. It is also prepared to make advances upon notes drawn payable ten days after demand, provided bank stock or other good security, to double the amount, is pledged as collateral. Its transactions, as heretofore, will be managed so as to afford security to the holders of its notes and credit to itself.
d2-8t W. RICHARDSON, Cashier.

This "savings fund" began operation in mid-1840 with an office at 10 Lombard St. It survived the heavy run on similar institutions in Baltimore in September of that year which resulted in the demise of a number of them. The fund was still operating in December, as evidenced by the illustrated advertisement which ran in the *Sun* December 2–9, 1840. Apparently the enterprise closed down in early 1841. All its recorded notes bear the printed date of August 1840; the 6 1/4c, 12 1/2c, and 25c denominations having the day in the date correctly expressed ("1st"), while the 50c and $1.00 notes have it "1th."

5.26.1 R-5
6 1/4c Printed date August 1st, 1840. Lithography, no imprint.

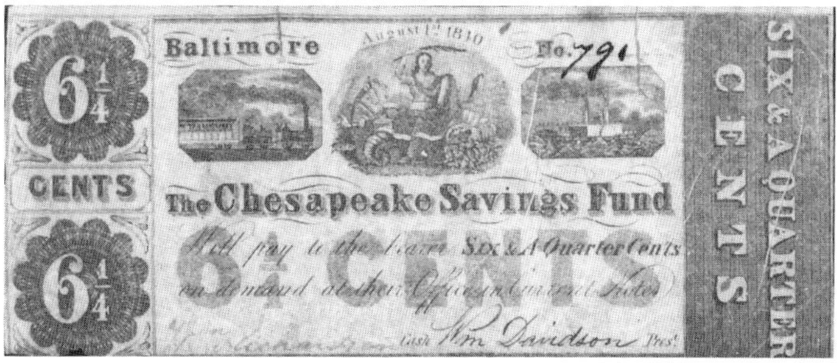

5.26.1

5.26.2 R-6
12 1/2c Printed date August 1st, 1840. Lithography, imprint: Lith by E. Weber & Co., Baltimore. Similar to 6 1/4c, No. 5.26.1.

5.26.3 R-5
25c Printed date August 1st, 1840. Lithography, imprint: Lith. by E. Weber & Co. Baltimore.

5.26.3

5.26.4 R-5
50c Printed date August 1th, 1840. Lithography, imprint: Lith. by Edw. Weber, Baltimore. The date reads "1th" instead of "1st."

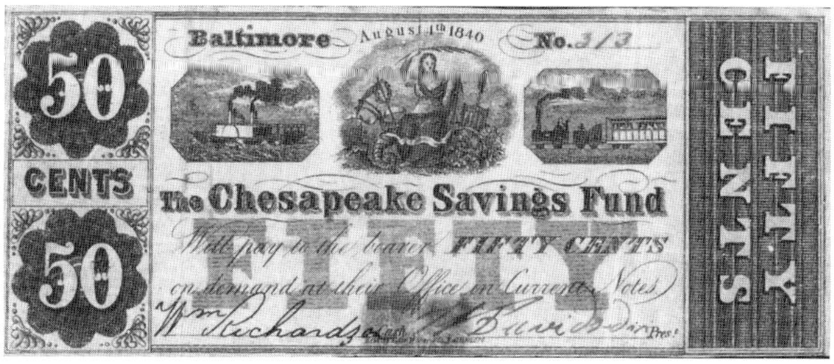

5.26.4

5.26.5 R-5
$1.00 Printed date August 1th, 1840. Lithography, imprint: Lith. by E. Weber & Co., Baltimore. Similar to 50c, No. 5.26.4.

5.26.5

5.27 The Citizens Bank of Baltimore

Charter approved April 2, 1836; voluntary liquidation in 1844; recommenced operations in 1850; converted to and became the Citizens National Bank of Baltimore in 1865; merged with the Merchants National Bank of Baltimore (Second) to form the First National Bank of Baltimore (Second) in 1928. During its note-issuing period the Citizen's Bank was initially located at 162 Baltimore St. and then in 1851 moved to the northeast corner of Pratt and Hanover streets.

5.27.1 A SENC

$1.00 Ca. 1840s. Engraving, imprint: Terry, Pelton. *Center:* 1; three allegorical women with eagle, pole and cap, shield, balance and book; 1. *Left:* ONE / two Indians reclining and smoking. *Right:* 1 / square portrait of Washington / ONE. *Between signatures:* Cattle. Altered from $1.00 Citizens Bank, Augusta, Maine, ME20G4, or from notes of other failed banks using the same plate. (MD24A5)

5.27.2 P R-7

$1.00 Printed partial date April 1st, 184_. Engraving, imprint: Underwood, Bald, Spencer & Hufty, Philada / Danforth, Underwood & Co., New York. Proof.

5.27.3 R-7

$1.00 Printed date April 1, 1850. Engraving, imprint: Rawdon, Wright & Hatch.

5.27.4 P R-7

$1.00 Printed date May 1, 1851. Engraving, imprint: Toppan, Carpenter, Casilear & Co. Phila. Similar to counterfeit No. 5.27.4 C. Proof. (MD25G20)

5.27.4 C R-5

$1.00 Printed date May 1, 1851. Engraving, imprint: Toppan, Carpenter, Casilear & Co., Phila. Counterfeit of same design as No. 5.27.4 P. (MD25C20)

5.27.2 P

5.27.3

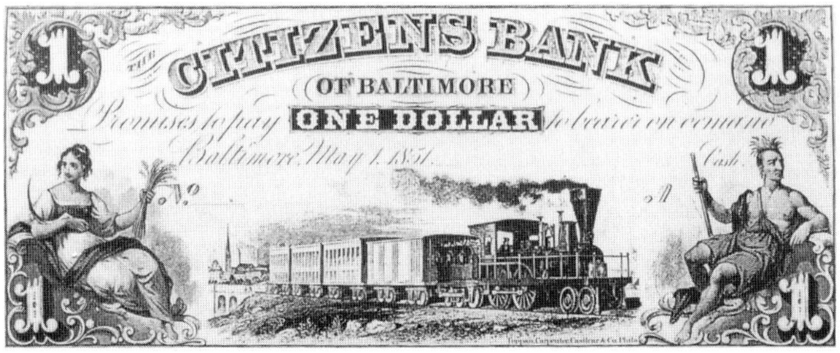

5.27.4 P

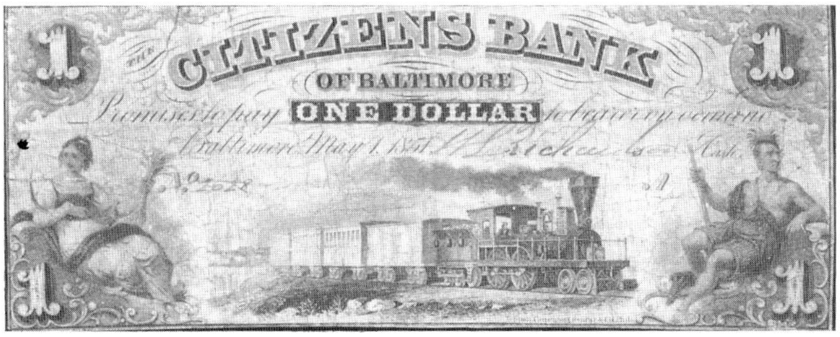

5.27.4 C

5.27.6 A R-6

$2.00 Ca. 1840s. Engraving, imprint: Terry, Pelton. Altered from $2.00 Citizens Bank, Augusta, Maine, ME20G12, or from notes of other failed banks using the same plate. (MD24A10)

5.27.7 A R-6

$2.00 Printed date Nov. 3rd, 1852. Engraving, imprint: Wellstood, Hanks, Hay, Whiting; New York. Altered from $2.00 Citizens Bank, Washington, D.C., DC180G4. (MD25A15)

5.27.8 R-7

$2.00 Printed date May 1st, 1862. Engraving, imprint: National Bank Note Co.

5.27.9 SENC

$2.00 Ca. 1860s. Engraving, imprint: National Bank Note Co. Same as No. 5.27.8, except date is only partially printed, ____ 18__. (MD25G24a)

5.27.10 A SENC

$3.00 Ca. late 1830s. Engraving, imprint: Terry, Pelton & Co. *Center:* Round female portrait; Ceres and Justice seated flanking shield bearing anchor and surmounted by eagle; round portrait of cherub. *Left:* 3 / woman standing with branch, trident, and oval bearing THREE / THREE. *Right:* 3 / Ceres seated in grain field / THREE. *Between signatures:* Anchor and implements. Altered from $3.00 Citizens Bank, Augusta, Maine, ME20G16, or from notes of other failed banks using the same plates. (MD24A15)

5.27.6 A

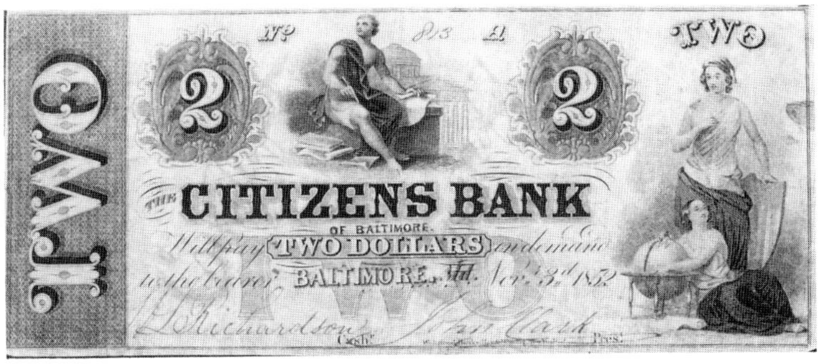

5.27.7 A

5.27.8

5.27.11 SENC

$3.00 Ca. 1860s. Engraving, imprint: National Bank Note Co. *Center:* 3; three children reading book, in circle. 3: *Left:* 3 / BALTIMORE. *Upper right:* 3. Tint was probably green. (MD25G28a)

5.27.12 R SENC

$5.00 Ca. 1830–40s. Engraving, imprint: Toppan, Carpenter & Casilear. Raised from $1.00 of same design as No. 5.27.4 P. (MD25R5)

5.27.13 A SENC

$5.00 Ca. late 1830s. Engraving, imprint: Terry, Pelton & Co. *Center:* 5; two allegorical women standing and one seated, agricultural items at left and ship at right. *Left:* FIVE / square portrait of Franklin / V. *Right:* V / square portrait of Lafayette / FIVE. *Between signatures:* Anchor and implements. Altered from $5.00 Citizens Bank, Augusta, Maine, ME20G20, or from notes of other failed banks using the same plate. (MD24A25—First of two identical numbers used by Haxby.)

5.27.14 R-7

$5.00 Ca. 1830s–60s. Engraving, imprint: Rawdon, Wright & Hatch, New York. The "B" of "Baltimore" in the bank title does not touch the shading of the "ze" above. Similar to No. 5.27.16 C. (MD25G2)

5.27.15 A SENC

$5.00 Ca. 1840s. Engraving, imprint: Rawdon, Wright, Hatch & Edson. *Center:* 5; woman seated with caduceus, left arm on shield; 5. *Right center:* Woman standing with branch in right hand, eagle on lap, cornucopia at right, ships in left background / V. *Left:* V / woman standing leaning on large square column at left, grain in left hand / V. *Between signatures:* Cherub riding on deer. Altered from $5.00 Bank of Monroe, Mich., MI280G28. (MD24A25—Second of two identical numbers used by Haxby.)

5.27.16 C R-5

$5.00 Ca. 1850s. Engraving, imprint: Rawdon, Wright, & Hatch, New York. Excellent imitation of genuine note. Imprint under right vignette: Designed, drawn and engraved by Freeman Rawdon. Counterfeit. (MD25C2)

5.27.17 R-6

$5.00 Ca. 1850s–60s. Engraving, imprint: Rawdon, Wright & Hatch. Same as No. 5.27.14, except for filled-in date. The "B" of "Baltimore" in the bank title does not touch the shading of the "ze" above. (MD25G30)

5.27.18 A R-6

$5.00 Printed date Nov. 3rd. 1852. Engraving, imprint: Wellstood, Hanks, Hay & Whiting; New York. Altered from $5.00 Citizens Bank, Washington, D.C., DC180G8. (MD25A30)

5.27.19 S R-6

$5.00 Printed date Aug. 10, 1859. Engraving, imprint: American Bank Note Company. Black on white with red network covering entire note. Spurious. (MD24S5)

5.27.20 R-7

$5.00 Ca. 1862. Engraving, imprint: American Bank Note Company. Black and red. (MD25G32a)

5.27.21 SENC

$10.00 Ca. 1830s–40s. Engraving, imprint: Rawdon, Wright & Hatch. *Center:* 10; bales on wharf, sailing ship in left background, steamship in right background; 10. *Left:* Laureated woman holding small sheaf at left, semi-nude mechanic, right hand on sledge, both standing flanking anvil, Mercury behind / 10. *Right:* 10 / Franklin standing with book and pen / 10. *Between signatures:* Clasped hands. (MD25G4)

5.27.16 C

5.27.18 A

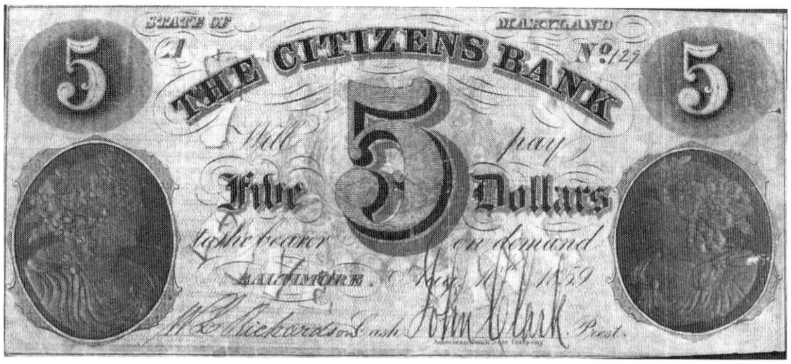

5.27.19 S

5.27.20

5.27.22 A R-6

$10.00 Ca. 1840–42. Engraving, imprint: TERRY, PELTON & CO., BOSTON & PROV. Altered from $10.00 Citizens Bank, Augusta, Maine, ME20G24. (MD24A30)

5.27.23 A R-6

$10.00 Ca. 1850s. Engraving, imprint: Wellstood, Hanks, Hay & Whiting, New York. Altered from $10.00 Citizens Bank, Washington, D.C., DC180G10. "Baltimore" in large block letters.

5.27.24 A R-6

$10.00 Ca. 1850s. Engraving, imprint: Wellstood, Hanks, Hay & Whiting, New York. Altered from $10.00 Citizens Bank, Washington, D.C., DC180G10. Same as No. 5.27.23 A, except "Baltimore" at lower center is in script letters, mixed upper- and lowercase. (MD25A45)

5.27.25 A R-7

$10.00 Ca. 1851–55. Engraving, imprint: Rawdon, Wright, Hatch & Edson, New York. Altered from $10.00 Bank of Monroe, Mich., MI280G30. (MD24A35)

5.27.26 SENC

$10.00 Ca. 1850s–60s. Engraving, imprint: Rawdon, Wright & Hatch. Same as No. 5.27.21, except for date. (MD25G34)

5.27.27 SENC

$20.00 Ca. 1830s–40s. Engraving, imprint: Rawdon, Wright & Hatch. *Center:* 20; sailing ship; 20. *Left:* Laureated woman holding small sheaf at left, semi-nude mechanic, right hand on sledge, both seated flanking anvil, Mercury behind / 20. *Right:* 20 / Justice, eagle on shield, bales, barrels, etc. / 20. *Between signatures:* Clasped hands. (MD25G6)

5.27.28 A SENC

$20.00 Ca. 1850s. Engraving, imprint: Wellstood, Hank, Hay & Whiting; New York. *Center:* 20; Mercury with cornucopia with produce in right arm, barrel and bale in background; 20. *Left:* Sailing ship / 20. *Right:* TWENTY / Mercury with cornucopia with coins. *Between signatures:* Schooner. Altered from $20.00 Citizens Bank, Washington, D.C., DC180G12. (MD25A55)

5.27.22 A

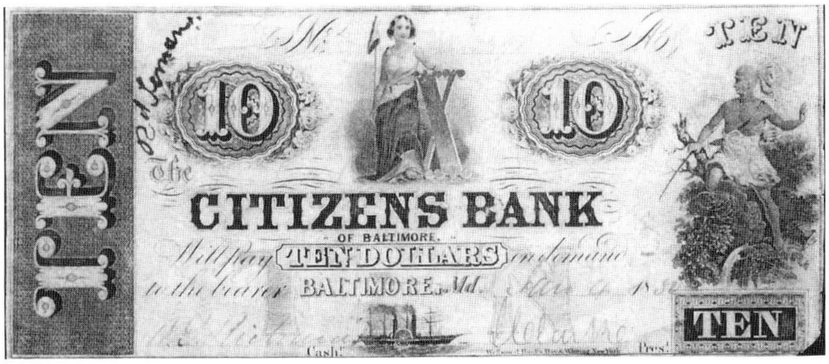

5.27.23 A

5.27.25 A

5.27.29 SENC

$20.00 Ca. 1850–60s. Engraving, imprint: Rawdon, Wright & Hatch. Same as No. 5.27.27, except for filled-in date. (MD25G38)

5.27.30 SENC

$50.00 Ca. 1830–40s. Engraving, imprint: Rawdon, Wright & Hatch. *Center:* 50; woman seated holding key and wand, arm resting on shield bearing building. *Left:* Laureated woman holding small sheaf at left, semi-nude mechanic, right hand on sledge, both seated flanking anvil, Mercury behind / 50. *Right:* L / woman standing in clouds holding torch, eagle bearing portrait of Washington on its breast. (MD25G8)

5.27.31 SENC

$50.00 Ca. 1850–60s. Engraving, imprint: Rawdon, Wright & Hatch. Same as No. 5.27.30, except for filled-in date. (MD25G40)

5.27.32 SENC

$100.00 Ca. 1830–40s. Engraving, imprint: Rawdon, Wright & Hatch. *Center:* Woman seated holding key & wand, arm resting on shield bearing building: 100. *Left:* C / Franklin standing with book and pen. *Right:* Laureated woman holding small sheaf at left, semi-nude mechanic, right hand on sledge, both seated flanking anvil, Mercury behind / 100. (MD25G10)

5.27.33 SENC

$100.00 Ca. 1850–60s. Engraving, imprint: Rawdon, Wright & Hatch. Same as No. 5.27.32, except for filled-in date. (MD25G42)

5.27.34 P R-7

$500.00 Ca. 1830s–40s. Engraving, imprint: Rawdon, Wright & Hatch, New York. Proof. (MD25G12)

5.27.35 P R-7

$1000.00 Ca. 1830s–40s. Engraving, imprint: Rawdon, Wright & Hatch, New York. Proof. (MD25G14)

5.27.34 P 5.27.35 P

5.28 The Citizens Savings Institution

According to the inscription on the few notes on record, the issuer was located at the "foot of the Market" in Fell's Point which was probably at the southern end of what is now Broadway, near Thames Street. If the institution was ever in operation, it would have been in late 1840 and survived probably for only a matter of a very few months.

5.28.1 R-7

6 1/4c Printed partial date, 184_. Lithography, no imprint.

5.28.2 R-7

12 1/2c Printed partial date 184_. Lithography, imprint: by E. Weber, Baltimore.

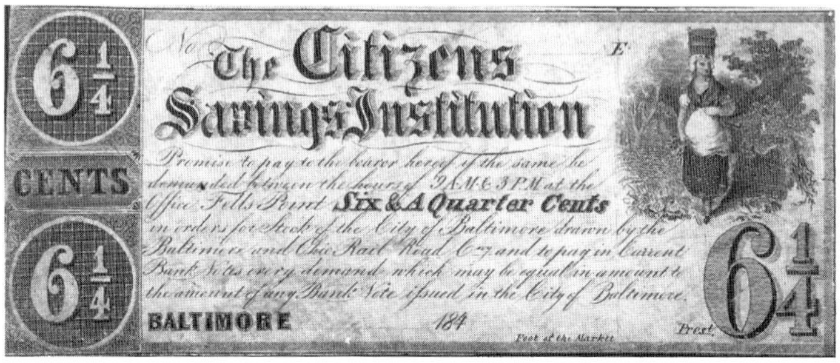

5.28.1

5.28.2

5.28.4 R-7

50c Printed partial date 184_. Lithography, imprint: E. Weber, Baltimore.

5.28.4

5.29 The City Bank of Baltimore

Charter approved December 31, 1812; voluntary liquidation in 1820. The bank was located at the northeast corner of Gay and Second streets.

5.29.1 R-7

6 1/4c Printed date 1st Nov. 1815. Letterpress, no imprint. (MD30G20)

5.29.2 R-7

10c Printed date October 7, 1816. Letterpress, no imprint.

5.29.3 R-6

12 1/2c Printed partial date November 1815. Letterpress, no imprint. (MD30G24)

5.29.4 R-6

25c Printed date 1st Nov. 1815. Letterpress, imprint: Robinson, Printer. (MD30G28)

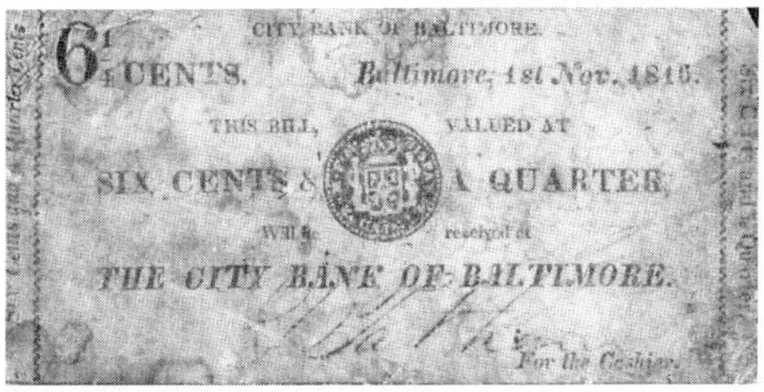

5.29.1

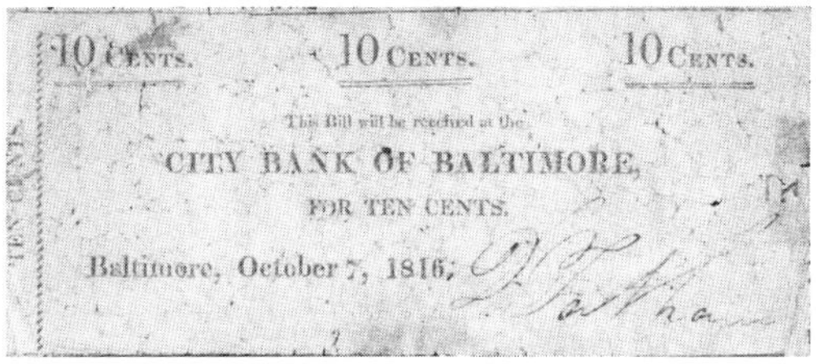

5.29.2

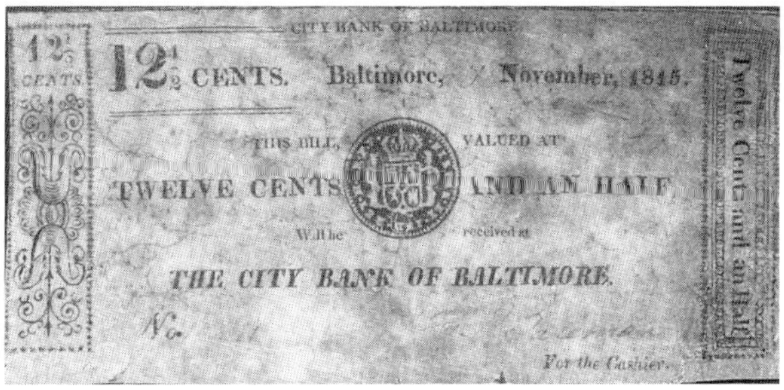

5.29.3

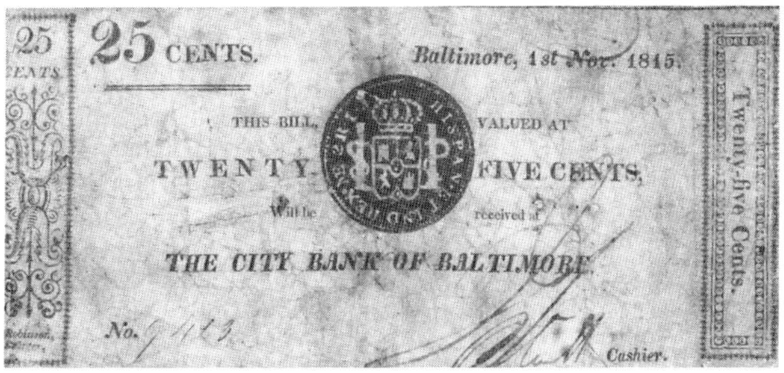

5.29.4

5.29.6 R-7

50c Ca. 1815–16. Letterpress, no imprint. (MD30G36)

5.29.7 R-6

$1.00 Ca. 1815–16. Letterpress, no imprint. (MD30G42)

5.29.8 R-6

$1.00 Printed year date 1816. Letterpress, imprint: J. Robinson, printer. (MD30G46)

5.29.9 R-7

$1.00 Printed year date 1818. Letterpress, imprint: J. Robinson, printer. Same as No. 5.29.8, except for date. (MD30G46b)

5.29.10 P R-7

$5.00 Ca. 1812–20. Engraving, imprint: Murray, Draper, Fairman & Co. Proof.

5.29.11 P R-7

$10.00 Ca. 1812–20. Engraving, no imprint. Proof.

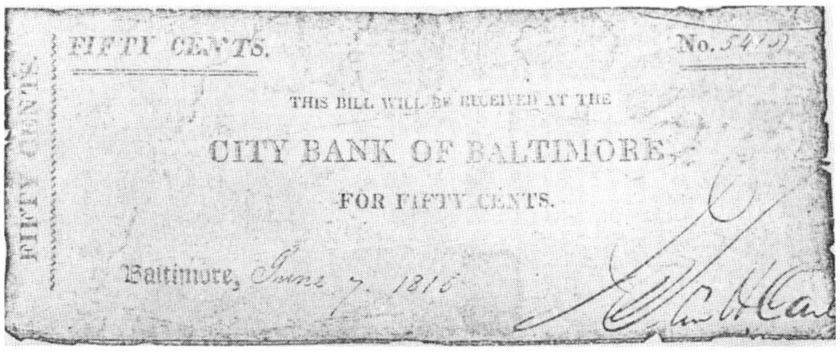

5.29.6

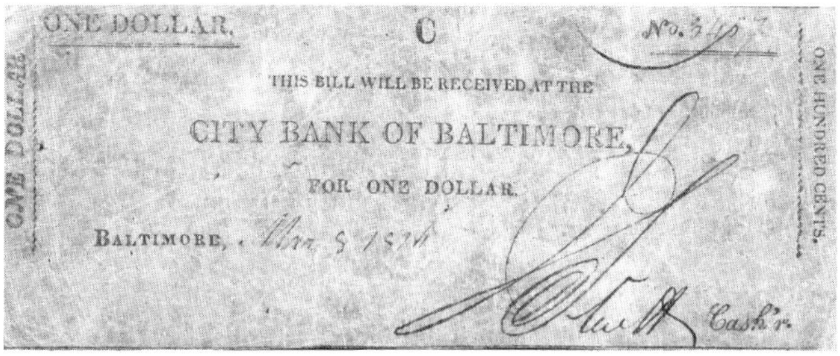

5.29.7

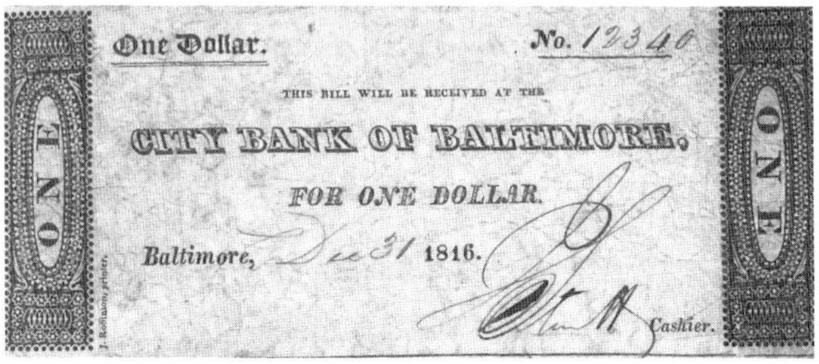

5.29.8

5.29.10 P

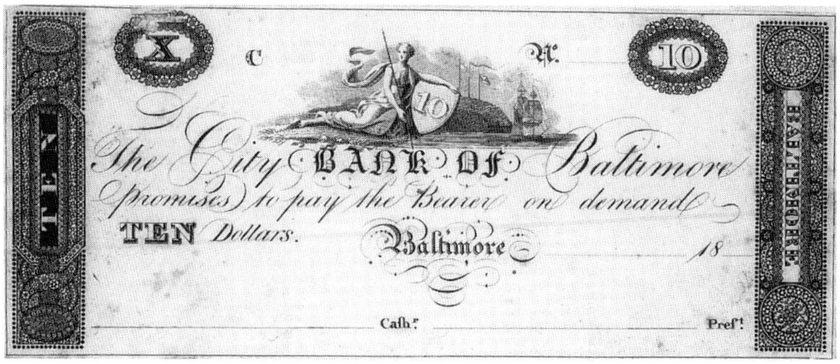

5.29.11 P

5.29.12 P R-7

$20.00 Ca. 1812–20. Engraving, imprint: Murray, Draper, Fairman & Co. Proof.

5.29.13 P R-7

$50.00 Ca. 1812–20. Engraving, imprint: Murray, Draper, Fairman & Co. Proof.

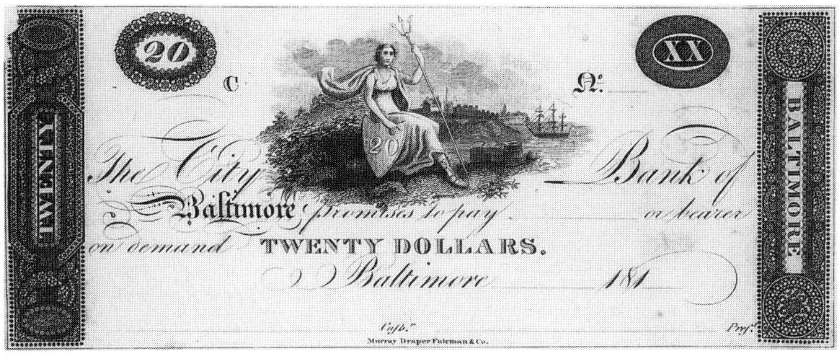

5.29.12 P

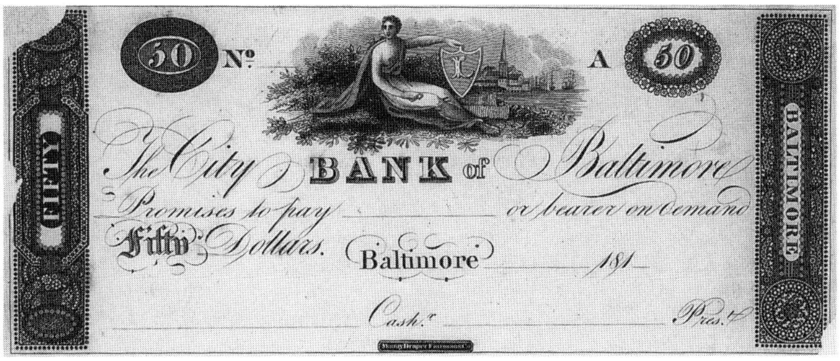

5.29.13 P

5.30 City Trust Savings Institution

There is no record of a charter approval. The Institution apparently began operation in July 1840 at 1 N. Howard St., and failed in early September of the same year.

5.30.1 R-6

6 1/4c Printed date July 25, 1840. Letterpress, imprint: Murphy, Printer, 146 Market Street. With reversed "4" on 6 1/4 die.

5.30.2 R-6

6 1/4c Printed date July 25, 1840. Letterpress, imprint: Murphy Printer, 146 Market St., Same as No. 5.30.1 with "1" corrected on 6 1/4 die.

5.30.3 R-5

12 1/2c Printed date July 25, 1840. Letterpress, imprint: MURPHY, PRINTER, 146 Market Street.

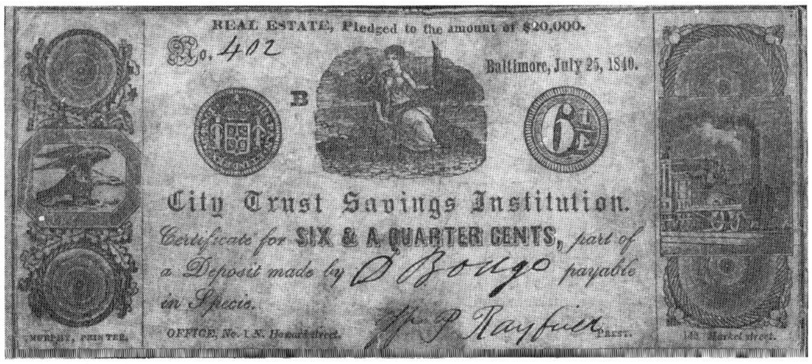

5.30.1

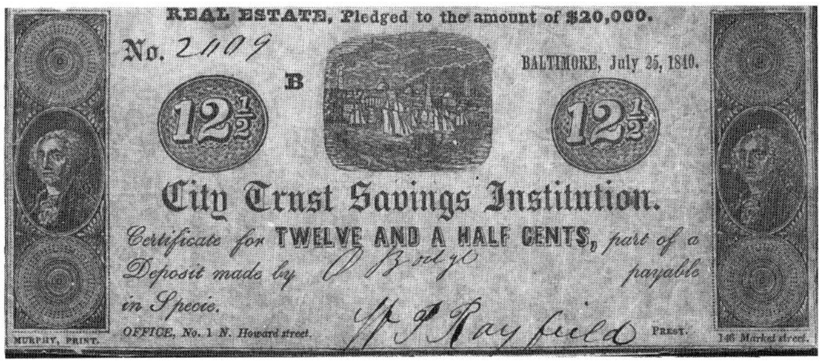

5.30.3

5.30.4 R-5

12 1/2c Printed date July 25, 1840. Letterpress, imprint: MURPHY, PRINT, 146 Market Street, with 12 1/2 die on left replaced with 1 real coin.

5.30.5 R-3

25c Printed date July 25, 1840. Letterpress, imprint: MURPHY, PRINTER, BALTIMORE.

5.30.6 R-6

25c Printed date July 25, 1840. Letterpress, imprint: MURPHY, PRINTER, BALTIMORE. Spelling error "Depisit" instead of "Deposit."

5.30.7 R-5

50c Printed date July 25, 1840. Letterpress, imprint: MURPHY PRINTER BALTIMORE. Vignette of Baltimore looking north from Federal Hill.

5.30.8 R-5

$1.00 Printed date July 25, 1840. Letterpress, imprint: MURPHY PRINTER BALTIMORE. Vignette of Baltimore looking north from Federal Hill.

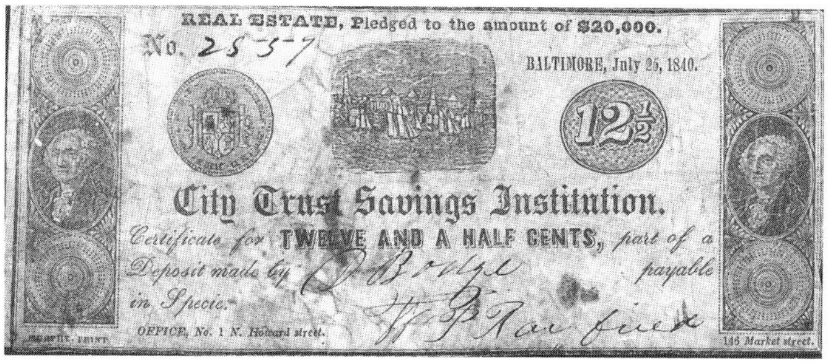

5.30.4

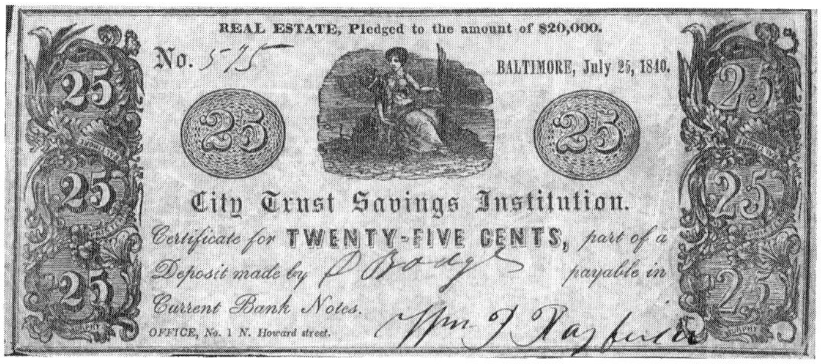

5.30.5

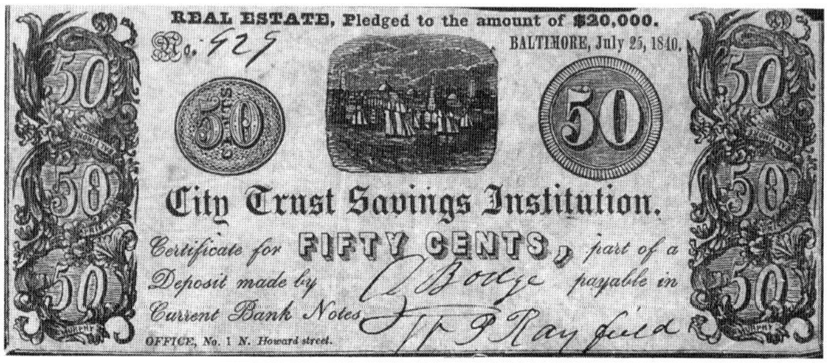

5.30.7

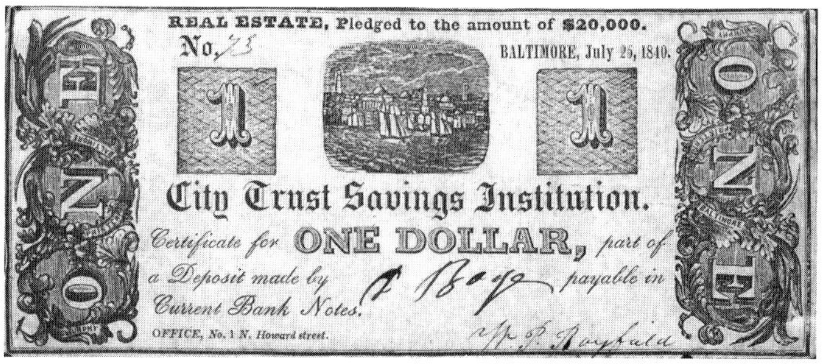

5.30.8

5.31 J. M. Clark

The identity of this issuer has not as yet been established, nor has the status of the notes themselves.

5.31.2 R-7
12 1/2c Printed year date 1840. Lithography, no imprint

5.31.3 R-7
25c Printed year date 1840. Lithography, no imprint.

5.31.4 R-7
50c Printed year date 1840. Lithography, imprint: E Weber.

5.31.2

5.31.3

5.31.4

5.32 J. S. Clark

The identity of the issuer has not as yet been established, nor has the status of the notes themselves.

5.32.1 R-7
6 1/4c Printed partial date 184_. Lithography, no imprint.

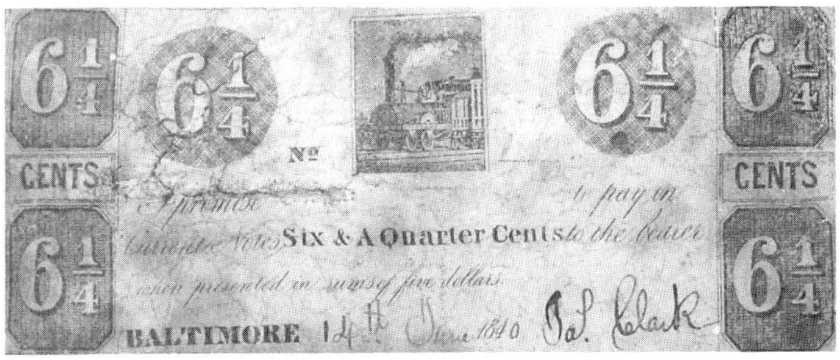

5.32.1

5.33 John Clark

According to directory listings and occasional newspaper notes, Clark conducted a lottery and exchange business "under the museum" at the northwest corner of Baltimore and Calvert streets between 1835 and 1845. His lower denomination "small change" notes are not infrequently found bearing a red handstamped overprint: REISSUED / PAYABLE IN CITY STOCK / ORDERS of the BALTO. / & OHIO R.R. CO. The dollar denomination notes all bear the promise to pay "in City stock orders of The Baltimore & Ohio Railroad or their equivalent in Baltimore bank notes" as a part of the printed promissory legend. The purpose of the handstamp was to lend credence to the circulating notes that were already under considerable pressure from the public. Several "shinplaster bankers" utilized similar handstamps.

5.33.1 R-3
6 1/4c Ca. 1840 (manuscript date). Engraving, imprint: Underwood, Bald, Spencer & Hufty, Philada. / Danforth, Underwood and Co., New York.

5.33.1 P R-6
6 1/4c Ca. 1840 (manuscript date). Engraving, imprint: Underwood, Bald, Spencer & Hufty, Philada. / Danforth, Underwood and Co., New York. Proof.

5.33.2 R-3
6 1/4c Ca. 1840 (manuscript date). Engraving, imprint: Underwood, Bald, Spencer & Hufty, Philada. / Danforth, Underwood and Co., New York. Same as No. 5.33.1, except with red handstamp reissue overprint.

5.33.3 R-3
6 1/4c Printed date Jany 1st. 1841. Engraving, imprint: Underwood, Bald, Spencer & Hufty, Philada. / Danforth, Underwood and Co., New York.

5.33.4 R-3
6 1/4c Printed date Jany 1st. 1841. Engraving, imprint: Underwood, Bald, Spencer & Hufty, Philada. / Danforth, Underwood and Co., New York. Same as No. 5.33.3, except with red handstamp reissue overprint.

5.33.5 R-3
12 1/2c Ca. 1840 (manuscript date). Engraving, imprint: Underwood, Bald, Spencer & Hufty, Philada. / Danforth, Underwood and Co., New York.

5.33.1

5.33.3

5.33.5

5.33.5 P R-7

12 1/2c Ca. 1840 (manuscript date). Engraving, imprint: Underwood, Bald, Spencer & Hufty, Philada. / Danforth, Underwood and Co., New York. Proof.

5.33.6 R-3

12 1/2c Ca. 1840 (manuscript date). Engraving, imprint: Underwood, Bald, Spencer & Hufty, Philada. / Danforth, Underwood and Co., New York. Same as No. 5.33.5, except with red handstamp reissue overprint.

5.33.7 R-3

12 1/2c Printed date Jany 1st. 1841. Engraving, imprint: Underwood, Bald, Spencer & Hufty, Philada. / Danforth, Underwood & Co., New York. Similar to No. 5.33.5 except for date.

5.33.8 R-3

12 1/2c Printed date Jany 1st. 1841. Engraving, imprint: Underwood, Bald, Spencer & Hufty, Philada. / Danforth, Underwood & Co., New York. Same as No. 5.33.7, except with red handstamp reissue overprint.

5.33.9

5.33.14

5.33.9 R-3

25c Ca. 1840 (manuscript date). Engraving, imprint: Underwood, Bald, Spencer & Hufty, Philada. / Danforth, Underwood & Co., New York.

5.33.9 P R-7

25c Ca. 1840 (manuscript date). Engraving, imprint: Underwood, Bald, Spencer & Hufty, Philada. / Danforth, Underwood, & Co., New York. Proof.

5.33.10 R-3

25c Ca. 1840 (manuscript date). Engraving, imprint: Underwood, Bald, Spencer & Hufty, Philada. / Danforth, Underwood, & Co., New York. Same as No. 5.33.9, except with red handstamp reissue overprint.

5.33.11 R-3

25c Printed date Jany 1st. 1841. Engraving, imprint: Underwood, Bald, Spencer & Hufty, Philada. / Danforth, Underwood, & Co., New York. Similar to No. 5.33.9 except for date.

5.33.12 R-3

25c Printed date Jany 1st. 1841. Engraving, imprint: Underwood, Bald, Spencer & Hufty, Philada. / Danforth, Underwood, & Co., New York. Same as No. 5.33.11, except with red handstamp reissue overprint.

5.33.13 R-3

50c Ca. 1840 (manuscript date). Engraving, imprint: Underwood, Bald, Spencer & Hufty, Philada. / Danforth, Underwood, & Co., New York. Similar to No. 5.33.14 except without handstamp.

5.33.13 P R-7

50c Ca. 1840 (manuscript date). Engraving, imprint: Underwood, Bald, Spencer & Hufty, Philada. / Danforth, Underwood, & Co., New York. Proof.

5.33.14 R-3

50c Ca. 1840 (manuscript date). Engraving, imprint: Underwood, Bald, Spencer & Hufty, Philada. / Danforth, Underwood, & Co., New York. Same as No. 5.33.13, except with red handstamp reissue overprint.

5.33.15 R-3

50c Printed date Jan 1st. 1841. Engraving, imprint: Underwood, Bald, Spencer & Hufty, Philada. / Danforth, Underwood & Co., New York. Similar to No. 5.33.13 except for date.

5.33.16 R-3

50c Printed date Jan. 1st. 1841. Engraving, imprint: Underwood, Bald, Spencer & Hufty, Philada. / Danforth, Underwood & Co., New York. Same as No. 5.33.15, except with red handstamp reissue overprint.

5.33.17 P R-7
$1.00 Ca. 1841. Engraving, imprint: Underwood, Bald, Spencer & Hufty, Philada. / Danforth, Underwood & Co., New York. Proof

5.33.18 R-4
$1.00 Printed date Jany 1st, 1841. Engraving, imprint: Underwood, Bald, Spencer & Hufty, Philada. / Danforth, Underwood & Co., New York.

5.33.18 P R-7
$1.00 Printed date Jany 1st, 1841. Engraving, imprint: Underwood, Bald, Spencer & Hufty, Philada. / Danforth, Underwood & Co., New York. Proof.

5.33.19 R-5
$2.00 Printed date Jany 1st. 1841. Engraving, imprint: Underwood, Bald, Spencer & Hufty, Philada. / Danforth, Underwood & Co., New York.

5.33.19 P R-7
$2.00 Printed date Jany 1st. 1841. Engraving, imprint: Underwood, Bald, Spencer & Hufty, Philada. / Danforth, Underwood & Co., New York. Proof.

5.33.20 R-6
$3.00 Printed date Jany 1st. 1841. Engraving, imprint: Underwood, Bald, Spencer & Hufty, Philada. / Danforth, Underwood & Co., New York.

5.33.20 P R-7
$3.00 Printed date Jany 1st. 1841. Engraving, imprint: Underwood, Bald, Spencer & Hufty, Philada. / Danforth, Underwood & Co., New York. Proof.

5.33.17 P

5.33.18

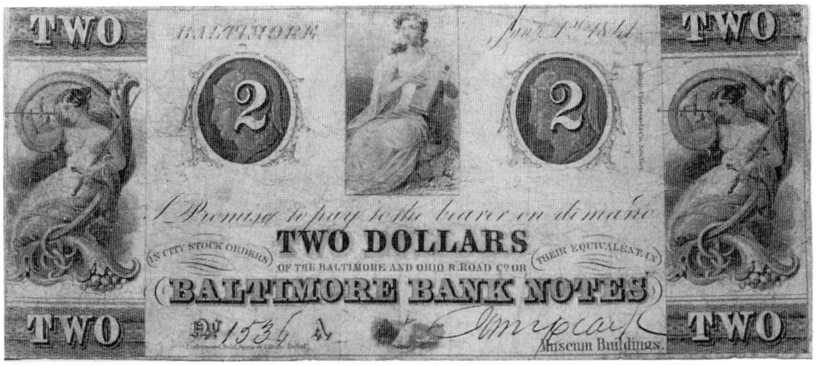

5.33.19

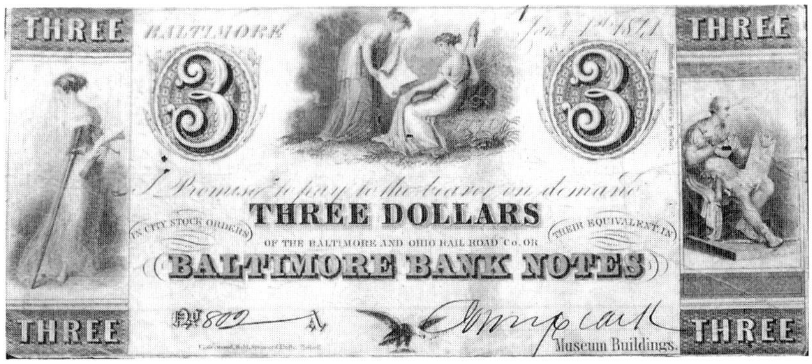

5.33.20

5.33.21 P R-7

$5.00 Ca. 1840. Engraving, imprint: Underwood, Bald, Spencer & Hufty, Philada. / Danforth, Underwood & Co., New York. Proof.

Notes in denominations of one, two, three, and five dollars, with the redemption legend, IN VIRGINIA MONEY OR ITS EQUIVALENT IN BALTIMORE BANK NOTES, were apparently prepared for Clark, but have not been recorded bearing his signature.

5.33.25 P R-7

$1.00 Printed date Sept 1, 1841. Engraving, imprint: Underwood, Bald, Spencer & Hufty, Philada. / Danforth, Underwood & Co., New York. The manuscript "signatures," 'Dixon, Cash' and 'Brown, Pres,' were probably written in an attempt to gain acceptance of a note not actually issued. Proof.

5.33.26 P R-7

$2.00 Printed date Sept. 1, 1841. Engraving, imprint: Underwood, Bald, Spencer & Hufty, Philada. / Danforth, Underwood & Co., New York. Proof.

5.33.27 P R-7

$3.00 Printed date Sept. 1, 1841. Engraving, imprint: Underwood, Bald, Spencer & Hufty, Philada. / Danforth, Underwood & Co., New York. Proof.

5.33.21 P

5.33.25 P

5.33.26 P

5.33.27 P

5.33.30 R-7

$5.00 Ca. 1841. Engraving, imprint: Underwood, Bald, Spencer & Hufty, Philada. / Danforth, Underwood & Co., New York.

5.33.30

5.34 **W. E. Coale**

In the "List of Small Notes Circulating in Baltimore," published in the *Baltimore Clipper* of September 12, 1840, the above name appeared as a broker with an office on South Charles Street near Baltimore Street. As none of Coale's notes have as yet been recorded by the authors, their designs and denominations are unknown.

5.35 **J. I. Cohen & Brothers**

Established about 1814 as a lottery and exchange office at 110 Baltimore St., this firm gradually phased out its lottery operations until in the 1831 city directory it listed itself as an exchange office. The next edition of the directory described the business as a banking house that was located at the northeast corner of Baltimore and Calvert streets and continued in use until the firm disappeared from the listings about 1870, a surviving family member, Israel Cohen, having become a stock and bond broker. Cohen notes are rare as the business was a successful one and regularly redeemed its notes in specie even during the "hard times" of 1837–41.

For a number of years the identification of the Cohen firm as the issuer of the higher denomination notes, of which only proofs were on record, had not been ascertained. During the preparation of this book, one of the authors saw a piece of sheet music, the cover of which included the unmistak-

Cover of sheet music, "The Very Last Polka" by Francois Bernard, lithographed by E. Weber & Co., Baltimore. Looking north on Calvert Street from its intersection with Baltimore Street, the museum building is on the left corner and the corner of Cohen's marble banking house is in the right foreground.

able corner of the Cohen building which appears on the notes. The banking house, built about 1835–36, was located at the northeast corner of Baltimore and Calvert streets.

5.35.1 P R-7
$1.00 Ca. 1833–38. Engraving, imprint: Draper, Underwood, Bald & Spencer. Proof.

5.35.2 R-6
$1.00 Ca. 1840. Engraving, imprint: Underwood, Bald, Spencer & Hufty, Philada. / Danforth, Underwood & Co., New York.

5.35.2 P R-7
$1.00 Ca. 1840. Engraving, imprint: Underwood, Bald, Spencer & Hufty, Philada. / Danforth, Underwood & Co., New York. Proof.

5.35.3 R-7
$2.00 Ca. 1838. Engraving, imprint: Draper, Underwood, Bald & Spencer.

5.35.1 P

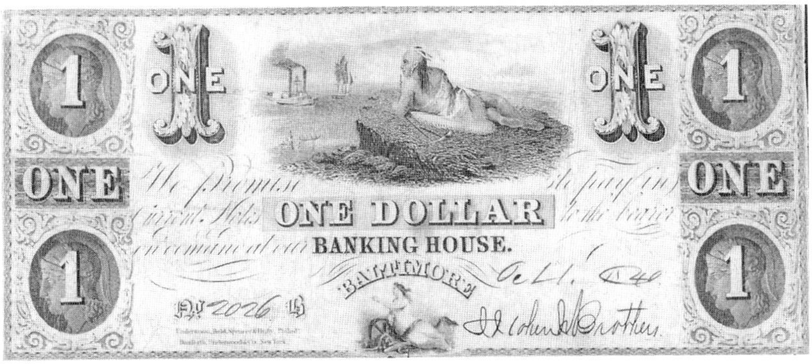

5.35.2

5.35.2 P

5.35.3

5.35.3 P R-7

$2.00 Ca. 1833–38. Engraving, imprint: Draper, Underwood, Bald & Spencer. Proof.

5.35.4 P R-7

$3.00 Ca. 1833–38. Engraving, imprint: Draper, Underwood, Bald & Spencer. Proof.

5.35.5 P R-7

$5.00 Ca. 1833–38. Engraving, imprint: Draper, Underwood, Bald & Spencer. Proof.

5.35.6 P R-7

$5.00 Ca. 1840. Engraving, imprint: Underwood, Bald, Spencer & Hufty. Vignette of the Cohen banking house. Proof.

According to a news item in the *Baltimore Sun* of May 18, 1840, a one-dollar note of J. I. Cohen & Brothers altered to a five had been presented in Philadelphia the previous week and detected. The item went on to say that all Cohen notes "above the denomination of three dollars have a view of the banking house upon them [and that] with a knowledge of this fact, it would be difficult to pass an altered note."

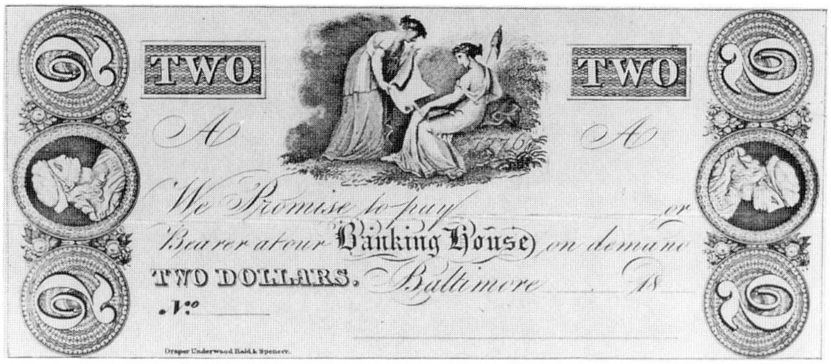

5.35.3 P

5.35.4 P

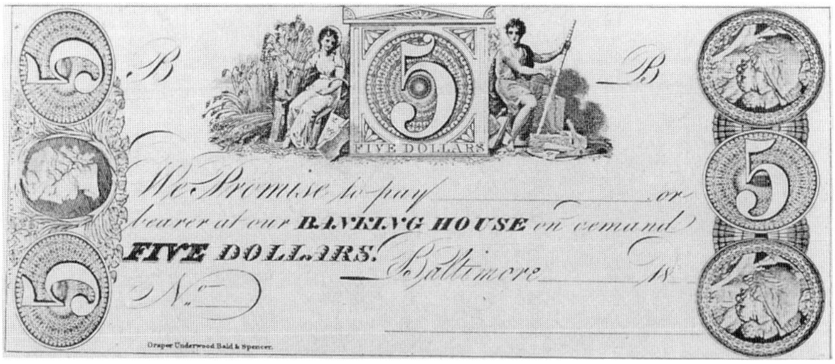

5.35.5 P

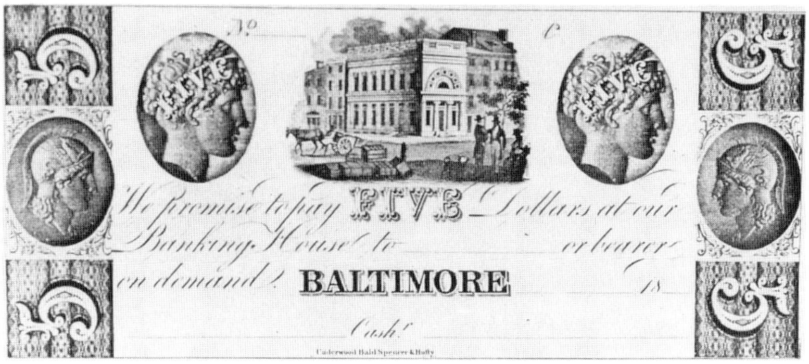

5.35.6 P

5.35.7 P R-7

$10.00 Ca. 1833–38. Engraving, imprint: Draper, Underwood, Bald & Spencer. Proof.

5.35.8 P R-7

$10.00 Ca. 1840. Engraving, imprint: Underwood, Bald, Spencer & Hufty. Vignette of the Cohen banking house. Proof.

5.35.9 P R-7

$20.00 Ca. 1833–38. Engraving, imprint: Draper, Underwood, Bald & Spencer. Proof.

5.35.10 P R-7

$20.00 Ca. 1840. Engraving, imprint: Underwood, Bald, Spencer & Hufty. Vignette of the Cohen banking house. Proof.

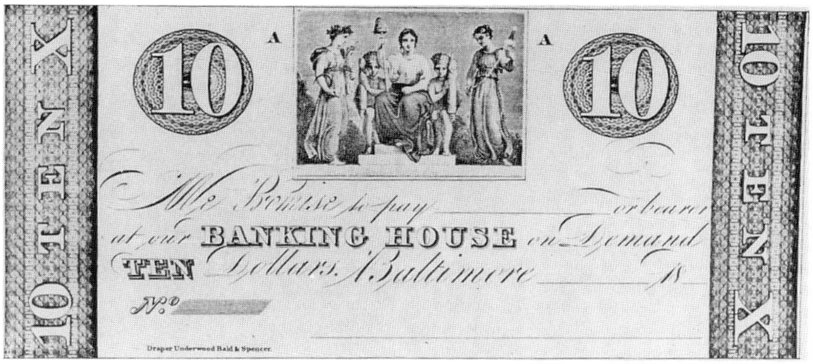

5.35.7 P

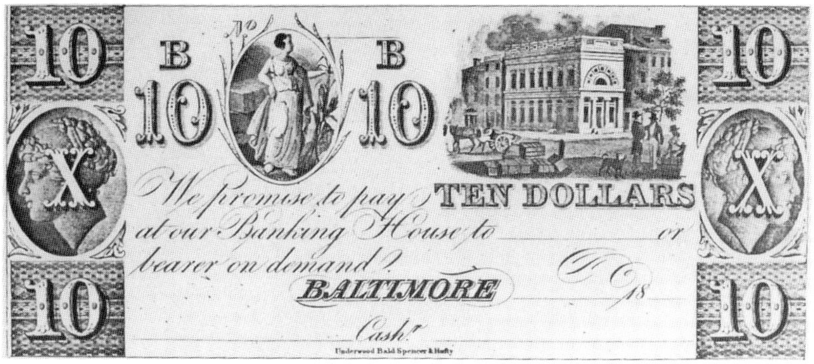

5.35.8 P

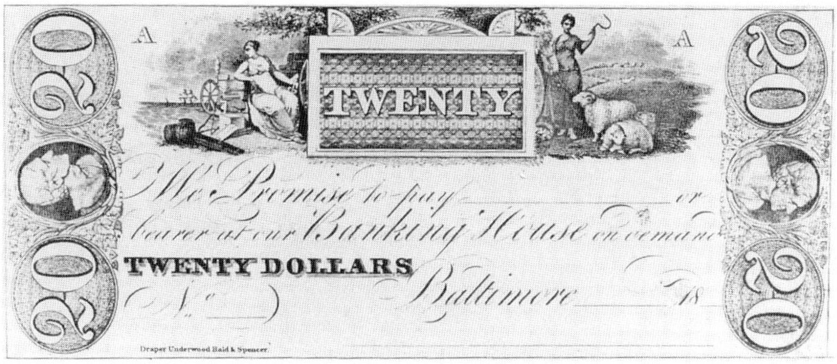

5.35.9 P

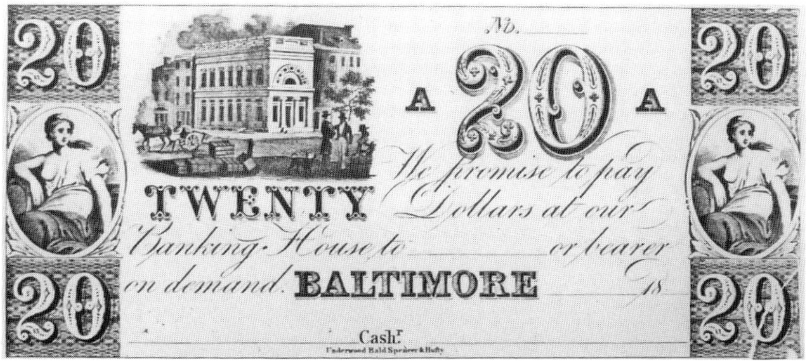

5.35.10 P

5.35.11 P R-7

$50.00 Ca. 1833–38. Engraving, imprint: Draper, Underwood, Bald & Spencer. Proof.

5.35.12 P R-7

$50.00 Ca. 1840. Engraving, imprint: Underwood, Bald, Spencer & Hufty. Vignette of the Cohen banking house. Proof.

5.35.13 P R-7

$50.00 Ca. 1840. Engraving, imprint: Underwood, Bald, Spencer & Hufty. Vignette of the Cohen banking house. Proof.

5.35.14 P R-7

$100.00 Ca. 1833–38. Engraving, imprint: Draper, Underwood, Bald & Spencer. Proof.

5.35.11 P

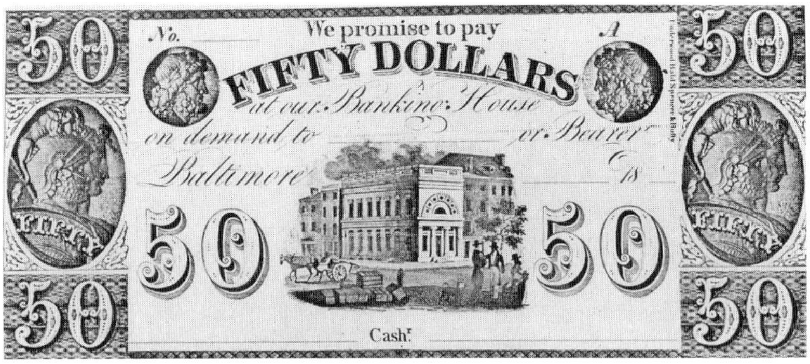

5.35.12 P

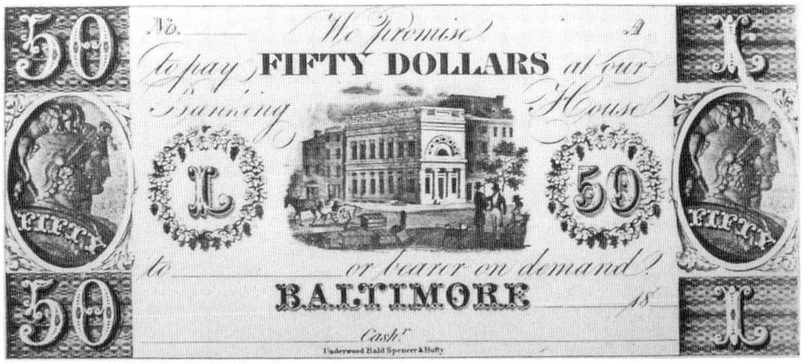

5.35.13 P

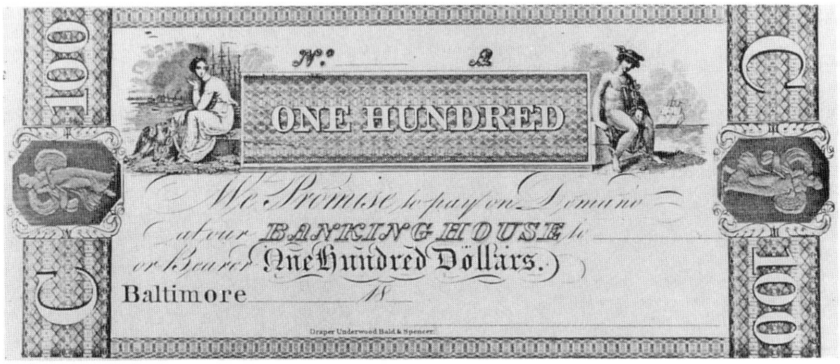

5.35.14 P

5.35.15 P R-7

$100.00 Ca. 1840. Engraving, imprint: Underwood, Bald, Spencer & Hufty. Vignette of the Cohen banking house. Proof.

5.35.16 P R-7

$500.00 Ca. 1840. Engraving, imprint: Underwood, Bald, Spencer & Hufty. Vignette of the Cohen banking house. Proof.

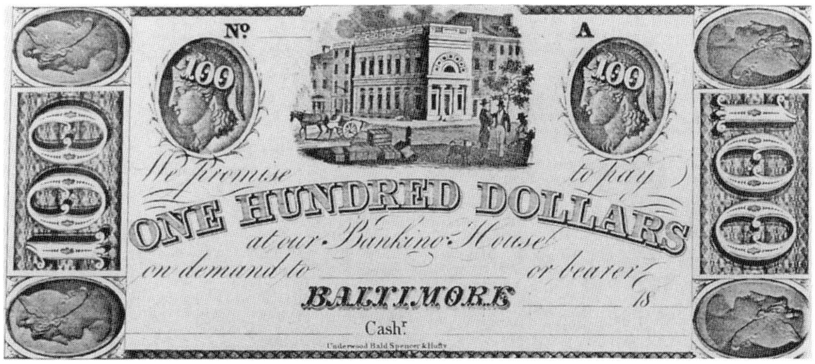

5.35.15 P

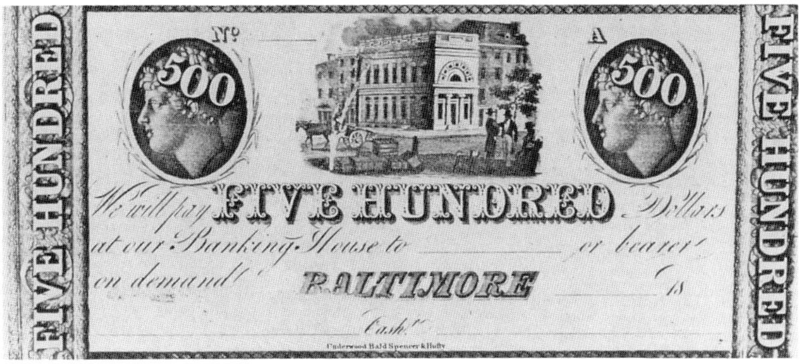

5.35.16 P

5.36 The Colonnade Baths

This institution, which included a public bathhouse and reading rooms, was located at the corner of Davis and Saratoga streets being so listed in the 1840–41 edition of the Baltimore city directory. The proprietor was Lew Milhau, who also conducted an adjoining tavern. He apparently moved on to other endeavors by 1845 when his directory listing showed him as the proprietor of the Washington Coffee House at nearby 2 N. Gay St., the Colonnade having come under the management of John Finlay by the time the 1847–48 directory was published. In 1850 Finlay was still the proprietor of the Colonnade, but succeeding editions contained no listings for the two men or the bathhouse.

5.36.1 R-7

6 1/4c Printed year date 1840. Letterpress, imprint: Printed by Bull & Tuttle, Baltimore.

5.36.1

5.36.2 R-7

6 1/4c Printed date May 1st, 1841. Lithography, imprint: Lith. by E. Weber & Co., Balt. The vignette depicts the Colonnade Baths. Similar to 6 1/4c, No. 5.36.2.

5.36.3 R-7

12 1/2c Printed date May 1st, 1841. Lithography, imprint: Lith. by E. Weber & Co., Balt. The vignette depicts the Colonnade Baths.

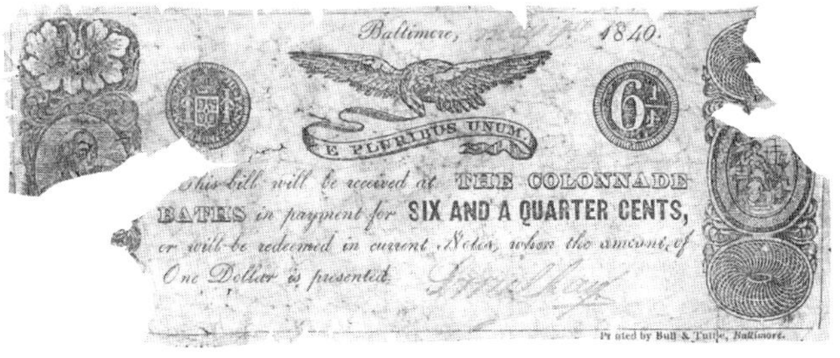

5.36.2

5.37 The Bank of Commerce

Charter approved March 10, 1854; converted to and became the National Bank of Commerce of Baltimore in 1890. The bank was located at 26 South St., near Baltimore St.

5.37.2 R-6

$1.00 Printed date March 15, 1862. Engraving, imprint: American Bank Note Company. (MD35G2)

5.37.3 A SENC

$2.00 Ca. 1856. Engraving, no imprint. *Left center:* Two women seated, left one pointing at ship in left background. *Right center:* Train, in oval. *Left:* Oval female portrait / medallion head bearing white TWO. *Right:* 2 on TWO / oval portrait of Washington / TWO. Altered. (MD35A10)

5.37.4 A R-6

$2.00 Printed partial date March 1st 18__. Ca. 1862. Engraving, imprint: Danforth, Wright & Co., New York & Philada. Altered from the Southern Bank of Georgia, Bainridge. Red background network to produce large negative TWO. Red die at "2" in both upper corners. (MD35A5a).

5.37.2

5.37.4 A

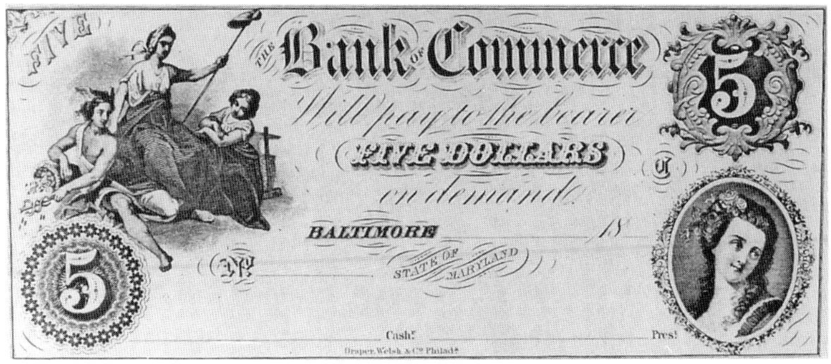

5.37.6 P

5.37.5 A R-6

$2.00 Printed partial date March 1st 18__. Ca. 1862. Engraving, imprint: Danforth, Wright & Co., New York & Philada. Same as No. 5.37.4 A, without TWO at center, with TWO DOLLARS in red. Altered. (MD35A5)

5.37.6 SENC

$5.00 Ca. 1850s. Engraving, imprint: Draper, Welsh & Co., Phila. Same as proof No. 5.37.6 P. (MD35G6)

5.37.6 P R-6

$5.00 Ca. 1850s. Engraving, imprint: Draper, Welsh & Co., Phila. Proof.

5.37.7 S SENC

$5.00 Ca. 1850s. Engraving, imprint: Unknown. *Center:* Eagle and shield. Spurious. (MD35N5)

5.37.9 S R-5

$5.00 Ca. 1854–55. Engraving, imprint: Wellstood, Hanks & Co., New York. Imitation of a genuine note (Clapp, Fuller & Browne's banknote reporter, March 1859, New York). Spurious. (MD35S5)

5.37.10 P R-7

$5.00 Ca. 1856–61. Engraving, imprint: Toppan, Carpenter & Co., Philada. & New York. Proof.

5.37.11 P R-7

$5.00 Ca. 1856–61. Engraving, imprint: Toppan, Carpenter & Co., Philada. & New York. Dark red network over lower portion of note producing negative FIVE. Proof. (MD35G8a)

5.37.12 S R-6

$5.00 Ca. 1860s. Engraving, imprint: Danforth, Bald & Co., Phila. & New York. Red orange security print, negative FIVE on micro-type background FIVE DOLLARS. From a modified fraudulent plate, originally for a counterfeit $5.00 (PA485C132a) on the Philadelphia Bank. Spurious. (MD35S10)

5.37.9 S

5.37.10 P

5.37.11 P

5.37.12 S

5.37.13 S R-7

$5.00 Ca. 1860s. Engraving, imprint: Danforth, Bald & Co., Phila. & New York. Same as No. 5.37.12 S, except without red-orange tint. Spurious.

5.37.15 P R-7

$10.00 Ca. 1850s. Engraving, imprint: Draper, Welsh & Co. Philadelphia. Proof. (MD35G10)

5.37.16 S SENC

$10.00 Ca. 1850s. Engraving, imprint: Unknown. *Center:* Eagle and shield. Spurious. (MD35N10)

5.37.17 S SENC

$10.00 Ca. 1850s. Engraving, imprint: Unknown. *Center:* Ship under sail. *Left:* 10 / oval portrait of Webster. *Right:* 10 / oval female portrait. Spurious. (MD35N15)

5.37.18 P R-7

$10.00 Ca. 1850–60s. Engraving, imprint: Toppan, Carpenter & Co., Philada & New York. Red-orange network over entire note producing negative TEN. Proof. (MD35G12a)

5.37.19 SENC

$20.00 Ca. 1850s. Engraving, imprint: Draper, Welsh & Co. Phila. *Center:* Steamship moving to right, other ships in background. *Left:* 20 / half-length figure of mechanic reclining on boiler, cogwheel, foundry in background. *Right:* 20 / sailor seated, box, bales and barrels. *Between signatures:* Woman's head. (MD35G14)

5.37.20 S SENC

$20.00 Ca. 1850s Engraving, imprint: Unknown. Eagle and shield at center. Spurious. (MD35N20)

5.37.21 P R-7

$50.00 Ca. 1850s. Engraving, imprint: Draper, Welsh & Co., Phila. Henry Clay at center. Proof. (MD35G16)

5.37.13 S

5.37.15 P

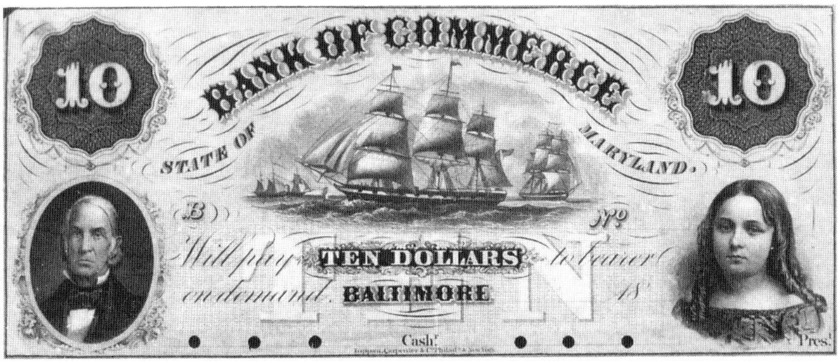

5.37.18 P

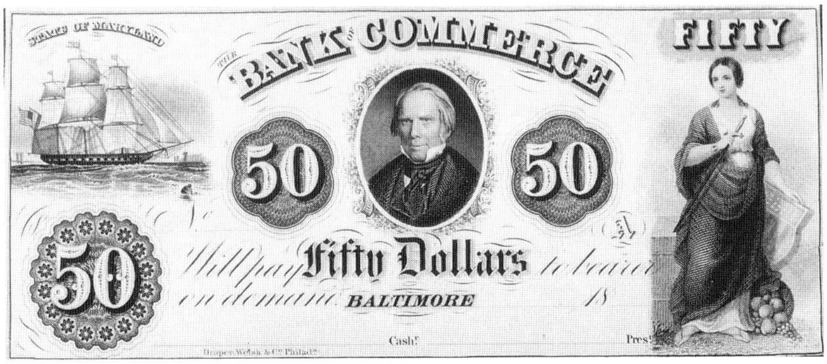

5.37.21 P

5.37.22 P R-7

$100.00 Ca. 1850s. Engraving, imprint: Draper, Welsh & Co., Philada. Proof. (MD35G18)

5.37.23 P R-7

$500.00 Ca. 1850s. Engraving, imprint: Toppan, Carpenter & Co., New York & Philada. Proof. (MD35G20)

5.37.24 SENC

$1000.00 Ca. 1850s. Engraving, imprint: Toppan, Carpenter & Co., New York & Philada. *Upper left/left center:* View of railroad depot, and wharf with steamboat docking, passengers, bales, etc., city in background. *Upper right corner:* Oval male portrait. *Lower left:* M. *Right:* 1000 / sailing ship, buildings, etc. (MD35G22)

5.37.22 P

5.37.23 P

5.38 The Commercial Bank of Baltimore

Charter approved March 30, 1836; closed in 1840.

5.38.4 SENC

$5.00 Ca. 1836–40. Engraving, imprint: Rawdon, Wright & Hatch. No other information available. (MD40G2)

5.38.5 S R-5

$5.00 Ca. 1838. Engraving, imprint: Rawdon, Wright & Hatch New York. Spurious. (MD40S5)

5.38.6 A R-7

$5.00 Ca. 1840. Engraving, imprint: Rawdon, Wright & Hatch, New York. Altered from $5.00 note of the Commercial Bank, Millington, Md., with the original Millington signatures still in place. (MD39A5)

5.38.5 S

5.38.6 A

5.38.7 SENC

$10.00 Ca. 1836–40. Engraving, imprint: Rawdon, Wright & Hatch. No other information available. (MD40G4)

5.38.9 SENC

$20.00 Ca. 1836–40. Engraving, imprint: Rawdon, Wright & Hatch. No other information available. (MD40G6)

5.38.11 SENC

$50.00 Ca. 1836–40. Engraving, imprint: Rawdon, Wright & Hatch. No other information available. (MD40G8)

5.39 The Commercial & Farmers Bank of Baltimore

Operated as an unchartered association during part of 1810. Charter approved December 23, 1810. Converted to and became the Commercial & Farmers National Bank in 1865. In its earliest years the bank was located at 235 Baltimore St., corner of Howard Street; about 1814–15 it moved to the southwest corner of Howard and German streets. (An item in the *Baltimore Republican & Argus,* March 15, 1842, stated that the small-note issue of the Commercial & Farmers Bank had been printed "during the last war" and "carefully laid away . . . and were now being circulated"; and that other banks in the city were using old plates.)

5.39.1 R-7

$1.00 Ca. 1850s. Engraving, imprint: Draper & Co., Phila. (MD45G20)

5.39.1 P R-7

$1.00 Ca. 1850s. Engraving, imprint: Draper & Co., Phila. Without engraved signature of president. Proof.

5.39.1 C R-6

$1.00 Ca. 1850s. Engraving, imprint: Draper & Co., Phila. Counterfeit of No. 5.39.1.

5.39.2 P R-7

$1.00 Ca. 1850s. Engraving, imprint: Draper & Co., Phila. With engraved signature of president. Proof.

5.39.3 P R-7

$1.00 Ca. 1850s. Engraving, imprint: Draper & Co., Phila. Same as No. 5.39.2 P, except without engraved president's signature. Proof.

5.39.1 P

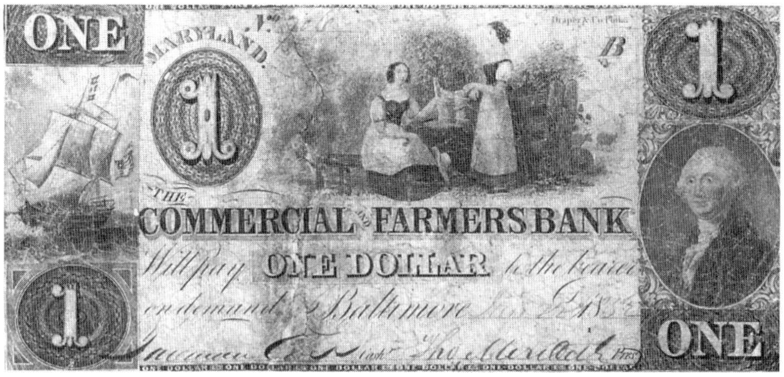

5.39.1 C

5.39.2 P

5.39.4 P R-7

$1.00 Ca. 1850s. Engraving, imprint: Draper & Co., Phila. With engraved signature of president. Proof.

5.39.10 R-6

$1.00 Printed partial date May 12th, 18__. Ca. 1860s. Engraving, imprint: National Bank Note Company. (MD45G22)

5.39.11 SENC

$2.00 Printed partial date May 12, 18__. Ca. 1860s. Engraving, imprint: National Bank Note Company. *Center:* Sailor, ship in background. On left and right is "2" on ornate die. Tint is green "2 2." (MD45G26a)

5.39.12 SENC

$3.00 Printed partial date May 12, 18__. Ca. 1860s. Engraving, imprint: National Bank Note Co. *Center:* Three children reading books. *Left and right:* 3 on ornate die. Tint is green "3 3." (MD45G30a)

5.39.13 SENC

$5.00 Ca. 1810. Engraving, imprint: Murray & Draper. Association issue. Text reads "pay out of their joint funds." (MD45G8)

5.39.14 SENC

$5.00 Ca. 1810s. Engraving, imprint: Murray & Draper. Similar to 5.39.13, but "out of their joint funds" deleted. (MD45G34)

5.39.15 R-7

$5.00 Ca. 1810s–30s. Engraving, no imprint. (MD45G36)

5.39.16 P R-5

$5.00 Ca. 1830s–50s. Engraving, imprint: Chas. Toppan. Proof. (MD45G38)

5.39.4 P

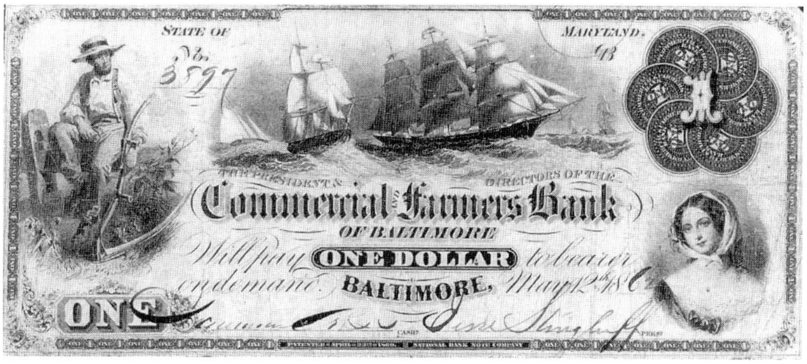

5.39.10

5.39.15

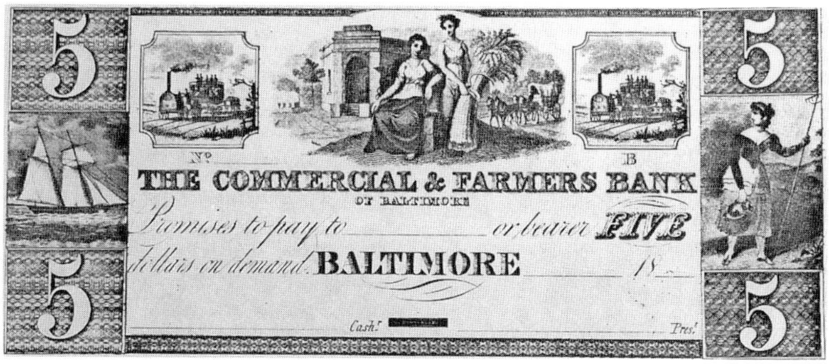

5.39.16 P

5.39.17 P R-7

$10.00 Ca. 1810. Engraving, imprint: Murray & Draper. Association issue. Text reads "pay out of their Joint Funds." Similar to No. 5.39.18. Proof. (MD45G10)

5.39.18 SENC

$10.00 Ca. 1810. Engraving, imprint: Murray & Draper. Similar to No. 5.39.17 P, but "out of their Joint Funds" deleted. (MD45G42)

5.39.19 SENC

$10.00 Ca. 1810s–30s. Engraving, imprint: Murray, Draper, Fairman, Brewster & Co. Similar to counterfeit No. 5.39.19 C. (MD45G44)

5.39.19 C R-5

$10.00 Ca. 1820s–30s. Engraving, imprint: Murray, Draper, Fairman, Brewster & Co. Counterfeit. (MD45C44)

5.39.21 P R-5

$10.00 Ca. 1830s–50s. Engraving, imprint: Chas. Toppan. Proof. (MD45G46)

5.39.22 S SENC

$10.00 Ca. 1840s. Engraving, imprint: Unknown. Oxen and plow at center. Probably spurious. (MD45N5)

5.39.23 C SENC

$10.00 Ca. 1850s. Engraving, imprint: Chas. Toppan. Counterfeit of same design as No. 5.39.21 P. (MD45C46)

5.39.24 P R-7

$10.00 Ca. 1856–61. Engraving, imprint: Toppan, Carpenter & Co., Philadelphia. Red borders around "10"s, large red "X" at center, red TEN DOLLARS at bottom. The portrait in the lower right corner is that of George Peabody. Proof. (MD45G48a)

5.39.25 R SENC

$10.00 Printed partial date March 12, 18__. Ca. 1860s. Engraving, imprint: National Bank Note Co. Raised from $1.00, No. 5.39.10. (MD45R5)

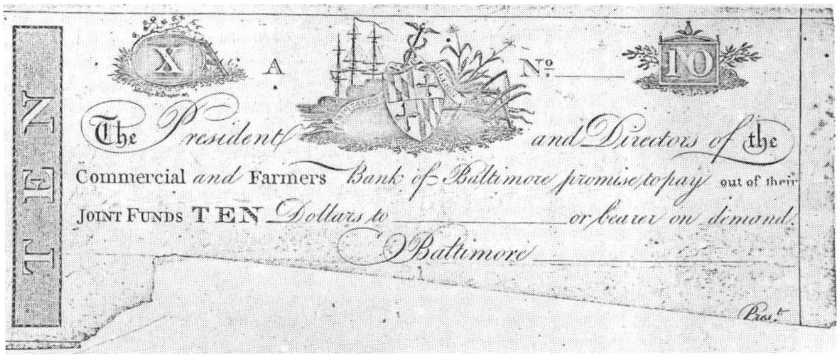

5.39.17 P

5.39.19 C

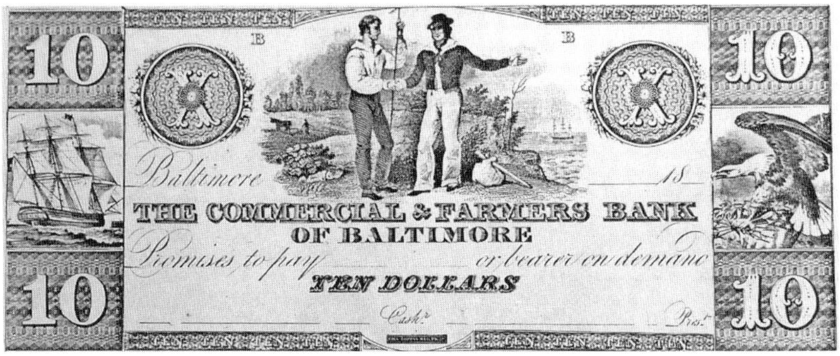

5.39.21 P

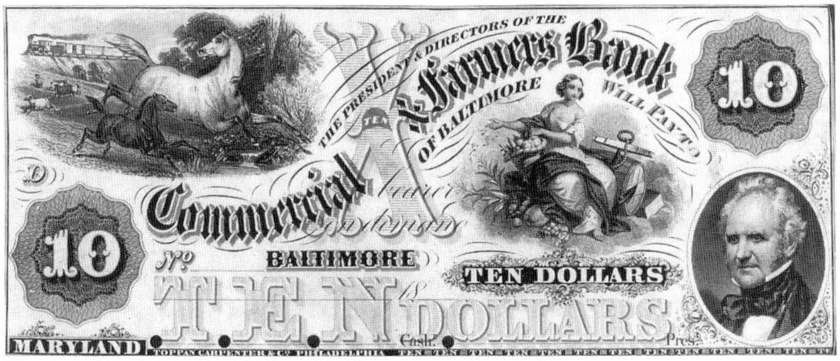

5.39.24 P

5.39.26 SENC

$20.00 Ca. 1810. Engraving, imprint: Murray & Draper. Association issue. Text reads "pay out of their joint funds." Similar to $10.00, No. 5.39.17 P. (MD45G12)

5.39.27 SENC

$20.00 Ca. 1810s. Engraving, imprint: Murray & Draper. Similar to No. 5.39.26, except for text from which "pay out of their Joint Funds" has been deleted. (MD45G50)

5.39.28 SENC

$20.00 Ca. 1810–30s. Engraving, no imprint. Similar to $5.00, No. 5.39.15. (MD45G52)

5.39.29 P R-7

$20.00 Ca. 1830s–50s. Engraving, imprint: Draper, Toppan, Longacre & Co., Phila. & New York. Proof. (MD45G54)

5.39.30 SENC

$50.00 Ca. 1810. Engraving, imprint: Murray & Draper. Association issue. Text reads "out of their Joint Funds." Similar to $10.00, No. 5.39.17 P. (MD45G14)

5.39.31 SENC

$50.00 Ca. 1810s. Engraving, imprint: Murray & Draper. Similar to $50.00, No. 5.39.30, except for text from which "pay out of their Joint Funds" has been deleted. (MD45G58)

5.39.32 SENC

$50.00 Ca. Early 1810s–early 1830s. Engraving, imprint: Unknown. Similar to $5.00, No. 5.39.15. (MD45G60)

5.39.33 P R-7

$50.00 Ca. 1830s–50s. Engraving, imprint: Draper, Toppan Longacre & Co., Phila. & N.Y. Proof. (MD45G62)

5.39.34 SENC

$100.00 Ca. 1810s. Engraving, imprint: Murray & Draper. Similar to $10.00, No. 5.39.18. (MD45G66)

5.39.35 SENC

$100.00 Ca. early 1810s–early 1830s. Engraving, imprint: None. Similar to $5.00, No. 5.39.15. (MD45G68)

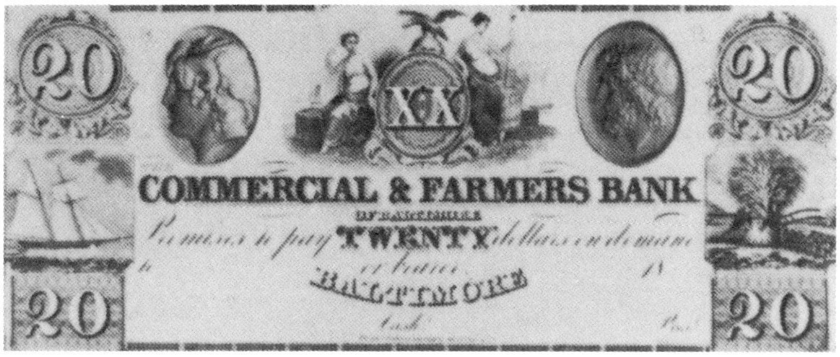

5.39.29 P

5.39.33 P

5.39.36 P

5.39.37 P

5.39.36 P R-7

$100.00 Ca. early 1810s–30s. Engraving, imprint: Murray, Draper, Fairman & Co. Proof.

5.39.37 P R-7

$100.00 Ca. 1830s–50s. Engraving, imprint: Draper, Toppan, Longacre & Co., Phila. & N.Y. Proof. (MD45G70)

5.39.38 P R-7

$500.00 Ca. 1830s–50s. Engraving, imprint: Draper, Toppan, Longacre & Co., Phila. & N.Y. Proof. (MD45G74)

5.39.39 P R-7

$1000.00 Ca. 1830s–50s. Engraving, imprint: Draper, Toppan, Longacre & Co., Phila. & N.Y. Proof. (MD45G78)

5.39.38 P

5.39.39 P

5.40 T. N. Conrad

The issuer was a resident of Fairfax Court House, Virginia, who obviously made business trips to Baltimore with sufficient frequency to justify the convenience of using his own small-change scrip.

5.40.3 R-3

25c Printed partial date June 1842. Letterpress, imprint: Murphy, print. (Va.#PF10-04)

5.40.3

5.41 I. Cooke

The issuer was the proprietor of a cotton mill on Paca Street.

5.41.3 R-7

25c Printed date August __, 1840. Letterpress, imprint: Matchett, Printer.

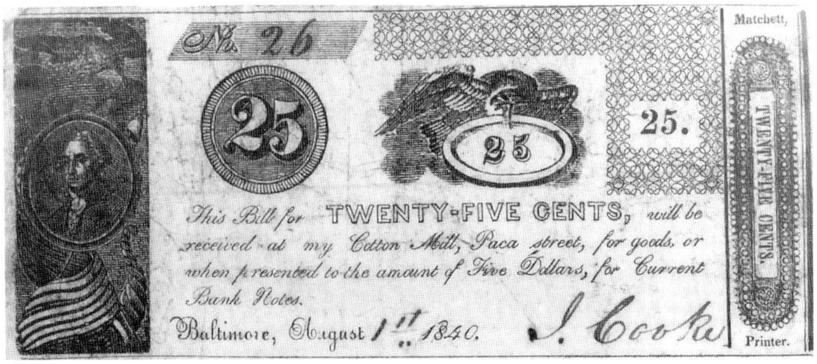

5.41.3

5.42 Calvin Cooper

The issuer was a grocer at 57 Bond St., Fells Point, being so listed in the 1814–15 and 1816 editions of the city directory. The only other listing for Calvin Cooper was in 1810 when he was shown as a hack owner at 23 W. Lancaster St., also in Fells Point.

5.42.1 R-7
6 1/4c Printed partial date, Sept. 1815. Letterpress, no imprint.

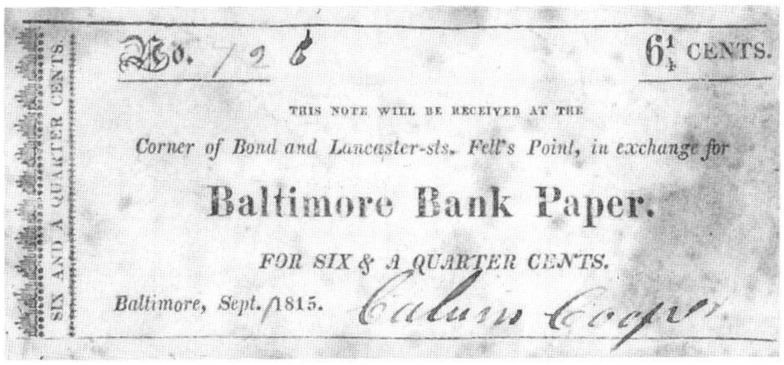

5.42.1

5.43 John Corse

5.43.5 R-7
$1.00 Printed date October 31, 1845. Engraving, no imprint. Bill of exchange drawn on John Corse, a private banker in Alexandria, Va., in which the signer directs the banker to pay his creditor $1.00 in current Virginia bank notes. The signature is unreadable, so the issuer has not been identified. Corse obviously supplied the printed bills to his clients. This note has been listed under his name, which is printed on the bill.

5.43.5

5.44 J. R. Crandall

In the "List of Small Notes Circulating in Baltimore," published in the *Baltimore Clipper* of September 12, 1840, there appeared "J.R. Crandall, Tavern Keeper, Camden st. near R.R. Depot." None of Crandall's notes have been recorded, thus neither denominations nor descriptions are currently available.

5.45 C. H. Creamer

Creamer was the proprietor of a tavern in Marsh Market Space. He issued a small number of scrip notes that he ultimately offered to redeem. None have been seen by the authors. Two articles from the *Sun* are partially reproduced below; they give all the facts known to date.
Thursday, August 8, 1840:

> A FREE BANKER. —Marcus Charles H. Creamer, the keeper of a tavern in Marsh Market Space, was yesterday brought before Justice Schaeffer. The action upon which he was arrested was for a debt of one dollar, which he had refused to pay the holder of a shinplaster which it was alleged he had issued. Some curious facts relating to the manufacture of paper money were developed in this case. It appears that sometime in April, Creamer, accompanied by two other persons, called on Mr. Weber, the lithographer, and asked him to print for them some blank notes, which they required to be done in a short time.

> Mr. W., being busy, referred them to a gentlemen of the name of Smith, and they applied to him. He executed the work, and it was delivered to Creamer.

There follows an account of Creamer's refusal to redeem 44 cents worth for a broker, Geo. McElfresh; then his decision to redeem. Before the justice of the peace Creamer said he had issued only $20 worth altogether since July 1 and that his application for the benefit of insolvency laws had canceled the debt. The magistrate gave judgment for the amount of the claim and bound him over, for $500 bond, to appear at October session of City Court. He was jailed for want of security.

From the *Sun,* Saturday, September 19, 1840:

> PUBLIC NOTICE.—Notice is hereby given to the public in general that whoever shall be in possession of notes signed C. H. CREAMER, and dated March 27, 1840, are respectfully requested to send them in for Redemption, forthwith at 7 fish market space.
>
> N.B. Of these notes, there have been issued $193.75, part on the 4th of May last $66, of which amount has been redeemed up to this date $38.50 remaining outstanding, $27.50 being numbered from No. 200 up to 300.
>
> s/9/t C. H. CREAMER

Only one example of Creamer's notes has been recorded by the authors and it had not been identified for a number of years due to the very neat but almost undecipherable penmanship of the Creamer signature. The date of the note, March 27, 1840, and its serial number 286 (within the "200 up to 300" range) fit Creamer's redemption notice of September 19, 1840, precisely.

5.45.5 R-7

$1.00 Printed year date 1840. Lithography, no imprint.

5.45.5

5.49 W. A. Danskin

Washington A. Danskin was the proprietor of a "gentlemen's furnishing store" at 194 Baltimore St. in 1840. Similar listings, with several different numbers, continued through the 1854–55 edition of the city directory.

5.49.2 R-7

12 1/2c Printed year date 1840. Letterpress, imprint: Murphy, Printer, 146 Market Street. Vignette is a view of Baltimore Harbor from Federal Hill.

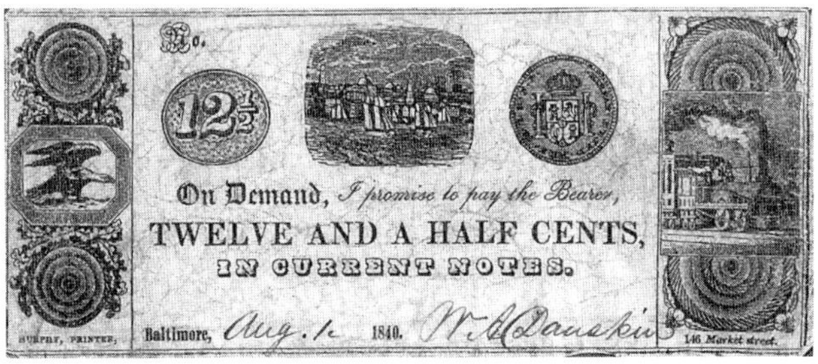

5.49.2

5.49.4 R-7

50c Printed date May 1, 1840. Letterpress, imprint: MURPHY PRINTER BALTIMORE. Vignette is a view of Baltimore Harbor from Federal Hill.

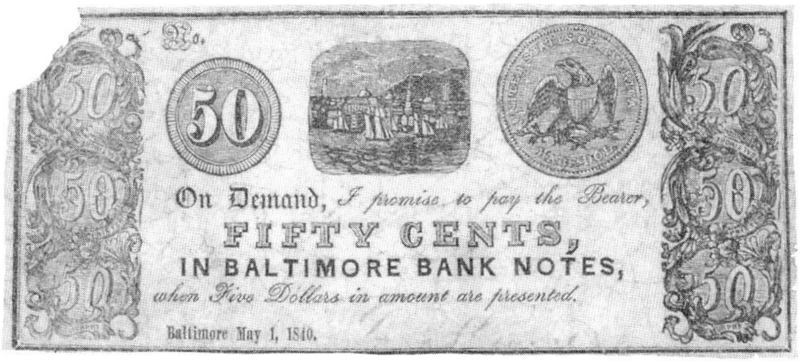

5.49.4

5.50 John Davis

A boot- and shoemaker, listed in the city directory of 1840 at 14 Holliday St., south of Fayette Street, and in 1842 on the east side of Eutaw Street, south of Franklin Street, Davis disappeared from listings thereafter. In the *Sun* of August 4, 5, 6, 1840, there appeared an advertisement that small notes issued by John Davis would be "redeemed in bankable money on presentation at his counter, No. 70, Franklin St."

5.50.1 R-7

6 1/4c Ca. 1840–42. Letterpress, no imprint (probably Bull & Tuttle). Similar to 12 1/2c, No. 5.50.2.

5.50.2 R-7

12 1/2c Ca. 1840–42. Letterpress, no imprint (probably Bull & Tuttle). Note the similarity to the 6 1/4c note issued by the Colonnade Baths in 1840, printed by Bull & Tuttle.

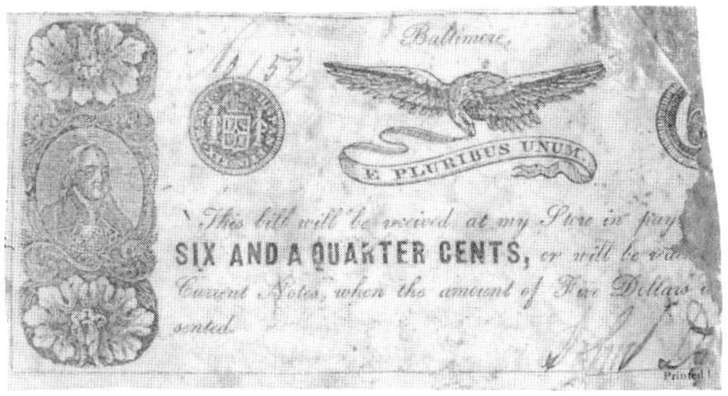

5.50.1

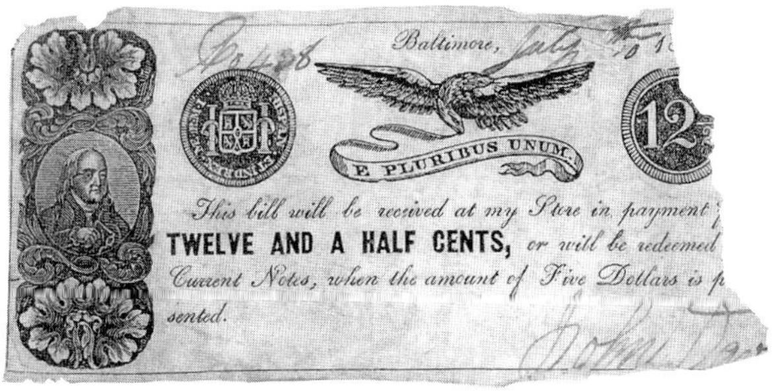

5.50.2

5.51 Joseph A. D—— ?

The identity of this issuer has not as yet been established due to illegible penmanship. He was obviously a storekeeper at the corner of Fleet Street and Strawberry Alley where the scrip could be received for either "goods or notes of the banks of Maryland."

5.51.2 R-7

12 1/2c Printed date November 21, 1815. Letterpress, no imprint.

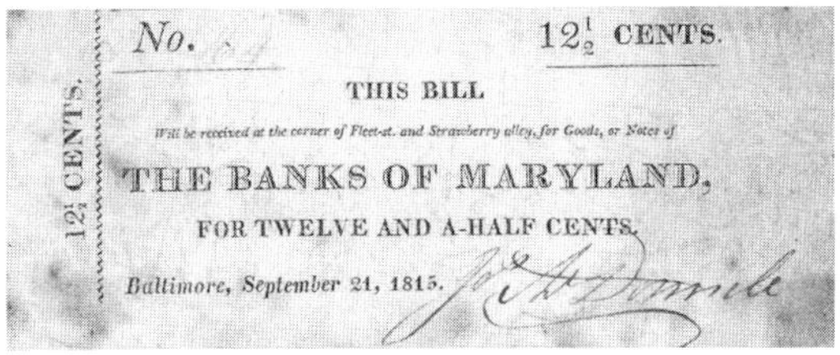

5.51.2

5.52 M. Denison

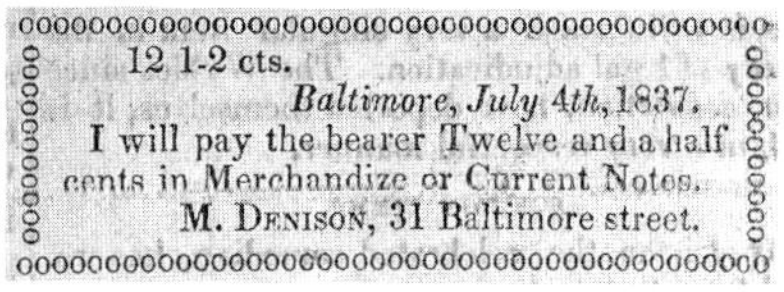

12 1-2 cts.
Baltimore, July 4th, 1837.
I will pay the bearer Twelve and a half cents in Merchandize or Current Notes.
M. Denison, 31 Baltimore street.

In the *Sun* of July 13, 1837, there appeared a long tongue-in-cheek article on the subject of the ills of shinplasters and the "suicide" of one T. Polyglot Tompkins, which contained a "sketch" in type of a note that had been offered to "Tompkins" by his barber. If there ever was such a note, and probably there was, it would have been issued by Marcus Denison, 31 Baltimore St., whose dwelling was in North Frederick Street, and who is listed thus in the 1835 city directory. In the 1837 edition, he is listed as a grocer, 31 Baltimore St., dw. 13 n Frederick. He does not appear in succeeding issues.

5.53 Dixon & Baker

No city directory listings of such a firm or individuals who would appear to be likely issuers of such scrip have as yet been found. "Stock" notes of this type were sold in large quantities by John Murphy, the printer, and it may well be that Dixon & Baker were merely speculators cashing in on the local demand for small-change notes. (See Exchange Bank, No. 5.59, for a note signed Edward Dixon, Cashr., and Thos. Baker, Banker.) The redemption clause includes the phrase "at my Banking House" although no such names appear in the 1837–42 city directories.

5.53.3 R-7

25c Ca. 1840. Letterpress, imprint: MURPHY PRINT. BALT. *Center:* Ceres, Spanish 2 reales piece at right, 25 at left. *Right:* Ship, 25 above and below. *Left:* 25 above and below. The actual listing for this note comes from the records of a collector who accumulated information over many years. His record card is listed as Smith & Baker; however, since the description matches the $1.00 note of Dixon and Baker, it is assumed that they were the issuers.

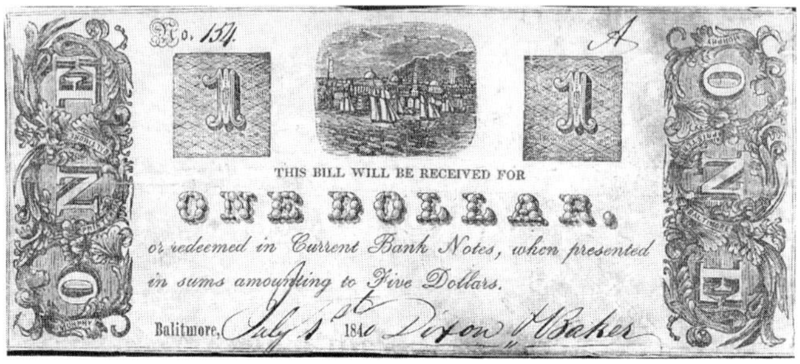

5.53.5

5.53.5 R-7

$1.00 Ca. 1840. Letterpress, imprint: MURPHY PRINTER BALTIMORE. Vignette is a view of Baltimore Harbor from Federal Hill.

5.54 Doyle's Lottery & Exchange Office

Michael Doyle conducted a lottery and exchange office at 26 Pratt St., opposite the Baltimore & Ohio Railroad depot, between 1837 and 1842 according to listings in the Baltimore city directories of that period. In 1845 he had moved his business to 144 Pratt St., and to 148 W. Pratt St. in 1847. His name did not appear thereafter. He advertised for several days in late September 1840 in the *Sun* that his small-change notes would be promptly redeemed on presentation at his office on Pratt Street.

5.54.1 R-7

6 1/4c Printed date Sept. 25, 1840. Letterpress, imprint: MURPHY PRINTER, 146 Market street.

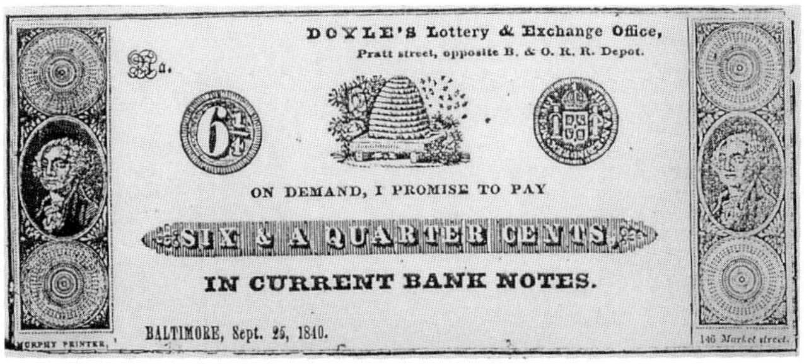

5.54.1

5.58 B. Egerton

Notes bearing the signature "B. Egerton" were issued by J. B. Egerton, the proprietor of a lottery office at the corner of South and Lombard streets, who lived at the corner of Exeter and Salisbury streets.

5.58.1 R-7

6 1/4c Printed year date 1840. Letterpress, no imprint. (The printers were probably Bull & Tuttle.)

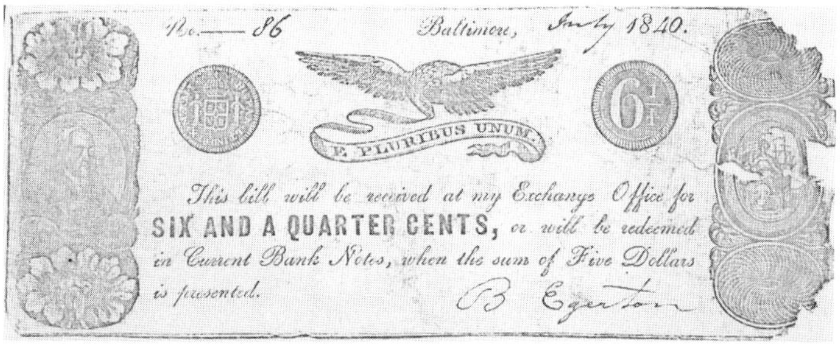

5.58.1

5.59 Exchange Bank (1840)

No record of such an institution or of the signers, Edward Dixon and Thos. Baker, has as yet been discovered. The same surnames, Dixon and Baker, appear as the signers on a $1.00 note, No. 5.53.5, with a manuscript date of July 1, 1840.

5.59.4 R-7

$1.00 Undated. Letterpress and lithography, no imprint.

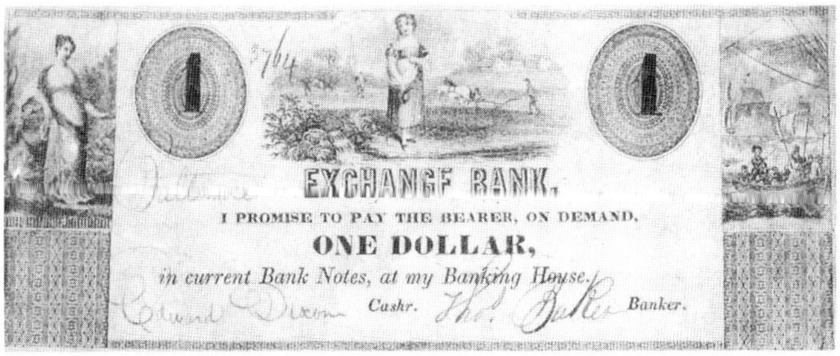

5.59.4

5.60 Exchange Bank (1856)

Charter amendment approved March 6, 1856. Listed in Baltimore city directories through 1860 with no record thereafter. Formerly Mechanics Exchange & Savings Company, Baltimore 1852.

5.60.3 SENC

$5.00 Ca. 1850s. Engraving, imprint: Unknown. No data available. (MD56G6)

5.60.4 SENC

$10.00 Ca. 1850s. Engraving, imprint: Unknown. No data available. (MD56G8)

5.60.5 SENC

$20.00 Ca. 1850s. Engraving, imprint: Unknown. No data available. (MD56G10)

5.60.6 SENC

$50.00 Ca. 1850s. Engraving, imprint: Unknown. No data available. (MD56G12)

5.61 Exchange Place Banking Co.

No city directory listings of either the company or the signers have been found, nor is there a record of the incorporation of such a company among the indexes of such actions by the General Assembly of Maryland. Presumably this was another "shinplaster" office whose purpose was primarily to circulate worthless paper.

5.61.1 R-7
6 1/4c Ca. 1832–33. Lithography, no imprint.

5.61.2 R-7
12 1/2c Ca. 1832–33. Lithography, no imprint.

5.61.3 R-7
25c Ca. 1832–33. Lithography, no imprint.

5.61.1

5.61.2

5.61.3

5.63 Peter Faddle

The identity of the signer of this "stock note" has not been established.

5.63.2 R-7
12 1/2c Printed date May 1, 1840. Letterpress, imprint: Murphy, Printer, Baltimore.

5.63.2

5.64 The Farmers & Merchants Bank of Baltimore

Prior to charter approval, the bank operated for a few months in 1810 as an unchartered association. Charter approved December 24, 1810; converted to and became the Farmers & Merchants National Bank of Baltimore in 1865. During the bank's note-issuing period it was successively located at 252 Baltimore St. (1810), Calvert Street, corner of Bank Lane (1849), and South and Lombard streets. (1857).

5.64.3 R-7

25c Printed year date 1815. Letterpress. This note was recorded "on the floor" at the Memphis show in 1992. Illustration not available.

5.64.5 A SENC

$1.00 Ca. 1840s. Engraving, imprint: Rawdon, Wright, Hatch. *Center:* 1; Hercules wrestling with lion; 1. *Left:* ONE / cherub in clouds, in circle / ONE. *Right:* Small ONE / Ceres and Vulcan seated flanking anvil, Mercury in clouds behind them, in large circle. Altered from $1.00 Farmers & Merchants Bank of St. Joseph, St. Joseph, Mich., MI380G2. (MD60A10)

5.64.6

5.64.6 R-7

$1.00 Ca. 1861. Engraving, imprint: Underwood, Bald, Spencer & Hufty, Philada.; Danforth, Underwood & Co., New York. (MD60N5)

5.64.6 P

5.64.6 P R-7

$1.00 Ca. 1840s. Engraving, imprint: Underwood, Bald, Spencer & Hufty, Philada / Danforth, Underwood & Co., New York. Proof.

5.64.7 A SENC

$1.00 Ca. 1854. Engraving, imprint: Rawdon, Wright, Hatch & Edson. *Center:* Reaper seated with cradle, basket of produce at left. *Left:* 1 / spread eagle with shield / ONE. *Right:* 1 / Indian woman as Liberty seated with right hand on ornate 1. *Between signatures:* Dog lying down. Overprint ONE. Altered from $1.00 Farmers & Merchants Bank of Memphis, Tenn., TN100G42 series. (MD60A5)

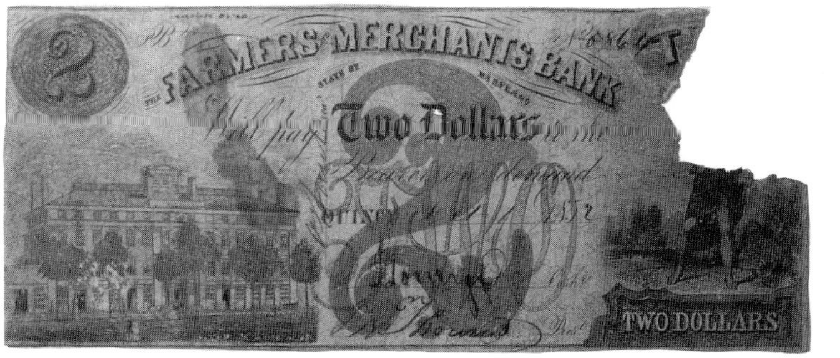

5.64.9 A

5.64.9 A R-7

$2.00 Printed partial date 185_. Ca. 1852. Engraving, no imprint. Altered to Maryland from a nonexistent bank in Quincy, Illinois, or Quincy, Mass. Large "2" in blue.

5.64.10 SENC

$3.00 Ca. 1850s. Engraving, imprint: Unknown. *Center:* Drove of cattle. *Left:* Portrait. *Right:* Coat of arms. (MD60N10)

5.64.11 SENC

$5.00 Ca. 1810. Engraving, imprint: Murray & Draper. Text reads "pay out of their joint funds." Association issue. No other data available. (MD60G8)

5.64.12 SENC

$5.00 Ca. early 1810s. Engraving, imprint: Murray & Draper. Similar to No. 5.64.11, except text reads "pay ____ or bearer on demand." (MD60G18)

5.64.13 P R-7

$5.00 Ca. 1810–20s. Engraving, imprint: Murray, Draper, Fairman, Brewster & Co. Printed on white paper. Proof. (MD60G20)

5.64.14 SENC

$5.00 Ca. 1810–20s. Engraving, imprint: Murray, Draper, Fairman, Brewster & Co. Same as No. 5.64.13 P, except printed on pink paper. (MD60G20a)

5.64.15 P R-7

$5.00 Ca. 1825–30. Engraving, imprint: Fairman, Draper, Underwood & Co. Apparently there is no particular significance to the word OHIO. The designer may have inserted it due to the attention being given to the founding of the Baltimore and Ohio Railroad. Proof.

5.64.16 P R-7

$5.00 Ca. 1835–50s. Engraving, imprint: Draper, Toppan & Longacre. Proof. (MD60G24)

5.64.17 S R-7

$5.00 Ca. 1840s. Engraving, imprint: Terry & Pelton, Boston. Spurious. (MD60S5)

5.64.18 A SENC

$5.00 Ca. 1854. Engraving, imprint: Rawdon, Wright, Hatch & Edson. *Center:* Reclining Indian woman and seated frontiersman flanking five gold dollars, three cherubs above. *Left:* 5 / script FIVE / FIVE. *Right:* 5 / oval female portrait / FIVE. Overprint FIVE. Altered from $5.00 Farmers & Merchants Bank of Memphis, Tenn., TN100G54. (MD60A15)

5.64.13 P

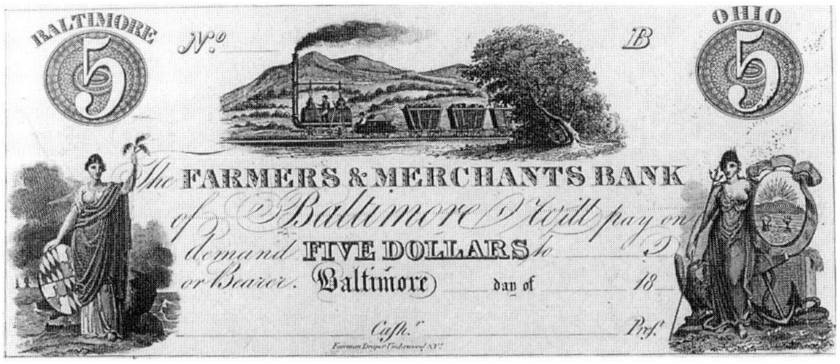

5.64.15 P

5.64.16 P

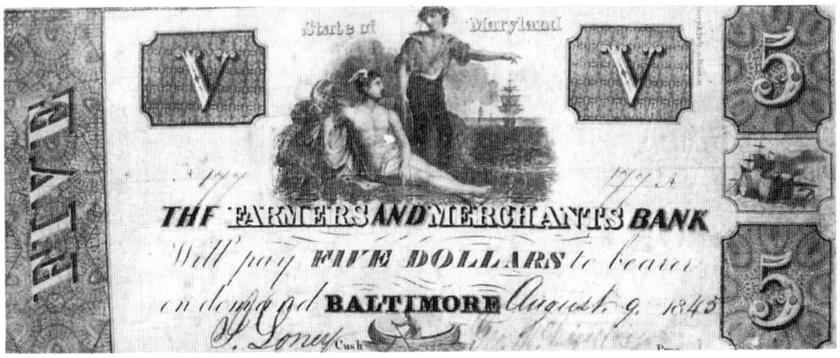

5.64.17 S

5.64.19 SENC

$5.00 Ca. 1856–60s. Engraving, imprint: Toppan, Carpenter & Co. *Center:* Farmer with sickle over shoulder, woman with grain under arm, and sailor with hands in pockets, horse and hay wagon, ship in left background; 5. *Left:* Portrait of girl. Tint is red "5" in each corner and FIVE and "5" in lower left corner and right corner. (MD60G28)

In the series of notes ($10.00, $20.00, $50.00, $100.00) in which the payment clause has been modified from the preceding "pay out of their joint funds" (association issue) to merely "pay ____ or bearer on demand" (chartered bank issue), each denomination has been seen, either in proof or uncirculated state, in which two printing plates, similar in design but actually differing in detail, were used. The engraving in each case is of such quality that counterfeiting would seem to be ruled out. Until further information is forthcoming, separate listings have not been made; it is hoped that this notation will stimulate others to do further research and report the results to the authors.

5.64.20 SENC

$10.00 Ca. 1810. Engraving, imprint: Murray & Draper. Text reads "pay out of their joint funds." Association issue. No other data available. (MD60G10)

5.64.21 SENC

$10.00 Ca. early 1810s. Engraving, imprint: Murray & Draper. Similar to No. 5.64.20, except text reads "pay ____ or bearer on demand." (MD60G30)

5.64.22 P

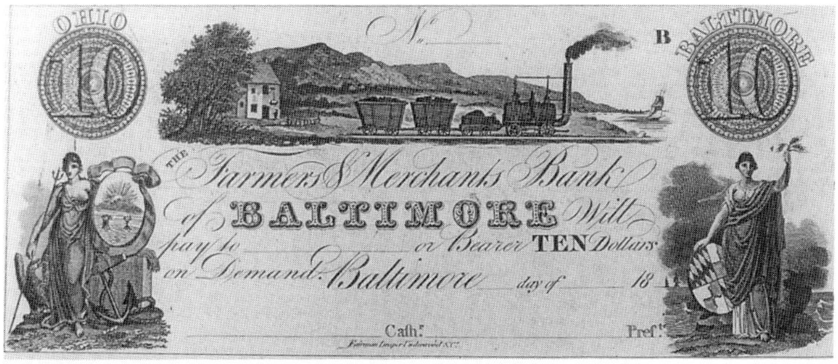

5.64.25 P

5.64.26 P

5.64.22 P R-7

$10.00 Ca. 1810–20s. Engraving, imprint: Murray, Draper, Fairman, Brewster & Co. Printed on white paper. Proof. (MD60G32)

5.64.23 SENC

$10.00 Ca. 1810s–20s. Engraving, imprint: Murray, Draper, Fairman, Brewster & Co. Same as No. 5.64.22 P, except printed on pink paper. (MD60G32a)

5.64.24 R SENC

$10.00 Ca. 1810–20s. Engraving, imprint: Murray, Draper, Fairman & Co. Raised from $5.00; similar to No. 5.64.13 P. (MD60R5)

5.64.25 P R-7

$10.00 Ca. 1825–30s. Engraving, imprint: Fairman, Draper, Underwood & Co. Apparently there is no particular significance to the word OHIO. The designer may have inserted it due to the attention being given to the founding of the Baltimore and Ohio Railroad. Proof.

5.64.26 P R-7

$10.00 Ca. 1835–50s. Engraving, imprint: Draper, Toppan, Longacre & Co., Phila & N.Y. Proof. (MD60G36)

5.64.27 A SENC

$10.00 Ca. 1840s. Engraving, imprint: Rawdon, Wright & Hatch. *Center:* 10; Ceres seated; 10. *Left:* Hebe and eagle / 10. *Right:* Commerce seated. *Between signatures:* Plow and sheaf. Altered from $10.00 Farmers & Merchants Bank of St. Joseph, St. Joseph, Mich., MI1380G10. (MD60A20)

5.64.28 N SENC

$10.00 Ca. 1840s–50s. Engraving, imprint: Unknown. *Center:* Woman with eagle. *Left:* Women with anchor. *Right:* Plow and sheaf. Nongenuine, unattributed. (MD60N15)

5.64.29 SENC

$10.00 Ca. 1856–60s. Engraving, imprint: Toppan, Carpenter & Co. *Upper left/left center:* Farmer with sickle over shoulder, woman with grain under arm, and sailor with hands in pocket, horse and hay wagon, ship in left background. *Right:* 10 / milkmaid, cow, calf and duck. Tint is red die bearing white "X" at right center. (MD60G40)

5.64.30 SENC

$20.00 Ca. 1810. Engraving, imprint: Murray & Draper. Text reads "pay out of their joint funds." Association issue. No other data available. (MD60G12)

5.64.31 SENC

$20.00 Ca. early 1810s. Engraving, imprint: Murray & Draper. Similar to No. 5.64.30, except text reads, "pay ____ or bearer on demand." (MD60G42)

5.64.32

5.64.34 P

5.64.36

5.64.32 R-3

$20.00 Ca. 1810s–20s. Engraving, imprint: Murray, Draper, Fairman & Co. Printed on white paper. Remainder. (MD60G44)

5.64.32 P R-7

$20.00 Ca. 1810s–20s. Engraving, imprint: Murray, Draper, Fairman & Co. Proof.

5.64.33 R-7

$20.00 Ca. 1810–20s. Engraving, imprint: Murray, Draper, Fairman & Co. Similar to No. 5.64.32, except printed on pink paper. (MD60G44a)

5.64.34 P R-7

$20.00 Ca. 1835–50s. Engraving, imprint: Draper, Toppan, Longacre & Co., Phila. Proof. (MD60G48)

5.64.35 A SENC

$20.00 Ca. 1840s. Engraving, imprint: Rawdon, Wright & Hatch. *Center:* XX, Ceres seated, XX. *Left:* Semi-nude allegorical male standing with staff in left hand, right hand raised holding thunderbolts / 20. *Right:* Semi-nude allegorical woman seated. *Between signatures:* Plow and sheaf. Altered from $20.00 Farmers & Merchants Bank of St. Joseph, St. Joseph, Mich., MI1380G12. (MD60A25)

5.64.36 R-7

$20.00 Ca. late 1850s. Engraving, imprint: Toppan, Carpenter & Co., Philada. & New York. Brown-orange tint. (MD60G52a)

5.64.37 SENC

$50.00 Ca. 1810. Engraving, imprint: Murray & Draper. Text reads "pay out of their joint funds." Association issue. No other data available. (MD60G14)

5.64.38 SENC

$50.00 Ca. early 1810s. Engraving, imprint: Murray & Draper. Similar to No. 5.64.37, except text reads "pay ____ or bearer on demand." (MD60G54)

5.64.39 R-4

$50.00 Ca. 1810s–20s. Engraving, imprint: Murray, Draper, Fairman & Co. Printed on white paper. Remainder. (MD60G56a)

5.64.39 P R-7

$50.00 Ca. 1810s–20s. Engraving, imprint: Murray, Draper, Fairman & Co. Proof.

5.64.40 R-7

$50.00 Ca. 1810s–20s. Engraving, imprint: Murray, Draper, Fairman & Co. Same No. 5.64.39, except printed on pink paper. (MD60G56a)

5.64.39 P

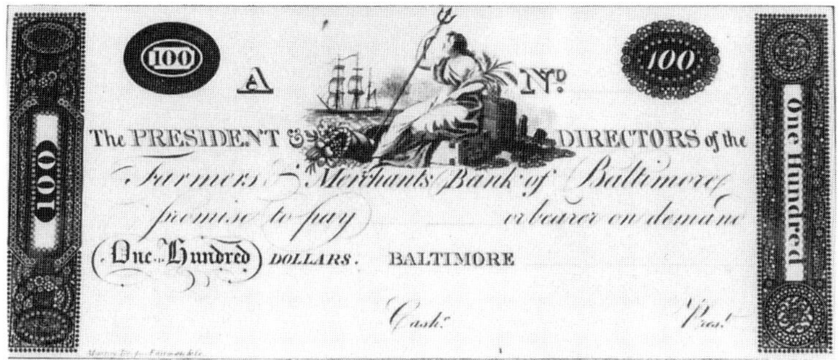

5.64.43

5.64.41 SENC

$50.00 Ca. 1835–50s. Engraving, imprint: Draper, Toppan, Longacre & Co. No other information available. (MD60G60)

5.64.42 SENC

$50.00 Ca. late 1850s. Engraving, imprint: Unknown. *Center:* 50; surveyor and three assistants. *Left:* Cherub on scroll / oval female portrait. *Right:* 50 / anchor, box, barrel, and bale. Tint is red. (MD60G64a)

5.64.43 R-4

$100.00 Ca. 1810s–20s. Engraving, imprint: Murray, Draper, Fairman & Co. Printed on white paper. Remainder. (MD60G68)

5.64.43 P R-7

$100.00 Ca. 1810s–20s. Engraving, imprint: Murray, Draper, Fairman & Co. Proof.

5.64.44 R-7

$100.00 Ca. 1810s–20s. Engraving, imprint: Murray, Draper, Fairman & Co. Similar to No. 5.64.43, except printed on pink paper. (MD60G68a)

5.64.45 SENC

$100.00 Ca. late 1850s. Engraving, imprint: Unknown. *Center:* 1/2-length figure of sailor boy, in oval; coast scene, three sailors, one looking through telescope, one seated on broken mast, third resting head on hand, men in left background, ships in right background. *Left:* 100 / farmer carrying corn. *Right:* 100 / woman feeding chickens. Tint is red. (MD60G72a)

5.64.46 SENC

$500.00 Ca. late 1850s. Engraving, imprint: Unknown. *Upper left/left center:* Men loading hay onto oxcart. *Lower left:* 500. *Right center:* Portrait of girl. *Right:* 500 / sailor boy, sailors in left background, ship in right background. Tint is red. (MD60G76a)

5.64.47 SENC

$1000.00 Ca. late 1850s. Engraving, imprint: Unknown. *Center:* Farmer plowing, boy carrying branch leading horses, dog, basket, etc. *Left:* 1000 / sailor leaning on capstan, ship in background. *Right:* 1000 / MARYLAND / portrait of girl. Tint is red. (MD60G80a)

Composite sheet of two $20.00 (No. 5.64.33), $50.00 (No. 5.64.40), $100.00 (No. 5.64.44), denominations, pink paper.

5.65 The Farmers & Planters Bank

This nonexistent bank was represented only by spurious notes and notes altered from those of other banks which were intended to pass for those of the Farmers & Planters Bank of Baltimore.

5.65.4 S R-7

$5.00 Ca. 1850s–60s. Engraved, no imprint. Spurious. (MD64S5)

5.65.4 S

5.65.8 A R-7

$50.00 Ca. 1840s. Engraving, imprint: Underwood, Bald, Spencer and Hufty, Philada.; Danforth, Underwood & Co., New York. Altered. (MD64A5)

5.65.8 A

5.66 The Farmers & Planters Bank of Baltimore

Charter approved April 4, 1836; converted to and became the National Farmers & Planters Bank of Baltimore in 1865. The bank was located at 17 South St., near Baltimore Street, the former location of the ill-fated Bank of Maryland, which had failed in 1834.

5.66.1 SENC

$1.00 Ca. 1836–40s. Engraving, imprint: Rawdon, Wright & Hatch, New York. *Center:* Three women. (MD65G2)

5.66.2 R-7

$1.00 Printed partial date April 2nd 18__. Ca. 1850. Engraving, imprint: Rawdon, Wright & Hatch, New York. Certificate of deposit with printed name of the depositor, William E. Mayhew, payable to bearer on demand. Mayhew, a prominent dry goods merchant, was president of the bank from 1842 until his death in 1860, when he was succeeded by Enoch Pratt.

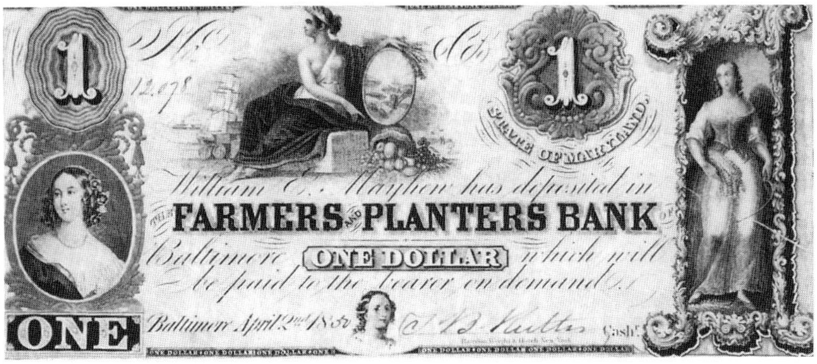

5.66.2

5.66.3 SENC

$1.00 Printed date Apr. 2, 18__. Ca. 1860s. Engraving, imprint: Rawdon, Wright & Hatch, New York. Same as No. 5.66.1, except imprint American Bank Note Co. (MD65G4)

5.66.4 R SENC

$5.00 Ca. 1836–40s. Engraving, imprint: Rawdon, Wright, & Hatch. Raised from $1.00, No. 5.66.1. (MD65R5)

5.66.6 A

5.66.5 SENC

$5.00 Ca. 1836–50s. Engraving, imprint: Rawdon, Wright & Hatch, New York. *Center:* 5; woman seated holding sickle, arm resting on sheaf, cows in left background; 5. *Left:* Lathework panel bearing 5, across. *Right:* Statue of Washington / FIVE. *Between signatures:* Schooner. (MD65G12)

5.66.6 A R-5

$5.00 Ca. 1850. Engraving, imprint: Rawdon, Wright & Hatch, New York. Altered from $5.00, Farmers & Mechanics Bank at Pontiac, Mich., MI335G8. (MD65A5)

5.66.7 R SENC

$10.00 Ca. 1836–40s. Engraving, imprint: Rawdon, Wright & Hatch, New York. Raised from $1.00, No. 5.66.1. (MD65R10)

5.66.8 SENC

$10.00 Ca. 1836–50s. Engraving, imprint: Rawdon, Wright & Hatch, New York. *Center:* X; two men reaping with scythes; X. *Left:* Panel with TEN across. *Right:* Woman carrying one sheaf on head and another under left arm / livestock and drovers in circle. *Between signatures:* Sailing ship. Similar to spurious note No. 5.66.8 s.

5.66.8 S R-6

$10.00 Ca. 1836–50s. Engraving, imprint: Rawdon, Wright & Hatch. Similar to No. 5.66.8. Spurious issue from genuine plate, with president's name spelled "Chaston" instead of "Cheston." (MD65G16)

5.66.10 R SENC

$20.00 Ca. 1836–40s. Engraving, imprint: Rawdon, Wright & Hatch, New York. Raised from $1.00, No. 5.66.1. (MD65R15)

5.66.11 SENC

$20.00 Ca. 1836–50s. Engraving, imprint: Rawdon, Wright & Hatch, New York. *Center:* XX; woman seated with rake at left, and woman standing with sheaf at right, flanking shield bearing plow. *Left:* Lathework panel bearing TWENTY. *Right:* Man cradling grain, house in background / man plowing with two horses. *Between signatures:* Ship. (MD65G20)

5.66.8 S

5.66.15 P

5.66.12 A SENC

$20.00 Ca. 1840s. Engraving, imprint: Rawdon, Wright & Hatch. *Center:* 20; farm implements, sheaves and produce. *Left:* Nude Hebe standing in clouds, large eagle behind her at right. *Right:* 20 / small eagle / XX. *Between signatures:* Pledge, in circle. Altered from $20.00 Chippeway County Bank, Sault De St. Mary, Mich., MI390G12. (MD65A10)

5.66.13 R SENC

$50.00 Ca. 1836–40s. Engraving, imprint: Rawdon, Wright & Hatch, New York. Raised from $1.00, No. 5.66.1. (MD65R20)

5.66.14 SENC

$50.00 Ca. 1836–50s. Engraving, imprint: Rawdon, Wright & Hatch, New York. *Center:* Two men cradling grain, one at right facing away from viewer, house in right background. *Left:* FIFTY, across. *Right:* Man plowing with two horses / farmers at work with two horses, house in background. *Between signatures:* Schooner. (MD65G24)

5.66.15 P R-7

$100.00 Ca. 1836–50s. Engraving, imprint: Rawdon, Wright & Hatch. Proof. (MD65G28)

5.66.16 SENC

$500.00 Ca. 1836–50s. Engraving, imprint: Rawdon, Wright & Hatch. *Center:* 50; woman seated with rake, at left, and woman standing with sheaf at right, flanking shield bearing plow. *Left:* 500, across. *Right:* Woman churning in dairy. *Between signatures:* Schooner. (MD65G32)

5.66.17 SENC

$1000.00 Ca. 1836–50s. Engraving, imprint: Rawdon, Wright & Hatch. *Center:* 1000; two women floating in clouds with wand, bag, grain and sickle; 1000. *Left:* 1000, across. *Right:* Woman holding scroll / 1000. *Between signatures:* Schooner. (MD65G36)

5.67 Federal Hill Boys Meeting

Neither the identity of the issuer nor the purpose for which this "note" was prepared have been established.

5.67.1 R-7

5c Letterpress, no imprint.

5.67.1

5.68 The Fells Point Bank of Baltimore

Charter amendment approved February 1, 1862 (formerly Fells Point Savings Institution of Baltimore); converted to and became the Second National Bank of Baltimore in 1864. It was located on Broadway between Canton and Eastern avenues.

5.68.1 R-7

$1.00 Ca. 1862–64. Engraving, imprint: American Bank Note Co. Security overprint in green. (MD70G2a)

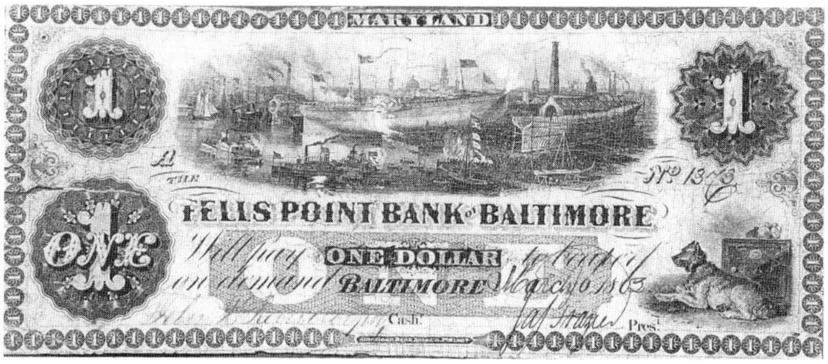

5.68.1

5.68.4 SENC

$5.00 Ca. 1862–64. Engraving, imprint: Unknown. *Center:* Two sailors, one seated on bale, other smoking pipe, rope, anchor, trumpet, etc., ships in background. *Left:* 5 / oval portrait of Clay. *Right:* Oval portrait of Washington. (MD70G4)

5.68.5 SENC

$10.00 Ca. 1862–64. Engraving, imprint: Unknown. *Left center:* 10. *Right center:* Steamship moving to right, ship in background. *Left:* Woman standing with cornucopia on shoulder / TEN. *Lower right:* TEN. (MD70G6)

5.68.6 SENC

$20.00 Ca. 1862–64. Engraving, imprint: Unknown. *Center:* Two white women with anchor, sickle and sheaf at left and Indian woman with pole and cap, and eagle, at right, flanking shield. *Left:* 20 / oval portrait of Jefferson. *Right:* 20 / oval female portrait. (MD70G8)

5.68.7 SENC

$50.00 Ca. 1862–64. Engraving, imprint: Unknown. *Upper left/left center:* Sailing ship, steamship and other ships in background. *Right center:* Female portrait. *Lower left:* 50. *Right:* 50 / eagle on shield. (MD70G10)

5.68.8 SENC

$100.00 Ca. 1862–64. Engraving, imprint: Unknown. *Center:* View of U.S. Capitol. *Left:* 100 / girl holding hen and chickens, in oval. *Right:* 100 / sailor holding telescope and seated on bale, capstan and ship. (MD70G12)

5.69 **Fells Point Savings Institution**

Chartered March 6, 1833 (Ch. 140, Acts of 1832). Attempt made to recharter as "Eastern Bank of Baltimore" (Ch. 298, Acts of 1835), but action not approved by membership. Name changed to Fells Point Bank of Baltimore in 1862. Originally located on Thames Street between Market and Bond streets, the institution moved in 1852 to Broadway between Canton and Eastern Avenue.

5.69.3 R-7

25c Ca. 1837–40. Engraving, imprint: Burton, Gurley & Edmonds, N. York.

5.69.4 R-7

25c Printed partial date 184_. Engraving, imprint: Danforth, Underwood & Co., New York / Underwood, Bald, Spencer & Hufty, Philada.

5.69.4 P R-7

25c Printed partial date 184_. Engraving, imprint: Danforth, Underwood & Co., New York / Underwood, Bald, Spencer & Hufty, Philada. Proof.

5.69.5 R-7

50c Ca. 1840. Engraving, no imprint. Printed by Burton, Gurley & Co., N. York.

5.69.6 P R-7

50c Printed partial year date 184_. Engraving, imprint: Underwood, Bald, Spencer & Hufty, Philada / Danforth, Underwood & Co., New York. Proof.

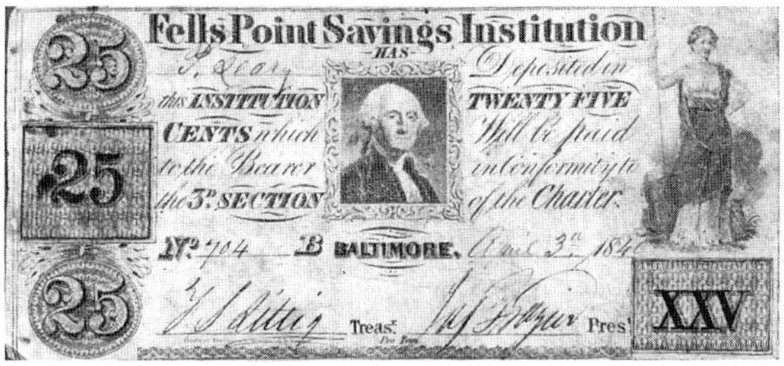

5.69.3

5.69.4P

5.69.5

5.69.6 P

5.69.7 R-7

$1.00 Ca. 1840. Engraving, imprint: Burton, Gurley & Co. Similar to 50c, No. 5.69.5

5.69.8 R-7

$1.00 Ca. 1844–45. Engraving, imprint: Danforth, Spencer & Hufty, New York / Spencer, Hufty & Danforth, Philada.

5.69.8 P R-7

$1.00 Ca. 1844–45. Engraving, imprint: Danforth, Spencer & Hufty, New York / Spencer, Hufty & Danforth, Philada. Proof.

5.69.9 P R-7

$5.00 Ca. 1844–50. Engraving, imprint: Danforth, Spencer & Hufty, New York / Spencer, Hufty & Danforth, Philada. Proof.

5.69.10 P R-7

$5.00 Ca. 1850s. Engraving, imprint: Draper, Welsh & Co., Phila. Henry Clay at lower left. Overprint "5-FIVE-5" in brick red. Proof.

5.69.11 P R-7

$10.00 Ca. 1844–50. Engraving, imprint: Danforth, Spencer & Hufty, New York / Spencer, Hufty & Danforth, Philada. Proof.

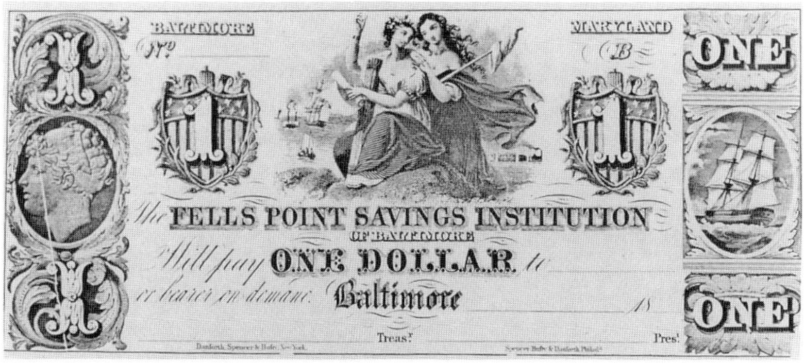

5.69.8 P

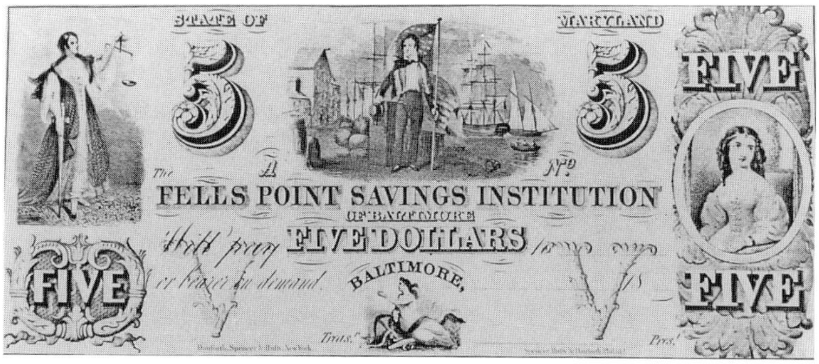

5.69.9 P

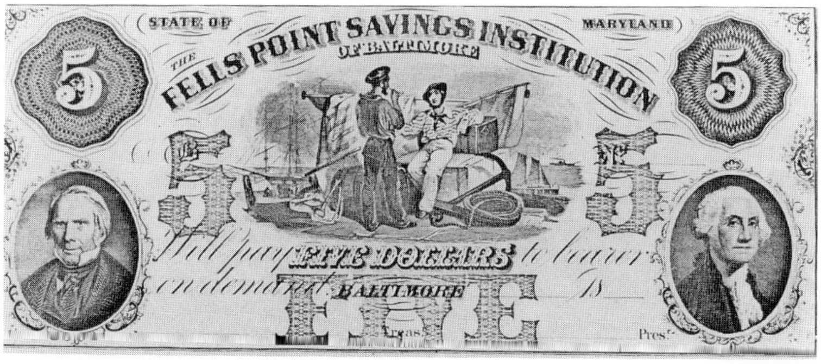

5.69.10 P

5.69.11 P

5.69.12 P R-7

$10.00 Ca. 1850s. Engraving, imprint: Draper, Welsh & Co., Phila. Overprint "10-TEN-10" in brick red. Proof.

5.69.13 P R-7

$20.00 Ca. 1844–50. Engraving, imprint: Hufty & Danforth, Philada. & New York. Proof.

5.69.14 P R-7

$20.00 Ca. 1850s. Engraving, imprint: Draper, Welsh & Co., Phila. Thomas Jefferson at left. Proof.

5.69.15 P R-7

$50.00 Ca. 1848–50s. Engraving, imprint: Hufty & Danforth, Philada. & New York. Daniel Webster at left. Proof.

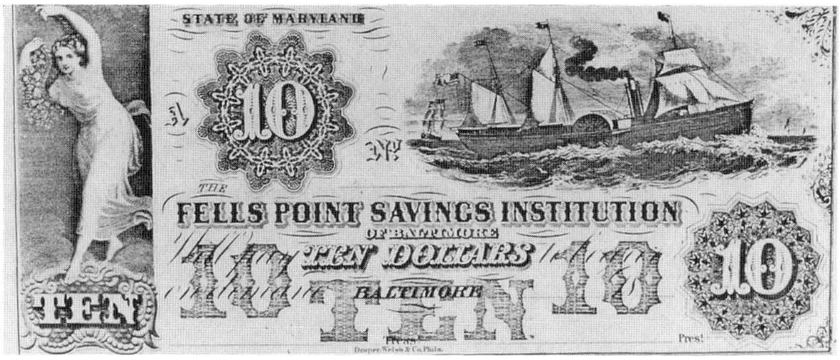

5.69.12 P

5.69.13 P

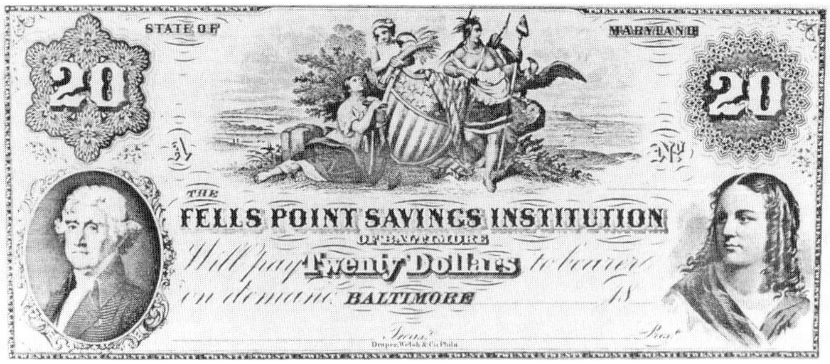

5.69.14 P

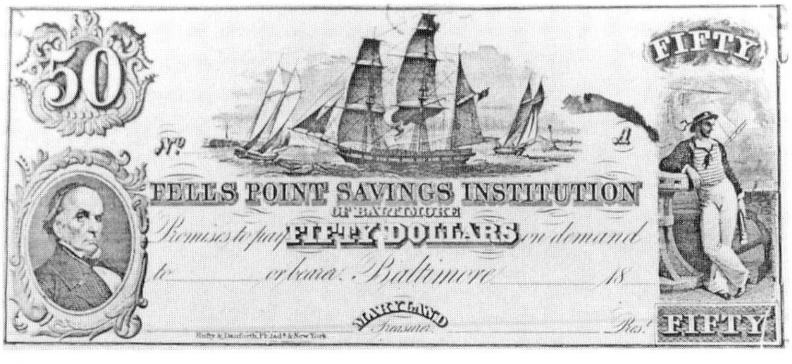

5.69.15 P

5.69.16 P R-7

$50.00 Ca. 1850s. Engraving, imprint: Draper, Welsh & Co., Phila. Proof.

5.69.17 P R-7

$100.00 Ca. 1850s. Engraving, imprint: Draper, Welsh & Co., Phila. Overprint HUNDRED in brick red. Proof.

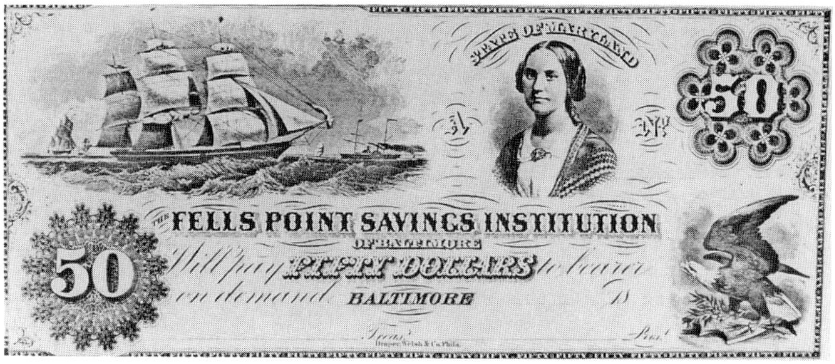

5.69.16 P

5.69.17 P

5.70 Paul Fillinger

The issuer was the proprietor of a grocery store at 20 Pennsylvania Ave., west of Franklin Street.

5.70.2 R-7

12 1/2c Ca. 1839–41. Lithography, no imprint.

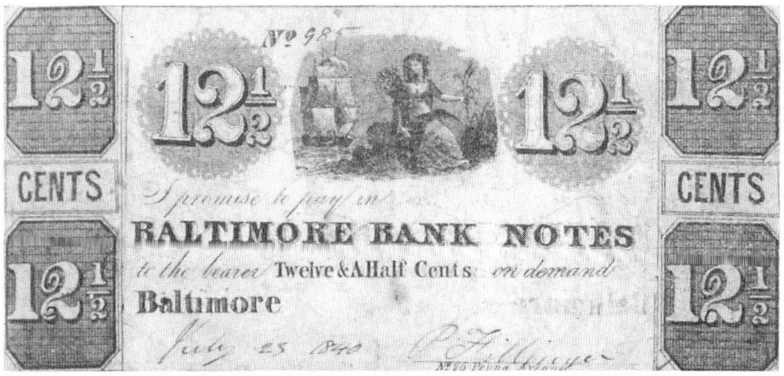

5.70.2

5.71 Thomas C. Ford

In the "List of Small Notes Circulating in Baltimore," published in the *Baltimore Clipper* of September 12, 1840, Ford's name appeared as a storekeeper in the Maryland Arcade. A similar listing appears in the 1840–41 city directory. None of Ford's notes have been recorded by the authors.

5.72 Foreign, Domestic Exchange Institution

The date of the opening of this exchange office is not known, but it ceased operations in July 1840. Its office was located at 37 Lombard St. An advertisement in the *Sun,* June 25, 1840, offered prompt redemption of its notes.

5.72.1 R-7

6 1/4c Ca. 1840. Lithography, no imprint (Ed Weber & Co.). Same design as 12 1/2c, No. 5.72.2.

5.72.2 R-7

12 1/2c Ca. 1840. Lithography, no imprint (Ed Weber & Co.).

5.72.3 R-7

25c Ca. 1840. Lithography, imprint: Lith. Ed. Weber & Co., Baltimore.

5.72.4 R-7

50c Ca. 1840. Lithography, imprint: Lithogr. by Ed Weber, Baltimore.

5.72.2

5.72.3

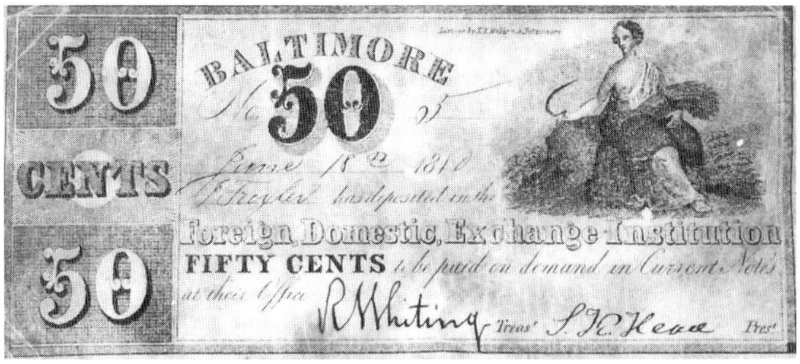

5.72.4

5.73 Daniel Fowble

The issuer was a grocer at the corner of Caroline and Wilkes streets in Fells Point.

5.73.3 R-7

3c Printed date September 10, 1815. Letterpress, no imprint.

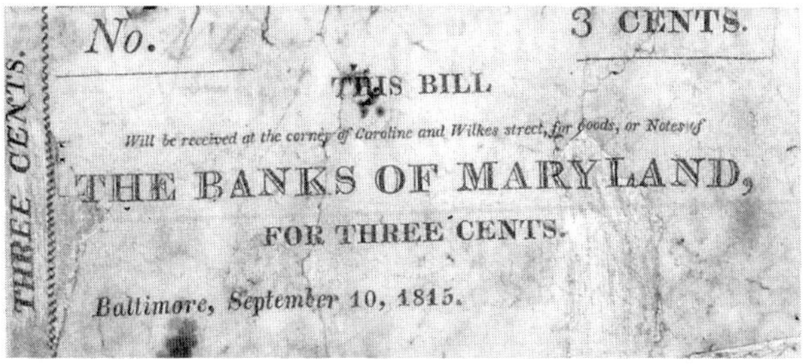

5.73.3

5.74 S. L. Fowler & Bros. Exchange Office

S. L. Fowler & Bros., Exchange Brokers, had offices in Baltimore at 170 Baltimore St., and in Washington, between 1837 and 1841.

5.74.3 R-3
25c Ca. 1840–41. Engraving, imprint: Draper, Toppan & Co., Phila. & New York.

5.74.3 P R-7
25c Ca. 1840–41. Engraving, imprint: Draper, Toppan & Co., Phila. & New York. Proof.

5.74.4 R-3
50c Ca. 1840–41. Engraving, imprint: Draper, Toppan & Co., Phila. & New York.

5.74.5 R-3
$1.00 Ca. 1840–41. Engraving, imprint: Draper, Toppan & Co., Phila. Payable in Virginia notes at the Washington office.

5.74.5 P R-7
$1.00 Ca. 1840–41. Engraving, imprint: Draper, Toppan & Co., Phila. Payable in Virginia notes at the Washington office. Proof.

5.74.6 R-3
$1.00 Ca. 1840–41. Engraving, imprint: Draper, Toppan & Co., Phila. & New York. Payable in current notes at the Baltimore office.

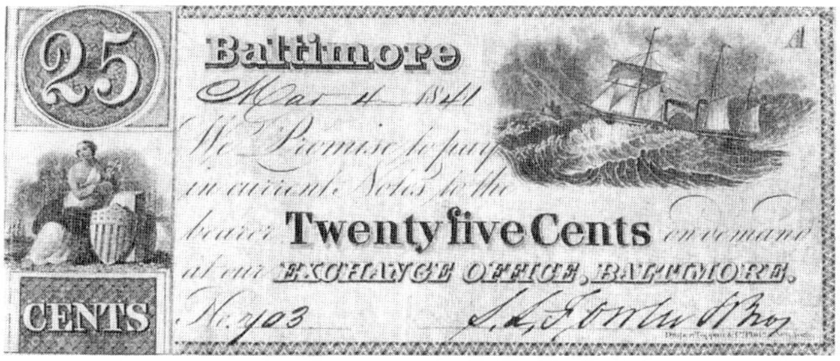

5.74.3

5.74.4

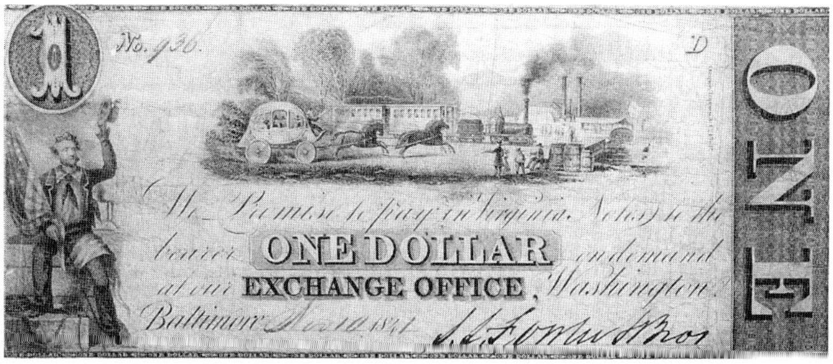

5.74.5

5.74.6

5.74.7 R-4

$2.00 Ca. 1840–41. Engraving, imprint: Draper, Toppan & Co., Phila. & New York. Payable in Virginia notes at the Washington office.

5.74.8 R-4

$2.00 Ca. 1840–41. Engraving, imprint: Draper, Toppan & Co., Phila. & New York. Payable in current notes at the Baltimore office.

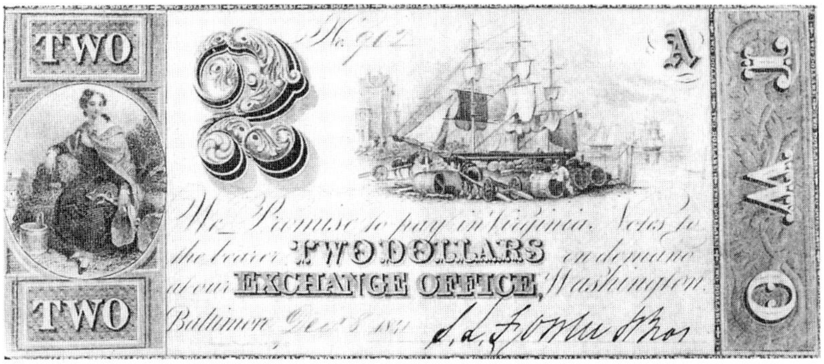

5.74.7

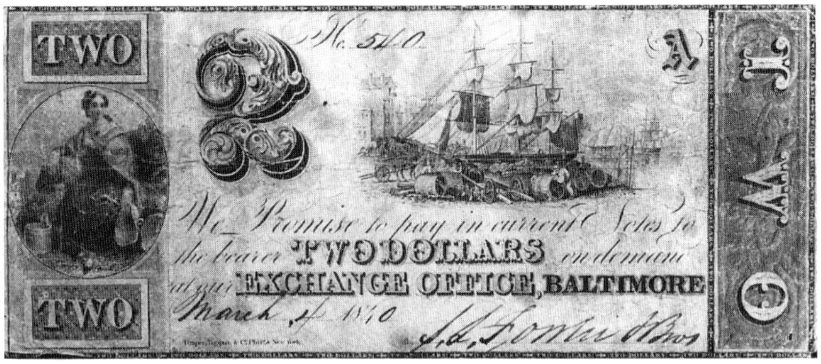

5.74.8

5.75 The Franklin Bank of Baltimore

Operated as an unchartered association until 1810. Charter approved December 23, 1810; succeeded by the Equitable National Bank of Baltimore in 1891; purchased the First National Bank of Baltimore (First) and operated under that name; voluntary liquidation in 1900. Originally located at 88 Baltimore St., the bank was at 13 North St. between Fayette and Baltimore streets from 1842 to 1860, when it relocated to 15 South St.

5.75.1 SENC

6 1/4c Ca. 1814. Letterpress, no imprint. Similar to 50c, No. 5.75.7. (MD75G20)

5.75.2 R-6

6 1/4c Printed date 1815. Letterpress, imprint: J. Robinson, Printer. (MD75G24)

5.75.3 SENC

12 1/2c Ca. 1810s. Letterpress, no imprint. Similar to 50c, No. 5.75.7. (MD75G28)

5.75.4 SENC

12 1/2c Printed date 1815. Letterpress, imprint: J. Robinson, Printer. Similar to 6 1/4c, No. 5.75.2. (MD75G32)

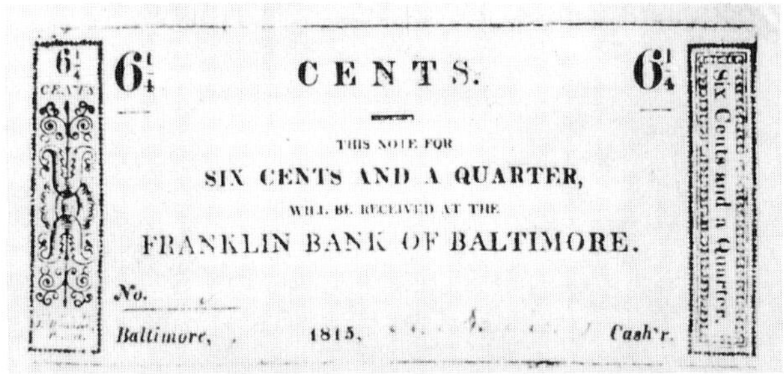

5.75.2

5.75.5 SENC

25c Ca. 1810s. Letterpress, no imprint. Similar to 50c, No. 5.75.7. (MD75G36)

5.75.6 R-7

25c Printed date 1815. Letterpress, imprint: J. Robinson, Printer. (MD75G40)

5.75.7 R-7

50c Ca. 1810s. Letterpress, no imprint. (MD75G44)

5.75.8 R-6

50c Printed date 1815. Letterpress, imprint: J. Robinson, Printer. Similar to 25c, No. 5.75.6. (MD75G48)

5.75.9 SENC

$1.00 Ca. 1810s. Engraving, imprint: Cone, Freeman & Co. Baltimore. *Center:* Franklin. Similar to counterfeit No. 5.75.9 C. (MD75G56)

5.75.9 C R-7

$1.00 Ca. 1810s. Engraving, imprint: Cone, Freeman & Co., Baltimore, Counterfeit of 5.75.9. (MD75C56)

5.75.11 P R-7

$1.00 Printed partial date March 1, 18__. Ca. 1840s and 1860s. Engraving, imprint: Danforth, Spencer & Hufty, New York / Spencer, Hufty & Danforth, Philada. Proof. (MD75G60)

5.75.11 C R-6

$1.00 Printed date March 1, 18__. Ca. 1840s and 1860s. Engraving, imprint: Danforth, Spencer & Hufty, New York / Spencer, Hufty & Danforth, Philada. Counterfeit of No. 5.75.11 P. (MD75G60)

5.75.12 SENC

$2.00 Ca. 1810s. Engraving, imprint: Cone, Freeman & Co. Baltimore, *Center:* Franklin. Similar to counterfeit No. 5.75.12 C. (MD75G64)

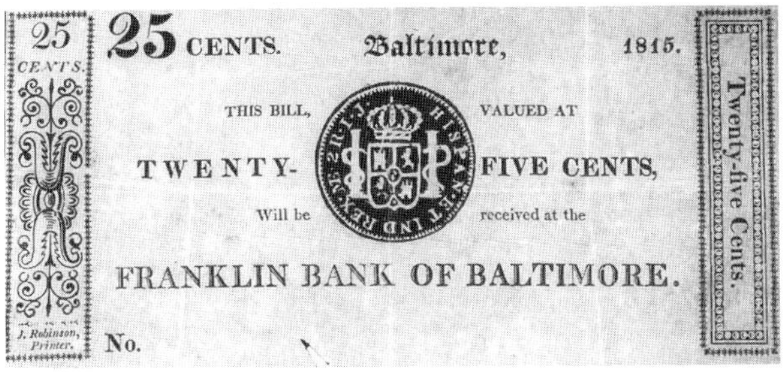

5.75.6

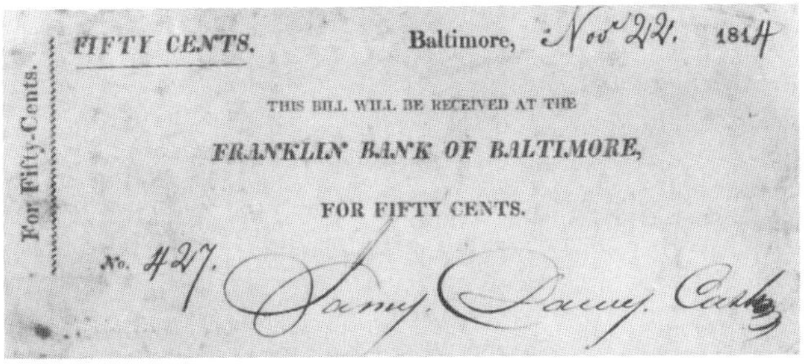

5.75.7

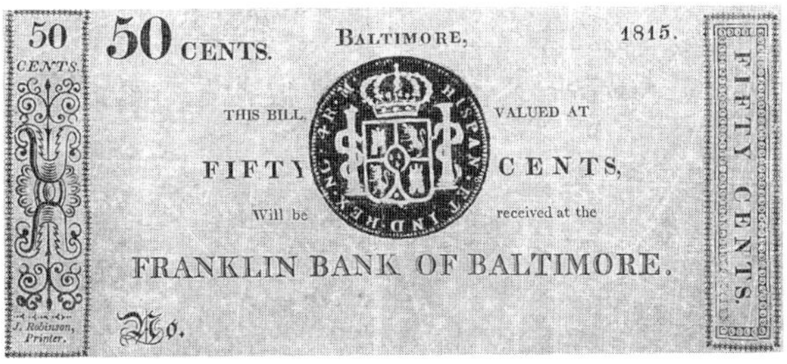

5.75.8

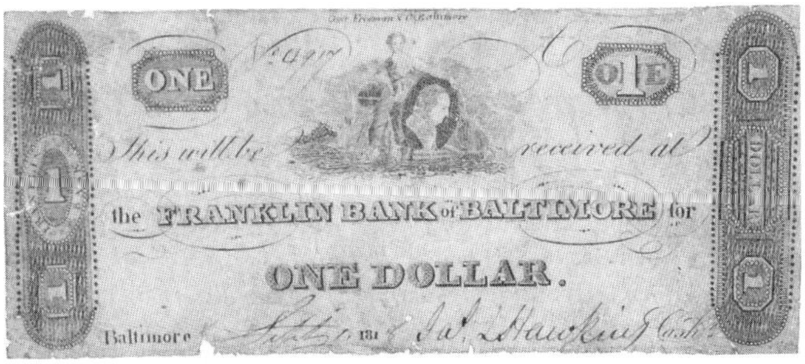

5.75.9 C

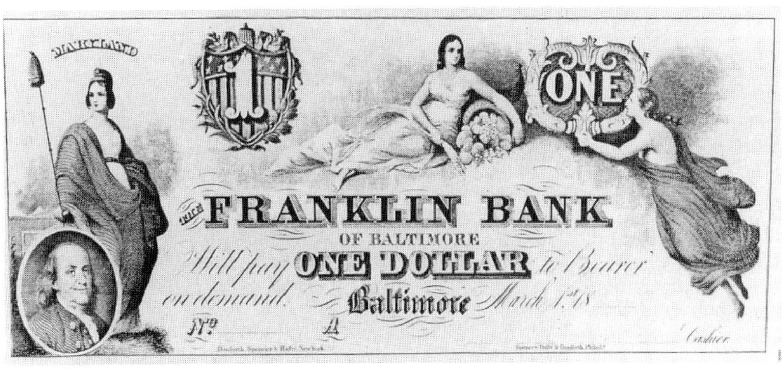

5.75.11 P

5.75.12 C R-5

$2.00 Ca. 1810s. Engraving, imprint: Cone, Freeman & Co., Baltimore. Counterfeit of No. 5.75.12. (MD75C64)

5.75.14 SENC

$5.00 Ca. 1810. Engraving, imprint: Unknown. Text reads "pay out of their joint funds." Association issue. No other data available. (MD75G8)

5.75.15 SENC

$5.00 Ca. early 1810s. Engraving, imprint: Unknown. Same as No. 5.75.14, except for text. Haxby catalog number MD75G60 is also assigned to $1.00 note. (MD75G60)

5.75.16 R-5

$5.00 Ca. early 1810s–20s. Engraving, imprint: Murray, Draper, Fairman & Co. Similar to counterfeit No. 5.75.16 C. (MD75G68)

5.75.16 C R-5

$5.00 Ca. 1820s. Engraving, imprint: Murray, Draper, Fairman & Co. Counterfeit of No. 5.75.16. (MD75C68)

5.75.17 P R-7

$5.00 Ca. 1810s–20s. Engraving, imprint: Murray, Draper, Fairman & Co. Proof. (MD75G72)

5.75.19 R-7

$5.00 Ca. 1830s–40s. Engraving, imprint: C. Toppan & Co., Philada. (MD75G76)

5.75.19 P R-6

$5.00 Ca. 1830s–40s. Engraving, imprint: C. Toppan & Co., Philada. Proof.

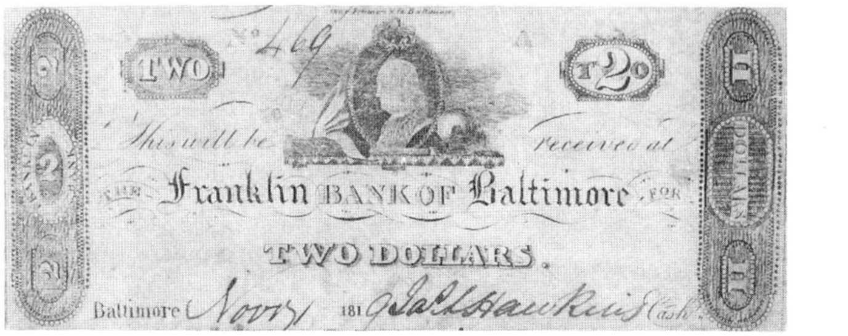

5.75.12 C

5.75.16 C

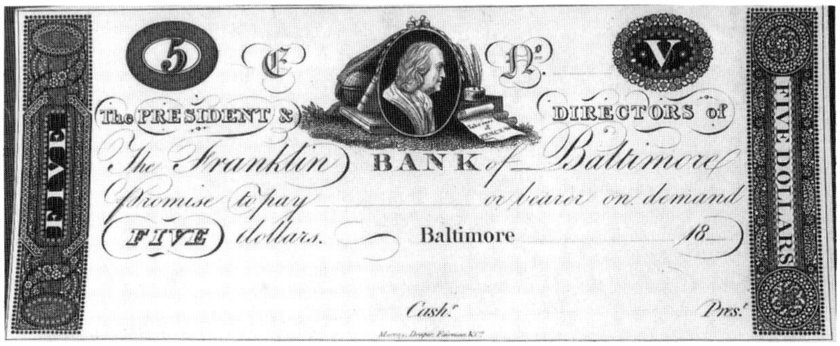

5.75.17 P

5.75.19 P

5.75.20 P R-7

$5.00 Ca. 1844–early 1850s. Engraving, imprint: Danforth, Spencer & Hufty, New York / Spencer, Hufty & Danforth, Philada. Proof. (MD75G80)

5.75.20 C R-5

$5.00 Ca. 1844–50s. Engraving, imprint: Danforth, Spencer & Hufty, New York / Spencer, Hufty & Danforth, Philada. Counterfeit of No. 5.75.20 P. (MD75C80)

5.75.22 R-7

$5.00 Ca. 1850–63. Engraving, imprint: Danforth, Bald & Co., Philada. & New York. Red security print of tiny repetitive FIVE covering entire note except vignettes.

5.75.22 P R-7

$5.00 Ca. 1850s. Engraving, imprint: Danforth, Bald & Co., Philada. & New York. Red security print. Same as No. 5.75.22. Proof.

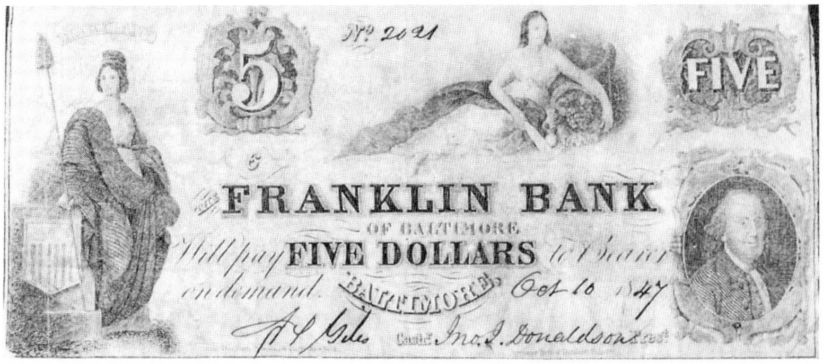

5.75.20 P

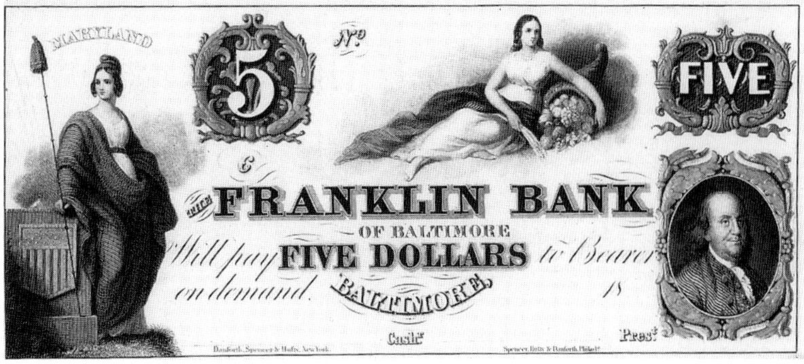

5.75.20 C

5.75.22

5.75.22 P

5.75.23 P R-7
$5.00 Ca. 1850s. Engraving, imprint: Danforth, Bald & Co. Philada & New York. Similar to No. 5.75.22 with red "5-5" security overprint, but no oval FIVE dies on either side of central vignette or overall miniature FIVE print. Proof. (MD75G84)

5.75.25 SENC
$10.00 Ca. 1810. Engraving, imprint: Unknown. Text reads "pay out of their joint funds." Association issue. No other data available. (MD75G10)

5.75.26 SENC
$10.00 Ca. early 1810s. Engraving, imprint: Unknown. Similar to $10.00, No. 5.75.25, except for text. (MD75G86)

5.75.27 P R-7
$10.00 Ca. 1810s–20s. Engraving, imprint: Murray, Draper Fairman & Co. Proof. (MD75G88)

5.75.28 P R-7
$10.00 Ca. 1830s–40s. Engraving, imprint: C. Toppan & Co., Philada. Proof. (MD75G92)

5.75.29 P R-7
$10.00 Ca. 1850s. Engraving, imprint: Danforth, Spencer & Hufty, New York / Spencer, Hufty & Danforth, Philada. Proof. (MD75G96)

5.75.30 SENC
$20.00 Ca. 1810. Engraving, imprint: Unknown. Text reads "pay out of their joint funds." Association issue. No other data available. (MD75G12)

5.75.31 SENC
$20.00 Ca. early 1810s. Engraving, imprint: Unknown. Similar to $20.00, No. 5.75.30, except for text. (MD75G98)

5.75.23 P

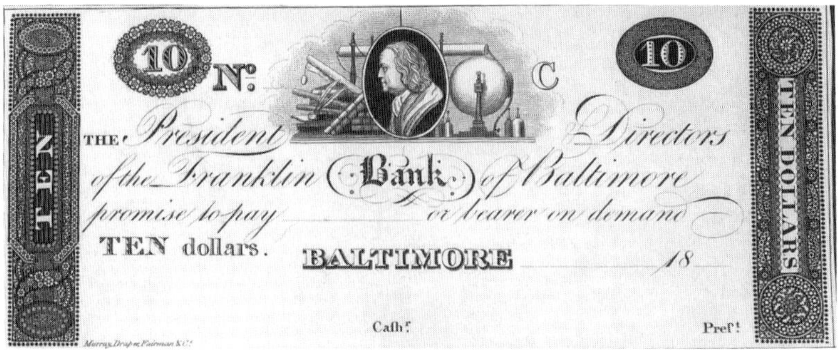

5.75.27 P

5.75.28 P

5.75.29 P

5.75.32 P R-7
$20.00 Ca. 1810s–20s. Engraving, imprint: Murray, Draper, Fairman & Co. Proof. (MD75G100)

5.75.33 P R-6
$20.00 Ca. 1830s–50s. Engraving, imprint: Toppan & Co. Proof. (MD75G104)

5.75.34 P R-7
$20.00 Ca. 1856–60. Engraving, imprint: Danforth, Wright & Co., Philada & New York. Red "XX 20" dies. Proof. (MD75G108)

5.75.35 SENC
$50.00 Ca. 1810. Engraving, imprint: Unknown. Text reads "pay out of their joint funds." Association issue. No other data available. (MD75G14)

5.75.36 SENC
$50.00 Ca. early 1810s. Engraving, imprint: Unknown. Similar to $50.00, No. 5.75.35, except for text. (MD75G110)

5.75.37 P R-7
$50.00 Ca. 1810s–20s. Engraving, imprint: Murray, Draper, Fairman & Co. Proof. (MD75G112)

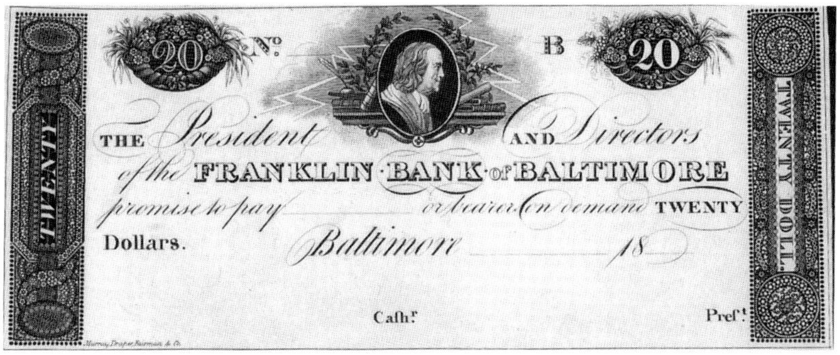

5.75.32 P

5.75.33 P

5.75.34 P

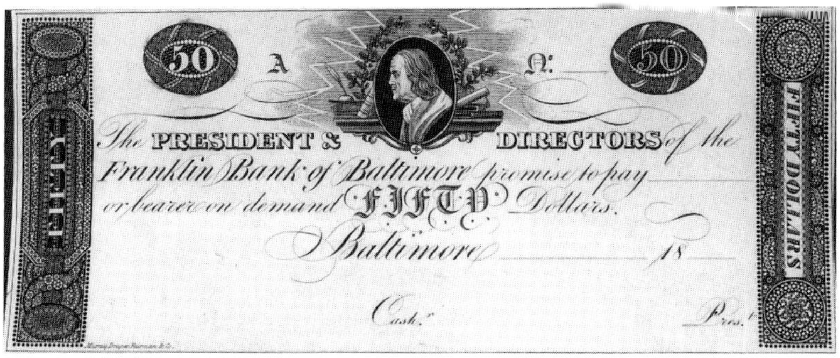

5.75.37 P

5.75.38 P R-7

$50.00 Ca. 1830s–50s. Engraving, imprint: C. Toppan & Co., Philada. Proof. (MD75G116)

5.75.39 P R-7

$50.00 Ca. 1856–60. Engraving, imprint: Danforth, Wright & Co., Philada & New York. Tint is three large red dies bearing "50" and FIFTY DOLLARS. Proof. (MD75G120)

5.75.40 SENC

$100.00 Ca. 1810s–20s. Engraving, imprint: Murray, Draper, Fairman & Co. Similar to counterfeit No. 5.75.40 C. (MD75G124)

5.75.40 C R-5

$100.00 Ca. 1812–19. Engraving, imprint: Murray, Draper, Fairman & Co. Counterfeit of No. 5.75.40. (MD75C124)

5.75.42 P R-7

$100.00 Ca. 1830s–50s. Engraving, imprint: Chas. Toppan & Co., Phila. Proof. (MD75G128)

5.75.38 P

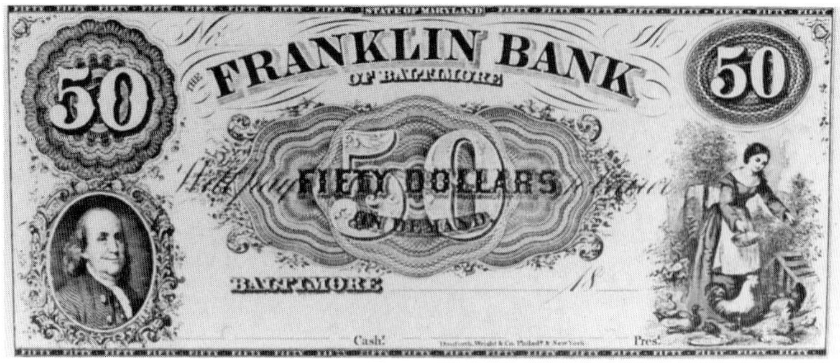

5.75.39 P

5.75.40 C

5.75.42 P

5.75.43 P R-7

$100.00 Ca. 1856–60. Engraving, imprint: Danforth, Wright & Co., Philada. & New York. Tint is red panel in center bearing ONE HUNDRED. Proof. (MD75G132)

5.75.44 P R-7

$500.00 Ca. 1850s. Engraving, imprint: C. Toppan & Co., Philada. Proof. (MD75G136)

5.75.45 P R-7

$1000.00 Ca. 1850s. Engraving, imprint: C. Toppan & Co., Philada. Proof. (MD75G140)

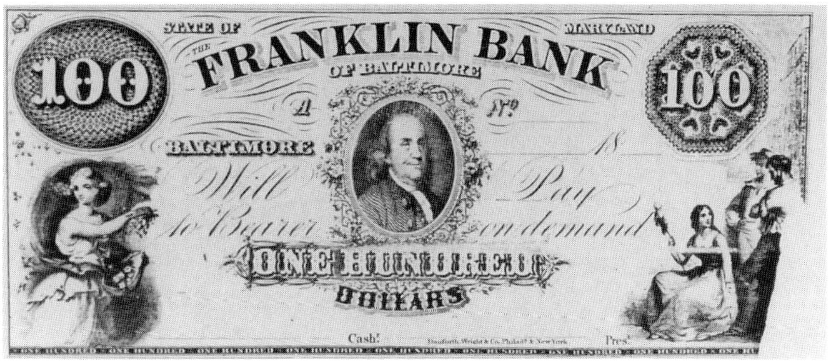

5.75.43 P

5.75.44 P

5.75.45 P

Wm. O'C. Fritschler (Black Horse Tavern)

See Western Franklin Savings Institution, No. 5.168, and Black Horse Tavern, No. 5.18.

5.80 **S. R. Gassaway**

The issuer was apparently Noah Gassaway, a produce dealer whose store was located on the west side of Pennsylvania Avenue, north of Franklin Street, being so listed in the city directories from 1837 through 1842. The signature "S. R. Gassaway" on the recorded notes was probably that of a family member who worked in the store, a Sam R. Gassaway appearing in the 1850 census index.

5.80.1 R-7
6 1/4c Printed year date 1841. Letterpress, no imprint.

5.80.2 R-7
12 1/2c Printed year date 1841. Letterpress, no imprint. *Center:* 12 1/2 circular die, primitive locomotive and passenger car. *Left:* Eagle; George Washington; flag. *Right:* Ship; Battle Monument; locomotive.

5.80.4 R-7
50c Printed year date 1841. Letterpress, no imprint.

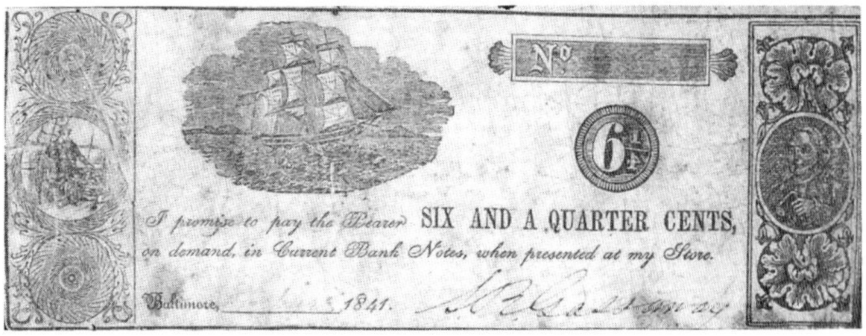

5.80.1

5.80.4

5.81 **Charles W. Geekie**

The issuer was the proprietor of a liquor and billiard saloon at 123 W. Baltimore St.

5.81.3 R-7
25c Printed partial date July 186 . Lithography, no imprint.

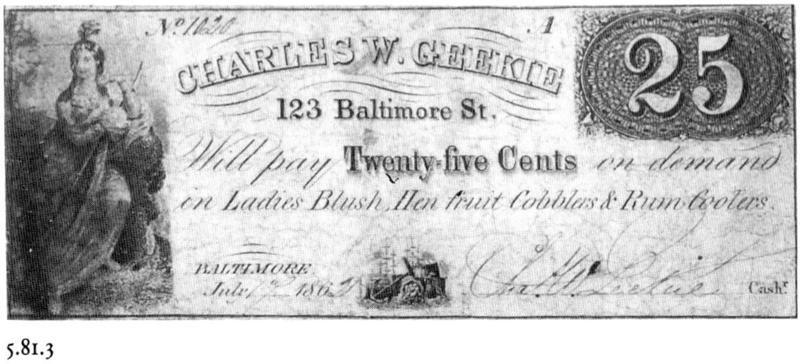

5.81.3

5.82 **Francis R. Gillmeyer**

Gillmeyer was a grocer and produce merchant whose store was at the corner of Pennsylvania Avenue and Pearl Street, being so listed in the 1840–45 editions of the city directories.

5.82.1 R-7

6 1/4c Ca. 1840–41. Lithography, no imprint.

5.82.2 R-7

12 1/2c Ca. 1840–41. Lithography, no imprint.

5.82.3 R-7

25c Printed year date 1840. Lithography, no imprint. *Left:* Primitive locomotive. *Center left:* Large 25. *Center right:* Oval view of Federal Hill, harbor.

5.82.4 R-7

25c Ca. 1840–41. Lithography, no imprint. Numeral in center, ships at right, locomotive and denomination at left.

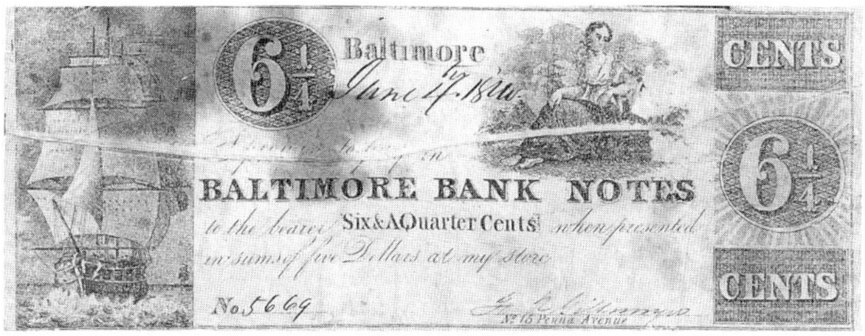

5.82.1

5.83 B. C. Goodhue

The issuer, Benjamin C. Goodhue, was a "dealer in general" according to the 1840 city directory, on Eden Street south of Jefferson Street. The advertisement by Goodhue appeared in the *Sun* of July 21, 1840, and speaks for itself.

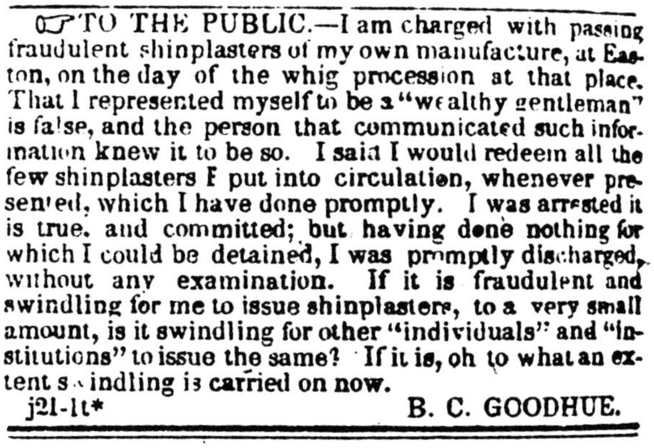

☞TO THE PUBLIC.—I am charged with passing fraudulent shinplasters of my own manufacture, at Easton, on the day of the whig procession at that place. That I represented myself to be a "wealthy gentleman" is false, and the person that communicated such information knew it to be so. I said I would redeem all the few shinplasters I put into circulation, whenever presented, which I have done promptly. I was arrested it is true, and committed; but having done nothing for which I could be detained, I was promptly discharged, without any examination. If it is fraudulent and swindling for me to issue shinplasters, to a very small amount, is it swindling for other "individuals" and "institutions" to issue the same? If it is, oh to what an extent swindling is carried on now.

j21-1t* B. C. GOODHUE.

5.83.5 R-7

$1.00 Ca. 1840. Letterpress, imprint: MURPHY, PRINTER, BALTIMORE. Central vignette of ships in harbor (probably the small woodcut of Baltimore inner harbor viewed from Federal Hill).

5.84 Good Intent Stage Co.

Based upon city directory listings and dates on the relatively few notes recorded, the Good Intent Stage Co. began running daily stagecoaches from Baltimore to Cumberland and Wheeling, via the National Road, in 1839. By early 1845, the stagecoaches from Baltimore to Cumberland had been supplanted by the Baltimore & Ohio R.R. Co. trains, the coaches still being used at least from Cumberland to Wheeling. Tickets for the entire journey, including the stagecoach portion, were sold by the B&O ticket agent in Baltimore. The Good Intent scrip notes so far recorded all show either Cumberland or Wheeling as the company offices for redemption. All recorded notes are signed "Hutchinson & Weart, Agents." J. A. Weart's name appeared in an 1842 Baltimore city directory advertisement, with an address at "14 Pratt street opposite the Rail road depot, the stages leaving daily at 3 1/2 P.M."

5.84.1 R-7

6 1/4c Printed year date ____ 1840. Lithography by E. Weber, Baltimore. Payable "at our Office, Cumberland, Maryland." (Va.#PW40-09)

5.84.2 R-7

6 1/4c Printed year date ____ 1840. Lithography, imprint: none. Similar to 6 1/4c, No. 5.84.1. Payable at Wheeling, Virginia. (Va.#PW40-08)

5.84.3 R-7

12 1/2c Printed year date ____ 1840. Lithography, imprint: Lith. by E. Weber, Baltimore. Payable "at our Office, Cumberland, Maryland." (Va.#PW40-13)

5.84.4 R-7

12 1/2c Printed year date ____ 1840. Similar to 12 1/2c, No. 5.84.3, but payable "at our office in Wheeling, Virginia." (Va.#PW40-12)

5.84.5 R-6

25c Printed date May 4th, 1841. Engraving, imprint: Draper, Toppan & Co., Phila. & New York. Payable "at our Office, Cumberland, Maryland." (Va.#PW40-21)

5.84.6 R-7

25c Partial printed date May 4, 18__. Engraving, imprint: Draper, Toppan & Co., Phila. & New York. Payable "at our Office, Cumberland, Maryland." Similar to No. 5.84.5 except for date.

5.84.7 R-7

50c Printed date May 4th, 1841. Engraving, imprint: Draper, Toppan & Co., Phila. & New York. Payable "at our Office, Cumberland, Maryland." (Va.#PW40-29)

5.84.8 R-7

50c Printed date May 4th, 1841. Engraving, imprint: Draper, Toppan & Co., Phila. & New York. Payable "at our Office, Wheeling, Virginia." Similar to No. 5.84.7 except for place of issue. (Va.#PW40-26)

5.84.1

5.84.3

5.84.5

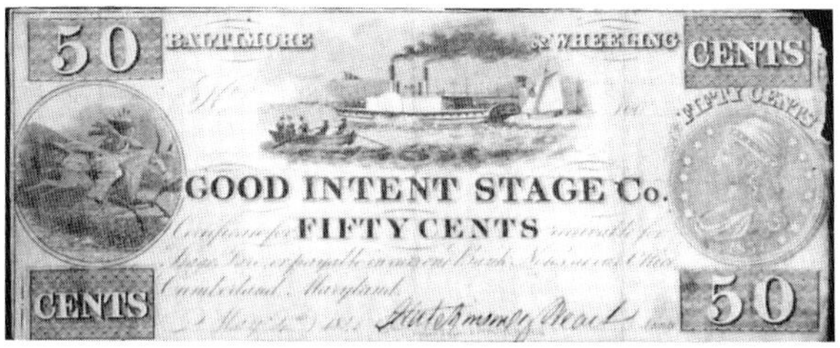

5.84.7

5.84.9 R-7

$1.00 Printed year date ____ 1839. Engraving, imprint: Draper, Toppan & Co., Phila. & New York. Payable "at our Office, Cumberland, Maryland." (Va.#PW40-36)

5.84.9 P R-7

$1.00 Printed year date ____ 1839. Same as No. 5.84.9. Proof. (Va.#PW40-36)

5.84.9

5.84.10 R-7

$1.00 Printed date June 10, 1840. Similar to No. 5.84.9, but payable "at our Office, Wheeling, Va." (Va.#PW40-32)

5.84.11 R-7

$1.00 Printed date June 10th 1840. Similar to No. 5.8471.10, except that "Wheeling, Virginia" is lined out and "Cumberland, Maryland" is inserted in manuscript above the agent's signature.

5.84.12 P

5.84.12 P R-7

$2.00 Printed year date ____, 1839. Engraved, imprint: Draper, Toppan & Co., Phila. & New York. Payable "at our Office, Cumberland, Maryland." Proof. (Va.#PW40-44)

5.85 Wm. Grames

The issuer was the proprietor of a grocery store at 17 Market St., at the corner of Lancaster Street.

5.85.3 R-7

3c Printed date September 21, 1815. Letterpress, no imprint.

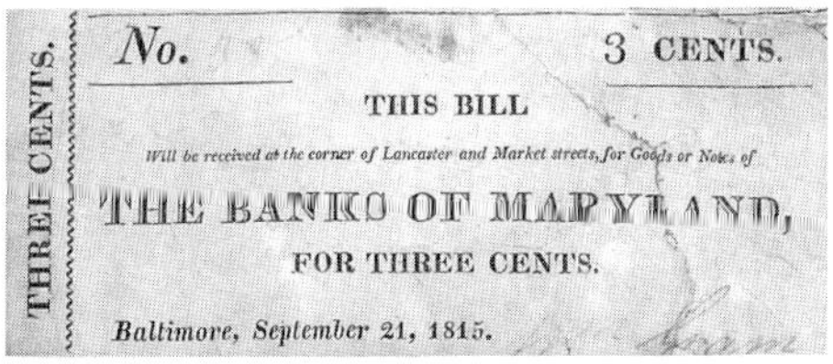
No. 3 CENTS.

THIS BILL

Will be received at the corner of Lancaster and Market streets, for Goods or Notes of

THE BANKS OF MARYLAND,

FOR THREE CENTS.

Baltimore, September 21, 1815.

THREE CENTS.

5.85.3

5.86 Thos. M. Groves & Co.

The issuers apparently conducted a currency exchange business for only a short time in 1840 as they do not appear in any of the city directories from 1837 to 1845. However, in the "List of Small Notes Circulating in Baltimore" published in the *Baltimore Clipper* of September 12, 1840, there is a listing for Thos. M. Groves & Co., at the corner of Fayette and St. Paul streets.

5.86.1 R-7
6 1/4c Printed date May 1, 1840. Letterpress, imprint: Murphy, Printer. Central vignette is a view of Baltimore Harbor from Federal Hill. The "4" in "6 1/4" on the value die is reversed.

5.86.2 R-7
12 1/2c Printed date May 1, 1840. Letterpress, imprint MURPHY, PRINTER. Center vignette is a view of Baltimore Harbor from Federal Hill.

5.86.3 R-7
25c Printed date May 1, 1840. Letterpress, imprint: MURPHY, PRINTER.

5.86.4 R-7
50c Printed date May 1, 1840. Letterpress, imprint: MURPHY, PRINTER. Center vignette is a view of Baltimore Harbor from Federal Hill.

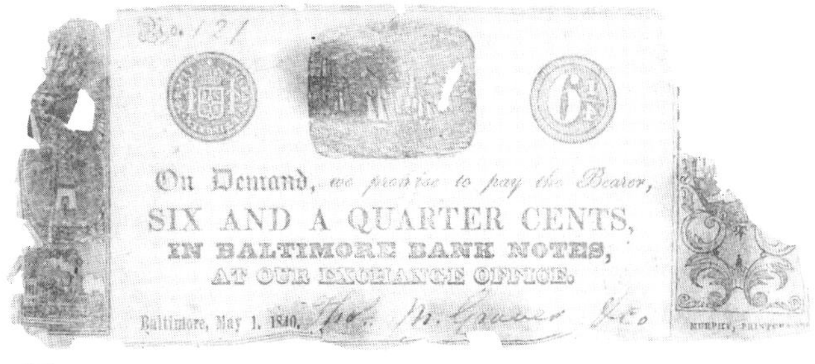

5.86.1

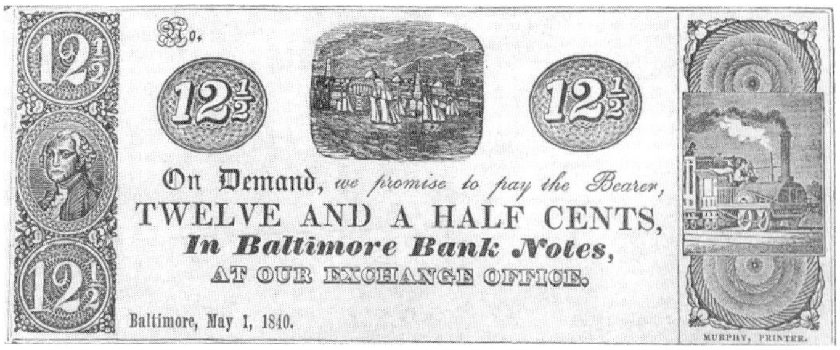

5.86.2

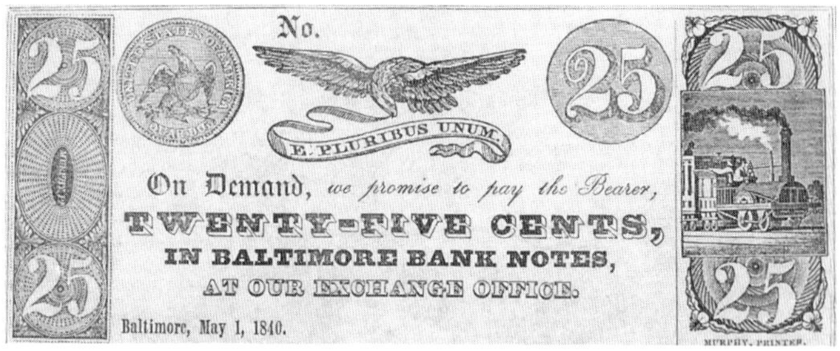

5.86.3

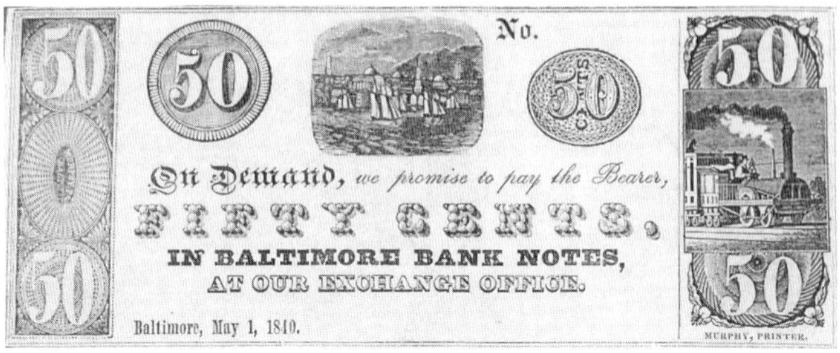

5.86.4

5.87 J. W. Hall

Although the handwriting on the fragmentary note illustrated below precludes the establishment of its date of issue, the two pictorial vignettes, Justice on the left end panel and Commerce at the upper right of the center panel, can be precisely identified as the work of Edw. W. Weber, a lithographer active in Baltimore in the 1837–42 period. The note's serial number, 2345, which is visible, indicates a rather high issue, which would be typical for a low-denomination scrip note issued by a small merchant. A search of contemporary Baltimore directories discloses a particularly likely candidate in John Hall, a grocer whose store was located at 7 S. Calvert St. The signature on the note is discernible as J. W. Hall.

5.87.1 R-7

6 1/4c Ca. 1840–42. Lithography, no imprint, although undoubtedly the work of Edw. W. Weber.

5.87.1

5.88 The Hamilton Bank

Charter approved April 1, 1836. First located in Savage, Md., the corporate office was moved to Baltimore in 1837. Charter forfeited in 1840 because of failure to pay notes in specie.

5.88.4 R-6

$5.00 Ca. 1837–40. Engraving, imprint: Draper, Toppan, Longacre & Co. Phila. & New York. *Center:* Hamilton. *Left:* Charles Carroll / Washington / Robert Fulton. *Right:* Unknown male portrait / Franklin / Robert Morris. Dates on known circulated notes are 1857–61, along with various signatures that were probably not genuine, but filled in on remainder notes. (MD80G4)

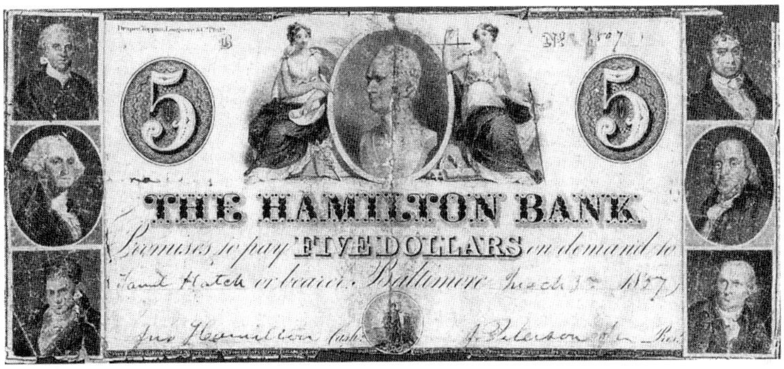

5.88.4

5.88.4 P R-7

$5.00 Ca. 1837–40. Engraving, imprint: Draper, Toppan, Longacre & Co., Phila. & New York. *Center:* Hamilton. *Left:* Charles Carroll / Washington / Robert Fulton. *Right:* Unknown male portrait / Franklin / Robert Morris. Proof.

5.88.5

5.88.5 R-7

$10.00 Ca. 1837–40. Engraving, imprint: Draper, Toppan, Longacre & Co., Phila. & New York. *Center:* Hamilton. *Left:* Charles Carroll / Washington / Robert Fulton. *Right:* Unknown male portrait / Franklin / Robert Morris. Dates on known circulated notes are 1857–61, along with various signatures which were probably not genuine, but filled in on remainder notes. (MD80G6)

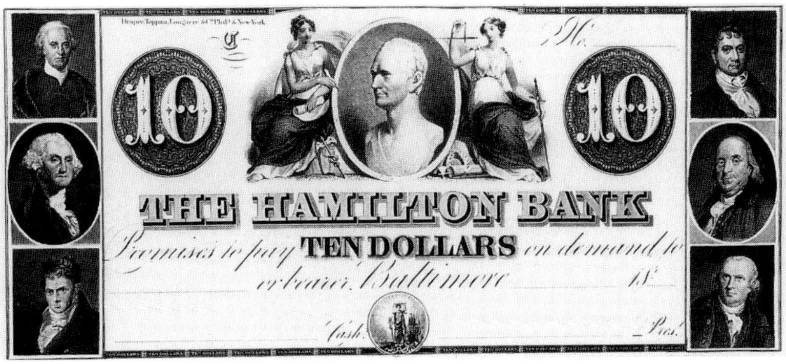

5.88.5 P

5.88.5 P R-7

$10.00 Ca. 1837–40. Engraving, imprint: Draper, Toppan, Longacre & co., Phila. & New York. *Center:* Hamilton. *Left:* Charles Carroll / Washington / Robert Fulton. *Right:* Unknown male portrait / Franklin / Robert Morris. Proof.

5.88.6 P   R-7

$20.00 Ca. 1837–40. Engraving, no imprint (Probably Draper, Toppan, Longacre & Co.). *Center:* Hamilton. *Left:* Charles Carroll / Washington / Robert Fulton. *Right:* Unknown male portrait / Franklin / Robert Morris. Proof. (MD80G8)

5.88.7   SENC

$50.00 Ca. 1837–40. Engraving, imprint: Draper, Toppan, Longacre & Co., Phila. & New York. No other information available. (MD80G10).

5.88.8   SENC

$100.00 Ca. 1837–40. Engraving, imprint: Draper, Toppan, Longacre & Co., Phila. & New York. No other information available. (MD80G12)

5.89 Harper & Lucas

The issuers have not been positively identified, but may have been Pete Harper and Thos. W. Lucas, who were boot- and shoemakers in East Baltimore, listed individually in the city directory for 1837 but not thereafter.

5.89.5   R-7

$1.00 Ca. 1840. Letterpress, imprint: MURPHY / PRINTER / BALTIMORE. Center vignette is a view of the city looking north from Federal Hill.

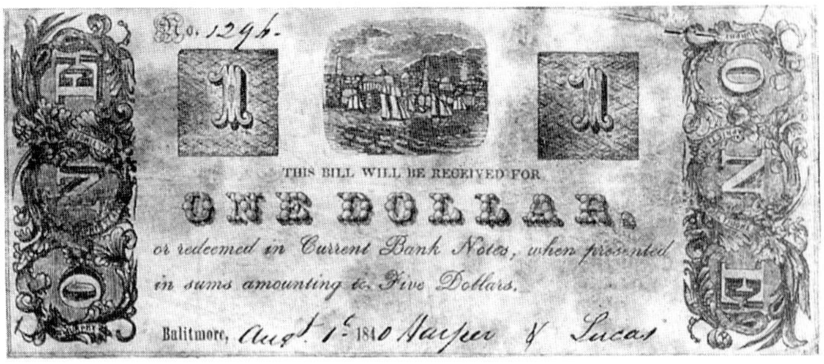

5.89.5

5.90 Charles Hinkle, Restauranteur

The issuer was the proprietor of a restaurant at the corner of Charles and Market streets in 1840. Prior to that time, he had operated the Greenhouse Hotel and Tavern at 11 Franklin St. in 1835–38, and later, in 1840–41, the Theatre Tavern, Holliday Street.

5.90.2   R-7

12 1/2c Printed date July 1, 1840. Letterpress, imprint: MURPHY / PRINTER / BALTIMORE. Central vignette is a view of Baltimore Harbor looking north from Federal Hill.

5.90.3   R-7

25c Printed date July 1, 1840. Letterpress, imprint: MURPHY / PRINTER / BALTIMORE.

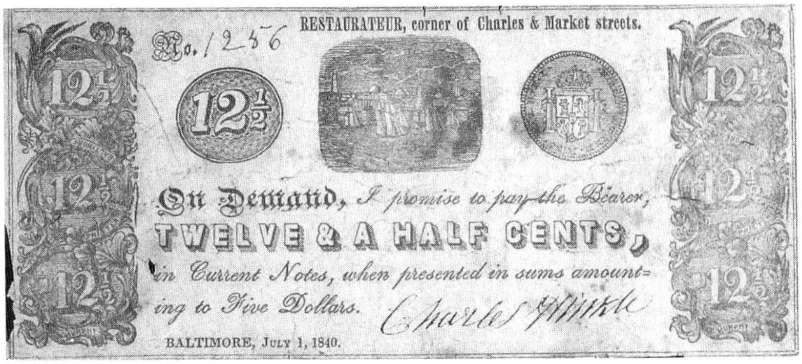

5.90.2

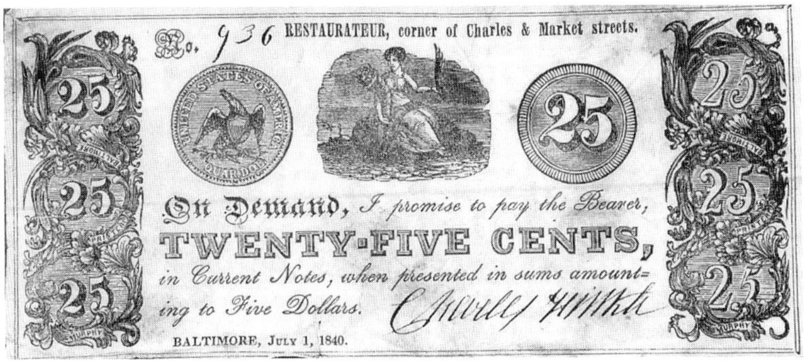

5.90.3

5.91 James Hodges

According to the "List of Small Notes Circulating in Baltimore" published in the *Baltimore Clipper* of September 12, 1840, Hodges was the barkeeper in Davis' Hotel on Pratt Street near South Street.

5.91.3 R-7
25c Printed date, 1840. Lithography, no imprint.

5.91.3

5.92 The Howard Bank

Chartered in 1848 as the Howard Street Savings Bank, the name was changed to the Howard Bank by charter amendment approved March 10, 1854; converted to and became the National Howard Bank of Baltimore in 1890. It was located initially at 81 N. Howard St. and changed its address in the 1864 city directory to NW corner, Howard and Fayette streets.

5.92.1 R-7
$1.00 Ca. 1850s–60s. Engraving, imprint: Danforth, Bald & Co., Phila. & New York. Vignette of the Battle Monument. Baltimore at center. No overprint. (MD85G2)

5.92.2 R-6
$1.00 Ca. 1860s. Engraving, imprint: American Bank Note Co. Similar to No. 5.92.1, except for imprint and ONE security overprint in green. (MD852b)

5.92.4 A SENC
$3.00 Ca. 1840. Engraving, imprint: Durand & Co. *Center:* 3; Indian man standing on rock with right knee raised, left hand on bow, dog at left; 3. *Left:* Three cherubs in clouds, one at right with stone tablet, on wide panel. *Right:* Panel with THREE, across. Altered from $3.00 Globe Bank, New York City, NY1625G8. (MD85A5)

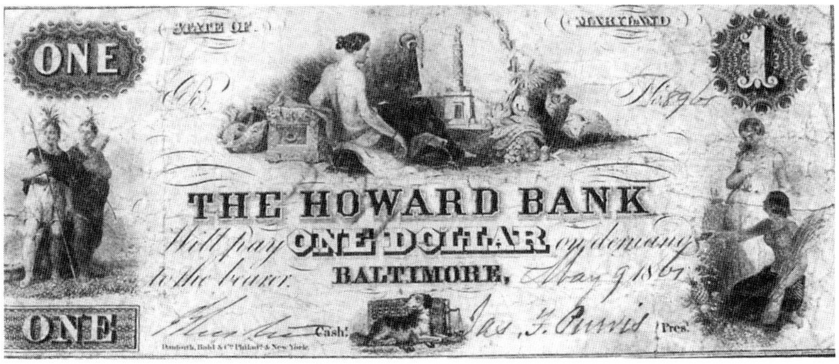

5.92.1

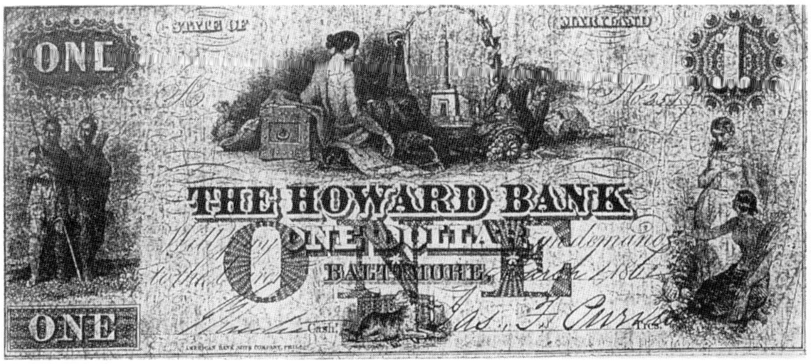

5.92.2

5.92.5 A SENC

$5.00 Ca. 1840. Engraving, imprint: Durand & Co. *Center:* Ships in harbor, large warehouse at left; 5. *Left:* Indian male standing on rock with right knee raised, left hand on bow, dog at left, all in square. *Right:* FIVE on die, on panel of wheat ears and fruit. Altered from $5.00 Globe Bank, New York City, NY1625G10 or 10a. (MD85A10)

5.92.6 P R-7

$5.00 Ca. 1850s. Engraving, imprint: Danforth, Bald & Co., Phila. & New York. Portrait of Col. John Eager Howard at center and Charles Carroll of Carrollton at left. Proof. (MD85G4)

5.92.7 P R-7

$10.00 Ca. 1850s–60s. Engraving, imprint: Danforth, Bald & Co., Phila. & New York. Portrait of Henry Clay at left. Proof. (MD85G6)

5.92.8 R-7

$20.00 Ca. 1850s–60s. Engraving, imprint: Danforth, Bald & Co., Phila. & New York. Portrait of Daniel Webster at left. Illustrated example was accepted for payment on May 3, 1915, by a successor bank, the National Exchange Bank of Baltimore. (MD85G8)

5.92.8 P R-7

$20.00 Ca. 1850s–60s. Engraving, imprint: Danforth, Bald & Co., Phila. & New York. Similar to No. 5.92.8. Proof.

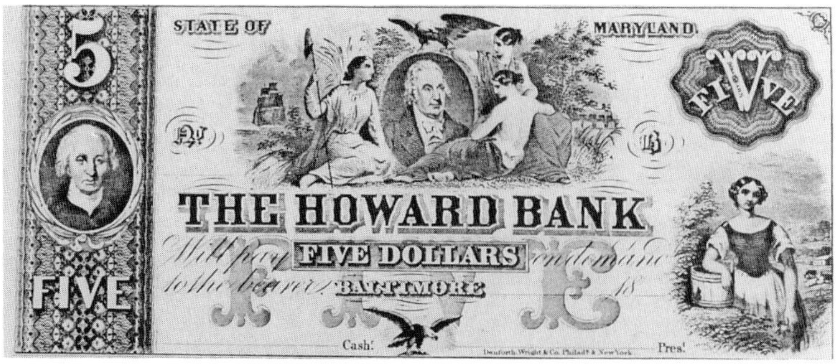

5.92.6 P

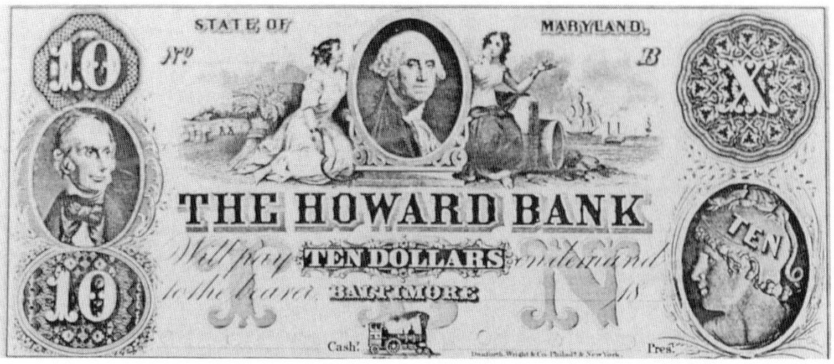

5.92.7 P

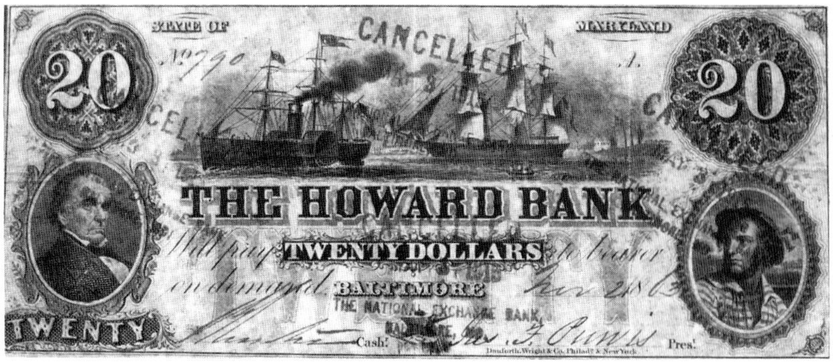

5.92.8

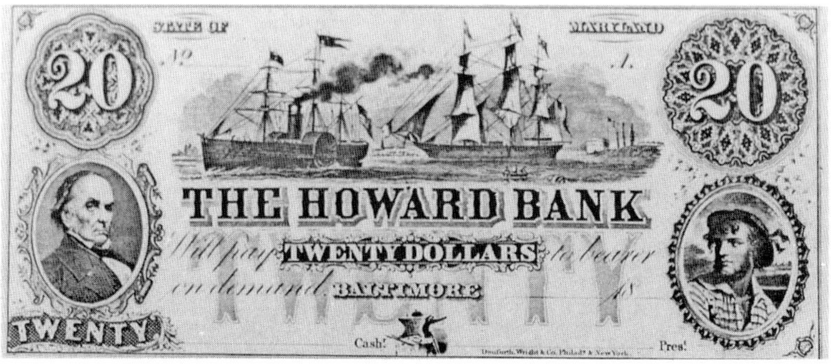

5.92.8 P

5.92.9 P R-7

$50.00 Ca. 1850s–60s. Engraving, imprint: Danforth, Bald & Co., Phila & New York. Vignette of the Battle Monument, Baltimore, at center. Proof. (MD85G10)

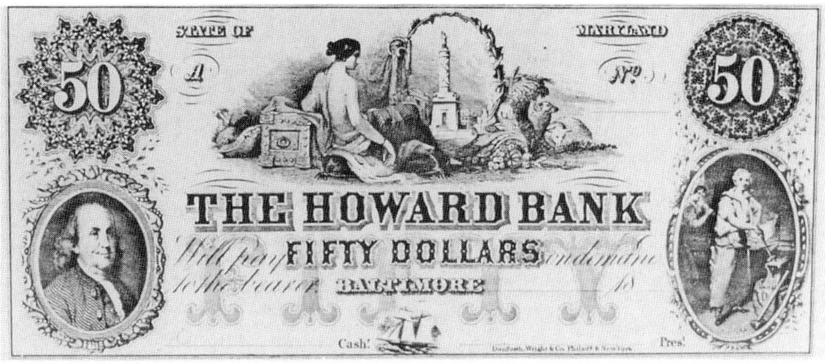

5.92.9 P

5.92.10 P R-7

$100.00 Ca. 1850s–60s. Engraving, imprint: Danforth, Bald & Co., Phila. & New York. Portrait of Andrew Jackson at right. Proof. (MD85G12)

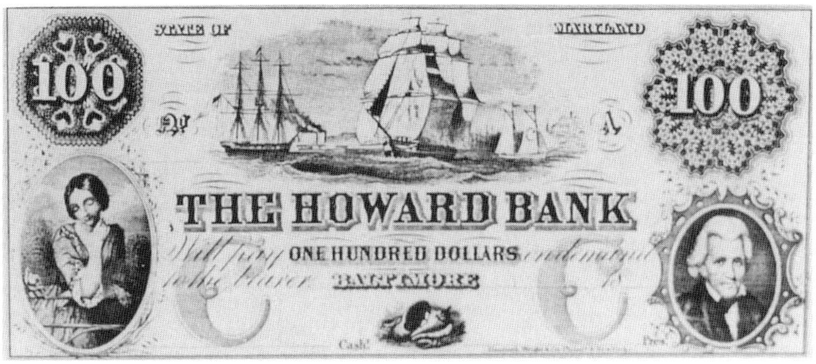

5.92.10 P

5.93 Howard Park Steam Cotton Factory

Howard Park Steam Cotton Factory is apparently a descriptive rather than corporate name, as contemporary city directory listings are under the name of the proprietor, Thomas H. Fulton. In the 1837 and 1840–41 directories his "wadding manufactory" was at French Street, near Potter Street. In 1842, Fulton was identified merely as a "cotton man," Howard Street north of Richmond. A full-page advertisement in the 1845 edition referred simply to the "Howard Factory," with the office at 8 Liberty St., at the corner of German Street, under the name of David A. Martin, Agent. Finally, the 1847 directory showed the "Howard Cotton Mills. F. H. Fulton, proprietor, Bolton Lane near Tyson Street." Arsonists attempted to burn the building near the Richmond Armory in mid-September 1844. It was closed and in the hands of trustees when it finally burned in late 1851.

5.93.1 R-7

6 1/4c Printed date August 20, 1840. Letterpress, imprint: MURPHY PRINTER. Left-end panel vignette of Battle Monument, Baltimore.

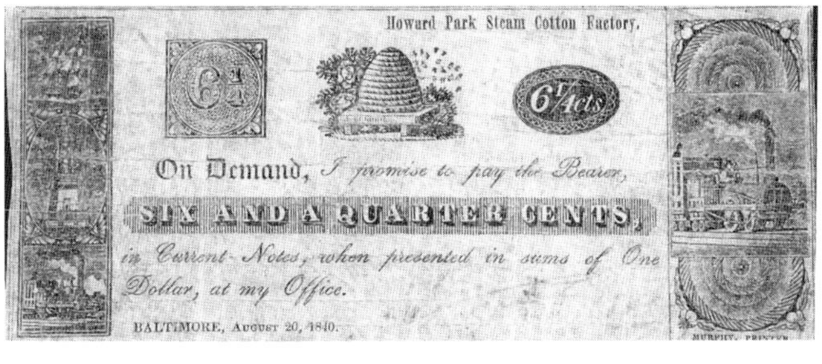

5.93.1

5.93.2 R-7

12 1/2c Printed date August 20, 1840. Letterpress, imprint: MURPHY PRINTER BALTIMORE. Central vignette of Baltimore, looking north from Federal Hill.

5.93.3 R-7

25c Printed date August 20, 1840. Letterpress, imprint: MURPHY PRINTER BALTIMORE. Similar to 50c, No. 5.93.4.

5.93.4 R-7

50c Printed date August 20, 1840. Letterpress, imprint: MURPHY PRINTER, BALTIMORE.

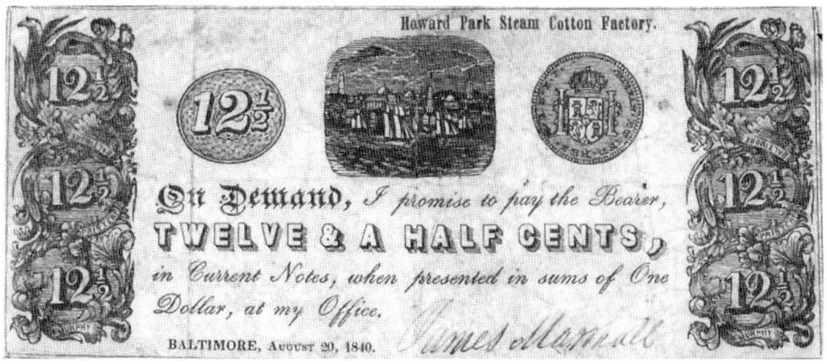

5.93.2

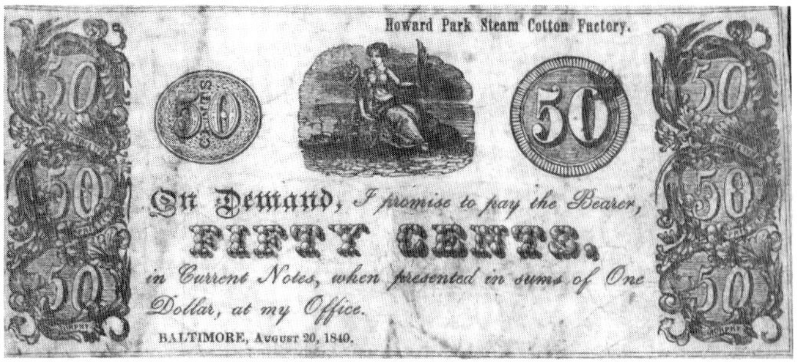

5.93.4

5.94 The Howard Street Savings Bank

Charter approved February 5, 1848; amended to change the name to the Howard Bank in 1854. Converted to and became the National Howard Bank of Baltimore in 1890. The bank was located at 81 N. Howard St., the address being changed to the NW corner, Howard and Fayette streets, in the 1864 city directory.

5.94.1 R-7

$1.00 Ca. 1848. Engraving, imprint: Hufty & Danforth, Philada. & New York.

5.94.1 P R-7

$1.00 Ca. 1848. Engraving, imprint: Hufty & Danforth, Philada. & New York. Proof.

5.94.2 P R-7

$1.00 Ca. 1850–52. Engraving, imprint: Danforth, Bald & Co., Philada. and New York. Battle Monument, Baltimore, at center. Proof.

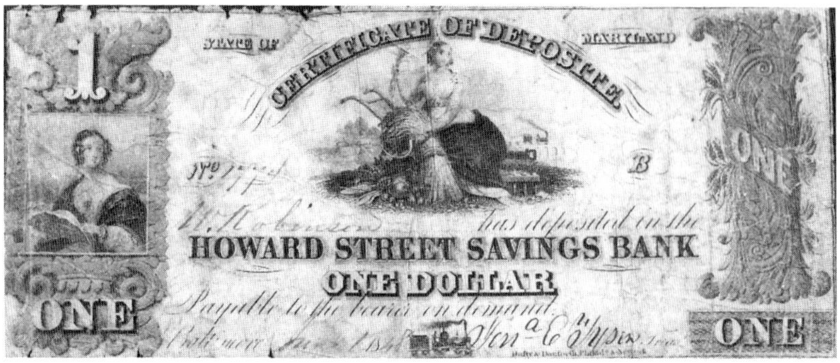

5.94.1

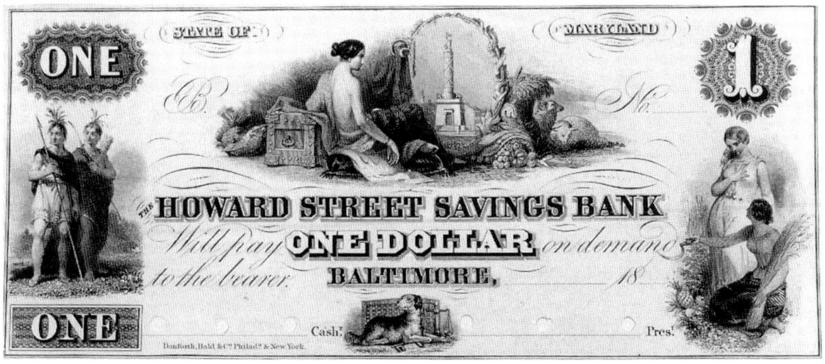

5.94.2 P

5.94.4 P R-7

$3.00 Ca. 1850–52. Engraving, imprint: Danforth, Bald & Co., Philada. & New York. Proof.

5.94.5 P R-7

$5.00 Ca. 1850–52. Engraving, imprint: Danforth, Bald & Co., Philada. & New York. Portrait of Col. John Eager Howard at center. Proof.

5.94.7 P R-7

$20.00 Ca. 1850–52. Engraving, imprint: Danforth, Bald & Co., Philada & New York. Portrait of Col. John Eager Howard at center. Proof.

5.94.8 P R-7

$50.00 Ca. 1850–52. Engraving, imprint: Danforth, Bald & Co., Philada. & New York. Proof.

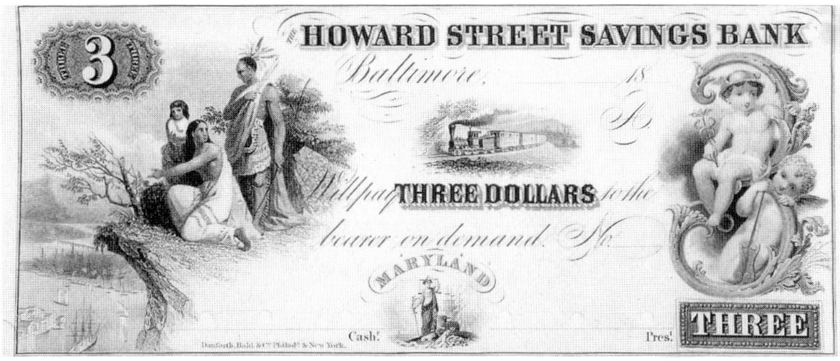

5.94.4 P

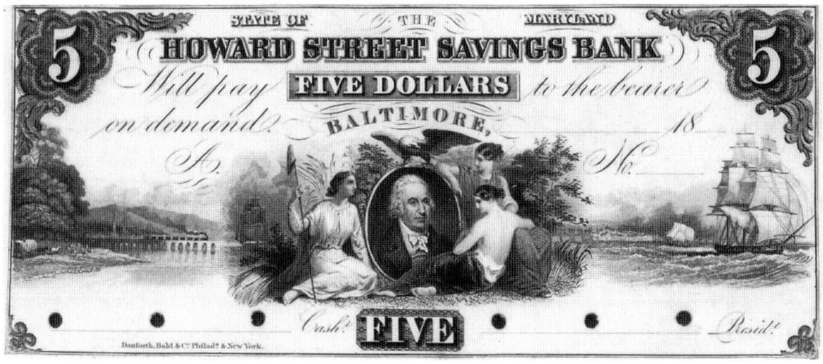

5.94.5 P

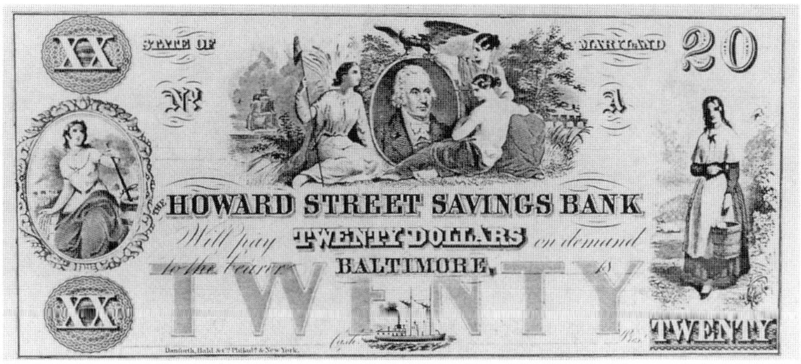

5.94.7 P

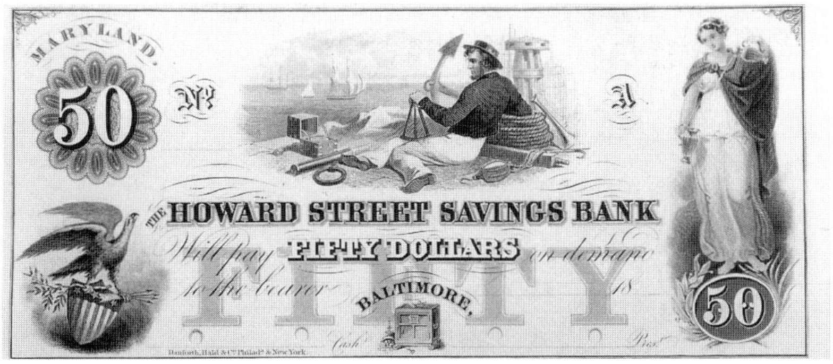

5.94.8 P

5.95 H. Hughes

A Hugh Hughes was listed in the 1840–41 city directory only at the "Lanvale Factory" on Jones's Falls, "near the city limits." In the 1842 and 1845 directories, he appeared as a machinist on Lombard Street. The only other possible listed Hughes is Hugh C. T. Hughes, a grocer and commission merchant at 4 Dugan's Wharf. Neither of the foregoing shows an address near 98 Baltimore St., which appears on the recorded scrip notes. Exactly similar notes are recorded bearing the signature "M. Jones." It is possible that Hughes and Jones were the proprietors of the store at 98 Baltimore St., but equally possible that both signatures were applied to unsigned remainders.

5.95.1 R-7

6 1/4c Printed date 1840. Letterpress, no imprint. The number "4" on the circular "6 1/4" value dies is reversed.

5.95.2 R-7

6 1/4c Printed date 1840. Letterpress, no imprint.

5.95.3 R-7

12 1/2c Printed date 1840. Letterpress, no imprint.

5.95.4 R-7

25c Printed date 1840. Letterpress, no imprint.

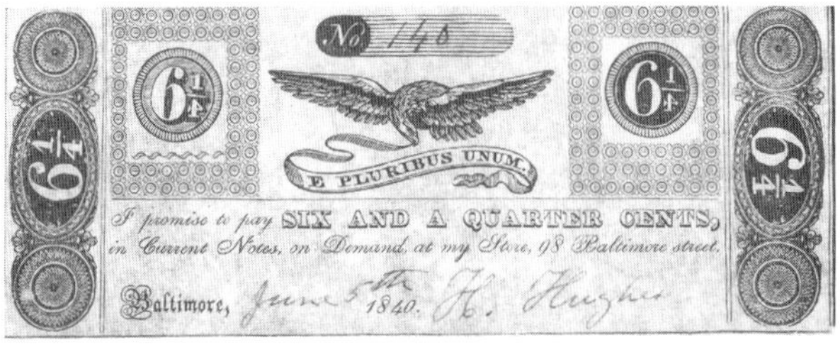

5.95.1

5.95.2

5.95.3

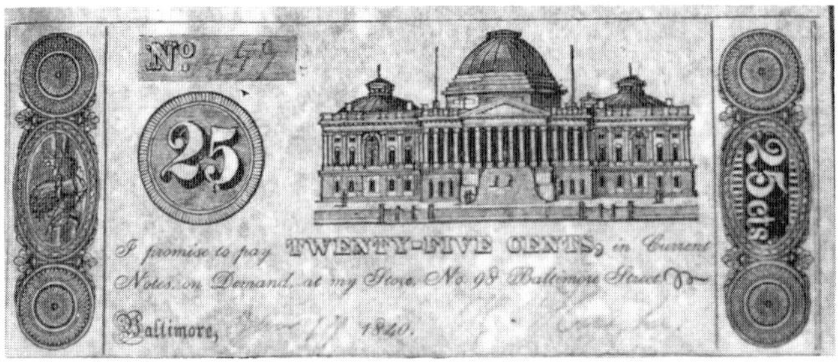

5.95.4

5.98 The Independent Manufacturing Company of Baltimore

Chartered by an act of the General Assembly of Maryland on December 17, 1816, the company being incorporated for the purpose of manufacturing cotton and woolen goods. The company itself did not manufacture such goods, but rather provided a market for the products of its members, which it either bought outright or accepted on consignment and then resold for their account. The basic idea was to encourage the domestic production of good quality woolens and cottons rather than have Americans remain dependent upon England for such goods. There were thirteen original incorporators of whom one, Andrew Ray, a lace weaver, was a signer (as president) of the few notes currently on record. The other signer, Edward Gillespy (treasurer), appears in the 1819 directory as a conveyancer. The company's warehouse was at 54 Howard St., according to the 1817–18 city directory. No other directory listings have been found. Apparently the project was short-lived.

5.98.4 R-7
$5.00 Ca. 1817. Engraving, no imprint.

5.98.6 R-7
$20.00 Ca. 1817. Engraving, no imprint.

5.98.8 R-7
$100.00 Ca. 1817. Engraving, no imprint. Post note with payment time to be filled in.

5.98.4

5.98.6

5.98.8

5.100 The Indian Queen Hotel

This hotel was listed in four city directory editions, 1814–15, 1816, 1817–18, and 1819, with an address of Baltimore and Hanover streets. The proprietor was John Gadsby.

5.100.2 R-7
12 1/2c Ca. 1815. Engraving, no imprint.

5.100.2

5.101 J. R. Jackson

This name appears in a listing of issuers of "Small Notes Circulating in Baltimore" published in the *Baltimore Clipper* of September 12, 1840. Jackson was identified as a grocer at 22 Light St. No examples of his notes have as yet been recorded.

5.102 Wm. James & Co.

The identity of this issuer has not as yet been definitely established, no pertinent directory listings having been found.

5.102.4 R-7
50c Ca. 1840. Letterpress, imprint: MURPHY, PRINTER.

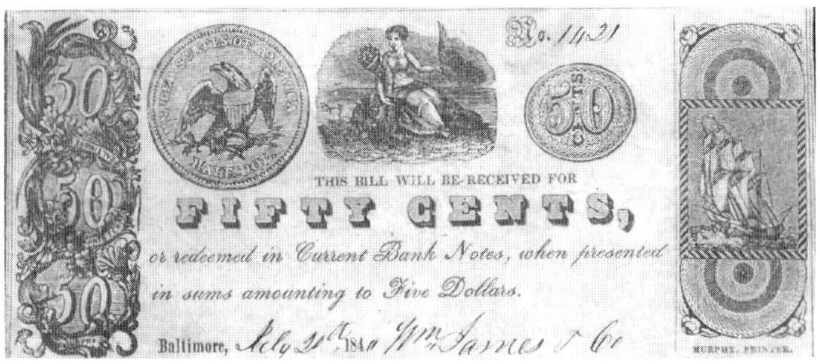

5.102.4

5.103 M. Jones

The identity of this issuer is not as yet established, no city directory listings bearing relationship to the address on the notes, 98 Baltimore St., having been found. See the exactly similar notes signed "H. Hughes."

5.103.1 R-7
6 1/4c Printed date 1840. Letterpress, no imprint. *Center:* Three men cutting wheat, one man binding. *Right and left:* 6 1/4.

5.103.1

5.103.2 R-7

12 1/2c Printed date 1840. Letterpress, no imprint.

5.103.3 R-7

25c Printed date 1840. Letterpress, no imprint.

5.103.2

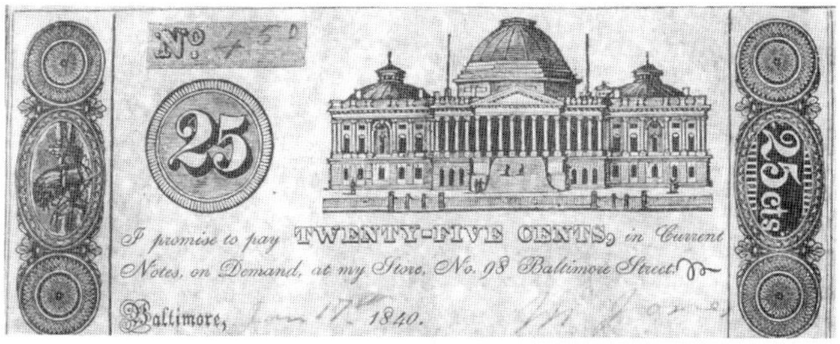

5.103.3

5.104 A. E. Kendall

Andrew E. Kendall was a baker, his place of business on Eden Street near Orleans Street in Old Town. His notes were also redeemable "at his wagon."

5.104.1 R-7

6 1/4c Printed date July 1, 1840. Letterpress, imprint: MURPHY, PRINTER, 146 Market street. Center vignette on left side is the Battle Monument, Baltimore.

5.104.2 R-7

12 1/2c Printed date July 1, 1840. Letterpress, imprint: MURPHY, PRINTER, BALTIMORE. Center vignette is view of Baltimore Harbor from Federal Hill.

5.104.3 R-7

25c Printed date July 1, 1840. Letterpress, imprint: MURPHY, PRINTER, BALTIMORE. Center vignette is view of Baltimore Harbor from Federal Hill.

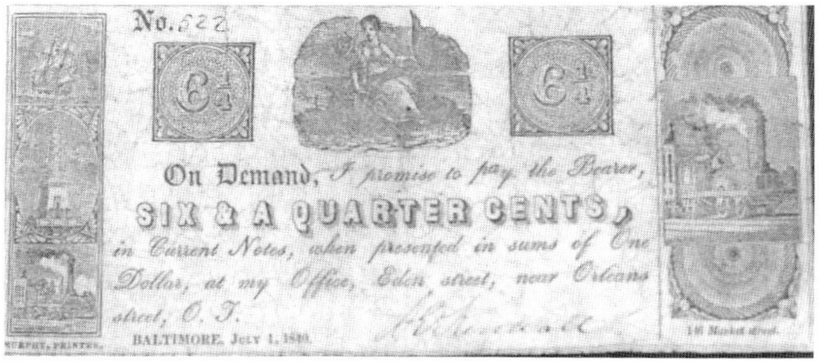

5.104.1

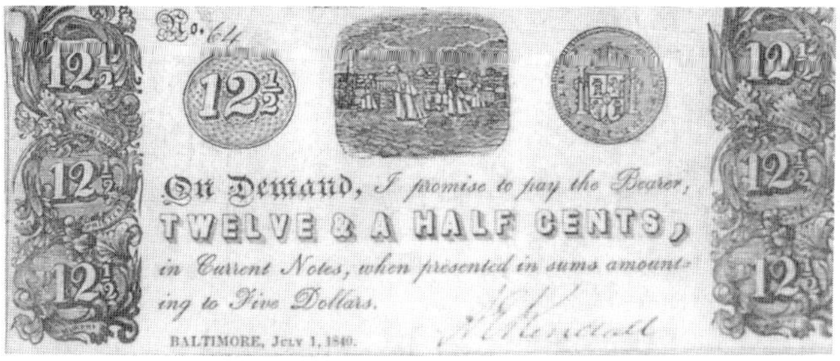

5.104.2

5.104.3

5.105 M. Kneass

The issuer, Michael Kneass, was a grocer at 5 S. Howard St., opposite the Commercial & Farmers Bank of Baltimore, which was located at the southwest corner of Howard and German streets.

5.105.1 R-7

5c Ca. 1814–16. Letterpress, no imprint. Similar to 6 1/4c, No. 5.105.2.

5.105.2 R-7

6 1/4c Ca. 1814–16. Letterpress, no imprint.

5.105.3 R-6

12 1/2c Ca. 1814–16. Letterpress, no imprint.

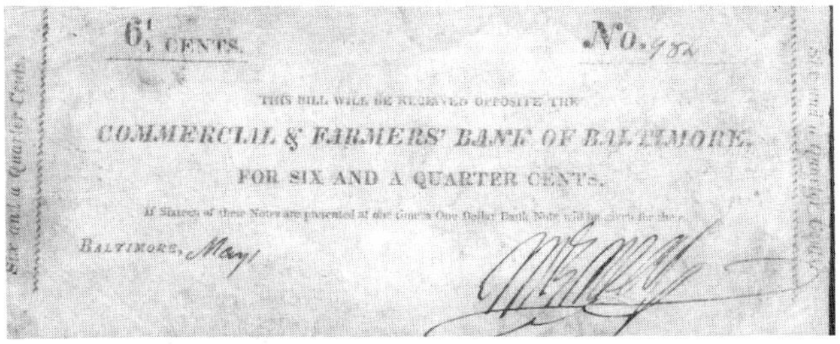

5.105.2

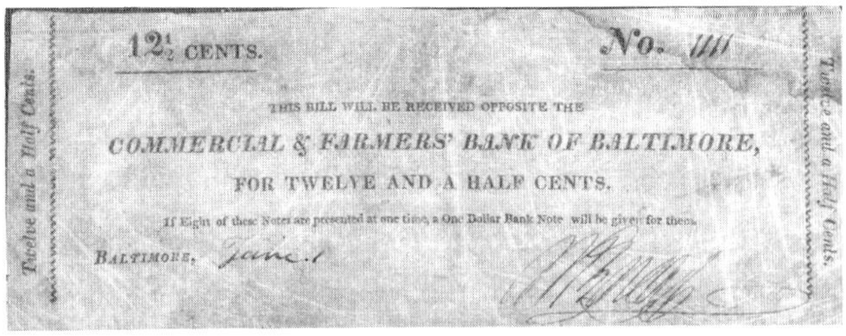

5.105.3

5.108 R. W. Latham & Co.

A private banking house in Washington, D.C., this company had a representative in Baltimore at 110 Fayette St. for a short time in 1844–45.

5.108.1 P R-7

$1.00 Ca. 1845–48. Engraving, imprint: Danforth, Spencer & Hufty, New York / Spencer, Hufty & Danforth, Philada. Proof.

5.108.2 P R-7

$2.00 Ca. 1844–48. Engraving, imprint: Spencer, Hufty & Danforth, Philada. / Danforth, Spencer & Hufty, New York. Proof.

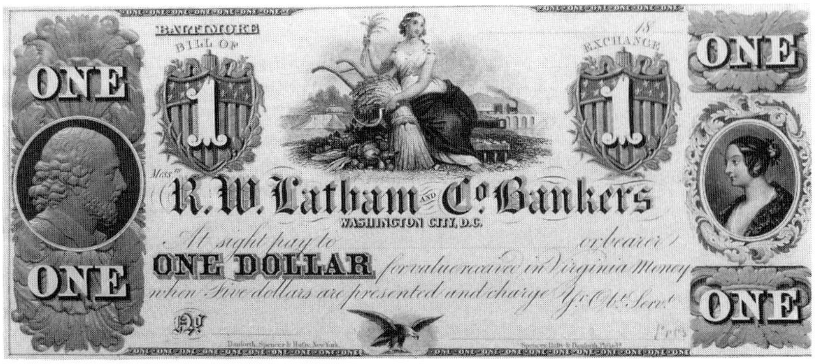

5.108.1 P

5.108.2 P

5.109 Jacob Laudenslager

A butcher and innkeeper, Laudenslager operated a tavern on Chinquapin Hill and a butcher's stall in Center Market in 1814–15.

5.109.2 R-7

12 1/2c Printed date September, 1815. Letterpress, no imprint.

5.109.3 R-7

25c Printed date September, 1815. Letterpress, no imprint. Similar to 12 1/2c, No. 5.109.2.

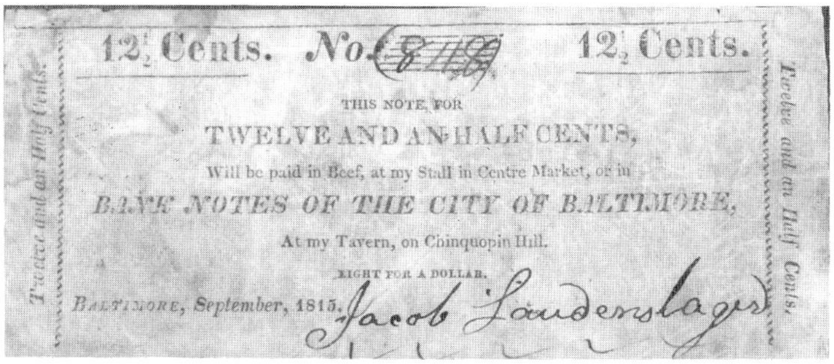

5.109.2

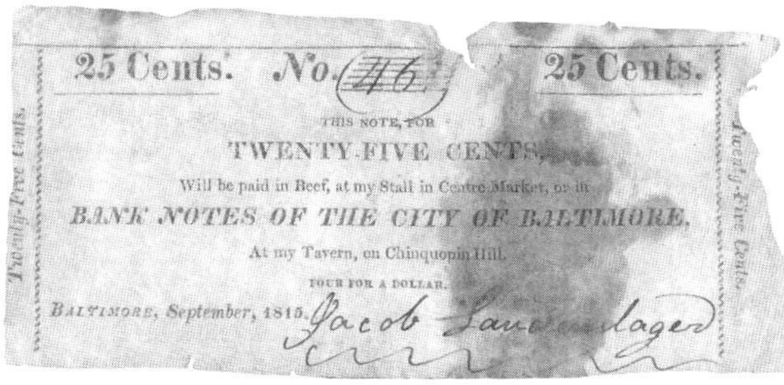

5.109.3

5.110 L. Lawrick

This name appears in a "List of Small Notes Circulating in Baltimore" published in the *Baltimore Clipper* of September 12, 1840. Lawrick was identified as a storekeeper at the corner of Caroline and Gough streets. No examples of his notes have been recorded as yet.

5.111 Josiah Lee & Co.

A lottery and exchange broker, Lee had his office at the southeast corner of Baltimore and Calvert streets, diagonally across the street from the office of John Clark in the Museum Buildings at the northwest corner of the intersection. Later, in 1845, Lee moved across Baltimore Street to the northeast corner of the same intersection. Note 5.111.5, printed from the same engraved plate as that used to produce John Clark's $1.00 note and signed "Josiah Lee & Co.," may indicate that Lee acquired Clark's business.

5.111.5 R-7

$1.00 Printed date Jany. 1st, 1841. Engraving, imprint: Danforth, Underwood & Co., New York / Underwood, Bald, Spencer & Hufty, Philada.

5.111.5

5.112 Morris Lee & Co.

The identity of this issuer has not as yet been definitely established, no pertinent directory listings having been found.

5.112.4 R-7

50c Partial printed date 184_. The only example of this note recorded to date has the date completed in manuscript, "Jan. 10, 1840." Letterpress, imprint: MURPHY, PRINTER.

5.112.4

5.113 Wm. Longton

The identity of this issuer has not as yet been definitely established, no pertinent directory listings having been found.

5.113.4 R-7

50c Printed partial date 184_. Ca. 1840–41. Letterpress, imprint: MURPHY, PRINTER, BALTIMORE.

5.113.4

5.115 The Marine Bank of Baltimore

Operated as an unchartered association until 1810. Charter approved December 23, 1810; converted to and became the National Marine Bank of Baltimore in 1880. Initially located at the corner of Alisanna and Market streets, Fells Point, the bank moved later to the northeast corner of Gay and Second streets at least as early as 1842.

5.115.1 SENC

6 1/4c Printed date 1814. Letterpress, no imprint. Similar to 25c, No. 5.115.5. (MD90G20)

5.115.2 SENC

6 1/4c Printed date 1815. Letterpress, no imprint. Similar to 50c, No. 5.115.8. (MD90G22)

5.115.3 SENC

12 1/2c Printed date 1814. Letterpress, no imprint. Similar to 25c, No. 5.115.5. (MD90G24)

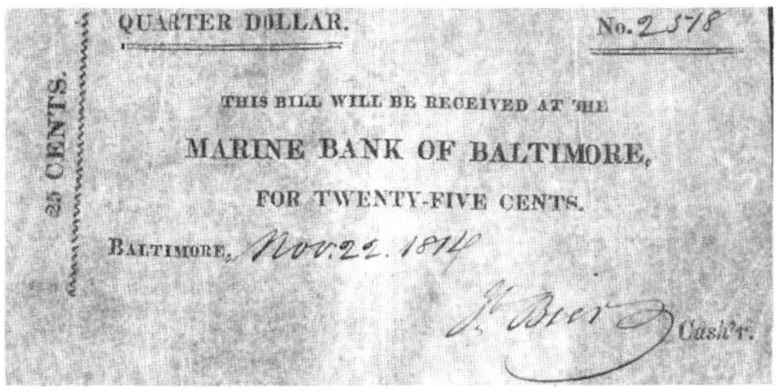

5.115.5

5.115.4 SENC

12 1/2c Printed date 1815. Letterpress, no imprint. Similar to 50c, No. 5.115.8. (MD90G26)

5.115.5 R-7

25c Ca. 1814. Letterpress, no imprint. (MD90G28)

5.115.6 SENC

25c Printed date 1815. Letterpress, no imprint. Similar to 50c, No. 5.115.8. (MD90G30)

5.115.7 SENC

50c Printed date 1814. Letterpress, no imprint. Similar to 25c, No. 5.115.5. (MD90G32)

5.115.8 R-7

50c Printed partial year date 181_. Ca. 1815. Letterpress, no imprint. (MD90G34)

5.115.9 P SENC

$1.00 Ca. 1810. Engraving, imprint: Murray & Draper. Association issue. Promissory inscription reads "The President, Directors & Company . . . promise to pay out of the JOINT FUNDS thereof and NO OTHER according to the Articles of the Association . . . " No other information available. Proof. (MD90G2)

5.115.10 R-7

$1.00 Printed partial year date 181_. Ca. 1810–15. Letterpress, no imprint.

5.115.11 SENC

$1.00 Ca. 1810s. Engraving, imprint: Cone, Freeman & Co. Baltimore. Similar to $2.00, No. 5.115.15. (MD90G36)

5.115.12 R-7

$1.00 Ca. 1810s. Engraving, imprint: Cone, Freeman & Co., Baltimore.

5.115.13 P R-7

$1.00 Ca. 1840s and 1860s. Engraving, imprint: Underwood, Bald, Spencer & Hufty, Philada. / Danforth, Underwood & Co., New York. Proof. (MD90G38)

5.115.14 SENC

$2.00 Ca. 1810. Engraving, imprint: Murray & Draper. Association issue. Promissory inscription reads "The President, Directors & Company . . . promise to pay out of the JOINT FUNDS thereof and NO OTHER according to the Articles of the Association . . . " No other information available. (MD90G4)

5.115.8

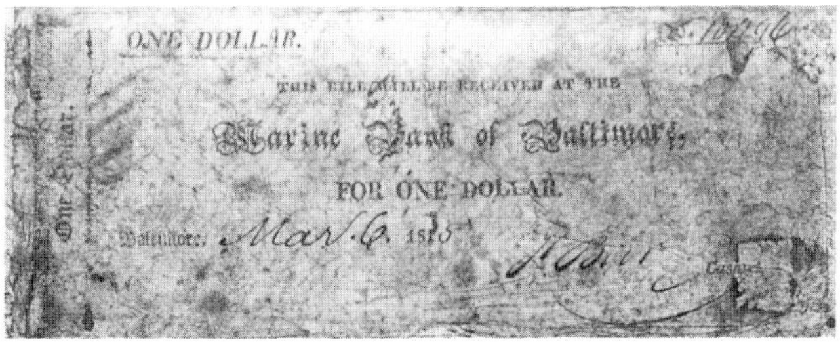

5.115.10

5.115.12

5.115.13 P

5.115.15 SENC

$2.00 Ca. 1810s. Engraving, imprint: Cone, Freeman & Co., Baltimore. Similar to counterfeit No. 5.115.15 C. (MD90G42)

5.115.15 C R-6

$2.00 Ca. 1810s. Engraving, imprint: Cone, Freeman & Co., Baltimore. Counterfeit of No. 5.115.15. (MD90C42)

5.115.16 P R-7

$2.00 Ca. 1840s and 1860s. Engraving, imprint: Underwood, Bald, Spencer & Hufty, Philada. / Danforth, Underwood & Co., New York. Proof. (MD90G40)

5.115.17 N SENC

$3.00 Ca. 1840s. Engraving, imprint: Durand & Co. *Center:* Sailing ship. *Left:* Two children. *Right:* Denomination. Nongenuine, unattributed. (MD90N5)

5.115.18 S SENC

$3.00 Printed partial date May 1, 185_. Engraving, imprint: Baldwin, Adams & Co. *Center:* St. George on horse fighting dragon. *Left:* 3 / square portrait of Washington / 3. *Right:* Lathework panel with 3 / THREE. *Between signatures:* Road, trees, signpost. Altered from spurious $3.00 (RI335S15a) on the Marine Bank, Providence, R.I. (MD90S3)

5.115.19 R-7

$5.00 Ca. 1810. Engraving, imprint: Murray & Draper. Association issue. Promissory inscription reads "The President, Directors & Company . . . promise to pay out of the JOINT FUNDS thereof and NO OTHER according to the articles of the association . . . " (MD90G8)

5.115.20 SENC

$5.00 Ca. 1810s. Engraving, imprint: Murray & Draper. Similar to counterfeit No. 5.115.20 C. (MD90G46)

5.115.20 C R-5

$5.00 Ca. 1810s. Engraving, imprint: Murray & Draper. Promissory inscription reads "The President and Directors . . . promise to pay . . . " Counterfeit of No. 5.115.20. (MD90C46)

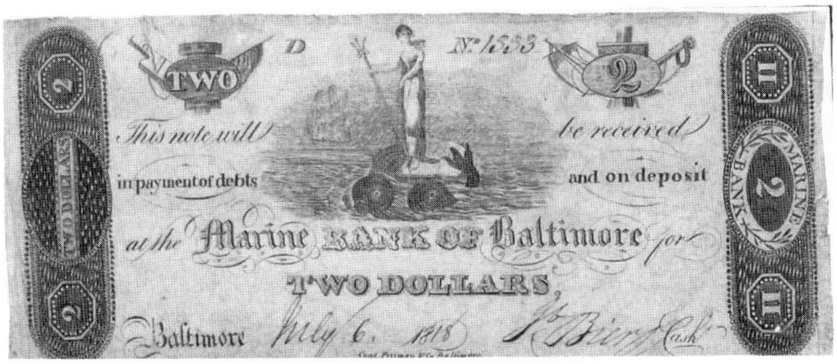

5.115.15 C

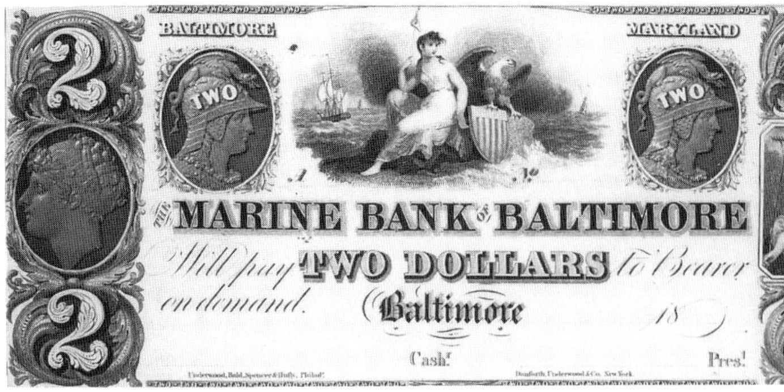

5.115.16 P

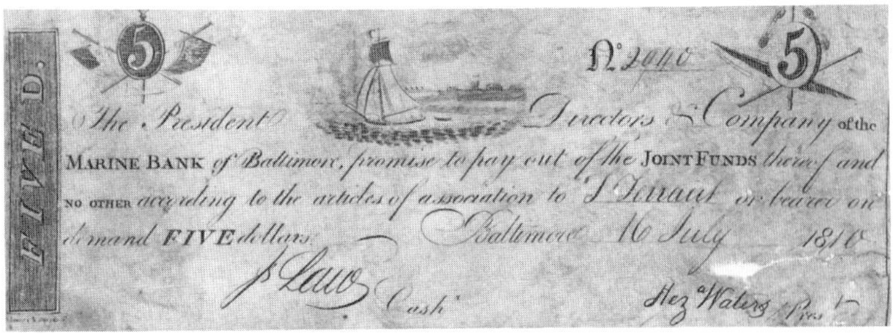

5.115.19

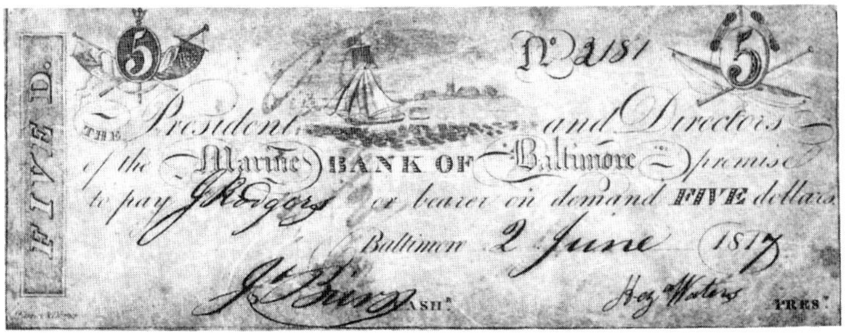

5.115.20 C

5.115.21 P R-7

$5.00 Ca. 1810s–20s. Engraving, imprint: Murray, Draper, Fairman & Co. Similar to counterfeit No. 5.115.21 C. Proof. (MD90G50)

5.115.21 C R-5

$5.00 Ca. 1810s–20s. Engraving, imprint: Murray, Draper, Fairman & Co. Counterfeit of note similar to No. 5.115.21 P. (MD90C50)

5.115.21 C

5.115.22 S SENC

$5.00 Ca. 1839. Engraving, imprint: Rawdon, Wright & Hatch. *Center:* Steamboat, sailing ship, and sloop; 5. *Left:* Ornate panel with 5 / 5, both across. *Right:* FIVE / bust of Franklin / FIVE. See spurious $5.00, No. 5.38.5 S, on the Commercial Bank of Baltimore for an illustration of the design. (MD90S10)

5.115.23 P R-7

$5.00 Ca. 1825–50s. Engraving, imprint: Fairman, Draper, Underwood & Co. Portrait of Columbus at left. Proof. (MD90G54)

5.115.23 P

5.115.24 N R-7

$5.00 Ca. 1844–48. Engraving, imprint: Draper, Toppan & Co. Phila. Nongenuine, unattributed. (MD90N10)

5.115.24 N

5.115.25 N SENC

$5.00 Ca. 1850s. Engraving, imprint: Unknown. *Center:* V; vessels; V. *Left:* Female portrait. *Lower right:* Sailors hauling on rope. Nongenuine, unattributed. (MD90N15)

5.115.26 SENC

$5.00 Ca. 1860s. Engraving, imprint: American Bank Note Co. *Center:* Two sailing ships. *Left:* Portrait of girl. *Right:* Two sailors hauling on rope. Tint is red, including die bearing "5" at upper left and right. (MD90G56)

5.115.27 P R-7

$10.00 Ca. 1810. Engraving, imprint: MURRAY & DRAPER. Association issue. Promissory inscription reads "The President, Directors & Company of the MARINE BANK OF BALTIMORE promise to pay out of the JOINT FUNDS thereof and no other according to the articles of association . . . " Proof. (MD90G10)

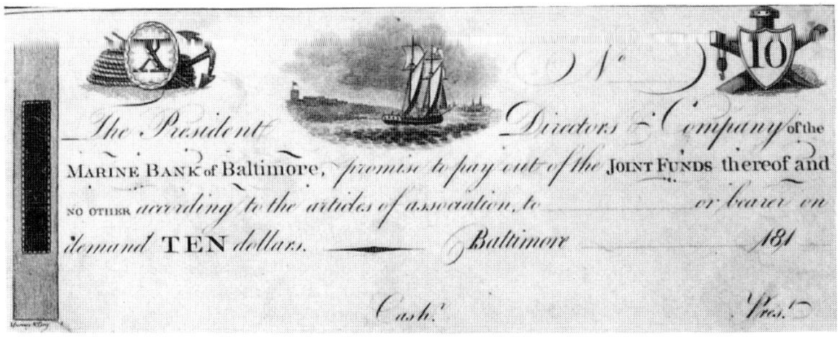

5.115.27 P

5.115.28 SENC

$10.00 Ca. 1810s. Engraving, imprint: Murray & Draper. Similar to counterfeit No. 5.115.28 c. (MD90G60)

5.115.28 c R-6

$10.00 Ca. 1810s. Engraving, imprint: Murray & Draper. Counterfeit of No. 5.115.28. (MD90C60)

5.115.29 p R-7

$10.00 Ca. 1810s–20s. Engraving, no imprint. Probably Murray, Draper, Fairman & Co. Proof.

5.115.30 p R-7

$10.00 Ca. 1825–30s. Engraving, imprint: Fairman, Draper, Underwood & Co. Similar to counterfeit No. 5.115.30 c. Proof. (MD90G64)

5.115.30 c R-6

$10.00 Ca. 1825–30s. Engraving, imprint: Fairman, Draper, Underwood & Co. Counterfeit of note similar to No. 5.115.30 p. (MD90C64)

5.115.31 p R-7

$10.00 Ca. 1835–50s. Engraving, imprint: Underwood, Bald & Spencer. Proof. (MD90G68)

5.115.32 n SENC

$10.00 Ca. 1840s. Engraving, imprint: Durand & Co. *Center:* Allegorical male reclining with water jug. *Left:* Ships. Nongenuine, unattributed. (MD90N20)

5.115.33 SENC

$10.00 Ca. 1860s. Engraving, imprint: American Bank Note Co. *Lower center:* X; eagle holding shield on rock in sea, ship in left and right background; X. *Left:* Sailor leaning on capstan, bale and barrel. *Right:* Woman seated leaning on bale, ship in background. Tint is red, including die bearing "5" at left and right. (MD90G70)

5.115.28 c

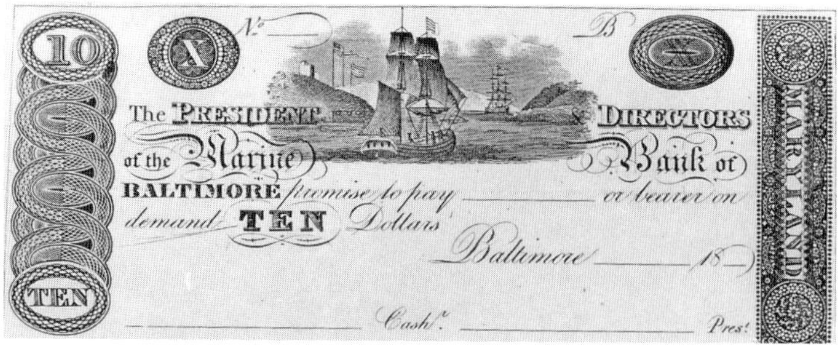

5.115.29 p

5.115.30 c

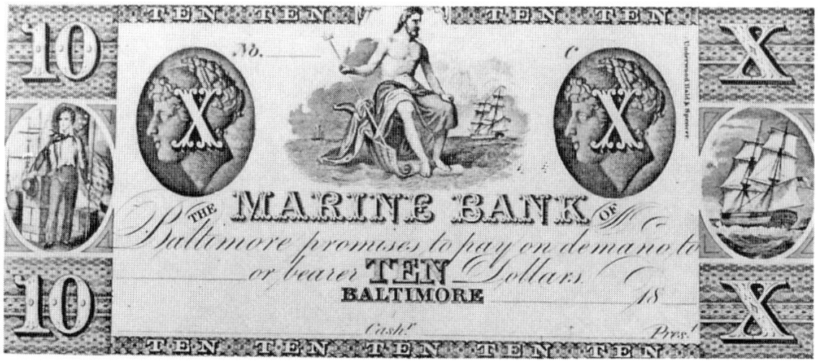

5.115.31 p

5.115.34 SENC

$20.00 Ca. 1810. Engraving, imprint: Murray & Draper. Association issue. Promissory inscription reads "The President, Directors & Company . . . promise to pay out of the JOINT FUNDS thereof and NO OTHER according to the Articles of the Association . . . " Probably similar to $20.00, No. 5.115.35 P. (MD90G12)

5.115.35 P R-7

$20.00 Ca. 1810s. Engraving, imprint: Murray & Draper. Proof. (MD90G72)

5.115.36 P R-7

$20.00 Ca. 1810s–20s. Engraving, no imprint. (Probably Murray, Draper, Fairman & Co.) Proof.

5.115.37 P R-7

$20.00 Ca. 1825–30s. Engraving, imprint. Fairman, Draper, Underwood & Co. At bottom, portrait of Jefferson between signatures. Proof. (MD90G76)

5.115.38 P R-7

$20.00 Ca. 1835–50s. Engraving, imprint: Underwood, Bald & Spencer. Proof. (MD90G80)

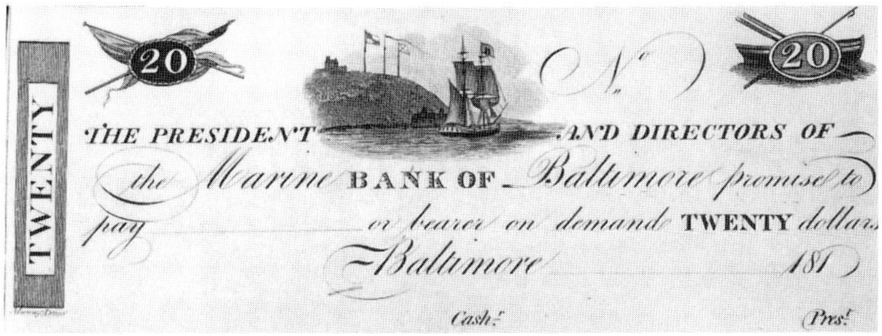

5.115.35 P

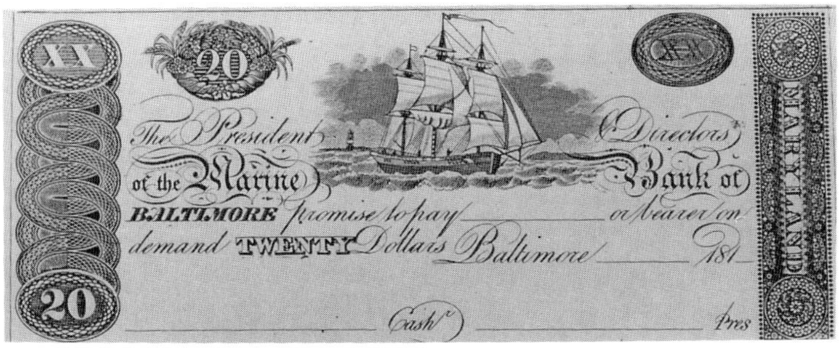

5.115.36 P

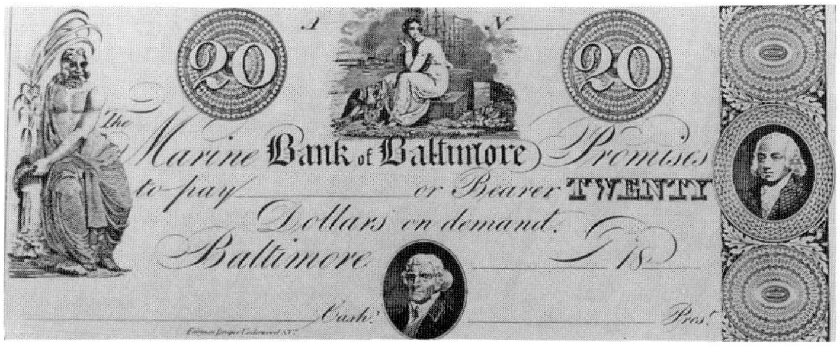

5.115.37 P

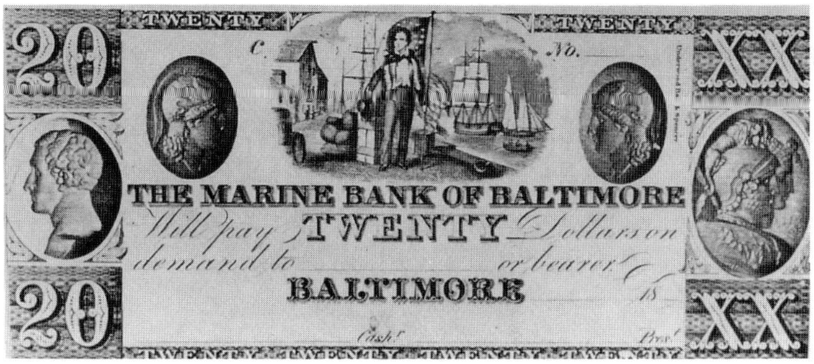

5.115.38 P

5.115.39 A R-7

$20.00 Ca. 1840s–50s. Engraving, imprint: Durand & Co., New York. Red TWENTY. Altered from $20.00 note, Globe Bank, New York City, NY1625G14. (MD90A5)

5.115.40 SENC

$20.00 Ca. 1860s. Engraving, imprint: American Bank Note Co. *Lower left corner:* 2 XX 0. *Lower right corner/right:* Dr. Kane's Arctic expedition, men, dogs, boat, etc. *Left:* 1/2-length figure of girl seated in chair / TWENTY. Tint is red, including die bearing "20" at upper right. (MD90G82)

5.115.41 SENC

$50.00 Ca. 1810. Engraving, imprint: Murray & Draper. Association issue. Promissory inscription reads "The President, Directors & Company . . . promise to pay out of the JOINT FUNDS thereof and NO OTHER according to the Articles of the Association . . . " (MD90G14)

5.115.42 P R-7

$50.00 Ca. 1810s. Engraving, imprint: Murray & Draper. Proof. (MD90G84)

5.115.43 P R-7

$50.00 Ca. 1825–30s. Engraving, imprint: Fairman, Draper, Underwood & Co. Proof. (MD90G88)

5.115.44 SENC

$50.00 Ca. 1850s. Engraving, imprint: Unknown. *Center:* 50; woman seated with anchor, ships in background; 50. *Left:* 50 / medallion head / 50, all across. *Right:* 50 / medallion head bearing 50 / FIFTY. *Between signatures:* Dog and safe. (MD90G92)

5.115.45 SENC

$50.00 Ca. 1860s. Engraving, imprint: American Bank Note Co. *Lower left/left corner:* Allegorical woman, ships in background. *Lower right corner:* Female portrait / 50. *Upper left:* 50. *Right:* 50 / anchor, bales, etc. Tint is red. (MD90G94)

5.115.46 SENC

$100.00 Ca. 1810s. Engraving, imprint: Murray & Draper. *Center right:* 100; sailing ship; 100. *Left:* Panel with HUNDRED, across. (MD90G96)

5.115.39 A

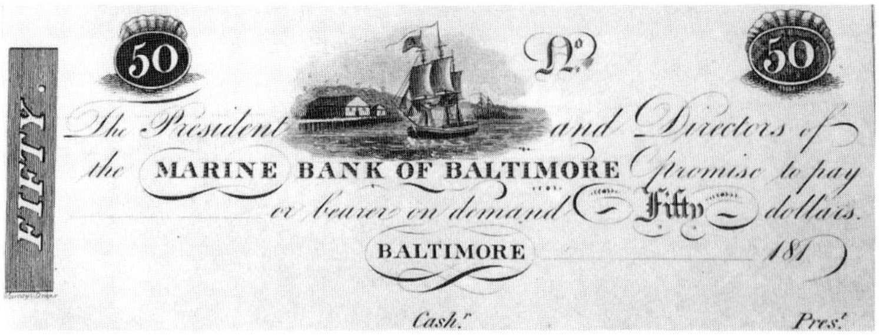

5.115.42 P

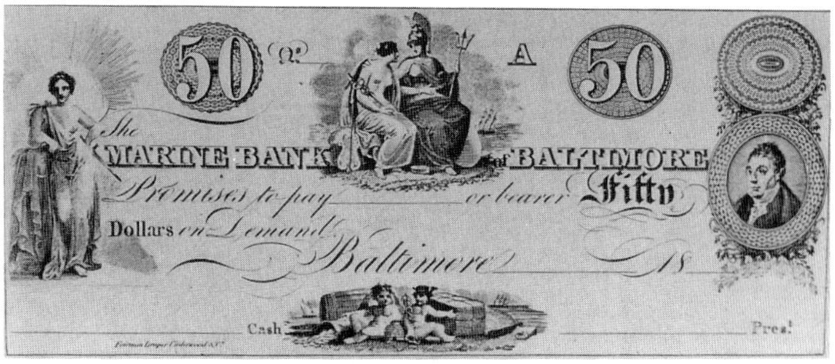

5.115.43 P

5.115.47 P R-7

$100.00 Ca. 1825–30s. Engraving, imprint: Fairman, Draper, Underwood & Co. Proof. (MD90G98)

5.115.47 C R-7

$100.00 Ca. 1825–30s. Engraving, imprint: Fairman, Draper, Underwood & Co. Counterfeit of note similar to No. 5.115.47 P. (MD90C98)

5.115.48 SENC

$100.00 Ca. 1850s. Engraving, imprint: Unknown. *Center:* 100 on medallion head; woman with wand seated on bales, ships in left background; 100 on medallion head. *Left:* 100 on medallion head / male portrait / 100 on medallion head, all across. *Right:* Full-length portrait of Lafayette. *Between signatures:* Two cherubs in boat. (MD90G100)

5.115.49 SENC

$100.00 Ca. 1860s. Engraving, imprint: American Bank Note Co. *Upper left center:* Shipyard scene. *Right center:* Sailor seated on anchor holding flag. *Right:* Eagle / 100. Red tint, including "C" at lower left and right corner. (MD90G102)

5.115.47 P

5.115.47 C

5.116 Marine Exchange Office of Baltimore

The issuer, Capt. M. Vicente, was listed in the 1840–41 city directory as a general agent at 42 1/2 Gay St., near the Shot Tower; and in 1842 as the "superintendent and general agent of ship and steamboat building, 42 north Gay Street," opposite Odd Fellows Hall.

5.116.3 R-7

25c Printed partial year date 184_. Ca. 1840. Lithography, imprint: Lith. by E. Weber & Co., Balto. Similar to 50c, No. 5.116.4. One-half of a 25c note has been recorded, possibly used in lieu of 12 1/2c needed for small change.

5.116.4 R-7

50c Printed partial year date 184_. Ca. 1840. Lithography, imprint: Lith. by E. Weber & Co., Balto.

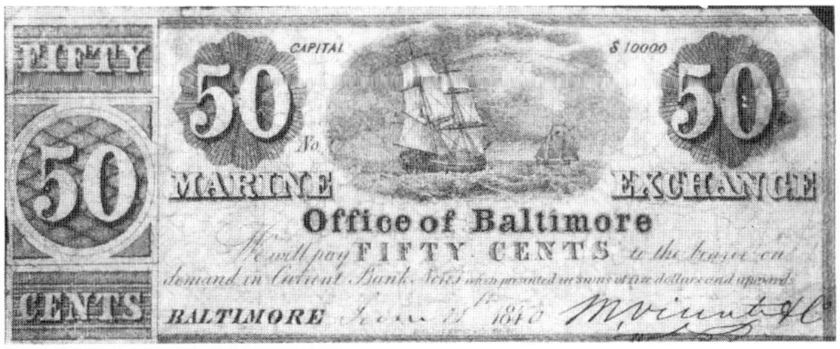

5.116.4

5.116.5 R-7

$1.00 Printed partial year date 184_. Ca. 1840. Lithography, imprint: Lith. by E. Weber & Co., Balto.

5.116.5

5.117 T. T. Martin & Co.

The issuer was an importer of wines and liquors and a general commission merchant, located at 72 S. Calvert St. from 1858 to 1864.

5.117.3 R-7

3c Printed date January 20th, 1863. Lithography, imprint: Lith. by A. Hoen & Co., Balto. Same design as 3c, No. 5.117.5.

5.117.4 R-7

3c Printed date February 4th, 1863. Lithography, imprint: Lith. by A. Hoen & Co., Balto. Same design as 3c, No. 5.117.5.

5.117.5 R-6

3c Printed date February 20th 1863. Lithography, imprint: Lith. by A. Hoen & Co., Balto.

5.117.6 R-6

10c Printed partial year date 186_. Lithography, imprint: Lith by A. Hoen & Co., Balto. Similar to 3c note, No. 5.117.5, with "No. ____" added at top.

5.117.5

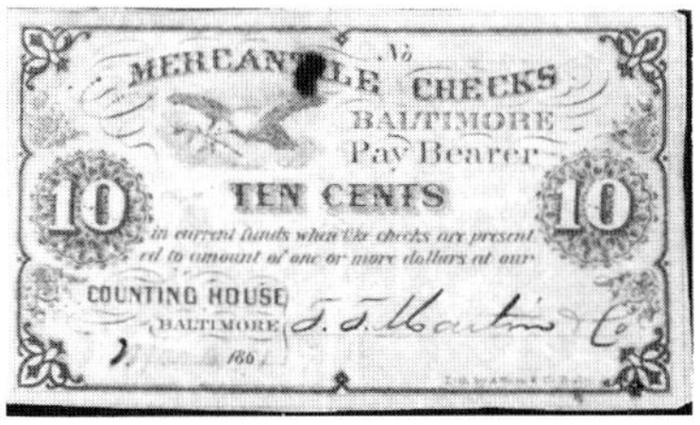

5.117.6

5.118 The Bank of Maryland

Charter approved December 14, 1790, opened for business July 1, 1791. In 1833, the president of the bank, Evan Poultney, together with Reverdy Johnson, Evan T. Ellicott, Hugh McElderry, and John Glenn, all prominent Baltimore citizens, allegedly manipulated the bank stock to their personal advantage. The bank failed in 1834. Its location was at 17 South St.

5.118.1 SENC

6 1/4c Printed partial date Oct. 1815. Letterpress, no imprint. Similar to 6 1/4c, No. 5.118.2, except for date. (MD95G4)

5.118.2 R-5

6 1/4c Printed partial date September 1816. Letterpress, no imprint. (MD95G4a)

5.118.3 R-7

12 1/2c Printed partial date October 1815. Letterpress, no imprint. Similar to 12 1/2c, No. 5.118.4, except for date. (MD95G8)

5.118.4 R-5

12 1/2c Printed partial date September 1816. Letterpress, no imprint. (MD95G8a)

5.118.5 SENC

25c Printed partial date Oct. 1815. Letterpress, no imprint. Similar to 25c, No. 5.118.6, except for date. (MD95G12)

5.118.6 R-5

25c Printed partial date September 1816. Letterpress, no imprint. (MD95G12a)

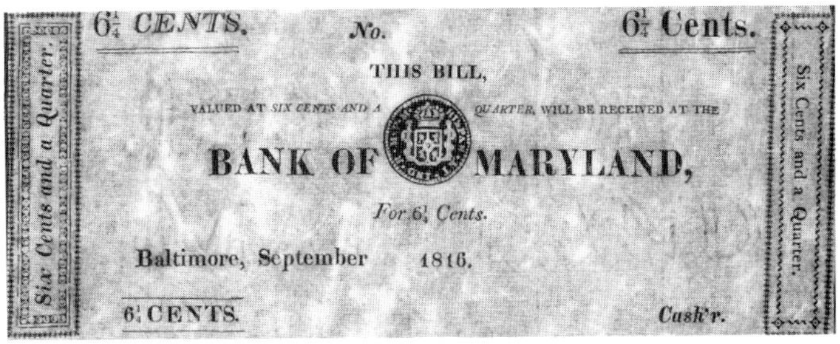

5.118.2

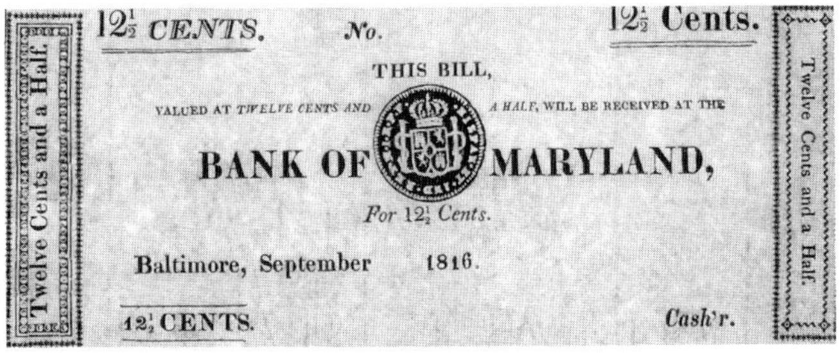

5.118.4

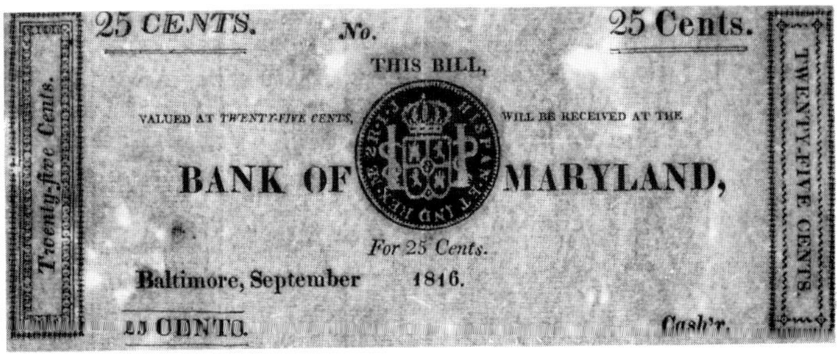

5.118.6

5.118.7 R-5

50c Printed partial date October 1815. Letterpress, no imprint. (MD95G16)

5.118.8 SENC

50c Printed partial date September 1816. Letterpress, no imprint. Similar to 50c, No. 5.118.7, except for date. (MD95G16a)

5.118.9 R-7

$1.00 Printed year date 1814. Letterpress, no imprint. (MD95G20)

5.118.10 R-6

$1.00 Ca. 1810s–30s. Engraving, imprint: MURRAY, DRAPER, FAIRMAN & CO. Thin pink paper with red silk threads, watermarked nine interlocking circles. (MD95G24a)

5.118.10 P R-7

$1.00 Ca. 1810s–30s. Engraving, imprint: MURRAY, DRAPER, FAIRMAN & CO. Similar to No. 5.118.10, except on white paper. Proof.

5.118.11 R-6

$2.00 Ca. 1810s–30s. Engraving, imprint: MURRAY, DRAPER, FAIRMAN & CO. Thin pink paper with red silk threads, watermarked nine interlocking circles. (MD95G28a)

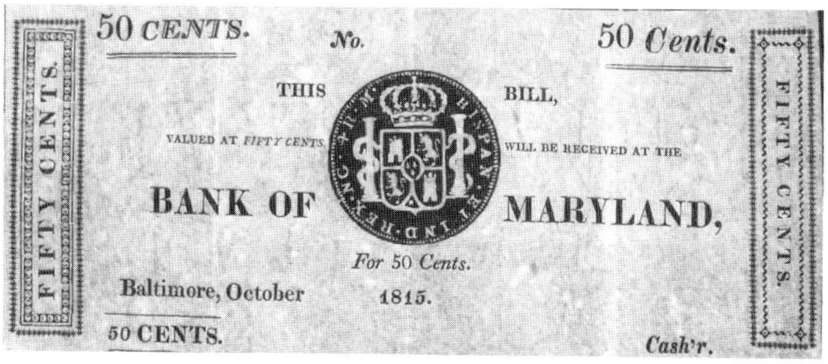

5.118.7

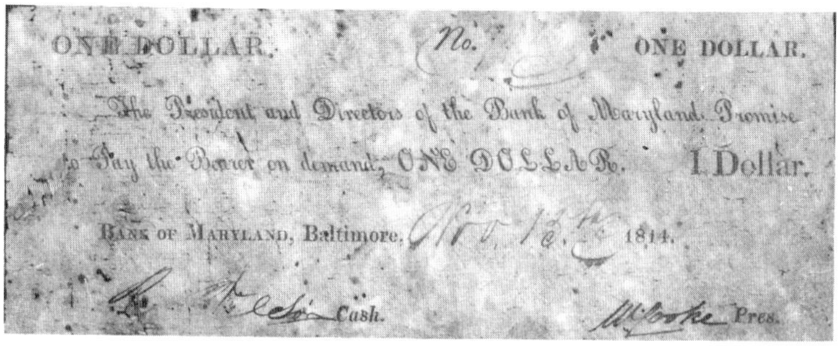

5.118.9

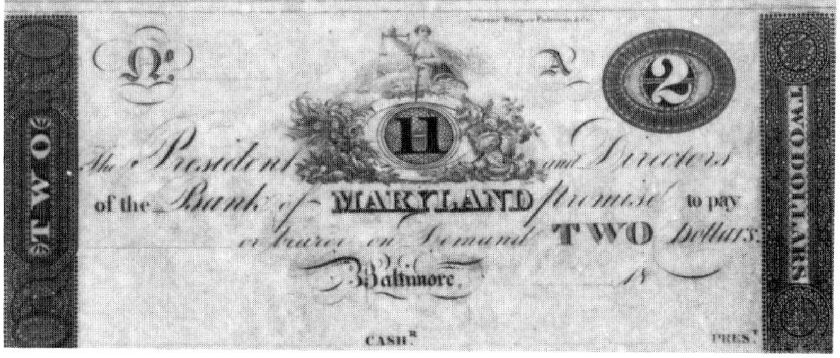

5.118.10 5.118.11

5.118.11 P R-7

$2.00 Ca. 1810s–30s. Engraving, imprint: MURRAY, DRAPER, FAIRMAN & CO. Similar to No. 5.118.11, except on white paper. Proof.

5.118.12 SENC

$2.00 Ca. 1814. Engraving, no imprint. Similar to $1.00, No. 5.118.9. (MD95G28)

5.118.13 R-7

$5.00 Ca. 1790s–1810s. Engraving, no imprint. Similar to counterfeit No. 5.118.13 C. (MD95G32)

5.118.13 C R-7

$5.00 Ca. 1790s–1810s. Engraving, no imprint. Counterfeit of No. 5.118.13. (MD95C32)

5.118.14 R-3

$5.00 Ca. 1810s–30s. Engraving: MURRAY, DRAPER, FAIRMAN & CO. (MD95G36)

5.118.14 P R-7

$5.00 Ca. 1810s–30s. Engraving, imprint: MURRAY, DRAPER, FAIRMAN & CO. Proof.

5.118.15 R-3

$5.00 Ca. 1825–30s. Engraving, imprint: FAIRMAN, DRAPER, UNDERWOOD & CO. (MD95G40)

5.118.11. P

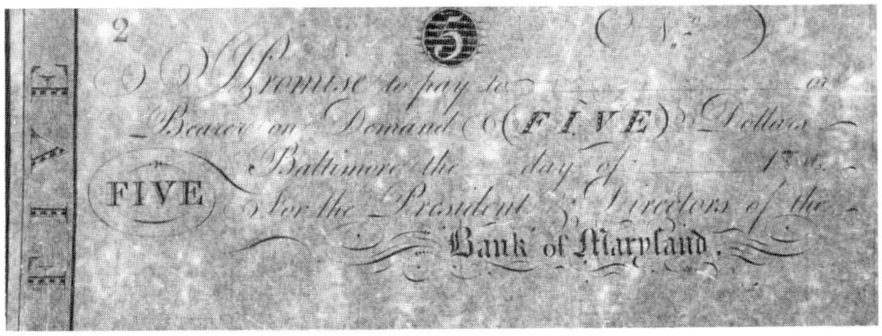

5.118.13 C

5.118.14

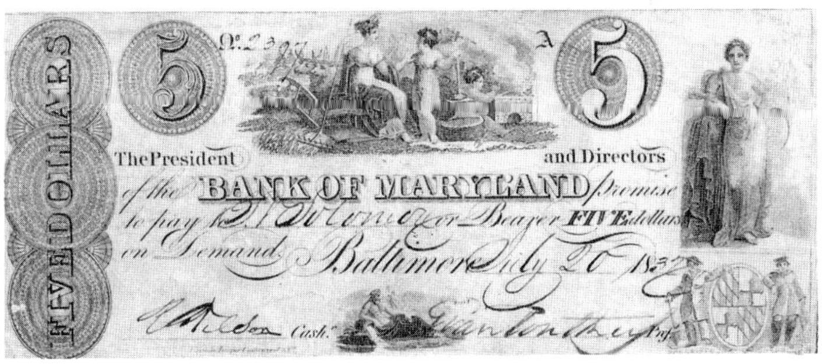

5.118.15

5.118.15 P R-7

$5.00 Ca. 1825–30s. Engraving, imprint: FAIRMAN, DRAPER, UNDERWOOD & CO. Proof.

5.118.16 R-3

$5.00 Ca. 1830s. Engraving, imprint: CHAS. TOPPAN & CO., Phila. (MD95G44)

5.118.16 P R-6

$5.00 Ca. 1830s. Engraving, imprint: CHAS TOPPAN & CO., Phila. Proof.

5.118.18 SENC

$10.00 Ca. late 1790s–1810s. Engraving, no imprint. Similar to counterfeit No. 5.118.18 C. (MD95G48)

5.118.18 C R-7

$10.00 Ca. late 1790s–1810s. Engraving, no imprint. Counterfeit of No. 5.118.18. (MD95C48)

5.118.19 R-5

$10.00 Ca. 1810s–30s. Engraving, imprint: MURRAY, DRAPER, FAIRMAN & CO. (MD95G52)

5.118.19 P R-7

$10.00 Ca. 1810s–30s. Engraving, imprint: MURRAY, DRAPER, FAIRMAN & CO. Proof.

5.118.20 SENC

$20.00 Ca. late 1790s–1810s. Engraving, no imprint. Similar to No. 5.118.18. (MD95G56)

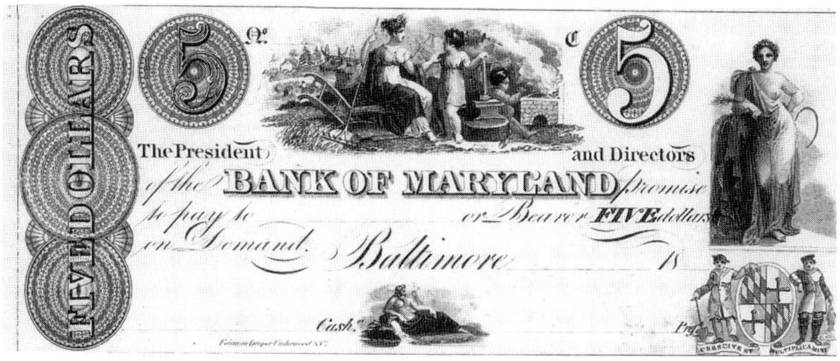

5.118.15 P

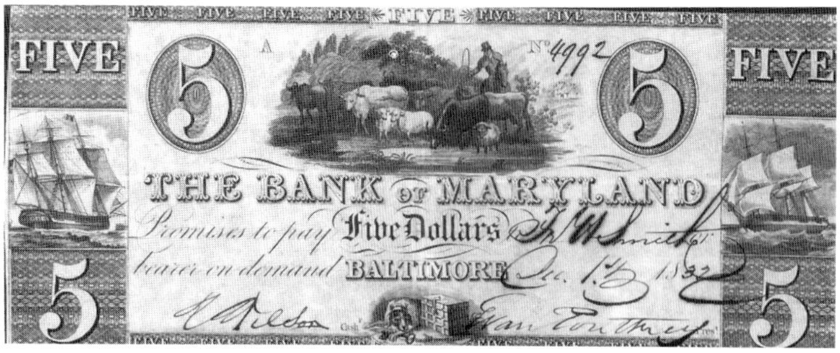

5.118.16

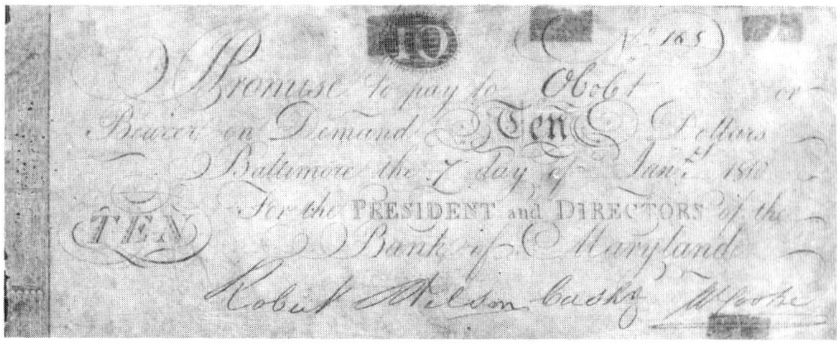

5.118.18 C

5.118.19

5.118.21 R-5

$20.00 Ca. 1810s–30s. Engraving, imprint: MURRAY, DRAPER, FAIRMAN & CO. (MD95G60)

5.118.21 P R-7

$20.00 Ca. 1810s–30s. Engraving, imprint: MURRAY, DRAPER, FAIRMAN & CO. Proof.

5.118.22 SENC

$50.00 Ca. late 1790s–1810s. Engraving, no imprint. Similar to $100.00, No. 5.118.24 (MD95G64)

5.118.23 R-5

$50.00 Ca. 1810s–30s. Engraving, imprint: MURRAY, DRAPER, FAIRMAN & CO. (MD95G68)

5.118.23 P R-7

$50.00 Ca. 1810s–30s. Engraving, imprint: MURRAY, DRAPER, FAIRMAN & CO. Proof.

5.118.21

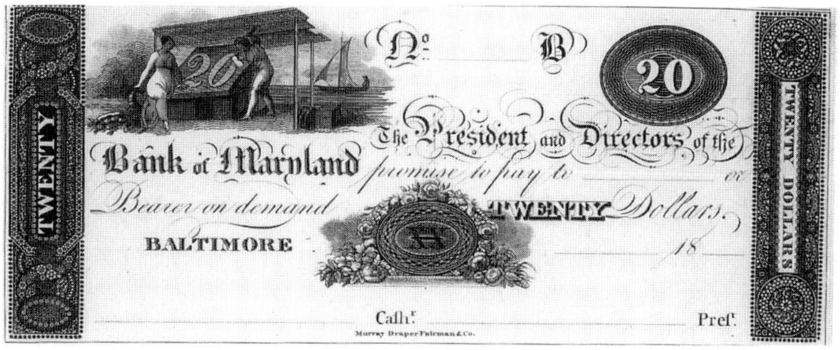

5.118.21 P

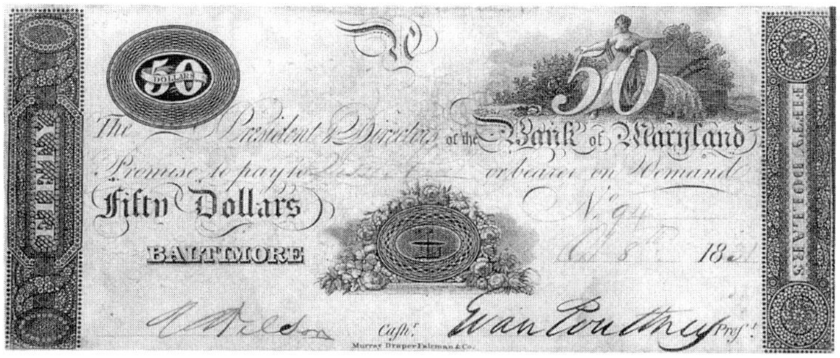

5.118.23

5.118.23 P

5.118.24 R-7

$100.00 Ca. late 1790s–1810s. Engraving, no imprint. (MD95G72)

5.118.24 C R-7

$100.00 Ca. late 1790s–1810s. Engraving, no imprint. Counterfeit of No. 5.118.24. (MD95C72)

5.118.25 R-7

$100.00 Ca. 1810s–30s. Engraving, imprint: MURRAY, DRAPER, FAIRMAN & CO. (MD95G76)

5.118.25 P R-7

$100.00 Ca. 1810s–30s. Engraving, imprint: MURRAY, DRAPER, FAIRMAN & CO. Proof.

5.118.26 R-7

$500.00 Ca. 1830s. Engraving, imprint: CHAS. TOPPAN & CO., Phila. (MD95G80)

5.118.26 P R-7

$500.00 Ca. 1830s. Engraving, imprint: CHAS. TOPPAN & CO., Phila. Proof.

5.118.27 R-7

$1000.00 Ca. 1830s. Engraving, imprint: CHAS. TOPPAN & CO., Phila. (MD95G84)

5.118.27 P R-7

$1000.00 Ca. 1830s. Engraving, imprint: CHAS. TOPPAN & CO., Phila. Proof.

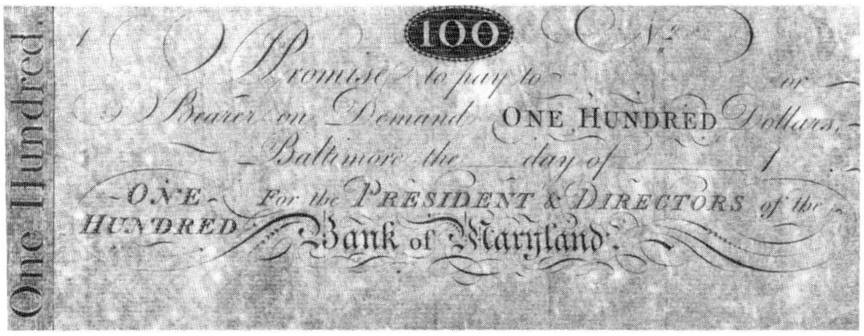

5.118.24

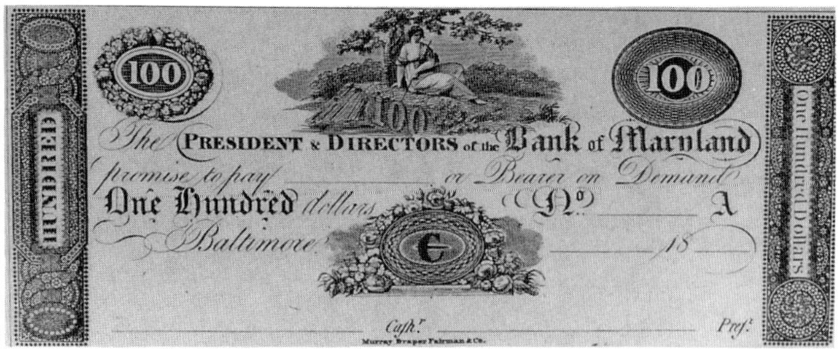

5.118.25 P

5.118.26 P

5.118.27 P

5.118.29 R-7

Post Note. Ca. 1791–95. Engraving, no imprint. The denominations of these notes were written in.

5.118.35 P R-7

$5.00 Ca. 1833–35. Engraving, imprint: Draper, Underwood, Bald & Spencer. Issued by the Union Bank of the State of Tennessee in Nashville. Payable at the Bank of Maryland in Baltimore. Proof. (TN210G190)

5.118.36 P R-7

$10.00 Ca. 1833–35. Engraving, imprint: Draper, Underwood, Bald & Spencer. Issued by the Union Bank of the State of Tennessee in Nashville, payable at the Bank of Maryland in Baltimore. Proof.

5.118.37 P R-7

$20.00 Ca. 1833–35. Engraving, imprint: Draper, Underwood, Bald & Spencer. Issued by the Union Bank of the State of Tennessee in Nashville. Payable at the Bank of Maryland in Baltimore. Proof. (TN210G194)

5.118.29

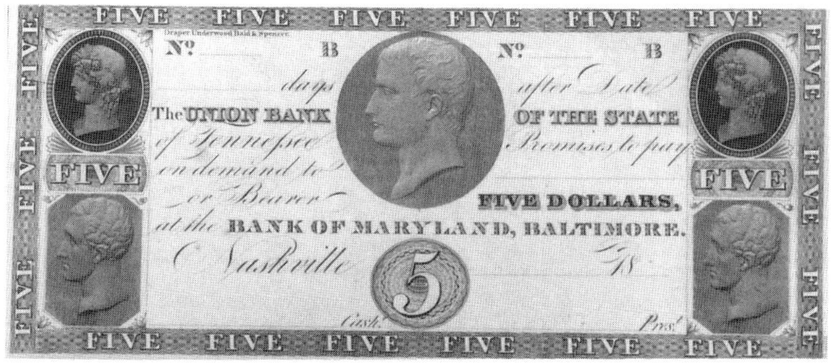

5.118.35 P

5.118.36 P

5.119 Maryland State Colonization Society

Founded in 1832 for the purpose of returning freed American Negro slaves to Africa, the society issued paper currency dated 1837 to provide a circulating medium for the colony Maryland in Liberia. The notes constituted the currency of the colony for many years. Prior to shipment to the colony, the notes were signed by the society's president, John H. B. Latrobe, and before issuance they were countersigned by the governor of Maryland in Liberia. The underprints at the ends and the ovals under the figures of value were lithographed. Facsimiles of the notes were printed on thin pink paper in 1885 for inclusion in a pamphlet "Maryland in Liberia," a reprint of a paper read before the Maryland Historical Society by John H. B. Latrobe on March 9, 1885. Sheets of the facsimiles were folded vertically for binding into the Latrobe pamphlets.

5.119.1 R-6

5c Printed partial date Novem. 1837. Letterpress, no imprint. Genuine note never shipped to Liberia. Black and light orange brown on thin white wove paper.

5.119.2 R-6

10c Printed partial date November 1837. Letterpress, no imprint. Genuine note never shipped to Liberia. Black and light orange brown on thin white wove paper.

5.119.3 R-6

25c Printed partial date November 1837. Letterpress, no imprint. Genuine note never shipped to Liberia. Black and light orange brown on thin white wove paper.

5.119.4 R-7

50c Printed partial date Nov. 1837. Letterpress, no imprint. Photograph of original note not available. See illustration of facsimile, No. 5.1194 F, for design.

5.119.5 R-7

$1.00 Printed partial date November, 1837. Letterpress, no imprint. Photograph of original note not available. See illustration of facsimile No. 5.119.5 F for design.

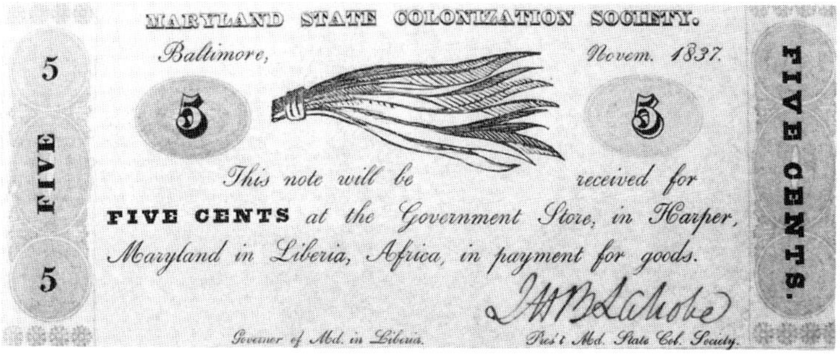

5.119.1

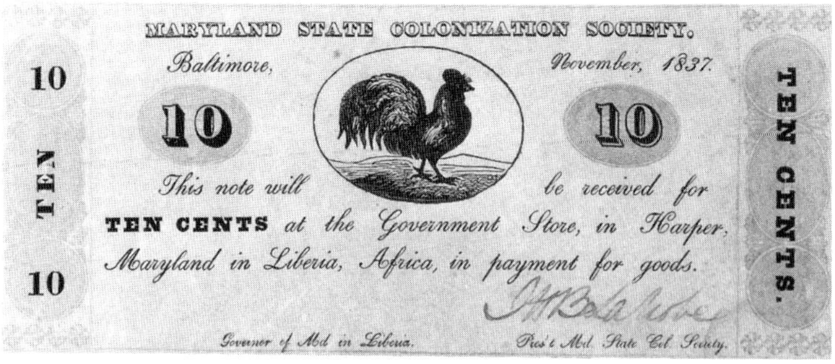

5.119.2

5.119.3

5.119.1 F–5 F

1885. Letterpress, no imprint. Facsimiles printed on thin pink bond paper, watermarked vertically in the sheet, double-lined CRANE & CO. BOSTON MASS 1883. Buff and black. The facsimiles were *not* produced from the plates used to print the original notes in 1837, there being numerous small differences in the details of the designs.

5.119.1 F R-4

5c Printed partial date Novem. 1837. Letterpress, no imprint. Facsimile of No. 5.119.1.

5.119.2 F R-4

10c Printed partial date Novem. 1837. Letterpress, no imprint. Facsimile of No. 5.119.2.

5.119.3 F R-4

25c Printed partial date Novem. 1837. Letterpress, no imprint. Facsimile of No. 5.119.3.

5.119.4 F R-4

50c Printed partial date Novem. 1837. Letterpress, no imprint. Facsimile of No. 5.119.4.

5.119.5 F R-4

$1.00 Printed partial date Novem. 1837. Letterpress, no imprint. Facsimile of No. 5.119.5.

5.119.1 F 5.119.2 F 5.119.3 F

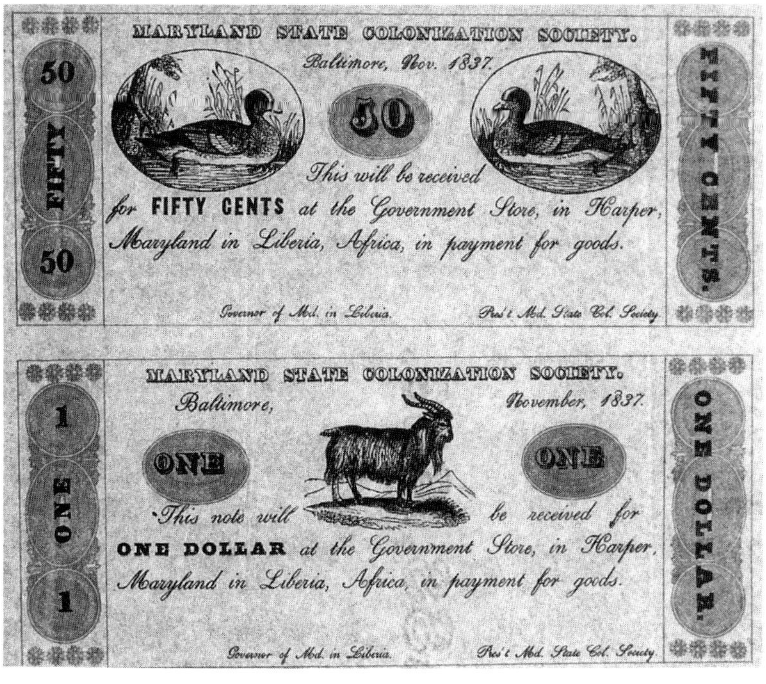

5.119.4 F 5.119.5 F

5.120 Charles McClean

The issuer was the proprietor of the Union Tavern at 6 Camden St., being so listed in the 1814 city directory.

5.120.3 R-7
3c Printed date September 12, 1815. Letterpress, no imprint.

5.120.4 R-7
6 1/4c Printed date September 12, 1815. Letterpress, no imprint.

5.120.3

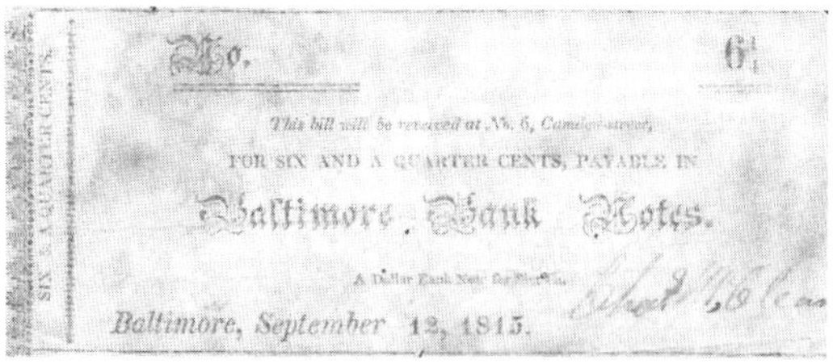

5.120.4

5.121 J. N. McCormick

John McCormick was a grocer on Harford Avenue "south of the church," according to the 1840–41 directory.

5.121.5 R-7
$1.00 Printed partial year date 184_. Ca. 1840. Lithography, no imprint (probably printed by E. Weber & Co., Baltimore).

5.121.5

5.122 Jas. McDonnell

The issuer was a grocer at the corner of Strawberry Alley and Fleet Street, Fells Point, being so listed in the 1816 city directory.

5.122.2 R-7
12 1/2c Printed date September 21, 1815. Letterpress, no imprint. The typeset inscription reads "This bill will be received at the corner of Fleet St. and Strawberry Alley, for goods, or notes of the banks of Maryland for twelve and a-half cents. Baltimore, September 21, 1815."

5.123 **Geo. & A. McNeal**

This name appears in the "List of Small Notes Circulating in Baltimore" published in the *Baltimore Clipper* of September 12, 1840. The issuers were listed as commission merchants at the southwest corner of Pratt and Frederick streets. No examples of their notes have as yet been recorded.

5.124 **The Mechanics Bank of Baltimore**

Operated as an unchartered association until 1806. Charter approved December 31, 1806. Converted to and became the National Mechanics Bank of Baltimore in 1865. The bank was located on the southeast corner of Calvert and Fayette streets.

5.124.1 SENC
6 1/4c Printed year date 1816. Letterpress, imprint: J. Robinson, Printer. Similar to 25c, No. 5.124.3. (MD100G20)

5.124.2 SENC
12 1/2c Printed year date 1816. Letterpress, imprint: J. Robinson, Printer. Similar to 25c, No. 5.124.3. (MD100G22)

5.124.3 R-7
25c Printed year date 1816. Letterpress, imprint: J. Robinson, Printer. (MD100G24)

5.124.4 SENC
50c Printed year date 1816. Letterpress, imprint: J. Robinson, Printer. Similar to $1.00, No. 5.124.5. (MD100G26)

5.124.5 SENC
$1.00 Printed partial year date 181_. Letterpress, imprint: J. Robinson, Printer. Similar to 25c, No. 5.124.3. No other information available. (MD100G28)

5.124.6 R-7
$1.00 Printed year date 1816. Letterpress, imprint: J. Robinson, Printer. (MD100G30)

5.124.7 P R-7
$1.00 Ca. 1817–20s. Engraving, imprint: CONE, FREEMAN & CO., BALTIMORE. Proof. (MD100G32)

5.124.7 C R-7
$1.00 Ca. late 1810s. Engraving, imprint: CONE, FREEMAN & CO., BALTIMORE. Counterfeit of note of similar design to No. 5.124.7 P. (MD100C32)

5.124.3

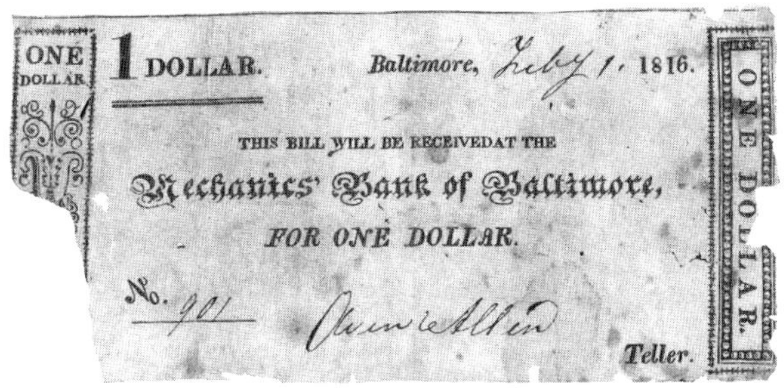

5.124.6

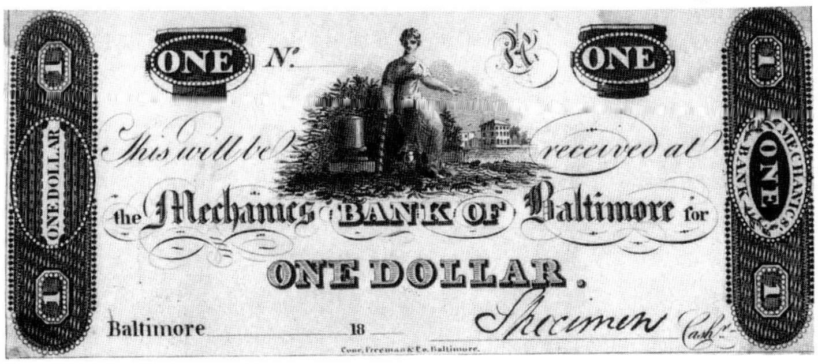

5.124.7 P

5.124.8 R-7

$1.00 Printed date May 4, 1844. Engraving, imprint: TOPPAN, CARPENTER & CO. See $1.00, No. 5.124.10, for similar note dated 1861. (MD100G36)

5.124.9 N SENC

$1.00 Ca. 1850s. Engraving, imprint: Unknown. *Center:* Three mechanics at work. Nongenuine, unattributed. (MD100N5)

5.124.10 R-7

$1.00 Printed date May 4, 1861. Engraving, imprint: Toppan, Carpenter & Co. Same as No. 5.124.8, except for 1861 date. Reissued during the Civil War utilizing the original plate. (MD100G36a)

5.124.11 R-6

$2.00 Printed partial year date, 181_. Ca. 1814–15. Letterpress, no imprint. (MD100G40)

5.124.12 R-5

$2.00 Printed date 1816. Letterpress, imprint: J. Robinson, Printer. (MD100G42)

5.124.13 SENC

$2.00 Ca. 1817–20s. Engraving, imprint: Cone, Freeman & Co., Baltimore. Similar to counterfeit No. 5.124.13 C. (MD100G44)

5.124.8

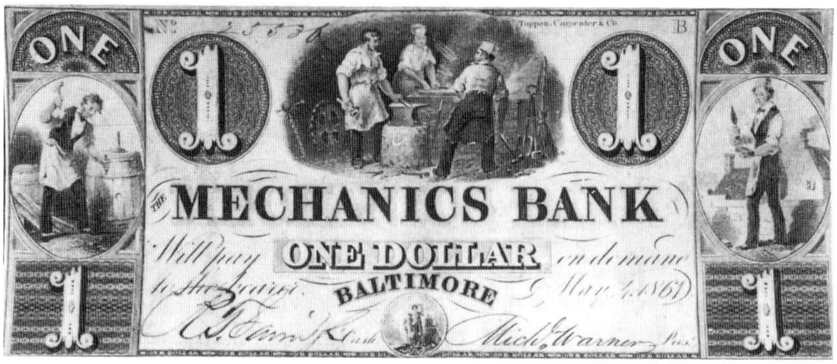

5.124.10

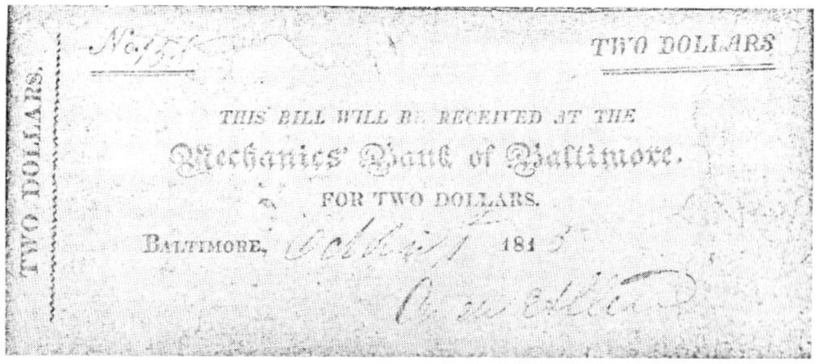

5.124.11

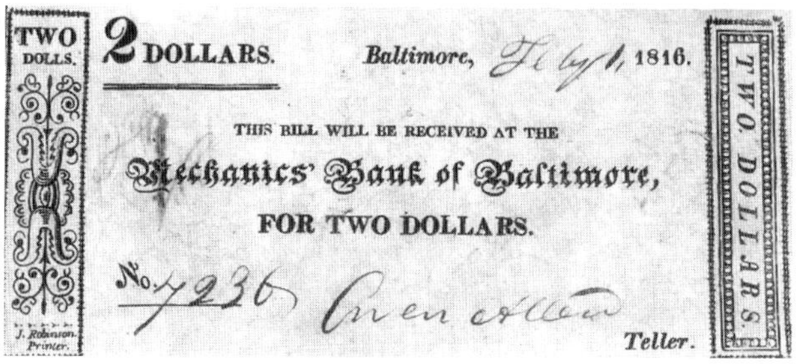

5.124.12

5.124.13 C R-4

$2.00 Ca. 1817–20s. Engraving, imprint: CONE, FREEMAN & CO., BALTIMORE. Counterfeit of No. 5.124.13. (MD100C44)

5.124.14 A SENC

$2.00 Ca. 1840. Engraving, imprint: Durand & Co., New York. *Center:* Manhattan reclining with his left hand on a water urn, right hand on staff; 2. *Left:* 2 on large die. *Right:* Half-length figure of woman, in circle, on panel of wheat and corn ears. Altered from $2.00 Globe Bank, New York City, NY1625G2. (MD100A5)

5.124.15 A R-7

$2.00 Ca. 1840s. Engraving, imprint: DURAND & CO., NEW YORK. Altered from $2.00 Globe Bank, New York City, NY1625G4. (MD100A10)

5.124.16 A SENC

$3.00 Ca. 1825–30s. Engraving, imprint: Fairman, Draper, Underwood & Co. *Center:* 3; Liberty and Prosperity seated flanking shield bearing three plows and surmounted by horse's head; oval portrait of Washington. *Left:* THREE, across. *Right:* 3 / Justice standing, right arm with balance resting on column, left hand on hip. *Between signatures:* Two jockeys on racehorses. Altered from $3.00 State Bank at Trenton, N.J., NJ560G16. (MD100A25)

5.124.17 A SENC

$3.00 Ca. 1840. Engraving, imprint: Durand and Co., New York. *Center:* Manhattan reclining with his left hand on a water urn, right hand on staff; 3. *Left:* 3 on large die. *Right:* 3 on die, on panel of wheat and corn ears. Altered from $3.00 Globe Bank, New York City, NY1625G6. (MD100A15)

5.124.18 A R-6

$3.00 Ca. 1840s. Engraving, imprint: DURAND AND COMP. NEW YORK. Altered from $3.00 Globe Bank, New York City, NY1625G8. (MD100A20)

5.124.19 S R-7

$3.00 Ca. 1849. Engraving, no imprint. Probably spurious.

5.124.13 C

5.124.15 A

5.124.18 A

5.124.19 S

5.124.20 s R-6

$3.00 Printed date October 18, 1862. Engraving, imprint: Rawdon, Wright, Hatch & Edson, New York. Overprint THREE and "3 3" in orange. Spurious note. (MD100S5)

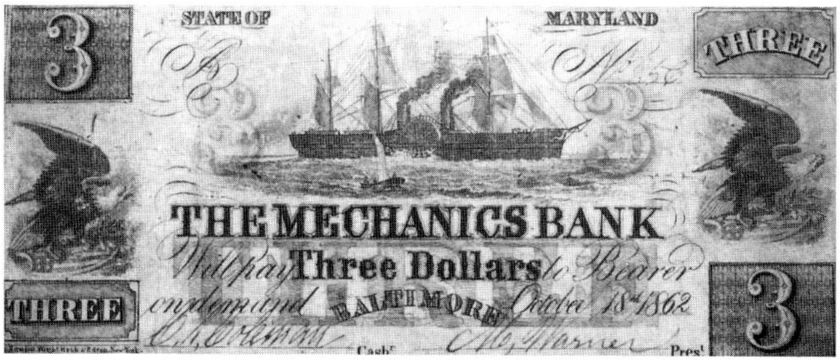

5.124.20 s

5.124.21 SENC

$5.00 Ca. 1806. Engraving, imprint: Unknown. Association issue. Text reads "pay out of their joint funds." No other information available. (MD100G8)

5.124.22 SENC

$5.00 Ca. 1806–10. Engraving, imprint: Unknown. Similar to counterfeit No. 5.124.22 C. (MD100G48)

5.124.22 C R-5

$5.00 Printed partial year date 180_. Ca. 1806–10. Engraving, no imprint. Counterfeit of No. 5.124.22. (MD100C48)

5.124.22 C

5.124.23 P SENC

$5.00 Ca. 1810s–20s. Engraving, imprint: Murray, Draper, Fairman & Co. Proof. (MD100G50)

5.124.23 P

5.124.24 P R-7

$5.00 Ca. 1820s. Engraving, no imprint (probably Fairman, Draper, Underwood & Co.). Proof.

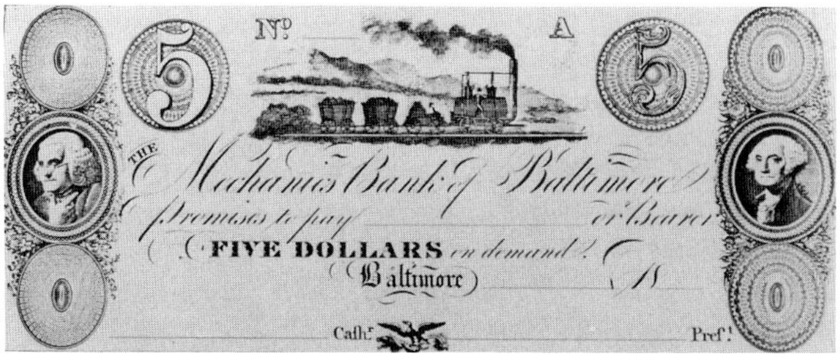

5.124.24 P

5.124.25 P R-7

$5.00 Ca. 1820s. Engraving, no imprint (probably Fairman, Draper, Underwood & Co.). Proof.

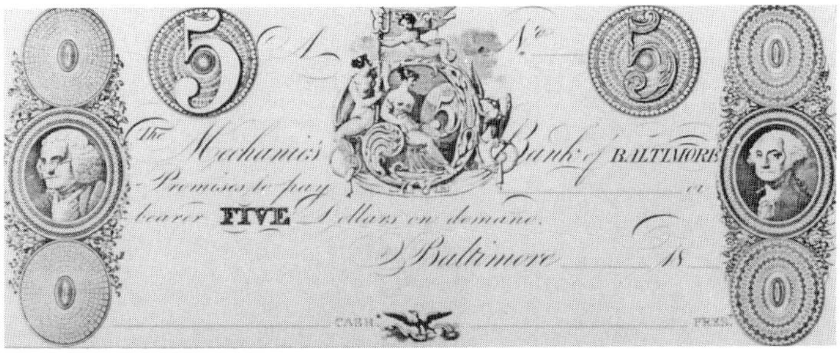

5.124.25 P

5.124.26 A SENC

$5.00 Ca. 1830s. Engraving, imprint: Rawdon, Wright & Hatch. *Center:* 5; woman seated with left elbow on large cogwheel at right; 5. *Left:* FIVE / semi-nude male seated with staff / V. *Right:* V / Vulcan standing at anvil / V. *Between signatures:* Arm and hammer. Altered from $5.00 Mechanics Bank, Montreal, Lower Canada, AS483G4. (MD100A35)

5.124.27 A SENC

$5.00 Ca. late 1830s–40s. Engraving, imprint: Rawdon, Wright & Hatch. *Center:* 5; Amphitrite & Neptune in shell drawn by seahorses; 5. *Left:* FIVE, across. *Right:* V / canal scene in circle / V. *Between signatures:* Steamboat. Altered from $5.00 Commercial Bank of Millington, Millington, Md., No. 83.1.3. (MD100A30)

5.124.28 P R-7

$5.00 Ca. early 1830s–50s. Engraving, imprint: C. Toppan & Co., Philada. Proof. (MD100G52)

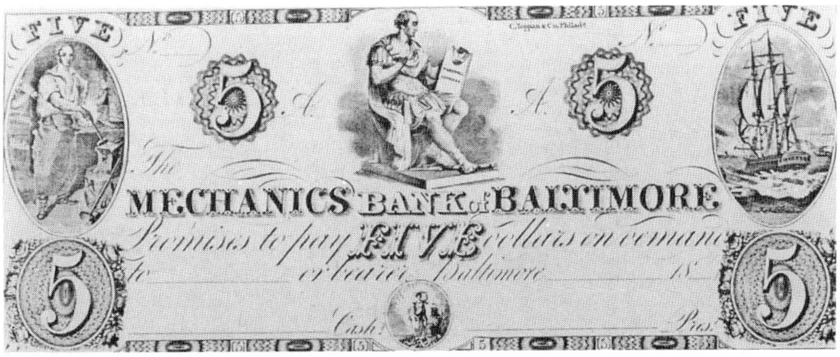

5.124.28 P

5.124.29 P R-7

$5.00 Ca. early 1830s–50s. Engraving, imprint: Chas. Toppan & Co., Philada. Proof.

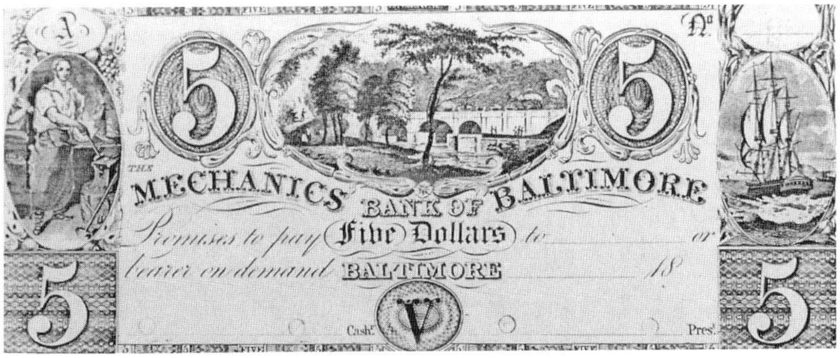

5.124.29 P

5,124.30 SENC

$5.00 Ca. 1840s. Engraving, imprint: Unknown. *Center:* Moneta seated receiving bag of coins from Mercury in clouds at right, griffin on chest at left. (MD100N10)

5.124.31 N SENC

$5.00 Ca. 1840s. Engraving, imprint: Unknown. *Center:* Sailing ship. Nongenuine, unattributed. (MD100N15)

5.124.32 SENC

$10.00 Ca. 1806. Engraving, imprint: Unknown. Association issue. Text reads "Pay out of their joint funds." No other information available. (MD100G10)

5.124.33 SENC

$10.00 Ca. 1806–10. No other information available. Similar to $5.00, No. 5.124.22 C. (MD100G54)

5.124.34 P R-7

$10.00 Ca. 1810s–20s. Engraving, imprint: MURRAY, DRAPER, FAIRMAN & CO. Same as No. 5.124.35 P, but with position letter, imprint, and signer's title. Proof. (MD100G58)

5.124.35 P R-7

$10.00 Ca. 1810s–20s. Engraving, imprint: Murray, Draper, Fairman & Co. Same as No. 5.124.34 P, but without position letter, imprint, or signers' titles. Proof.

5.124.36 P R-7

$10.00 Ca. 1820s. Engraving, no imprint (probably Murray, Draper, Fairman & Co.). Proof.

5.124.37 P R-7

$10.00 Ca. 1830s. Engraving, imprint: FAIRMAN, DRAPER, UNDERWOOD & CO. Proof. Possibly Haxby No. MD100N20.

5.124.38 P R-6

$10.00 Ca. early 1830s–40s. Engraving, imprint: Chas. Toppan & Co., Phila. Similar to counterfeit $10.00, No. 5.124.38 C. Proof. (MD100G60).

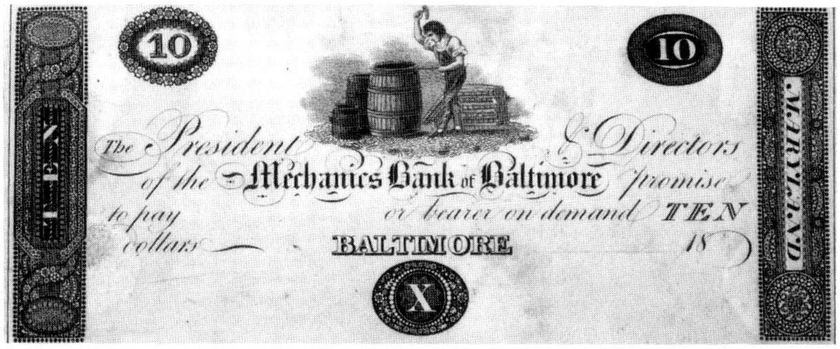

5.124.35 P

5.124.36 P

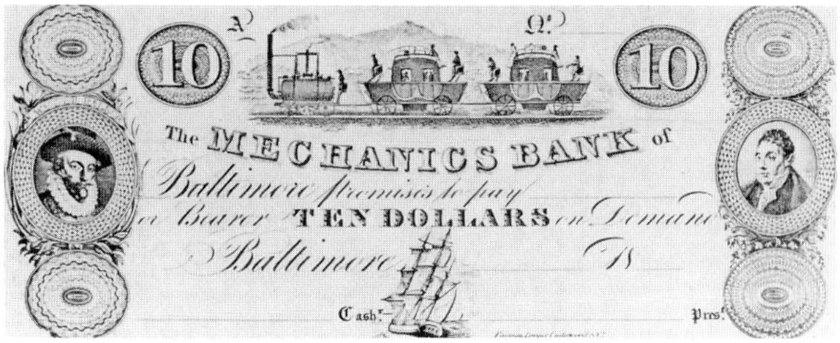

5.124.37 P

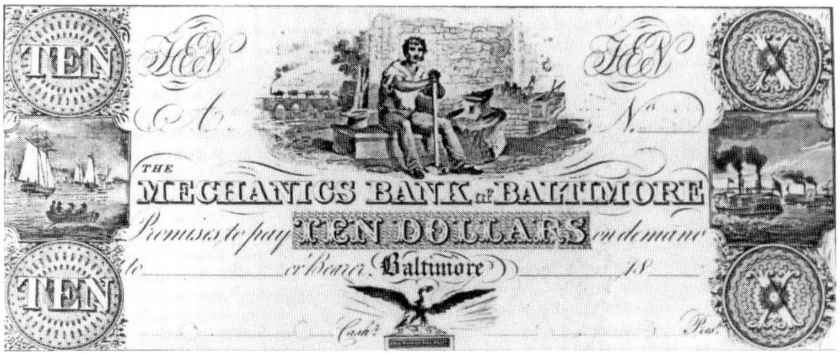

5.124.38 P

5.124.38 C R-6

$10.00 Ca. 1830s–40s. Engraving, imprint: Chas. Toppan & Co., Phila. Counterfeit of note of design similar to No. 5.124.38 P. (MD100C60)

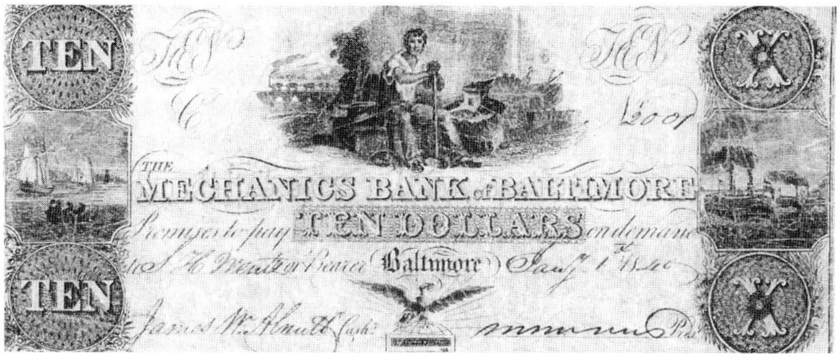

5.124.38 C

5.124.39 A SENC

$10.00 Ca. 1840. Engraving, imprint: Durand & Co. *Center:* X; ships in harbor, large warehouse at left. *Left:* Female artist standing, resting on easel, in square. *Right:* 10 / medallion head in oval / 10. Altered from $10.00 Globe Bank, New York City, NY1625G12. (MD100A50)

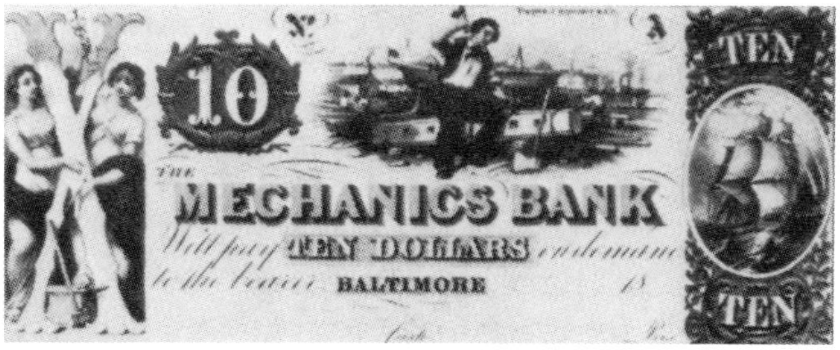

5.124.40 P

5.124.40 P R-7

$10.00 Ca. 1840s–50s. Engraving, imprint: Toppan, Carpenter & Co. Proof. (MD100G62)

5.124.42 A

5.124.41 A SENC

$10.00 Ca. 1840s. Engraving, imprint: Danforth, Underwood, Bald & Spencer. Altered from $10.00 Commercial Bank of Millington, Millington, Md., No. 83.1.6. (MD100A40)

5.124.42 A R-7

$10.00 Ca. 1840s. Engraving, imprint: Rawdon, Wright & Hatch. Altered from $10.00 Commercial Bank of Millington, Millington, Md., No. 83.1.7. (MD100A45)

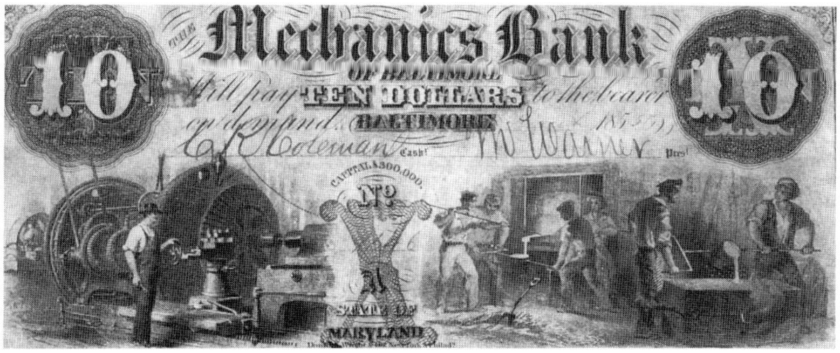

5.124.43 A

5.124.43 A R-7

$10.00 Printed partial date 185_. Ca. 1856–60. Engraving, imprint: Danforth, Wright & Co. New York & Phila. Altered from $10.00 Mechanics Bank, Memphis, Tenn., TN105G8. Green "X" at lower center. (MD100A55)

5.124.44 SENC

$20.00 Ca. 1806. Engraving, imprint: Unknown. Association issue. Text reads "Pay out of their joint funds." (MD100G12)

5.124.45 SENC

$20.00 Ca. 1806–10. No other information available. Similar to $5.00, No. 5.124.22 C. (MD100G64)

5.124.46 P R-7

$20.00 Ca. 1810s–20s. Engraving, imprint: Murray, Draper, Fairman & Co. Proof. (MD100G68)

5.124.47 P R-7

$20.00 Ca. 1820s. Engraving, no imprint (probably Murray, Draper, Fairman & Co.). Similar to No. 5.124.46 P. Proof.

5.124.48 P R-7

$20.00 Ca. early 1830s–40s. Engraving, imprint: C. Toppan & Co., Phila. Proof. (MD100G72)

5.124.48 C R-7

$20.00 Ca. 1830s–40s. Engraving, imprint: Charles Toppan & Co., Phila. Counterfeit of note of similar design to No. 5.124.48 P. (MD100C72)

5.124.49 P R-7

$20.00 Ca. early 1830s–40s. Engraving, no imprint. Same as $20.00, No. 5.124.48 P, except without imprint. Proof.

5.124.50 A SENC

$20.00 Ca. 1830s–40s. Engraving, imprint: Terry Pelton. *Center:* Beehive in oval; Indian man standing with tomahawk in raised right hand, dog and dead deer at right; plowman and two horses in oval. *Left:* XX / canal scene, in square / XX. *Right:* 20 / reaper with sheaf standing under tree, in square / 20. Altered from $20.00 East Bridgewater Bank, East Bridgewater, Mass., MA545G18. (MD100A60)

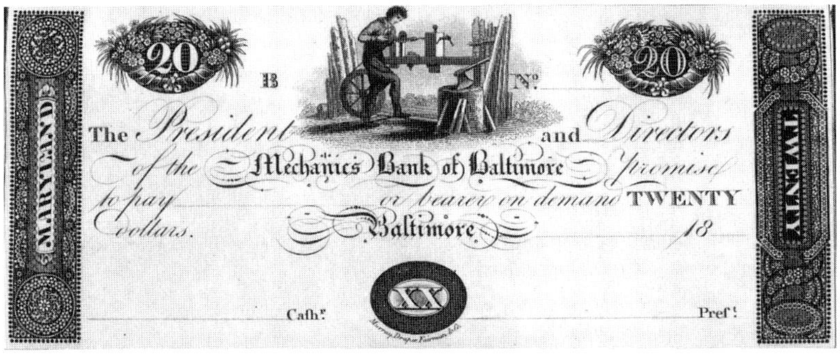

5.124.46 P

5.124.48 P

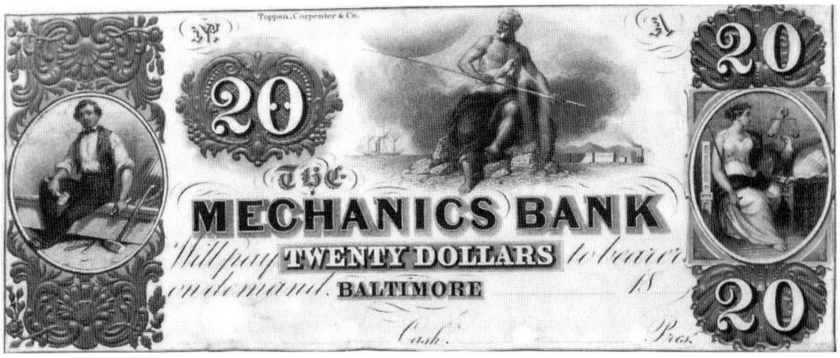

5.124.53 P

5.124.51 A SENC

$20.00 Ca. 1836–40s. Engraving, imprint: Danforth, Underwood & Co.; Underwood, Bald, Spencer & Hufty. *Center:* Diagonal 20, on medallion head; Pat Lyon standing by forge; diagonal 20, on medallion head. *Left:* 20 / primitive train, in oval / XX. *Right:* 20 / cattle, man at right, in oval / XX. Altered from $20.00 Tenth Ward Bank, New York City, NY1935G20. (MD100A65)

5.124.52 N SENC

$20.00 Ca. 1850s. Engraving, imprint: Unknown. *Center:* Deer in stream. Non-genuine, unattributed. (MD100N25)

5.124.53 P R-7

$20.00 Ca. 1856–60s. Engraving, imprint: Toppan, Carpenter, & Co. Proof. (MD100G74)

5.124.54 SENC

$50.00 Ca. 1806. Engraving, imprint: Unknown. Association issue. Text reads "pay out of their joint funds." (MD100G14)

5.124.55 SENC

$50.00 Ca. 1806–10s. No information available. Similar to $5.00, No. 5.124.22. (MD100G78)

5.124.56 P R-7

$50.00 Ca. 1812–20s. Engraving, imprint: Murray, Draper, Fairman & Co. Proof. (MD100G82)

5.124.57 R SENC

$50.00 Ca. 1820s. Engraving, imprint: Murray, Draper, Fairman & Co. Raised from note of design similar to $5.00, No. 5.124.23 P. (MD100R5)

5.124.58 P R-7

$50.00 Ca. 1830s–50s. Engraving, imprint: Charles Toppan & Co., Phila. Proof. (MD100G86)

5.124.59 SENC

$50.00 Ca. 1850s. Engraving, imprint: Unknown. *Center:* Steamship, city in background. *Left and right:* 50 / FIFTY across. *Between signatures:* 50; Indian head; 50. (MD100G88)

5.124.60 SENC

$100.00 Ca. 1850s. Engraving, imprint: Unknown. *Center:* Train, rocks, trees, etc. *Left:* 100 / landscape, arched bridge in background. *Right:* 100 / train crossing bridge / 100. (MD100G92)

5.124.61 SENC

$100.00 Ca. 1850s. Engraving, imprint: Unknown. *Center:* Train, factory, cow, and dog / C, C. *Left:* Indian head / 100. *Right:* 100 / 100. *Between signatures:* Wheels. (MD100G94)

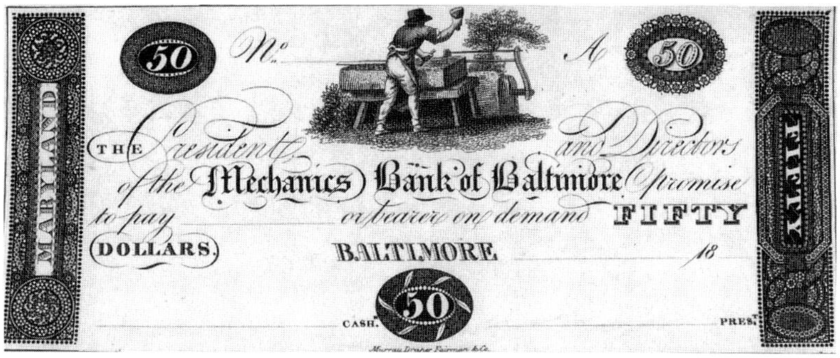

5.124.56 P

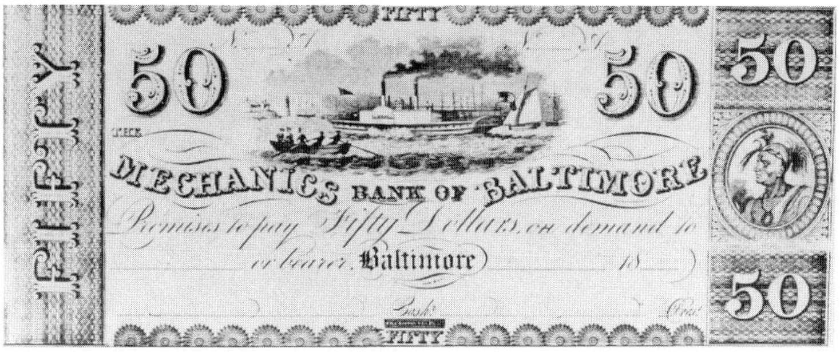

5.124.58 P

5.124.62 SENC

$500.00 Ca. 1850s. Engraving, imprint: Unknown. *Center:* 500; man seated, machinery, ships in left background; 500. *Left:* 500 / railway track cutting through rock / 500. *Right:* View of monument. *Between signatures:* Head of Indian. (MD100G98)

5.124.63 SENC

$1000.00 Ca. 1850s. Engraving, imprint: Unknown. *Center:* Woman seated, left arm on cogwheel, pedestal at left. *Left:* 1000 / statue of Washington. *Right:* 1000 / railroad tracks, rocks, trees, etc. *Between signatures:* Eagle. (MD100G102)

5.125 Mechanics Savings Fund

Opening for business in early May 1840, this "Savings Fund" was little more than a "shinplaster shop" that issued its small-change notes in exchange for larger denomination notes or coins. It suspended payments early in September 1840. The office was on Light Street near Baltimore Street until July 14, 1840, when it was moved to 12 South St., "one door from Lovely Lane."

5.125.1 R-6
6 1/4c Printed date May 2, 1840. Letterpress, imprint: MURPHY PRINTER BALTIMORE 146 Market street. Reversed "4" in die, upper right.

5.125.2 R-6
6 1/4c Ca. 1840. Lithography, no imprint.

5.125.3 R-6
6 1/4c Printed year date 1840. Lithography, no imprint.

5.125.4 R-5
12 1/2c Printed date May 2, 1840. Letterpress, imprint: MURPHY PRINTER BALTIMORE.

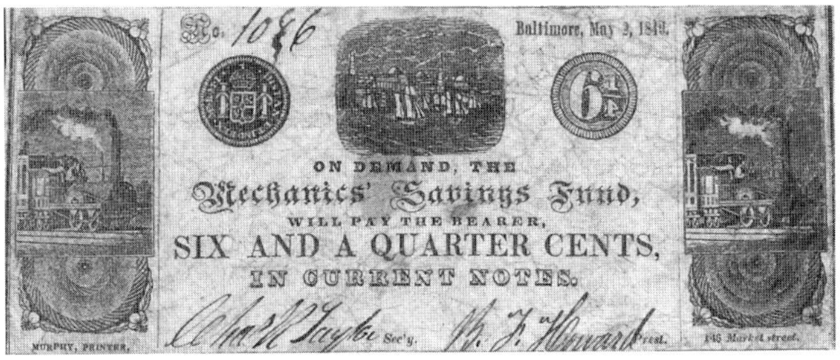

5.125.1

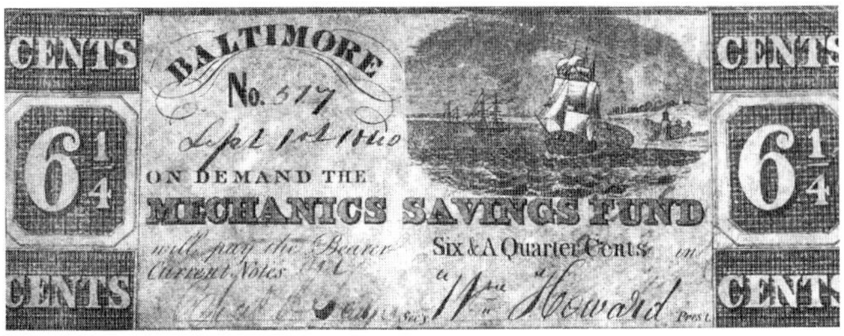

5.125.2

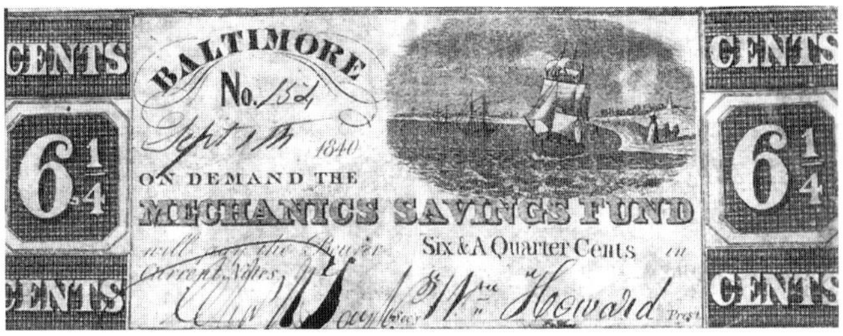

5.125.3

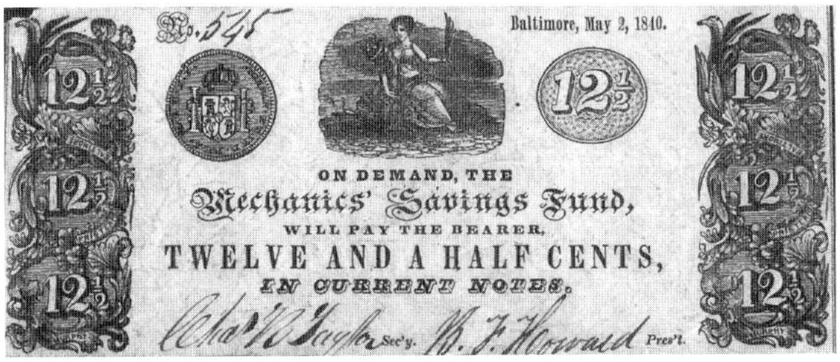

5.125.4

5.125.5 R-5
12 1/2c Printed year date 1840. Lithography, no imprint.

5.125.7 R-5
25c Printed date May 2, 1840. Letterpress, imprint: MURPHY PRINTER BALTIMORE. Center vignette is woodcut of Baltimore inner harbor.

5.125.8 R-5
25c Printed partial date 1840. Lithography, imprint: by E. Weber & Co. TWENTY FIVE CENTS in small typeface.

5.125.9 R-5
25c Printed partial year date 184_. Ca. 1840. Lithography, no imprint, but undoubtedly by E. Weber & Co. TWENTY FIVE CENTS in large typeface.

5.125.10 R-5
50c Printed date May 2, 1840. Letterpress, imprint: MURPHY PRINTER BALTIMORE.

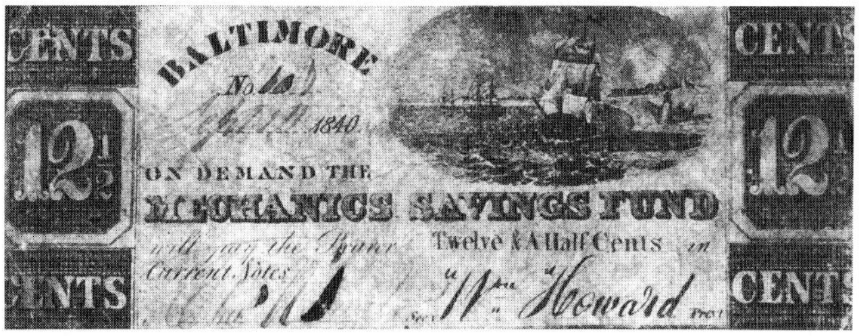

5.125.5

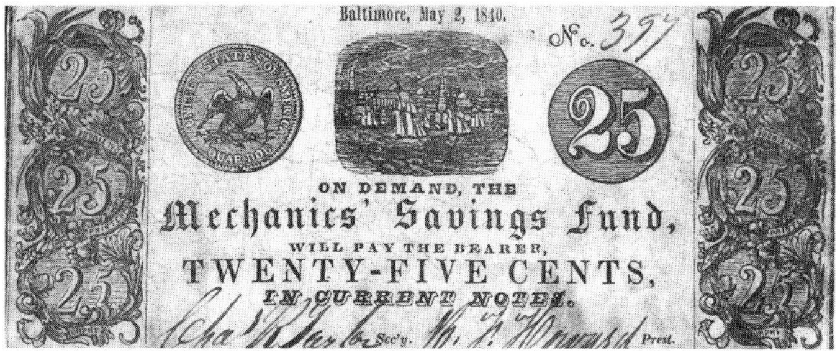

5.125.7

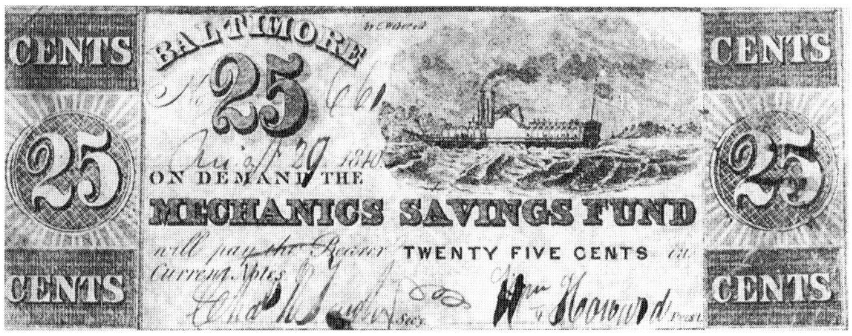

5.125.8

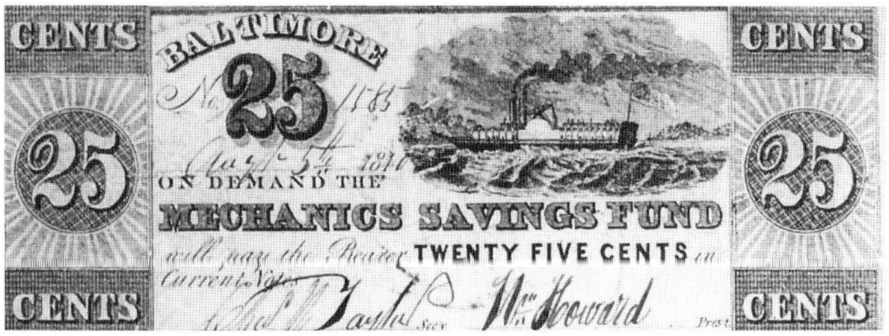

5.125.9

5.125.10

5.125.11 R-5

50c Printed partial year date 184_. Ca. 1840. Lithography, imprint: by E. Weber & Co. FIFTY CENTS in delicate serifed letters.

5.125.12 R-6

50c Printed partial date 184_. Lithography, no imprint, but undoubtedly by E. Weber & Co. FIFTY CENTS in large block letters.

5.125.13 R-6

$1.00 Ca. 1840. Lithography, no imprint, but undoubtedly by E. Weber & Co.

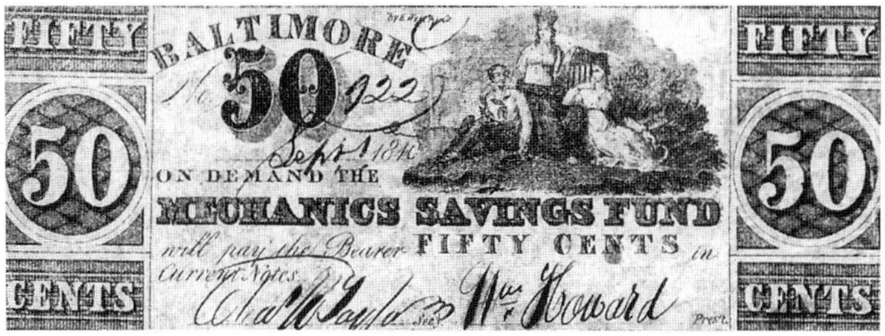

5.125.11

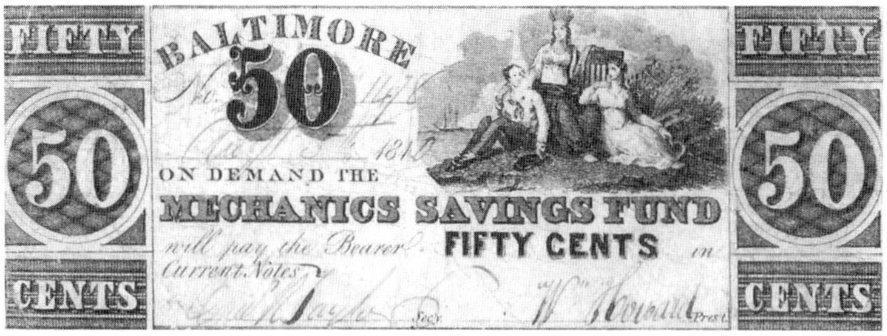

5.125.12

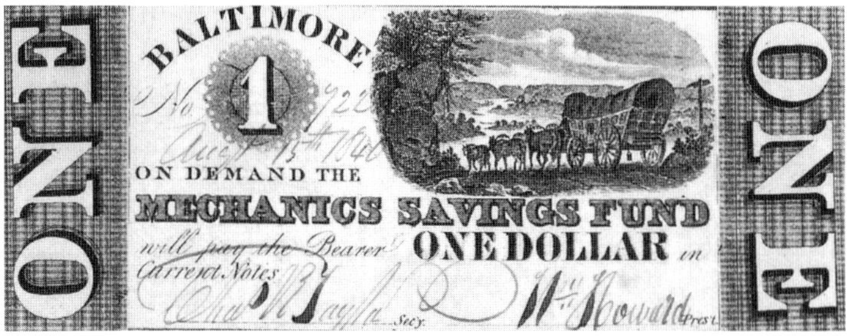

5.125.13

5.127 The Merchants Bank of Baltimore

Charter approved March 11, 1835; converted to and became the Merchants National Bank of Baltimore in 1865. The bank was located on the southwest corner of Gay and Second streets.

5.127.1 N SENC

$1.00 Ca. 1840s. Engraving, imprint: Unknown. *Center:* Two females and blacksmith. Not genuine, unattributed. (MD105N5)

5.127.2 P R-7

$1.00 Printed date March 12th 1842. Engraving, imprint: Underwood, Bald, Spencer & Hufty, Philada. / Danforth, Underwood & Co., New York. Proof.

5.127.2 P

5.127.3 P R-7

$1.00 Ca. 1848–50. Engraving, imprint: Hufty & Danforth, Philada. & New York. Proof. (MD105G12).

5.127.4 R-4

$1.00 Printed date January 6, 1862. Engraving, imprint: Hufty & Danforth, Philada. & New York. Red handstamped serial numbers. This note was apparently extensively counterfeited, although not listed as such by Haxby. Similar to No. 5.127.4 C. (MD105G12a)

5.127.4 C R-4

$1.00 Printed date January 6, 1862. Engraving, imprint: Hufty & Danforth, Philada & New York. Poorer quality of impression, perhaps from worn plate. Counterfeit.

5.127.5 R-7

$1.00 Printed date January 6, 1862. Engraving, imprint: Hufty & Danforth, Philada. & New York. Red handstamped serial numbers. This may be a counterfeit, although not listed as such by Haxby. Same as No. 5.127.4 C, but with green security tint left vignette and counters, counter at upper right and green tint underneath the bank's name. Green three-circle security tint on back.

5.127.6 A SENC

$2.00 Ca. late 1835–40s. Engraving, imprint: Rawdon, Wright & Hatch. *Center:* Mercury in clouds, facing right, scattering coins from cornucopia; 2 on large die. *Left:* TWO / cherub kneeling, writing on stone slab at left / TWO. *Right:* Girl seated at left with sheaf on head and basket on left arm, boy seated with sickle / 2. *Between signatures:* Pledge, in circle. Altered from $2.00 Chippeway County Bank, Sault De St. Mary, Mich., MI390G4. (MD105A5)

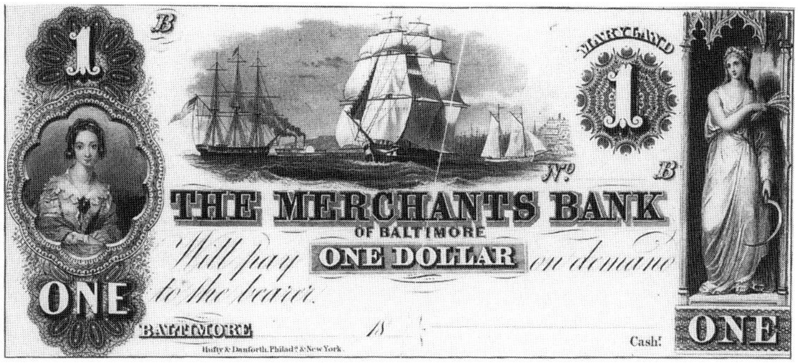

5.127.3 P

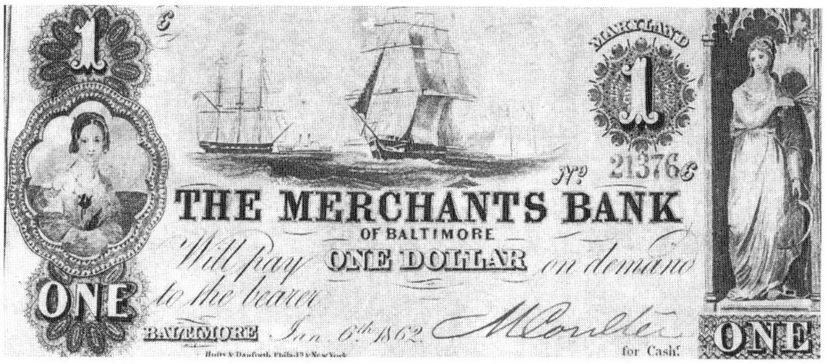

5.127.4

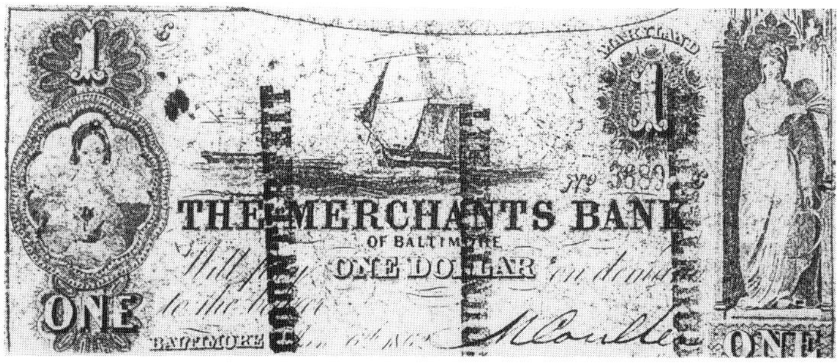

5.127.4 C

5.127.7 R-7

$2.00 Printed date March 12th, 1842. Engraving, imprint: Underwood, Bald, Spencer & Hufty, Philad.; Danforth, Underwood & Co. New York. Similar to proof, $2.00, No. 5.127.7 P, except that the title at the signature line has been changed to "Prest," replacing "Cashr." The signer's name, J. Swan, is correct, although the genuineness of the signature has not been verified.

5.127.7 P R-7

$2.00 Printed date March 12th, 1842. Engraving, imprint: Underwood, Bald, Spencer & Hufty, Philada. / Danforth, Underwood & Co., New York. Proof.

5.127.8 S R-5

$2.00 Ca. 1860s. Engraving, no imprint. Spurious. (MD104S5)

5.127.9 A SENC

$3.00 Printed date Dec. 20, 1841. Engraving, imprint: Durand & Co. *Center:* 3; train going left; 3. *Left:* Floral panel with square vignette of standing woman, leaning on column. *Right:* Panel of corn and wheat, with bull's head in circle. *Between signatures:* Steamship. Altered from the Exchange and Banking Co. of Apalachicola, Fla., FL10G6. (MD105A10)

5.127.10 A SENC

$5.00 Ca. 1835–40. Engraving, imprint: Rawdon, Wright & Hatch. *Center:* 5; woman standing with left elbow on large cogwheel at right; 5. *Left:* FIVE / semi-nude male standing with staff / V. *Right:* V / Vulcan standing at anvil / V. *Between signatures:* Arm and hammer. Altered from $5.00 Mechanics Bank, Montreal, Lower Canada, AS483G4. (MD105A20)

5.127.11 P SENC

$5.00 Ca. 1835–50s. Engraving, Rawdon, Wright, Hatch & Edson, New York. Small circular view of Baltimore Harbor in left end panel. Proof. (MD105G18)

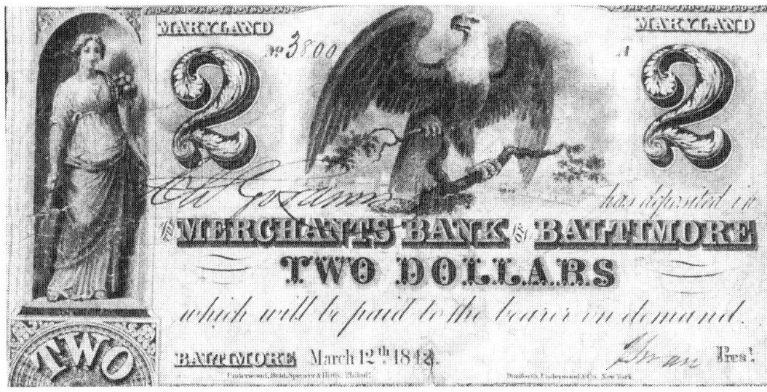

5.127.7

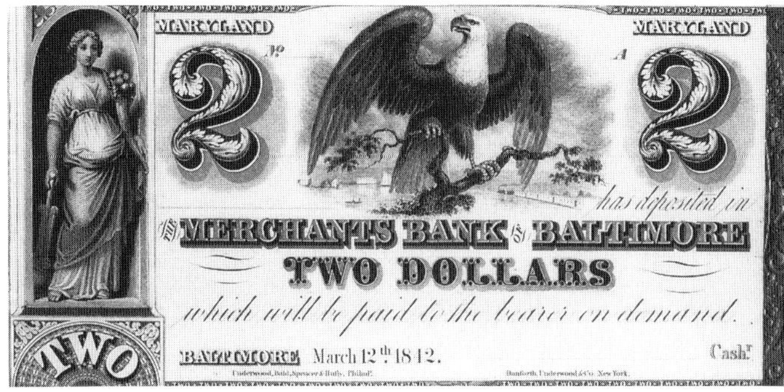

5.127.7 P

5.127.8 S

5.127.11 P

5.127.12 A R-7

$5.00 Ca. 1840. Engraving, Draper, Underwood, Bald & Spencer. Altered from a $5.00 note of the Commercial Bank of Millington, Md., No. 83.1.2. (MD105A15)

5.127.13 S R-7

$5.00 Ca. 1840s. Engraving, no imprint. Spurious. (MD104SA10)

5.127.14 R-7

$5.00 Ca. 1850s–1860s. Engraving, imprint: Rawdon, Wright, Hatch & Edson, New York. Patented: 30 June 1857. Bright blue and black. "CAPITAL $1,500,000" at bottom. (MD105G20a)

5.127.14 P R-7

$5.00 Ca. 1850s. Engraving, imprint: Rawdon, Wright, Hatch & Edson, New York. Patented: 30 June 1857. Bright blue and black "CAPITAL $1,500.000" at bottom. Proof. (MD105G20a).

5.127.15 P R-7

$5.00 Ca. 1850s. Engraving, imprint: Rawdon, Wright, Hatch & Edson, New York. Same as No. 5.127.14 P, except bright green and black. "CAPITAL $2,000,000" at bottom. Proof. (MD105G20b)

5.127.16 N SENC

$5.00 Ca. 1850s. Engraving, imprint: Unknown. *Center:* Vessels. *Left:* Liberty seated. *Right:* Woman reaping. Nongenuine, unattributed. (MD105N10)

5.127.18 SENC

$5.00 Ca. 1860s. Engraving, imprint: American Bank Note Co. Same as No. 5.127.15 P, except for imprint. (MD105G20d)

5.127.19 A SENC

$10.00 Ca. late 1835–40s. Engraving, imprint: Rawdon, Wright & Hatch. *Center:* Amphitrite and Neptune in shell drawn by seahorses; X on large die. *Left:* 10 on large die / small primitive train / 10. *Right:* X / farm produce and implements / 10. *Between signatures:* Pledge, in circle. Altered from $10.00 Chippeway County Bank, Sault De St. Mary, Mich., MI390G10. (MD105A25)

5.127.12 A

5.127.13 S

5.127.14

5.127.15 P

5.127.20 P R-7

$10.00 Ca. 1835–50s. Engraving, imprint: Rawdon, Wright, Hatch & Edson, New York. *Center:* Moneta seated receiving a bag of coins from Mercury in clouds at right, griffin on chest at left. Proof. (MD105G22)

5.127.21 A SENC

$10.00 Ca. 1840s. Engraving, imprint: Danforth, Underwood & Co.; Underwood, Bald, Spencer & Hufty. *Center:* Diagonal 10 on medallion head; presentation of the Declaration of Independence; diagonal 10 on medallion head. *Left:* 10 / sailor standing with U.S. flag in left hand, in oval / X. *Right:* X / Pat Lyon standing by forge, in oval / 10. *Between signatures:* Eagle. Altered from $10.00 Tenth Ward Bank, New York City, NY1935G18. (MD105A30).

5.127.22 R-7

$10.00 Ca. 1842. Engraving, imprint: Rawdon, Wright & Hatch, N.Y. STATE OF MARYLAND in double-lined slanting capital letters across top; *upper center:* TEN and X in oval dies on either side of reclining woman; *across center:* MERCHANTS BANK in large, fancy, slanting double-lined capitals.

5.127.23 SENC

$10.00 Ca. 1850s. Engraving, imprint: Rawdon, Wright, Hatch & Edson. *Center:* 10 and X; woman reclining, right arm on cornucopia of coins. *Left:* Sailor, barrel and shield. *Right:* 10 and X / weighing cotton bales. Tint in blue. (MD105G24a)

5.127.24 SENC

$10.00 Ca. 1850s. Engraving, Rawdon, Wright, Hatch & Edson. Same as No. 5.127.23, except tint in green. (MD105G24b)

5.127.25 A SENC

$10.00 Ca. 1850s. Engraving, imprint: Unknown. *Center:* 10; semi-nude Mercury seated on shore with caduceus, ship at left; 10. *Left:* Lathework panel with TEN, across. *Right:* Minerva standing with spear and shield / TEN. *Between signatures:* British arms. Altered from $10.00 Bank of Lower Canada, Quebec, Canada, AS488G10a. (MD105A35)

5.127.27

5.127.30

5.127.31 P

5.127.26 SENC

$10.00 Ca. 1860s. Engraving, imprint: American Bank Note Co. Same as No. 5.127.24, except for imprint. (MD105G24d)

5.127.27 R-6

$20.00 Ca. 1835–50s. Engraving, imprint: Rawdon, Wright, Hatch & Edson, New York. (MD105G26)

5.127.28 A SENC

$20.00 Ca. 1840s. Engraving, imprint: Danforth, Underwood & Co.; Underwood, Bald, Spencer & Hufty. *Center:* Diagonal 20, on medallion head. *Left:* 20 / primitive train, in oval / XX. *Right:* 20 / cattle, man at right in oval / XX. Altered from $20.00 Tenth Ward Bank, New York City, NY1935G20. (MD105A40)

5.127.29 SENC

$20.00 Ca. 1850s. Engraving, imprint: Rawdon, Wright, Hatch & Co., New York. Same as No. 5.127.30, except for imprint. (MD105G28b)

5.127.30 R-7

$20.00 Ca. 1860s. Engraving, imprint: American Bank Note Co., Phila. Patented 30 June 1857. Green overprint. Red serial numbers. (MD105G28d)

5.127.31 P R-7

$50.00 Ca. 1835–50s. Engraving, imprint: Rawdon, Wright, Hatch & Co., New York. Proof of circulating note. (MD105G30)

5.127.32 SENC

$50.00 Ca. 1835–50. Engraving, imprint: Rawdon, Wright, Hatch & Edson. *Center:* Woman reclining, right arm on cornucopia of coins, sceptre in upraised left hand. *Left:* FIFTY DOLLARS across; 50. *Right:* 50. Tint in green, including "50" at lower left. (MD105G30b)

5.127.33 SENC

$50.00 Ca. 1860s. Engraving, imprint: American Bank Note Co. Same as No. 5.127.32, except for imprint. (MD105G30d)

5.127.34 SENC

$100.00 Ca. 1835–50s. Engraving, imprint: Rawdon, Wright & Hatch. *Center:* C; Moneta seated receiving bag of coins from Mercury in clouds at right, griffin on chest at left. *Left and right:* 100. (MD105G32)

5.127.35 SENC

$100.00 Ca. 1850s. Engraving, imprint: Rawdon, Wright, Hatch & Edson. *Center:* Woman reclining, right arm on cornucopia of coins, sceptre in upraised left hand. *Left:* 100 / sailor seated on bale and woman with cornucopia. *Right:* C / 100. Tint in green. (MD105G34b)

5.127.36 SENC

$100.00 Ca. 1860s. Engraving, imprint: American Bank Note Co. Same as No. 5.127.35, except for imprint. (MD105G34d)

5.127.37 SENC

$500.00 Ca. 1835–50s. Engraving, imprint: Rawdon, Wright, Hatch & Co., New York. *Center:* 500; Moneta seated receiving bag of coins from Mercury in clouds at right, griffin on chest at left; 500. *Left and right:* 500. (MD105G36)

5.127.38 SENC

$500.00 Ca. 1850s. Engraving, imprint: Rawdon, Wright, Hatch & Edson. *Right corner:* D. *Left:* $500 / woman reclining, right arm on cornucopia of coins, sceptre in upraised left hand. *Right:* 500. Tint probably green. (MD105G38b)

5.127.39 SENC

$1000.00 Ca. 1835–50s. Engraving, imprint: Rawdon, Wright, Hatch & Co., New York. *Center:* 1000; Moneta seated receiving bag of coins from Mercury in clouds at right, griffin on chest at left; 1000. *Left and right:* 1000. (MD105G40)

5.127.40 SENC

$1000.00 Ca. 1850s. Engraving, imprint: Rawdon, Wright, Hatch & Edson. *Lower center:* M; woman reclining, right arm on cornucopia of coins, sceptre in upraised left hand. *Right center:* $1000. *Left:* ONE THOUSAND, across; 1000. *Right:* STATE OF MARYLAND, across. Tint probably in green. (MD105G44b)

5.128 The National Road Stage Company

Contemporary portrait of Lucius W. Stockton, president and cosigner of the company's scrip.

This stagecoach company provided daily service from Baltimore to Wheeling, via Frederick, Hagerstown, and Cumberland. An advertisement in the Baltimore city directory of 1833 showed daily departures at 5:00 A.M. from the office of the proprietors, Stockton & Stokes, adjoining Barnum's City Hotel at the southwest corner of Calvert and Fayette streets. The through trip was scheduled for 48 hours in summer and 60 hours in the winter season. Special post coaches were also available for travelers wishing "to cross the mountains with ease, traveling the entire route by daylight, going through in three and a half days." The proprietors, Stockton & Stokes, were also harnessmakers and builders of fine stagecoaches. Their notes can be found with the inserted names of the cities in which the firm had offices and would redeem the notes. The principal owner of the company was Lucius W. Stockton (1799–1844), a prominent mail contractor as well as a stagecoach operator. He had also been the president of the Washington & Fredericksburg Steamboat Company prior to 1841.

5.128.6 P R-7

$2.00 Ca. 1841–44. Engraving, imprint: Underwood, Bald, Spencer & Hufty, Philada. / Danforth, Underwood & Co., New York. Proof. (Va.#PW40-55)

5.128.7 P R-7

$5.00 Ca. 1841–44. Progress proof, company name and text lightly penciled in.

5.128.8 P R-7

$5.00 Ca. 1841–44. Engraving, imprint: Underwood, Bald, Spencer & Hufty, Philada. / Danforth, Underwood & Co., N.Y. Proof. (Va.#PW40-56)

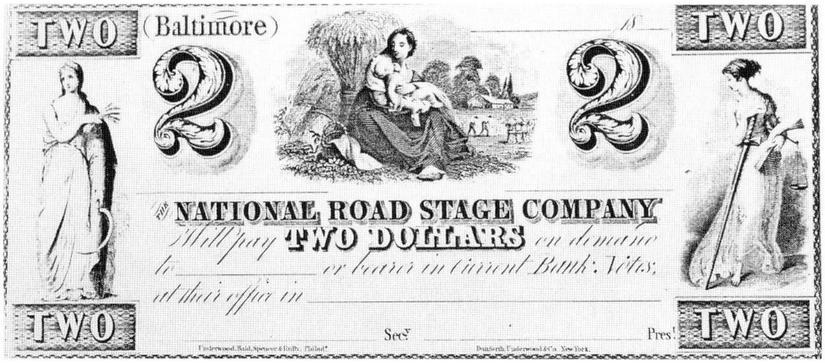

5.128.6 P

5.128.7 P

5.128.8 P

CUMBERLAND OFFICE

Scrip issued by the Cumberland office was redeemable at the Cumberland, Hagerstown, or Wheeling offices.

5.128.12 R-7

25c Printed partial date June 1837. Engraving, imprint: Underwood, Bald, Spencer & Hufty.

5.128.12

UNIONTOWN, PA. OFFICE

The Uniontown office issued scrip redeemable at the stage offices in Wheeling, Uniontown, Cumberland, and Hagerstown as evidenced by the notes illustrated below.

5.128.16 P R-7

25c Printed partial date June 1837. Engraving, imprint: Underwood, Bald, Spencer & Hufty. Proof. (Va.#PW40-65)

5.128.17 P R-7

50c Printed partial date June 1837. Engraving, imprint: Underwood, Bald, Spencer & Hufty. Proof. (Va.#PW40-66)

5.128.18 R-7

50c Printed partial date November 1837. Engraving, imprint: E. Morris, Philadelphia. (Va.#PW40-60)

5.128.19 R-7

$1.00 Printed partial date June 1837. Engraving, imprint: Underwood, Bald, Spencer & Hufty. (Va.#PW40-67)

5.128.16 P

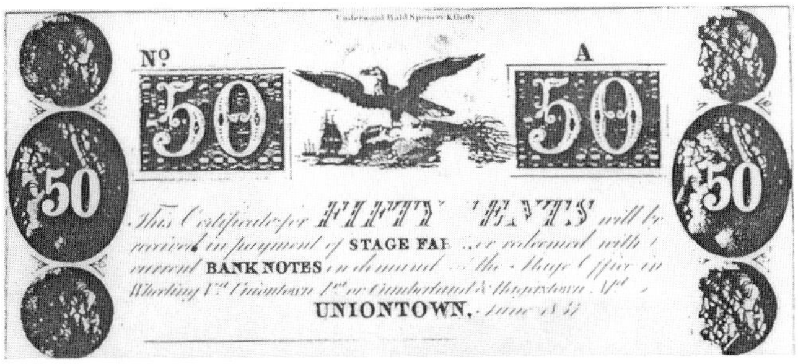

5.128.17 P

5.128.19

WHEELING OFFICE

The company's Wheeling office also issued scrip, as evidenced by the notes illustrated below, the imprint being the same as that on the notes prepared for the Baltimore office.

5.128.24 R-7

12 1/2c Printed date August 6th, 1841. Engraving, imprint: Underwood, Bald, Spencer & Hufty, Philada. / Danforth, Underwood & Co., New York. (Va.#PW40-50)

5.128.25 R-7

25c Printed date August 6th, 1841. Engraving, imprint: Underwood, Bald, Spencer & Hufty, Philada. / Danforth, Underwood & Co., New York. (Va.#PW40-51)

5.128.26 R-7

50c Printed date August 6th, 1841. Engraving, imprint: Underwood, Bald, Spencer & Hufty, Philada. / Danforth, Underwood & Co., New York. (Va.#PW40-52)

5.128.27 R-7

$1.00 Printed date August 10th, 1841. Engraving, imprint: Underwood, Bald, Spencer & Hufty, Philada. / Danforth, Underwood & Co., New York. (Va.#PW40-53)

5.128.24

5.132 New-Theatre Tavern

The issuer, James McConkey, was the proprietor of a tavern located on the east side of Holliday Street, across from the present City Hall, and next to the Holliday Street Theatre, which had recently been rebuilt.

5.132.2 R-7

12 1/2c Ca. 1815. Letterpress, no imprint. (For other scrip issued at this tavern, *see* John M. Barrett, No. 5.16, and F. A. Gibbons, No. 5.154, Theatre House.)

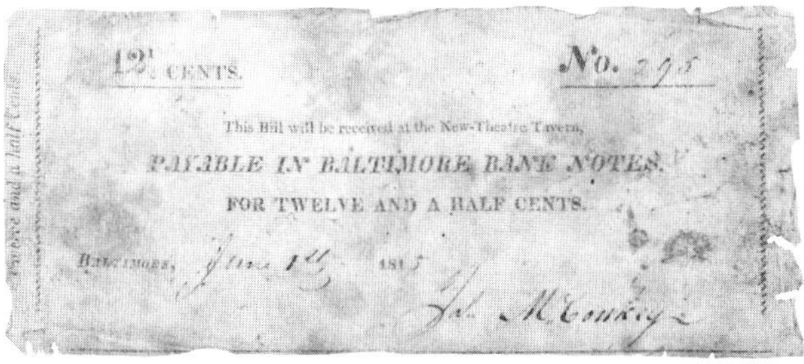

5.132.2

5.133 The Patapsco Savings Fund

Located at 10 Lombard St., just west of South Street, this "shinplaster shop" began operations in April or May 1840 and, to use the newspaper language of the day, "exploded sky high," September 9, 1840. The principals in the venture fled the city, one, Eber J. Cooke, being arrested about five miles away where he planned to board the train for Philadelphia and New York. The president, Thomas Pennington, escaped and made his way to New Orleans and then to Cincinnati, where by March 1841 he was operating a broker's office.

5.133.1 R-4

6 1/4c Ca. April–September 1840. Letterpress, imprint: Murphy, Printer, 146 Market street. Center vignette is a woodcut view of Baltimore, looking north from Federal Hill.

5.133.2 R-6

6 1/4c Ca. April–September 1840. Similar to 6 1/4c, No. 5.133.1, but left-center "6 1/4" on plain round die in place of square. Left vignette is ship at sea.

5.133.3 R-2

12 1/2c Ca. April–September 1840. Engraving, imprint: Underwood, Bald, Spencer & Hufty, Philada. / Danforth, Underwood & Co., New York.

5.133.4 R-2

25c Ca. April–September 1840. Engraving, imprint: Underwood, Bald, Spencer & Hufty, Philada. / Danforth, Underwood & Co., New York.

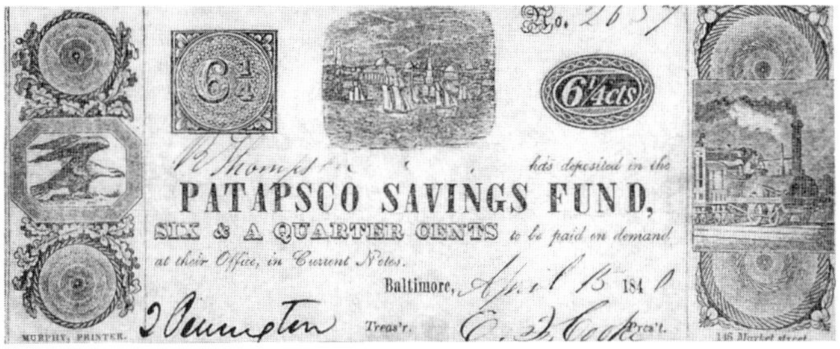

5.133.1

5.133.2

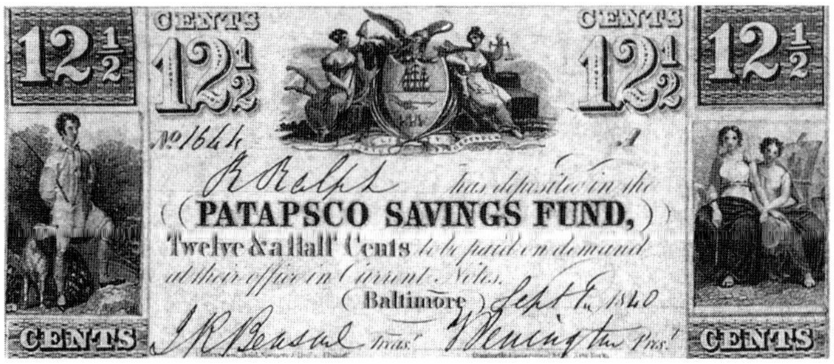

5.133.3

5.133.4

5.133.5 R-2

50c Ca. April–September 1840. Engraving, imprint: Underwood, Bald, Spencer & Hufty, Philada. / Danforth, Underwood & Co., New York.

5.133.6 R-2

$1.00 Ca. April–September 1840. Engraving, imprint: Underwood, Bald, Spencer & Hufty, Philada. / Danforth, Underwood & Co., New York.

5.133.6 P R-7

$1.00 Ca. April–September 1840. Engraving, imprint: Underwood, Bald, Spencer & Hufty, Philada. / Danforth, Underwood & Co., New York. Proof.

5.133.7 R-5

$2.00 Ca. April–September 1840. Engraving, imprint: Underwood, Bald, Spencer & Hufty, Philada. / Danforth, Underwood & Co., New York.

5.133.8 R-6

$3.00 Ca. April–September 1840. Engraving, imprint: Underwood, Bald, Spencer & Hufty, Philada. / Danforth, Underwood & Co., New York.

5.133.5

5.133.6

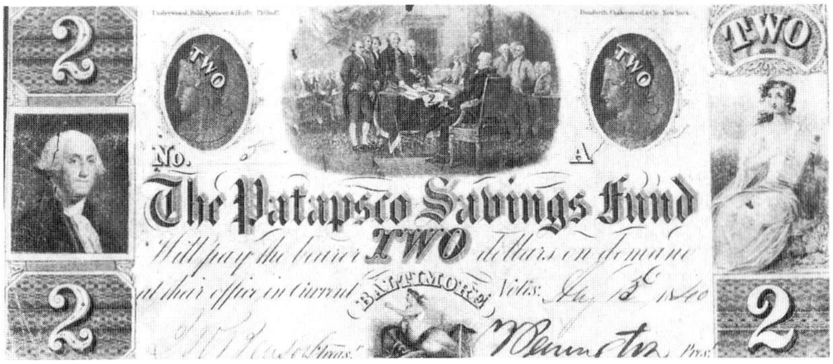

5.133.7

5.133.8

5.133.10 P R-7

Proof sheet of the vignettes and denomination dies for the 25c and 50c notes, Nos. 5.133.4 and 5.133.5, engraved by Underwood, Bald, Spencer & Hufty / Danforth, Underwood & Co.

5.133.10 P

5.134 The People's Bank

Charter amendment approved March 6, 1856; formerly the Fremont Savings Institution, which had been founded in 1853; converted to and became the Maryland National Bank of Baltimore in 1901. During the period in which it issued its own notes, the bank was located on the northeast corner of Baltimore and Paca streets.

5.134.1 R-5

$1.00 Ca. 1861. Engraving, imprint: Hufty & Danforth, Philada. & New York. Possibly spurious.

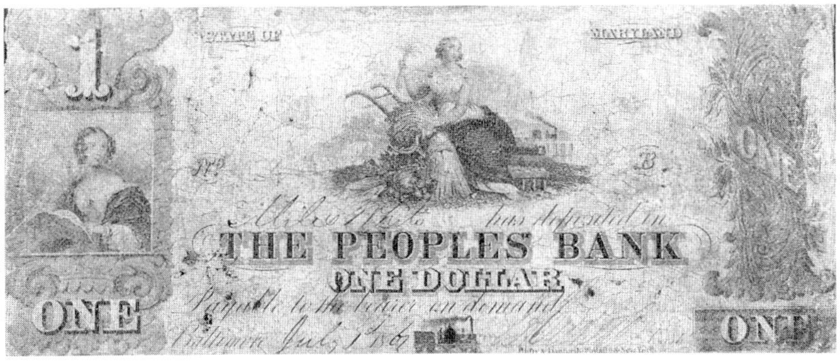

5.134.1

5.134.4 SENC

$5.00 Ca. 1856–60s. Engraving, imprint: Wellstood, Hay & Whiting, New York. Same as No. 5.134.5, except without American Bank Note Co. monogram. (MD110G6a)

5.134.5 R-7

$5.00 Ca. 1856–60s. Engraving, imprint: WELLSTOOD, HAY & WHITING, NEW YORK and American Bank Note Co. monogram. Portrait at left of Philip E. Thomas, first president of Baltimore & Ohio Railroad. Red security overprint and network. (MD110G6b)

5.134.6 A R-7

$5.00 Ca. 1860. Engraving, imprint: Danforth, Underwood & Co., N.Y. Printed from an altered plate originally prepared for the Commercial Bank of Millington, Millington, Md., in 1843–45. See $5.00, No. 83.1.2. (MD111A5)

5.134.7 A SENC

$5.00 Ca. 1860. Engraving, imprint: American Bank Note Co. *Center:* Train moving to left, buildings and hills in right background. *Lower left:* Oval male portrait. *Right:* 5 / Justice standing in small oval / FIVE. Tint in red-orange with white ornate FIVE, or overprint of red panel with white FIVE. Altered from $5.00, Clinton Bank, Westernport, Md., 146.1.1. (MD110A5)

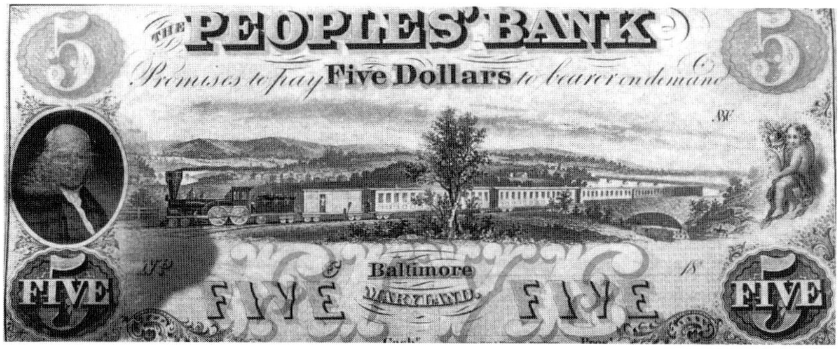

5.134.5

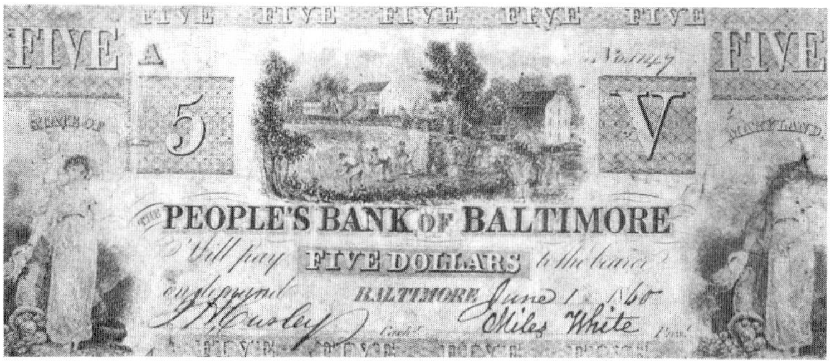

5.134.6 A

Uncut sheet of $10.00 (5.134.8), $20.00 (5.134.9), $50.00 (5.134.10), $100.00 (5.134.14).

5.134.8 R-7

$10.00 Ca. 1858–60s. Engraving, imprint: American Bank Note Company and WELLSTOOD, HAY & WHITING, NEW YORK. Red security overprint and network. See uncut sheet $10.00–20.00–50.00–100.00. (MD110G8b)

5.134.9 R-7

$20.00 Ca. 1858–60s. Engraving, imprint: American Bank Note Company and WELLSTOOD, HAY & WHITING, NEW YORK. Red security overprint and network. See uncut sheet $10.00–20.00–50.00–100.00. (MD110G10b)

5.134.10 R-7

$50.00 Ca. 1858–60s. Engraving, imprint: American Bank Note Company and WELLSTOOD, HAY & WHITING, NEW YORK. Red security overprint and network. See uncut sheet $10.00–20.00–50.00–100.00. (MD110G12b)

5.134.11 R-7

$100.00 Ca. 1858–60s. Engraving, imprint: American Bank Note Company and WELLSTOOD, HAY & WHITING, NEW YORK. Red security overprint and network. See uncut sheet $10.00–20–50–100. (MD110G14b)

5.136 John Pidgeon

The issuer was a printer in Vulcan Alley, near Liberty and McElderry streets in Old Town. It seems likely that Pidgeon designed and printed his own scrip.

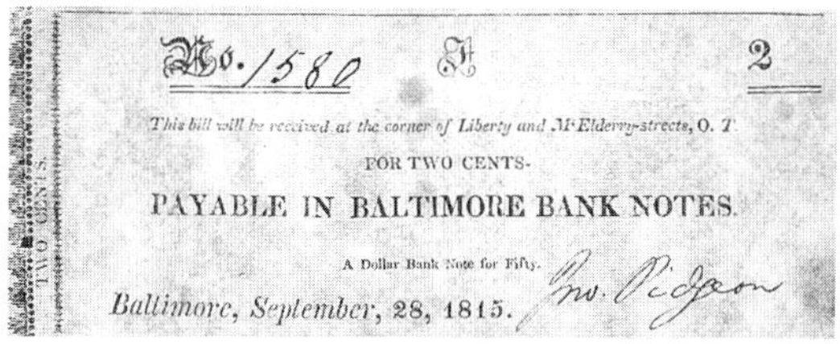

5.136.2

5.136.2 R-7

2c Printed date September 28, 1815. Letterpress, no imprint. Similar to 3c, No. 5.136.3. Inscribed "A Dollar Bank Note for 50."

5.136.3 R-7

3c Printed date September 28, 1815. Letterpress, no imprint. Inscribed, "A Dollar Bank Note for thirty-three." Similar to 2c, No. 5.136.2.

5.136.4 R-7

4c Printed date September 28, 1815. Letterpress, no imprint. Inscribed "A Dollar Bank Note for twenty-five." Similar to 2c, No. 5.136.2.

5.137 Post Office of Baltimore

Scrip issued by the post office to facilitate making change during the small-coin shortage incidental to the War of 1812. As the notes were issued they were handstamped in red with a circular date stamp also used to postmark mail.

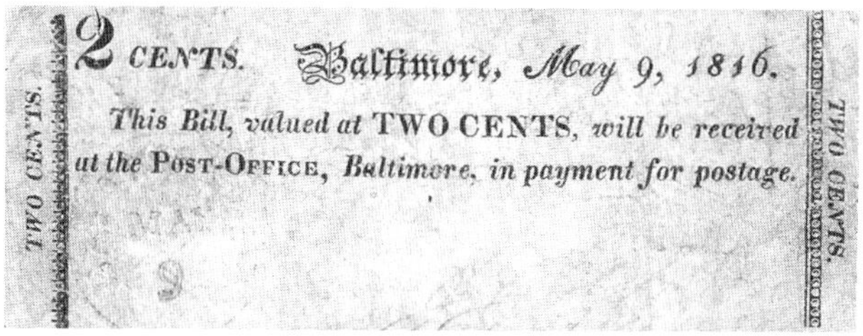

5.137.2

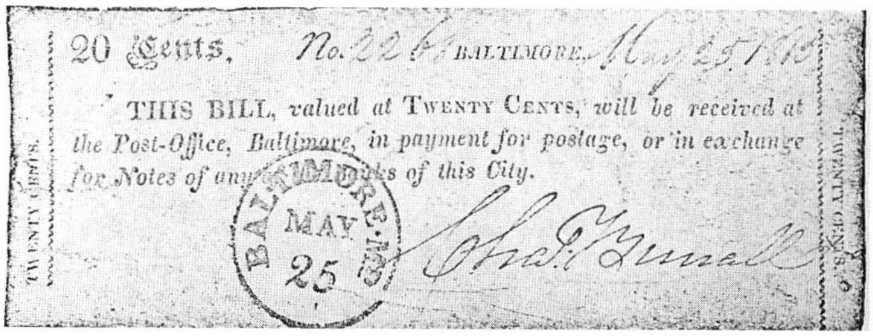

5.137.10

5.137.2 R-7

2c Printed date May 9, 1816. Letterpress, no imprint.

5.137.7 R-7

12 1/2c Ca. 1815–20. Letterpress, no imprint. Similar to 20c, No. 5.137.10.

5.137.10 R-7

20c Ca. 1815–20. Letterpress, no imprint.

5.138 The Real Estate Bank of Baltimore

Charter approved March 28, 1836. Due to inability to secure adequate capital through stock subscriptions, the bank never opened for business.

5.138.1 P R-7

$5.00 Ca. 1836. Engraving, imprint: Rawdon, Wright & Hatch. With decorative ornamentation under right portrait. Proof.

5.138.2 P R-7

$5.00 Ca. 1836. Engraving, imprint: Rawdon, Wright & Hatch. Without decorative ornamentation under right portrait. Proof. (MD115G2)

5.138.3 P R-7

$10.00 Ca. 1836. Engraving, imprint: Rawdon, Wright & Hatch. Proof. (MD115G4)

Proof sheet of essays, mounted on soft card, of proposed $5.00 and $10.00 notes (5.138.1–3 P). The top $5.00 note has floreate ornamentation under the oval portrait of Charles Carroll at right, while the ornamentation has been cut away on the next two subjects.

5.140 Russel Reynolds

The identity of this issuer has not as yet been definitely established.

5.140.2 R-7

12 1/2c Printed date June 1, 1840. Letterpress, imprint: S. Sands, Printer.

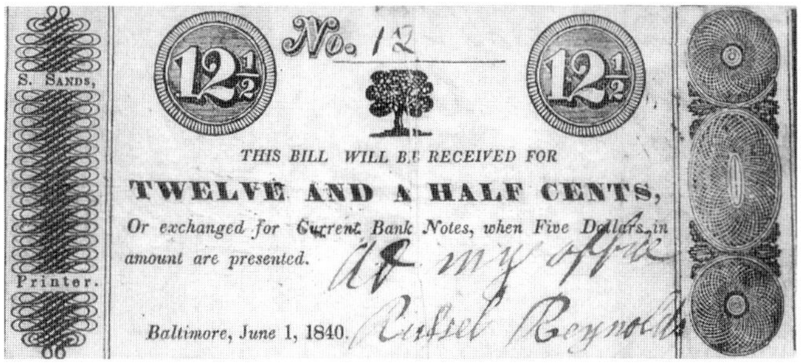

5.140.2

5.141 William Ridgaway Jr.

The issuer was a storekeeper on Baltimore Street above Charles in 1840. By September 1840 the store had closed.

5.141.2 R-7

12 1/2c Printed date May 2, 1840. Letterpress, imprint: MURPHY, PRINTER, BALTIMORE.

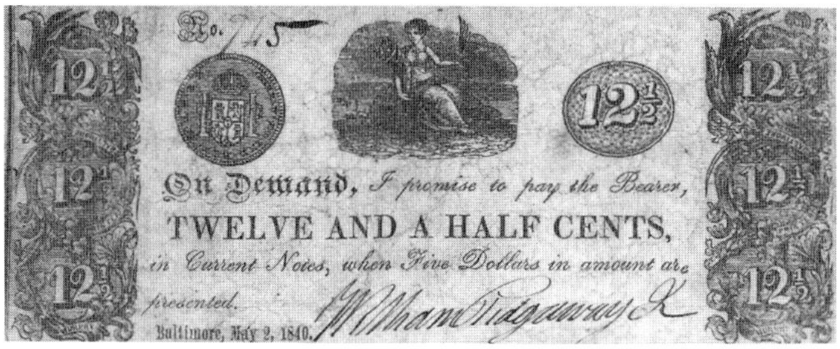

5.141.2

5.142 M. Ringrose & Co.

The issuer was the proprietor of a dry goods store at 27 N. Howard St.

5.142.1 R-7

6 1/4c Printed date July 1, 1837. Letterpress, no imprint.

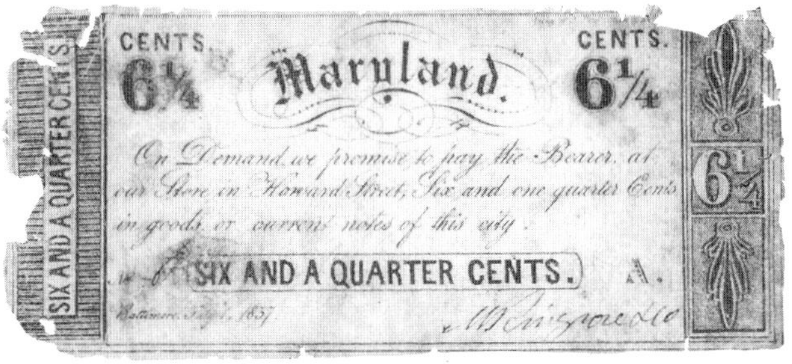

5.142.1

5.143 E. T. Roberson

The issuer has not as yet been identified with certainty, although it is highly probable that it was the Elizabeth Robertson listed in the 1842 city directory as the proprietor of a dry goods store at 57 Hanover St. The addition of a "T" in the surname was most likely the fault of the directory enumerator or the compositor.

5.143.3 R-7

25c Printed date May 1, 1840. Letterpress, imprint: MURPHY / PRINTER / BALTIMORE. Center vignette is a woodcut view of Baltimore and the inner harbor from Federal Hill.

5.143.4 R-7

50c Printed date May 1, 1840. Letterpress, imprint: MURPHY / PRINTER / BALTIMORE. Center vignette is a woodcut view of Baltimore and the inner harbor from Federal Hill.

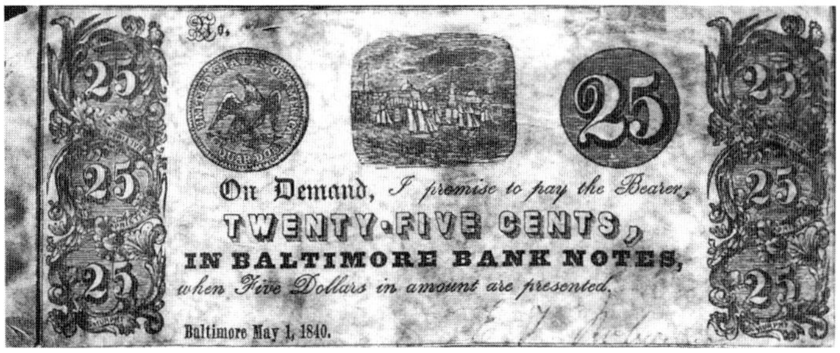

5.143.3

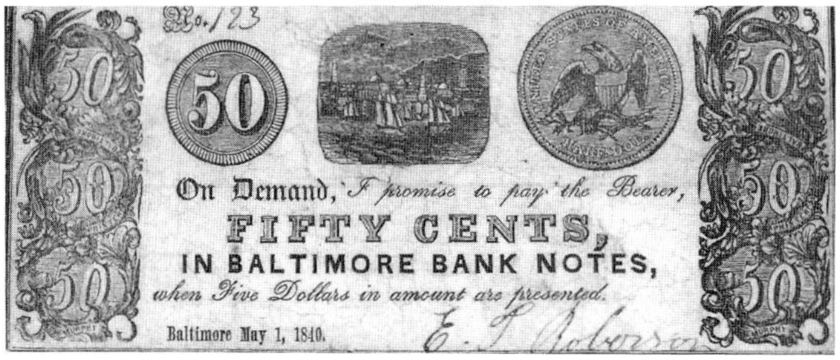

5.143.4

5.144 **E. W. Robinson Exchange Office**

The issuer conducted a lottery and exchange office at 80 Baltimore St. between Holliday and South streets from 1840 to 1845. Robinson notes have been found with a red, four-line, handstamped overprint: "Redeemable in / City Stock Orders / of the Baltimore & / Ohio Rail Road Co." See example on 50c, No. 5.144.4.

5.144.3 R-7
25c Ca. 1840–41. Lithography, imprint: Lith. of Ed. Weber & Co., Balt.

5.144.4 R-7
50c Ca. 1840–41. Lithography, imprint: Lith. by E. Weber & Co., Baltimore.

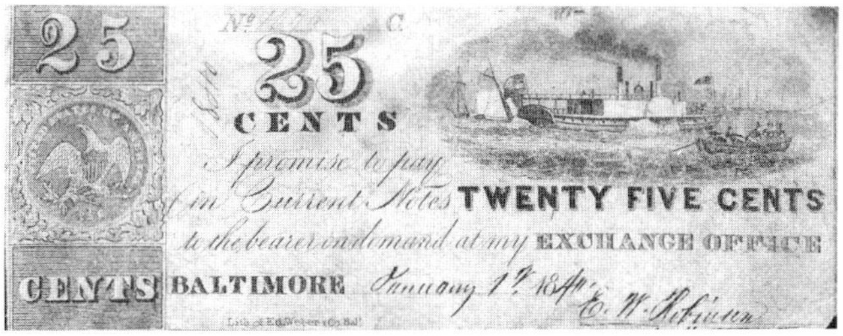

5.144.3

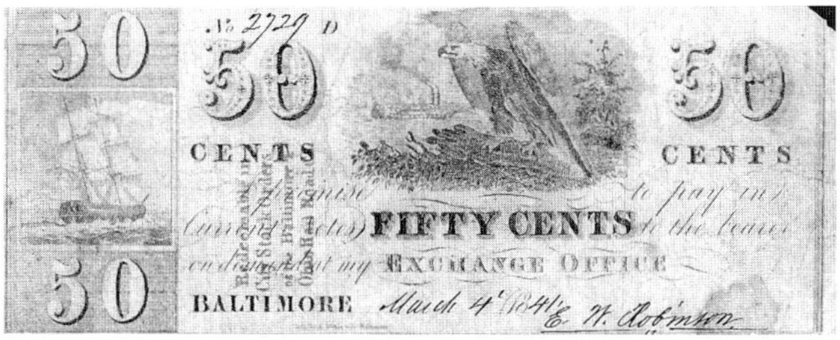

5.144.4

5.145 **T. Russell**

Thomas Russell conducted a variety store at several locations on Baltimore Street from 1837 to 1842.

5.145.1 R-7
6 1/4c Ca. 1837–42. Letterpress, imprint: S. Sands. Reversed "4" in the "6 1/4c" die.

5.145.1

5.146 **A. Shuck**

The issuer was a hat manufacturer on Holliday Street near Bath Street.

5.146.2 R-7
12 1/2c Printed date May 1, 1840. Letterpress, imprint: MURPHY, PRINTER, BALTIMORE.

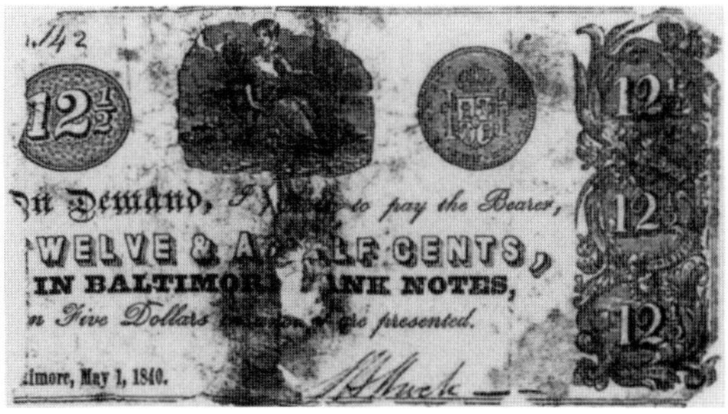

5.146.2

5.147 John P. Shultz

At the time of issue of the only recorded note of John P. Shultz, he was a grocer at the corner of Caroline and Wilk streets. According to directory listings he was a tavernkeeper at 31 Bond St. in 1817 and in 1819 had again become a grocer at "Caroline and Wilk streets (by the pump)." Between 1822 and 1824 he was listed as the proprietor of a grocery and liquor store at the same address. He disappeared from directory listings in subsequent editions.

5.147.2 R-7
12 1/2c Printed date September 21, 1815. Letterpress, no imprint.

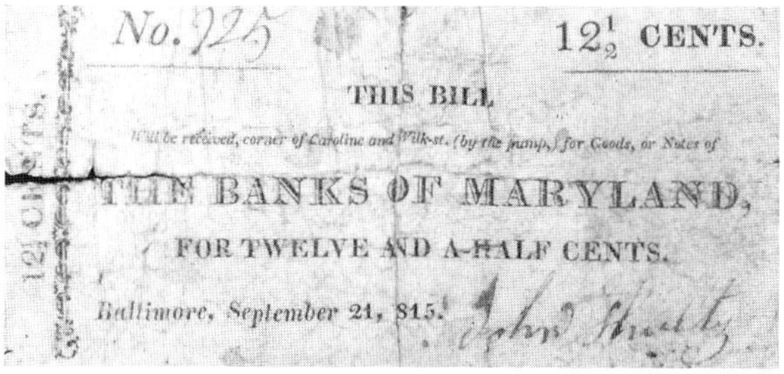

5.147.2

5.148 Christian Slemmer

The issuer was the proprietor of a domestic goods store on Queen Street near Pratt Street in Old Town.

5.148.2 R-7
12 1/2c Printed date March 2, 1815. Letterpress, no imprint. This bill valued at TWELVE AND AN HALF CENTS, will be received by the subscriber in payment for goods, or in exchange for notes of the Banks in the city of Baltimore Pratt street, near the bridge.

5.149 Jno. Smith

As would be expected there are a number of John Smiths listed in the Baltimore city directories of the 1839–42 period. Most of them were laborers or mechanics who would not normally issue scrip. The most likely candidate, in the authors' opinion, was John Smith, a grocer at Dugan's Wharf at the corner of Granby and High streets in Fell's Point.

5.149.4 R-7
50c Printed partial year date 184_. Lithography, no imprint.

5.149.4

5.150 Smith & Baker

Although the city or town where the illustrated note was issued is not indicated thereon, Baltimore is considered to be the most likely place. The printer, John Murphy, was a very active supplier of notes of this general design in the 1839–41 period. In addition to the production of such notes for specific issuers, Murphy produced "blank" or "stock" notes that could be personalized in manuscript by their purchasers. A search of Baltimore city directories for the years from 1837 through 1842 reveals no firm by the name of Smith and Baker, nor are any individuals listed who appear to be likely candidates for such a partnership. The illustrated note, the only one on record, has certainly been heavily circulated, having lost a large part of its left end, and bears the serial number 650, as well as a specific printed date, May 18, 1840. It is possible that the note was fraudulently placed in circulation by a fictitious partnership.

5.150.3 R-7
25c Printed date May 18, 1840. Letterpress, imprint: MURPHY PRINTER BALTIMORE / MURPHY, PRINT. BALT.

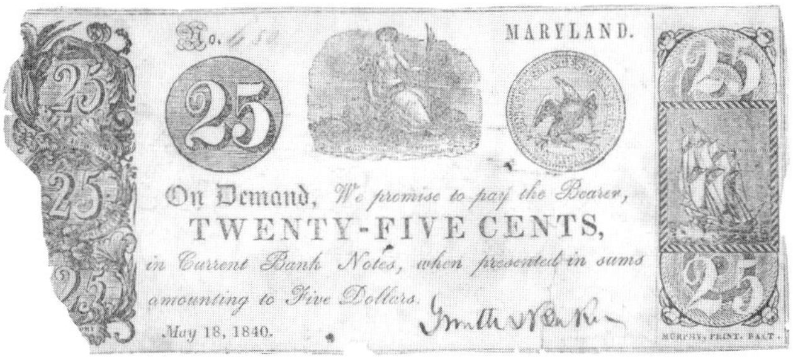

5.150.3

5.151 Thomas Stiff

The issuer was an innkeeper at 22 Fayette St., being so listed in the 1816 city directory.

5.151.2 R-7
12 1/2c Printed date August 28, 1815. Letterpress, no imprint.

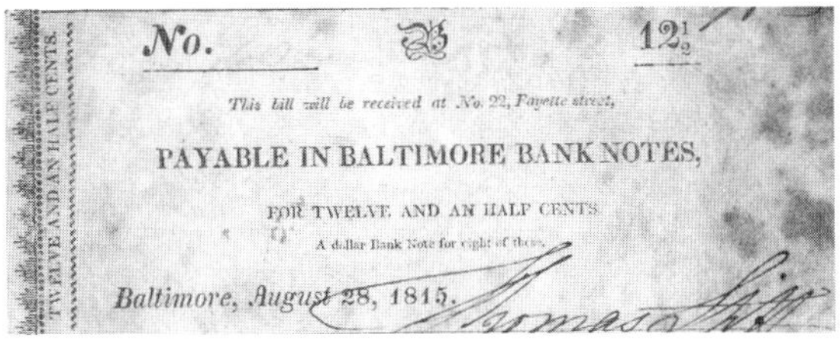

5.151.2

5.152 David Stirratt

The issuer was a grocer and domestic goods manufacturer, his store being at the corner of Bridge and Union streets. According to the statement on the note illustrated (5.152.1), Stirratt's note issue was predicated on the SAVINGS' BANK STOCK OF THE MANUFACTURING LOT, whatever that means.

5.152.1 R-7
6 1/4c Ca. 1826–27. Letterpress, imprint: Matchett, print.

5.152.2 R-7
12 1/2c Ca. 1826–27. Letterpress, imprint: Matchett, print.

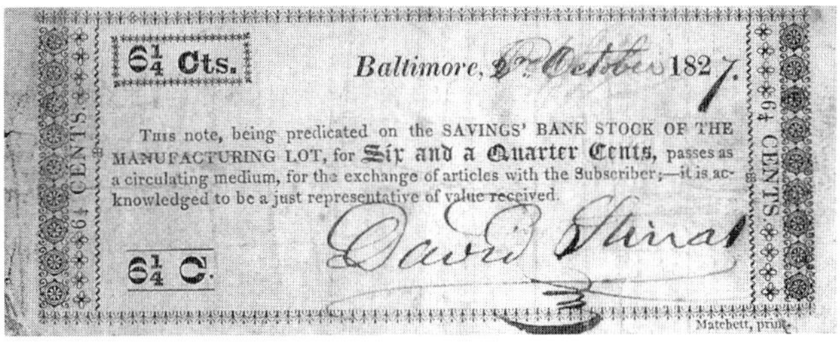

5.152.1

5.153 J. L. Stoner

This name appears in a listing of small notes circulating in Baltimore in early September 1840 published in the *Baltimore Clipper* of September 12, 1840. Stoner was identified as the proprietor of a lottery and exchange office on "East Baltimore st., near the bridge." No examples of his scrip have as yet been recorded.

5.154 Theatre House

The Theatre House, or Theatre Tavern, was located at 19 Holliday St., directly opposite the present City Hall, and next to the Holliday Street Theatre. The proprietor and signer of the notes was F. A. Gibbons. The following advertisement appeared in the *Sun,* November 21–23, 1840.

> SMALL NOTES!!—The subscriber respectfully informs the public that all NOTES bearing his signature will be redeemed in Current Bank Bills, when presented to the amount of $5, and also that any amount of his money will always be redeemed with the ordinary business paper.
>
> F. A. GIBBONS,
>
> n21-3+ Theatre Tavern, Holliday st.

5.154.1 R-7
6 1/4c Printed date July 25, 1840. Letterpress, imprint: MURPHY, PRINT. 146 MARKET street. Center vignette is a woodcut view of Baltimore and the inner harbor from Federal Hill.

5.154.2 R-7
12 1/2c Printed partial date 184_. Ca. 1840–42. Lithography, imprint: Lith. by E. Weber & Co., Balt.

5.154.3 R-7
25c Printed partial date 184_. Ca. 1840–42. Lithography, imprint: Lith. by E. Weber & Co., Baltimore. (For other scrip issued at this tavern, *see* New-Theatre Tavern, No. 5.132.)

5.154.1

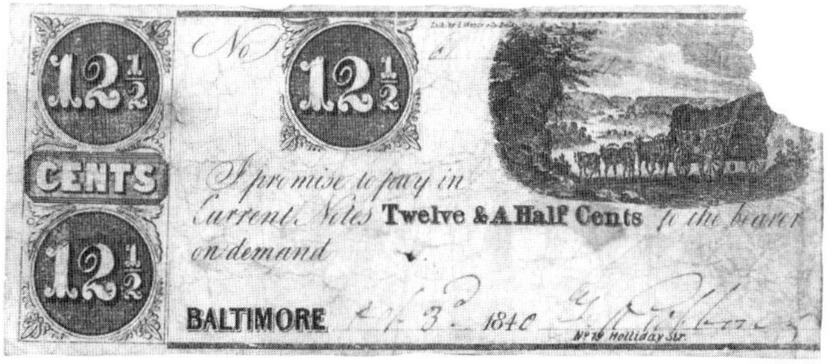

5.154.2

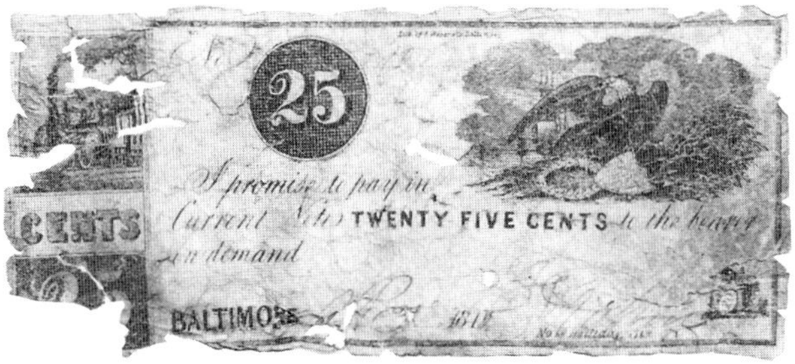

5.154.3

5.155 W. Thompson Exchange Office

The identity of this issuer has not as yet been definitely established.

5.155.2 R-7

12 1/2c Printed year date 1840. Letterpress, no imprint.

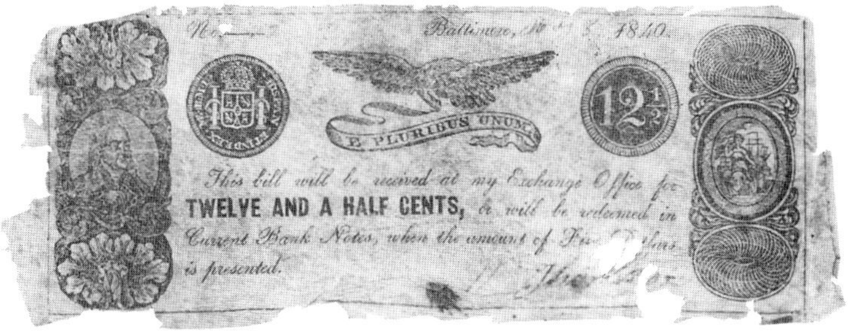

5.155.2

5.156 The Tide Water Canal Company

A company called "The Proprietors of the Susquehanna Canal," formed in 1783, built a waterway along the west shore of the Susquehanna River from tidewater north to the Maryland–Pennsylvania boundary. By 1803 the canal was usable, and by 1822 products valued at $1,300,000 per year were arriving at Port Deposit and Havre de Grace for transfer to Baltimore, but the operation was not profitable. In 1839, new owners, called the Susquehanna Tidewater Canal Company, finished building the waterway north from the state boundary to Columbia, Pa. This canal was 45 miles long, 50 feet wide, and 5 feet deep, and had 29 locks, of which 11 were in Maryland. Never really profitable, primarily because of railroad competition, the upper parts of the waterways were abandoned in 1890, and ten years later the lower section ended operations. Company scrip was issued in 1839–40 and was almost immediately substantially discounted in the financial market even though it was accepted at face value by the company for freight and passenger charges. The older issues of the company were noninterest-bearing and were "convertible into stock . . . at the pleasure of the holder." Reportedly they bore the signature of V. B. Palmer. When the company changed hands in 1839 new designs for notes were prepared which were redeemable in "current bank notes in the City of Baltimore." Whether notes in these designs were actually issued is not known as proofs are the only examples recorded by the authors. Finally, the last issue, bearing the printed date of May 1, 1840, appeared, circulated examples of the $1.00 and $2.00 denominations being rather frequently encountered.

5.156.3 P R-7

25c Undated proof or specimen. Engraving, no imprint, but probably by Draper, Toppan, Longacre & Co., whose successor firm was Draper, Toppan & Co., as the canal vignette is the same as that used for the left end vignette on the dollar denomination notes bearing the imprint of the latter firm and dated May 1, 1840. Proof.

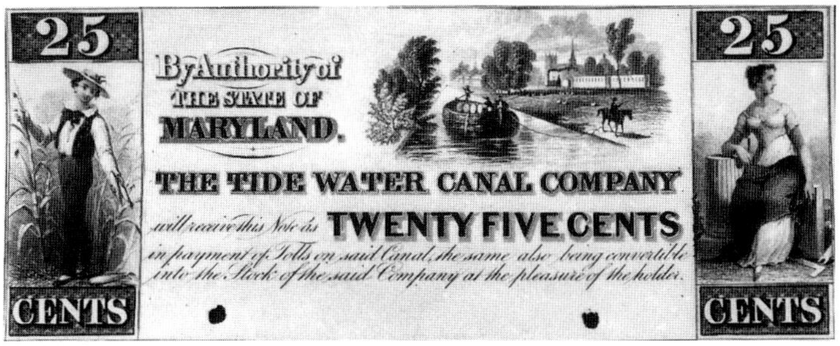

5.156.3 P

5.156.4 P R-7
$1.00 Undated proof or essay. Engraving, imprint: Draper, Toppan, Longacre & Co., Phila. & N.Y.

5.156.5 R-3
$1.00 Printed date May 1, 1840. Engraving, imprint: Draper, Toppan & Co., Phila. & New York. Similar to $2.00, No. 5.156.7. A $1.00 note handstamped ST. LOUIS is known; this was the name of one of the company's passenger and freight barges, applied presumably as a control by the boat's master.

5.156.6 P R-7
$2.00 Undated proof or essay. Engraving, imprint: Draper, Toppan, Longacre & Co., Phila. & N.Y.

5.156.7 R-3
$2.00 Printed date May 1, 1840. Engraving, imprint: Draper, Toppan & Co., Phila. & New York.

5.156.8 P R-7
$3.00 Undated proof or essay. Engraving, imprint: Draper, Toppan, Longacre & Co., Phila. & N.Y.

5.156.9 R-4
$3.00 Printed date May 1, 1840. Engraving, imprint: Draper, Toppan & Co., Phila. & New York. Similar to $2.00, No. 5.156.7.

5.156.10 R-4
$5.00 Printed date May 1, 1840. Engraving, imprint: Draper, Toppan & Co., Phila. & New York. Similar to $2.00, No. 5.156.7.

5.156.14 SENC
$20.00 Printed date Dec. 1, 1841. Surviving example not confirmed but recorded by D. C. Wismer in the *Coin Collectors Journal,* December 1940.

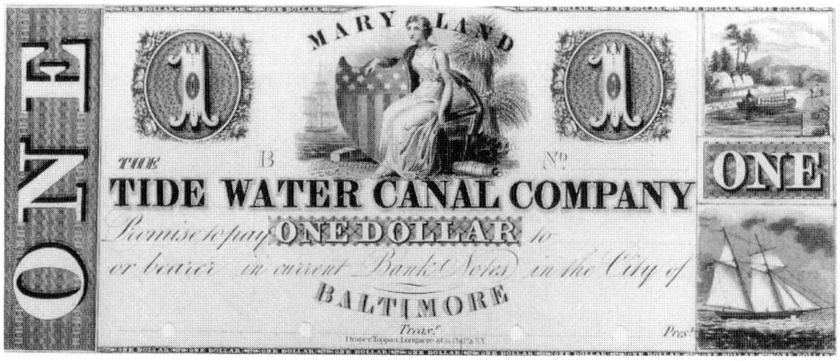

5.156.4 P

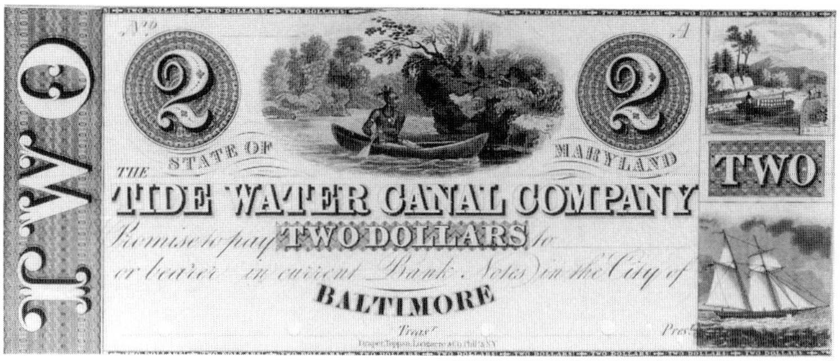

5.156.6 P

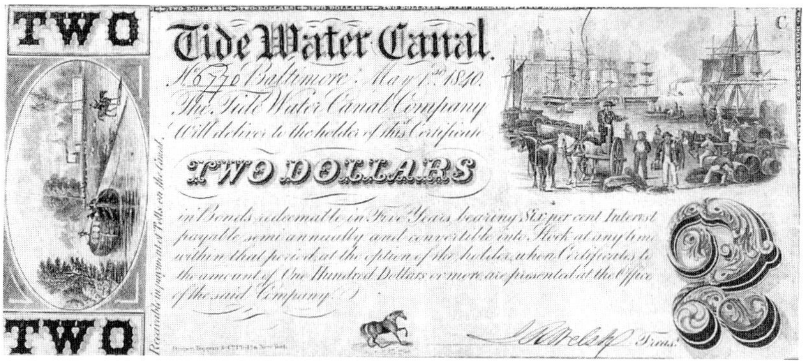

5.156.7

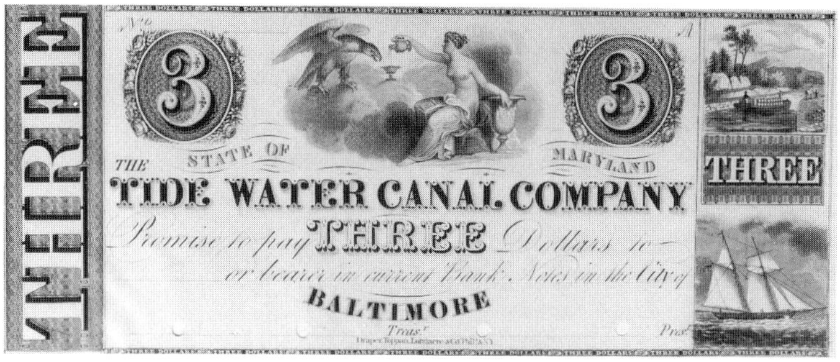

5.156.8 P

5.156.15 P R-7
$50.00 Undated proof or essay. Engraving, imprint: Draper, Toppan, Longacre & Co., Phila. & N.Y.

5.156.16 P R-7
$100.00 Undated proof or essay. Engraving, imprint: Draper, Toppan, Longacre & Co., Phila. & N.Y.

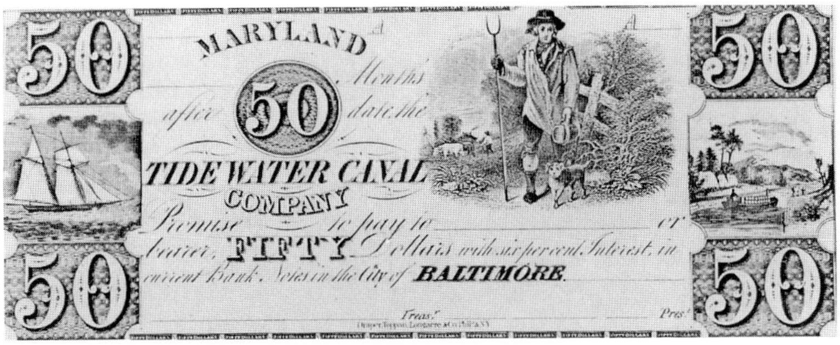

5.156.15 P

The $1.00, $2.00, $3.00, $50.00, and $100.00 essays were prepared by Draper, Toppan, Longacre & Co., Phila. & N.Y., probably in late 1839 when the canal company had just changed hands. The designs were not used, and in early 1840 the design and wording was completely changed to that which appears on the $1.00, $2.00, $3.00, and $5.00 notes dated May 1, 1840, imprinted Draper, Toppan & Co., Phila & New York (Longacre having left the firm).

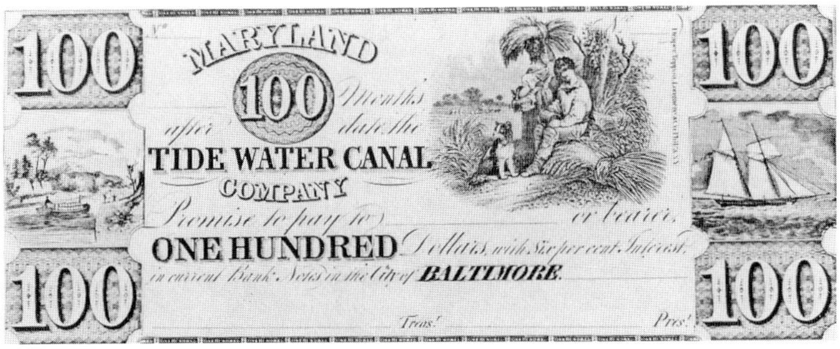

5.156.16 P

5.157 T. T. Tucker & Bros.

The issuers, Thomas T. Tucker & Brothers, conducted a lottery and exchange brokerage business at the southeast corner of Baltimore Street and Centre Market Space from 1837 to 1840. This scrip was redeemable in stock orders of the Baltimore & Ohio Railroad Co.

5.157.1 R-6
6 1/4c Ca. 1840. Lithography, no imprint. Similar to 12 1/2c, No. 5.157.2.

5.157.2 R-6
12 1/2c Ca. 1840. Lithography, no imprint.

5.157.2

5.158 The Union Bank of Maryland

Operated as an unchartered association until 1805. Charter approved January 12, 1805; converted to and became the National Union Bank of Baltimore in 1865. In 1833 President Jackson ordered public funds withdrawn from the Bank of the United States and its branches in whose places the administration chose twenty-three state-chartered banks as places of deposit. Since it was quickly alleged that the banks selected were favored because of party loyalty, they were nicknamed "pet banks." The Union Bank of Maryland received this "honor." During the period in which the bank issued its own currency, its addresses were North Charles near Baltimore Street (1810); Charles and Chatham streets (1814–15); and the SE corner of Charles and Fayette Street (1842–47).

5.158.1 SENC

6 1/4c Ca. 1814–15. Letterpress, no imprint. Similar to 50c, No. 5.158.8. (MD120G18)

5.158.2 SENC

6 1/4c Printed date 1815. Letterpress, no imprint. Similar to 25c, No. 5.158.7. (MD120G20).

5.158.3 R-7

12 1/2c Ca. 1814–15. Letterpress, no imprint. (MD120G22)

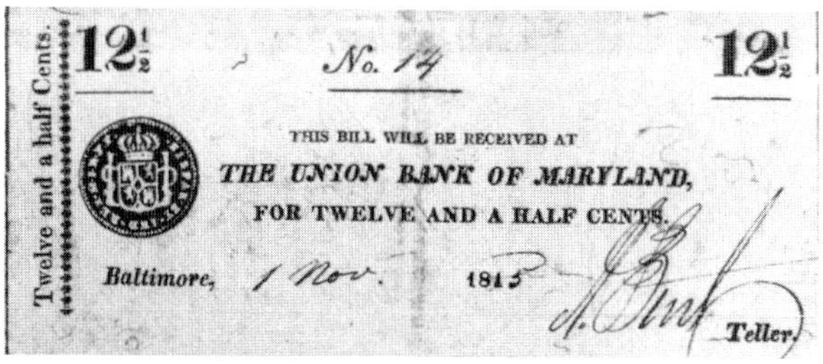

5.158.3

5.158.4 SENC

12 1/2c Printed year date 1815. Similar to 25c, No. 5.158.7. (MD120G24)

5.158.7

5.158.5 R-7

12 1/2c Printed year date 1816. Letterpress, no imprint.

5.158.6 SENC

25c Ca. 1814–15. Letterpress, no imprint. Similar to 50c, No. 5.158.8. (MD120G26)

5.158.7 R-7

25c Printed date 1815. Letterpress, no imprint. (MD120G28)

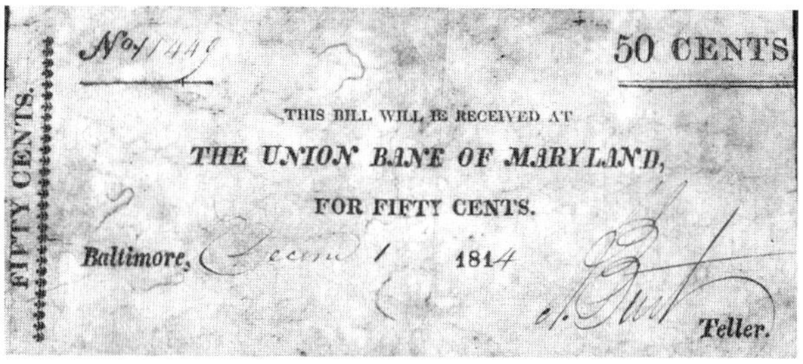

5.158.8

5.158.8 R-7

50c Ca. 1814–15. Letterpress, no imprint. (MD120G30)

5.158.9 R-7

50c Printed date 1815. Letterpress, no imprint. (MD120G32)

5.158.10 A

5.158.10 A R-6

$1.00 Ca. 1820s–50s. Engraving, imprint: Fairman, Draper, Underwood & Co. Altered from $1.00 State Bank at Trenton, Trenton, N.J., NJ560G6. (MD120A5)

5.158.11 P R-7

$1.00 Printed date March 10, 1842. Engraving, imprint: Draper, Toppan & Co. Similar to $1.00, No. 5.158.14, except for printed date and imprint. Proof. (MD120G36)

5.158.12 R-7

$1.00 Printed date March 10, 1842. Engraving, imprint: Toppan, Carpenter & Co. Same as $1.00, No. 5.158.11 P, except for imprint. (MD120G36a)

5.158.13 R-7

$1.00 Printed date May 1st, 1861. Engraving, imprint: American Bank Note Co. Same as $1.00, No. 5.158.11 P, except for date and imprint. (MD120G36b)

5.158.14 R-6

$1.00 Printed date May 1, 1861. Engraving, imprint: American Bank Note Co., Phila. Same as $1.00, No. 5.158.13, except it has printed serial number. (MD120G36c)

5.158.15 A SENC

$2.00 Ca. 1840. Engraving, imprint: Durand & Co. *Center:* Manhattan reclining with his left hand on a water urn, right hand on staff; 2. *Left:* 2 on large die. *Right:* 1/2-length figure of woman in circle, on panel of wheat and corn ears. Altered from $2.00 Globe Bank, New York City, NY1625G2. (MD120A10)

5.158.16 A SENC

$2.00 Ca. 1840. Engraving, imprint: Durand & Co. *Center:* 2; woman in clouds, holding cornucopia at right. *Left:* TWO / woman artist standing leaning on column at right / TWO. *Right:* 2 / two cherubs with book and flute / 2. Altered from $2.00 Globe Bank, New York City, NY1625G4. (MD120A15)

5.158.17 S R-7

$2.00 Printed partial date Dec. 1st, 185_. Engraving, imprint: American Bank Note Co., Boston. Spurious. (MD120S5)

5.158.18 A SENC

$3.00 Ca. 1840. Engraving, imprint: Durand & Co. *Center:* Manhattan reclining with his left hand on a water urn, right hand on staff; 3. *Left:* 3 on large die. *Right:* 3 on die, on panel of wheat and corn ears. Altered from $3.00 Globe Bank, New York City, NY1625G6. (MD120A20)

5.158.19 A SENC

$3.00 Ca. 1840. Engraving, imprint: Durand & Co. *Center:* 3; Indian man seated on rock with right knee raised, left hand on bow, dog at left; 3. *Left:* three cherubs in clouds, one at right with stone tablet, on wide panel. *Right:* Panel with THREE, across. Altered from $3.00 Globe Bank, New York City, NY1625G8. (MD120A25)

5.158.20 SENC

$5.00 Ca. 1803–5. Engraving, no imprint. Association issue. Probably reads "Pay out of their joint funds." No other information available. Probably similar to $20.00, No. 5.158.36. (MD120G8)

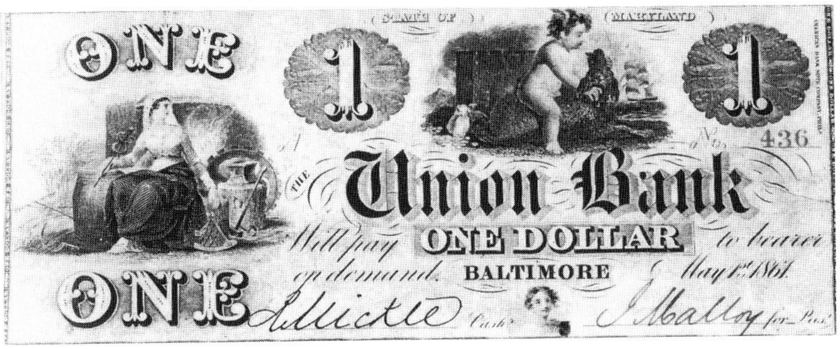

5.158.14

5.158.17 S

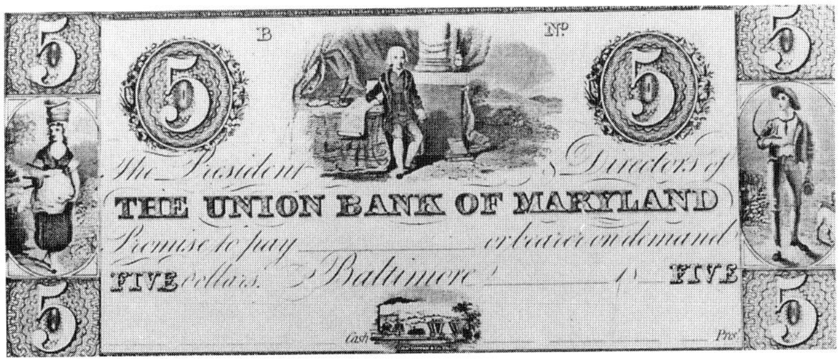

5.158.24 P

5.158.21 SENC

$5.00 Ca. 1805–10s. No information available. Similar to $10.00, No. 5.158.30. (MD120G40)

5.158.22 SENC

$5.00 Ca. 1810s. Engraving, imprint: W. Harrison. Similar to $20.00, No. 5.158.37. (MD120G44)

5.158.23 SENC

$5.00 Ca. 1820s. No information available. (MD120G48)

5.158.24 P R-5

$5.00 Ca. early 1830s–50s. Engraving, imprint: Toppan & Co. *Center:* Charles Carroll. Proof. (MD120G50)

5.158.25 A SENC

$5.00 Printed date June 1, 1841. Engraving, imprint: Draper, Toppan & Co. *Center:* Ornate 5; white horse and black horse flanking shield surmounted by eagle; ornate 5. *Left:* Three-quarters length figure of Liberty standing / eagle on limb / three-quarters length figure of nude Indian woman, all in ovals. *Right:* Woman with cornucopia / eagle on limb / one-half length figure of Indian man, all in ovals. *Between signatures:* Dog, key, and strongbox. Relief note. Altered from $5.00, Towanda Bank, Towanda, Pa., PA650G28. (MD120A30)

5.158.26 SENC

$5.00 Ca. 1850s. Engraving, imprint: Rawdon, Wright, Hatch & Edson. *Center:* Woman seated on rock, arm on shield at right. *Left:* Woman with right arm raised / 5. *Right:* Lathework panel with FIVE, across. *Between signatures:* V. See spurious $5.00 (CT320SIO) on the Union Bank, New London, for an illustration of the design. (MD120S10)

5.158.27 SENC

$5.00 Ca. 1850s. Engraving, imprint: Unknown. *Center:* Allegorical male reclining, monument in background. *Left:* 5 / milkmaid with pail / 5. *Right:* 5 / male reaper / 5. (MD120N5)

5.158.28 R-7

$5.00 Ca. 1856–60s. Engraving: Toppan, Carpenter & Co., Philad. *Left center:* Charles Carroll. Tint is red-orange overall, outlining white "V V" at the bottom. (MD120G52a)

5.158.28 P R-7

$5.00 Ca. 1856–60s. Engraving: Toppan, Carpenter & Co., Philad. *Left center:* Charles Carroll. Tint is red-orange overall, outlining white "V V" at the bottom. Proof.

5.158.29 SENC

$10.00 Ca. 1803–5. Association issue. Probably reads "Pay out of their joint funds." No other information available. Probably similar to $20.00, No. 5.158.36. (MD120G10)

5.158.30 SENC

$10.00 Ca. 1805–10s. Engraving, no imprint. Similar to counterfeit $10.00, No. 5.158.30 C. (MD120G54)

5.158.30 C R-7

$10.00 Ca. 1805–10s. Engraving, no imprint. Counterfeit of $10.00, No. 5.158.30 (MD120C54)

5.158.31 SENC

$10.00 Ca. 1810s. Engraving, imprint: W. Harrison. No other information available. Similar to $20.00, No. 5.158.37. (MD120G58)

5.158.28 P

5.158.30 C

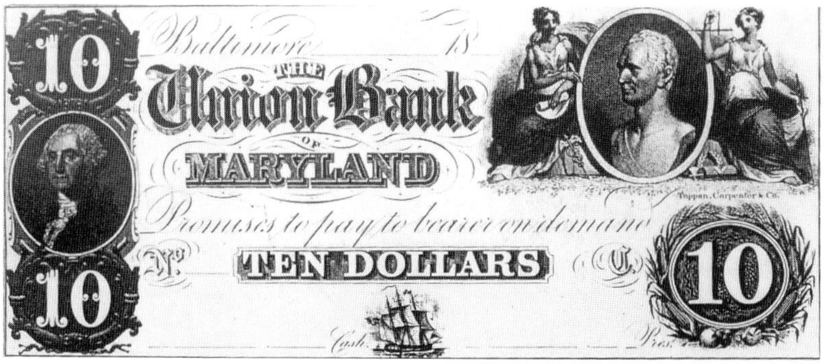

5.158.34 P

5.158.32 SENC

$10.00 Ca. 1820s–30s. Engraving, imprint: Unknown. No other information available. (MD120G62)

5.158.33 SENC

$10.00 Ca. 1850s. Engraving, imprint: Unknown. *Center:* Southern farm scene. (MD120N10)

5.158.34 R-6

$10.00 Ca. 1856–60s. Engraving, imprint: Toppan, Carpenter & Co. Similar to proof, No. 5.158.34 P. (MD120G64)

5.158.34 P R-7

$10.00 Ca. 1856–60s. Engraving, imprint: Toppan, Carpenter & Co. Proof.

5.158.34 C SENC

$10.00 Ca. 1856–60s. Engraving, imprint: Toppan, Carpenter & Co. Counterfeit of $10.00, No. 5.158.34. (MD120C64).

5.158.35 R-7

$10.00 Ca. 1858. Engraving, imprint: Toppan, Carpenter & Co., Philada. Same as No. 5.158.34, except with large TEN overprint in brick red at center.

5.158.36 SENC

$20.00 Ca. 1803–5. Engraving, no imprint. Association issue. Probably reads "Pay out of their joint funds." No other information available. Probably similar to counterfeit $20.00, No. 5.158.36 C. (MD120G12)

5.158.36 C R-7

$20.00 Ca. 1805–10s. Engraving, no imprint. Counterfeit of $20.00, No. 5.158.36. (MD120C12)

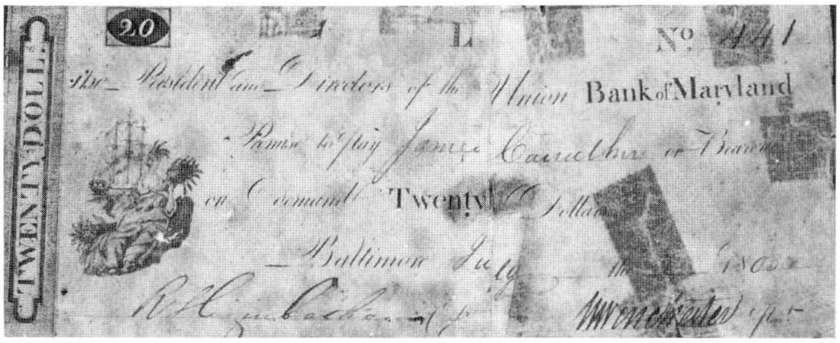

5.158.36 C

5.158.37 SENC

$20.00 Ca. 1805–10s. Engraving, imprint. W. Harrison. Similar to counterfeit $20.00, No. 5.158.37 C. (MD120G68)

5.158.37 C R-6

$20.00 Ca. 1810s. Engraving, imprint: W. Harrison. Counterfeit of $20.00, No. 5.158.37. (MD120C68)

5.158.37 C

5.158.38 SENC

$20.00 Ca. 1820s–30s. No other information available. (MD120G72)

5.158.39 A SENC

$20.00 Ca. 1840s. Engraving, imprint: Danforth, Underwood, & Co.; Underwood, Bald, Spencer & Hufty. *Center:* Diagonal 20 on medallion head; Pat Lyon standing by forge; diagonal 20, on medallion head. *Left:* 20 / primitive train, in oval / XX. *Right:* 20 / cattle, man at right, in oval / XX. Altered from $20.00 Tenth Ward Bank, New York City, NY1935G20. (MD120A35)

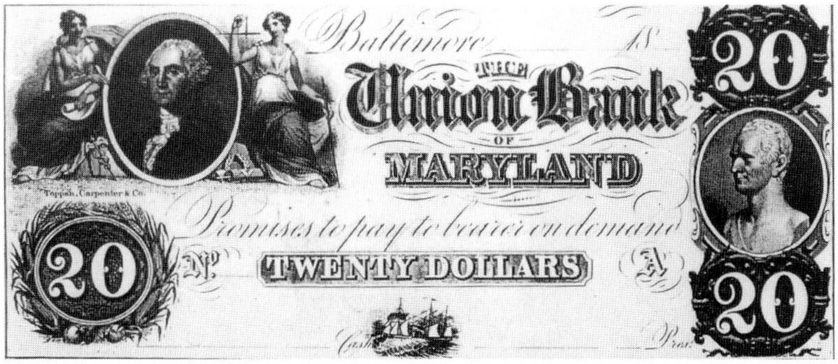

5.158.40 P

5.158.40 P R-7

$20.00 Ca. 1856–60s. Engraving, imprint: Toppan, Carpenter & Co. Proof. (MD120G74)

5.158.41 SENC

$50.00 Ca. 1803–05. No information available. Association issue. Probably reads "Pay out of their joint funds." Probably similar to counterfeit $20.00, No. 5.158.36 C. (MD120G14)

5.158.42 SENC

$50.00 Ca. 1805–10s. No other information available. Probably similar to counterfeit $10.00, No. 5.158.30 C. (MD120G78)

5.158.43 SENC

$50.00 Ca. 1810s. Engraving, imprint: W. Harrison. Similar to counterfeit $50.00, No. 5.158.43 C. (MD120G80)

5.158.43 C R-7

$50.00 Ca. 1815. Engraving, no imprint. Counterfeit of $50.00, No. 5.158.43. (MD120C80)

5.158.44 SENC

$50.00 Ca. 1820s. No other information available. (MD120G82)

5.158.45 P R-7

$50.00 Ca. 1825–30s. Engraving, imprint: Fairman, Draper, Underwood & Co. Portrait of Charles Carroll at right. Proof. (MD120G84)

5.158.46 P R-7

$100.00 Ca. 1825–30s. Engraving, imprint: Fairman, Draper, Underwood & Co. Portrait of Charles Carroll at left. Proof. (MD120G88)

5.158.47 S SENC

$100.00 Ca. 1840s. Engraving, imprint: Draper, Toppan & Co. *Upper right center:* Two women seated, one pointing at train in background. *Left:* 100 / portrait of Washington / 100. *Right:* 100 / medallion head / 100. Spurious. See spurious $100.00 note of Western Bank of Baltimore (5.167.18 s) for an illustration of the design. (MD120S20)

5.158.48 A SENC

$100.00 Ca. 1840s. Engraving, imprint: Terry Pelton. *Center:* Sampson wrestling the lion: C. *Left:* 100 / farmer standing with rake / 100. *Right:* 100 / Washington at Dorchester Heights, 1775 / 100. *Between signatures:* Raft in harbor. Altered from $100.00 Citizens Bank, Augusta, Maine, ME25G32. (MD120A40)

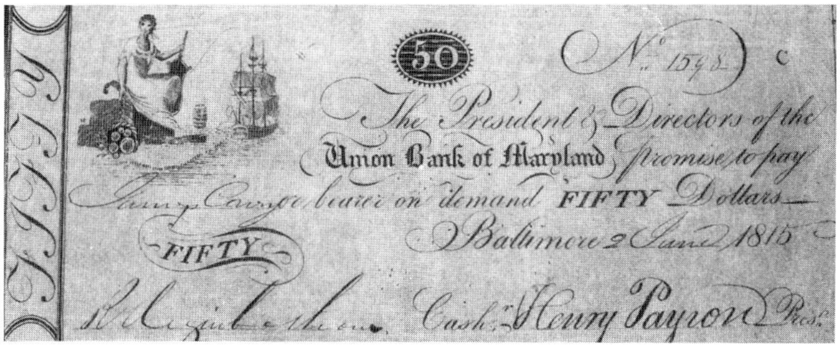

5.158.43 C

5.158.45 P

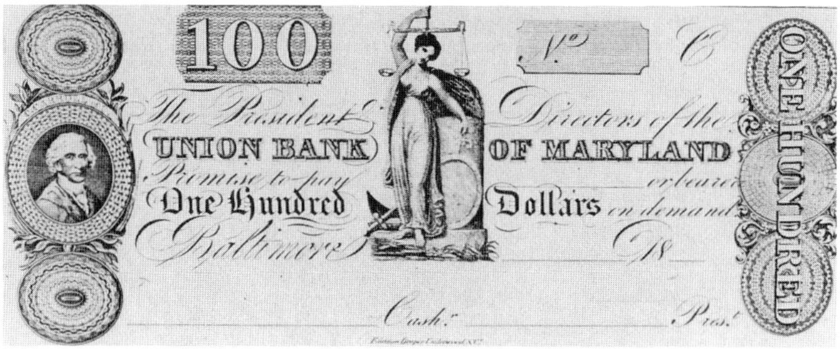

5.158.46 P

POST NOTES

5.158.49 P R-7

$20.00 Ca. 1833–50s. Engraving, imprint: Fairman, Draper, Underwood & Co. Post note. Proof.

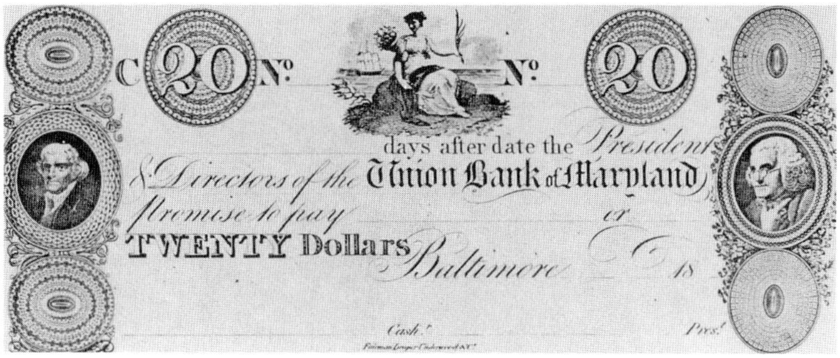

5.158.49 P

5.158.50 P R-7

$50.00 Ca. 1833–50s. Engraving, imprint: Fairman, Draper, Underwood & Co. Post note. Proof.

5.158.51 P R-7

$100.00 Ca. 1833–50s. Engraving, imprint: Fairman, Draper, Underwood & Co. Post note. Proof.

5.158.52 P R-7

$500.00 Ca. 1833–50s. Engraving, imprint: Draper, Underwood, Bald & Spencer. Post note. Proof. (MD120G92)

5.158.53 P R-7

$1000.00 Ca. 1833–50s. Engraving, imprint: Draper, Underwood, Bald & Spencer. Post note. Proof. (MD120G96)

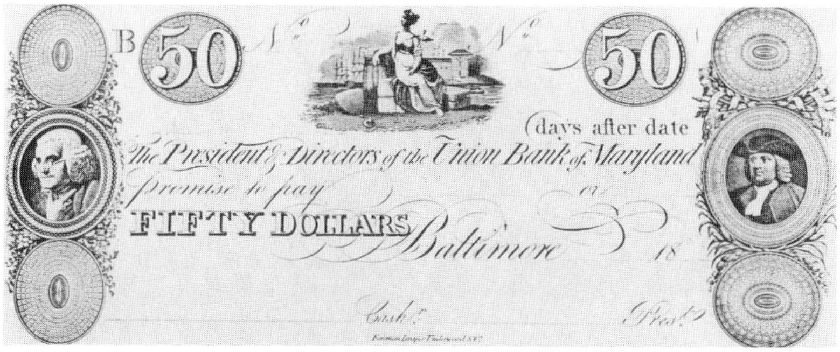

5.158.50 P

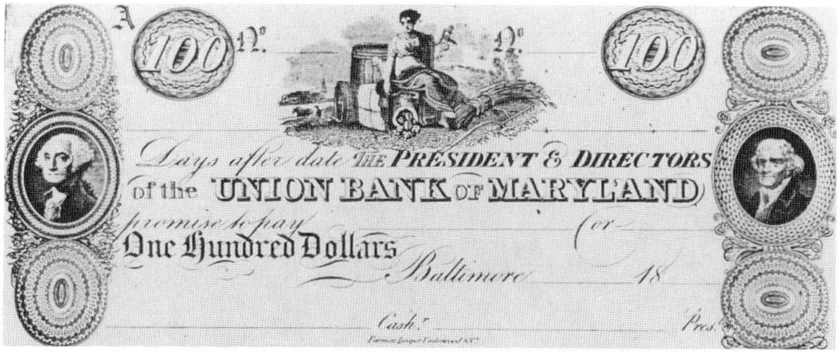

5.158.51 P

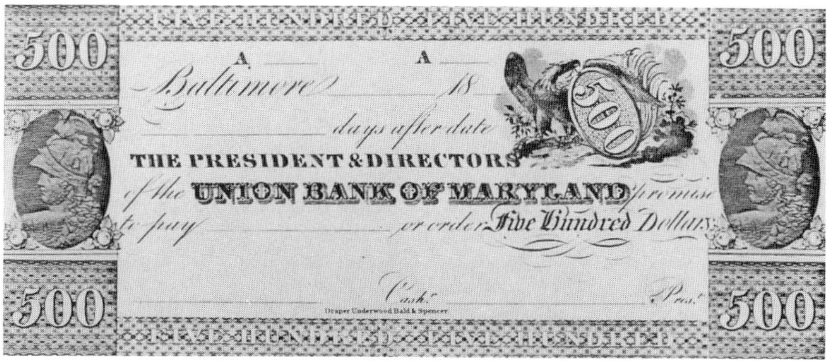

5.158.52 P

5.158.53 P

5.159 **Bank of the United States**

BALTIMORE OFFICE OF DISCOUNT AND DEPOSIT

The First Bank of the United States, created under an exclusive federal charter in 1791, operated until 1811 when renewal bills were defeated by one vote in both the Senate and the House of Representatives. The bank headquarters was in Philadelphia and branches eventually were opened in New York, Boston, Baltimore, Washington, Norfolk, Charleston, Savannah, and New Orleans. The Baltimore branch, known as the Office of Discount and Deposit, was located at the corner of Gay and Second streets. The Second Bank of the United States, again under federal charter and based in Philadelphia, opened for business on January 1, 1817, and by 1825 had eighteen branches, that in Baltimore being the third most important. When Congress refused to renew the bank's charter, its entire business in Baltimore, together with the banking house, was transferred to the Merchants' Bank of Baltimore on October 1, 1836.

LOCAL PRINCIPAL OFFICERS

	President	*Cashier*
1795–1799	Archibald Campbell	David Harris
1800–11	John Swan	David Harris
1817–ca. 1828	John Donnell	John White
1828–36	William Patterson	John White

The authors know of no banknotes that were issued by the Baltimore Office of Discount and Deposit. Notes issued by the bank's Philadelphia home office specified the Office of Discount and Deposit at which they could be redeemed, a space for the city name to be inserted in manuscript appearing on each note. Those notes in this category that have come to our attention are illustrated and recorded in the following listing.

5.159.1 C R-7

$5.00 Ca. 1819. Engraving, imprint: Tanner, Kearney & Tiebout & Co. "Comm. & Farmers Bank Baltimore" written in above date line. Counterfeit.

5.159.3 R-7

$10.00 Ca. 1835. Engraving, imprint: Murray, Draper, Fairman & Co. Payable at the Office of Discount & Deposit in Baltimore.

5.159.1 C

5.159.3

5.159.6 R-7
$50.00 Ca. 1804. Engraving, no imprint: Payable at the Office of Discount & Deposit in Baltimore.

5.159.7 R-7
$50.00 Ca. 1828. Engraving, imprint. Fairman, Draper, Underwood & Co. Payable at the Office of Discount and Deposit in Baltimore.

5.159.6

5.159.7

5.160 U.S. Army Life Insurance Co.

No information is available about this company, not even directory listings for the 1860–64 period having been found. The notes are listed as a Sutlers emission in "Sutler Issues of the Civil War" by James J. Curto in the *Numismatist* of 1959.

5.160.2 R-6
5c Printed partial date Dec. 186_. Lithography, imprint: Ferd. Meyer & Co., Lith., 96 Fulton St., New York. Light green.

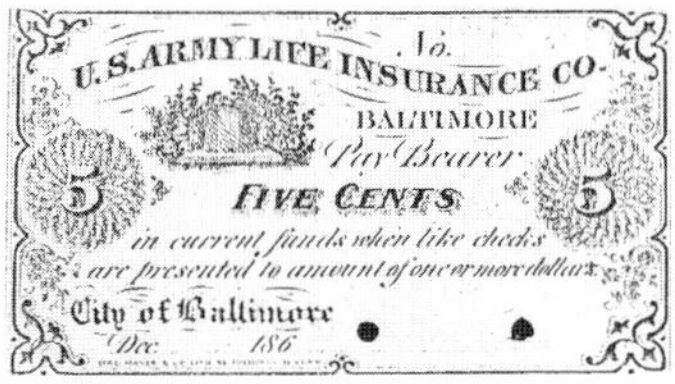

5.160.2

5.160.3 R-6
10c Printed partial date Dec. 186_. Lithography, imprint: Ferd. Meyer & Co., Lith., 96 Fulton St., New York. Light green. Similar to 5c, No. 5.160.2.

5.160.4 R-6
25c Printed partial date Dec. 186_. Lithography, imprint: Ferd. Meyer & Co., Lith., 96 Fulton St., New York. Light green. Similar to 5c, No. 5.160.2.

5.161 The United States Insurance Company of Baltimore

Incorporated by an act of the General Assembly of Maryland passed February 24, 1833 (Chapter 191, Acts of 1833), the company was authorized to underwrite both casualty and life insurance as soon as at least 5,000 shares of stock valued at $20 each, a total of $200,000, had been subscribed and paid for. This amount was apparently reached by late 1833 or early 1834 as "policies" "payable to bearer" of the type illustrated below are to be found bearing early 1834 dates. The company's offices were "on South Street, opposite Lovely Lane" according to the 1833 Baltimore city directory, the only edition in which such a listing appeared. Peter Neff, the president of the company, was listed at a residential address and at his "counting house, 108 Baltimore street"; in the 1835 directory he had only a residential listing and in succeeding editions was not shown at all. Joshua J. Atkinson was listed in 1833 as the company's secretary and signed the "policies" as such. Like Neff, he showed only a residential listing in 1835. In the 1837 directory, Atkinson was listed as the secretary of the Baltimore & Ohio Rail Road Co. The company must have terminated its activities by 1835 at the latest. Short-term "policies" of the type illustrated below, made out for varying amounts and payable to bearer, with the amount in manuscript, apparently circulated in Baltimore to some degree during the life of the company, probably being considered to be equivalent to post notes.

5.161.1 R-4

Ca. 1833–34. Engraving, imprint: Chas. Toppan & Co.

5.161.1

5.162 James Urie

The issuer was probably James Urie, listed in the 1814–15 city directory as a blockmaker at the corner of South and Pratt streets, the address printed on the one note recorded to date.

5.162.3 R-7

25c Printed date October 9, 1815. Letterpress, no imprint.

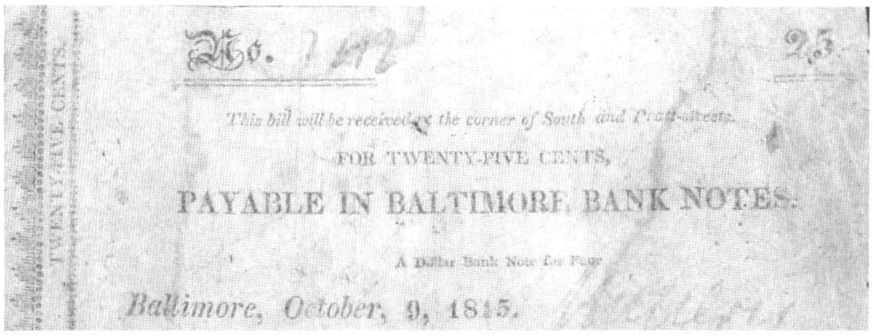

5.162.3

5.163 The Utopian Bank

Little definitive information on this institution, if it was ever in actual operation, is known. An engraved copperplate, from which the relatively few recorded notes were printed, has been in the collection of the Maryland Historical Society for many years, along with a proof-like impression on thick, soft paper without watermark. Another impression on similar paper watermarked CRANE DOESKIN in double-lined uppercase letters is known. Impressions are also known on thin, hard, unwatermarked paper. Some numismatists think that the notes were prepared for a Utopian community planned for the Baltimore area which never came to fruition. Others consider that they may have been prepared for a book on the Utopian system, in which there was a resurgence in interest in the early nineteenth century in America. The imprint of the engraver of the plate appears in the lower right corner of the printed note as "J. Sands. sc." John Sands was working in Baltimore as an engraver and copperplate printer between 1824 and 1827 according to city directories.

5.163.1 R-6
$5.00 Ca. 1824–27. Engraving, imprint: J. Sands, Sc. Thin hard unwatermarked wove paper. Similar to No. 5.163.2.

5.163.2 R-6
$5.00 Ca. 1824–27. Engraving, imprint: J. Sands, Sc. Similar to No. 5.163.1, except on thick, soft paper watermarked in the sheet, CRANE DOESKIN in double-lined uppercase letters.

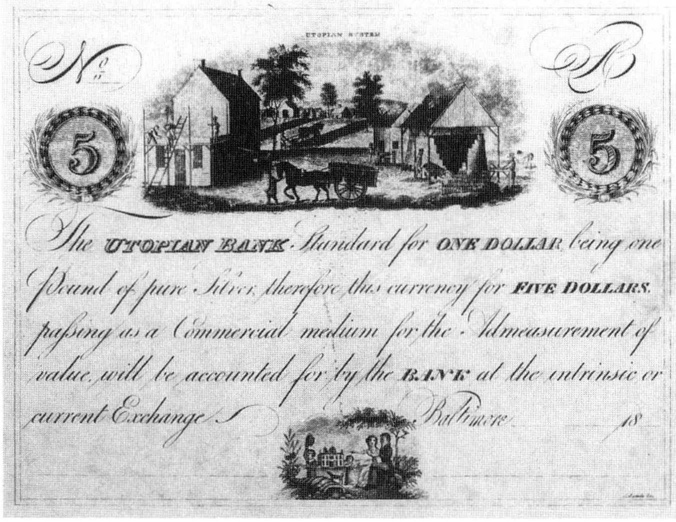

5.163.2

5.164 H. Vanderford

The issuer, Henry Vanderford, is listed in the 1816 city directory as a grocer at 1 County Wharf, Fell's Point. He is similarly listed in the 1817–18 edition and in the 1819 edition at a new address, just two doors away at 5 County Wharf.

5.164.3 R-7
18 3/4–18 1/4c. Printed date Oct. 7, 1815. Letterpress, no imprint. This "double denomination" note was undoubtedly the result of an error on the part of the printer who, when setting the type for the text of the body of the note carefully spelled out EIGHTEEN AND A QUARTER CENTS instead of the "18 3/4" which appears in two other places. The correct denomination of 18 3/4c is, of course, exactly three times the basic 6 1/4c denomination.

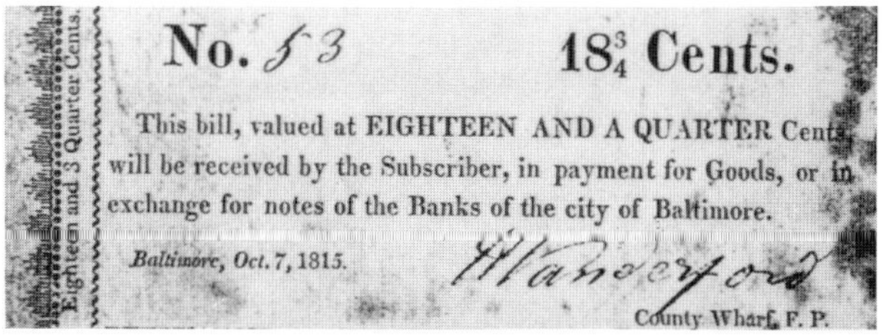

5.164.3

5.165 Vauxhall Drinking Institution

The issuer, whose whimsy is evident in the "firm name" and the depositor's name, Jonathan Slick, he selected to appear on his small-change scrip, was one Robert Saulsby, whose name appears in city directory listings from 1837 through 1845 as the proprietor of the Vauxhall Tavern, Vauxhall Hotel, and Vauxhall Gardens on the east side of Light Street "three doors south of York." This location would have been near the southern end of the Light Street pavillion of Baltimore's present-day Harbor Place.

5.165.1 R-7

6 1/4c Printed date Nov. 8, 1839. Letterpress, no imprint.

5.165.1

5.166 Wm. G. Wade

The identity of this issuer has not as yet been definitely established as no listings have been found in the city directory editions of 1814–15, 1816, and 1817–18. However, the full printed date and specific street address, as well as the statement that the note will be received "in payment for goods or in exchange for notes of the banks of the city of Baltimore" certainly indicate that Wade was a shopkeeper in business in August 1815, at 69 Bond St.

5.166.2 R-7

12 1/2c Printed date August 17, 1815. Letterpress, no imprint.

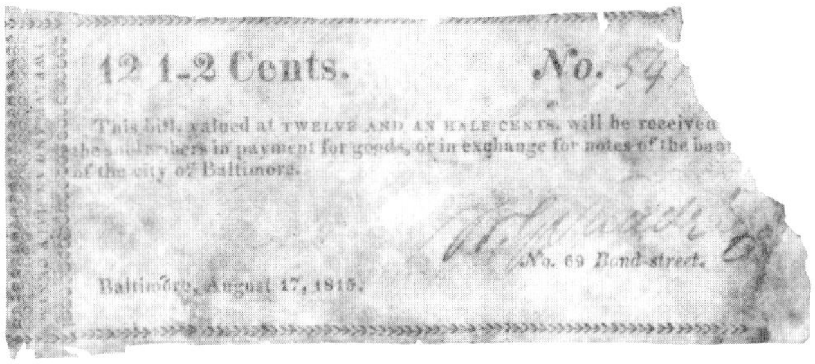

5.166.2

5.167 The Western Bank of Baltimore

Charter approved March 28, 1836, the bank having succeeded the Mechanic's Savings Fund Society of Baltimore, which had been founded in 1832 and Converted to and became the Western National Bank of Baltimore in 1865. The bank was located on the west side of Eutaw Street, at the corner of Marion Street, between Baltimore and Fayette streets.

5.167.1 R-7

$1.00 Printed date July 1st, 1845. Engraving, imprint: Danforth, Spencer & Hufty, New York / Spencer, Hufty & Danforth, Philada. (MD125G4)

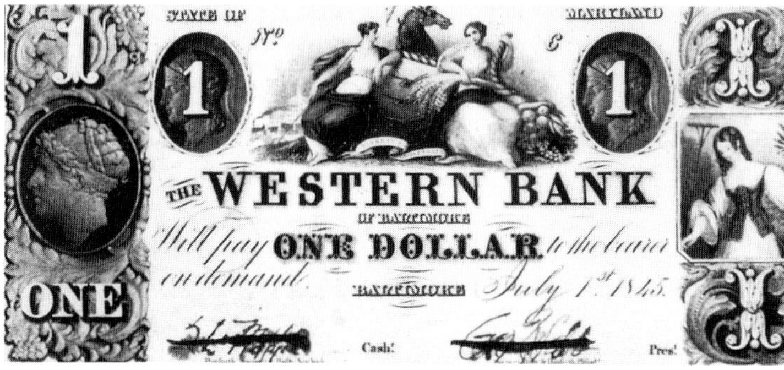

5.167.1

5.167.1 P R-7

$1.00 Printed date July 1st, 1845. Engraving, imprint: Danforth, Spencer & Hufty, New York / Spencer, Hufty & Danforth, Philada. Proof.

5.167.2 R-6

$1.00 Printed date July 1st, 185_. Engraving, imprint: Danforth, Spencer & Hufty, New York / Spencer, Hufty & Danforth, Philada. Similar to $1.00, No. 5.167.1, except signature space for cashier only. (MD125G4a)

5.167.3 R-7

$1.00 Printed date July 1st, 1862. Engraving, imprint: Danforth, Spencer & Hufty, New York / Spencer, Hufty & Danforth, Philada. Similar to $1.00, No. 5.167.2, with additional imprint A.B.N. Co. (MD125G4b)

5.167.4 R-7

$2.00 Ca. 1862. Engraving, imprint: Spencer, Hufty & Danforth. No other information available.

5.167.5 S R-5

$3.00 Ca. 1840s. Engraving, imprint: Durand & Compy, New York. Spurious. (MD125GS5)

5.167.6 A R-7

$3.00 Ca. 1840s. Engraving, imprint: Durand & Company, New York. Altered note. (MD125A5)

5.167.7 SENC

$5.00 Ca. 1836–40s. Engraving, imprint: Draper, Toppan, Longacre. Center vignette is the Exchange building, Baltimore. Right vignette is the Battle Monument, Baltimore. (MD125G12)

5.167.7 C R-5

$5.00 Ca. 1836–40s. Engraving, imprint: Draper, Toppan, Longacre & Co., New York. Counterfeit of $5.00, No. 5.167.7. (MD125C12)

5.167.8 A R-7

$5.00 Ca. 1836–40s. Engraving, imprint: Danforth, Underwood, & Co.; Underwood, Bald, Spencer & Hufty. Altered from $5.00 Tenth Ward Bank, New York City, NY1935G16. (MD125A10)

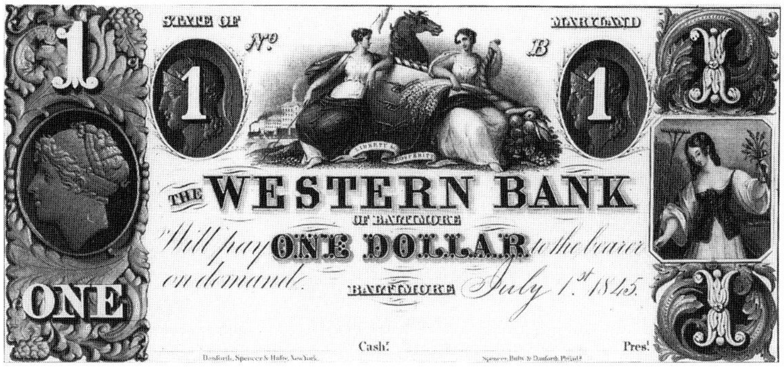

5.167.1 P

5.167.5 S

5.167.7 C

5.167.8 A

5.167.9 SENC
$5.00 Ca. 1850s. Engraving, imprint: Unknown. *Center:* 5; Mercury seated on bale, holding wand and cornucopia, balance, strong box and lion at right; 5. *Left:* 5 / medallion head / 5. *Right:* Statue of Washington in large 5. *Between signatures:* Dog's head. (MD125G16)

5.167.10 A R-7
$10.00 Ca. 1836–40s. Engraving, imprint: Danforth, Underwood & Co.; Underwood, Bald, Spencer & Hufty. *Center:* Presentation of the Declaration of Independence. *Right:* Pat Lyon standing by forge. Altered from $10.00 Tenth Ward Bank, New York City, NY1935G18. (MD125A15)

5.167.11 N SENC
$10.00 Ca. 1840s. Engraving, imprint: Unknown. *Center:* Mercury on wharf, ships in background. Nongenuine. (MD125N5)

5.167.12 N SENC
$10.00 Ca. 1840s. Engraving, imprint: Unknown. *Center:* Woman with ships in background. Nongenuine. (MD124N10)

5.167.13 R-7
$10.00 Ca. 1850s. Engraving, imprints: Toppan, Carpenter & Co., N.Y., and ABCo. *Center:* Mercury seated on bale, holding wand and cornucopia, balance, strongbox and lion at right. *Left:* boy seated holding sickle, girl carrying basket and sheaf. *Between signatures:* Dog's head. (MD125G20)

5.167.14 A SENC
$20.00 Ca. 1836–40s. Engraving, imprint: Danforth, Underwood & Co.; Underwood, Bald, Spencer & Hufty. *Center:* Diagonal 20, on medallion head; Pat Lyon standing by forge; diagonal 20, on medallion head. *Left:* 20 / primitive train, in oval / XX. *Right:* 20 / cattle, man at right, in oval / XX. Altered from $20.00 Tenth Ward Bank, New York City, NY1935G20. (MD125A20)

5.167.18 S

5.167.15 SENC
$20.00 Ca. 1850s. Engraving, imprint: Unknown. *Left corner:* 20 / two farmers at lunch, woman pouring water from pitcher. *Left:* Winged female head surrounded by flags, anchor, etc., eagle at top / XX / male head and hammer on shield. *Lower right:* 20. *Between signatures:* Dog's head. (MD125G24)

5.167.16 N SENC
$50.00 Ca. 1836–40s. Engraving, imprint: Terry, Pelton. No other information available. Nongenuine. (MD125N15)

5.167.17 SENC
$50.00 Ca. 1850s. Engraving, imprint: Unknown. *Center:* L; village scene, men, horses, cattle, etc.; L. *Left:* 50 / canal scene / FIFTY. *Right:* 50 / allegorical woman / FIFTY. *Between signatures:* Sheaves. (MD125G28)

5.167.18 S R-7
$100.00 Ca. 1840. Engraving, imprint: Draper, Toppan & Co., New York & Phila. Spurious note. (MD125S10)

5.167.19 N SENC
$100.00 Ca. 1840s. Engraving, imprint: Unknown. *Center:* Sampson and the lion. Nongenuine, unattributed. (MD125N20)

5.167.20 SENC
$100.00 Ca. 1850s. Engraving, imprint: Unknown. *Center:* C; woman seated, eagle at right with medal in beak, barrels, bales, etc.; C. *Left:* 100 / sloop, city in background / 100. *Right:* 100 / woman standing carving male bust / 100. (MD125G32)

5.167.21 SENC
$500.00 Ca. 1850s. Engraving, imprint: Unknown. *Center:* Cherub; 500; cherub. *Left and right:* 500, across. *Between signatures:* Ship. (MD125G36)

5.168 Western Franklin Savings Institution

This institution may have begun operation about 1833 as a charter was approved January 16, 1833, for a Franklin Savings Company, and a notice of a 5% dividend was published in the January 7, 1834, issue of the *American and Commercial Daily Advertiser.* No record thereafter has been located, and the charter expired in 1845 and was not renewed. However, on March 10, 1843, a charter was approved for the Franklin Savings Institution of Baltimore, the sole purpose of this incorporation being the liquidation of that institution. The title in this 1843 act differs from that passed in 1833 only in that "Institution" is substituted for "Company." It seems likely that the 1843 act was intended to apply to the Western Franklin Savings Institution because the incorporators, with two exceptions, were all directors of Western Franklin. The identification of the recorded signers of the Western Franklin scrip, James Dixon (treasurer) and John Rothrock (president), has not been definitely established, although individuals with those names are to be found in city directories, Dixon as a carpenter on Pratt Street west of Sharp in 1840–41 and 1842, and Rothrock (without occupation) on Paca Street south of Lombard. The Western Franklin appears in a bank list in the 1842 directory as being on Baltimore Street, west of Eutaw. Both addresses are in the same general neighborhood as that of the Western Franklin.

5.168.1 R-7

6 1/4c Ca. 1839–40. Engraving, imprint: Underwood, Bald, Spencer & Hufty, Philada / Danforth, Underwood & Co., New York.

5.168.1 P R-7

6 1/4c Ca. 1839–40. Engraving, imprint: Underwood, Bald, Spencer & Hufty, Philada / Danforth, Underwood & Co., New York. Proof.

5.168.2 P R-7

12 1/2c Ca. 1839–40. Engraving, imprint: Underwood, Bald, Spencer & Hufty, Philada / Danforth, Underwood & Co., New York. Proof.

5.168.3 R-7

25c Ca. 1839–40. Engraving, imprint: Underwood, Bald, Spencer & Hufty, Philada. / Danforth, Underwood & Co., New York.

5.168.3 P R-7

25c Ca. 1839–40. Engraving, imprint: Underwood, Bald, Spencer & Hufty, Philada. / Danforth, Underwood & Co., New York. Proof.

5.168.4 R-6

25c Ca. 1839–40. Engraving, imprint: Draper, Toppan & Co., Philada.

5.168.1

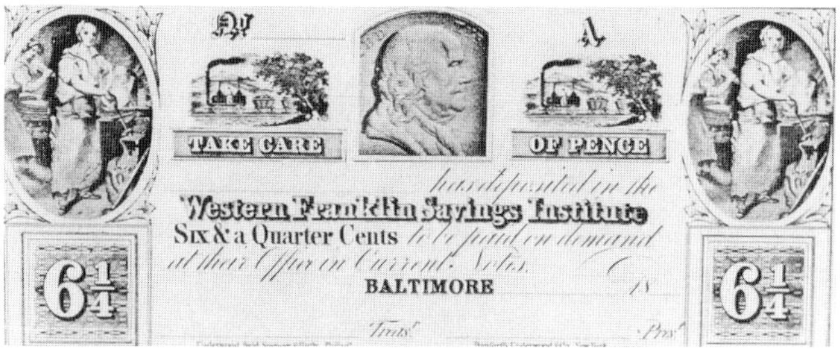

5.168.1 P

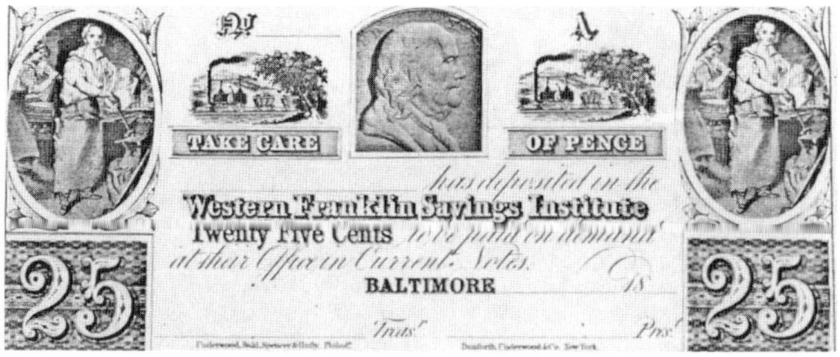

5.168.3 P

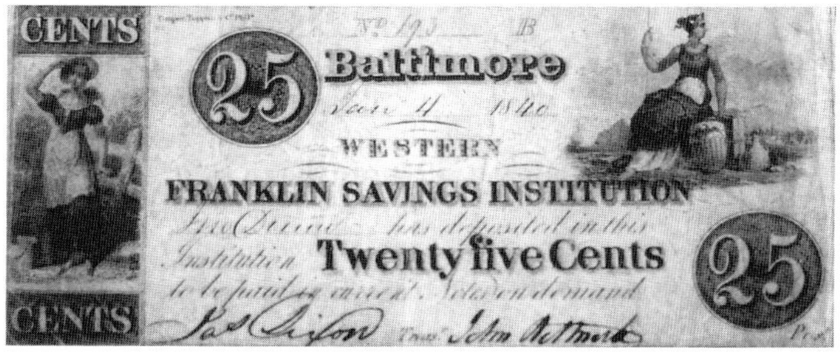

5.168.4

5.168.5 P R-7

50c Ca. 1839–40. Engraving, imprint: Underwood, Bald, Spencer & Hufty, Philada. / Danforth, Underwood & Co., New York. Proof.

5.168.6 R-7

$1.00 Ca. 1839–40. Engraving, imprint: Underwood, Bald, Spencer & Hufty, Philada. / Danforth, Underwood & Co., New York.

5.168.6 P R-7

$1.00 Ca. 1839–40. Engraving, imprint: Underwood, Bald, Spencer & Hufty, Philada. / Danforth, Underwood & Co., New York. Proof.

5.168.7 R-7

$2.00 Ca. 1839–40. Engraving, imprint: Draper, Toppan & Co., Philada.

5.168.5 P

5.168.6 P

5.168.7

5.169 Western Mechanics Savings Institution

Charter approved March 5, 1830. The sole directory listing for this institution, located at the corner of Baltimore and Pearl streets, was in the 1842 edition, indicating that the enterprise ceased operations in early 1841, after which no other listings have been found. M. Perine, who signed the notes as treasurer, was Maulden Perine, who operated a pottery at the corner of Pine and Lexington streets and lived nearby on Lexington Street, west of Pine Street. John Feast, who signed as treasurer pro tem, was a florist and seedsman on Lexington Street west of Pine Street.

5.169.1 R-7

6 1/4c Ca. 1839–41. Engraving, imprint: Underwood, Bald, Spencer & Hufty, Philada. / Danforth, Underwood & Co., New York.

5.169.3 R-7

12 1/2c Ca. 1839–41. Letterpress, no imprint. Vignette in upper left corner of Battle Monument, Baltimore.

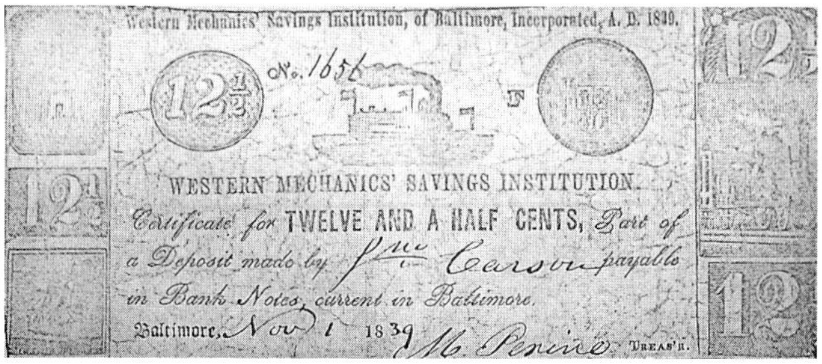

5.169.3

5.169.4 R-7

12 1/2c Ca. 1839–41. Engraving, imprint: Draper, Toppan & Co., Phila. Similar to 12 1/2c, No. 5.169.5, but year date partially printed, 18__, and title of signer, "Treas'r."

5.169.5 R-6

12 1/2c Printed year date 1839. Engraving, imprint: Draper, Toppan & Co., Phila. Title of signer, "Treas'r. Pro tem."

5.169.5 P R-7

12 1/2c Printed year date 1839. Engraving, imprint: Draper, Toppan & Co., Phila. Title of signer, "Treas'r. Pro tem." See proof sheet No. 5.169 A for example.

5.169.6 R-7

25c Ca. 1839. Letterpress, no imprint. Vignette in upper left corner of the Battle Monument, Baltimore.

5.169.7 R-7

25c Printed year date 1839. Engraving, imprint: Draper, Toppan & Co., Phila. Vignette at left of the Battle Monument, Baltimore.

5.169.8 R-7

25c Printed year date 1839. Engraving, imprint: Draper, Toppan & Co., Phila. Title of signer, "Treas'r. Pro tem."

5.169.8 P R-7

25c Printed year date 1839. Engraving, imprint: Draper, Toppan & Co., Phila. Title of signer, "Treas'r. Pro tem." See proof sheet No. 5.169 A for example.

5.169.9 R-7

25c Printed year date 1839. Engraving, imprint: Draper, Toppan & Co., Phila. Red, three-line, handstamped overprint, BALT. & OHIO RAILROAD STOCK ORDERS, over "Bank notes" in redemption clause. Signature block inscribed "Treasr."

5.169.10 R-7

50c Ca. 1839. Letterpress, imprint: MURPHY, PRINTER. Vignette in upper left corner of the Battle Monument, Baltimore.

5.169.5

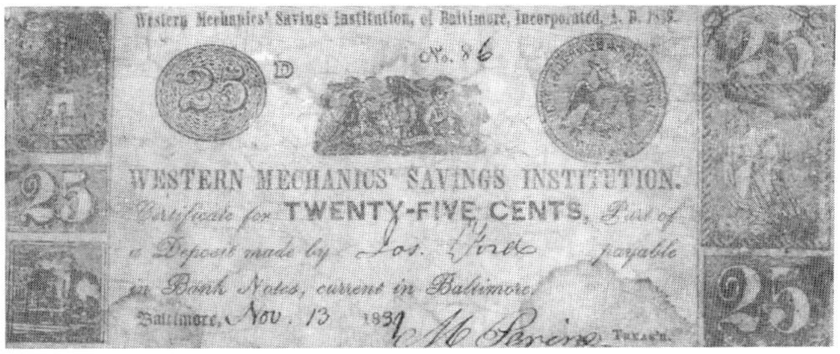

5.169.6

5.169.7

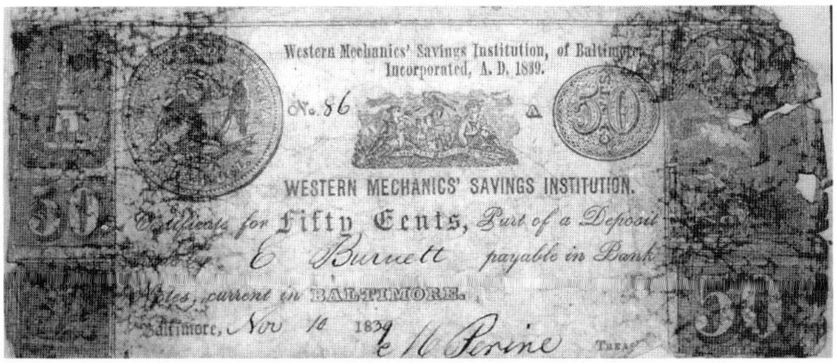

5.169.10

5.169.11

5.169.11 R-6

50c Printed year date 1839. Engraving, imprint: Draper, Toppan & Co., Phila. Red, three-line, handstamped overprint, BALT. & OHIO RAILROAD STOCK ORDERS, over "Bank Notes" in redemption clause. Signature block inscribed "Treasr."

5.169.12 R-7

50c Printed year date 1839. Engraving, imprint: Draper, Toppan and Co. Phila. Signature block inscribed "Treasr. Pro tem."

5.169.12 P R-7

50c Printed year date 1839. Engraving, imprint: Draper, Toppan and Co., Phila. Signature block inscribed "Treasr. Pro tem." See proof sheet No. 5.169 A for example.

5.169.13 R-6

$1.00 Printed year date 1839. Engraving, imprint: Draper, Toppan & Co., Philada. Red, three-line, handstamped overprint, BALT. & OHIO RAILROAD STOCK ORDERS, over "Bank Notes" in redemption clause. Signature block inscribed "Treasr." Similar to $1.00, No. 5.169.15.

5.169.12

5.169.14

5.169.14 R-6

$1.00 Printed year date 1840. Engraving, imprint: Draper, Toppan & Co., Phila. Signature block inscribed "Treasr." Without red overprint.

5.169.15 R-6

$1.00 Printed year date 1840. Engraving, imprint: Draper, Toppan & Co., Philada. Red, three-line, handstamped overprint, BALT. & OHIO RAILROAD STOCK ORDERS over "Bank Notes" in redemption clause. Signature block inscribed "Treasr." Similar to No. 5.169.16 except for handstamp.

Proofs of the 12 1/2c, 25c, and 50c notes with full printed year date and "Treas. Pro tem" (Nos. 5.169.5 P, 5.169.8 P, 5.169.12 P).

5.169.16 R-7

$1.00 Printed year date 1840. Engraving, imprint. Draper, Toppan & Co., Phila. Red, oval, handstamped overprint, BALT. & OHIO RAILROAD STOCK ORDERS, over "Bank Notes" in redemption clause.

5.169.17 R-7

$2.00 Printed year date 1840. Engraving, imprint: Draper, Toppan & Co., Phila. Red, three-line, handstamped overprint, BALT. & OHIO RAIL ROAD STOCK ORDERS, over "Bank Notes" in redemption clause.

5.169.18 R-7

$2.00 Printed year date 1840. Engraving, imprint: Draper, Toppan & Co., Phila. Without overprint.

5.169.16

5.169.17

5.170 Western Savings Institution of Baltimore

In the *Sun* of Wednesday, November 1, 1837, there appeared the following news item:

> Banking Extraordinary.—We understand that a fellow on the Eastern Shore of Maryland, has attempted an emission of notes of the "Western Savings Institution of Baltimore." His notes passed well enough at first, and he supplied himself with a horse and gig, a watch, etc. The thing took so well that he resolved to dip deeper, and bought a farm; but the sight of such a quantity of bran [*sic*] new notes, all of them the same, as was counted out to pay for it, excited the suspicion of the seller, and on inquiry he found that the Western Savings Institution had not a local habitation. At his suggestion, the officers of justice put a period to our banker's further operations.

No further information has been found as to the identity or fate of the self-appointed "banker." However, some two years later, in July 1840, the following two advertisements appeared in the *Sun*.

Thursday, July 9, 1840:

> NOTICE.—Having associated myself with the WESTERN SAVINGS INSTITUTION, I am desirous of to call in all my other notes. All persons holding any of the above notes will please present them for redemption.
>
> O. C. FRITSCHLER
>
> N.B. The notes of the western savings institution will at all times be redeemed in current notes of this city, at their office, No. 60 PENNSYLVANIA AVENUE.
>
> j4-1ws

Wednesday, July 22, 1840.

> NOTICE. - All persons holding notes on the "WESTERN SAVINGS INSTITUTION," are earnestly requested to present the same for redemption as soon as convenient, at their office, No. 60 Pennsylvania Avenue.
>
> J22-3ts W.O. C. Fritschler President

According to the 1840–42 city directories, Wm. Fritschler was a tavernkeeper on Pennsylvania Avenue, east of Biddle Street. He was so listed in only this one directory, his name not appearing in prior or succeeding editions. For information on the tavern operation and scrip note, see Black Horse Tavern, No. 5.18.

5.170.1 R-7
6 1/4c Printed date July 1, 1840. Letterpress, imprint: Murphy, Printer. The "4" in "6 1/4" on the value die is reversed. Vignette in center of left panel is the Battle Monument, Baltimore.

5.170.3 R-7
25c Printed date July 1, 1840. Letterpress, imprint: Murphy, Printer, Baltimore. Center vignette is a view of Baltimore Harbor from Federal Hill.

5.170.1

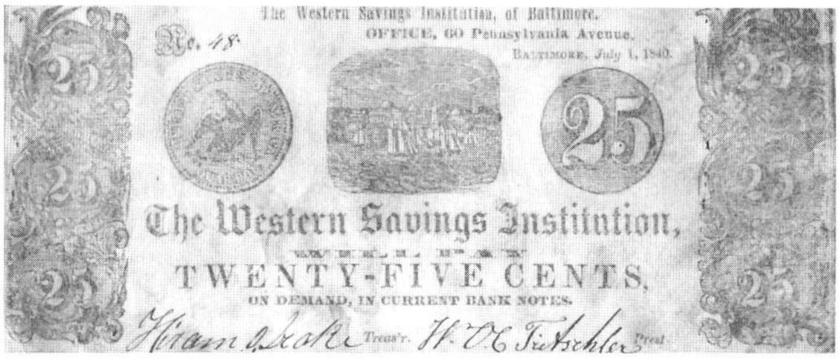

5.170.3

5.171 George White

The issuer was a grocer at the corner of Wilk and Caroline streets, Fell's Point, being so listed in the 1816 city directory.

5.171.3 R-7
3c Printed date September 11, 1815. Letterpress, no imprint.

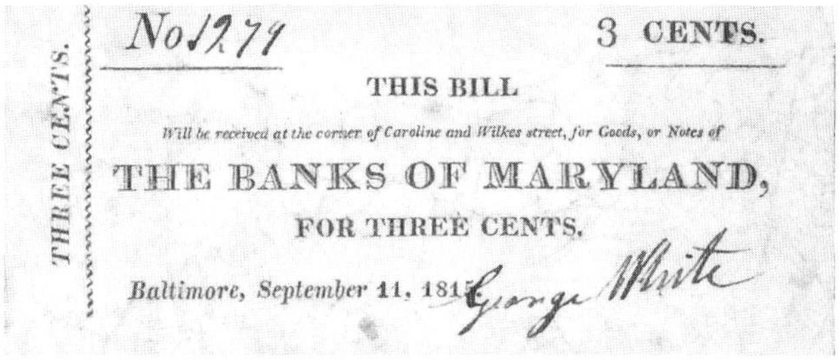

5.171.3

5.172 William Wilkens & Co.

The issuer was a processor of animal hair from the tails of cattle, horses, and hogs, the springiness of which made it ideal for stuffing mattresses, sofas, chairs, and carriage seats. Later the company produced bristles, glue, and hair cloth. Founded in the late 1830s, the company built the plant illustrated on its scrip in the mid-1850s. The company remained in business until well into the twentieth century.

Complete sheet of fourteen with six impressions of the 5c note arranged se tenant to a vertical column of two 50c, two 25c, three 10c, and an extra 5c. This sheet layout is a perfect example of the way that lithographers would make maximum use of available space on a lithographic stone when laying down transfers from a matrix (master die) stone.

5.172.1 R-5

5c Printed date Dec. 1st, 1862. Lithography, imprint: Hunckel & Son, Balto.

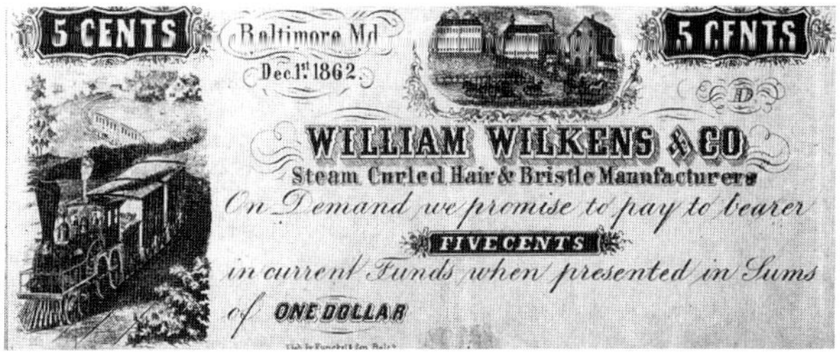

5.172.1

5.172.2 R-5

10c Printed date Dec. 1st, 1862. Lithography, imprint: Hunckel & Son, Balto. Similar to 5c, No. 5.172.1.

5.172.3 R-6

25c Printed date Dec. 1st, 1862. Lithography, imprint: Hunckel & Son, Balto. Similar to 5c, No. 5.172.1.

5.172.4 R-6

50c Printed date Dec. 1st, 1862. Lithography, imprint: Hunckel & Son, Balto. Similar to 5c, No. 5.172.1.

5.173 **John W. Wilmer**

For several days in early to mid-September 1840, a small notice over the name of John W. Wilmer appeared in the *Sun* to the effect that those holding his notes could have them redeemed at his office. Wilmer was a commission merchant and dealer in grain and produce at No. 5 Bowley's Wharf. No surviving examples of his scrip have as yet been recorded.

5.174 **J. F. Winchell**

The issuer, James F. Winchell, was a baker whose shop was at 59 South St., being so listed in city directories from 1812 to 1819.

5.174.1 R-7
6 1/4c Printed date August 26, 1815. Letterpress, no imprint.

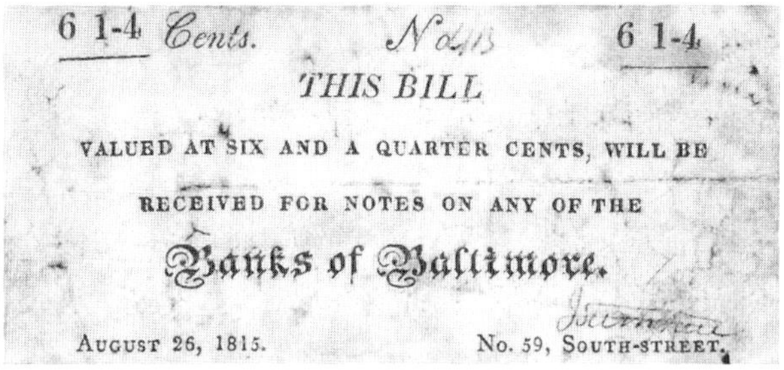

5.174.1

5.175 **Thomas Winwood**

In the collection of the Maryland Historical Society there is a small copper plate engraved for a 6 1/4c note, dated June 10, 1815, which is inscribed:

> This Bill will be received at No. 13 North Liberty St for six and a quarter cents in exchange for goods or bank notes
>
> Balt- June 10th 1815 ____
>
> W. Robinson, Sc Printed by J. Dainty 36 Market St.

The 1814–15 Baltimore City directory contains a listing for a Thomas Winwood, grocer, 13 N. Liberty St., who was obviously the issuer. The engraver has been identified as William Robinson who was working in Philadelphia in the 1815–18 period, and the printer was John Dainty, a copperplate printer in Philadelphia in the same period. No examples of this note have been recorded by the authors.

A recent gift to the Society included a fragmented example of a 10c note of the same issuer, whose signature is identifiable under ultraviolet light.

5.175.3 R-7
10c Ca. 1816. Letterpress, no imprint.

5.175.3

5.176 Unidentified Issuer

The notes illustrated below appeared as Lot No. 636 in the NASCA auction sale of R. M. Smythe & Co. on March 31, 1989, being geographically attributed to Philadelphia. In contemporary Philadelphia city directories of the period, no Light Street is listed. There was, and is, a prominent business street of that name in Baltimore, at the western edge of the Inner Harbor. As yet, the issuer, obviously a storekeeper, for whom these notes were prepared has not been identified, but in the opinion of the authors, the notes are of Baltimore origin.

5.176.3 R-7
25c Printed partial date 186_. Engraving, imprint: Unknown.

5.176.4 R-7
50c Printed partial date 186_. Engraving, imprint: Unknown.

5.176.3

5.176.4

5.177 Unidentified Issuer

This note is considered to be a remainder from an actual issue by an as-yet-unidentified individual. Had it been a salesman's sample or an unused so-called stock note, it is highly unlikely that a complete day, month, and year date would have been printed thereon.

5.177.5 R-7
$1.00 Printed date Dec. 6, 1839. Letter-press, no imprint.

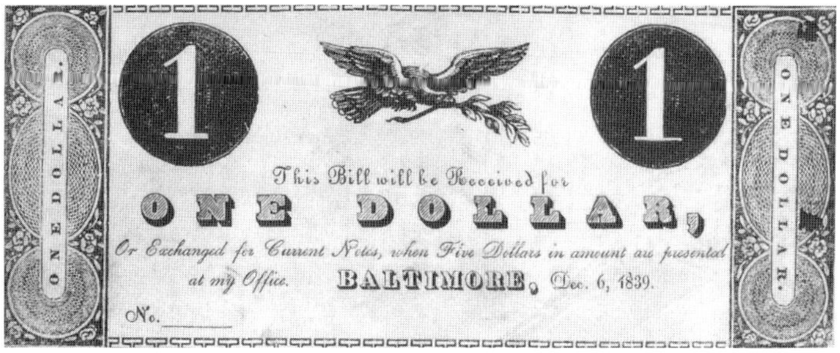

5.177.5

5.181 Unidentified Issuer

The proofs illustrated below were discovered in the Christie's 1990 sale of the American Bank Note Co. archival material. The potential issuer of these notes, if ever produced, has not been discovered as yet. These proofs bear the imprint, "Chas. Toppan & Co., Phila." who were using this wording from about 1834 to 1837. Prior to 1829 the usual imprint was simply "Charles Toppan," and an 1837 merger produced the firm name, "Draper, Toppan, Longacre & Co." Thus, these proofs were probably produced in the 1834–37 period. In the same Christie's sale were proofs that had been produced by Underwood, Bald, Spencer & Hufty for J. I. Cohen, Jr. & Brothers, private bankers in Baltimore. On all issues attributed to Cohen the promissory legend begins, "We promise to pay . . . at our Banking House" (see Nos. 5.35.1 P–16 P). The comparable wording on the proofs shown below is "I promise to pay . . . at my Banking House." Researching contemporary Baltimore city directories reveals only two private bank listings during the entire 1829–41 period: J. I. Cohen Jr. & Brothers, and Evan Poultney's Bank. The latter firm changed its name to Poultney, Ellicott & Co. in 1833. Based upon the foregoing, it is the authors' assumption that Toppan submitted the proofs to the Cohen firm, which rejected them, ultimately deciding upon the "we-our" wording used on the notes produced by Underwood, Bald, Spencer & Hufty.

5.181.1 P R-7

$5.00 Ca. 1837. Engraving, imprint: Chas. Toppan & Co., Phila. Vignette, right end panel, Battle Monument, Baltimore. Proof.

5.181.2 P R-7

$10.00 Ca. 1837. Engraving, imprint: Chas. Toppan & Co., Phila. Proof.

5.181.3 P R-7

$20.00 Ca. 1837. Engraving, imprint: Chas. Toppan & Co., Phila. Proof.

5.181.1 P

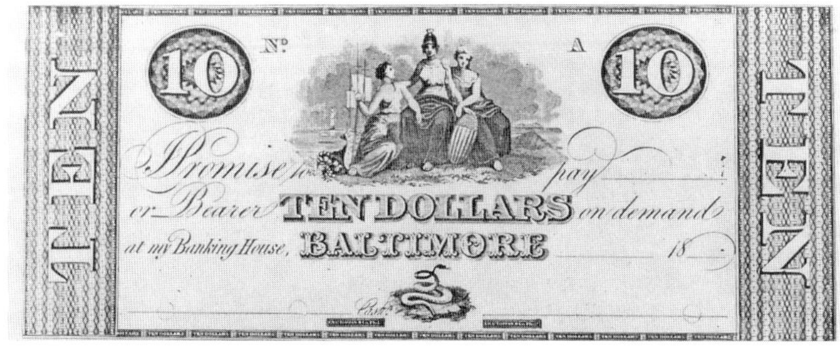

5.181.2 P

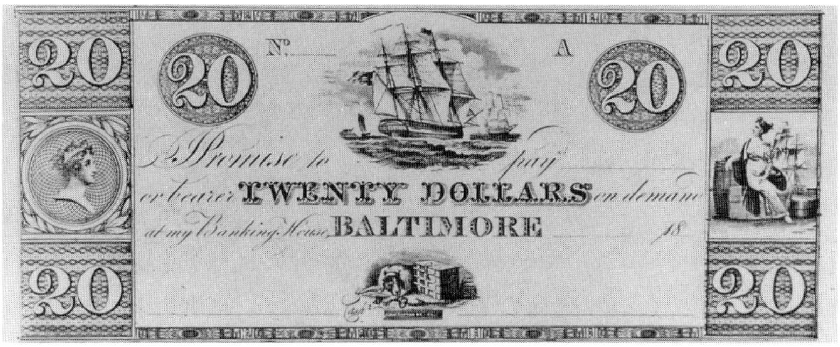

5.181.3 P

5.181.4 P R-7
$20.00 Ca. 1837. Engraving, imprint: Chas. Toppan & Co., Phila. Proof.

5.181.5 P R-7
$50.00 Ca. 1837. Engraving, imprint: Chas. Toppan & Co., Phila. Proof.

5.181.6 P R-7
$100.00 Ca. 1837. Engraving, imprint: Chas. Toppan & Co., Phila. Vignette, right end panel, Battle Monument, Baltimore. Proof.

5.181.7 P R-7
$500.00 Ca. 1837. Engraving, imprint: Chas. Toppan & Co., Phila. Proof.

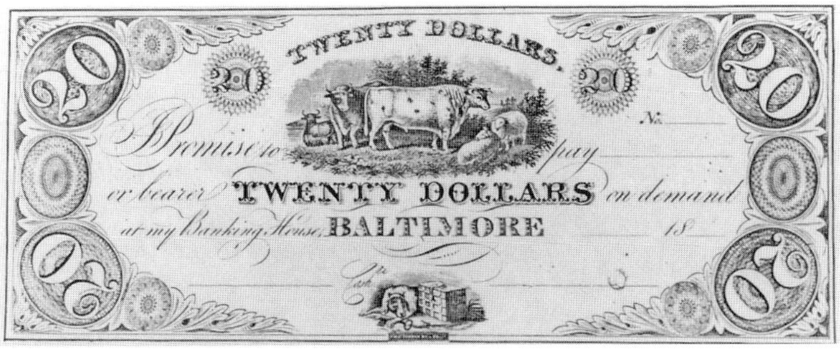

5.181.4 P

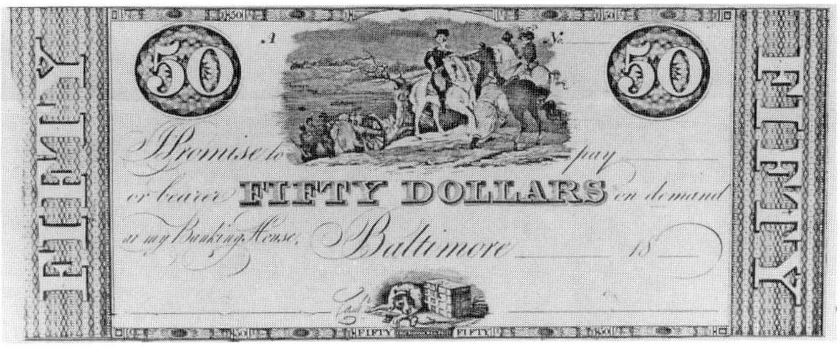

5.181.5 P

5.181.6 P

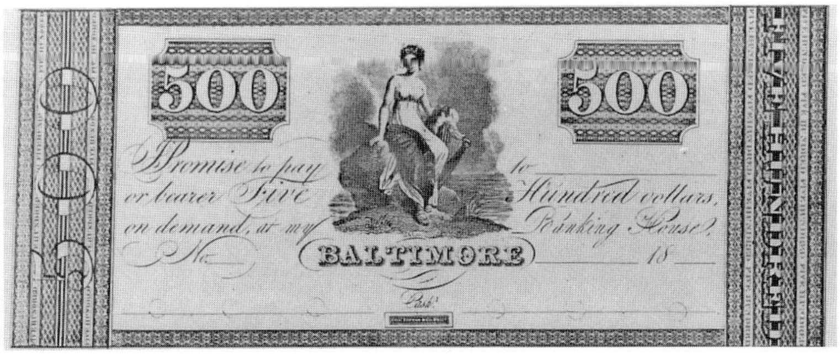

5.181.7 P

5.181.8 P R-7

$1000.00 Ca. 1837. Engraving, imprint: Chas. Toppan & Co., Phila. Proof.

5.181.8 P

5.182 Unidentified Issuer

The proofs illustrated here were discovered in the Christie's 1990 sale of the American Bank Note Co. archival material. The potential issuer of these notes, if ever produced, has not been determined.

5.182.1 P R-7

$1.00 Ca. 1836–43. Engraving, imprint: Underwood, Bald, Spencer & Hufty, Philada. / Danforth, Underwood & Co., New York. Proof.

5.182.2 P R-7

$2.00 Ca. 1836–43. Engraving, imprint: Underwood, Bald, Spencer & Hufty, Philada. / Danforth, Underwood & Co., New York. Proof.

5.182.1 P

5.182.2 P

6 BALTIMORE COUNTY

6.1 E. T. J. Woodward

The issuer was Emanuel T. J. Woodward, a real estate agent and gentleman farmer whose home and office were at Providence, three miles north of Baltimore on Bel Air Road. On January 8, 1840, he advertised in the *Sun* that he would attend to the duties of coroner and magistrate for Baltimore County at his residence and that when in the city he could be found at the store of Adam Ross at the corner of Baltimore Street and Centre Market Space.

6.1.3 R-7

25c Ca. 1840. Lithography, no imprint. "County" inserted in manuscript after BALTIMORE in date line.

6.1.5 R-7

$1.00 Printed partial year date 184_. Lithography, no imprint. Payable "at Conine's Office." Conine was the proprietor of a prominent lottery and exchange office in Baltimore, by whom Woodward had arranged to have his scrip redeemed.

6.1.3

6.1.5

7 BARREN CREEK / BARREN CREEK SPRINGS, WICOMICO COUNTY

This small farming community, prior to 1865 in Somerset County, was noted from Indian times for the healing powers of its foul-smelling spring water. In the early nineteenth century, when the town was a stagecoach stop, its fame spread and large numbers of people came to procure the sulphurous mineral waters. The spring-water prosperity peaked in the latter part of the nineteenth and early twentieth centuries, and terminated by 1920. The spring has still not run dry. Today the town is known as Mardela Springs or simply Mardela.

7.1 John H. Bacon

The issuer was the proprietor of a general store.

7.1.2 R-7

10c Printed date November 4, 1862. Letterpress, no imprint.

7.1.3 R-7

25c Printed date November 4, 1862. Letterpress, no imprint.

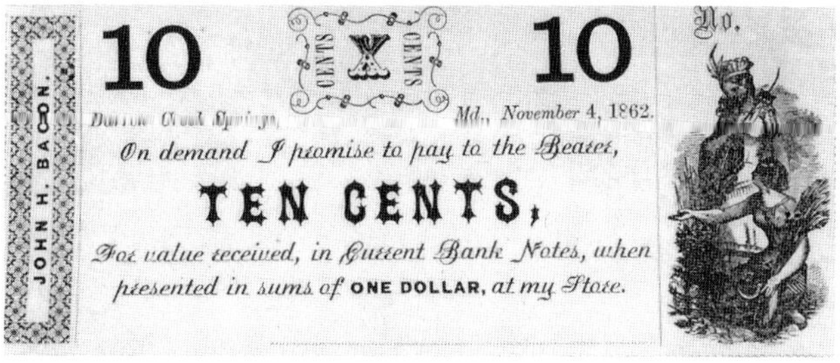

7.1.2

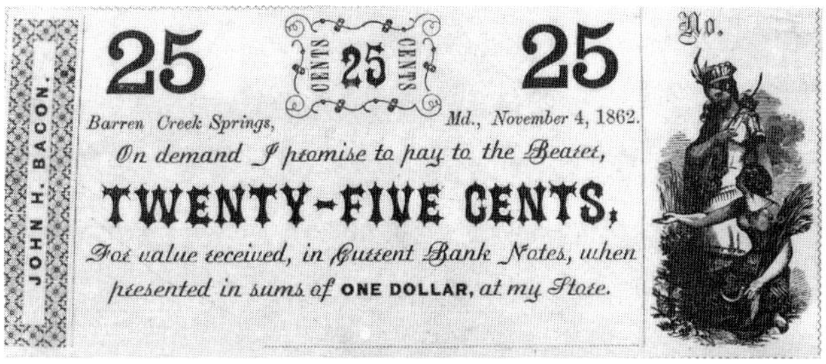

7.1.3

7.2 A. S. D. Evans

The issuer was the proprietor of a general store.

7.2.2 R-7
10c Printed date Nov. 15, 1839. Letterpress, imprint: MURPHY, PRINT. BALT. / MURPHY PRINTER BALTIMORE.

7.2.3 R-7
25c Printed date Nov. 15, 1839. Letterpress, imprint: MURPHY, PRINT. BALT.

7.2.4 R-7
50c Printed date Nov. 15, 1839. Letterpress, imprint: MURPHY, PRINT. BALT.

7.2.2

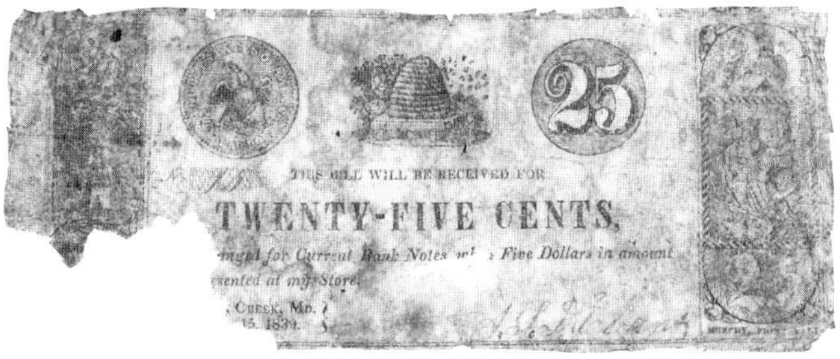

7.2.3

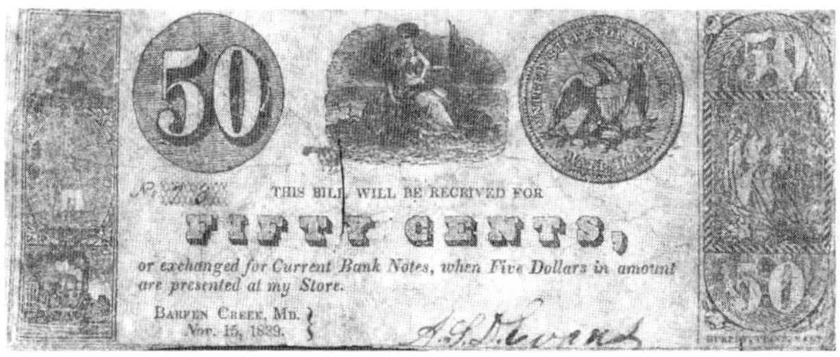

7.2.4

8 BEAVER DAMS, WORCESTER COUNTY

8.1 Unidentified Issuer

The only note recorded from this small village southeast of Newtown (now Pocomoke City) is illustrated below, photographed from a poor photocopy made some years ago. The signature of the issuer, obviously the proprietor of a country store, has not as yet been deciphered. The locality took its name from a nearby stream called Beaver Dams Branch as early as 1759.

8.1.4 R-7
50c Printed date Nov. 1, 1840. Letterpress, imprint: MURPHY PRINTER BALTIMORE.

8.1.4

9 BELTSVILLE, PRINCE GEORGE'S COUNTY

Previously called Vannsville, the name of this small town was changed to Beltsville in 1835 in honor of Truman Belt, the landowner who had provided a right-of-way for the Baltimore & Ohio Railroad.

9.1 C. C. Hoffman

The issuer was apparently the proprietor of a general store.

9.1.2 R-7

12 1/2c Printed date Feb. 8, 1842. Letterpress, no imprint. Redeemable in Virginia bank notes by W. H. Tenney, Georgetown, D.C.

9.1.2

10 BERLIN, WORCESTER COUNTY

The town was built on land originally patented as "Burleigh" in 1677. The town name is probably a combination of the words Burleigh and Inn.

10.1 G. & J. W. Staton

The issuers, George and John W. Staton, were the proprietors of a general store located for many years at the corner of Main and Market streets.

10.1.2 R-7

10c Ca. 1863. Lithography, no imprint. Blue face, dull rose-red back. Vignette of the Maryland state seal on the face. Notes of this type, bearing the Maryland state seal, are known with the printed date, December 10, 1862, imprinted Pottsville, Pa., instead of Berlin, Maryland.

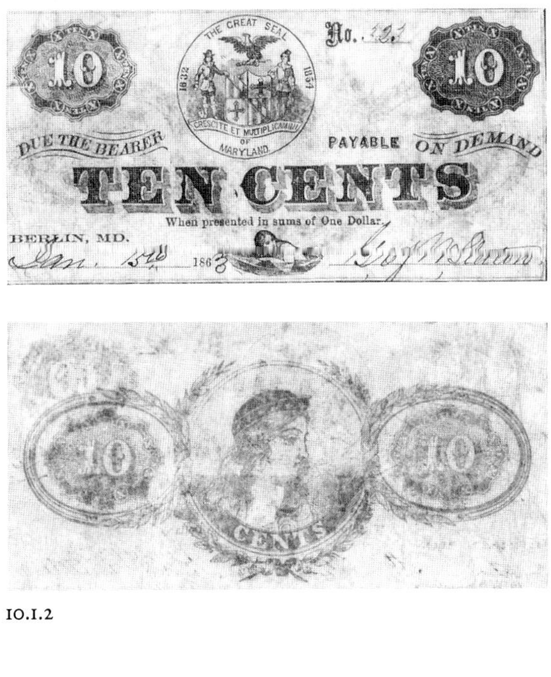

10.1.2

10.2 Unidentified Issuer

Unissued sheet of six denominations. Vignettes and end plates engraved, denominations and texts printed by letterpress. Imprint: E. Morris, Printer, Philad.

10.2.1 R-7
5c Ca. 1837. Engraving/letterpress, imprint: E. Morris, Printer, Philad.

10.2.2 R-7
10c Ca. 1837. Engraving/letterpress, imprint: E. Morris, Printer, Philad.

10.2.3 R-7
25c Ca. 1837. Engraving/letterpress, imprint: E. Morris, Printer, Philad.

10.2.4 R-7
50c Ca. 1837. Engraving/letterpress, imprint: E. Morris, Printer, Philad.

10.2.5 R-7
$1.00 Ca. 1837. Engraving/letterpress, imprint: E. Morris, Printer, Philad.

10.2.6 R-7
$2.00 Ca. 1837. Engraving/letterpress, imprint: E. Morris, Printer, Philad.

11 BLADENSBURG, PRINCE GEORGE'S COUNTY

Originally Beall Town, Bladensburg was laid out in 1742 and named for Thomas Bladen, governor of Maryland from 1742 to 1747.

11.1 D. W. Ferrall

The issuer, Dennis W. Ferrall, was the proprietor of a general store.

11.1.4 R-7
50c Printed date January 1, 1842. Letterpress, imprint: Murphy, print. Balt.

11.1.4

11.2 **Jno. McKnew**

The issuer was the proprietor of a general store.

11.2.2 R-7

12 1/2c Ca. 1837. Letterpress, imprint: P. Haas, Lithr.

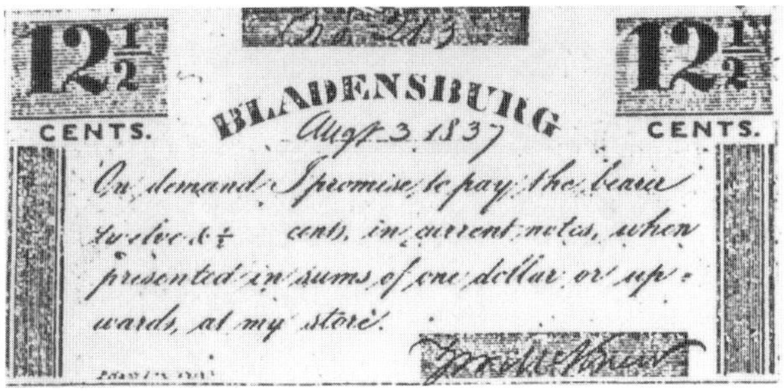

11.2.2

13 BOONSBORO, WASHINGTON COUNTY

Settled in 1774 by George and William Boone, in 1801 this was the post office of Boonesburg. Town lots were laid out in 1829. The town is about 21 miles northwest of Frederick, near Keedysville.

13.1 **Town of Boonsboro**

Small-change scrip issued by the burgess and commissioners of the town.

13.1.2 R-7

12 1/2c Ca. 1837. Letterpress, imprint: Unclear, probably P. Haas.

13.1.3 R-7

25c Printed partial year date, 184 . Lithography, imprint: Lith. by Ed. Weber & Co., Balt.

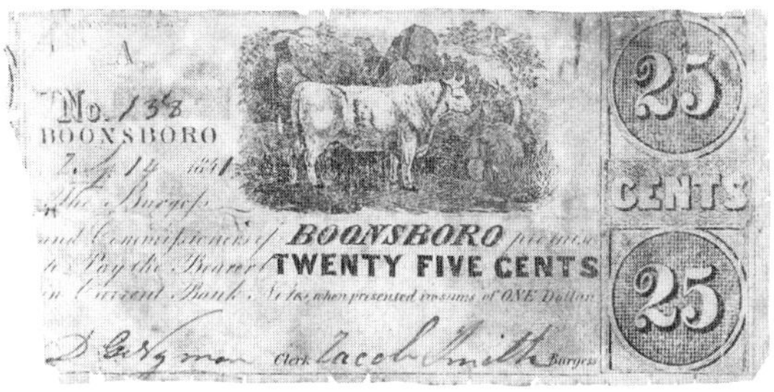

13.1.3

13.3 **J. A. & S. Pentz & Co.**

The issuers were apparently proprietors of a general store.

13.3.4 R-7

50c Printed year date 1837. Letterpress, imprint: Beaver & Dainty, Philadelphia.

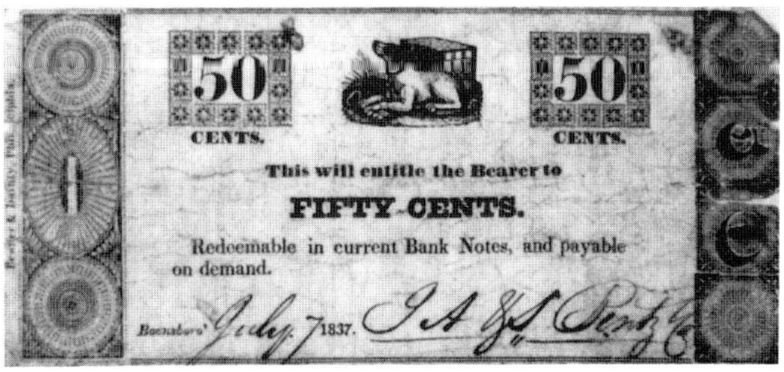

13.3.4

13.5 Unidentified Issuer

13.5.4 R-7

50c Printed partial date July ___ 1837. Letterpress, imprint: Robinson, PRINTER, Baltimore. Town name spelled Boonesboro.

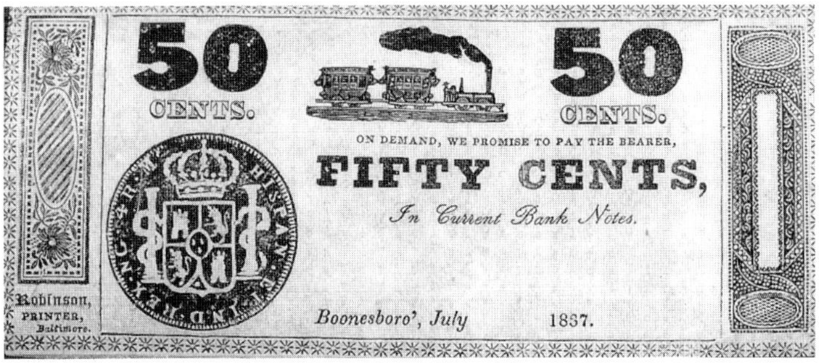

13.5.4

14 BROAD CREEK, HARFORD COUNTY

Broad Creek runs from its headwaters just south of the Maryland-Pennsylvania line southeast through Pylesville to the Mill Green area where it turns northeast and flows into the Susquehanna River at Ross's Landing. It provided power to a number of mills in the early to mid-nineteenth century.

14.1 James T. Bond

The issuer's "Tan Bark Yard and Tannery" was on Prospect Road one-half mile below Mill Green, at Carr's Run. According to Bond's surviving accounts ledgers he skinned, tanned, and sold all kinds of skins "from squirrel to bull hides."

14.1.2 R-7

10c Printed year date 1841. Letterpress, no imprint.

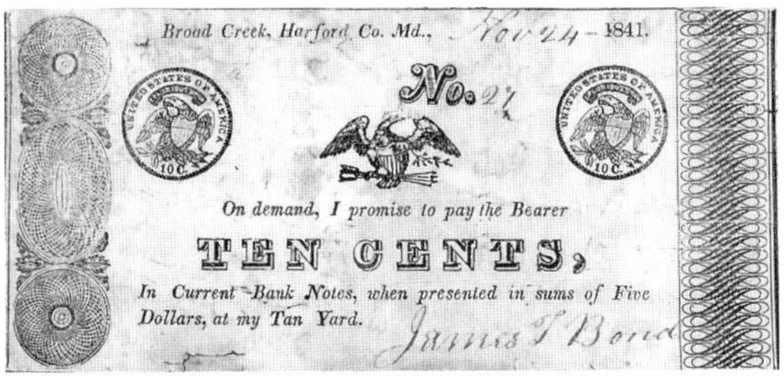

14.1.2

16 CAMBRIDGE, DORCHESTER COUNTY

Established by the Maryland Assembly in 1684 and named for the English university town. Located on the Choptank River, 16 miles south of Easton.

16.1 Town of Cambridge

The town's commissioners issued small-change scrip during the 1837–41 period and again during the Civil War to alleviate acute shortages of coins.

16.1.1 R-5

5c Printed date December 3, 1862. Letterpress, imprint: Murphy, pr. Balt. Pale green network and large red double-lined FIVE CENTS security underprint on face. Ornate red design surrounding oval enclosing denomination and town name on back.

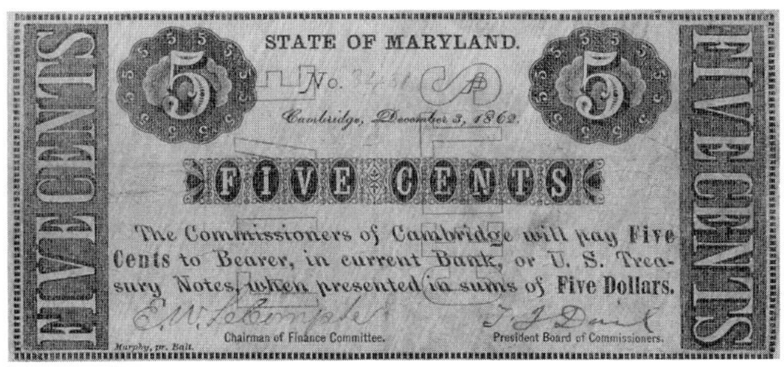

16.1.1

16.1.3 R-5

10c Printed date December 3, 1862. Similar to 5c, No. 16.1.1, in design, security underprint, and back.

16.1.4 R-7

12 1/2c Ca. 1839–40. Letterpress, imprint: MURPHY, PRINT. BALT. Blue.

16.1.5 R-5

25c Printed date December 3, 1862. Similar to 5c, No. 16.1.1, in design, security underprint, and back.

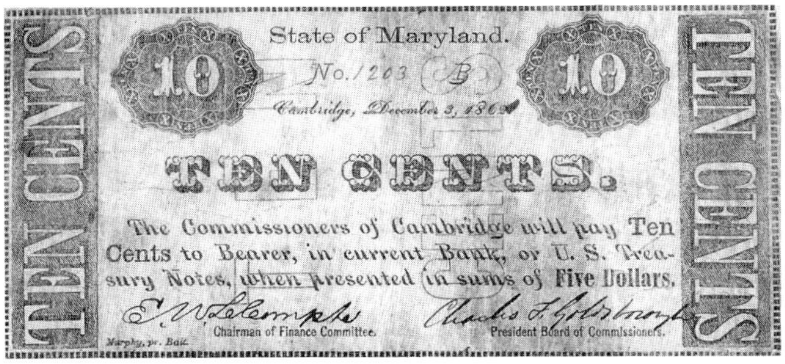

16.1.3

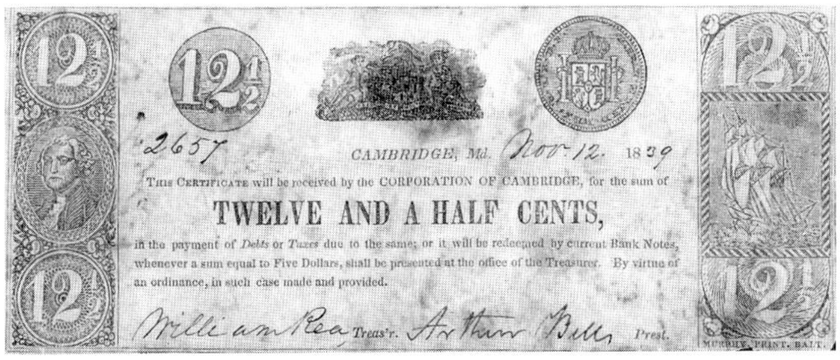

16.1.4

Unissued sheet, showing minor differences in design of the 5c (16.1.1), 10c (16.1.3), and 25c (16.1.5) notes of December 3, 1862.

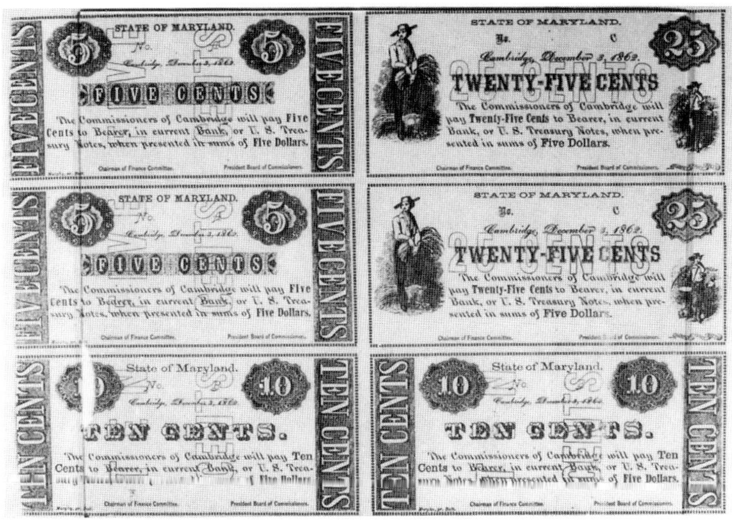

16.1.6 R-6

50c Printed date December 3, 1862. Pale green network and red double-lined FIVE CENTS security underprint on face, and ornate red design surrounding oval enclosing denomination and town name on back.

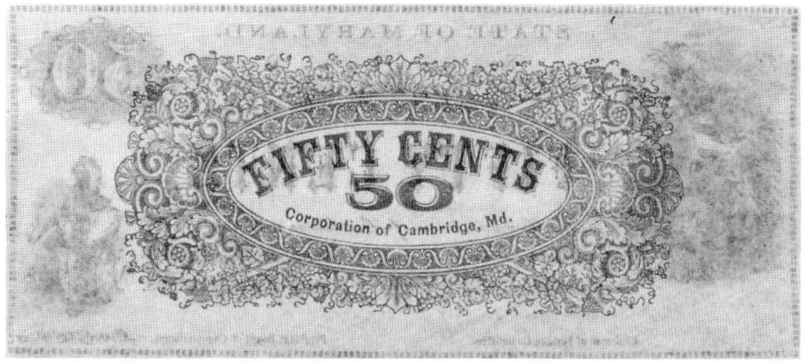

16.1.6

16.2 **Bank of Dorchester**

This bank was chartered in 1817, but did not go into operation. It is not clear whether notes were prepared in anticipation of its opening.

---

17 CARROLL COUNTY

17.1 **J. & E. LeGore**

The issuers were probably Jacob and Ezra Legore and Ezra's daughter, Elizabeth, who appear in the 1840 and 1850 census indexes and resided in the Uniontown district of Carroll County. They were the proprietors of a general store, the precise location of which has not as yet been determined.

17.1.1 R-7

6 1/4c Printed partial year date 184_. Letterpress, no imprint. Vignette of the Battle Monument, Baltimore, at left. The sailing ship vignette at upper right bears the imprint "Horton" of John S. Horton, an engraver active in Baltimore from 1833 to about 1843.

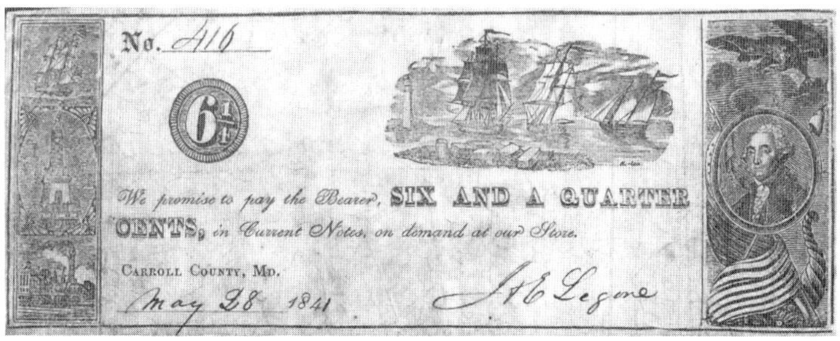

17.1.1

---

18 CARTER'S CROSS ROADS, CARROLL COUNTY

This place, now known as Dorsey's Cross Roads, is located at the intersection of Liberty Road and Washington Road approximately 3 1/2 miles northwest of Eldersburg.

18.1 Henry Holland

The issuer was the proprietor of a hotel and general store at this crossroads. By 1863 the proprietor of the store and hotel was A. E. Dorsey, hence the change in the place name.

18.1.1 R-7
6 1/4c Printed date September 1, 1841. Letterpress, imprint: MURPHY, PRINTER, 146 market st. Balt. Green.

18.1.2 R-7
12 1/2c Printed date September 1, 1841. Letterpress, imprint: MURPHY PRINTER BALTIMORE. Green.

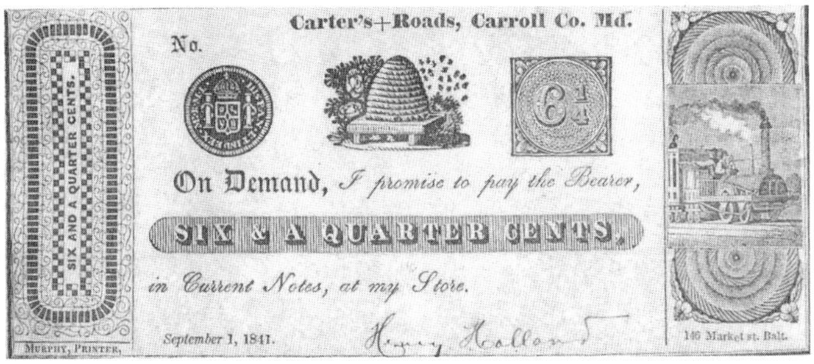

18.1.1

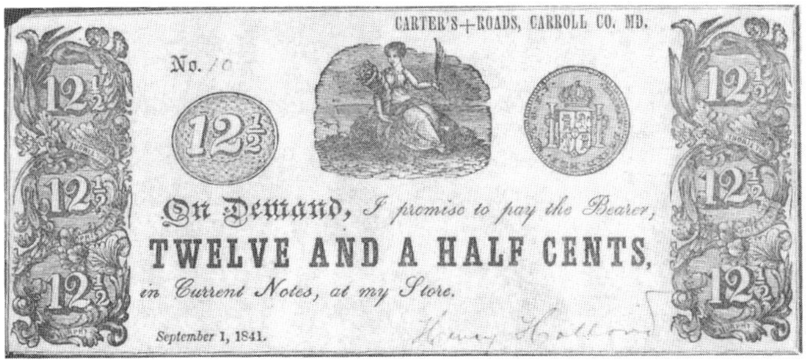

18.1.2

20 CENTREVILLE, QUEEN ANNE'S COUNTY

Originally Chester Mills, the name was changed to Centreville in 1797 and it became the county seat of Queen Anne's County. Located about 6 miles northeast of Wye Mills.

20.1 Centreville Bank

This bank was chartered in 1817 but did not go into operation. It is not clear whether notes were prepared in anticipation of its opening.

20.2 Daniel Newnam

The issuer was the proprietor of a carriage manufacturing and repairing business.

20.2.7 R-7
$2.00 Printed date April 18, 1840. Letterpress, imprint: MURPHY PRINTER BALTIMORE. Minimum redemption amount changed in manuscript from $5.00 to $50.00.

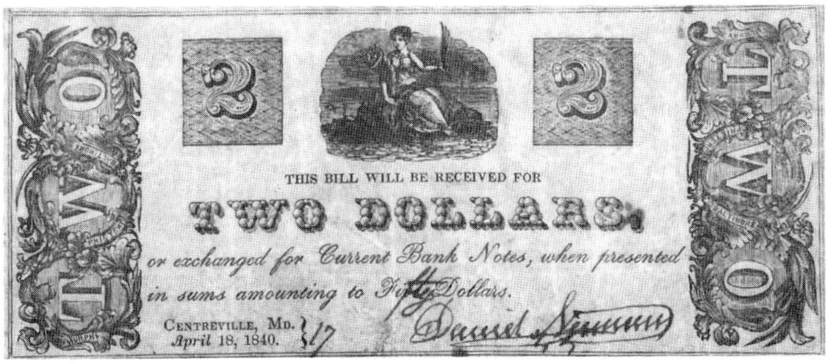

20.2.7

20.3 Unidentified Issuer

20.3.4 R-7
5c Printed partial year dated 186_. Letterpress, imprint: TIMES, PRINT.

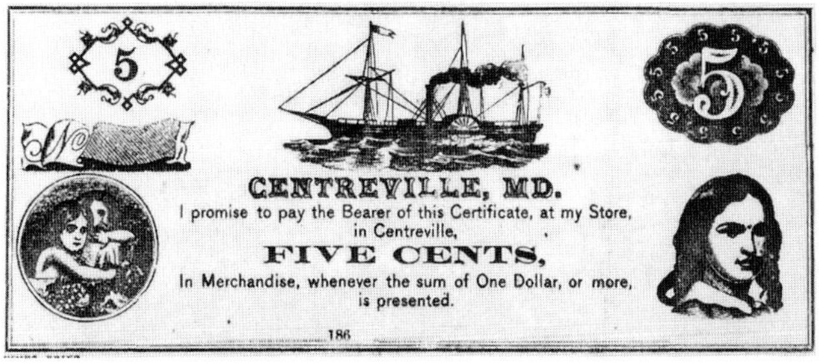

20.3.4

21 CHAPTICO, ST. MARY'S COUNTY

This small village is situated about three miles northeast of Maddox and about ten miles from Leonardtown. The name of the village and a creek and a bay derives from Algonquin linguistic sources, its approximate meaning being "a big (or deep) stream." The bay itself is an inlet of the Wicomico River.

21.1 Phil Turner

The issuer, while not yet specifically identified, was almost certainly the proprietor of a country store.

21.1.3 R-7
25c Printed date Nov. 1, 1839. Letterpress, imprint: MURPHY, PRINT. BALT. Vignette, left end panel, is Battle Monument, Baltimore.

21.1.3

22 CHARLESTOWN, CECIL COUNTY

Incorporated in 1742 and named to commemorate the fifth Lord Baltimore, this town is located on the west side of the Northeast River, about three miles south of the town of North East.

22.1 Fisherman's Bank of Charlestown

The *Federal Gazette & Baltimore Advertiser* of August 7, 1804, reported that the people of "Charlestown at the head of our bay being anxious to help poor fishermen who are poorly treated in Baltimore, plan to erect a bank at Turkey Point, with its parent institution in Charlestown." A search of 1800–1813 legislative records reveals no incorporation of such a bank. No examples of notes or scrip supposedly issued by such an institution have been reported. It is highly unlikely that such an institution was ever in existence.

22.2 Unidentified Issuer

The issuer, as yet unidentified, was the proprietor of a general store.

22.2.1 R-7

6 1/4c Printed date February, 1841. Engraving, imprint: Manly & Orr, Printers, Philadelphia.

22.2.4 R-7

50c Printed date February 1841. Engraving, imprint: Manly & Orr, Printers, Philadelphia.

22.2.1

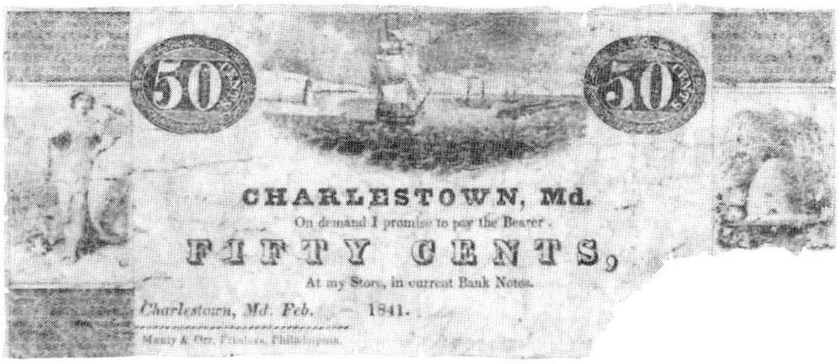

22.2.4

23 THE CHESAPEAKE & OHIO CANAL COMPANY

The canal was begun as a proposed waterway along the established Potomac and trans-Allegheny trade route to the Ohio River. It was the economic heir of the old Potomack Company, which had attempted unsuccessfully from 1785 to 1828 to fulfill George Washington's dream of developing a practical water route through the Potomac Valley. Construction of the canal started on July 4, 1828, the same day that construction of the Baltimore & Ohio Railroad began in Baltimore. Legal, economic, and labor problems beset the company from the beginning, culminating in very serious financial problems in 1838–39.

The canal was used as each section was completed; first from Georgetown to Seneca in 1831; then to Harpers Ferry in 1833; and to near Hancock in 1839, 134 miles from its beginning in Georgetown. The final 50.5 miles to Cumberland were not completed until 1850—eight years after the B&O Railroad had reached that point. The canal never attained any great measure of economic success and a great flood that swept the Potomac Valley in 1889 left it in ruin. It was rebuilt and used until 1924 when another flood seriously damaged the canal and the already financially troubled company. The canal and its property were sold by the receivers of the company in 1938 to the United States, under the stewardship of the National Park Service; ultimately, in 1972, it became a National Historical Park.

Small-denomination scrip was issued in 1837 by the Washington office of the company and notes in $5.00, $10.00, and $20.00 denominations in 1840–41 by both the Frederick and Washington offices.

23.1 Frederick Office

These $5.00, $10.00, and $20.00 notes were payable "nine months after date . . . with interest from date." Ca. 1840–41. Engraving, imprint: Danforth, Underwood & Co., New York / Underwood, Bald, Spencer & Hufty, Philada. The payee's name on all notes issued in Frederick was Jacob Markell, a director of the company in 1840–41. Prior to October 8, 1840, the name was written in by hand on a line of printer's rule; on that date and thereafter the name was engraved and printed as an integral part of the design. The enlarged photographs illustrate the Jacob Markell name in both handwritten and engraved form. See below for individual listings. Handwritten name of payee, Jacob Markell, on line of printer's rule. Engraved name of payee, Jacob Markell, line of printer's rule deleted.

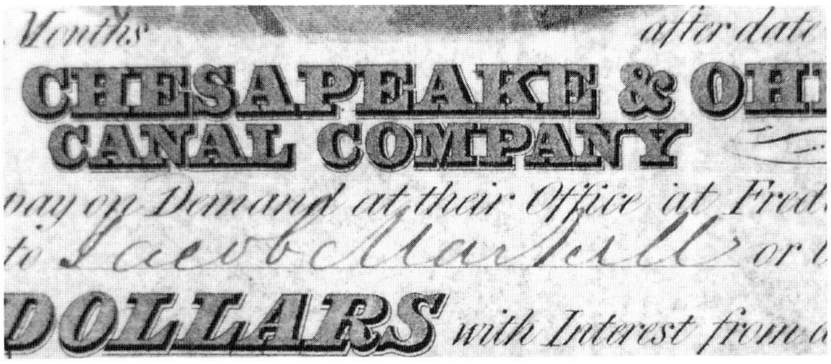

23.1.1 R-1
$5.00 Handwritten payee's name.

23.1.2 R-1
$5.00 Engraved payee's name.

23.1.3 R-1
$10.00 Handwritten payee's name.

23.1.4 R-1
$10.00 Engraved payee's name.

23.1.2

23.1.4

23.1.5 R-1

$20.00 Handwritten payee's name.

23.1.6 R-1

$20.00 Engraved payee's name.

23.1.5

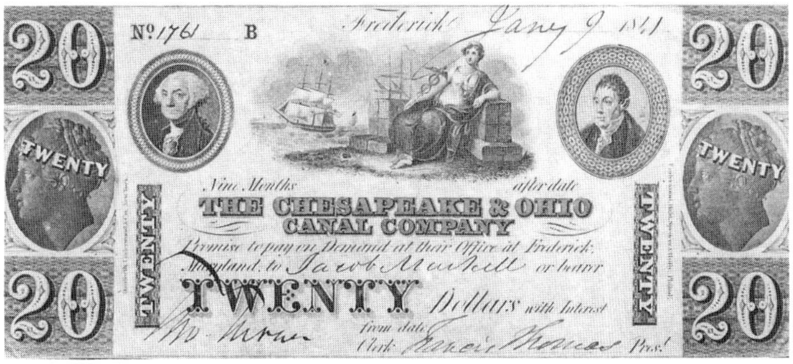

23.1.6

23.2 Washington Office

23.2.1 R-6

25c Printed date Augt. 10, 1837. Engraving, imprint: Underwood, Bald, Spencer & Hufty.

23.2.2 P R-6

50c Printed partial year date 183_. Engraving, imprint: Underwood, Bald, Spencer & Hufty.

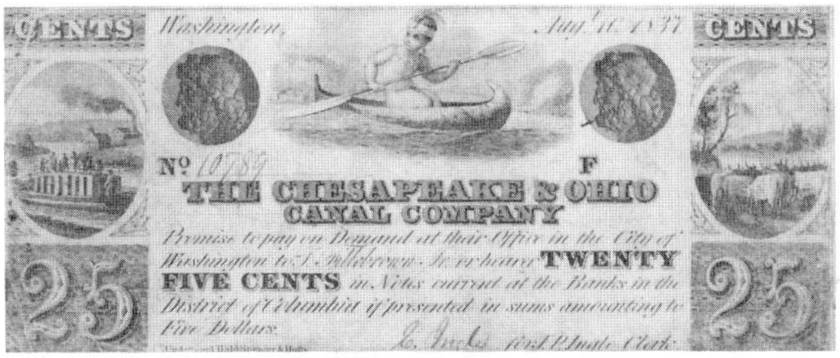

23.2.1

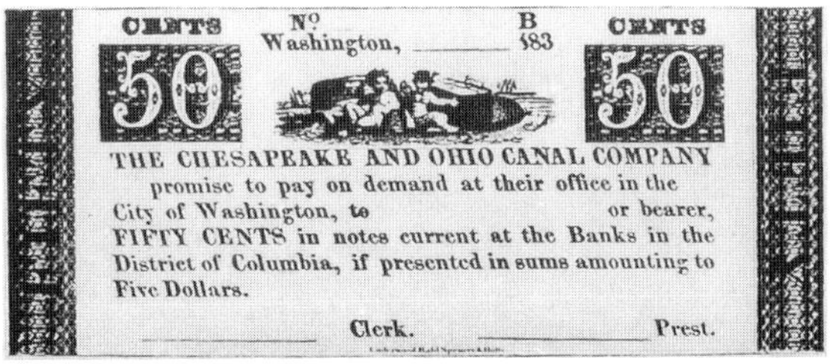

23.2.2 P

23.2.3 P R-6

$1.00 Printed partial year date 183 . Engraving, imprint: Underwood, Bald, Spencer & Hufty.

23.2.4 P R-7

$2.00 Printed partial year date 183 . Engraving, imprint: Underwood, Bald, Spencer & Hufty. Proof.

23.2.5 P R-7

$3.00 Printed partial year date 183 . Engraving, imprint: Underwood, Bald, Spencer & Hufty. Proof.

$5.00, $10.00, $20.00 Ca. 1840–41. Engraving, imprint: Underwood, Bald, Spencer & Hufty. Similar to the notes issued at the Frederick office. All notes have the payee's name, T. Fillebronn Jr., printed, and bear the printed partial year date 184_. See below for individual listings.

23.2.6 R-1

$5.00 Inscribed "Nine Months after date . . . with Interest from date."

23.2.7 R-1

$5.00 Inscribed "Six months after date . . . with legal interest thereon."

23.2.8 R-1

$10.00 Inscribed "Nine Months after date . . . with Interest from date."

23.2.9 R-1

$10.00 Inscribed "Six months after date . . . with legal interest thereon."

23.2.10 R-1

$20.00 Inscribed "nine months after date . . . with Interest from date."

23.2.11 R-1

$20.00 Inscribed "Six months after date . . . with legal interest thereon."

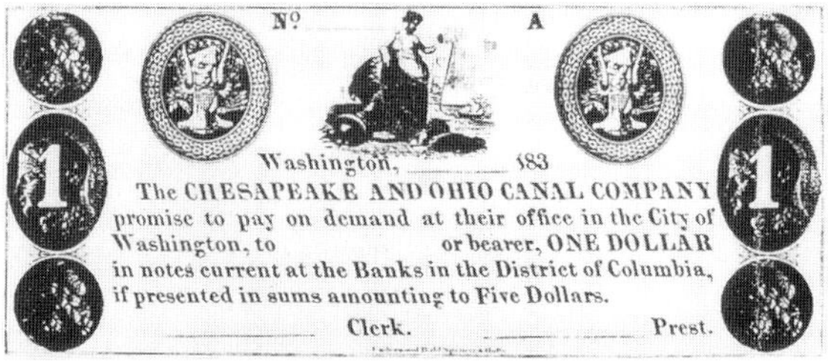

23.2.3 P

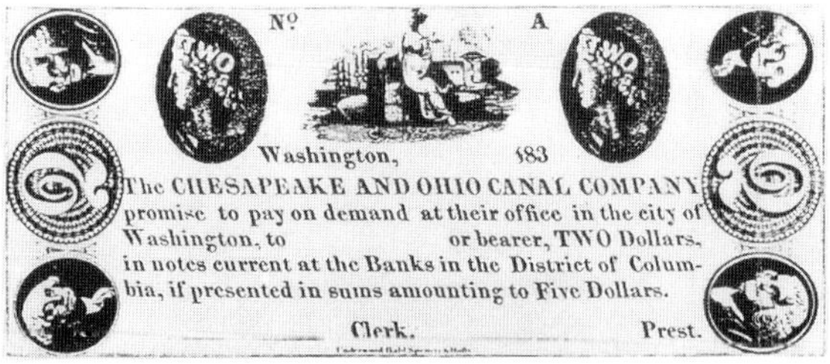

23.2.4 P

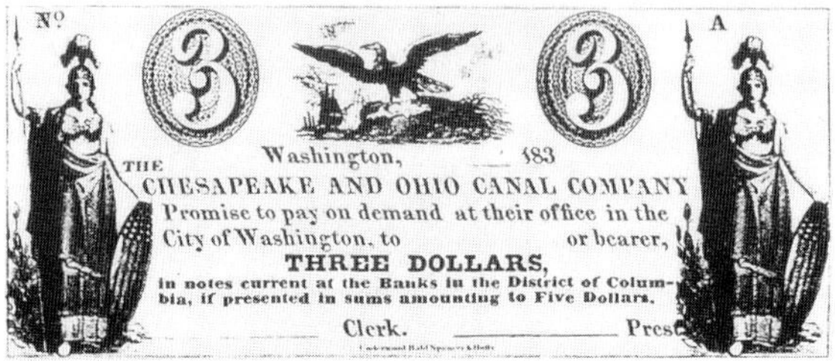

23.2.5 P

23.2.6

23.2.11

24 THE CHESAPEAKE & OHIO CANAL

Small-change scrip was issued by a number of construction contractors and merchants along the route of the canal during the 1837–41 period. Such notes are distinguishable from those issued by the company as its issues always bear the full corporate name, including the word "Company."

24.1 Jim Bauermann

The issuer was a construction contractor on sections 366 and 367.

24.1.1 R-7
6 1/4c Printed date Jan. 1, 1838. Letterpress, imprint: Robinson, PRINTER, Baltimore.

24.1.3 R-7
25c Printed date January 1, 1838. Letterpress, imprint: Robinson, PRINTER, Baltimore.

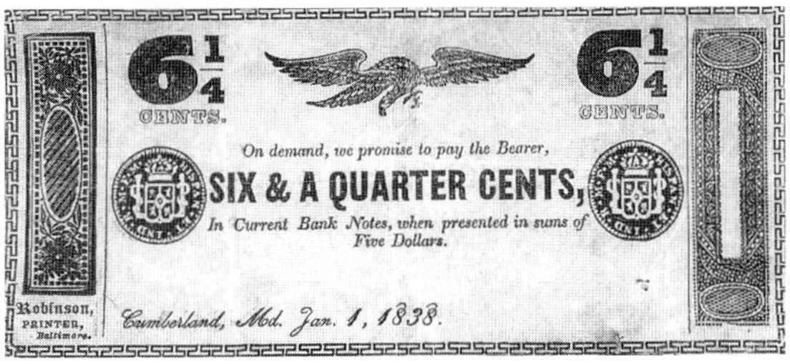

24.1.1

24.1.3

24.3 Garlic & Woodward

The issuers were construction contractors on sections 333 and 334 at Deep Cut near Old Town.

24.3.3 R-7
25c Printed date August 1, 1837. Letterpress, imprint: E. Morris, Pr., Philadelphia.

24.3.3

24.4 Hallman and Cushwa

The issuers were proprietors of a general store in sections 243 and 244. They obviously used a stock of notes prepared with the erroneous heading of the canal company, which was crossed out and "We" written in.

24.4.2 R-7
12 1/2c Ca. 1837. Letterpress, imprint: Toy, Printer, Baltimore.

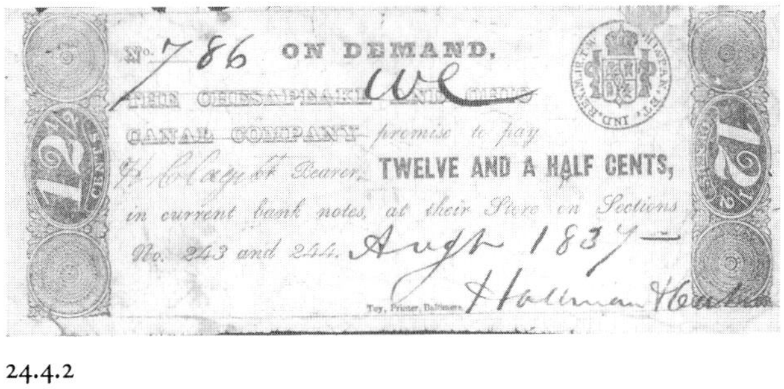

24.4.2

24.5 Hatch, Negus & Rexford

The issuers were contractors for Section 323 of the canal near Town Creek.

Partial sheet of three denominations, printed date May 25, 1838.

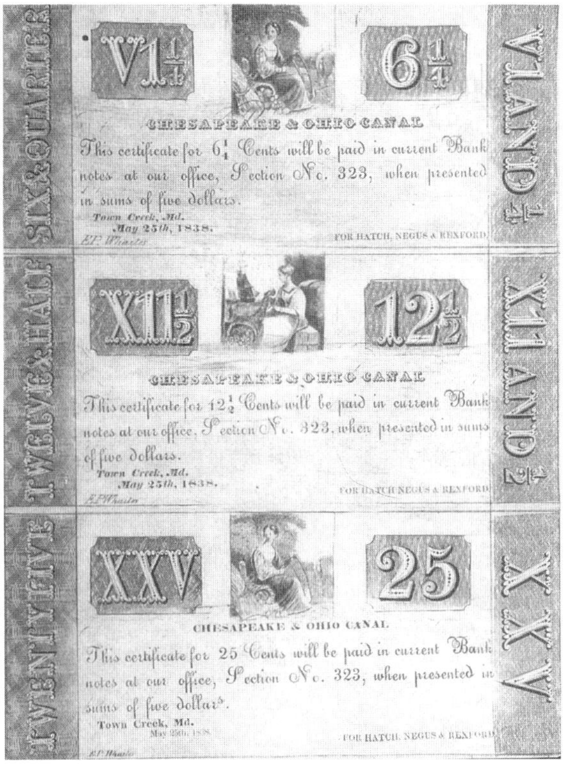

24.5.1 R-7
6 1/4c Printed date May 25, 1838. Engraving, imprint: E. P. Whaites.

24.5.2 R-7
12 1/2c Printed date May 25, 1838. Engraving, imprint: E. P. Whaites.

24.5.3 R-7
25c Printed date May 25, 1838. Engraving, imprint: E. P. Whaites

24.5.4 P R-7
75c Similar to nos. 24.5.1, 2, and 3, except for the absence of redemption text and the name of the issuer. Probably a proof of an unfinished design or essay.

24.5.4 P

24.6 Geo. Hoblitzell

The issuer was a contractor on sections 353 and 356 as well as the proprietor of a store in Cumberland.

24.6.6 R-7
$2.00 Printed date May 1, 1838. Letterpress, imprint: Murphy & Spalding, printers, Baltimore. Redemption medium changed in manuscript from "Current Notes" to "in Scrip."

24.6.6

24.7 MacCubbin & Lowe

The issuers were proprietors of a general store at some point on the canal in Allegany County between Hancock and Cumberland.

24.7.2 R-7
12 1/2c Printed date, December 10, 1839. Letterpress, imprint: MURPHY, PRINT. BALT.

24.7.5 R-7
$1.00 Printed date December 10, 1839. Letterpress, imprint: MURPHY, PRINTER, BALTIMORE. Vignette is a woodcut view of Baltimore harbor.

24.7.2

24.7.5

24.9 Geo. G. McPherson

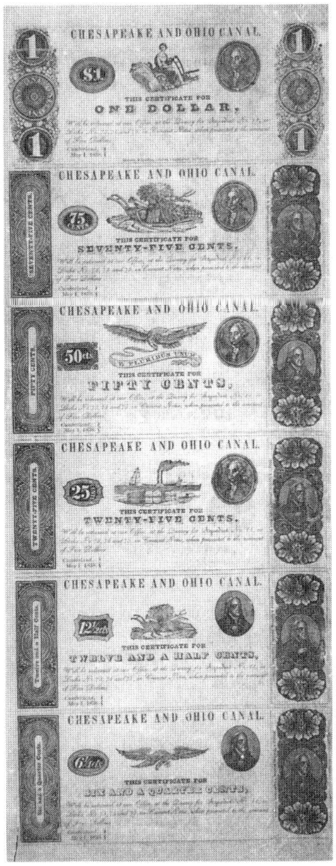

Complete sheet, unsigned.

The issuer was the contractor at the quarry for Aqueduct 11 and locks 73, 74, and 75.

24.9.1 R-7
6 1/4c Printed date May 1, 1838. Letterpress, no imprint.

24.9.2 R-7
12 1/2c Printed date May 1, 1838. Letterpress, no imprint.

24.9.3 R-7
25c Printed date May 1, 1838. Letterpress, no imprint.

24.9.4 R-7
50c Printed date May 1, 1838. Letterpress, no imprint.

24.9.5 R-7
75c Printed date May 1, 1838. Letterpress, no imprint.

24.9.6 R-7
$1.00 Printed date May 1, 1838. Letterpress, imprint: Murphy & Spalding, printer, 1 Light street, Baltimore.

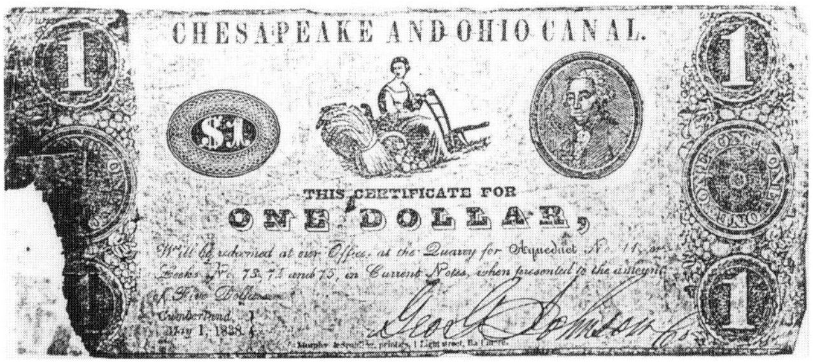

24.9.6

Signed and circulated 50c note, establishing the identity of the owner.

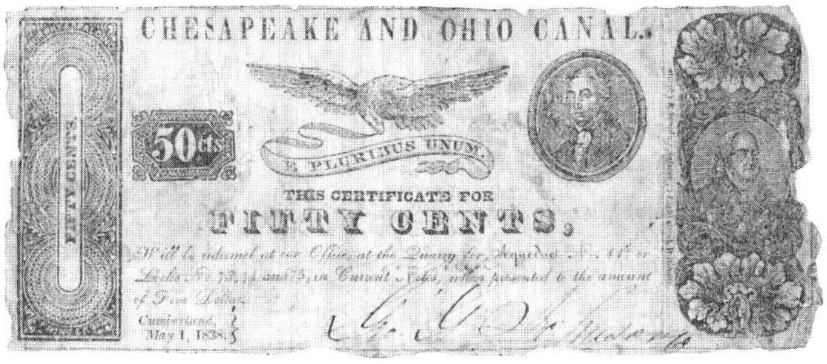

24.11 L. Montgomery

The issuer, Lee Montgomery, was the contractor for the construction of the tunnel at the Paw Paw bends, being referred to in the "Report of the General Committee of the Stockholders of the C. & O. Canal Co.," July 21, 1840.

Portion of an unissued sheet, showing the designs of the 12 1/2c, 50c, and $1.00 denominations. The faint penciled signature, J. Annall, is probably that of the Morris Salesman.

24.11.2 R-7

12 1/2c Printed date, April 10, 1838. Lithography, imprint: E. Morris, Philadelphia; text printed by letterpress.

24.11.3 R-7

25c Printed date April 10, 1838. Lithography, imprint: E. Morris, Philadelphia; text printed by letterpress.

24.11.4 R-7

50c Printed date April 10, 1838. Lithography, imprint: E. Morris, Philadelphia; text printed by letterpress.

24.11.5 R-7

$1.00 Printed date April 10, 1838. Lithography, imprint: E. Morris, Philadelphia; text printed by letterpress.

25c circulated note showing Montgomery's signature.

24.13 Galton Murray

The issuer was the proprietor of a general store on the canal near Old Town.

24.13.4 R-7
50c Printed date Dec. 10, 1839. Letterpress, imprint: MURPHY PRINT BALT. Redemption statement changed in manuscript from "Current Bank Notes" to "Current Scrip."

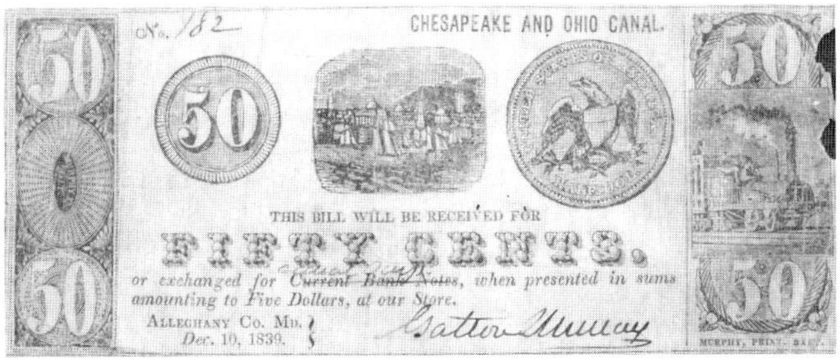

24.13.4

24.15 J. Noble Nisbet

The issuer was the contractor for Section 329 and Lock 68 at Rock Difficult.

24.15.3 R-7
25c Printed date April 16, 1838. Letterpress, imprint: W. D. Bell, Pr. Hagerstown, Md.

24.15.4 R-7
50c Printed date April 18, 1838. Letterpress, no imprint.

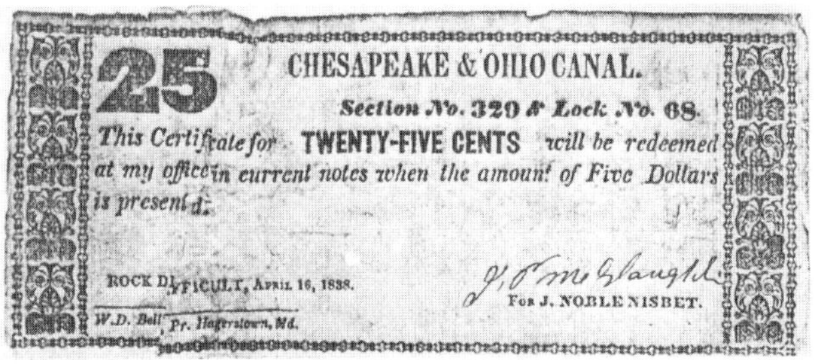

24.15.3

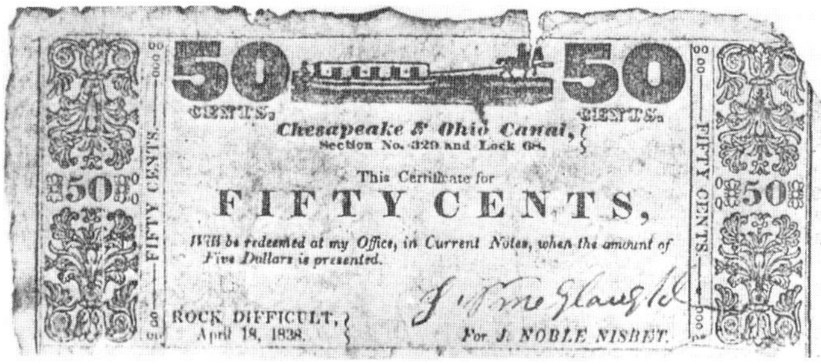

24.15.4

24.15.5 R-7

$1.00 Printed date April 16, 1838. Letterpress, imprint: W. D. Bell, Pr. Hagerstown, Md.

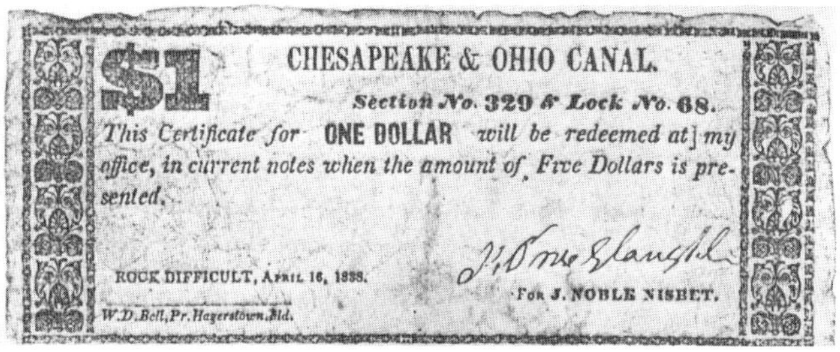

24.15.5

24.18 Unidentified Issuer

The issuer was probably a contractor on the canal.

24.18.1 R-7

12 1/2c Ca. 1837. Mentions sections 243 and 244. Surviving example not confirmed but recorded by D. C. Wismer in the *Coin Collectors Journal,* December 1940.

25 CHESTERTOWN, KENT COUNTY

Originally called New Town in 1708, it is located on the Chester River, near Radcliff Creek. An act in 1730 provided for a new town to be laid out and to be called Chestertown.

25.1 Bank of Chestertown

A bank of this name was reported to have opened in 1856. Whether this report is correct or not is unknown, as are any details of this supposed bank's issues.

25.2 The Farmers & Mechanics Bank of Kent County

Charter approved March 1, 1850; converted to and became the Kent National Bank of Chestertown in 1865.

25.2.1 P R-7

$1.00 Ca. 1856. Engraving, imprint: Toppan, Carpenter, Casilear & Co., Phila. & New York. Proof.

25.2.1 P

25.2.2 R-7

$5.00 Ca. 1856. Engraving, imprint: Toppan, Carpenter, Casilear & Co., New York and Phila. Red security print "5-5" in ornate type. (MD150G8b)

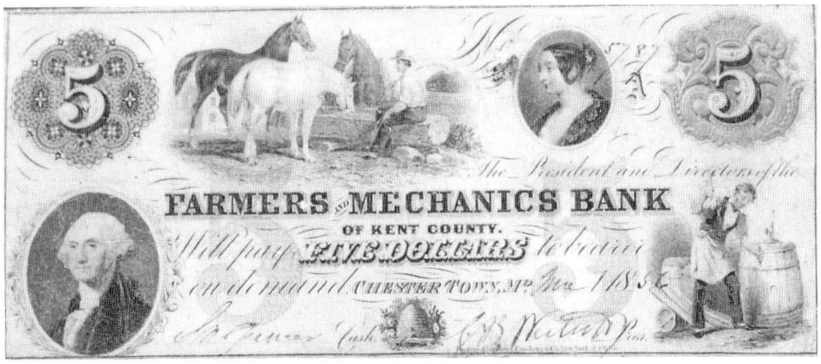

25.2.2

25.2.3 R-7

$5.00 Ca. 1856. Engraving, imprint: Toppan, Carpenter, Casilear & Co., New York and Phila. Same as No. 25.2.1, except red FIVE security print in large negative block letters. (MD150G8a)

25.2.4 S R-6

$5.00 Ca. 1860–61. Engraving, imprint: TOPPAN, CARPENTER & CO. PHILADELPHIA / AMERICAN BANK NOTE COMPANY. The 5s, Vs, and double-lined FIVE are printed in brick red. Spurious note, printed from a modified plate originally for a counterfeit $5.00 on the Farmer's & Mechanics Bank, Philadelphia, Pa. (MD150S5a)

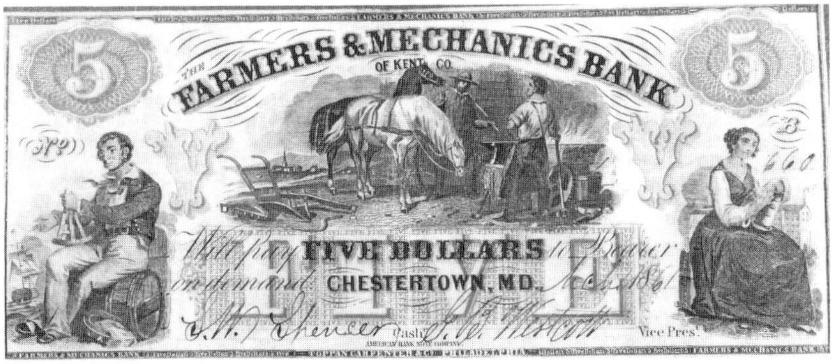

25.2.4 S

25.2.5 A SENC

$5.00 Printed date Aug. 6, 1865. Engraving, no imprint. *Upper center:* Oval portrait of Franklin. *Upper left and upper right:* 5. *Lower left-right* (whole-note vignette): Man standing by tree with jug; pair of oxen, two children standing on log, man felling tree with axe. Red ornate "V V" overprint. Altered from $5.00 Farmer's Bank, Wickford, R.I., RI565G8a. (MD150A5)

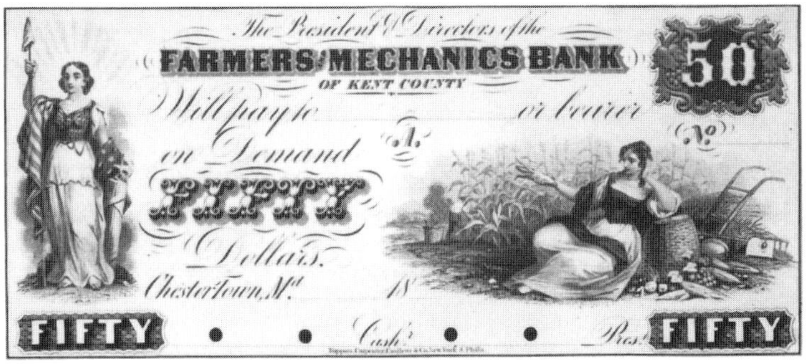

25.2.8 P

25.2.6 SENC

$10.00 Ca. 1850s. Engraving, imprint: Toppan, Carpenter, Casilear & Co. *Center:* Man on horse, reapers and wagon in right background. *Left:* 10 / woman seated, leaning on shield bearing X. *Right:* 10 / oval female portrait. *Bottom center:* Machinery. Red overprint. (MD150G10a)

25.2.7 SENC

$20.00 Ca. 1850s. Engraving, imprint: Unknown. *Center:* Woman seated, leaning on bale, ships in background. *Left:* 20 / oval female portrait. *Right:* 20 / oval portrait of Franklin. (MD150G12)

25.2.8 SENC

$50.00 Ca. 1850s. Engraving, imprint: Toppan, Carpenter, Casilear & Co., Phila. & New York.

25.2.8 P R-7

$50.00 Ca. 1856. Engraving, imprint: Toppan, Carpenter, Casilear & Co., Phila. & New York. Proof. (MD150G14)

25.2.9 SENC

$100.00 Ca. 1850s. Engraving, imprint: Unknown. *Center:* Woman seated holding ear of corn; men, boats, and village in background. *Left:* 100 / woman seated with sickle and sheaf. *Right:* 100 / oval female portrait. (MD150G16)

26 CHESTERTOWN AND MILLINGTON, KENT COUNTY

26.1 Watkins & Walker

The issuers were partners who operated general stores in the towns of Chestertown and Millington, which are about 11 miles apart in Kent County.

26.1.5 R-7

$1.00 Printed date Dec. 6, 1839. Letterpress, imprint: MURPHY, PRINTER 146 Market st. BALT.

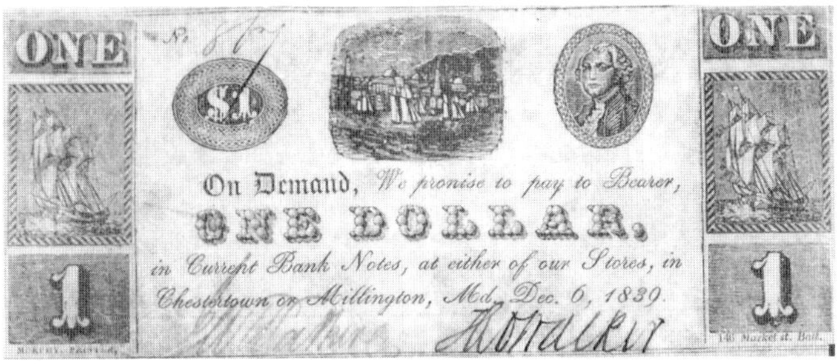

26.1.5

28 CLEAR SPRING, WASHINGTON COUNTY

This small town near Indian Spring, Big Spring, and Green Spring Furnace was founded in 1821 by Martin Meyers. The name is from a spring so large that at one time it turned a mill wheel.

28.1 Clear Spring Corporation

Corporation scrip issued to alleviate the shortage of coin during the "hard times" of 1837–41.

28.1.1 R-7

6 1/4c Printed date March 8, 1838. Letterpress, imprint: ROBINSON, PRINTER Baltimore.

28.1.1

29 CONOWINGO, CECIL COUNTY

A village located at Conowingo Creek where it enters the Susquehanna River near the present Conowingo Dam.

29.1 Conowingo Bridge Company

As far back as 1816 the General Assembly of Maryland approved the incorporation of a company to construct and operate a toll bridge at Conowingo, on the main road between Baltimore and Philadelphia. Notes were apparently issued by that company in 1840.

A sheet of six notes dated 1840 was recorded by D. C. Wismer in *Coin Collectors Journal*, December 1940. Denominations and descriptions are not available and no surviving examples have been confirmed.

30 CUMBERLAND, ALLEGANY COUNTY

This city on the Potomac River near Wills Mountain derives its name from Fort Cumberland, which was begun on July 4, 1754, and named to honor King George II's son, William Augustas, Duke of Cumberland.

30.1 Corporation of Cumberland

Issued by the municipality of Cumberland to alleviate a shortage of coin.

30.1.1 R-5

$1.00 Printed date January 1, 1849. Lithography, imprint: Lith. by E. Weber & Co., Balto.

30.1.1

30.2 Allegany County Bank

Charter approved March 8, 1858; closed in 1864.

30.2.1 R-1

$1.00 Printed date June 1, 1861. Engraving, imprint: AMERICAN BANK NOTE CO., NEW YORK. Plain back. (MD155G2)

30.2.2 R-1

$1.00 Printed date June 1, 1861. Engraving, imprint: AMERICAN BANK NOTE CO., NEW YORK. Same as No. 30.2.1, but with green back as illustrated. (MD155G2a)

30.2.3 R-1

$2.00 Printed date June 1, 1861. Engraving, imprint: AMERICAN BANK NOTE CO., NEW YORK. Plain back. (MD155G4)

30.2.1

30.2.2

30.2.3

30.2.4 R-1

$2.00 Printed date June 1, 1861. Engraving, imprint: AMERICAN BANK NOTE CO., NEW YORK. Same as No. 30.2.3, but with green back as illustrated. (MD155G4a)

30.2.5 R-5

$5.00 Ca. 1859. Engraving, imprint: AMERICAN BANK NOTE COMPANY. Red ends with large negative "5." Small script ABCo logo below; NO at upper left. (MD155G6a)

30.2.6 R-5

$5.00 Ca. 1859. Engraving, imprint: AMERICAN BANK NOTE COMPANY. Red ends with large negative "5." Same as No. 30.2.5, except without ABCo logo.

30.2.7 R-1

$5.00 Ca. 1859–60. Engraving, imprint: American Bank Note Company. Red security underprint. Without ABCo logo. Otherwise same as No. 30.2.8. (MD155G6b)

30.2.8 R-1

$5.00 Ca. 1859–61. Engraving, imprint: American Bank Note Company. Red security underprint. Small script ABCo logo at upper left. (MD155G6c)

30.2.9 R-1

$5.00 Ca. 1862–64. Engraving, imprint: American Bank Note company. Same as No. 30.2.8, except security underprint is in green. (MD155G6d)

30.2.4

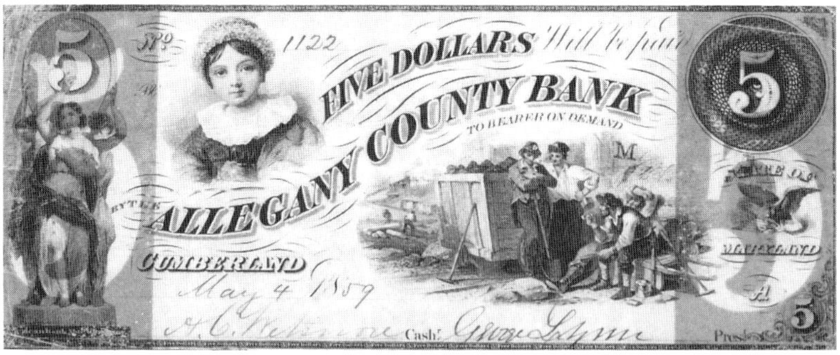

30.2.5

30.2.8

30.2.9

30.2.10 R-2

$10.00 Ca. 1859–61. Engraving, imprint: American Bank Note Company. Red security underprint of overall lathe work with ornate TEN on panel of microlettering. (MD155G8b)

30.2.11 R-2

$10.00 Ca. 1860s. Engraving, imprint: American Bank Note Company. Same as No. 30.2.10, except underprint is in green. (MD155G8d)

30.2.10

30.3 The Cumberland Bank of Allegany

Charter approved January 7, 1812; voluntary liquidation in 1821. Reopened in 1833, succeeded by the First National Bank of Cumberland in 1864.

30.3.1 R-7

6 1/4c Printed date October 25, 1815. Letterpress, imprint: Printed by S. Magill.

30.3.1

30.3.3 R-7

25c Printed date November 10, 1815. Letterpress, imprint: Printed by S. Magill. Similar to 6 1/4c, No. 30.3.1.

30.3.5 R-7

$1.00 Ca. 1810s. Engraving, imprint: Freeman, Balto. Similar to $2.00, No. 30.3.9. (MD160G20)

30.3.5 C SENC

$1.00 Ca. 1810s. Engraving, imprint: Freeman, Baltimore. Counterfeit of No. 30.3.5. (MD160C20)

30.3.6 P R-7

$1.00 Ca. 1836–43. Engraving, imprint: Underwood, Bald, Spencer & Hufty, Philada. / Danforth, Underwood & Co., New York. Proof. (MD160G50)

30.3.6 P

30.3.6 C SENC

$1.00 Ca. 1850s. Engraving, imprint: Underwood, Bald, Spencer & Hufty, Philada. / Danforth, Underwood & Co., New York. Counterfeit similar to No. 30.3.6 P. (MD160C50)

30.3.7 R-7

$1.00 Printed date May 25, 1861. Engraving, imprint: American Bank Note Co., Philada. Red ornate "1" and negative ONE security underprint. (MD160G50a)

30.3.7

30.3.9 SENC
$2.00 Ca. 1810s. Engraving, imprint: Freeman, Balto. Similar to counterfeit No. 30.3.9 C. (MD160G24)

30.3.9 C R-7
$2.00 Ca. 1812–21. Engraving, imprint: Freeman, Balto. Counterfeit of No. 30.3.9. (MD160C24)

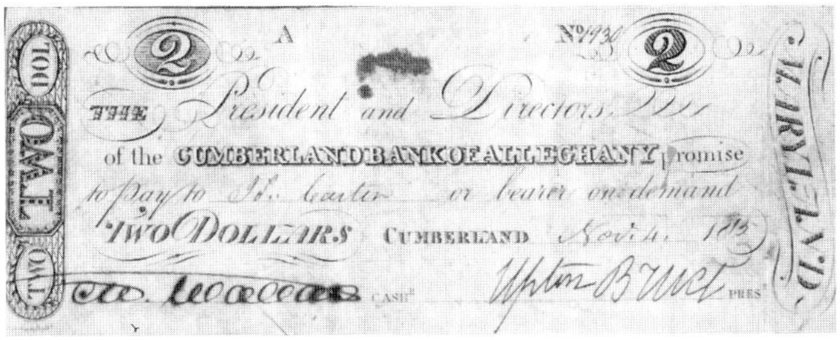

30.3.9 C

30.3.10 R-6
$5.00 Ca. 1812–21. Engraving, imprint: Murray, Draper, Fairman & Co. Circulated notes of this type normally bear the signatures of C. W. Wallace, cashier, and Upton Bruce, president. (MD160G30)

30.3.10 P R-7
$5.00 Ca. 1812–21. Engraving, imprint: Murray, Draper, Fairman & Co. Proof of No. 30.3.10.

30.3.10 P

30.3.10 C R-7
$5.00 Ca. 1812–21. Engraving, imprint: Murray, Draper, Fairman & Co. Counterfeit of No. 30.3.10. (MD160C30)

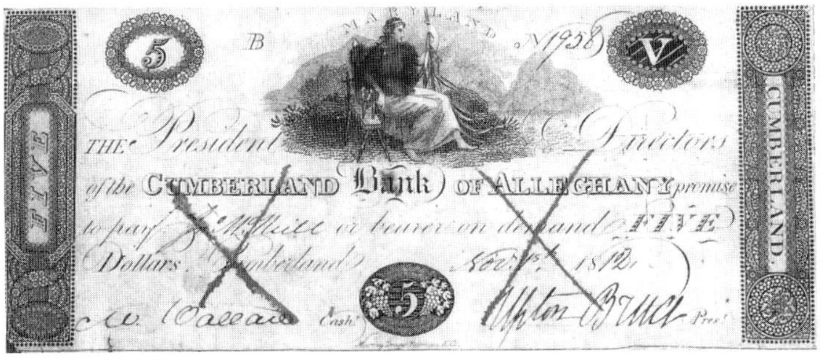

30.3.10 C

30.3.11 R-7
$5.00 Ca. 1833–50s. Engraving, imprint: Danforth, Underwood, Bald & Spencer. *Center:* Medallion head; view of Cumberland with drover and cattle in left foreground and wagon pulled by four horses in right background, both crossing stream; medallion head. *Left:* 5 / woman with cornucopia / 5. *Right:* FIVE / woman with cornucopia / FIVE. Letter A. (MD150G56)

30.3.11 P R-7
$5.00 Ca. 1833–50s. Engraving, imprint: Draper, Underwood, Bald & Spencer. Proof of No. 30.3.11.

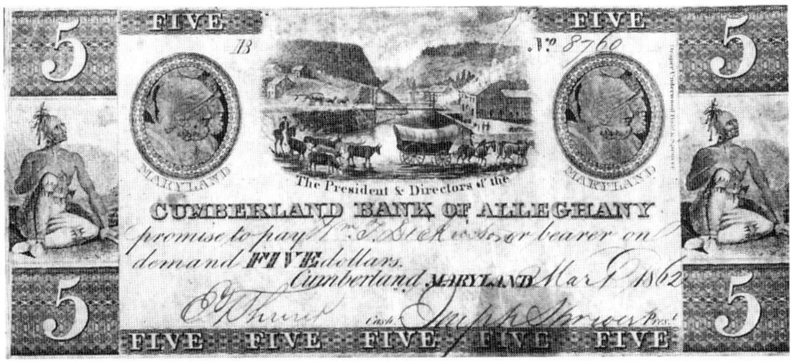

30.3.12

30.3.12 R-7
$5.00 Ca. 1833–63. Engraving, imprint: Draper, Underwood, Bald & Spencer. Center vignette is view of Cumberland, as in No. 30.3.11. Letter B. (MD160G57)

30.3.12 P R-7
$5.00 Ca. 1833–63. Engraving, imprint: Draper, Underwood, Bald & Spencer. Proof of No. 30.3.12.

30.3.13 R-7

$5.00 Ca. 1833–63. Engraving, imprint: Draper, Underwood, Bald & Spencer. Similar to No. 30.3.12, but with differing oval vignettes and end designs. Letter C. (MD160G58)

30.3.13 P R-7

$5.00 Ca. 1833–63. Engraving, imprint: Draper, Underwood, Bald & Spencer. Proof of No. 30.3.13.

30.3.14 A SENC

$5.00 Ca. 1860s. Engraving, imprint: American Bank Note Co. *Center:* Train moving to left, buildings and hills in right background. *Lower left:* Oval male portrait. *Right:* 5 / Justice standing in small oval / FIVE. Tint is red orange with white ornate FIVE. Overprint is red panel with white FIVE. Altered from $5.00, Clinton Bank, Westernport, Md., 146.1 series. (MD160A5)

30.3.16 SENC

$10.00 Ca. 1812–21. Engraving, imprint: Murray, Draper, Fairman & Co. Similar to No. 30.3.16 C. (MD160G34)

30.3.16 C R-7

$10.00 Ca. 1812–21. Engraving, imprint: Murray, Draper, Fairman & Co. Counterfeit of No. 30.3.16. (MD160C34)

30.3.17 R-7

$10.00 Ca. 1833–35. Engraving, imprint: Draper, Underwood, Bald & Spencer. Same as No. 30.3.18, except for ABCo. logo. (MD160G62)

30.3.17 P R-7

$10.00 Ca. 1833–35. Engraving, imprint: Draper, Underwood, Bald & Spencer. Same as No. 30.3.18, except for ABCo. logo. Proof of No. 30.3.17.

30.3.18 R-6

$10.00 Reissued 1860–63. Engraving, imprint: Draper, Underwood, Bald & Spencer at upper right and small script ABCo. logo at bottom center. (MD160G62a)

30.3.13

30.3.16 C

30.3.17

30.3.18

30.3.20 R-7
$20.00 Ca. 1812–21. Engraving, imprint: Murray, Draper, Fairman & Co. Similar to No. 30.3.20 C. (MD160G38)

30.3.20 C R-7
$20.00 Ca. 1812–21. Engraving, imprint: Murray, Draper, Fairman & Co. Counterfeit of No. 30.3.20. (MD160C38)

30.3.21 P R-7
$20.00 Ca. 1833–35. Engraving, imprint: Draper, Underwood, Bald & Spencer. Proof. (MD160G66)

30.3.22 SENC
$20.00 Ca. 1840s. Engraving, imprint: Unknown. TWENTY across left end. Woman at right. (MD160N5)

30.3.24 SENC
$50.00 Ca. 1812–21. Engraving, imprint: Murray, Draper, Fairman & Co. Similar to $20.00, No. 30.3.20 C. (MD160G40)

30.3.25 P R-7
$50.00 Ca. 1833–35. Engraving, imprint: Draper, Underwood, Bald & Spencer. Proof. Printings from a defaced plate are on record. (MD160G70)

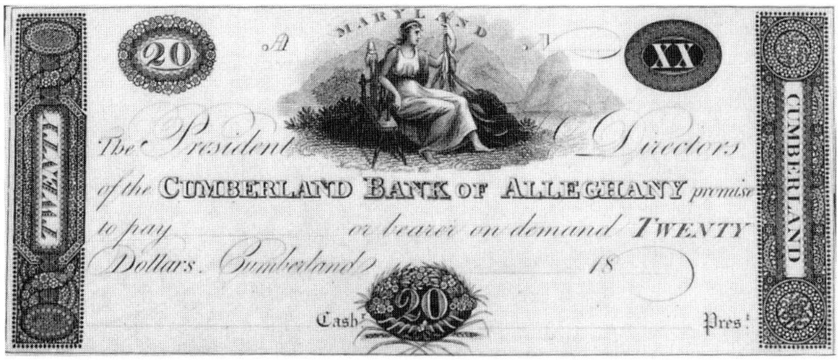

30.3.20

30.3.20 C

30.3.21 P

30.3.25 P

30.4 The Cumberland City Bank

Charter amendment approved March 10, 1858; formerly Cumberland Savings Institution (1848); Cumberland Savings Bank (first 1850). Closed and trustee appointed in 1858; apparently reopened in 1862.

30.4.1 R-5

$1.00 Printed date October 26, 1862. Engraving, imprint: American Bank Note Co., Phila. Green security overprint, lower center with green ONE. (MD160G6a)

30.4.2 R-7

$2.00 Printed date October 26, 1862. Engraving, imprint: American Bank Note Co., Phila. Green security underprint lower center outlining negative TWO. (MD165G8a)

30.4.3 R-7

$5.00 Ca. 1858. Engraving, imprint: Danforth, Bald & Co., Philada. & New York. Similar to $5.00, No. 30.4.4, but with brown-orange overall lathework with white "V V" in fancy letters and large die with ornate white FIVE. (MD165G2a)

30.4.3 P R-7

$5.00 Ca. 1858. Engraving, imprint: Danforth, Bald, & Co., Philada. & New York. Proof of No. 30.4.3.

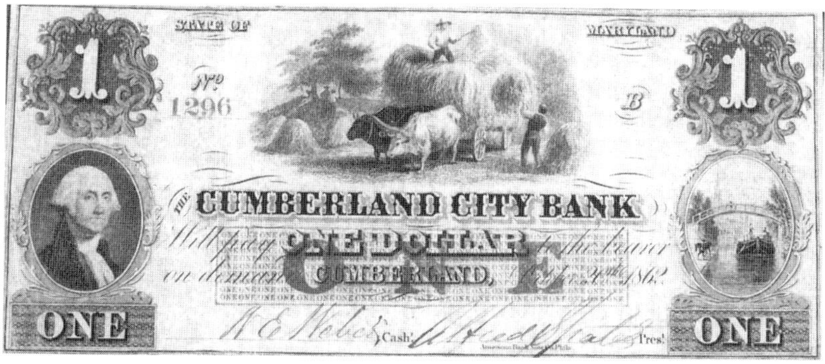

30.4.1

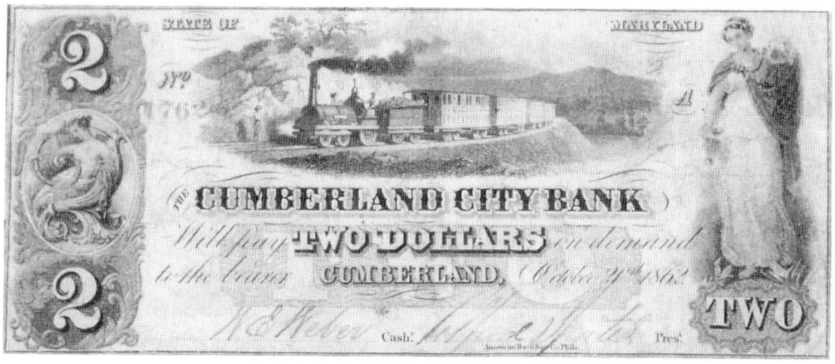

30.4.2

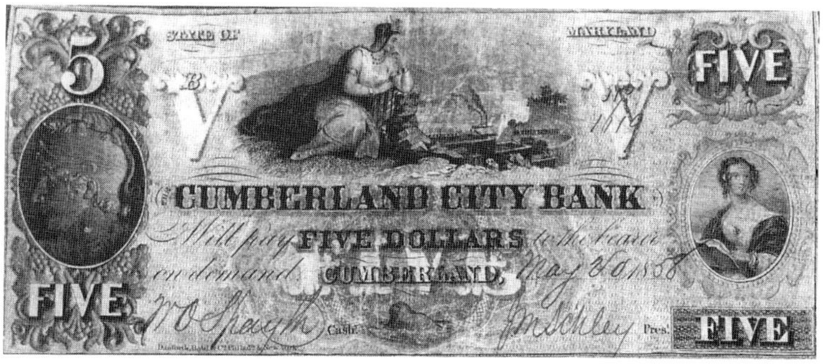

30.4.3

30.4.3 P

30.4.4 R-5

$5.00 Printed date October 20th, 1862. Engraving, imprint: American Bank Note Co., Phila. Green security underprint covering entire note. (MD165G10a)

30.4.5 R-7

$5.00 Printed date October 20th, 1862. Engraving, imprint: American Bank Note Co., Phila. Same as No. 30.4.4, except with red security underprint on entire note.

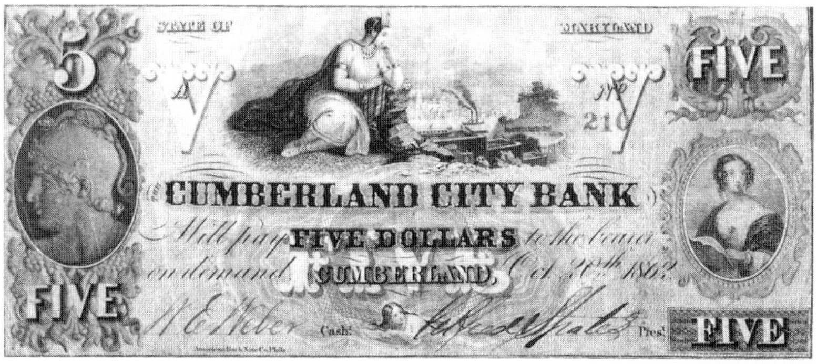

30.4.4

30.4.6 A R-7

$10.00 Ca. 1830s–40s. Engraving, imprint: Terry, Pelton & Co. *Center:* X; spread eagle with shield and arrows, motto E PLURIBUS UNUM above; X. *Left:* 10 / oval portrait of Washington, held by cherub at left / 10. *Right:* 10 / standing Indian male / 10. *Between signatures:* Ship. Altered from $10.00 Citizens Bank, Augusta, Maine, ME20G24, or from notes of other failed banks using the same plate. (MD160A5)

30.4.7 SENC

$10.00 Ca. 1858. Engraving, imprint: Danforth, Bald & Co., Philada & New York. *Center:* Ceres seated, sickle in left hand, right elbow resting on shield, flanked by ornate "1" and "0." *Left:* X / white cow, black one behind in oval / TEN. *Right:* 10 on medallion head / blacksmith standing at left watching second at right, swinging sledge, in square. *Between signatures:* Primitive train. Red-brown tint. (MD165G4a)

30.4.8 SENC

$10.00 Printed date October 20, 1862. Engraving, imprint: American Bank Note Co. Similar to No. 30.4.7, except for date, imprint, and tint, which is green. (MD165G12a)

30.5 The Cumberland Savings Bank

Charter amendment approved March 5, 1850; formerly Cumberland Savings Institution. Name changed to Cumberland City Bank in 1858.

30.5.1 P R-7

$1.00 Ca. 1850s. Engraving, imprint: Danforth, Bald & Co., Philada. & New York. Proof.

30.5.2 P R-7

$2.00 Ca. 1850s. Engraving, imprint: Danforth, Bald & Co., Philada. & New York. Proof.

30.5.1 P

30.5.2 P

30.5.3 R-6

$5.00 Ca. 1850–58. Engraving, imprint: Danforth, Bald & Co. Philada & New York.

30.5.3 P R-7

$5.00 Co. 1850–58. Engraving, imprint: Danforth, Bald & Co., Philada. & New York. Proof of No. 30.5.3.

30.5.4 R-3

$5.00 Ca. 1850–58. Engraving, imprint: Danforth, Bald & Co., New York. Brick red security underprint "5 FIVE 5."

30.5.4 P R-6

$5.00 Ca. 1850–58. Engraving, imprint: Danforth, Bald & Co., Philada. & New York. Brick red security underprint "5 FIVE 5." Proof.

30.5.3

30.5.3 P

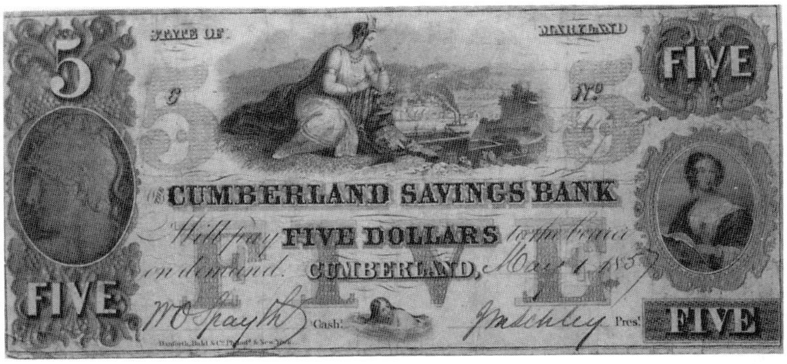

30.5.4

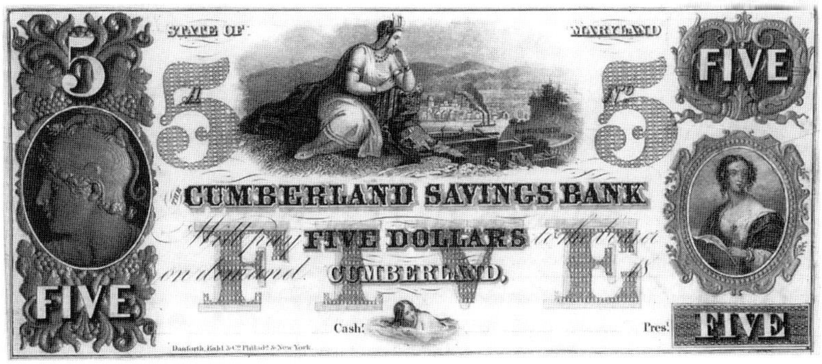

30.5.4 P

30.5.5 P R-6

$5.00 Ca. 1857–58. Engraving, imprint: Danforth, Bald & Co., Philada. & New York. Same as No. 30.5.4 P with only FIVE security underprint. Proof.

30.5.6 P R-7

$10.00 Ca. 1850. Engraving, imprint: Danforth, Bald & Co., Philada. & New York. Proof.

30.5.7 P R-7

$10.00 Ca. 1850–58. Engraving, imprint: Danforth, Bald & Co., Philada. & New York. Same as No. 30.5.6 P with security underprint "X TEN X" in brick red. Proof.

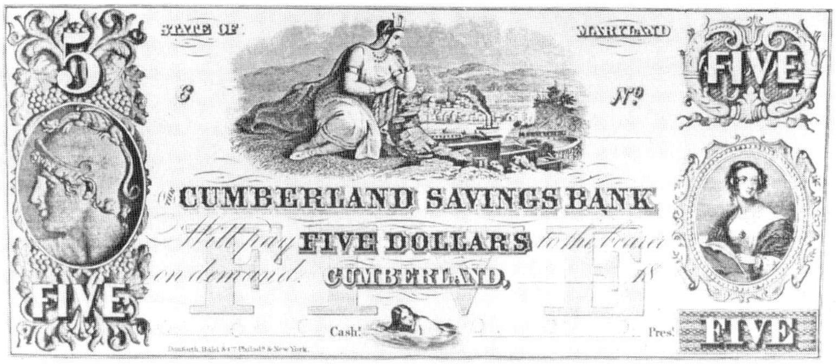

30.5.5 P

30.5.6 P

30.5.7 P

30.6 The Cumberland Savings Institution

Charter approved January 21, 1848; name changed to Cumberland Savings Bank in 1850.

30.6.1 P R-7

$1.00 Ca. 1848–50. Engraving, imprint: Hufty & Danforth, Philada. & New York. Proof.

30.6.1 P

30.6.2 P R-7

$2.00 Ca. 1848–50. Engraving, imprint: Hufty & Danforth, Philada. & New York. Proof.

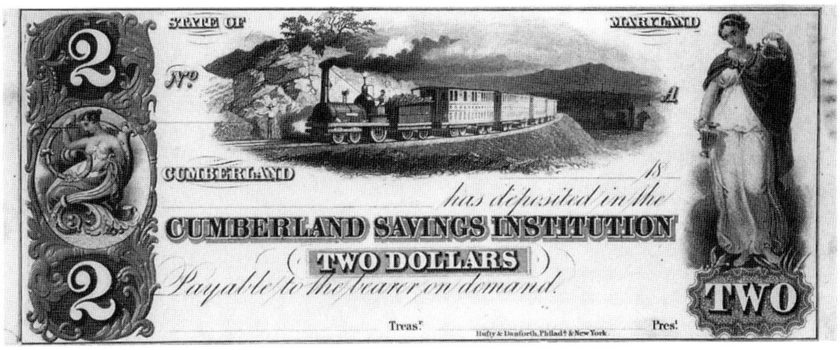

30.6.2 P

30.8 The Mineral Bank of Maryland

Charter approved March 25, 1836; liquidation in 1857.

30.8.1 R-7

$1.00 Printed date March 4, 1846. Engraving, imprint: Underwood, Bald, Spencer & Hufty, Philada; Danforth, Underwood & Co., New York. (MD170G2)

30.8.1 P R-7

Progressive die proof with bank name and city lightly inserted in pencil.

30.8.2 P R-7

$1.00 Printed partial date 184_. Engraving, imprint: Underwood, Bald, Spencer & Hufty, Philada; Danforth, Underwood & Co., New York. Same as No. 30.8.1, except for date. Proof.

30.8.3 R-5

$5.00 Ca. 1854. Engraving, imprint: Rawdon, Wright & Hatch, New York. (MD170C6)

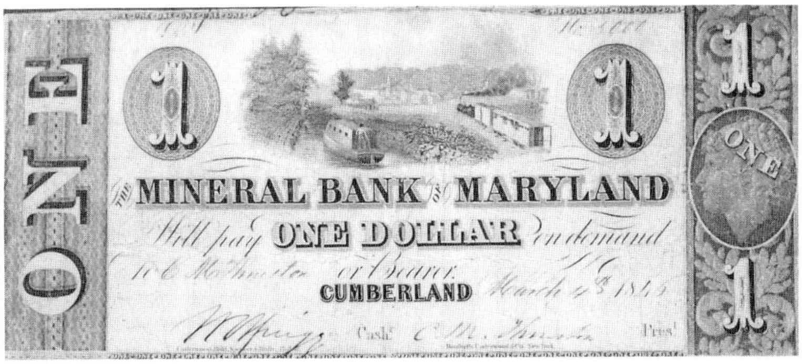

30.8.1

30.8.1 P

30.8.3

30.8.4 R-5

$5.00 Ca. 1856. Engraving, imprint: Rawdon, Wright, Hatch & Edson, New York. With ornate red FIVE security overprint. Similar to No. 30.8.3, but with different train at bottom center and engraved payee name. (MD170G6b)

30.8.5 SENC

$10.00 Ca. 1840s. Engraving, imprint: Unknown. Farmer plowing at center. (MD170A5)

30.8.6 A R-7

$10.00 Ca. 1849. Engraving, imprint: Terry, Pelton & Co., Boston & Prov. Altered from $10.00 Citizens Bank, Augusta, Maine, ME20G24. (MD169A5)

30.8.7 R-7

$10.00 Ca. 1855. Engraving, imprint: Rawdon, Wright & Hatch, New York. (MD170G8)

30.8.8 SENC

$20.00 Ca. 1832–50s. Engraving, imprint: Rawdon, Wright & Hatch. *Center:* XX; figure floating in clouds emptying cornucopia of gold / XX. *Left:* 20 / horse / 20. *Right:* TWENTY / woman seated with wand, man floating in clouds with cornucopia of gold. *Between signatures:* Dog's head. (MD170G10)

30.8.9 SENC

$50.00 Ca. 1832–50s. Engraving, imprint: Rawdon, Wright & Hatch. *Center:* L / woman reclining on globe holding lighted torch, eagle with portrait of Washington on its breast / L. *Left:* 50 / canal, railroad, factories and ships / 50. *Right:* 50 / steamboat / 50. *Between signatures:* Woman's head. (MD170G12)

30.8.4

30.8.6 A

30.8.7

31 CUMBERLAND & HAGERSTOWN

31.1 Stewart & Maguire

The issuers, proprietors of a general store in Cumberland, arranged for redemption of their notes in Hagerstown as well, at the bookstore of a relative, William Stewart.

31.1.1 R-7
6 1/4c Printed date April 26, 1841. Letterpress, imprint: W. D. Bell, Pr.

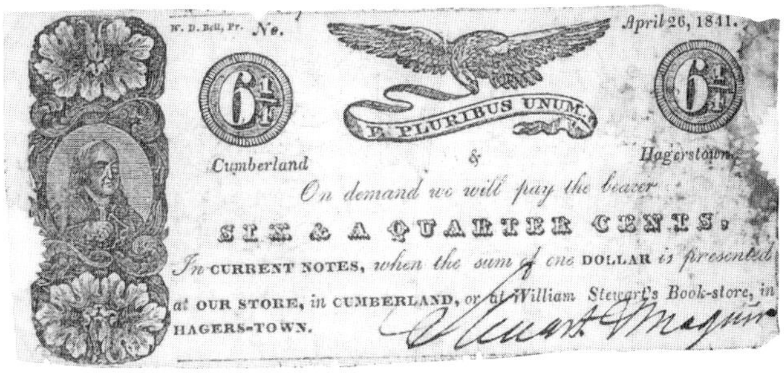

31.1.1

32 DARLINGTON, HARFORD COUNTY

This small town is situated equi-distant about 2 1/2 miles from the Susquehanna River and Deer Creek, 16 miles northwest of Belair. It was a post office as early as 1819. The name probably is attributed to Darlington, Durham, England, the home of an early settler.

32.1 John M. Hopkins & Co.

The issuer sold canned goods, which he personally processed, and also was a butcher.

32.1.2 R-7
12 1/2c Printed partial year date 183_. Letterpress, imprint: Murphy & Spalding, printers, NO. 1 Light street, Balt.

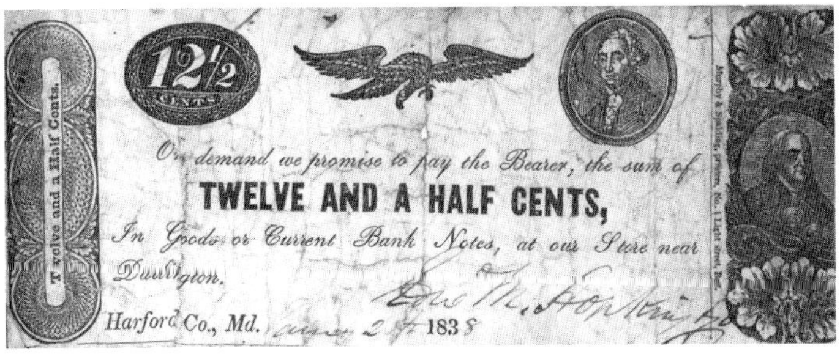

32.1.2

32.2 T. W. & B. Silver Jr.

The issuers were proprietors of a general store.

32.2.1 R-7
5c Printed date May 4, 1841. Engraving, imprint: Manly & Orr, Printers, Philad.

32.2.2 R-7
6 1/4c Printed date May 4, 1841. Engraving, imprint: Manly & Orr, Printers, Philad.

32.2.1

Complete sheet of six denominations. An example of the 5c denomination appearing in this sheet is on record which bears a penciled signature, "T. W. & B. Silver," which is suspect as it does not resemble that shown on No. 32.2.7, although it could have been signed by another member of the firm. Whether or not the sheet was prepared for the Silvers is not known, but it is tentatively assigned to that firm.

32.2.3 R-7
10c Printed date May 4, 1841. Engraving, imprint: Manly & Orr, Printers, Philad.

32.2.4 R-7
12 1/2c Printed date May 4, 1841. Engraving, imprint: Manly & Orr, Printers, Philad.

32.2.5 R-7
25c Printed date May 4, 1841. Engraving, imprint: Manly & Orr, Printers, Philad.

32.2.6 R-7
50c Printed date May 4, 1841. Engraving, imprint: Manly & Orr, Printers, Philad.

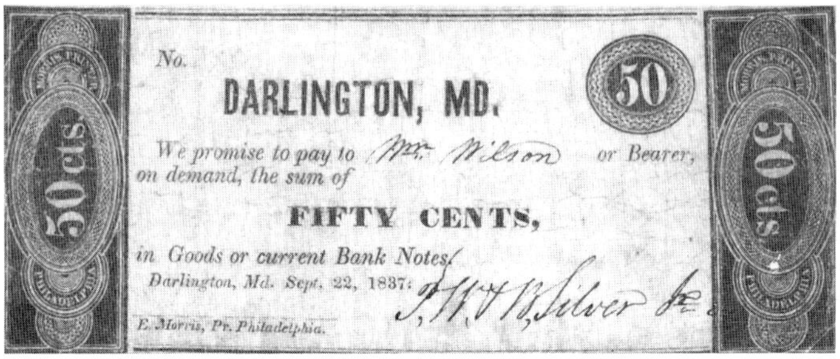

32.2.7

32.2.7 R-7
50c Printed date Sept. 22, 1837. Lithography, imprint: E. Morris, Pr., Philadelphia;

32.4 Unidentified Issuer

32.4.3 R-7
10c Printed partial year date 186_. Lithography, no imprint.

32.4.3

32.5 Unidentified Issuer

32.5.2 R-7

12 1/2c Ca. 1837–40. Letterpress, no imprint.

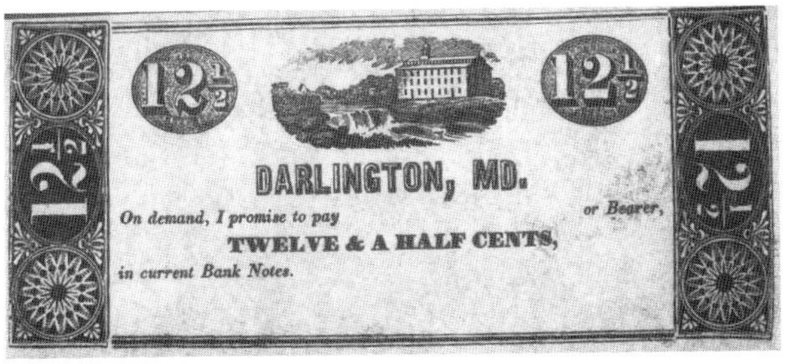

32.5.2

34 DEER CREEK WORKS, HARFORD COUNTY

The site of this iron forge was on Deer Creek at the present-day Forge Hill Road about 3/4 miles south of U.S. Route 1. Originally known as Lebanon Forge, the Deer Creek Works operated until 1878.

34.1 Deer Creek Works

Large remainders of the Deer Creek Works notes in complete unsigned sheets appeared on the market in the mid-1930s. The authors have never seen Deer Creek notes in circulated condition; it may well be that the notes were never put into circulation. "Signatures" such as "C. Clements," "C. Cousin," "C. Cummings," and "E. R. Threw" or "Thew," which are occasionally encountered on uncirculated notes, would seem to have no particular significance.

34.1.1 R-2

6 1/4c Printed date March 4, 1837. Engraving, imprint: Manly & Orr, Printers, Philadelphia.

34.1.2 R-5

6 1/4c Printed date March 4, 1837. Engraving, imprint: Manly & Orr, Printers, Philadelphia. This note differs from No. 34.1.1 in the central vignette and end plates; additionally the letter *A* appears above the right 6 1/4 die.

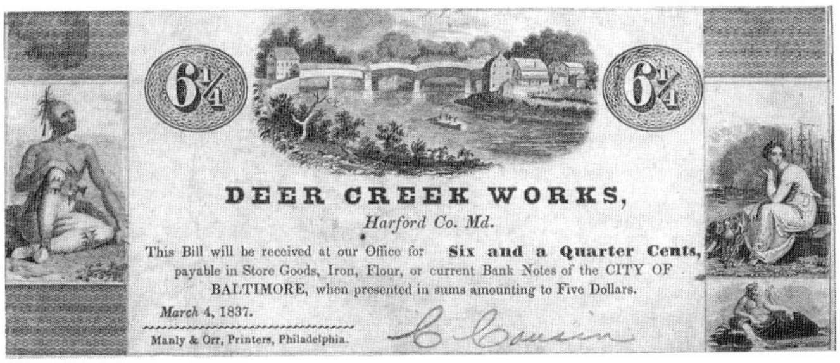

34.1.1

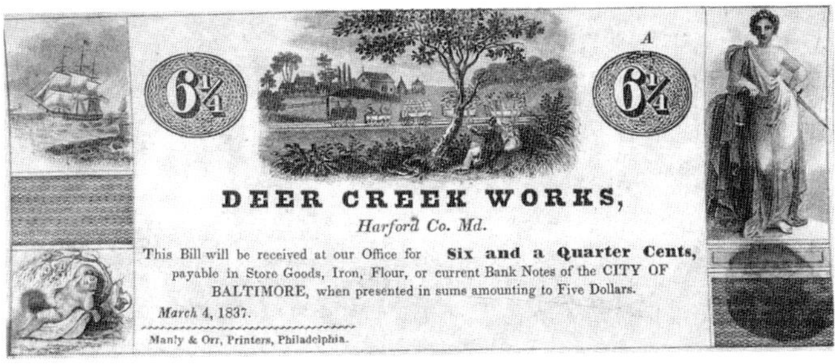

34.1.2

34.1.3 R-2

12 1/2c Printed date March 4, 1837. Engraving, imprint: Manly & Orr, Printers, Philadelphia.

34.1.4 R-2

25c Printed date March 4, 1837. Engraving, imprint: Manly & Orr, Printers, Philadelphia.

34.1.5 R-2

50c Printed date March 4, 1837. Engraving, imprint: Manly & Orr, Printers, Philadelphia.

34.1.6 R-2

$1.00 Printed date March 4, 1837. Engraving, imprint: Manly & Orr, Printers, Philadelphia.

34.1.7 R-2

$2.00 Printed date March 4, 1837. Engraving, imprint: Manly & Orr, Printers, Philadelphia.

34.1.3

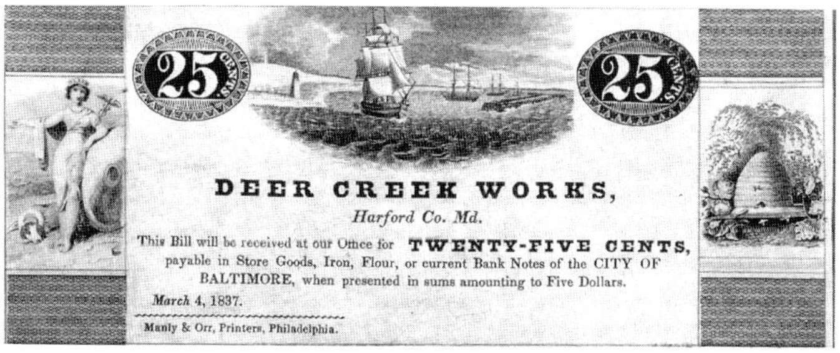

34.1.4

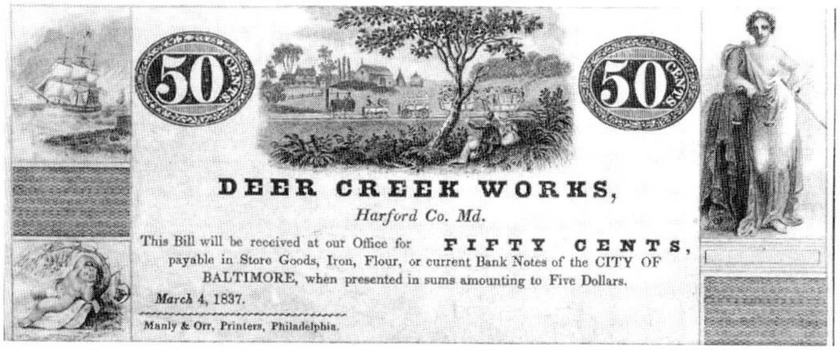

34.1.5

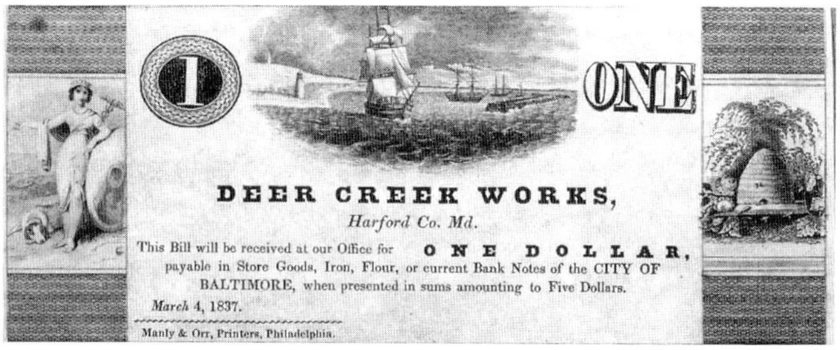

34.1.6

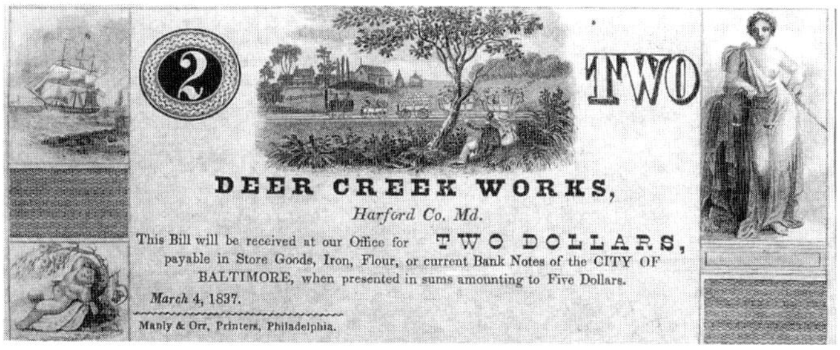

34.1.7

Complete remainder sheet showing the layout of the 12 1/2c (34.1.1), 25c (34.1.3), and 50c (34.1.5) denominations on the plate.

36 DENTON, CAROLINE COUNTY

This town on the Choptank River was called Eden-Town in 1793. The present name is derived from the surname of Sir Robert Eden, the last royal governor of Maryland (1769–74), who left for England shortly after the American Revolution.

36.1 Commissioners of Denton

Scrip issued by the town during the Civil War to alleviate the shortage of coins.

36.1.1 R-5

5c Printed partial date January 1863. Letterpress, imprint: MURPHY PRINT BALTO in scroll. Security underprint of dots in pale green and "5 CENTS" in red, double-lined uppercase lettering in upper center of face. Reverse design printed in brown.

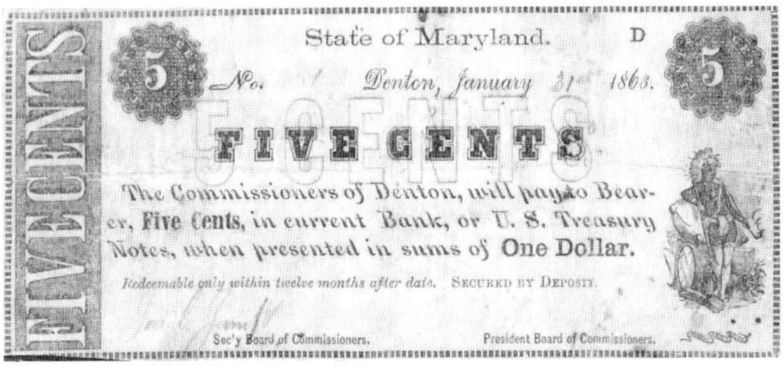

36.1.1

36.1.2 R-6

10c Printed partial date January 1863. Letterpress, imprint: Murphy, pr. Balt. Similar security underprint and reverse as on 5c, No. 36.1.1.

36.1.3 R-7

25c Printed partial date January 1863. Letterpress, imprint: MURPHY PRINT BALTO. Similar security underprint and reverse as on 5c, No. 36.1.1.

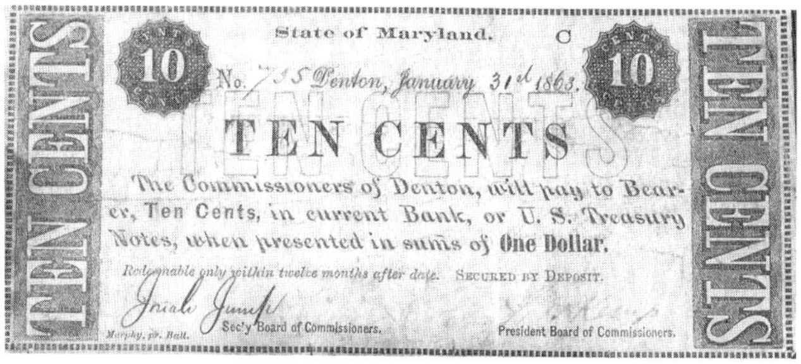

36.1.2

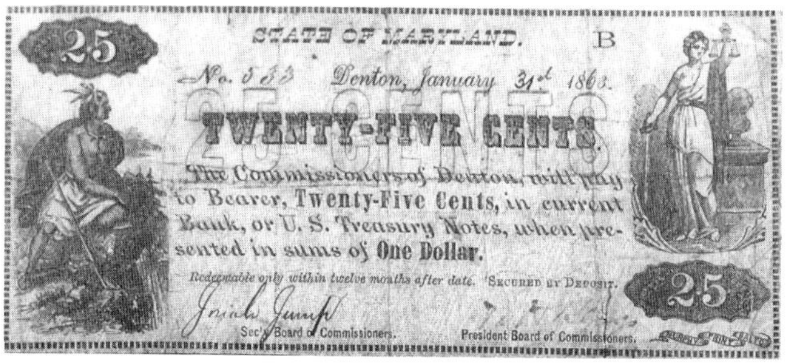

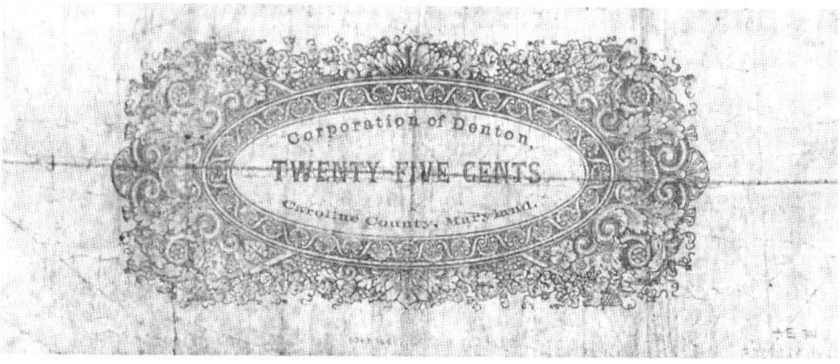

36.1.3

36.2 Bank of Caroline

Charter approved January 10, 1814; voluntary liquidation in 1821. With the exception of the $5.00, No. 36.2.9, the designs of the $10.00 (36.2.10 P), $20.00 (36.2.11 P), and $50.00 (36.2.12 P) notes have not as yet been determined. However, the subjects of their central vignettes are illustrated below although their specific match-ups have not been accomplished. These illustrations were found in the files of a senior collector.

36.2.3 SENC

25c Printed date Nov. 8, 1815. Engraving, imprint: Murray, Draper, Fairman & Co. Similar to 50c, No. 36.2.4. (MD175G8)

36.2.4 R-7

50c Printed date Nov. 8th 1815. Engraving, imprint: Murray, Draper, Fairman & Co. (MI75G10)

36.2.5 SENC

75c Printed date Nov. 8, 1815. Engraving, imprint: Murray, Draper, Fairman & Co. Similar to 50c, No. 36.2.4. (MD174G12)

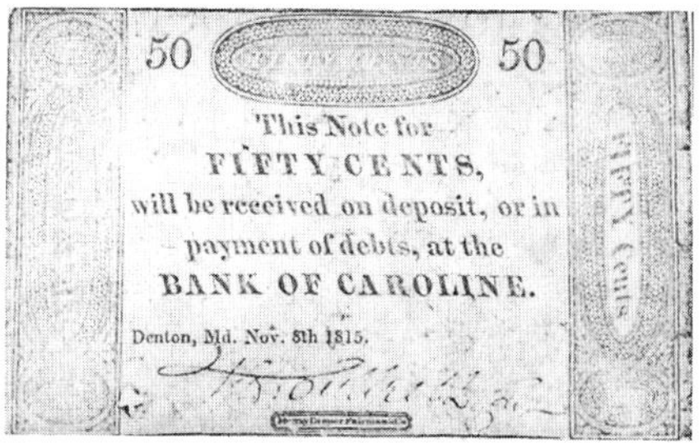

36.2.4

36.2.6 R-7

$1.00 Printed partial year date 181_. Engraving, imprint: Murray, Draper, Fairman & Co. (MD175G14)

36.2.7 SENC

$2.00 Ca. 1810s. Engraving, imprint: Murray, Draper, Fairman & Co. Similar to $1.00, No. 36.2.6 (MD175G16)

36.2.8 SENC

$3.00 Ca. 1810s. Engraving, imprint: Murray, Draper, Fairman & Co. Similar to $1.00, No. 36.2.6. (MD175G18)

36.2.9 P SENC

$5.00 Ca. 1810s. Engraving, imprint: Murray, Draper, Fairman & Co. Proof. (MD175G20)

36.2.10 P SENC

$10.00 Ca. 1810s. Engraving, imprint: Murray, Draper, Fairman & Co. Proof. (MD175G24)

36.2.11 P SENC

$20.00 Ca. 1810s. Engraving, imprint: Murray, Draper, Fairman & Co. Proof. (MD175G28)

36.2.12 P SENC

$50.00 Ca. 1810s. Engraving, imprint: Murray, Draper, Fairman & Co. Proof. (MD175G32)

36.2.6

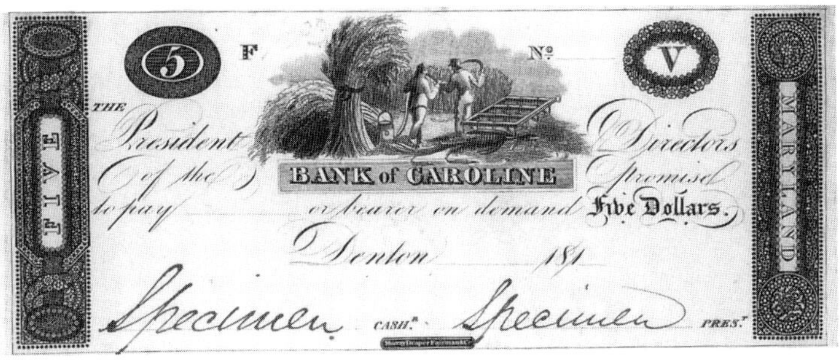

36.2.9 P

36.3 Thos. Culbreth

The issuer dealt in general merchandise in Denton, although his scrip was redeemable at the branch of the Farmers Bank of Maryland in Easton.

36.3.8 R-7

$3.00 Printed year date 1841. Letterpress, no imprint.

36.3.8

36.4 Walsh & Saulsbury

The issuers were proprietors of a general store.

36.4.4 R-7

50c Printed date April 8, 1840. Letterpress, imprint: MURPHY, PRINTER, BALTIMORE. Central vignette is a view of Baltimore and the inner harbor from Federal Hill.

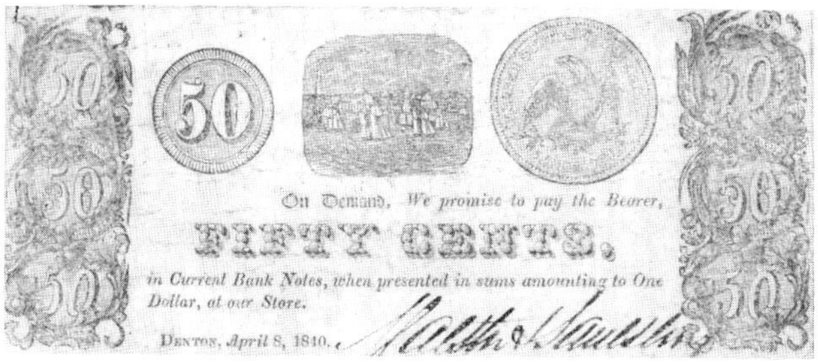

36.4.4

37 DIRICKSON'S CROSS ROADS, WICOMICO COUNTY

This village near Parsonsburg is now called Pittsville in honor of Dr. H. R. Pitts, who was the president of the Wicomico & Pocomoke Railroad, completed in 1868 from Salisbury to Berlin as a continuation of the line from Claiborne.

37.1 Jas. M & E. Fooks

The issuers were James Minas Fooks and Ebenezer Fooks, proprietors of a country store situated at or near the boundary line between the then-counties of Worcester and Somerset, now in Wicomico County.

37.1.3 R-6

25c Printed partial year date 184_. Letterpress, no imprint. Approximately a half dozen of these notes have been recorded, all but one bearing the same serial number, 40. The central vignette in the right end panel shows the Battle Monument in Baltimore.

37.1.3

39 EASTON, TALBOT COUNTY

On the Tred Avon River, Easton, then a mere hamlet, was first known as Pitts Bridge and then Talbot Town. In 1779 it became a post office and was named Easton, after a town in Somersetshire, England, the county in which one finds the Welsh river Avon.

39.1 The Easton Bank of Maryland

Succeeding the Easton branch of the Farmers Bank of Maryland in 1853 (see Annapolis, No. 2), the bank was converted to the Easton National Bank of Maryland in 1865.

39.1.1 SENC

$1.00 Ca. 1850s. Engraving, imprint: Unknown. *Center:* Woman; 1; woman. (MD180N5)

39.1.2 SENC

$1.00 Ca. 1860s. Engraving, imprint: American Bank Note Co. *Center:* Boy and girl seated under tree; cattle and sheep in background. *Left:* 1 / farmer leaning on fence petting dog. *Right:* 1 / ONE on 1. *Lower center:* ONE DOLLAR on ONE . Tint is "1 1," color unknown. (MD180G2).

39.1.3 A SENC

$2.00 Printed date Dec. 20, 1854. Engraving, imprint: Danforth, Bald & Co. *Center:* 2; Indian man standing on cliff watching train. *Left:* Laureated woman standing, leaning on ornate shield bearing large TWO, across. *Right:* 2 on oval die with small KAN below / stag on hill facing viewer. *Lower center:* Bear leaning against tree. Altered from $2.00 Delaware City Bank, Delaware, Kan., K520G4. (MD180A5)

39.1.4 P R-7

$5.00 Ca. 1856–58. Engraving, imprint: Danforth, Wright & Co., Philada. & New York. Proof. (MD180G4)

39.1.5 P R-7

$10.00 Ca. 1856–58. Engraving, imprint: Danforth, Wright & Co. Philada., & New York. Proof. (MD180G6)

39.1.6 P R-7

$20.00 Ca. 1856–58. Engraving, imprint: Danforth, Wright & Co. Philada., & New York. Proof. (MD180G8)

39.1.7 P R-7

$50.00 Ca. 1856–58. Engraving, imprint: Danforth, Wright & Co., Philada. & New York. Proof. (MD180G10)

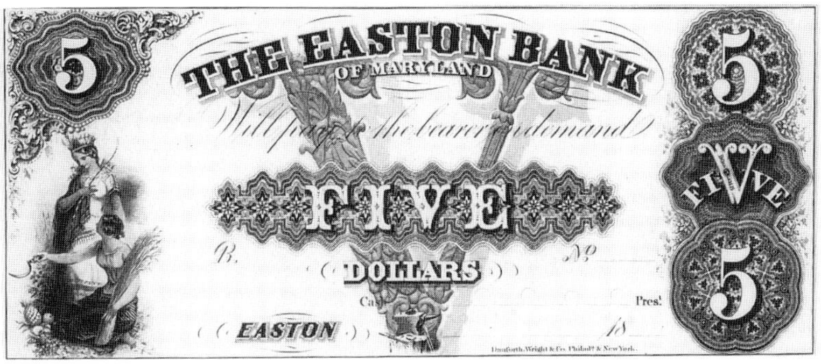

39.1.4 P

39.1.5 P

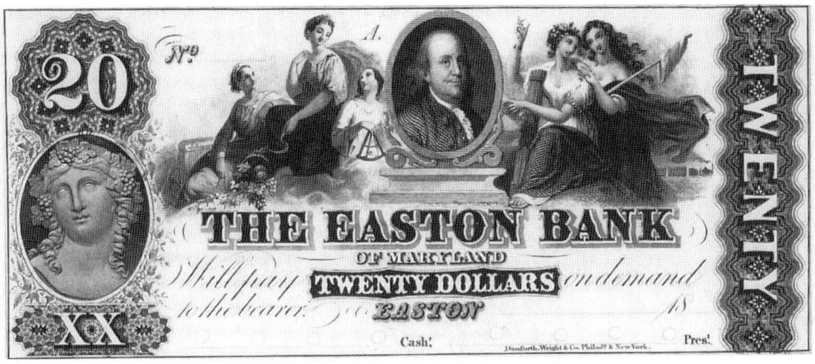

39.1.6 P

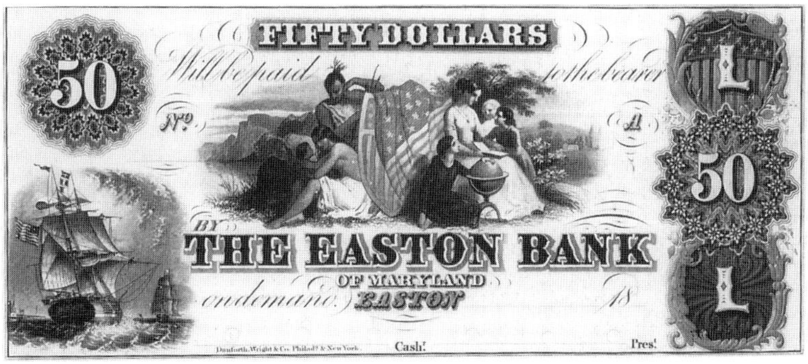

39.1.7 P

39.1.8 P R-7

$100.00 Ca. 1856–58. Engraving, imprint: Danforth, Wright & Co., Philada. & New York. Proof. (MD180G12)

39.1.8 P

39.2 Unidentified Issuer

39.2.4 R-7

50c Printed partial date June , 1841. Letterpress, no imprint. "June" has been lined out and "September" written in.

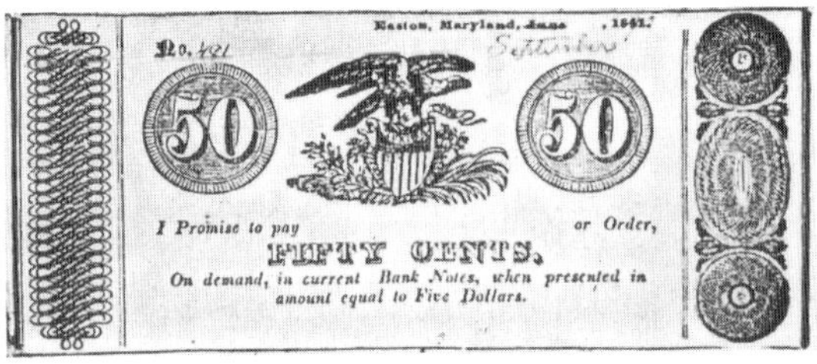

39.2.4

---

41 ELKTON, CECIL COUNTY

The land tract of this town was patented in 1681 as Friendship, the first name of the village being Head of Elk because of its location at the head of the Elk River. An act of the Maryland General Assembly formally named the town Elkton in 1787.

41.1 The Commissioners of Elkton

Small-change notes issued by the town to alleviate the shortage of coins during the Civil War. All notes headed ELKTON LOAN at top center in serifed uppercase letters.

41.1.1 R-5

5c Printed date Feb. 1st, 1863. Engraving, imprint: American Bank Note Co., Philada. Security underprint is large brick red CENTS on red panel of micro CENTS. Similar to No. 41.1.2, except date.

41.1.2

41.1.2 R-4

5c Printed date Feb. 10, 1863. Engraving, imprint: American Bank Note Co., Philada. Same as 5c, No. 41.1.1, except date.

41.1.3 R-5

10c Printed date Feb. 1st, 1863. Engraving, imprint: American Bank Note Co., Philada. Security underprint is similar to 5c, No. 41.1.1.

41.1.4 R-4
10c Printed date Feb. 10th, 1863. Engraving, imprint: American Bank Note Co., Philada. Same as 10c, No. 41.1.3, except date.

41.1.4

41.1.5 R-5
25c Printed date Feb 1st, 1863. Engraving, imprint: American Bank Note Co., Philada. Security underprint similar to 5c, No. 41.1.1, with addition of "25-25" at lower corners. Portrait of Gen. George B. McClelland in center oval.

41.1.5

41.1.6 R-4
25c Printed date Feb. 10th, 1863. Engraving, imprint: American Bank Note Co., Philada. Same as 25c, No. 41.1.5, except date.

41.1.7 R-6
50c Printed date Feb. 1st, 1863. Engraving, imprint: American Bank Note Co., Philada. Security underprint similar to 5c, No. 41.1.1.

41.1.8

41.1.8 R-5
50c Printed date of Feb. 10th, 1863. Engraving, imprint: American Bank Note Co, Philada. Same as 50c, No. 41.1.7, except date.

41.2 The Elkton Bank of Maryland

Charter approved December 23, 1810; voluntary liquidation in 1830.

41.2.1 R-5
6 1/4c Printed date Jan. 20, 1815. Letterpress, no imprint. Similar to 12 1/2c, No. 41.2.2. (MD185G4)

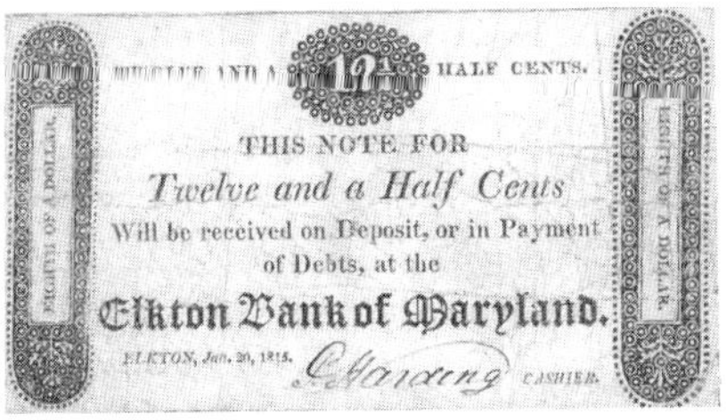

41.2.2

41.2.2 R-7
12 1/2c Printed date Jan. 20, 1815. Letterpress, no imprint. (MD185G8)

41.2.3 R-7
25c Printed date Jan. 20, 1815. Letterpress, no imprint. Similar to 12 1/2c, No. 41.2.2. (MD185G12)

41.2.4 SENC
50c Printed date Jan. 20, 1815. Letterpress, no imprint. Similar to 12 1/2c, No. 41.2.2. (MD185G16)

41.2.5 R-7

$1.00 Printed partial year date 181_. Engraving, imprint: W. Harrison, Sculpt.; C.P.H. Printed. (MD185G20)

41.2.6 R-7

$2.00 Printed partial year date 181_. Engraving, imprint: W. Harrison. Sculp.; C.P.H. printed. (MD185G24)

41.2.7 R-7

$3.00 Printed partial year date 181_. Engraving, imprint: W. Harrison, fct.; C.P.H. Printed. (MD185G28)

41.2.7 C R-7

$3.00 Printed partial year date 181_. Engraving, imprint: W. Harrison, C. P. Harrison. Counterfeit of same design as No. 41.2.7. (MD185C28)

41.2.8 R-7

$5.00 Ca. 1810s–20s. Engraving, no imprint. (MD185G32)

41.2.9 R-7

$5.00 Ca. 1810s–20s. Engraving, no imprint. Without letter *T* after "Pres."

41.2.9 C R-5

$5.00 Ca. 1810s–20s. Engraving, imprint: Murray fc / Printed by C. P. Harrison. Counterfeit of No. 41.2.9. Without letter *T* after "Pres." (MD185C32)

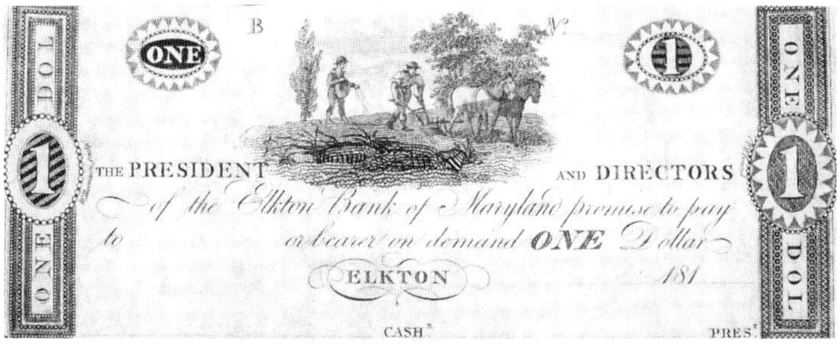

41.2.5

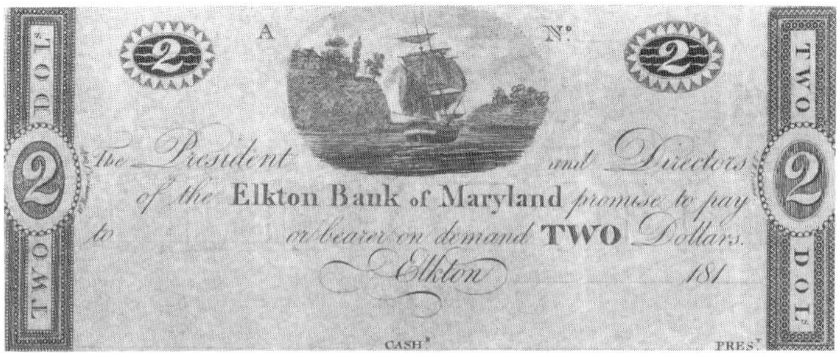

41.2.6

41.2.7

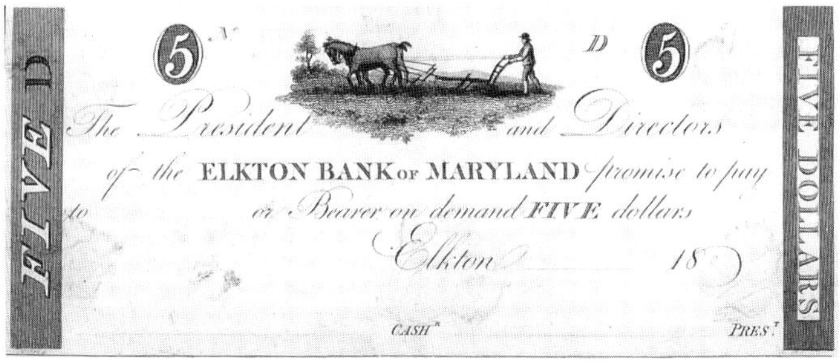

41.2.8

41.2.9 C

41.2.10 R-3

$5.00 Ca. 1825–32. Engraving, imprint: Fairman, Draper, Underwood & Co. (MD185G34)

41.2.11 R-5

$5.00 Ca. 1825–32. Engraving, imprint: Fairman, Draper, Underwood & Co. Payable at the Mechanics Bank in Philadelphia. (MD185G50)

41.2.12 R-7

$10.00 Ca. 1810s–20s. Engraving, imprint: Murray, fc (*left*) / Printed by C.P. Harrison (*right*). Similar to counterfeit No. 41.2.12 C. (MD185G36)

41.2.12 C R-6

$10.00 Ca. 1810s–20s. Engraving, no imprint. Counterfeit of No. 41.2.12. (MD185C36)

41.2.13 R-7

$10.00 Ca. 1825–32. Engraving, imprint: Fairman, Draper, Underwood & Co. Similar to No. 41.2.14, except for text. (MD185G38)

41.2.14 R-5

$10.00 Ca. 1825–32. Engraving, imprint: Fairman, Draper, Underwood & Co. Payable at the Mechanics Bank in Philadelphia. Similar to No. 41.2.13, except for text. (MD185G52)

41.2.15 SENC

$20.00 Ca. 1810s–20s. Engraving, imprint: Murray, fc (*left*) / Printed by C.P. Harrison (*right*). Similar to counterfeit No. 41.2.15 C. (MD185G40)

41.2.15 C R-7

$20.00 Ca. 1810s–20s. Engraving, no imprint. Counterfeit of No. 41.2.15. (MD185C40)

41.2.10

41.2.11

41.2.12 C

41.2.14

41.2.15 C

41.2.16 R-4

$20.00 Ca. 1825–32. Engraving, imprint: Fairman, Draper, Underwood & Co. (MD185G44)

41.2.17 SENC

$50.00 Ca. 1810s–20s. Engraving, imprint: Murray, fc (*left*) / Printed by C. P. Harrison (*right*). Similar to counterfeit No. 41.2.17 C. (MD185G46)

41.2.17 C R-7

$50.00 Ca. 1810s–20s. Engraving, no imprint. Counterfeit of No. 41.2.17. (MD185C46)

41.2.16

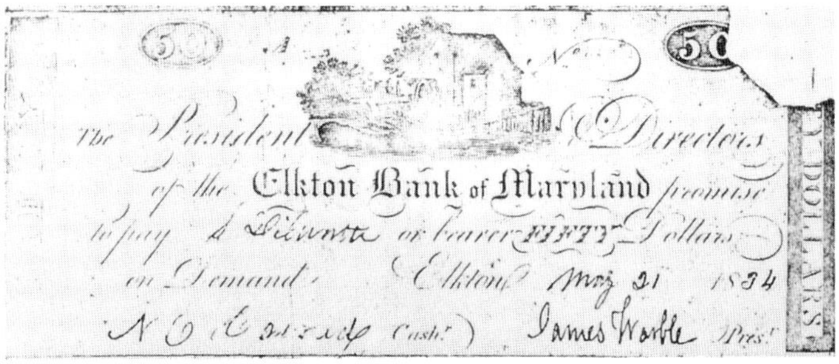

41.2.17 C

41.3 The Farmers & Merchants Bank of Cecil County

Charter approved March 10, 1862; voluntary liquidation in 1865 and probably absorbed by the National Bank of Elkton (1865).

41.3.1 R-2

$1.00 Printed partial year date 186_. Ca. 1862. Engraving, imprint: American Bank Note Co., New York. Green and black. Plain back. (MD190G2a)

41.3.2 R-3

$1.00 Printed partial year date 186_. Ca. 1862. Engraving, imprint: American Bank Note Co., New York. Same as No. 41.3.1, but light yellow green and black. Plain back.

41.3.3 R-2

$1.00 Printed partial year date 186_. Ca. 1862. Engraving, imprint: American Bank Note Co., New York. Same as No. 41.3.1 with green back as illustrated. (MD190G2b)

41.3.4 R-2

$1.00 Printed partial year date 186_. Ca. 1864. Engraving, imprint: American Bank Note Co., New York. Same as No. 41.3.3, except has a printed serial number and engraved president's signature. (MD190G2c)

41.3.1

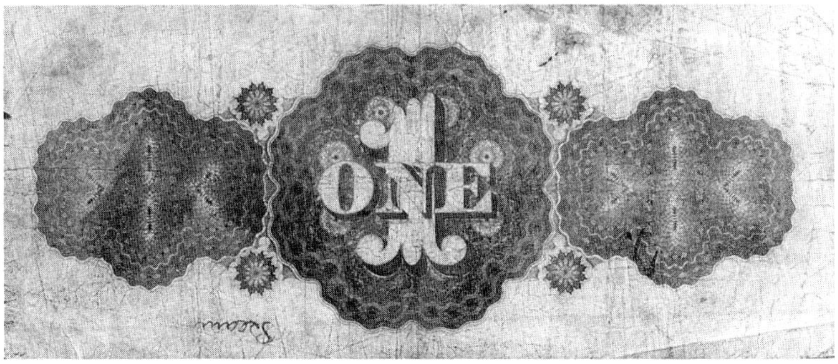

41.3.3

41.3.5 R-2

$2.00 Printed partial year date 186_. Ca. 1862. Engraving, imprint: American Bank Note Co., New York. Same as No. 41.3.7, with written serial number, plain back. (MD190G6a)

41.3.6 R-2

$2.00 Printed partial year date 186_. Ca. 1862–63. Engraving, imprint: American Bank Note Co., New York. Green and black. Plain back. (MD190G4a)

41.3.7 R-2

$2.00 Printed partial year date 186_. Ca. 1862–65. Engraving, imprint: American Bank Note Co., New York. Green and black. Plain back. (MD190G6c)

41.3.8 R-2

$2.00 Printed partial year date 186_. Ca. 1863. Engraving, imprint: American Bank Note Co., New York. Same as No. 41.3.5 with green back. (MD190G6b)

41.3.9 R-2

$2.00 Printed partial year date 186_. Ca. 1863. Engraving, imprint: American Bank Note Co., New York. Same as No. 41.3.6, except with green back. (MD190G4b)

41.3.10 R-2

$2.00 Printed partial year date 186_. Ca. 1863. Engraving, imprint: American Bank Note Co., New York. Same as No. 41.3.6, except with printed serial number and engraved president's signature. (MD190G4c)

41.3.5

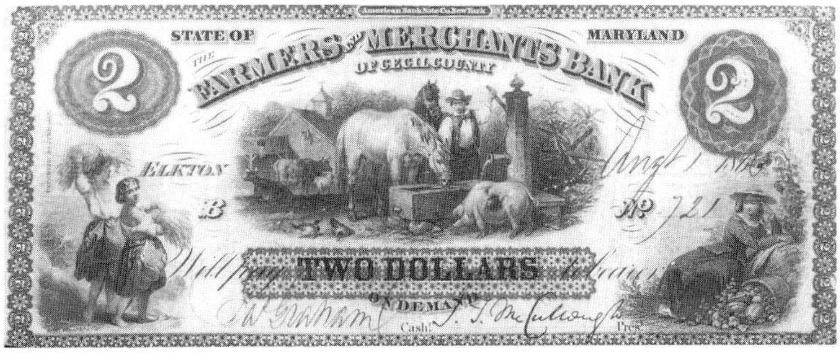

41.3.6

41.3.7

41.3.8

41.3.11 R-5
$5.00 Ca. 1862. Engraving, imprint: National Bank Note Company. Red and black. Andrew Jackson at left.

41.3.12 R-2
$5.00 Ca. 1862. Engraving, imprint: National Bank Note Co. Same as No. 41.3.11, except orange and black. (MD190G8a)

41.3.13 R-2
$5.00 Ca. 1862. Engraving, imprint: National Bank Note Co. Same as No. 41.3.12, except printed serial number. (MD190G8b)

41.3.14 R-5
$5.00 Ca. 1862. Engraving, imprint: National Bank Note Co. Same as No. 41.3.11, except green and black.

41.3.15 R-3
$10.00 Ca. 1862. Engraving, imprint: National Bank Note Company. Red and black.

41.3.16 R-2
$10.00 Ca. 1862. Engraving, imprint: National Bank Note Company. Same as No. 41.3.15, except orange and black. (MD190G10a)

41.3.17 R-2
$10.00 Ca. 1862. Engraving, imprint: National Bank Note Company. Same as No. 41.3.18, except printed serial number. (MD190G10b)

41.3.18 R-5
$10.00 Ca. 1862. Engraving, imprint: National Bank Note Company. Same as No. 41.3.15, except green and black.

41.3.19 R-3
$20.00 Printed partial year date 186_. Engraving, imprint: American Bank Note Co., New York. Green and black. Same design as $2.00, No. 41.3.6, except for denomination. (MD190G12a)

41.3.11

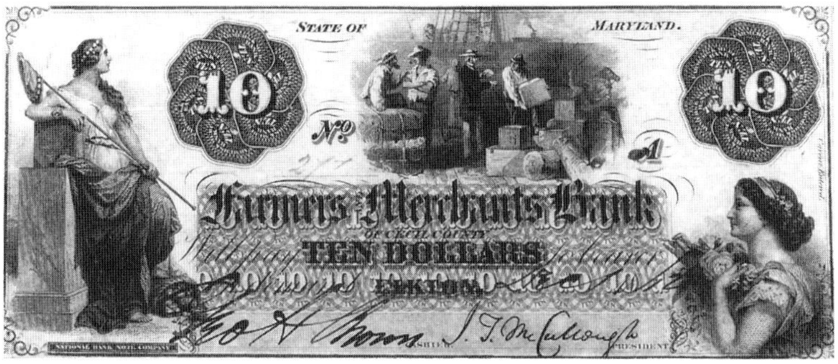

41.3.15

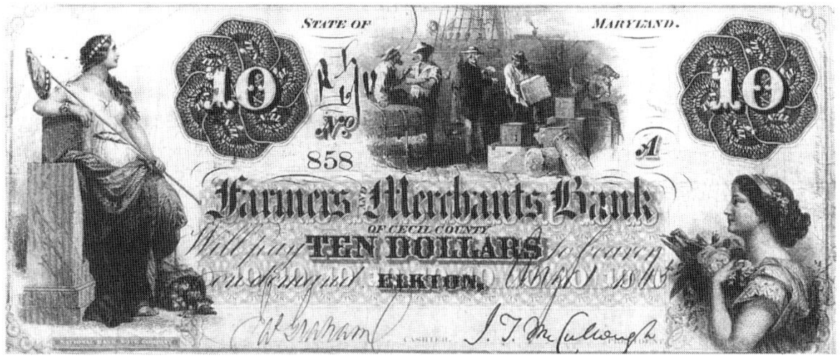

41.3.17

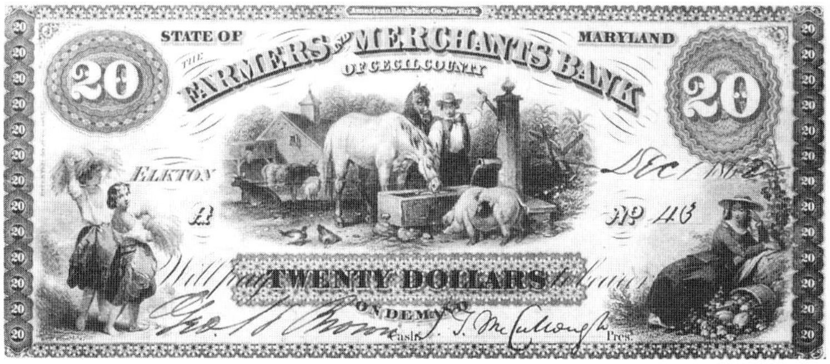

41.3.19

Farmers Bank of Maryland, Elkton Branch

See Farmers Bank of Maryland, No. 2.3.

42 ELLICOTT'S LOWER MILLS, HOWARD COUNTY

Situated on the Patapsco River three miles west of Catonsville, the present Ellicott City was first named Ellicott's Mills and then Ellicott's Lower Mills. The names derive from John, Joseph, and Andrew Ellicott who bought water rights and transported their milling machinery from Philadelphia to downstream Elkridge Landing in 1774.

42.1 Columbia Turnpike Company

42.1.3 R-7

25c Printed partial year date 181_. Letterpress, imprint: Printed by J. Robinson, 96 Market Street, Baltimore. Similar to 100c note, No. 42.1.5.

42.1.4 R-7

50c Printed partial year date 181_. Letterpress, imprint: Printed by J. Robinson, 96 Market Street, Baltimore. Similar to 100c note, No. 42.1.5.

42.1.5 R-7

100c (ONE DOLLAR) Printed partial year date 181_. Letterpress, imprint: Printed by J. Robinson, 96 Market street, Baltimore.

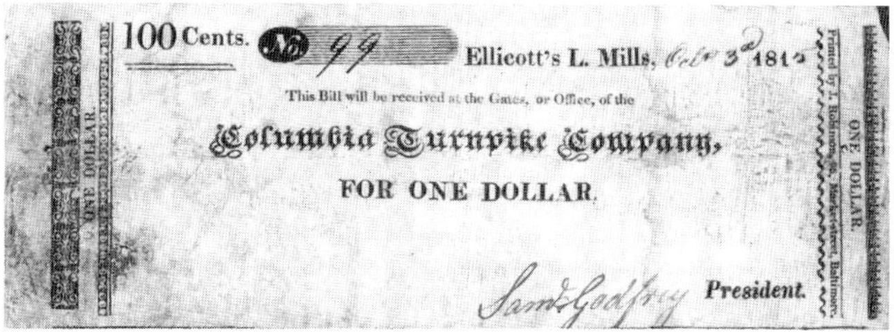

42.1.5

43 ELLICOTT'S MILLS, HOWARD COUNTY

43.1 The Bank of Howard County

Charter approved May 31, 1853. No record of operations has been found.

43.2 The Patapsco Bank of Maryland

Charter approved Feb. 21, 1834; voluntary liquidation in 1853.

43.2.3 P R-6

25c Engraved year date 1837. Engraving, imprint: Draper, Toppan, Longacre & Co. Proof.

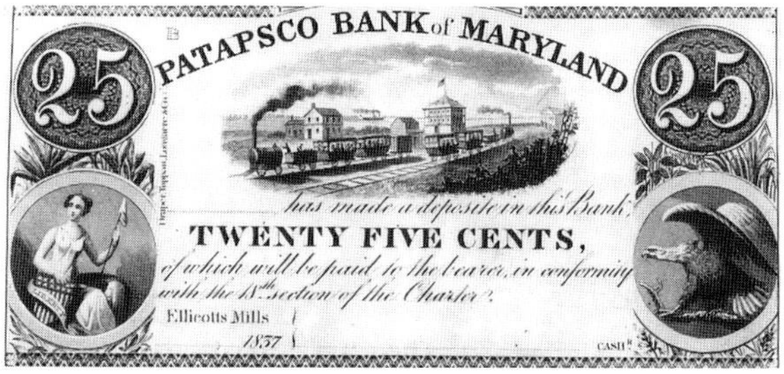

43.2.3 P

43.2.4 R-5

25c Engraved year date 1838. Engraving, imprint: Draper, Toppan, Longacre & Co. Same as No. 43.2.3, except date.

43.2.5 P R-6

50c Engraved year date 1837. Engraving, imprint: Draper, Toppan, Longacre & Co., Phila. Proof.

43.2.6 R-5

50c Engraved year date 1838. Engraving, imprint: Draper, Toppan, Longacre & Co., Phila.

43.2.7 SENC

$1.00 Ca. 1830s. No information available. (MD200G6)

43.2.8 R-7

$1.00 Engraved year date 1837 with "8" written over "7." Engraving, imprint: Draper, Toppan, Longacre & Co., Phila & N.Y.

43.2.9 R-7

$1.00 Engraved date March 15, 1845. Engraving, imprint: Toppan, Carpenter & Co.

43.2.10 R-7

$2.00 Printed year date 1837. Engraving, imprint: Draper, Toppan, Longacre & Co., Phila. & New York. (MD200G10)

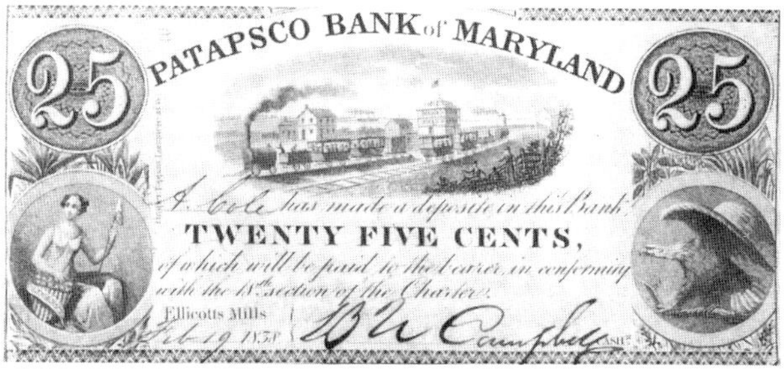

43.2.4

43.2.5 P

43.2.6

43.2.8

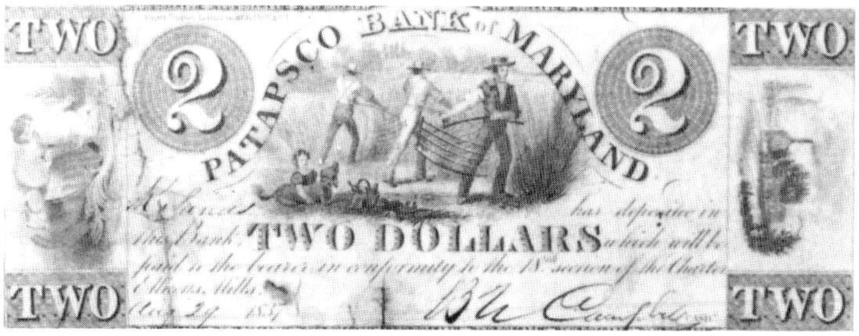

43.2.10

43.2.11 P R-7

$5.00 Ca. 1835–39. Engraving, imprint: Draper, Toppan, Longacre & Co., Phila & New York. Proof. (MD200G16)

43.2.12 S R-7

$5.00 Ca. 1840s. Engraving, imprint: Rawdon, Wright & Hatch. From a fraudently modified plate, originally for a $5.00 note (OH355G8) on the Geauga Insurance Co., Painesville, Ohio. (MD200S5)

43.2.13 P R-7

$10.00 Ca. 1835–39. Engraving, imprint: Draper, Toppan, Longacre & Co., Phila & New York. Proof. (MD200G22)

43.2.14 P R-7

$20.00 Ca. 1835–39. Engraving, imprint: Draper, Toppan, Longacre, Phila & New York. Proof. (MD200G28)

43.2.11 P

43.2.12 S

43.2.13 P

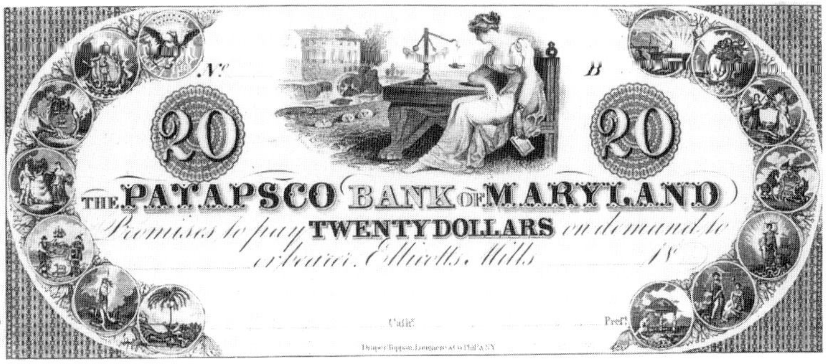

43.2.14 P

43.2.15 P R-7

$50.00 Ca. 1835–39. Engraving, imprint: Draper, Toppan, Longacre, Phila & New York. Proof. (MD200G32)

43.2.16 P R-7

$100.00 Ca. 1835–39. Engraving, imprint: Draper, Toppan, Longacre, Phila & New York. Proof. (MD200G36)

43.2.15 P

43.2.16 P

43.3 J. K. Swaine

The issuer was the proprietor of a general store.

43.3.2 R-6

12 1/2c Printed date Nov. 25, 1839. Letterpress, imprint: MURPHY, PRINT, BALT.

43.3.3 R-6

25c Printed date Nov. 25, 1839. Letterpress, imprint: MURPHY, PRINT, BALT.

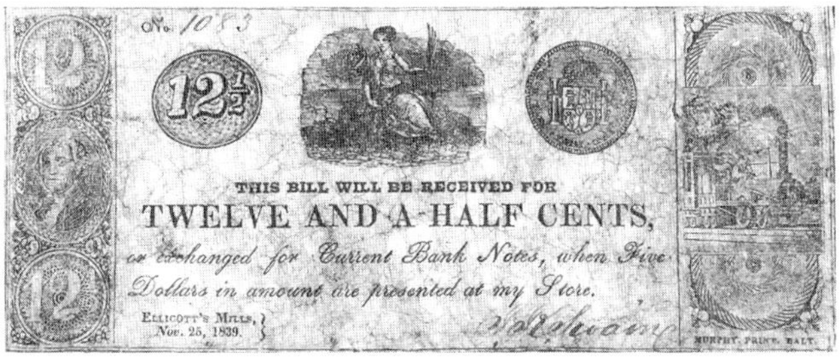

43.3.2

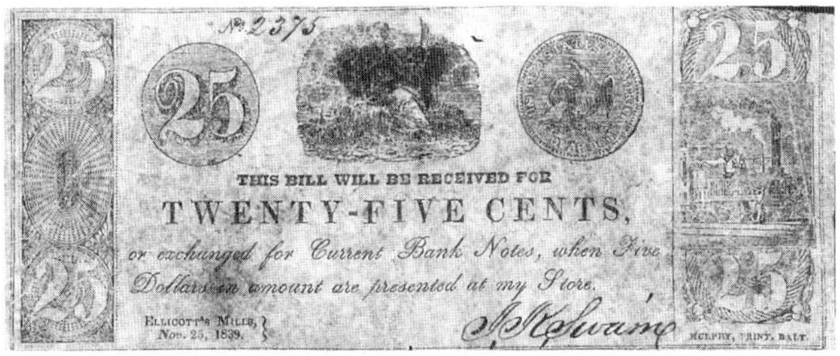

43.3.3

44 EMMITTSBURG, FREDERICK COUNTY

This town on Tom's Creek was a post office in 1800; in 1795 Emmitt's Mill was nearby. The attribution is to Samuel Emmit, an Irish immigrant who patented land in May 1757 and laid out the town in August 1785.

44.1 Corporation of Emmittsburg

The town issued scrip to alleviate the shortage of small change during the "hard times" of 1837–41.

44.1.1 R-7

6 1/4c Printed date Sept. 12, 1837. Letterpress, no imprint. Train at center.

44.1.2 R-7

6 1/4c Printed date Dec., 1837. Letterpress, no imprint. Train at center.

44.1.3 R-5

6 1/4c Printed partial date April __ 1840. Engraving, imprint: Manly & Orr, Printers, Philad. Town name spelled with one *t*.

44.1.4 R-7

12 1/2c Printed partial date Dec. 1837. Letterpress, no imprint. Town name spelled with two *t*s.

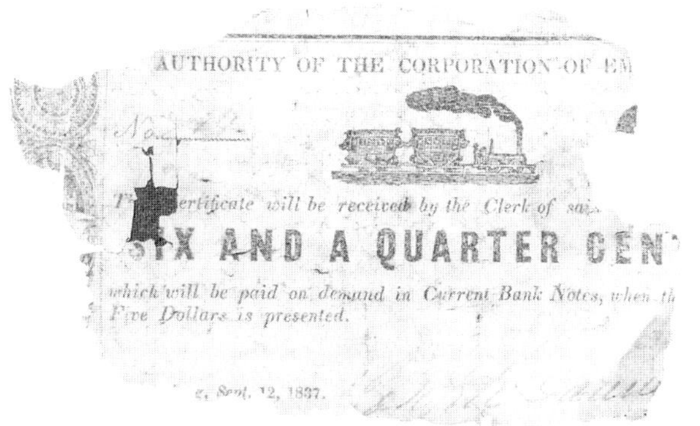

44.1.1

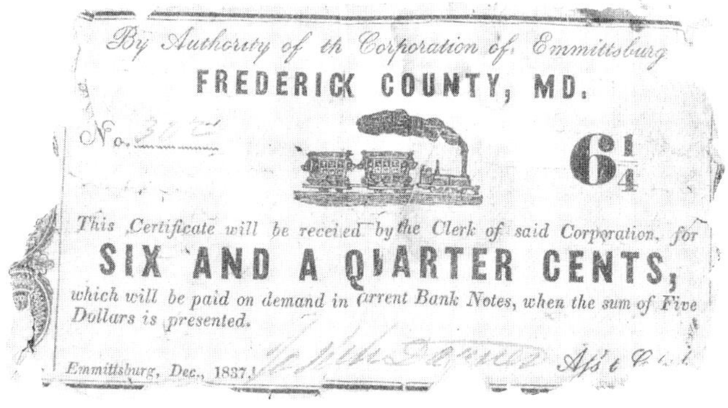

44.1.2

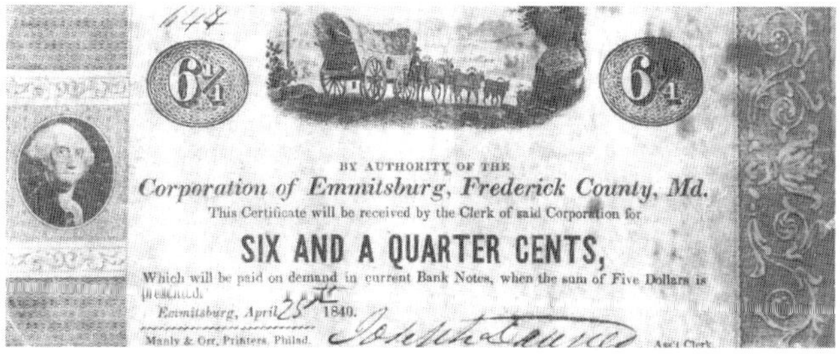

44.1.3

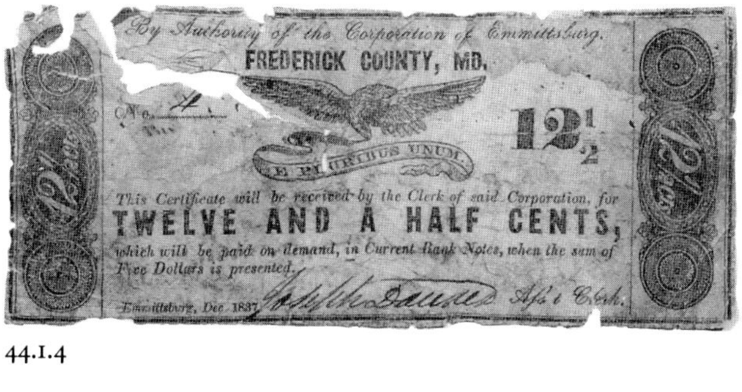

44.1.4

44.1.5 R-7

12 1/2c Printed partial date April __ 1840. Engraving, imprint: Manly & Orr, Printers, Philad. Town name spelled with one *t*.

44.1.6 R-7

25c Printed partial date Dec. 1837. Letterpress, no imprint. Town name spelled with two *t*s.

44.1.7 R-7

25c Printed partial date Dec. 1837. Letterpress, imprint: Woods, print. Baltimore. Town name spelled with two *t*s.

44.1.8 R-5

25c Printed partial date April __ 1840. Engraving, imprint: Manly & Orr, Printers, Philad. Town name spelled with one *t*.

44.1.9 R-7

50c Printed date August 9, 1837. Letterpress, imprint: Murphy & Spalding, printers, No. 1 Light street, Baltimore. Town name spelled Emmetsburg.

44.1.10 R-7

50c Printed partial date Dec. 1837. Letterpress, no imprint (undoubtedly printed by Woods, Baltimore). Town name spelled with two *t*s.

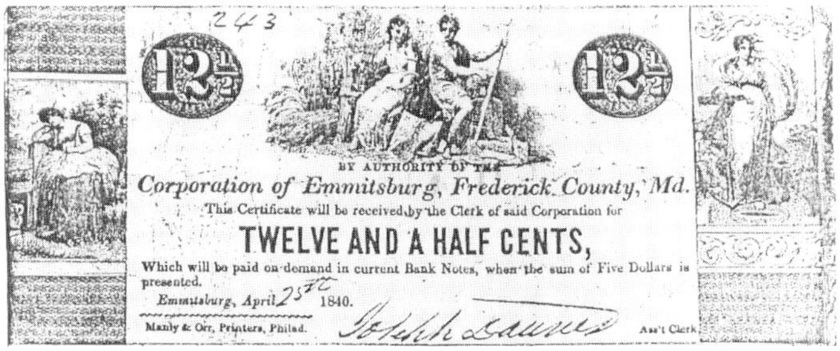

44.1.5

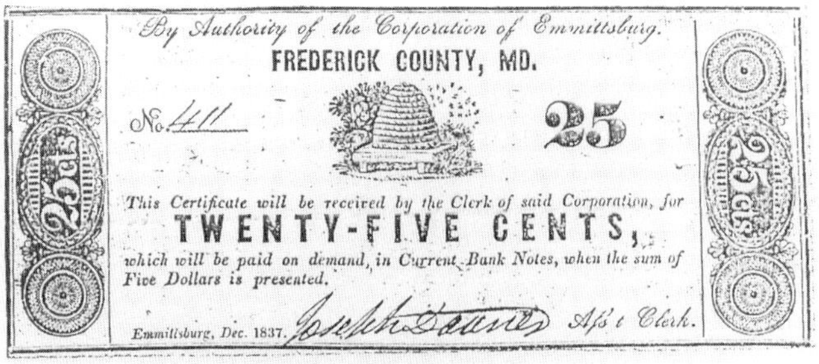

44.1.6

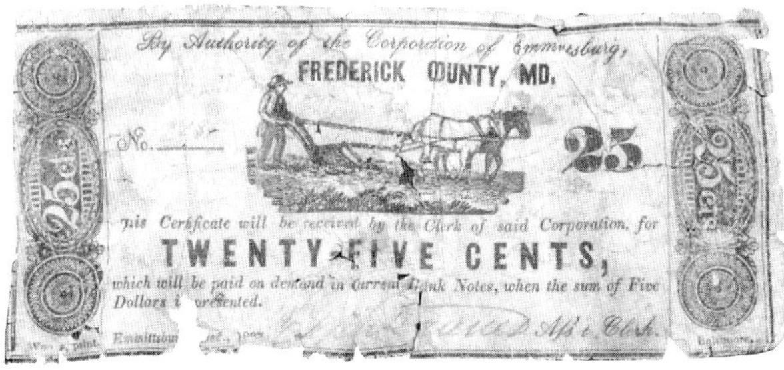

44.1.7

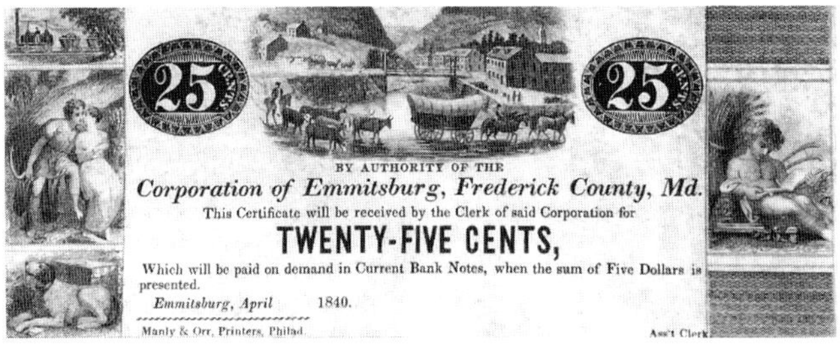

44.1.8

44.1.10

44.1.11 R-5

50c Printed partial date April __ 1840. Engraving, imprint: Manly & Orr, Printers, Philad. Town name spelled with one *t*.

44.1.12 R-7

$1.00 Printed date August 9, 1837. Letterpress, imprint: Murphy & Spalding printers, No. 1 Light st., Baltimore.

44.1.13 R-6

$1.00 Printed partial date Dec. 1837. No imprint (undoubtedly printed by Woods, Baltimore). Town name spelled with two *t*s.

44.1.14 R-5

$1.00 Printed partial date April __ 1840. Engraving, imprint: Manly & Orr, Printers, Philad. Town name spelled with one *t*.

44.1.15 R-5

$1.00 Printed partial date April __ 1840. Engraving, imprint: Manly & Orr, Printers, Philad. Town name spelled with one *t*.

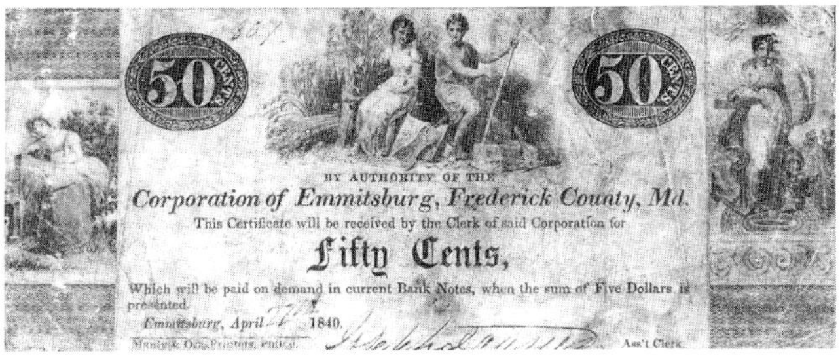

44.1.11

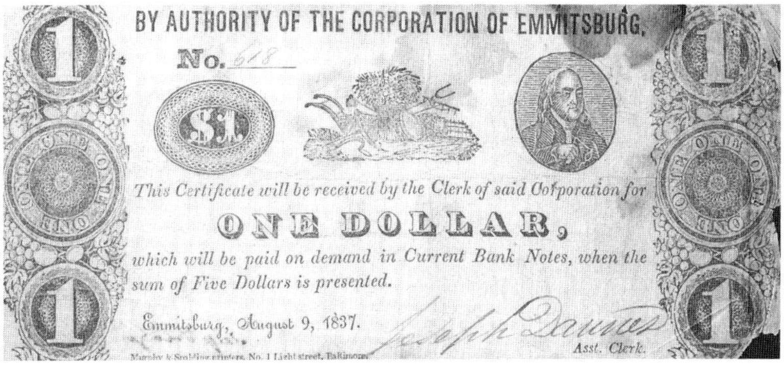

44.1.12

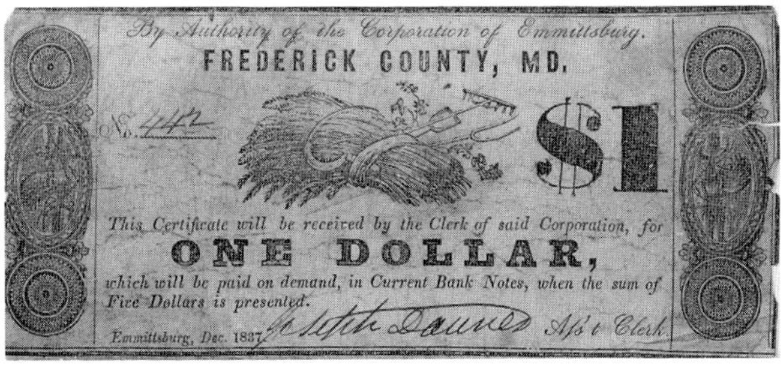

44.1.13

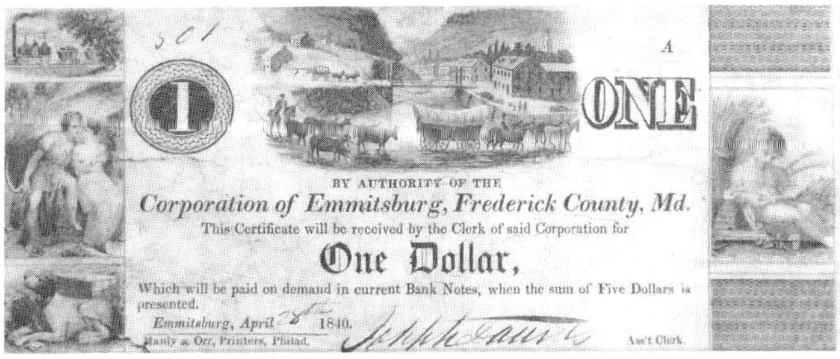

44.1.14

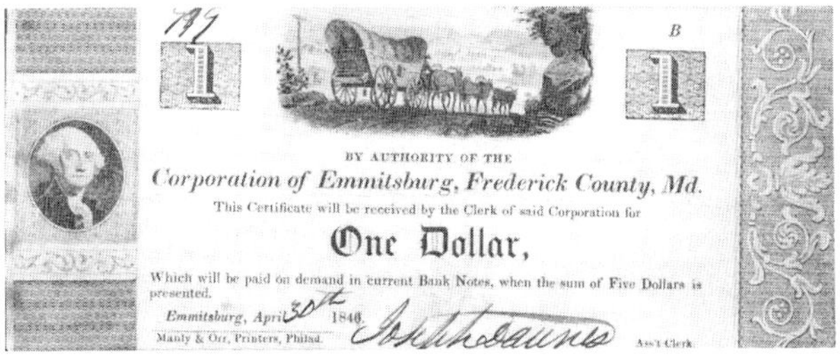

44.1.15

44.2 Grover & Pittinger

The issuers were the proprietors of a general store.

44.2.1 R-7
6 1/4c Printed date April 15, 1841. Letterpress, imprint: MURPHY, PRINTER, 146 Market St., Balt.

44.2.2 R-7
12 1/2c Printed date April 15, 1841. Letterpress, imprint: Murphy, Printer, Baltimore. Same as No. 44.2.3, except for date.

44.2.3 R-7
12 1/2c Printed date June 10, 1841. Letterpress, imprint: Murphy, Printer, Baltimore. Vignette is a woodcut view of Baltimore from Federal Hill.

44.2.4 R-6
25c Printed date April 15, 1841. Letterpress, imprint: Murphy, Printer, Baltimore. Vignette is a woodcut view of Baltimore from Federal Hill.

44.2.5 R-7
50c Printed date April 15, 1841. Letterpress, imprint: Murphy, Printer, Balt.

44.2.6 R-5
50c Printed date June 10, 1841. Letterpress, imprint: Murphy, Printer, Balt. Same as No. 44.2.5, except for date.

44.2.7 R-7
50c Printed date October 19, 1841. Letterpress, imprint: Murphy, Printer, Balto. Same as No. 44.2.5, except for date and payable in "Railroad Notes."

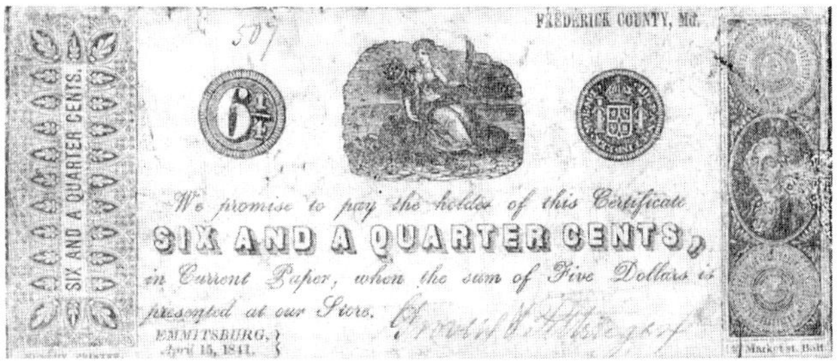

44.2.1

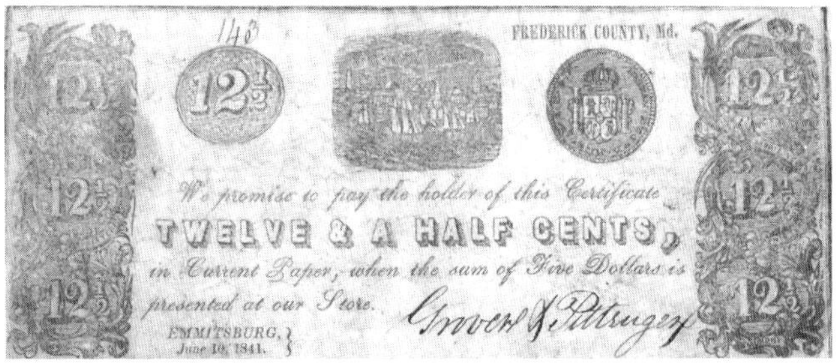

44.2.3

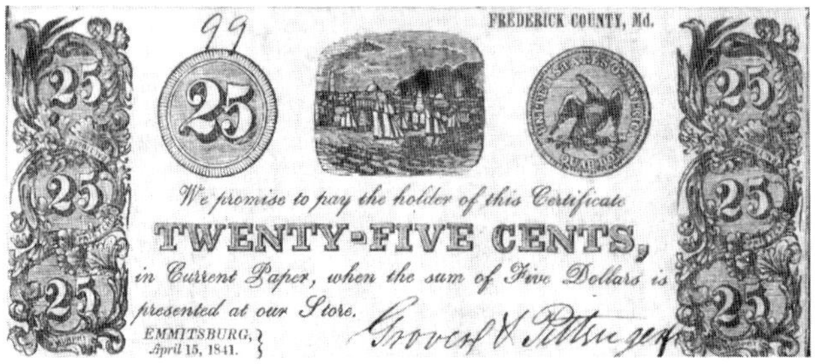

44.2.4

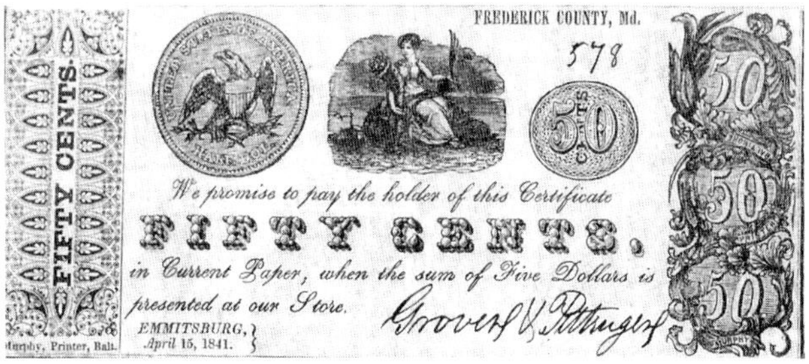

44.2.5

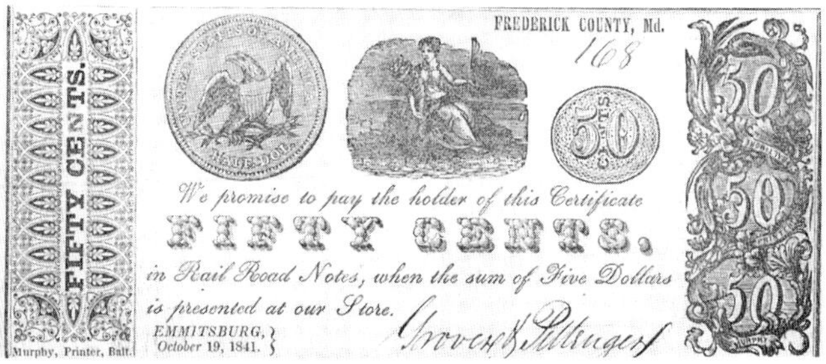

44.2.7

44.3 Unidentified Issuer

44.3.1 R-7

$1.00 Partial printed date 183_. Letterpress, imprint: Examiner Office, pr.

44.3.1

46 FIFTEEN MILE CREEK, ALLEGANY COUNTY

A branch of the Potomac River, Fifteen Mile Creek has its mouth at the village of Little Orleans about 6 1/2 miles southwest of Piney Grove in Allegany County.

46.1 James McGuire

The issuer was the proprietor of a general store at Fifteen Mile Creek, a small settlement near the mouth of the creek, a branch of the Potomac River with its mouth at Little Orleans.

46.1.3 R-7

25c Printed date January 20, 1840. Letterpress, imprint: MURPHY, PRINT., BALT.

46.1.3

47 FINKSBURG, CARROLL COUNTY

This village is located about four miles northwest of Reisterstown on the Reisterstown-Westminster Road.

47.1 The Finksburg Savings Institution

47.1.1 R-7

6 1/4c Ca. 1840–41. Lithography, imprint: Lith. by E. Weber & Co., Baltimore.

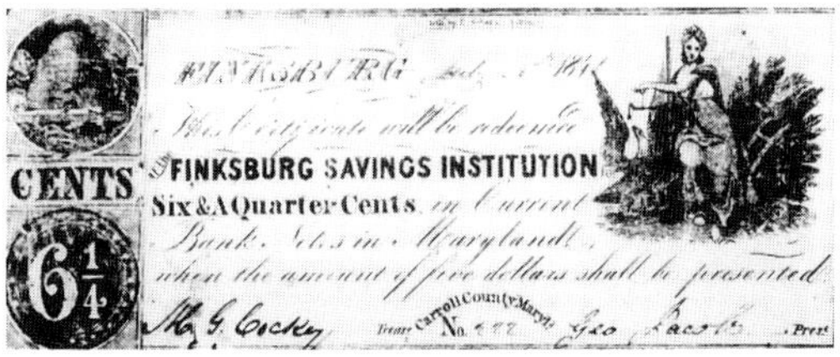

47.1.1

49 FORK-TOWN, SOMERSET COUNTY

This small community at the intersection of roads leading to Princess Anne, the Pocomoke River, and Salisbury was originally called Disharoon's Crossroads, the first house having been erected in 1772. About 1820 the name was changed to Forktown when the majority of the villagers no longer bore the name of Disharoon, and by 1840 the Forktown post office had been established. The name was again changed, to the present-day Fruitland, in 1873 to better reflect the agricultural character of the area, which had become a major railroad shipping point for berries and tomatoes to the Philadelphia and New York markets.

49.1 Unidentified Issuer

49.1.4 R-7

50c Printed date May 9th, 1838. Letterpress, imprint: Robinson, PRINTER, Baltimore.

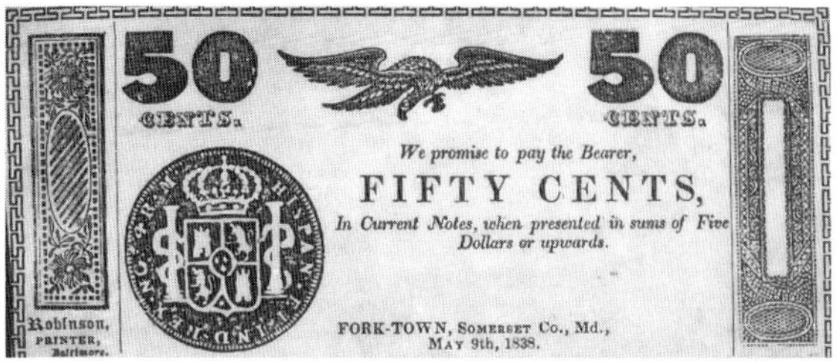

49.1.4

51 FREDERICK, FREDERICK COUNTY

This city, near the Monocacy River, was laid out in 1745 by Daniel Dulaney, a land speculator, and incorporated in 1817. The name is usually attributed to the sixth Lord Baltimore, Frederick Calvert, son of Charles Calvert, although it may have been named for Frederick, Prince of Wales, a friend of Lord Baltimore.

51.1 City of Frederick

Small-change scrip issued by the city to alleviate the acute shortage of coins during the "hard times" of 1837–41.

51.1.1 R-6

5c Printed date August 15, 1837. Letterpress, imprint: E. Morris, Printer.

51.1.2 R-7

5c Printed date July 10, 1841. Letterpress, imprint: Murphy, Print, Balt. "5-5" and FIVE CENTS vertical overprint in brick red. Payable at the FARMERS AND MECHANIC'S BANK OF FREDERICK CO.

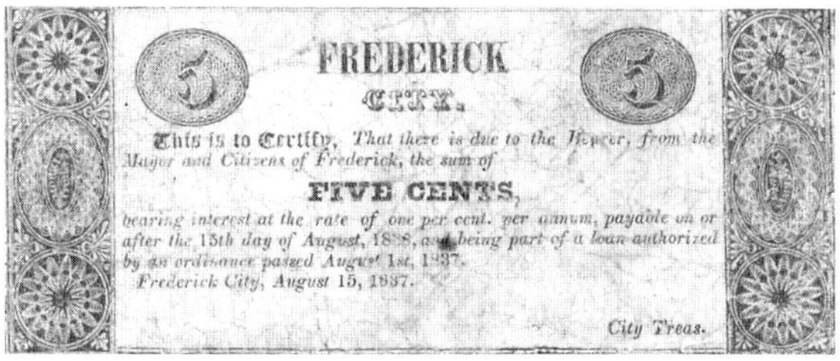

51.1.1

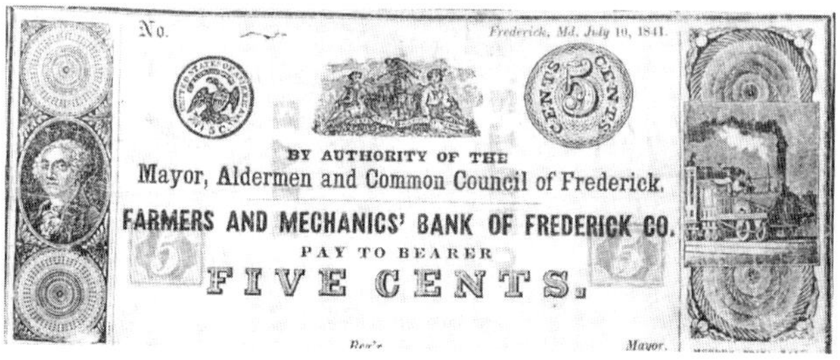

51.1.2

51.1.3 R-7

6 1/4c Printed partial date August __, 1837. Letterpress, imprint: Printed at the Herald Office, Frederick. Payable at the Frederick County Bank.

51.1.4 R-7

6 1/4c Printed partial date August __, 1837. Letterpress, imprint: Printed at the Herald Office, Frederick. Payable at the Frederick County Bank. Similar to No. 51.1.3, except imprint at top right.

51.1.5 R-7

6 1/4c Printed date July 10, 1841. Similar to 5c, No. 51.1.2, overprinted vertical SIX CENTS in brick red. Payable at the FARMERS AND MECHANICS' BANK OF FREDERICK CO.

51.1.6 R-7

10c Printed partial date July __ 1837. Letterpress, imprint: Printed at the Herald Office, Frederick. Payable at the FREDERICK-TOWN BRANCH BANK.

51.1.7 R-7

10c Printed date July 10, 1841. Letterpress, imprint: Murphy, Print., Balt. Overprinted "10-10" and vertical TEN CENTS in brick red. Payable at the FARMERS & MECHANICS' BANK OF FREDERICK CO.

51.1.8 R-7

12 1/2c Printed partial date April __ 1840. Engraving, no imprint. Payable at the FARMERS AND MECHANICS' BANK OF FREDERICK CO. Letter B.

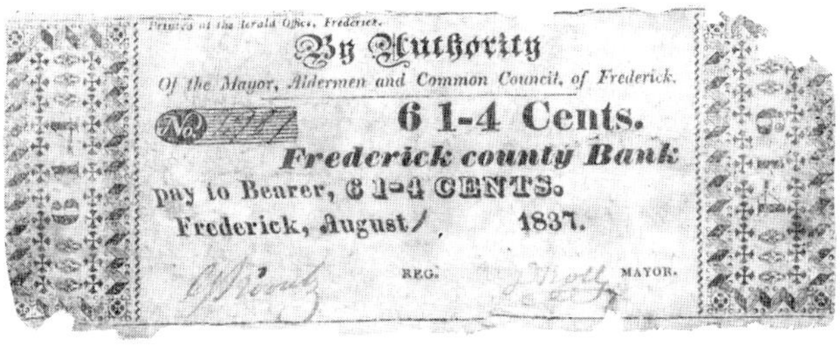

51.1.3

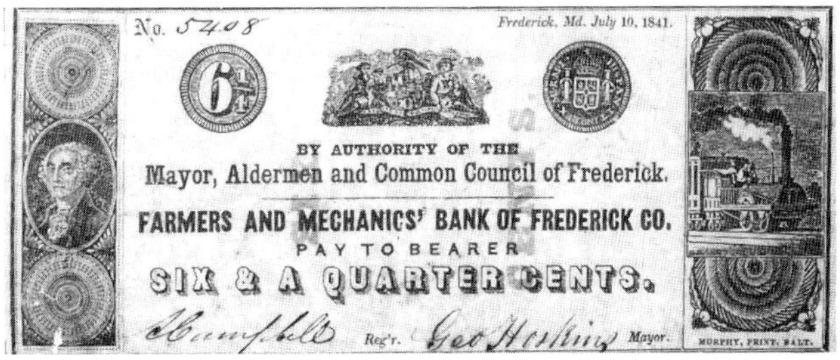

51.1.5

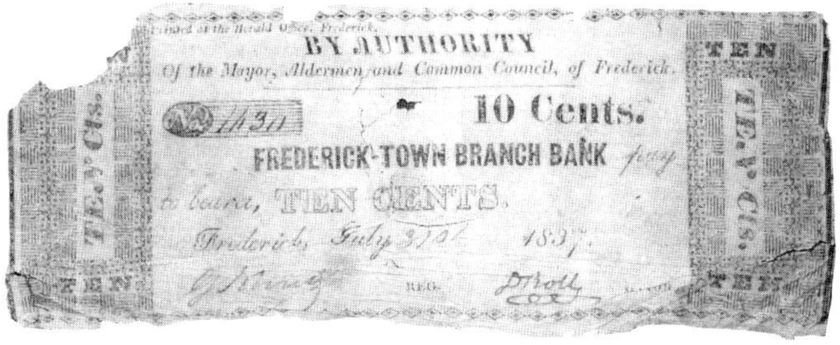

51.1.6

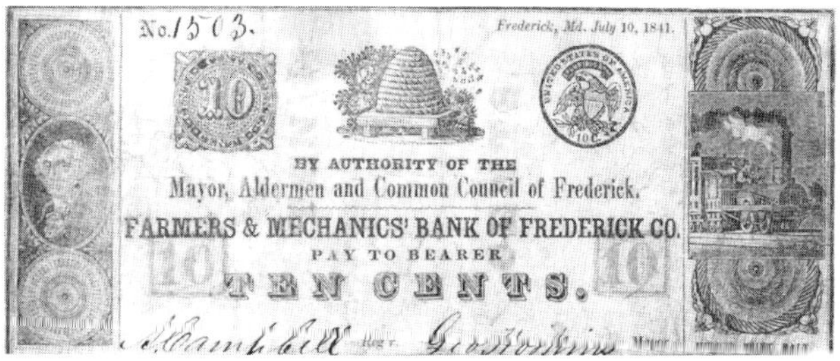

51.1.7

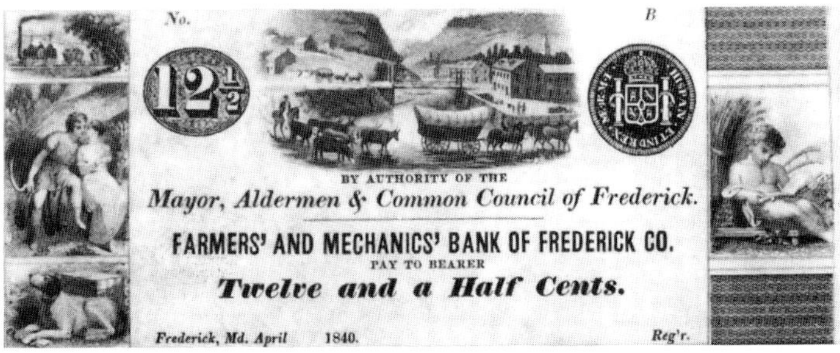

51.1.8

51.1.9 R-7

12 1/2c Printed partial date April __ 1840. Engraving, no imprint. Similar to No. 51.1.8 except for vignette and end plates. Letter A.

51.1.10 R-7

12 1/2c Printed partial date April __ 1840. Engraving, no imprint. Same as No. 51.1.8 except for vignette. Letter C.

51.1.11 R-7

12 1/2c Printed partial date April __ 1840. Engraving, no imprint. Same as No. 51.1.8, except payable at Frederick County Bank. Letter B.

51.1.12 R-7

12 1/2c Printed partial date April __ 1840. Engraving, no imprint. Same as No. 51.1.9, except payable at Frederick County Bank. Letter A.

51.1.13 R-7

12 1/2c Printed partial date April __ 1840. Engraving, no imprint. Same as No. 51.1.10, except payable at Fredericktown Branch Bank. Letter B.

51.1.14 R-7

12 1/2c Printed partial date April __ 1840. Engraving, no imprint. Same as No. 51.1.12, except payable at Fredericktown Branch Bank. Letter A.

51.1.15 R-7

25c Printed date August 15, 1837. Letterpress, imprint: E. Morris, Pr. Philadelphia.

51.1.9

51.1.11

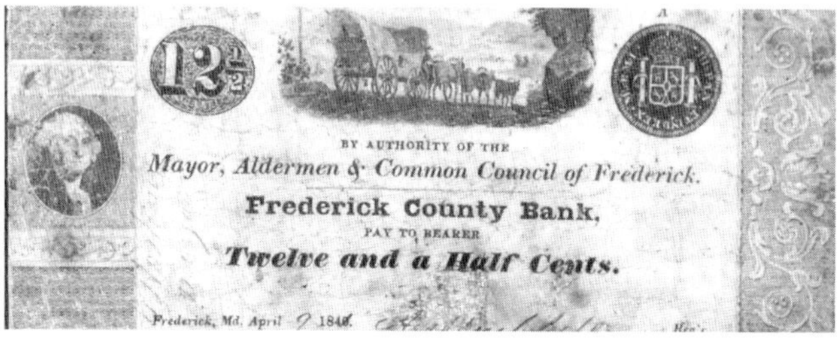

51.1.12

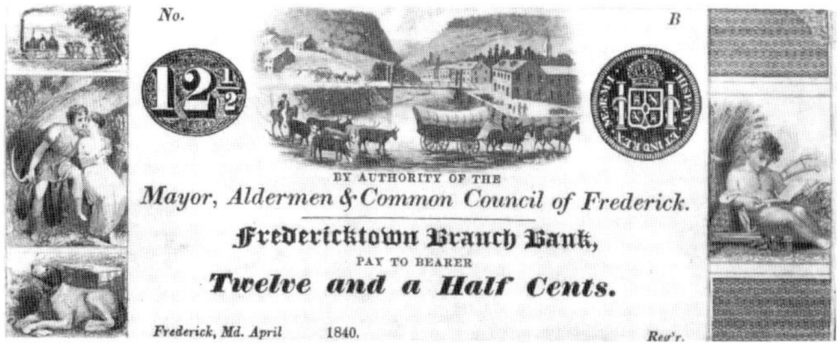

51.1.13

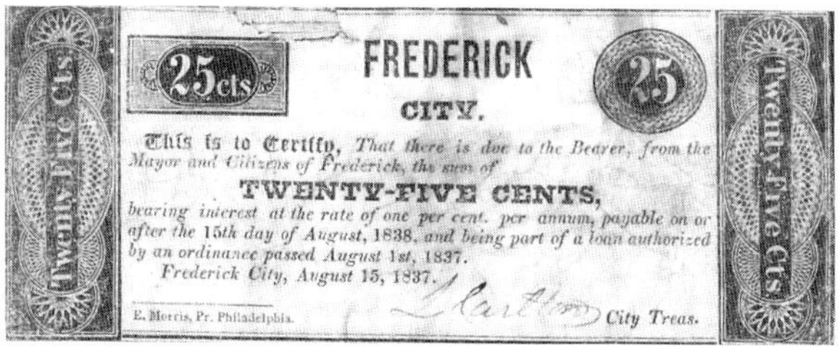

51.1.15

51.1.16 R-7

25c Printed partial date April 1840. Engraving, no imprint. Payable at the Fredericktown Branch Bank.

51.1.17 R-7

25c Printed partial date April 1840. Engraving, no imprint. Same as No. 51.1.16, except payable at the FARMERS AND MECHANICS' BANK OF FREDERICK CO.

51.1.18 R-7

25c Printed partial date April 1840. Engraving, no imprint. Same as No. 51.1.16, except payable at the Frederick County Bank.

51.1.19 R-5

50c Printed partial date July 1837. Letterpress, imprint: Printed at the Herld [*sic*] Office, Frederick. Payable at the FREDERICKTOWN BRANCH BANK.

51.1.20 R-7

50c Printed date August 15, 1837. Letterpress, imprint: E. Morris, Pr. Philadelphia.

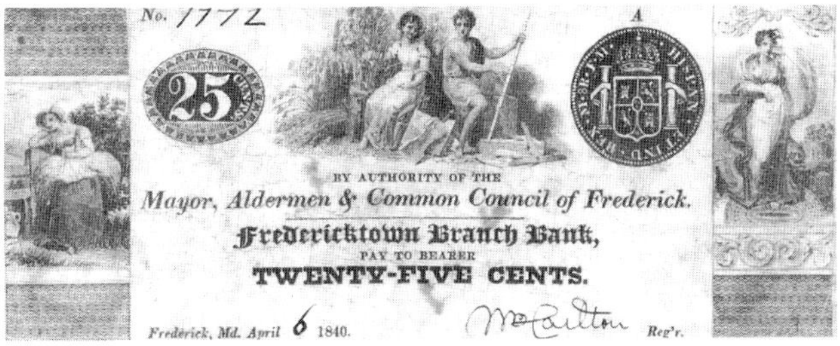

51.1.16

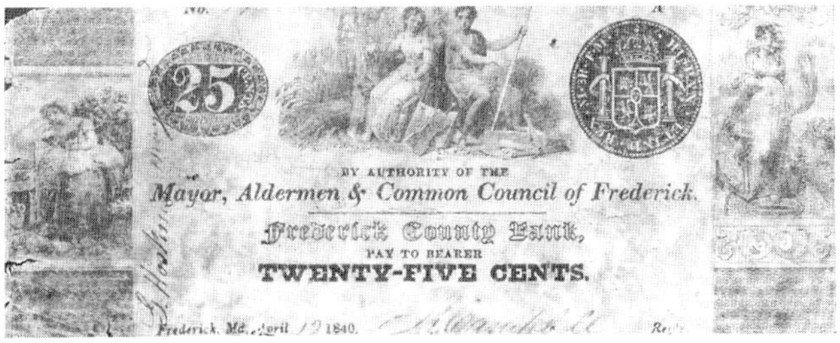

51.1.17

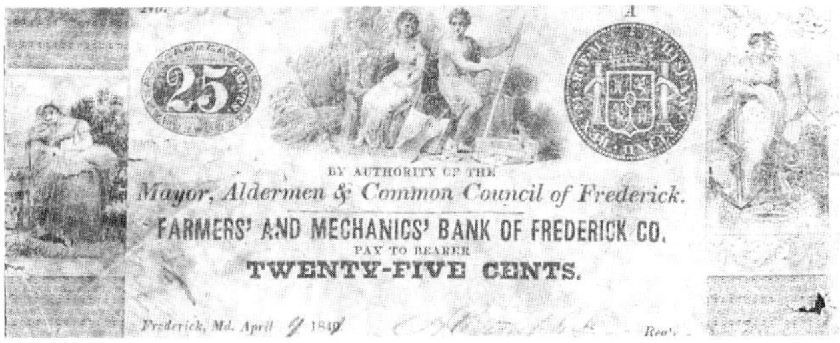

51.1.18

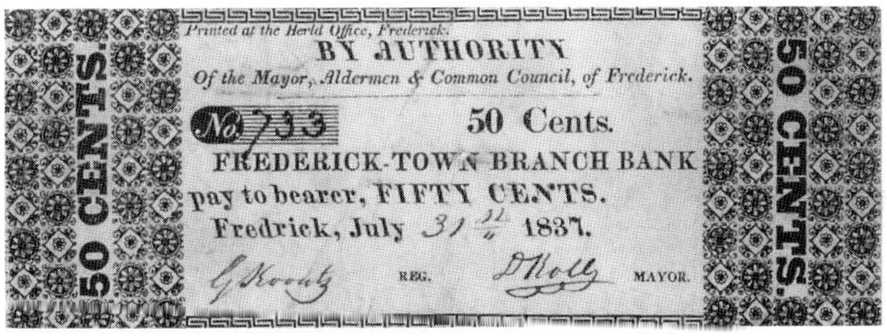

51.1.19

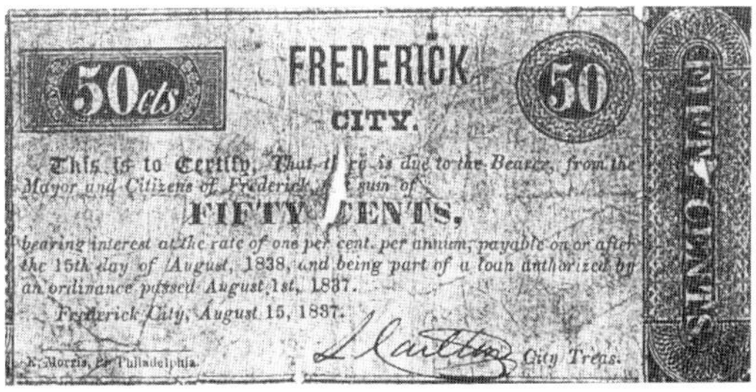

51.1.20

51.1.21 R-7

50c Printed partial date April 1840. Engraving, no imprint. Payable at the Frederick County Bank.

51.1.22 R-7

$1.00 Printed partial date April __ 1840. Engraving, no imprint. Payable at the FARMERS AND MECHANICS' BANK OF FREDERICK CO.

51.1.23 R-7

$1.00 Printed partial date April 1840. Engraving, no imprint. Same as 50c, No. 51.1.21, except payable at the Frederick-town Branch Bank.

51.1.26 R-7

$2.00 Printed date August 15, 1837. Letterpress, imprint: E. Morris, Pr. Philadelphia.

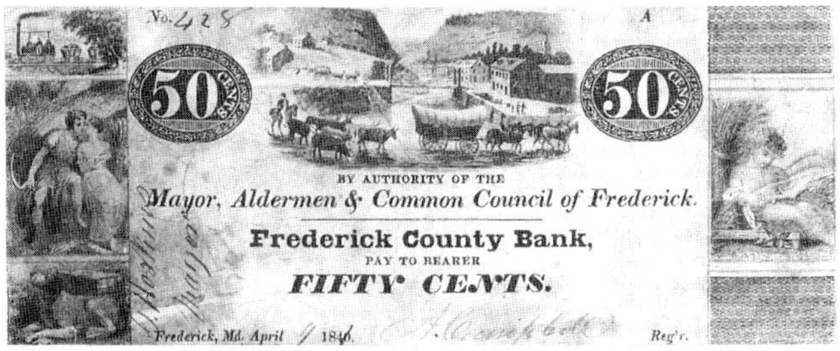

51.1.21

51.1.22

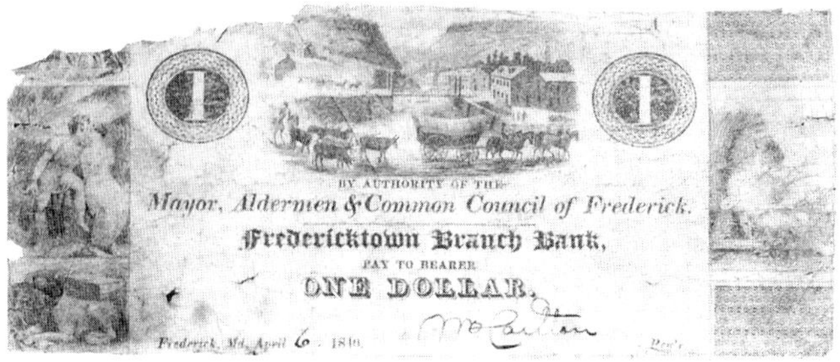

51.1.23

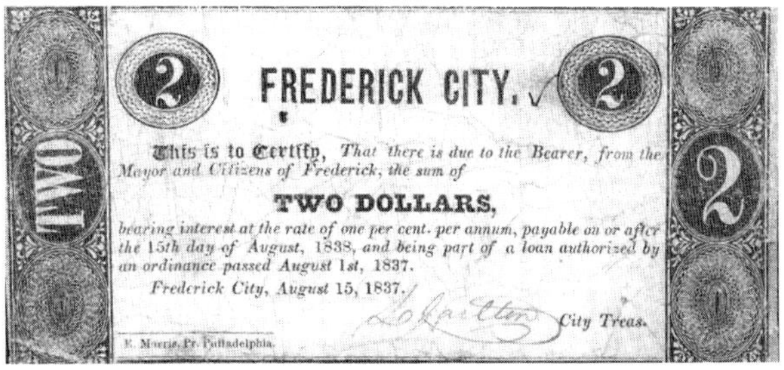

51.1.26

51.2 The Central Bank of Frederick

Charter approved May 30, 1853; converted to and became the Central National Bank of Frederick in 1865.

51.2.1 R-7

$1.00 Printed date May 20th, 1861. Engraving, imprint: American Bank Note Co., Philada. Security overprint: colorless ONE in brick red panel. (MD205G2a)

51.2.3 S R-6

$5.00 Ca. 1850s. Engraving, imprint: Wellstood, Hanks & Co., New York. Spurious. (MD204S5)

51.2.4 S R-7

$5.00 Ca. late 1850s. Engraving, imprint: Draper, Welsh & Co., Philada. Spurious. (MD205S10)

51.2.5 SENC

$5.00 Ca. 1853–60s. Engraving, imprint: Toppan, Carpenter, Casilear & Co., Phila. *Center:* Milkmaid seated, one hand on pail, two cows, farmhouse and trees in background. *Left:* 5 / oval female portrait. *Right:* 5 / oval portrait of Webster. Red FIVE overprint. (MD205G6a)

51.2.7 R-7

$10.00 Ca. 1850s–60s. Engraving, imprint: Toppan, Carpenter, Casilear & Co., Phila. Red TEN overprint. (MD205G8a)

51.2.9 SENC

$20.00 Ca. 1853–60s. Engraving, imprint: Toppan, Carpenter, Casilear & Co., Phila. *Center:* Three nude nymphs supporting cherub. *Left:* 20 / oval male portrait. *Right:* 20 / milkmaid milking cow, second cow lying down. (MD205G10a)

51.2.12 SENC

$50.00 Ca. 1853–60s. Engraving, imprint: Toppan, Carpenter, Casilear & Co., Phila. *Center:* Cattle, stream, three sheep in background. *Left:* 50, across / oval portrait of Pierce. *Right:* 50 / oval portrait of Fillmore. (MD205G12)

51.2.14 SENC

$100.00 Ca. 1853–60s. Engraving, imprint: Toppan, Carpenter, Casilear & Co., Phila. *Center:* Oval portrait of Washington. *Left:* Shield surmounted by eagle / C, across. *Upper right:* 100. (MD205G15)

51.2.1

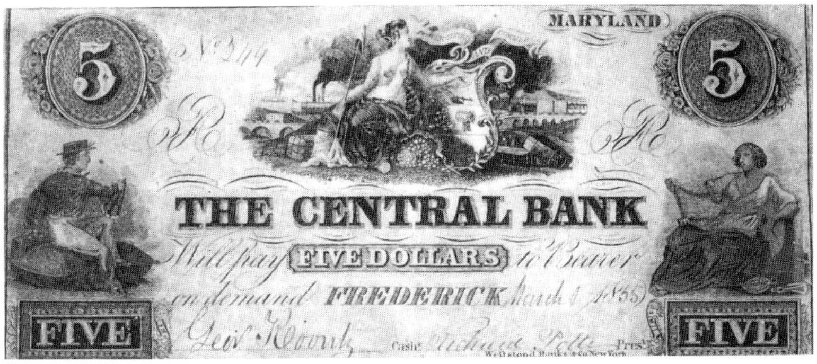

51.2.3 S

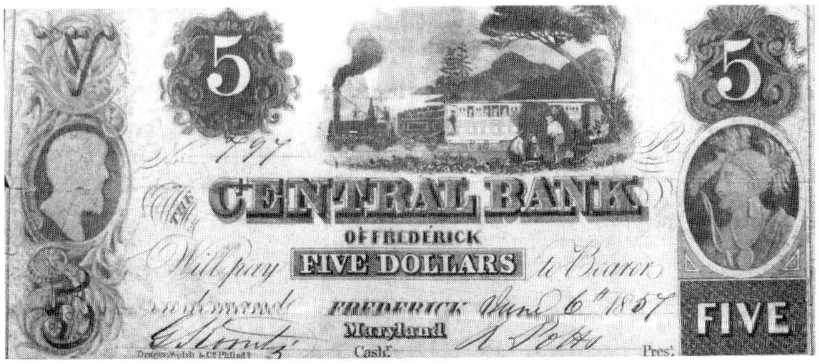

51.2.4 S

51.2.7

51.3 City Hotel

For many years the City Hotel was located on West Patrick Street near the corner of the square. The notes were signed by Daniel Dorsey, the proprietor.

51.3.2 R-7

12 1/2c Printed year date 1840. Letterpress, imprint: MURPHY PRINT. BALT.

51.3.3 R-7

12 1/2c Printed date April 26, 1841. Letterpress, imprint: MURPHY PRINTER BALTIMORE.

51.3.5 R-7

50c Printed date May 1, 1840. Letterpress, imprint: Murphy / Printer / Baltimore.

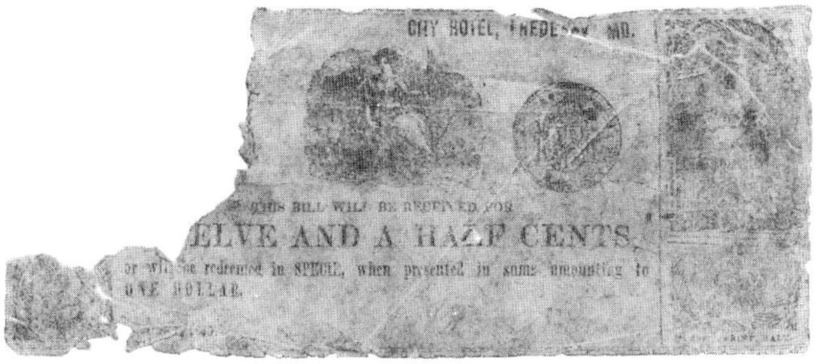

51.3.2

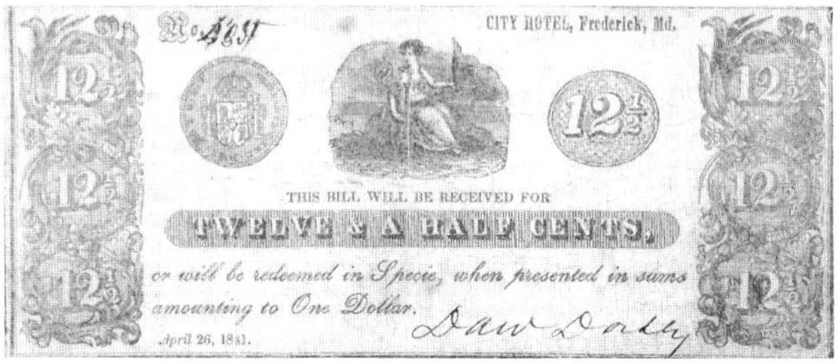

51.3.3

51.3.5

51.4 The Farmers & Mechanics Bank of Frederick County

Charter amendment approved February 24, 1827; formerly the Bank of Westminster (1816) and its Frederick branch (1817); converted to and became the Farmers & Mechanics National Bank of Frederick in 1865.

51.4.1 R-7

$1.00 Ca. 1850s–60s. Engraving, imprint: Underwood, Bald, Spencer & Hufty, Phila. / Danforth, Underwood & Co., New York. Originally thought to be a spurious note; identical proofs, No. 51.1.4 P, were found in the American Bank Note Co. archives. (MD210S5)

51.4.1 P R-7

$1.00 Ca. 1840s–50s. Engraving, imprint: Underwood, Bald, Spencer & Hufty, Phila. / Danforth, Underwood & Co., New York. Proof.

51.4.2 A R-7

$1.00 Ca. 1860s. Printed partial date May 1st 18__. Engraving, imprint: Danforth, Wright & Co., New York & Philada. Altered from $1.00 Bank of Washtenaw, Mich., MI50G40. (MD208A5)

51.4.3 A R-7

$1.00 Ca. 1860s. Engraving, imprint: Danforth, Wright & Co., New York & Philada. Altered from $1.00 Bank of Washtenaw, Mich., MI50G40. Same as No. 51.4.2 A, except written date.

51.4.4 A R-7

$1.00 Engraving, imprint: Danforth, Wright, & Co., New York & Philada. Same as No. 51.4.2 A, except written date, with red ONE overprint. Altered. (MD205A5a)

51.4.5 R-7

$2.00 Ca. 1861. Engraving, imprint: Underwood, Bald, Spencer & Hufty, Philada. / Danforth, Underwood & Co., New York. Originally thought to be a spurious note; identical proofs, No. 51.4.5 P, were found in the American Bank Note Co. archives. (MD210S10)

51.4.5 P R-7

$2.00 Ca. 1861. Engraving, imprint: Underwood, Bald, Spencer & Hufty, Philada. / Danforth, Underwood & Co., New York. Proof.

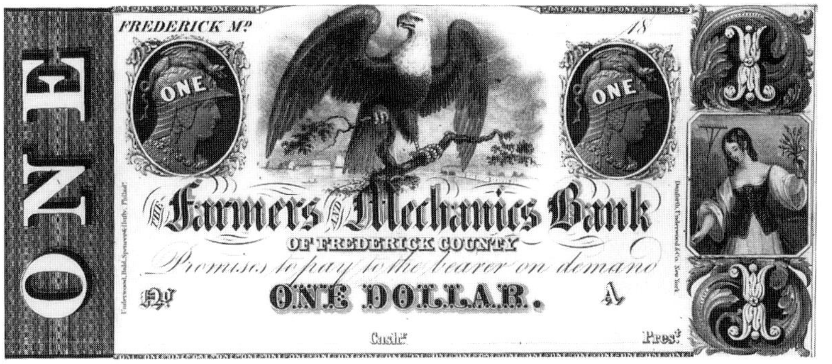

51.4.1 P

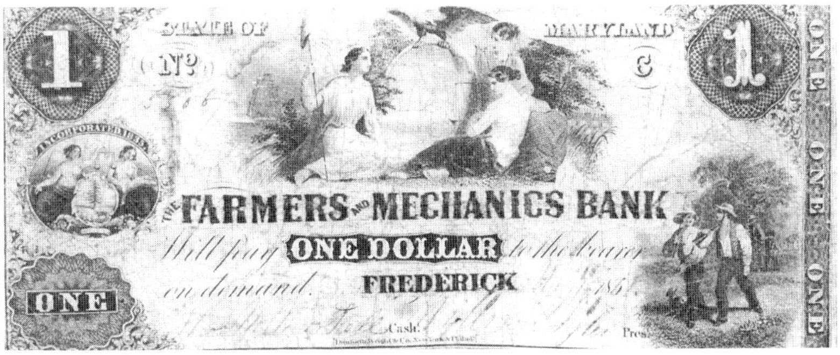

51.4.2 A

51.4.5

51.4.5 P

51.4.7 A R-7

$3.00 Printed date Dec. 1st, 1840. Engraving, imprint: Rawdon, Wright & Hatch. Altered. (MD208A10)

51.4.8 P R-7

$5.00 Ca. 1827–30. Engraving, imprint: Fairman, Draper, Underwood & Co. Payable at the Branch at Westminster. Proof.

51.4.9 R-7

$5.00 Ca. 1827–60s. Engraving, imprint: Fairman, Draper, Underwood & Co. (MD210G20)

51.4.9 P R-7

$5.00 Ca. 1827–60s. Engraving, imprint: Fairman, Draper, Underwood & Co. Proof.

51.4.7 A

51.4.8 P

51.4.9

51.4.9 P

51.4.10 A R-7

$5.00 Ca. 1830s–40s. Engraving, imprint: Burton & Gurley. Altered from Farmers & Mechanics Bank, Burlington, Wis. No other information known.

51.4.11 S R-6

$5.00 Ca. 1849. Engraving, imprint: Rawdon, Wright & Hatch, New York. From a modified fraudulent plate, originally for a counterfeit $5.00, PA205C104, on the Farmers Bank of Lancaster, Pa. Spurious. (MD209S5)

51.4.12 S R-7

$5.00 Ca. 1850s. Engraving, no imprint. Spurious and altered. (MD208S5)

51.4.13 A R-5

$5.00 Ca. 1854. Engraving, imprint: Danforth, Wright & Co., N. York. Altered from $5.00 Farmers & Mechanics Bank at Pontiac, Mich., MI335G8. FREDERICK, MD beneath FIVE DOLLARS. (MD209A5)

51.4.14 A R-7

$5.00 Ca. 1854. Engraving, imprint: Danforth, Wright & Co., N. York. Similar to No. 51.4.13 A, but only FREDERICK beneath FIVE DOLLARS. Altered.

51.4.15 A R-6

$5.00 Ca. 1859. Engraving, imprint: Baker and Kuykinick, N.Y.; W. L. Ormsby, New York. *Back:* Five portraits of Washington, each surrounded by a circle consisting of 5s. Altered from $5.00 Crawfordsville, Logansport & Northern R.R. Co., Logans port, Ind., IN355G6. (MD208A15)

51.4.11 S

51.4.12 S

51.4.13 A

51.4.15 A

51.4.16 P R-7

$10.00 Ca. 1827–30. Engraving, imprint: Fairman, Draper, Underwood & Co. Payable at the branch at Westminster. Proof.

51.4.17 A SENC

$10.00 Ca. 1830s–40s. Engraving, imprint: Burton & Gurley. *Center:* 10; Ceres seated leaning on sheaves at left, two cows at right; 10. *Left:* TEN / woman standing pouring from pitcher into cup / X. *Right:* Scrollwork panel with TEN across. Altered from $10.00 Farmers & Mechanic's Bank, Burlington, Wis., WI90G8. (MD208A35)

51.4.18 S R-7

$10.00 Ca. 1847. Engraving, imprint: Toppan, Carpenter & Co. Spurious. (MD208S15)

51.4.19 SENC

$10.00 Ca. 1840s. Engraving, imprint: Unknown. *Center:* Blacksmith shoeing horse. (MD208N5)

51.4.20 P R-7

$10.00 Ca. 1850s. Engraving, imprint: Fairman, Draper, Underwood & Co. Proof. (MD210G28)

51.4.21 A R-7

$10.00 Printed partial year date 185_. Engraving, imprint: Danforth, Wright & Co., New York & Philada. Altered and raised from $1.00 Bank of Washtenaw, Washtenaw, Mich., MI50G40. (MD208AR30)

51.4.22 A R-7

$10.00 Printed date May 1, 1854. Engraving, imprint: Danforth, Wright & Co., New York & Philada. Altered and raised from $1.00 Bank of Washtenaw, Washtenaw, Mich., MI50G40. Same as No. 51.4.21 A, except for date. (MD208AR30a)

51.4.23 A R-7

$10.00 Date unknown. Engraving, imprint: Rawdon, Wright & Hatch. *Center:* 10; Ceres seated; 10. *Left:* Train / X / steamboat. *Right:* 10 on ornate die. *Between signatures:* Pledge, in circle. Altered from $10.00 Farmers & Mechanics Bank at Pontiac, Pontiac, Mich., MI335G10. (MD209A10)

51.4.16 P

51.4.18 S

51.4.20 P

51.4.21 A

51.4.24 A R-7

$20.00 Ca. 1830s–40s. Engraving, imprint: BURTON & GURLEY. Altered from Farmers & Mechanics Bank, Burlington, Wis. No other information known.

51.4.25 P R-7

$20.00 Ca. 1850s. Engraving, imprint: Fairman, Draper, Underwood & Co. Proof. (MD210G36)

51.4.26 P R-7

$20.00 Ca. 1827–30. Engraving, imprint: Fairman, Draper, Underwood & Co. Payable at the branch at Westminster. Proof.

51.4.27 A SENC

$50.00 Ca. 1830s–40s. Engraving, imprint: Burton & Gurley. *Center:* Woman with one arm resting on anchor. *Left:* Woman with one foot resting on globe. *Right:* Stag. Altered from $50.00, Farmers & Mechanics Bank, Burlington, Wis., WI90G12. (MD208A40)

51.4.28 P R-7

$50.00 Ca. 1850s. Engraving, imprint: Fairman, Draper, Underwood & Co. Proof. (MD210G44)

51.4.29 A SENC

$100.00 Ca. 1830s–40s. Engraving, imprint: Burton & Gurley. *Center:* Woman with left arm around eagle. *Left:* Portrait of Washington. *Right:* Medallion head of Lafayette. Altered from $100.00, Farmers & Mechanics Bank, Burlington, Wis., WI90G14. (MD208A45)

51.4.30 P R-7

$100.00 Ca. 1850s. Engraving, imprint: Fairman, Draper, Underwood & Co. Proof. (MD210G52)

51.4.31 C SENC

$100.00 Ca. 1850s. Engraving, imprint: Unknown. Counterfeit of same design as No. 51.4.30 P. (MD210C52)

51.4.25 P

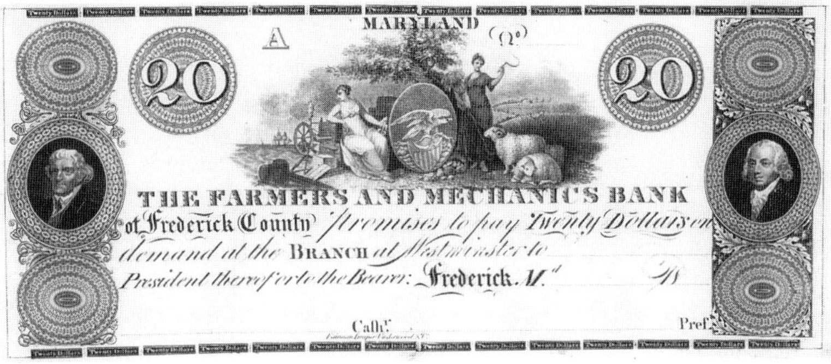

51.4.26 P

51.4.28 P

51.4.30 P

Farmers Bank of Maryland, Frederick Branch

See Farmer's Bank of Maryland, No. 2.3.

51.5 The Franklin Savings Bank of Frederick

Charter approved March 10, 1856; absorbed by the Commercial State Bank of Frederick in 1921.

51.5.1 R-7
$1.00 Printed partial date May __ 1861. Letterpress, imprint: Murphy & Co., Print. Balto.

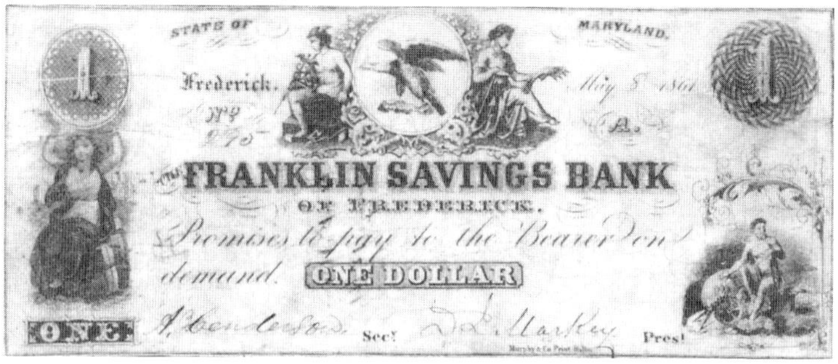

51.5.1

51.6 The Frederick County Bank

Charter approved January 29, 1818; converted to and became the Frederick County National Bank, Frederick, in 1865.

51.6.1 R-7
$1.00 Ca. 1818–30s. Engraving, imprint: Murray, Draper, Fairman & Co. Pale red overall security underprint.

51.6.1 P R-7
$1.00 Ca. 1818–30s. Engraving, imprint: Murray, Draper, Fairman & Co. Pale red overall security underprint. Proof. (MD215G12)

51.6.2 P R-7
$1.00 Ca. 1840s. Engraving, imprint: Draper, Toppan & Co., Phila. & New York. *Right:* Washington at Dorchester Heights, 1775. Proof. (MD215G16)

51.6.3 R-7
$1.00 Ca. 1860s. Engraving, imprint: American Bank Note Co., Phila. Same as No. 51.6.2 P, except for imprint.

51.6.1 P

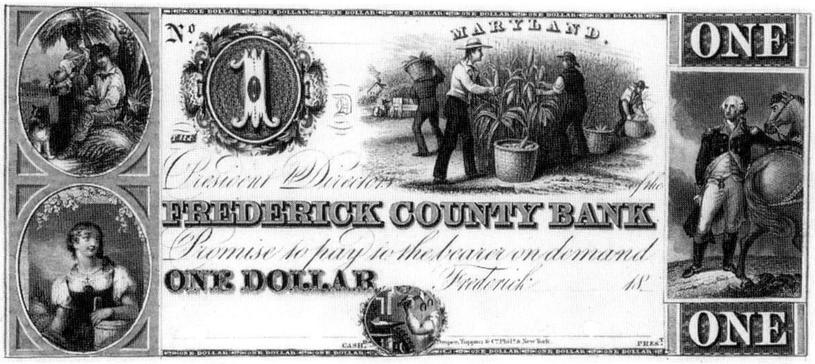

51.6.2 P

51.6.4 P R-7

$2.00 Ca. 1812–30s. Engraving, imprint: Murray, Draper, Fairman & Co. Proof. (MD215G18)

51.6.5 P R-7

$2.00 Ca. 1840. Engraving, imprint: Draper, Underwood, Bald, & Spencer. Proof.

51.6.6 P R-7

$3.00 Ca. 1812–30s. Engraving, imprint: Murray, Draper, Fairman & Co. Proof. (MD215G22)

51.6.6 C R-7

$3.00 Ca. 1812–30s. Engraving, imprint: Murray, Draper, Fairman & Co. Counterfeit of same design as No. 51.6.6 P. (MD215C22)

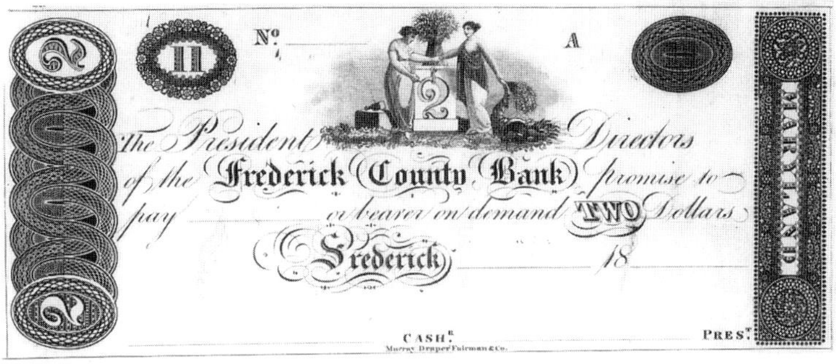

51.6.4 P

51.6.5 P

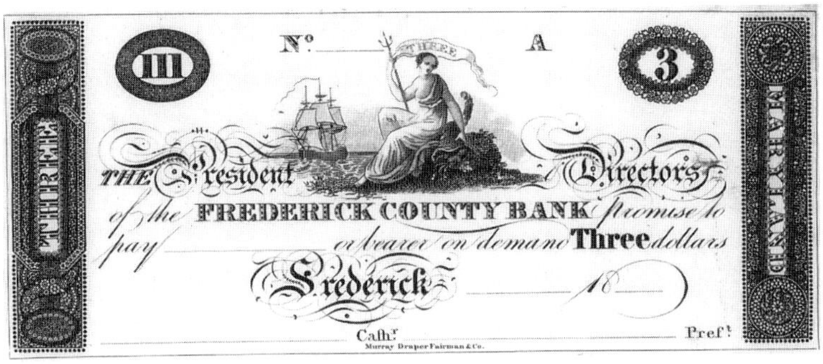

51.6.6 P

51.6.6 C

51.6.7 P R-7

$5.00 Ca. 1812–30s. Engraving, imprint: Murray, Draper, Fairman & Co. Proof. (MD215G24)

51.6.8 P

$5.00 Ca. 1812–30s. Engraving, imprint: Murray, Draper, Fairman & Co. Proof.

51.6.9 P R-7

$5.00 Ca. 1840. Engraving, imprint: Draper, Underwood, Bald & Spencer. Proof.

51.6.10 R SENC

$5.00 Ca. 1840s. Engraving, imprint: Draper, Toppan & Co. Raised from $1.00 of same design as No. 51.62 P. (MD215R5)

51.6.11 SENC

$5.00 Ca. 1850s. Engraving, imprint: Toppan, Carpenter, Casilear & Co. Phila. & New York. (MD215G28)

51.6.11 P R-7

$5.00 Ca. 1850s. Engraving, imprint: Toppan, Carpenter, Casilear & Co. Phila. & New York. Proof.

51.6.7 P

51.6.8 P

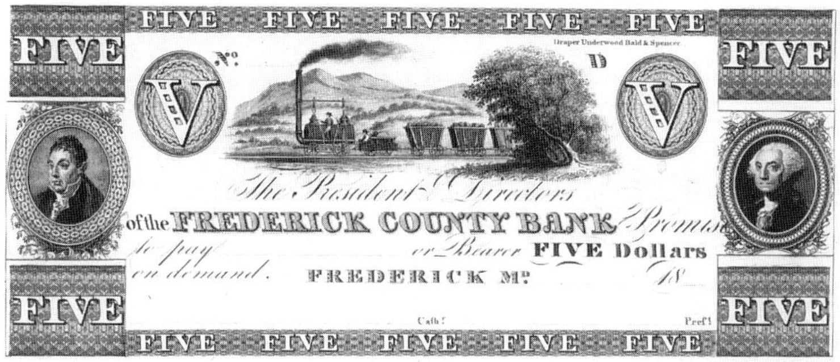

51.6.9 P

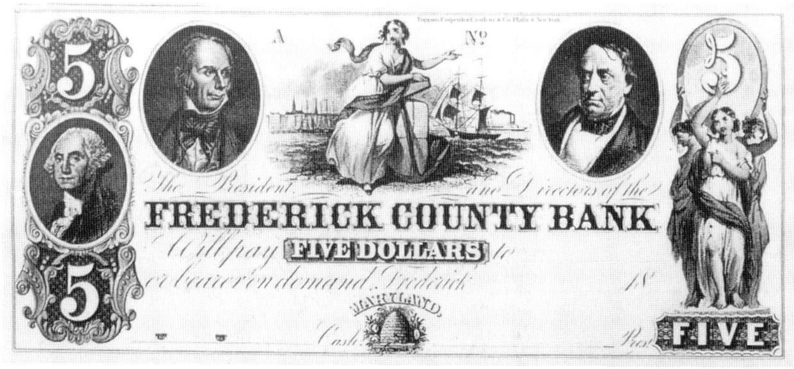

51.6.11 P

51.6.12 P R-7

$10.00 Ca. 1812–30s. Engraving, imprint: Murray, Draper, Fairman & Co. Proof. (MD215G32)

51.6.13 R R-7

$10.00 Ca. 1812–30s. Engraving, imprint: Murray, Draper, Fairman & Co. Raised from $1.00 of same design as No. 51.6.1 P. (MD215R10)

51.6.14 R SENC

$10.00 Ca. 1840s. Engraving, imprint: Draper, Toppan & Co. Raised from $1.00 of same design as No. 51.6.2 P. (MD215R15)

51.6.15 R R-7

$10.00 Ca. 1840s. Raised from unknown $1.00 with center vignette of a female resting on a bale of goods.

51.6.16 P R-6

$10.00 Ca. 1856–61. Engraving, imprint: Toppan, Carpenter & Co., Philad. Proof. (MD215G36)

51.6.12 P

51.6.13 R

51.6.16 P

51.6.17 P R-7

$20.00 Ca. 1812–30s. Engraving, imprint: Murray, Draper, Fairman & Co. Proof. (MD215G40)

51.6.18 R SENC

$20.00 Ca. 1812–30s. Engraving, imprint: Murray, Draper, Fairman & Co. Raised from $2.00 of same design as No. 51.6.4 P. (MD215R20)

51.6.19 R SENC

$20.00 Ca. 1840s. Engraving, imprint: Draper, Toppan & Co. Raised from $1.00 of same design as No. 51.6.2 P. (MD215R25)

51.6.20 SENC

$20.00 Ca. 1850s. Engraving, imprint: Unknown. *Center:* Justice standing, farmer plowing, house in background. *Left:* XX / 20. *Right:* MARYLAND, across. (MD215G44)

51.6.21 R SENC

$50.00 Ca. 1840s. Engraving, imprint: Draper, Toppan & Co. Raised from $1.00 of same design as No. 51.6.2 P. (MD215R30)

51.6.22 P R-7

$50.00 Ca. 1850s. Engraving, imprint: Fairman, Draper, Underwood & Co. Proof. (MD215G48)

51.6.23 P R-7

$100.00 Ca. 1850s. Engraving, no imprint, but printed by Fairman, Draper, Underwood & Co. in sheet with $50.00, No. 51.6.22 P. Proof. (MD215G52)

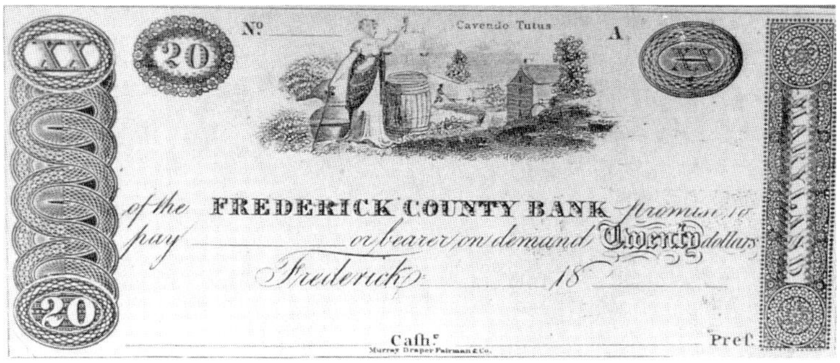

51.6.17 P

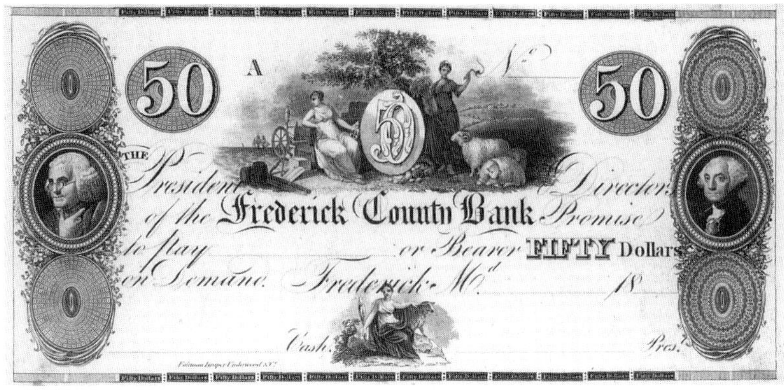

51.6.22 P

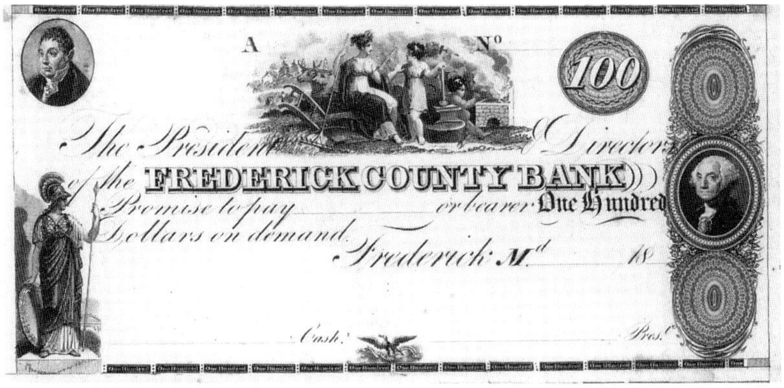

51.6.23 P

51.8 Frederick Town Savings Institution

Charter approved March 7, 1828; merged with the Fredericktown Trust Company to form the Fredericktown Savings & Trust Company in 1962.

51.8.3 R-7

25c Ca. 1840. Letterpress, imprint: Murphy, print. 146 Market st. Balt.

51.8.4 R-7

50c Ca. 1840. Letterpress, imprint: Murphy, print. 146 Market st., Balt. Similar to 25c, No. 51.8.3.

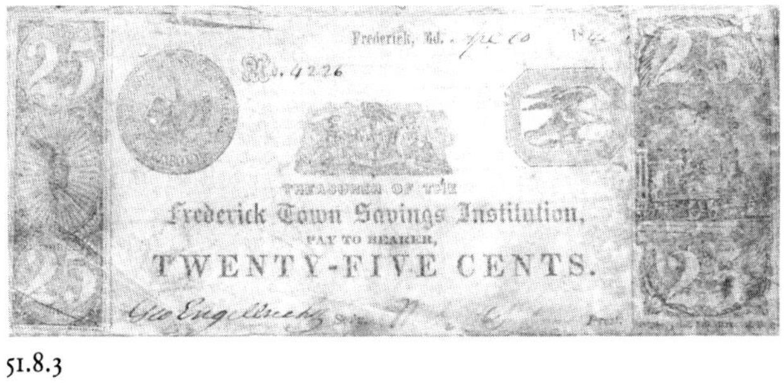

51.8.3

51.8.5 P R-7

$1.00 Ca. 1840. Engraving, imprint: Draper, Underwood, Bald & Spencer. Proof.

51.8.5 C R-7

$1.00 Ca. 1840. Engraving, imprint: Underwood, Bald & Spencer. Counterfeit of same design as No. 51.8.5 P.

51.8.6 SENC

$1.00 Date unknown. *Center:* Large "1" on ONE, female with basket of flowers at right, two females at left. *Right and left:* ONE on 1 above, 1 on ONE below. Surviving example not confirmed but recorded by D. C. Wismer in *The Numismatist,* September 1925. No other information available.

51.8.7 P R-7

$2.00 Ca. 1840. Engraving, imprint: Draper, Underwood, Bald & Spencer. Proof.

51.8.8 P R-7

$5.00 Ca. 1840. Engraving, imprint: Draper, Underwood, Bald & Spencer. Proof.

51.8.9 P R-7

$5.00 Ca. 1845–50. Engraving, imprint: Draper & Co., Phila. Proof.

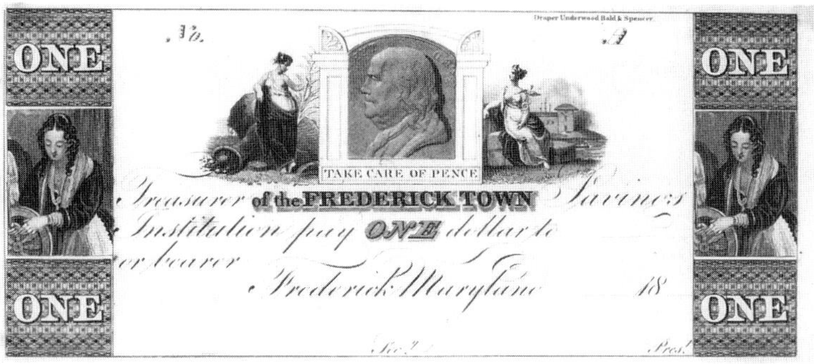

51.8.5 P

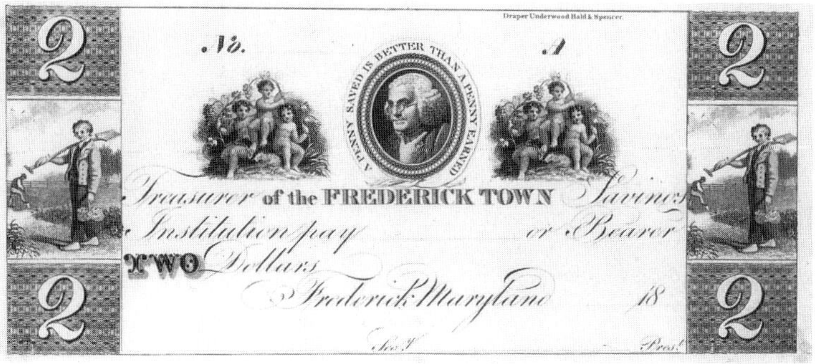

51.8.7 P

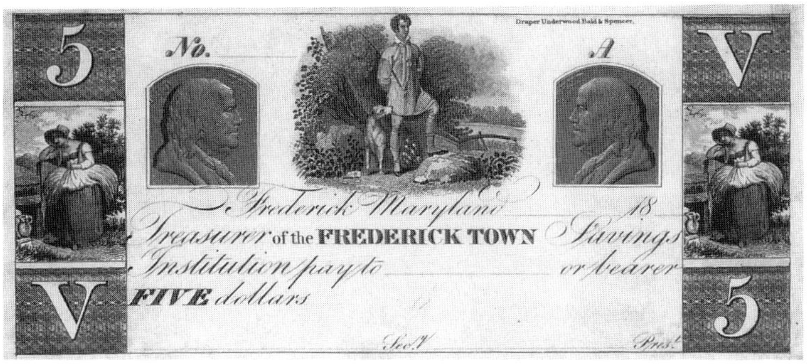

51.8.8 P

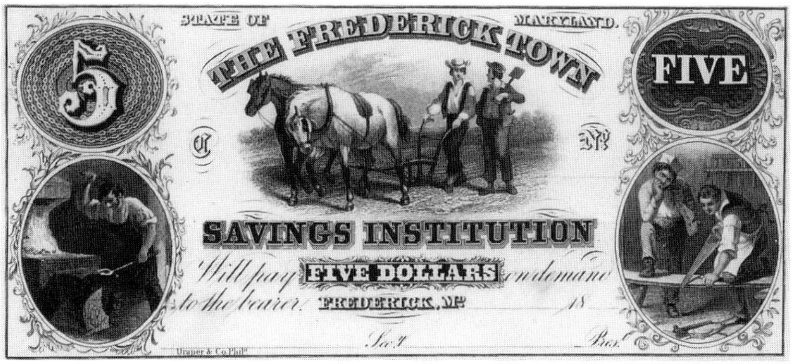

51.8.9 P

51.8.10 P R-7

$10.00 Ca. 1845–50. Engraving, imprint: Draper & Co., Phila. Proof.

51.8.11 P R-7

$20.00 Ca. 1845–50. Engraving, imprint: Draper & Co., Phila. Proof.

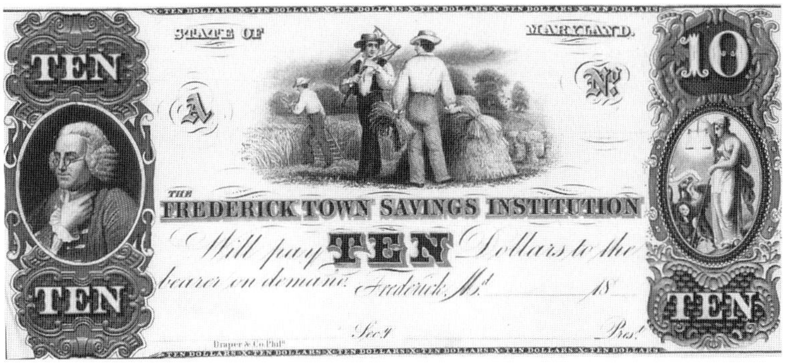

51.8.10 P

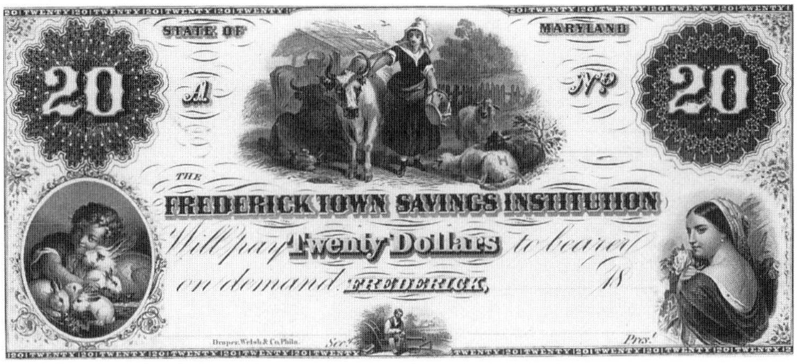

51.8.11 P

51.9 Hauer & Rohr

The 1820 Maryland census index lists Daniel, Daniel Jr., Elizabeth M., and George Hauer; and Christian, George, John, and Philip Rohr in Frederick. Which of these people conducted the store has not as yet been determined. Their scrip, with the denominations inserted in manuscript, was redeemable at the Frederick Town Branch Bank (of the Annapolis-domiciled Farmers Bank of Maryland). The issued notes were printed by letterpress and bear no imprint.

51.9.1 R-7

6 1/4c Printed partial date 181_. Ca. 1814.

51.9.2 R-7

12 1/2c Printed partial date 181_. Ca. 1814.

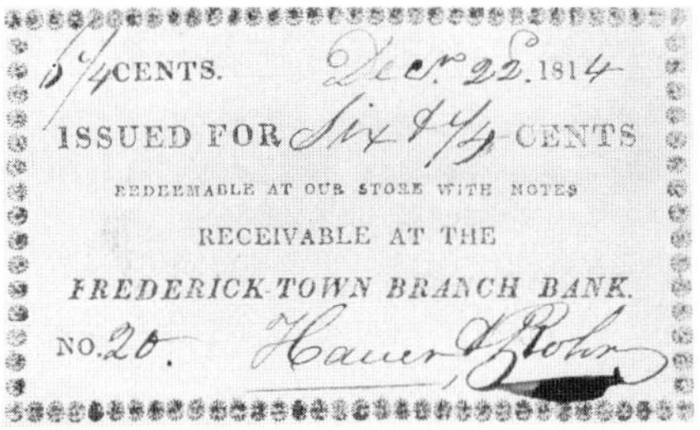

51.9.1

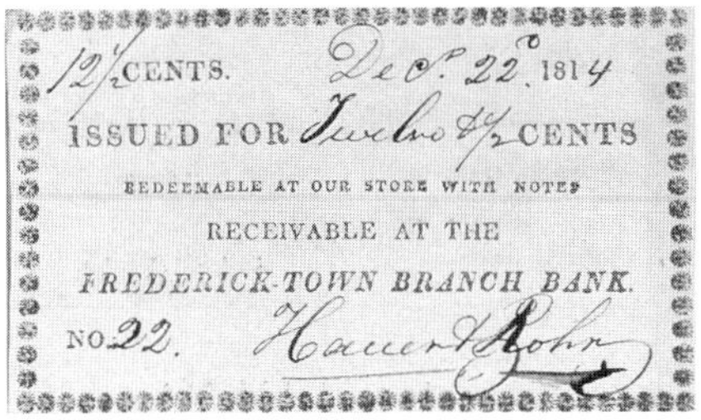

51.9.2

51.9.4 R-7

37 1/2c Printed partial date 181_. Ca. 1814.

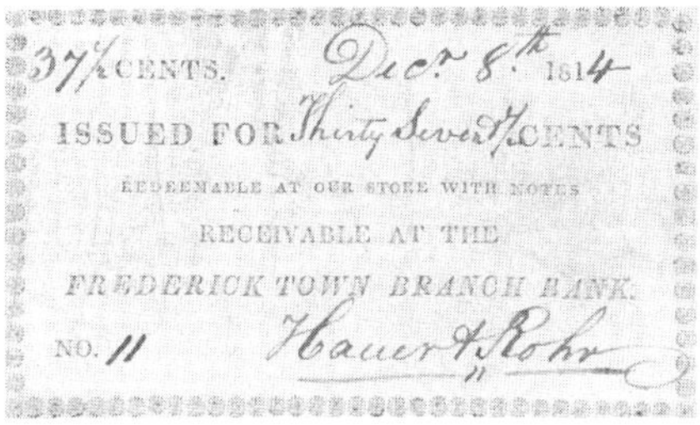

51.9.4

51.10 Wm. C. Hoffman

The issuer was the proprietor of a general store.

51.10.1 R-7

5c Printed date April 4th, 1840. Letterpress, no imprint. Center vignette of Ceres and farm implements.

51.10.2 R-7

5c Printed date April 11th, 1840. Letterpress, imprint: Printed at the "Herald" Office. Center vignette of balance scales.

51.10.3 R-7

6 1/4c Printed date April 4th, 1840. Letterpress, imprint: Printed at the Herald Office. Center vignette of barrel of vegetables and farm implements.

51.10.4 R-7

6 1/4c Printed date April 4th, 1840. Letterpress, no imprint. Center vignette same as No. 51.10.3; text slants to left.

51.10.1

51.10.2

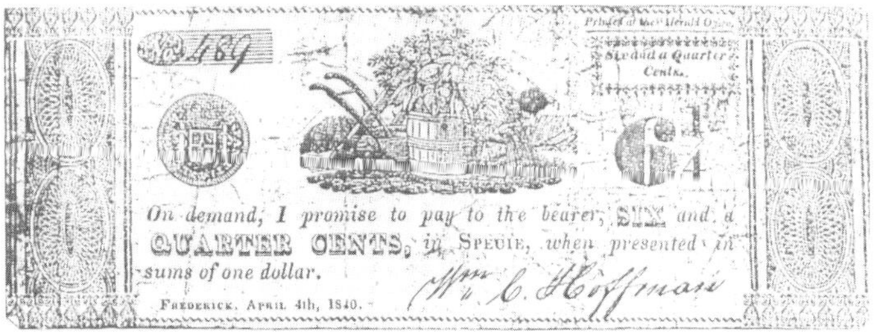

51.10.3

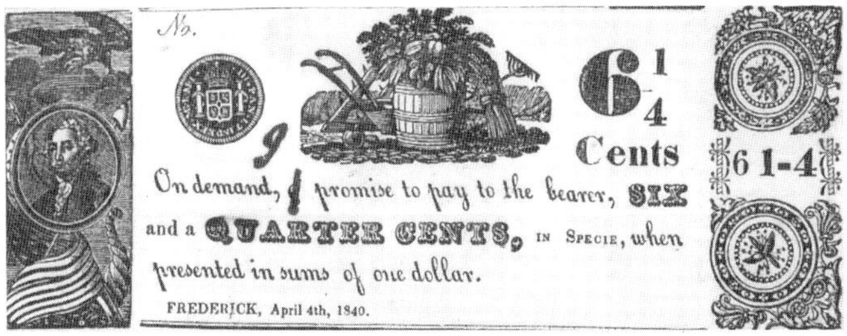

51.10.4

51.10.5 R-7

6 1/4c Printed date April 4th, 1840. Letterpress, no imprint. Center vignette same as No. 51.10.3; two ovals in each endplate.

51.10.6 R-7

6 1/4c Printed date April 4th, 1840. Letterpress, no imprint. Center vignette of sheaf of wheat and rake; "Six and a Quarter Cents" in left end plate.

51.10.7 R-7

6 1/4c Printed date April 4th, 1840. Letterpress, imprint: Printed at the "Herald Office." Center vignette same as No. 51.10.6; "6 1/4" in each end plate.

51.10.8 R-7

6 1/4c Printed date April 11th, 1840. Letterpress, imprint: Printed at the "Herald Office." Center vignette same as No. 51.10.3; "6 1/4" in right end plate.

51.10.9 R-7

10c Printed date April 4th, 1840. Letterpress, no imprint. Center vignette same as No. 51.10.3; small "10" in right end plate, Franklin in left end plate.

51.10.5

51.10.6

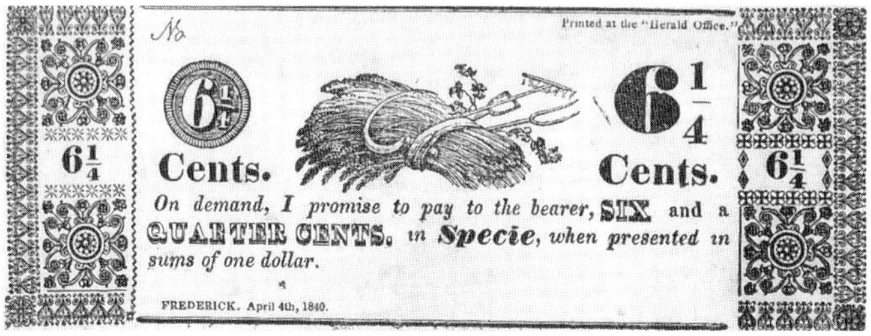

51.10.7

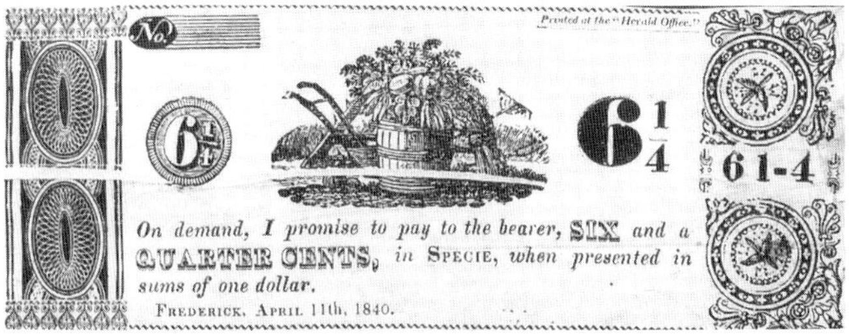

51.10.8

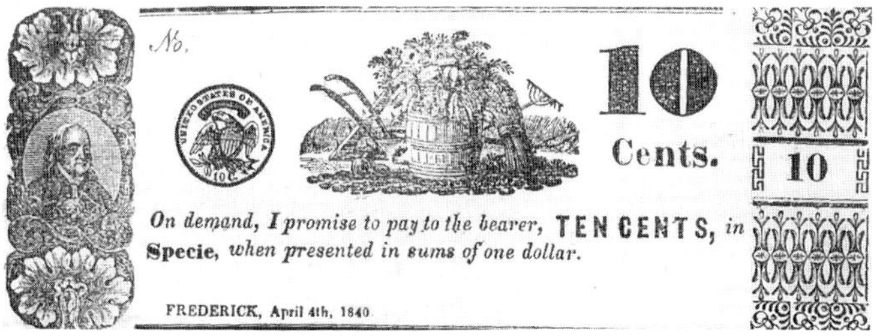

51.10.9

51.10.10 R-7

10c Printed date April 11th, 1840. Letterpress, imprint: Printed at the "Herald Office." Center vignette same as No. 51.10.3; Washington in left end plate.

51.10.10

51.10.11 R-7

10c Printed date April 11th, 1840. Letterpress, imprint: Printed at the "Herald Office." Center vignette same as No. 51.10.6; Franklin in left end plate.

51.10.11

51.10.12 R-7

20c Printed date April 11th, 1840. Letterpress, imprint: Printed at the "Herald Office." Center vignette same as No. 51.10.1.

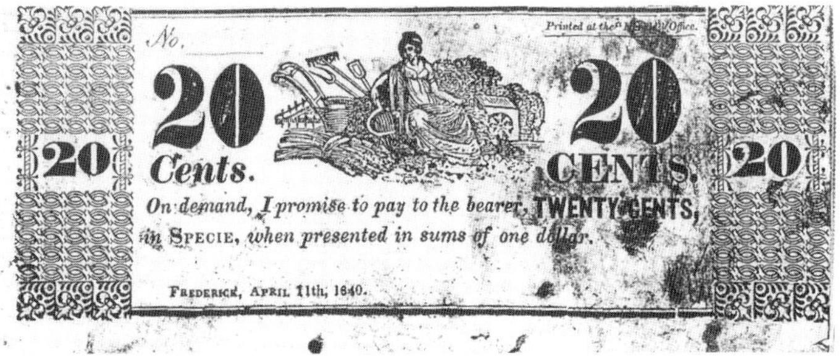

51.10.12

51.11 Real Estate Bank of Frederick County

Charter approved March 31, 1836. No record of operations has been found.

51.12 Thomas Shaw

The issuer is recorded in "History of Frederick County, Maryland" by T. J. C. Williams and Folger McKinsey (1910) as the manager of a lottery in 1814 to fund the rebuilding of All Saints Church in Fredericktown in 1814. He was a founding member of the Agricultural Society of Frederick City in 1820, and its treasurer in 1827. Shaw was also the treasurer of the nearby Libertytown Cattle Show in the same year. He obviously had arranged with the Frederick-Town Branch Bank of the Farmers Bank of Maryland in Annapolis (the branch operated in Frederick from 1807 to 1853) to redeem his scrip.

51.12.2 R-7

12 1/2c Printed date June 10, 1815. Letterpress, no imprint.

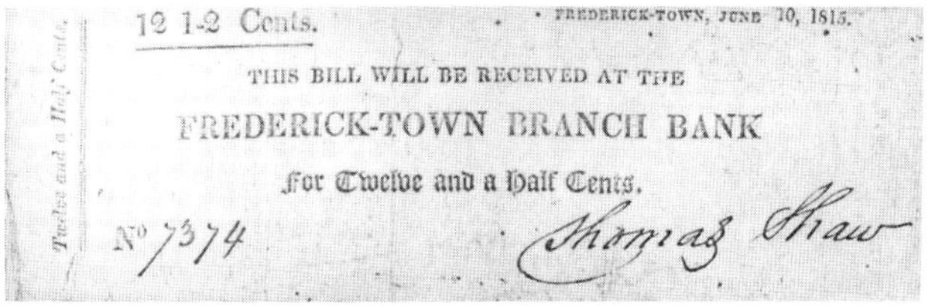

51.12.2

Bank of Westminster (First), Frederick Branch

See Bank of Westminster, Frederick Branch, No. 150.4 et seq.

51.13 Jacob Yeakle

The issuer was a member of a prominent family in Frederick and Hagerstown, largely involved in the retail shoe business.

51.13.1 R-7

5c Printed date Sept. 1st, 1841. Letterpress, imprint: Printed at the Herald Office.

51.13.2 R-7

6 1/4c Printed date Sept. 1st. 1841. Letterpress, imprint: Printed at the Herald Office. 12 in right end panel instead of 6 1/4.

51.13.3 R-7

10c Printed date Sept. 1st. 1841. Letterpress, imprint: Printed at the Herald Office. 50 in right end panel instead of 10.

51.13.4 R-7

12 1/2c Printed date Sept. 1st. 1841. Letterpress, imprint: Printed at the Herald Office. Lowercase *p* in "printed." 12 in right end panel instead of 12 1/2.

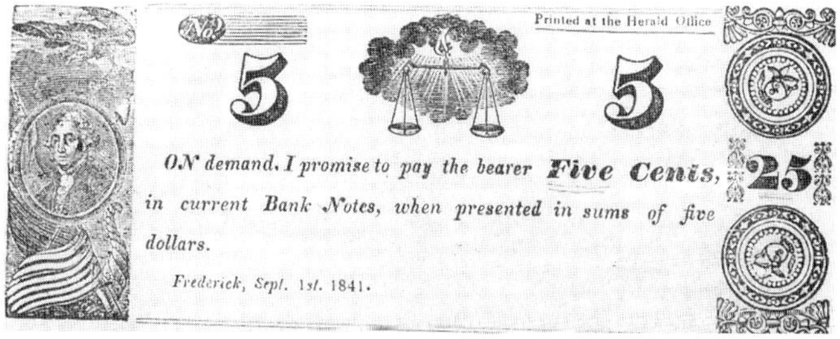

51.13.1

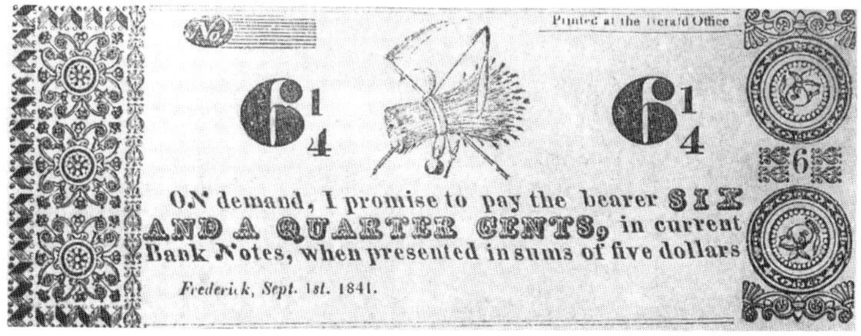

51.13.2

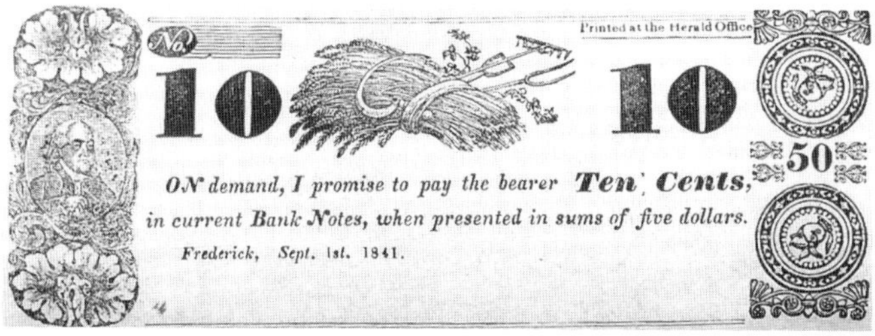

51.13.3

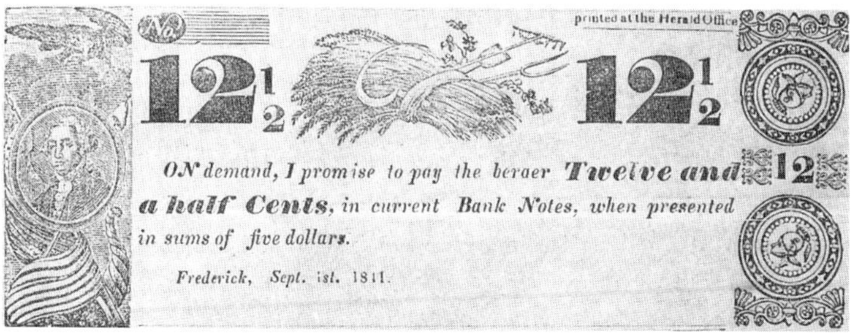

51.13.4

51.13.5 R-7

25c Printed date Sept. 1st. 1841. Letterpress, imprint: Printed at the Herald Office. Circulated note signed Jacob Yeakle. (Visible under ultraviolet light, the faded signature on this note established the identity of the issuer.)

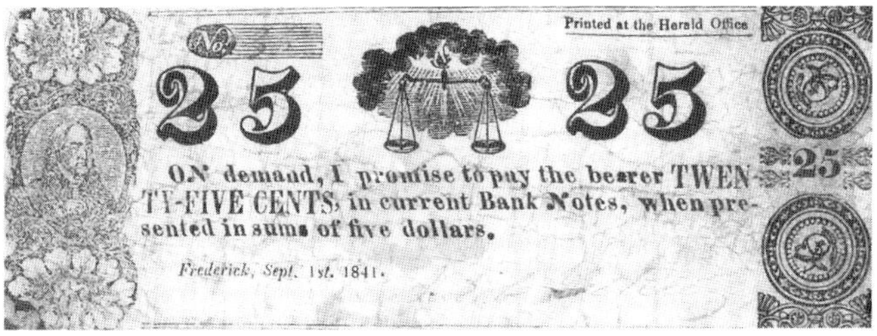

51.13.5

Complete sheet of three denominations, arranged vertically 25c (51.13.5), 12 1/2c (51.13.4), 6 1/4c (51.13.2).

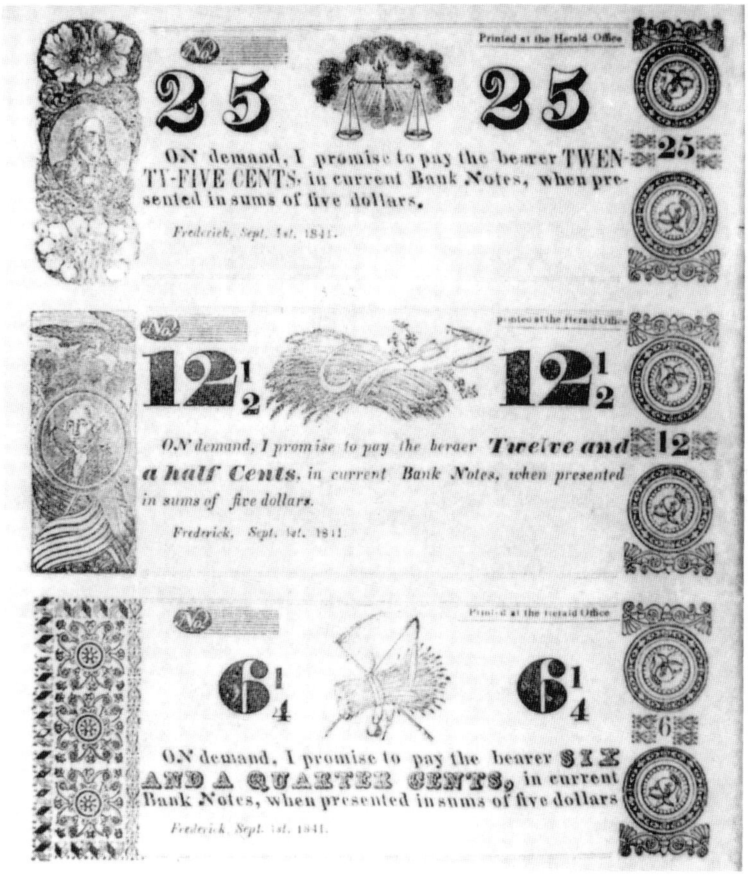

51.16 Unidentified Issuer

51.16.1 R-7

6 1/4c Printed date April 20, 1841. Letterpress, imprint: Murphy, Printer. 146 Market street.

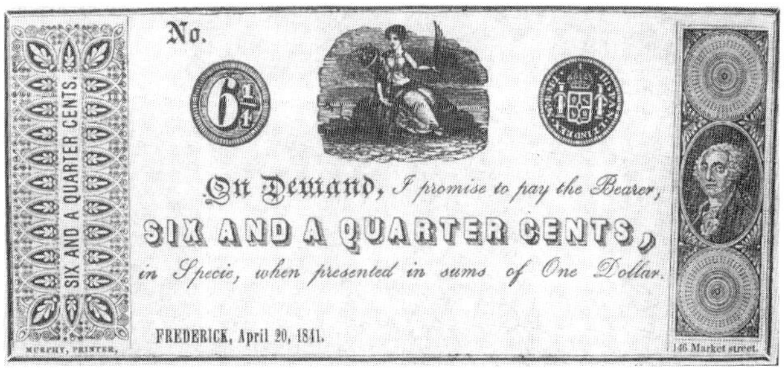

51.16.1

51.16.2 R-7

10c Printed date April 20, 1841. Letterpress, imprint: Murphy, Printer. 146 Market St., Balt.

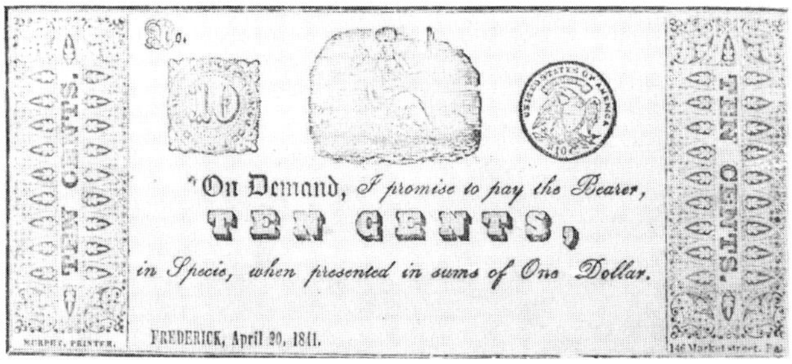

51.16.2

51.17 Unidentified Issuer

Inscribed "ONE SQUARE FROM THE FREDERICK COUNTY BANK I promise to pay in Specie." The issuer, whomever he was and if he ever materialized, obviously hoped to take advantage of the proximity of his location to that of the Frederick County Bank to lend further credence to his scrip.

In his "MASTER LIST of Uncut Sheets of Obsolete Bills and Old Bank Checks," Frank F. Sprinkle listed this illustrated sheet (*below*) as an emission of the Frederick County Bank. He had apparently overlooked the four words "ONE SQUARE FROM THE" in very small letters immediately above the name of the bank.

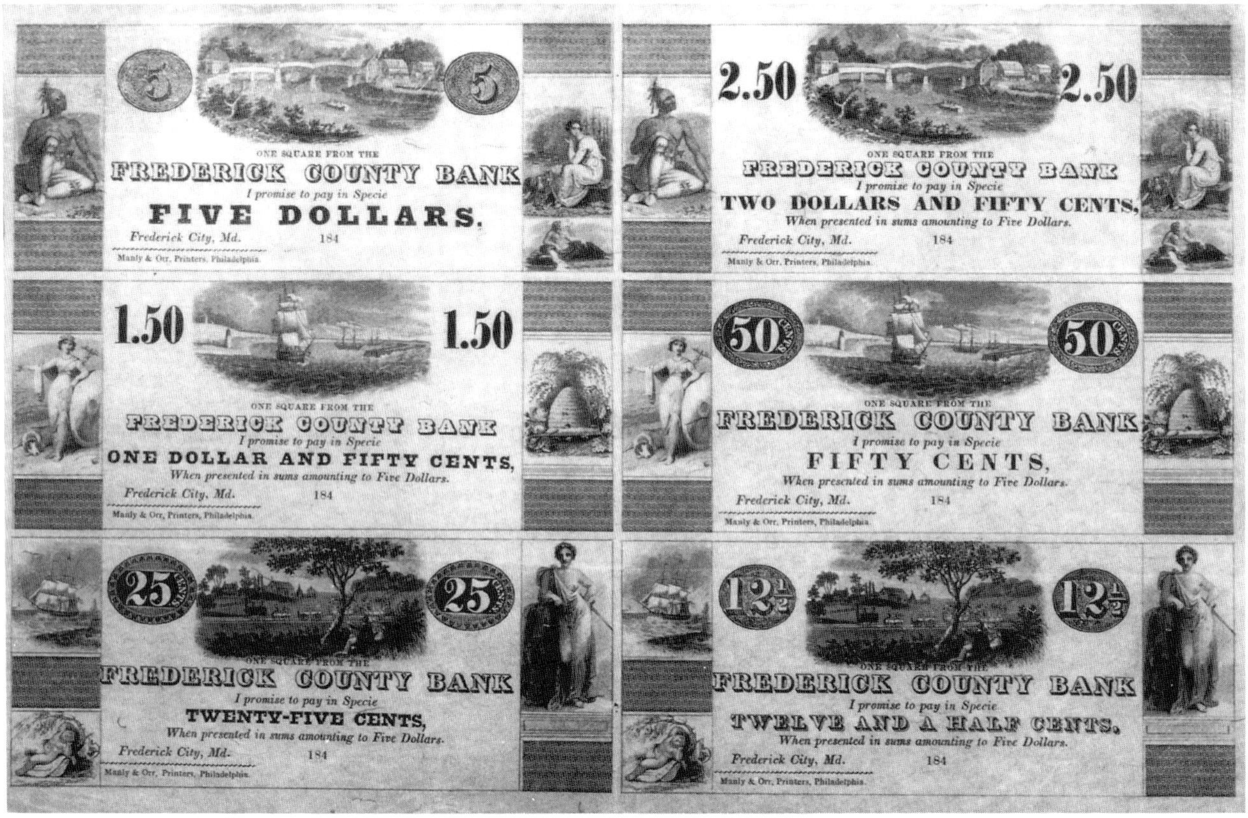

51.17.2 R-7

12 1/2c Printed partial year date 184_. Engraving, imprint: Manly & Orr, Printers, Philadelphia. Payable in specie one square from the Frederick County Bank.

51.17.3 R-7

25c Printed partial year date 184_. Engraving, imprint: Manly & Orr, Printers, Philadelphia. Payable in specie one square from the Frederick County Bank.

51.17.4 R-7

50c Printed partial year date 184_. Engraving, imprint: Manly & Orr, Printers, Philadelphia. Payable in specie one square from the Frederick County Bank.

51.17.5 R-7

$1.50 Printed partial year date 184_. Engraving, imprint: Manly & Orr, Printers, Philadelphia. Payable in specie one square from the Frederick County Bank.

51.17.8 R-7

$2.50 Printed partial year date 184_. Engraving, imprint: Manly & Orr, Printers, Philadelphia. Payable in specie one square from the Frederick County Bank.

51.17.9 R-7

$5.00 Printed partial year date 184_. Engraving, imprint: Manly & Orr, Printers, Philadelphia. Payable in specie one square from the Frederick County Bank.

53 FROSTBURG, ALLEGANY COUNTY

Located nine miles west of Cumberland on the National Road (now U.S. Route 40) Frostburg is named for Meshach and Catherine Frost who opened a tavern there in 1812.

53.1 The Frostburg Bank

Charter amendment approved March 10, 1856; formerly Frostburg Savings Bank (1854); converted to and became the First National Bank of Frostburg in 1865.

53.1.1 R-7

$1.00 Ca. 1861–64. Engraving, imprint: American Bank Note Co., New York. Orange red overprint "1-1" at top and negative ONE in negative fancy letters in lower center. (MD225G2)

53.1.2 P R-7

$5.00 Ca. 1853–60s. Engraving, imprint: Rawdon, Wright, Hatch & Edson. Red FIVE overprint in fancy letters. Proof. (MD225G6a)

53.1.3 P R-7

$10.00 Ca. 1853–60s. Engraving, imprint: Rawdon, Wright, Hatch & Edson. Overprinted "XX" and TEN in fancy letters. Proof. (MD225G8a)

53.1.4 SENC

$20.00 Ca. 1853–60s. Engraving, imprint: Rawdon, Wright, Hatch & Edson. *Center:* 20; farmer seated on grain, keg and grain cradle beside, two men cradling at left, two horses and hay loading at right; 20. *Left:* Oval female portrait / XX. *Right:* Oval female portrait / 20. (MD225G10a)

53.1.1

53.1.2 P

53.1.3 P

53.2 Geo. H. Krebs

The issuer was a coal, real estate, and lumber dealer.

53.2.1 R-7
6 1/4c Printed date June 8, 1840. Letterpress, no imprint. Pink paper.

53.2.2 R-7
6 1/4c Printed date June 8, 1840. Letterpress, no imprint. Pink paper. Similar in design to No. 53.2.1.

53.2.3 R-7
12 1/2c Printed date June 8, 1840. Letterpress, no imprint. Pink paper.

53.2.4 R-7
12 1/2c Printed date June 8, 1840. Letterpress, no imprint. Pink paper. Similar end design to 6 1/4c, No. 53.2.2.

53.2.5 R-7
25c Printed date June 8, 1840. Letterpress, no imprint. Pink paper.

53.2.6 R-6
50c Printed date June 8, 1840. Letterpress, no imprint. Numeral "50" in lower corners in single-lined shaded typeface. CENTS under "50" in upper left portion of body of note.

53.2.7 R-7
50c Printed date June 8, 1840. Letterpress, no imprint. Similar to No. 53.2.6, except all corner numerals in double-lined typeface. CENTS to right of "50" in upper left portion of body.

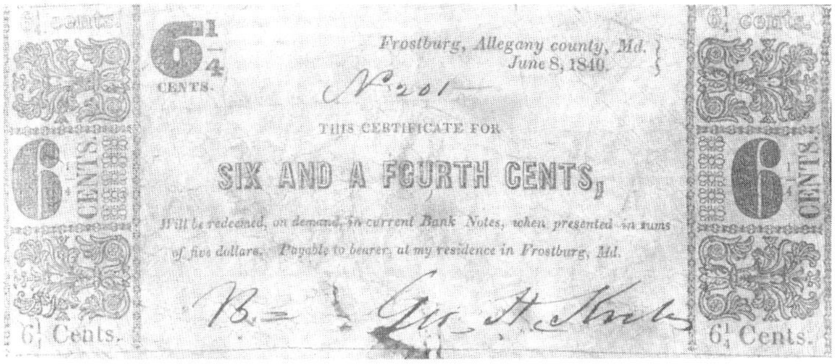

53.2.1

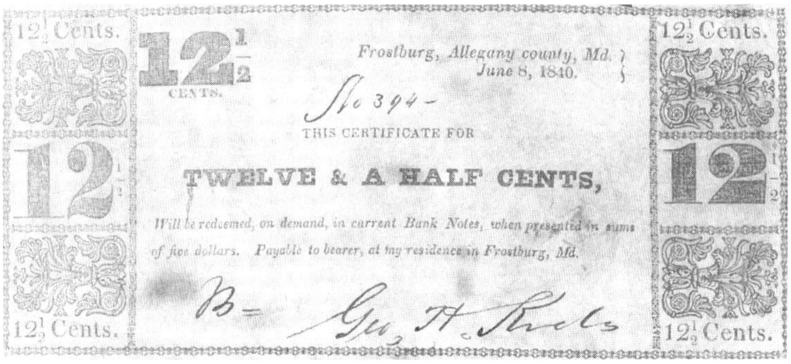

53.2.3

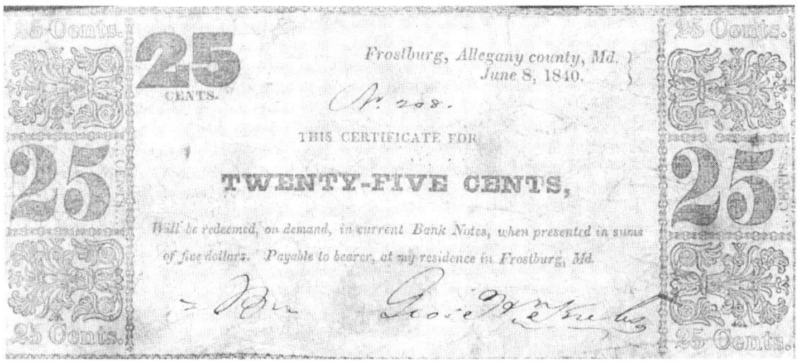

53.2.5

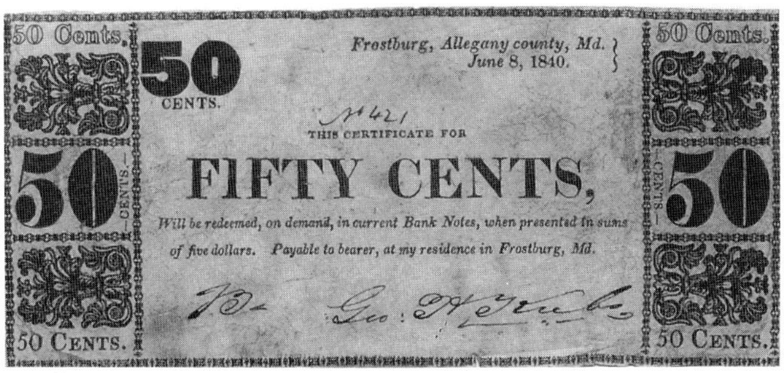

53.2.6

53.2.8 R-7

$1.00 Printed date June 8, 1840. Letterpress, no imprint. Shortened "1" in each side panel; "$" in lower corners reversed.

53.2.9 R-7

$1.00 Printed date June 8, 1840. Letterpress, no imprint. Similar to No. 53.2.8, except "1$" in lower left corner instead of "$1."

53.2.10 R-7

$1.00 Printed date June 8, 1840. Letterpress, no imprint. Similar to No. 53.2.8, except full-length "1" in each side panel; "One Doll." in all four corners.

53.2.11 R-7

$1.00 Printed date June 8, 1840. Letterpress, no imprint. Similar to No. 53.2.8, except single-lined "1" and slanted "$" in lower left corner.

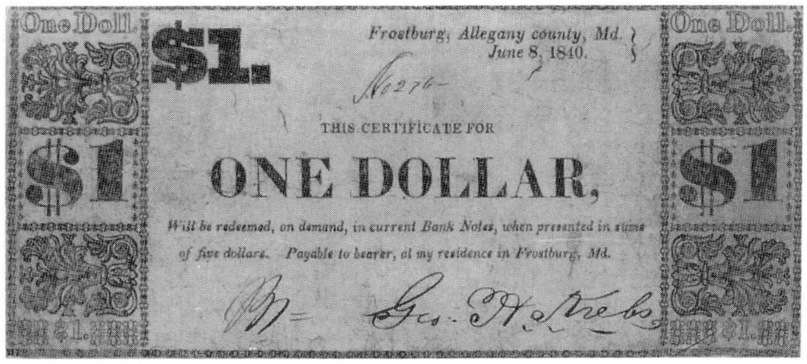

53.2.8

53.2.10

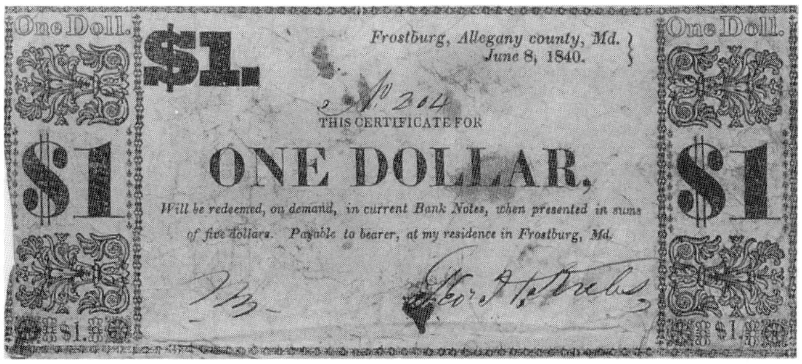

53.2.11

54 GEORGETOWN

This town was originally in Montgomery County and became a part of Washington, D.C., in 1801. The name is attributed to Ninian Beall's son, George, who owned the land on which the town was built.

54.1 Bank of Columbia

Bank operated from 1793 until 1820, when it suspended and made an assignment for the benefit of creditors. It became a District of Columbia bank when Georgetown became a part of the district in 1801.

54.1.1 SENC

$5.00 Ca. 1790s. No data available. (MD228G4)

54.1.2 SENC

$5.00 Ca. early 1800s. No data available. (MD228G8)

54.1.3 SENC

$10.00 Ca. 1790s. Engraving, imprint: Unknown. Similar to counterfeit, No. 54.1.3 C. (MD228G10)

54.1.3 C R-7

$10.00 Ca. 1790s. Engraving, imprint: Unknown. Counterfeit of No. 54.1.3. (MD228C10)

54.1.4 SENC

$10.00 Ca. early 1800s. No data available. (MD228G14)

54.1.5 SENC

$20.00 Ca. 1790s. Engraving, imprint: Unknown. Similar to $10.00, No. 54.1.3. (MD228G16)

56 GRACEHAM, FREDERICK COUNTY

This village, about 1 3/4 miles southeast of Thurmont, arose about 1750. The name is explained by the story that a visiting Lutheran minister exclaimed, "May this be a hamlet where the grace of God abounds."

56.1 Jn. A. Henning

The issuer, John A. Henning, was the proprietor of a general store.

56.1.3 R-7

25c Printed date October 19, 1841. Letterpress, imprint: Murphy, Printer, Balt. Vignette is a woodcut view of Baltimore looking north over the inner harbor.

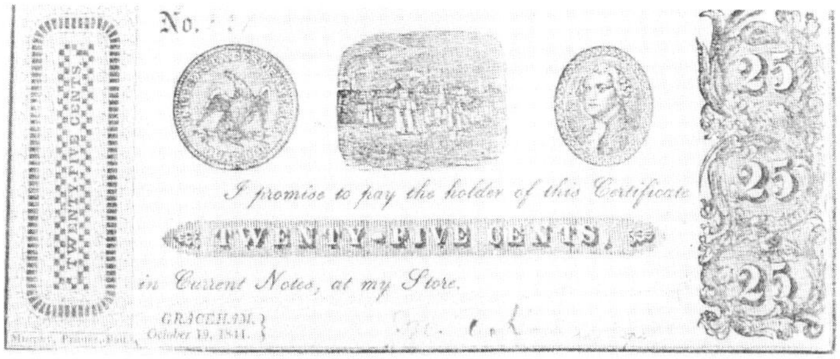

56.1.3

57 GREENFIELD MILLS, FREDERICK COUNTY

57.1 The Greenfield Mills

Dr. Meredith Davis, owner of the Greenfield Mills, was the leading miller in Frederick County in the 1830s. His flour mill was on the Monocacy River, 3 1/2 miles from Tuscarora Station on the Metropolitan Branch of the Baltimore & Ohio Railroad, 12 miles from Frederick. Scrip was issued by the Mills between 1832 and 1838, which directed the Fredericktown Branch Bank (of the Annapolis-domiciled Farmers Bank of Maryland) to pay the denominated amount to the bearer.

57.1.1 R-1

25c Ca. 1837. Letterpress, imprint: Printed at the Citizen Office. Vignette is horse-drawn two-wheel cart.

57.1.2 R-1

25c Ca. 1838. Letterpress, imprint: Printed at the "Citizon" Office, Frederick. No vignette.

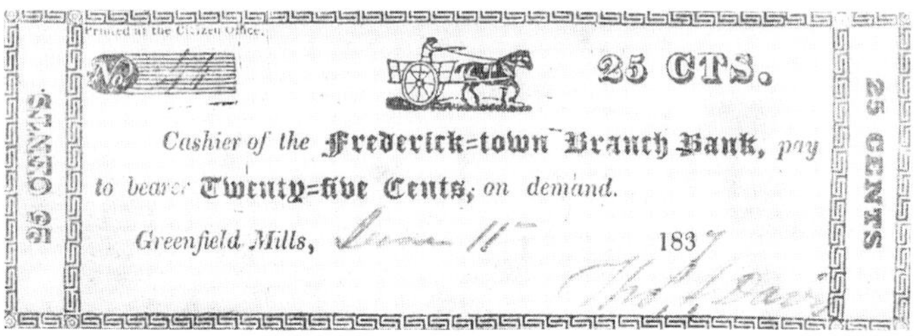

57.1.1

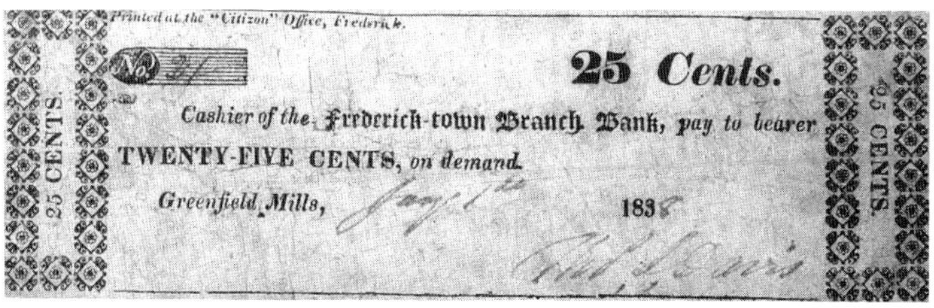

57.1.2

57.1.3 R-1

50c Ca. 1837. Letterpress, imprint: Printed at the Citizen Office, Frederick. Vignette is two horse-drawn covered wagon.

57.1.4 R-1

50c Ca. 1838. Letterpress, imprint: Printed at the "Citizen" Office, Frederick. No vignette.

57.1.5 R-3

$1.00 Ca. 1832. Letterpress, imprint: PRINTED AT THE CITIZEN "OFFICE" FREDERICK. Yellow paper. Similar to $3.00, No. 57.1.11.

57.1.6 R-1

$1.00 Ca. 1837. Letterpress, imprint: Printed at the Citizen Office, Frederick. Vignette of a house.

57.1.7 R-1

$1.00 Ca. 1838. Letterpress, imprint: Printed at the "Citizen" Office, Frederick. No vignette.

57.1.8 R-3

$2.00 Ca. 1832. Letterpress, imprint: PRINTED AT THE CITIZENS "OFFICE" FREDERICK. Similar to $3.00, No. 57.1.11. Yellow paper.

57.1.9 R-1

$2.00 Ca. 1837. Letterpress, imprint: Printed at the Citizen Office. Vignette is two horse-drawn covered wagon.

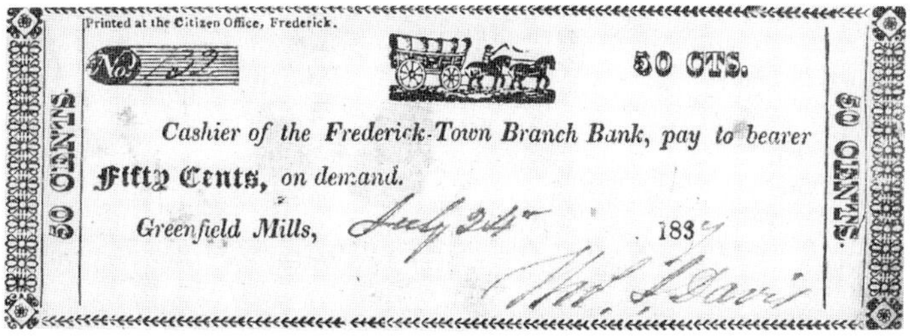

57.1.3

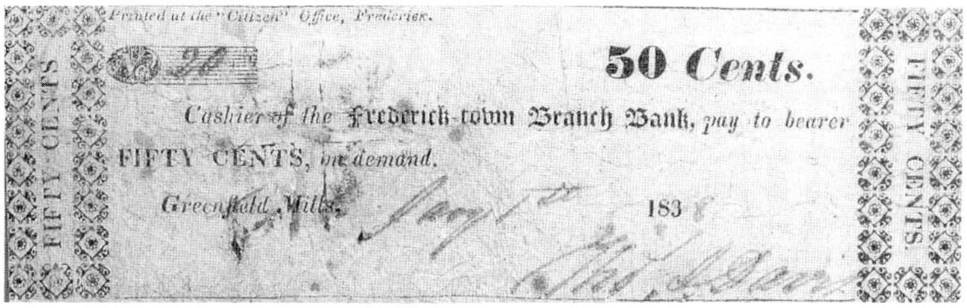

57.1.4

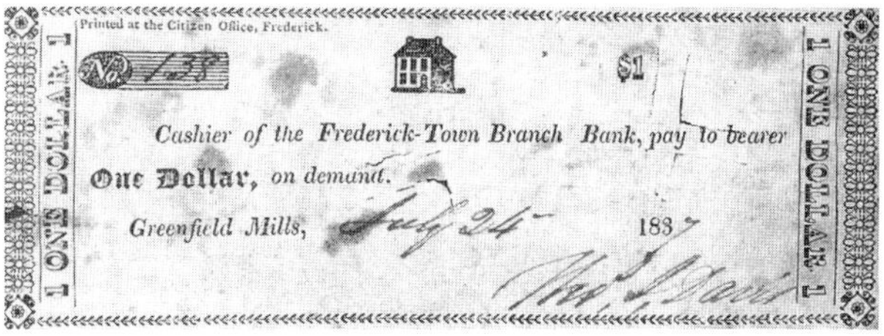

57.1.6

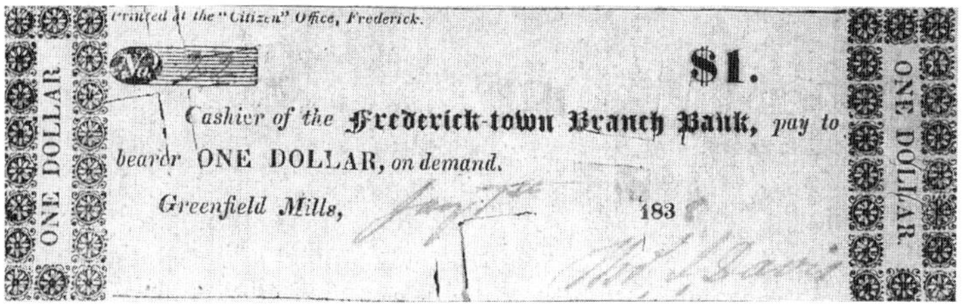

57.1.7

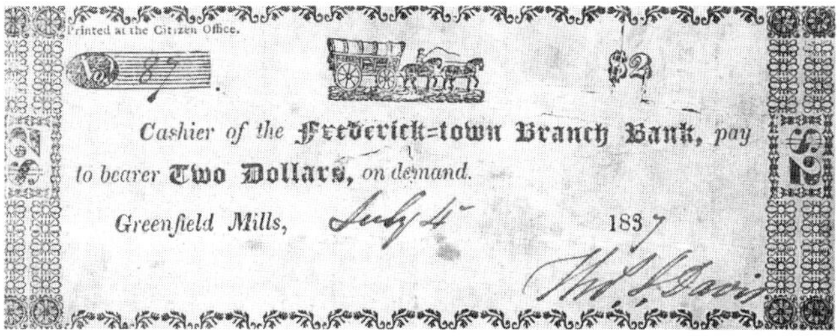

57.1.9

57.1.10 R-1

$2.00 Ca. 1838. Letterpress, imprint: Printed at the "Citizen" Office, Frederick. No vignette.

57.1.11 R-4

$3.00 Ca. 1832. Letterpress, imprint: PRINTED AT THE CITIZENS "OFFICE," FREDERICK. Yellow paper.

57.1.12 R-5

$5.00 Ca. 1835–36. Engraving, no imprint. No scrollwork surrounding "Patent" near lower left corner.

57.1.13 R-1

$5.00 Ca. 1835–36. Engraving, imprint (under left foreground of vignette): Medairy, Sc. Scroll work surrounding "Patent" near lower left corner.

57.1.14 R-1

$10.00 Ca. 1835–36. Engraving, imprint (under left foreground of vignette): Medairy, Sc. Scroll work surrounding "Patent" near lower left corner.

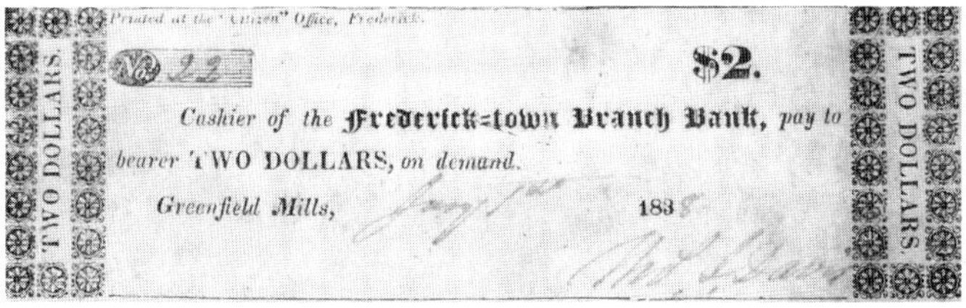

57.1.10

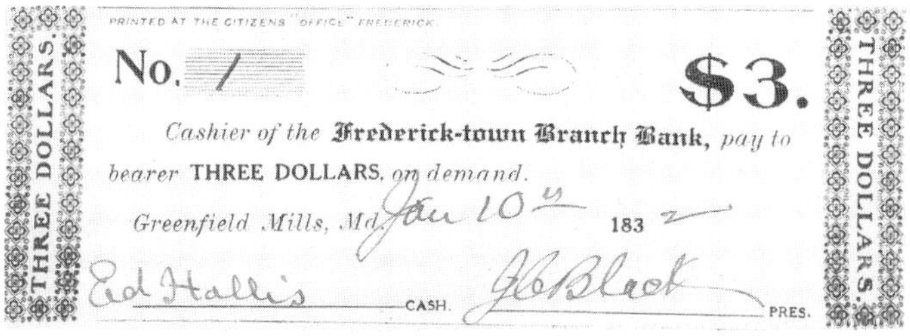

57.1.11

57.1.12

57.1.13

57.1.14

57.2 Unidentified Issuer

57.2.4 R-7

50c Printed date May 20, 1841. Letterpress, imprint: Murphy, printer, Baltimore.

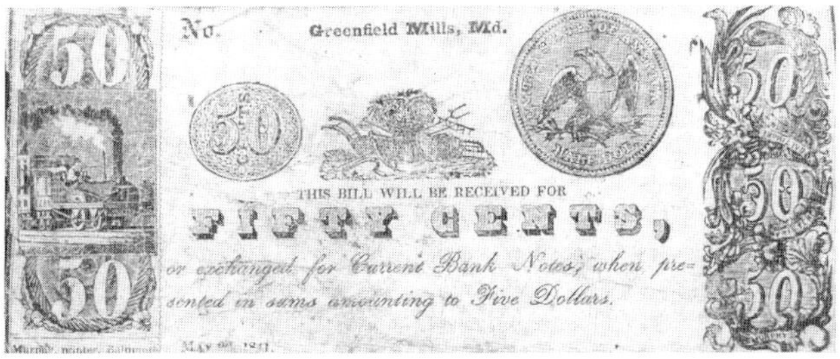

57.2.4

58 GREENSBOROUGH, CAROLINE COUNTY

Situated on the west bank of the Choptank River 4 1/2 miles northeast of Ridgely, this town was established by an act of the state legislature in 1732. Its first names were Choptank Bridge and Bridge Town; the change to Greensboro came after a resurvey in 1791.

58.1 The Farmers & Merchants Bank of Greensborough

Charter approved March 10, 1854, operations probably beginning in 1855. Voluntary liquidation completed September 16, 1865, and the charter repealed in 1867. Notes bearing the signatures of J. E. Hignutt, cashier, and S. H. Hazard, president, were apparently printed from original face plates that had fallen into improper hands, as there were never any such officers. The cashier and president during the entire life of the bank were A. E. Warner and Spencer Hitch, respectively.

58.1.1 R-2

$1.00 Printed date August 15, 1862. Engraving, imprint: American Bank Note Co., New York. STATE OF MARYLAND at top in double-lined uppercase letters. Black and yellowish green. Town name beneath that of the bank misspelled "Greensrobough." Also inscribed "PATENTED 30 JUNE 1857" in green immediately below Greensborough. (MD230G2a)

58.1.1

58.1.2 R-2

$1.00 Printed date August 15, 1862. Similar to No. 58.1.1, spelling of town name corrected. Handstamped serial number. (MD230G2b)

58.1.3 R-2

$1.00 Printed date August 15, 1862. Similar to No. 58.1.1, but "State of Md." at top in script lettering and with green engine-turned "1 ONE 1" design on the reverse. The green ink used for the security print and reverse design is darker in hue than that on the previous notes, Nos. 58.1.1 and 58.1.2. Patent inscription is eliminated. (MD230G2c)

58.1.3

58.1.4 R-2

$2.00 Printed date August 15, 1862. Engraving, imprint: American Bank Note Co., New York. Black and yellowish green. STATE OF MARYLAND at top in double-lined uppercase letters. Town name beneath that of the Bank misspelled "Greensrobough." (MD230G4a)

58.1.5 R-2

$2.00 Printed date August 15, 1862. Engraving, imprint: American Bank Note Co., New York. Similar to No. 58.1.4, spelling of town name corrected. Handstamped serial number. (MD230G4b)

58.1.6 R-2

$2.00 Printed date August 15, 1862. Engraving, imprint: American Bank Note Co., New York. Similar to No. 58.1.5, but STATE OF MARYLAND at top in script lettering. The green ink used to print the security portions of the design was of a much darker hue than that used for Nos. 58.1.4 and 58.1.5. Ornate engine-turned design on reverse. (MD230G4c)

58.1.7 R-3

$3.00 Printed date August 15, 1862. Engraving, imprint: American Bank Note Co., New York. Green security imprint "3 THREE 3" on engine-turned panels on face, also inscribed "PATENTED 30 JUNE 1857" in green immediately below the eagle vignette. Same as No. 58.1.8, except with handwritten serial number. (MD230G6a)

58.1.8 R-3

$3.00 Printed date August 15, 1862. Engraving, imprint: American Bank Note Co., New York. Similar to No. 58.1.7, except has handstamped serial number. (MD230G6b)

58.1.9 SENC

$3.00 Printed date August 15, 1862. Engraving, imprint: American Bank Note Co., New York. Similar to No. 58.1.8, with ornate green design on reverse—reported, not seen. (MD230G6c)

58.1.3 REV

58.1.4

58.1.6

58.1.10 A R-7

$5.00 Ca. 1854–58. Engraving, imprint: Rawdon, Wright, Hatch & Edson. Altered from the $5.00 Farmers & Merchants Bank of Memphis, Tenn., TN100G54. Security overprint FIVE in red. (MD229A5)

58.1.11 R-4

$5.00 Ca. 1855–63. Engraving, imprint: Danforth, Wright & Co., Philada. and New York. No overprint. The signatures on this particular note are not identifiable as those of any recorded officer of the bank. Similar to No. 58.1.12. (MD230G8)

58.1.12 R-3

$5.00 Ca. 1856–63. Engraving, imprint: Danforth, Wright & Co., Philada. and New York. Similar to No. 58.1.11, with red security overprint FIVE in engine-turned serifed uppercase letters. (MD230G8a)

58.1.12 P R-6

$5.00 Ca. 1856–63. Engraving, imprint: Danforth, Wright & Co., Philada. and New York. Similar to No. 58.1.11, with red security overprint FIVE in engine-turned serifed uppercase letters. Proof.

58.1.13 R-4

$5.00 Ca. 1862–63. Engraving, imprint: Danforth, Wright & Co., Philada. and New York. Similar to No. 58.1.12, with "ABCo" monogram of the American Bank Note Co. added below the numeral in the upper right corner. Red security imprint, colorless FIVE in engine-turned rectangular panel with chamfered corners. (MD230G8b)

58.1.8

58.1.10 A

58.1.12

58.1.12 P

58.1.14 R-5

$5.00 Ca. 1862–63. Engraving, imprint: Danforth, Wright & Co., Philada. and New York. Similar to No. 58.1.13, but with green security imprint FIVE in ornate engine-turned letters. (MD230G8c)

58.1.15 R-4

$10.00 Ca. 1862–63. Engraving, imprint: Danforth, Wright & Co., Philada. & New York. Red security imprint, colorless TEN in engine-turned rectangular panel with chamfered corners. ABCo monogram of the American Bank Note Co. to left of numeral in upper right corner. (MD230G10b)

58.1.16 SENC

$10.00 Ca. 1862–63. Engraving, imprint: Danforth, Wright & Co., Philada. & New York. No overprint. Similar to No. 58.1.17 P.

58.1.16 P R-7

$10.00 Ca. 1862–63. Engraving, imprint: Danforth, Wright & Co., Philada. & New York. No overprint. Proof. (MD230G10)

58.1.17 R-4

$10.00 Ca. 1862–63. Engraving, imprint: Danforth, Wright & Co., Philada. & New York. Similar to No. 58.1.16, but with red security overprint TEN in engine-turned serifed uppercase letters. (MD230G10a)

58.1.17 P R-7

$10.00 Ca. 1862–63. Engraving, imprint: Danforth, Wright & Co., Philada. & New York. Similar to No. 58.1.16, but with red security overprint TEN in engine-turned serifed uppercase letters. Proof.

58.1.18 R-5

$10.00 Ca. 1862–63. Engraving, imprint: American Bank Note Co., New York. Similar to No. 58.1.17, but with green security imprint TEN in ornate engine-turned letters. (MD230G10c)

58.1.18 P R-7

$10.00 Ca. 1862–63. Engraving, imprint: American Bank Note Co., New York. Similar to No. 58.1.17, but with green security imprint TEN in ornate engine-turned letters. Proof.

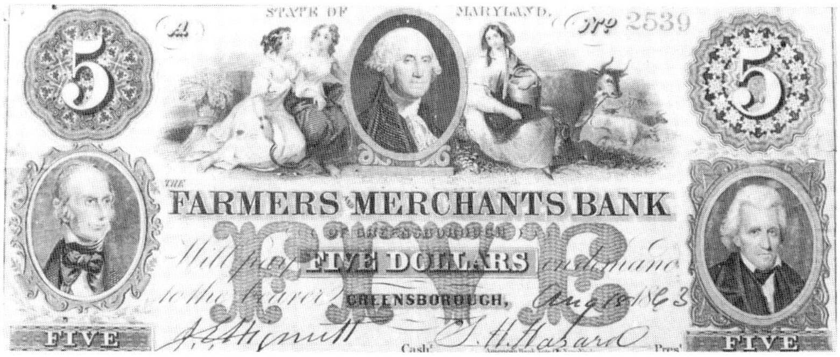

58.1.14

58.1.15

58.1.17 P

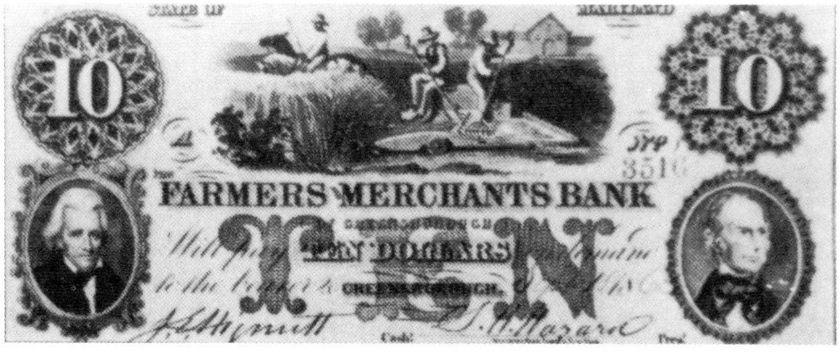

58.1.18 P

60 HAGERSTOWN, WASHINGTON COUNTY

Jonathan Hager (1719–75) patented Hager's Choice in December 1739 and Hager's Delight in 1753. The town was laid out in 1762 and named Elizabeth Town in honor of Hager's wife, Elizabeth Kershner Hager. However, the name was not popular and in January 1814 the assembly passed "an act to change the name of Elizabeth Town to Hager's Town, and incorporate the same." A post office was opened in 1792.

60.1 Corporation of Hagerstown

Scrip issued by the town of Hagerstown to help alleviate the difficulties caused by the disappearance of small change during the "hard times" of 1837–40, and again during the Civil War.

60.1.1 R-5
5c Printed partial year date 186_. Ca. 1862–63. Letterpress, imprint: Saml. S. Shryock, Chambersburg, Pa. Green security underprint. Payor inscription BY ORDER OF TOWN COUNCIL.

60.1.2 R-7
6 1/4c Printed date Oct. 1, 1841. Letterpress, imprint: C.D. Bell. Payor inscription THE MODERATOR AND OTHER COMMISSIONERS.

60.1.3 R-7
6 1/4c Printed date Dec. 10, 1841. Letterpress, imprint: C. D. Bell. Payor inscription THE MODERATOR AND OTHER COMMISSIONERS.

60.1.4 R-5
10c Printed partial year date 186_. Ca. 1862–63. Similar payor inscription to 5c, No. 60.1.1.

60.1.5 R-7
12 1/2c Printed date June 20, 1840. Engraving, no imprint. Similar payor inscription to 6 1/4c, No. 60.1.2.

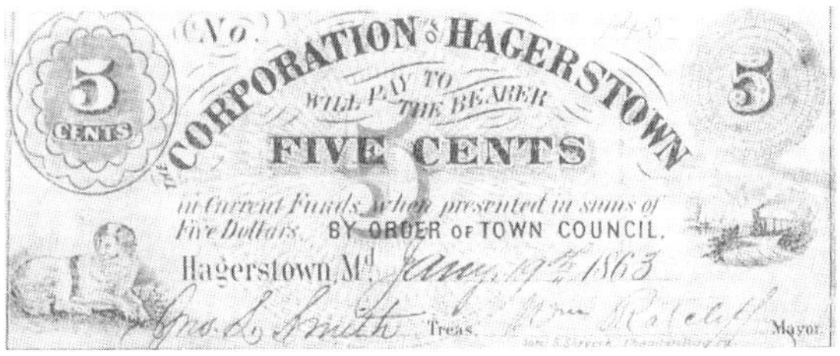

60.1.1

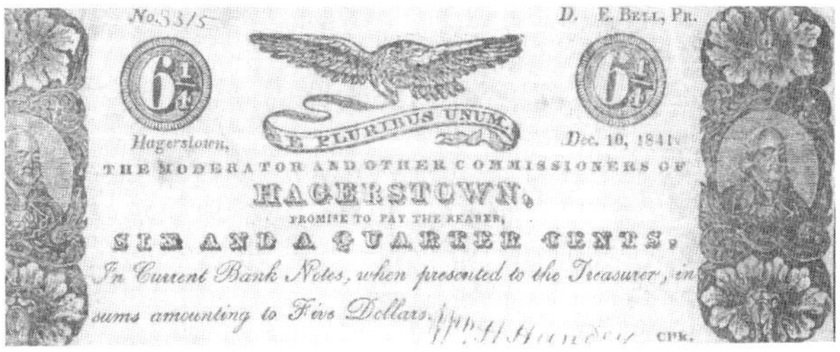

60.1.3

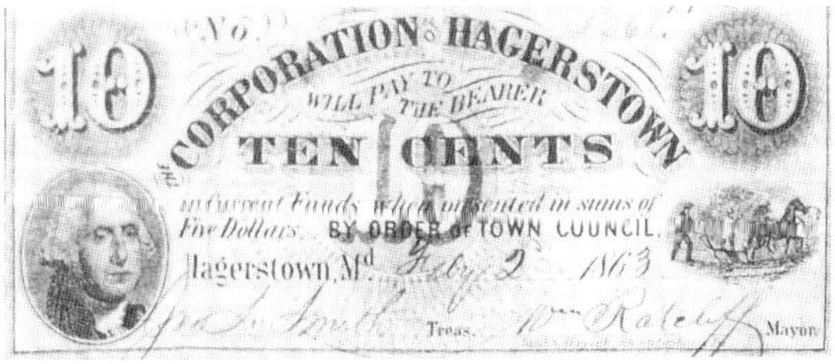

60.1.4

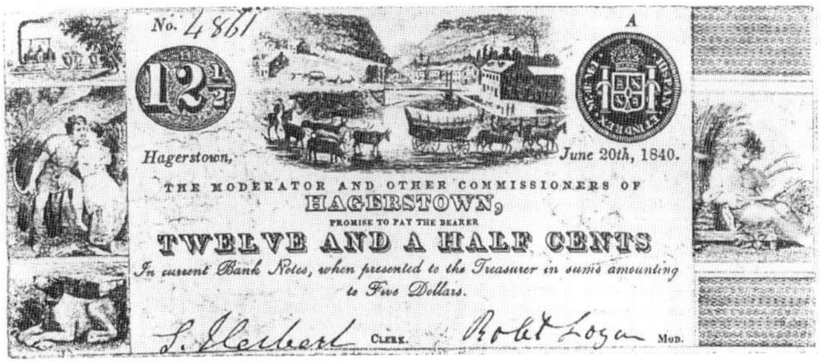

60.1.5

60.1.6 R-7

25c Printed date June 20, 1840. Engraving, no imprint. Similar payor inscription to 6 1/4c, No. 60.1.2.

60.1.7 R-6

25c Printed partial year date 186_. Ca. 1862–63. Letterpress, imprint: Saml. S. Shryock, Chambersburg, Pa. Green security underprint. Similar payor inscription to 5c, No. 60.1.1.

60.1.8 R-7

50c Printed date June 20, 1840. Engraving, no imprint. Similar payor inscription to 6 1/4c, No. 60.1.2.

60.1.9 R-7

$1.00 Printed date April 1, 1840. Engraving, no imprint. Similar payor inscription to 6 1/4c, No. 60.1.2.

60.1.10 R-7

$1.00 Printed date June 20, 1840. Engraving, no imprint. Similar payor inscription to 6 1/4c, No. 60.1.2.

60.1.6

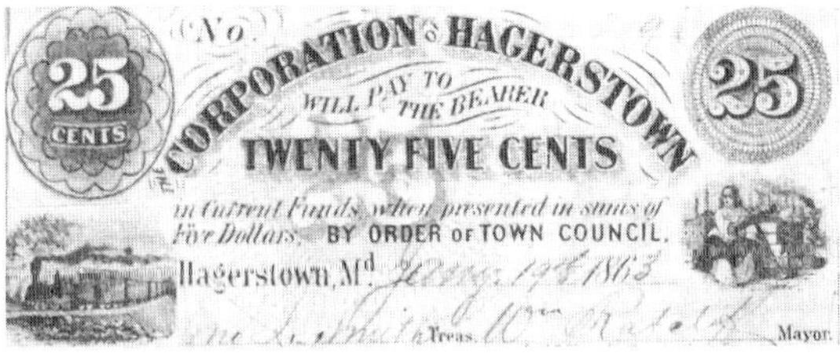

60.1.7

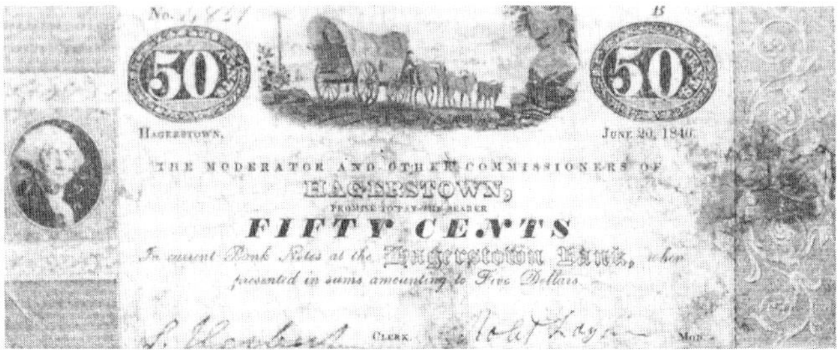

60.1.8

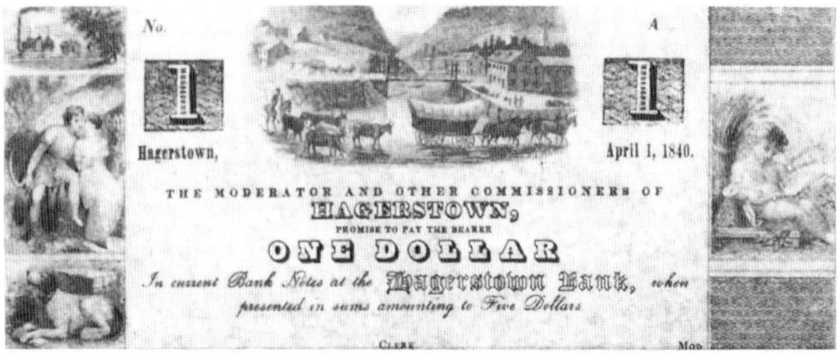

60.1.9

60.1.10

60.1.11 R-7

$1.00 Printed date June 20, 1840. Engraving, no imprint. Similar payor inscription to 6 1/4c, No. 60.1.2.

60.1.11

60.2 Jas. Allen (written in)

The identity of the signer, Jas. Allen, has not been established.

60.2.4 R-7

50c Printed date April __ 1840. Engraving, imprint: Manly & Orr, Printers, Philadelphia. Both the issuer's signature and the name of the place of issue, Hagerstown, are in manuscript.

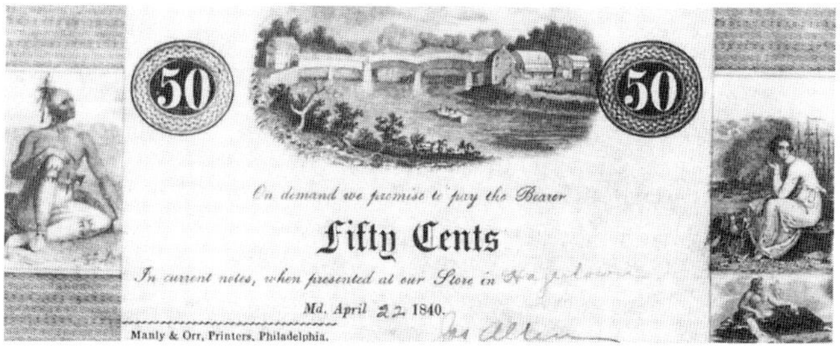

60.2.4

60.3. The Farmers & Millers Bank of Hagerstown

Charter approved March 31, 1836. Closed in 1843.

60.3.1 R-3

$1.00 Ca. 1836–43. Engraving, imprint: Underwood, Bald, Spencer & Hufty, Philada. / Danforth, Underwood & Co. New York. (MD235G2)

60.3.1 P R-7

$1.00 Ca. 1836–43. Engraving, imprint: Underwood, Bald, Spencer & Hufty, Philada. / Danforth, Underwood & Co. New York. Proof.

60.3.4 R-2

$1.00 Ca. 1836–43. Engraving, imprint: Underwood, Bald, Spencer & Hufty, Philada. / Danforth, Underwood & Co., New York. (MD235G4)

60.3.1

60.3.4

60.3.4 P R-7

$1.00 Ca. 1836–43. Engraving, imprint: Underwood, Bald, Spencer & Hufty, Philada. / Danforth, Underwood & Co., New York. Proof.

60.3.5 C SENC

$1.00 Sibbett's "WESTERN REVIEW AND COUNTERFEIT DETECTOR" of 1845 reports a badly executed counterfeit note. No other information available.

60.3.6 R-3

$2.00 Ca. 1840s. Engraving, imprint: Danforth, Spencer & Hufty, New York / Spencer, Hufty & Danforth, Philada. (MD235G8)

60.3.6 P R-7

$2.00 Ca. 1836–43. Engraving, imprint: Danforth, Spencer & Hufty, New York / Spencer, Hufty & Danforth, Philada. Proof.

60.3.8 R-5

$3.00 Ca. 1840s. Engraving, imprint: Danforth, Spencer & Hufty, New York / Spencer, Hufty & Danforth, Philada. (MD235G12)

60.3.4 P

60.3.6

60.3.6 P

60.3.8

60.3.8 P R-7

$3.00 Ca. 1840s. Engraving, imprint: Danforth, Spencer & Hufty, New York / Spencer, Hufty & Danforth, Philada. Proof.

60.3.10 R-6

$5.00 Ca. 1830s–40s. Engraving, imprint: Underwood, Bald, Spencer & Hufty, Philada / Danforth, Underwood & Co., New York. (MD235G14)

60.3.10 P R-7

$5.00 Ca. 1830s–40s. Engraving, imprint: Underwood, Bald, Spencer & Hufty, Philada / Danforth, Underwood & Co., New York. Proof.

60.3.12 R-6

$5.00 Ca. 1830s–40s. Engraving, imprint: Underwood, Bald, Spencer & Hufty, Philada. / Danforth, Underwood & Co., New York. (MD235G16)

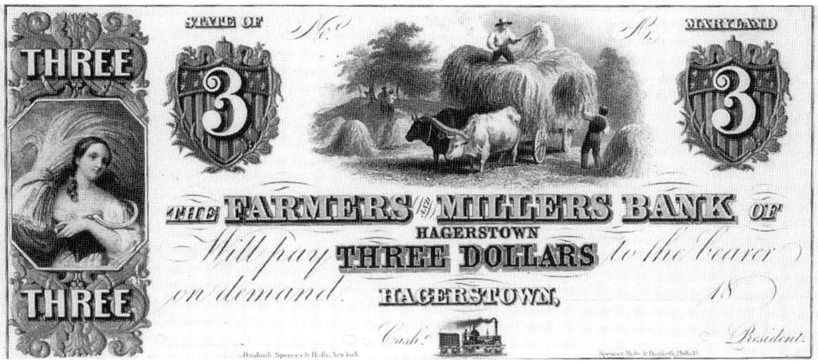

60.3.8 P

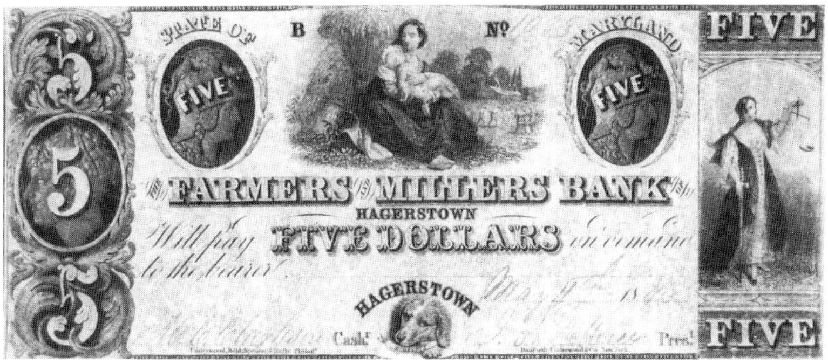

60.3.10

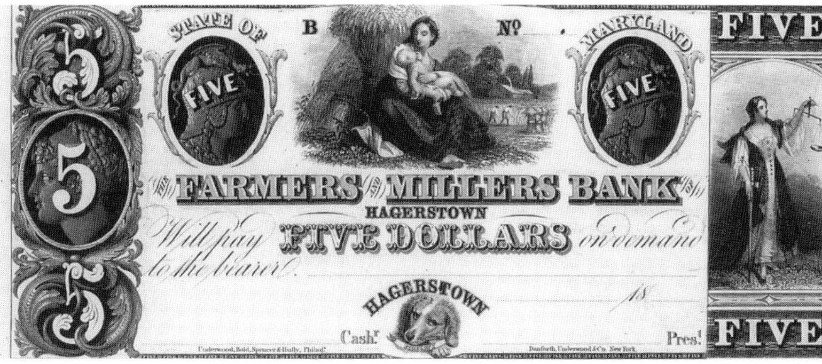

60.3.10 P

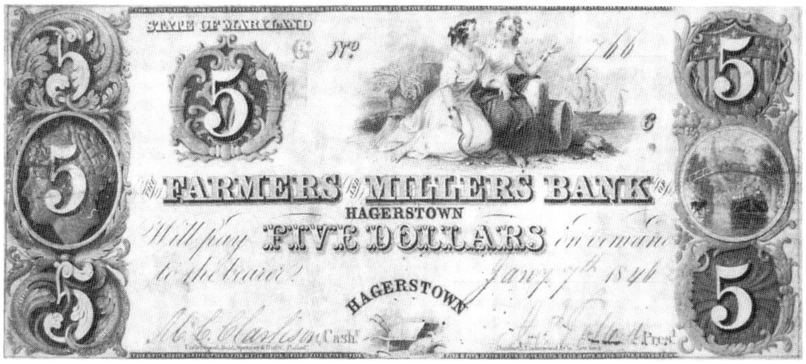

60.3.12

60.3.12 P R-7

$5.00 Ca. 1830s–40s. Engraving, imprint: Underwood, Bald, Spencer & Hufty, Philada. / Danforth, Underwood & Co., New York. Proof.

60.3.14 P R-7

$10.00 Ca. 1830s. Engraving, imprint: Underwood, Bald, Spencer & Hufty, Philada. / Danforth, Underwood & Co., New York. Proof. (MD235G18)

60.3.16 P R-7

$10.00 Ca. 1830s–40s. Engraving, imprint: Underwood, Bald, Spencer & Hufty, Philada. / Danforth, Underwood & Co., New York. Proof. (MD235G20)

60.3.18 P R-7

$20.00 Ca. 1830s–40s. Engraving, imprint: Underwood, Bald, Spencer & Hufty, Philada / Danforth, Underwood & Co., New York. Proof.

60.3.20 P R-7

$50.00 Ca. 1830s–40s. Engraving, imprint: Underwood, Bald, Spencer & Hufty, Philada / Danforth, Underwood & Co., New York. Proof.

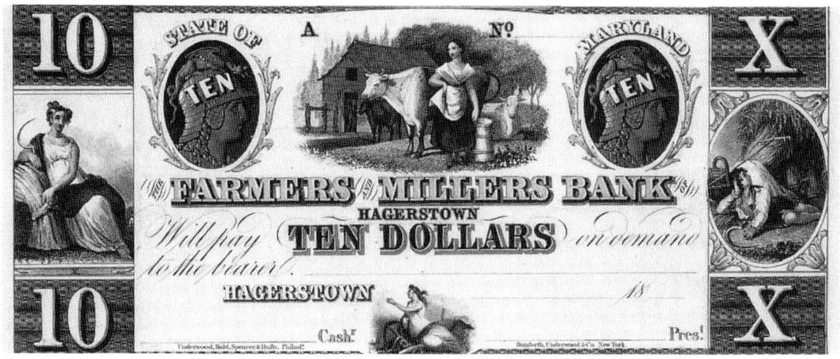

60.3.14 P

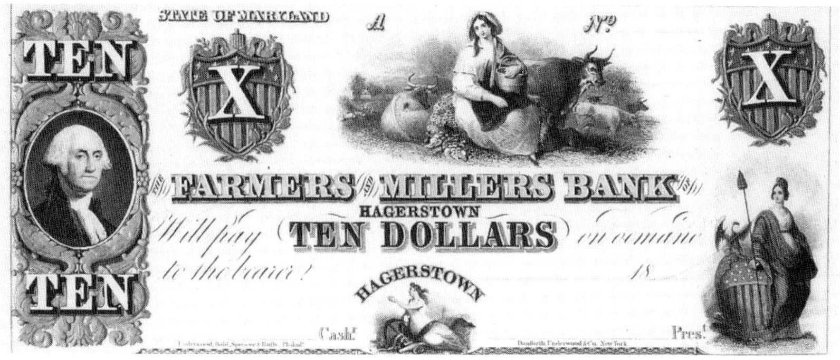

60.3.16 P

60.3.18 P

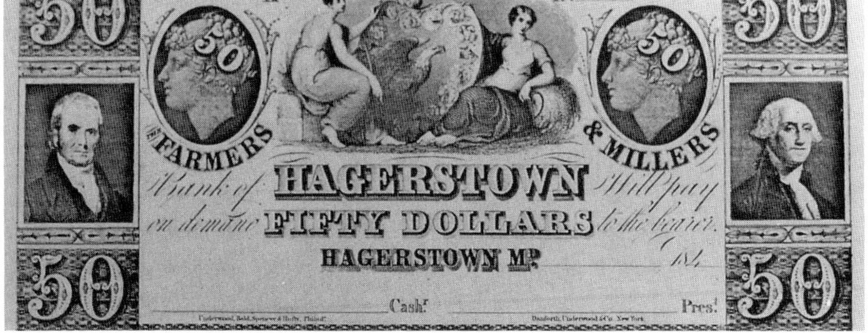

60.3.20 P

60.3.22 P   R-7

$100.00 Ca. 1830s–40s. Engraving, imprint: Underwood, Bald, Spencer & Hufty, Philada / Danforth, Underwood & Co., New York. Proof.

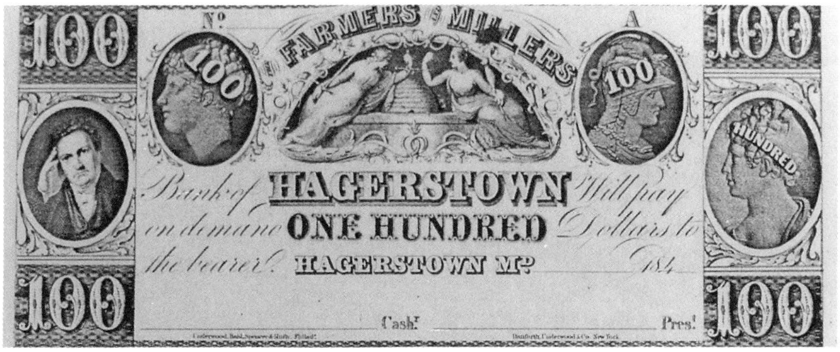

60.3.22 P

60.4 Franklin House

Small-change scrip issued by the Franklin House, a hotel located at the railroad depot.

60.4.2   R-7

12 1/2c Ca. 1840s. Engraving, imprint: Manly & Orr, Printers, Philadelphia.

60.4.2

60.5 The Franklin Rail Road Company

Incorporated under a special act of the legislature of Pennsylvania, March 12, 1832, and granted certain franchises and privileges under a special act of the legislature of Maryland, May 4, 1836, the railroad opened for operation between Hagerstown and Chambersburg, Pa. (22 miles), on February 3, 1841. Burdened with debt, the railroad was sold at auction in 1849 for $600, and was operated for a period as a horse tramway, using wooden rails with iron straps. Ultimately, it was sold again for $600 in 1855 to the Chambersburg, Greencastle & Franklin R.R. Co.

60.5.1   R-2

50c Printed partial year date 184_. Engraving, no imprint (probably by Manly & Orr, Philadelphia). Minor differences in the spacing of the central design and inscription have been found, resulting in greater distances between the value dies and the top and side frame lines and the proximity of the words HAGERSTOWN BANK and the side frame lines.

60.5.1

60.5.2 R-2

50c Printed partial year date 184_. Engraving, no imprint. Similar minor differences appear as on 50c, No. 60.5.1.

60.5.4 R-2

$1.00 Printed partial year date 184_. Engraving, no imprint. Similar minor differences appear as on 50c, No. 60.5.1.

60.5.6 R-2

$1.00 Printed partial year date 184_. Engraving, no imprint. Similar minor differences appear as on 50c, No. 60.5.1.

60.5.8 R-4

$5.00 Printed year date 184_. Engraving, imprint: Underwood, Bald, Spencer, & Hufty, Philada. / Danforth, Underwood & Co., New York.

60.5.8 P R-7

$5.00 Printed year date 1841. Engraving, imprint: Underwood, Bald, Spencer & Hufty, Philada. / Danforth, Underwood & Co., New York. Proof.

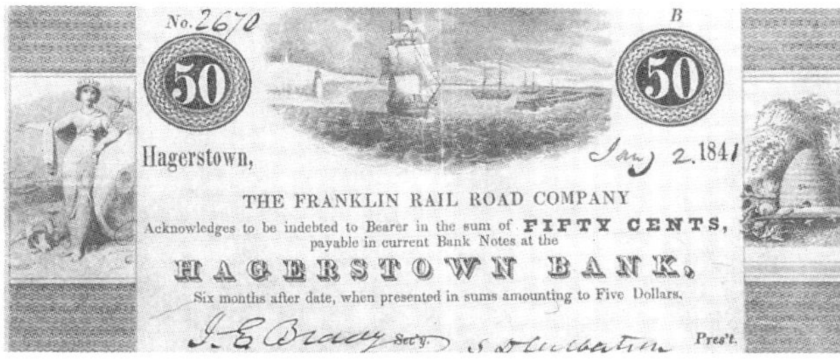

60.5.2

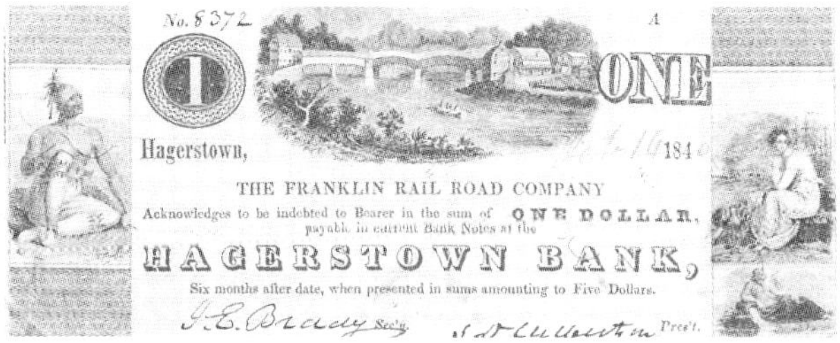

60.5.4

60.5.6

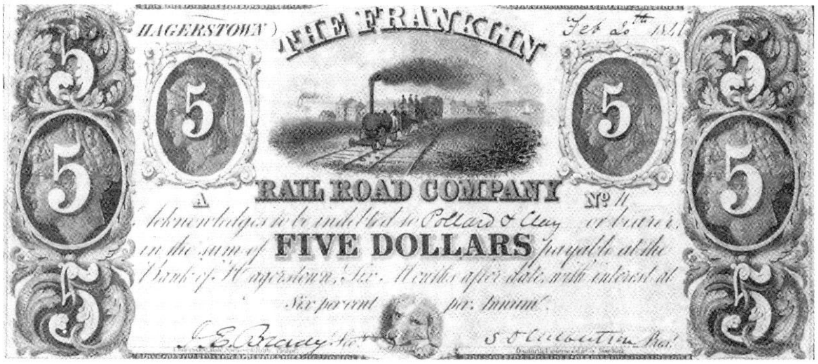

60.5.8

60.5.12 R-7

Probably a salesman's sample sheet showing design essays, none of which were used for notes ultimately placed in circulation. The manuscript wording inserted on the first note is that which was used on circulated notes. Ca. 1840. Engraving, no imprint. Probably printed by Manly & Orr, Philadelphia.

60.5.12

60.6 Robert P. Gustin

Scrip issued by Robert P. Gustin, a merchant in nearby Berkley Springs, Virginia (now West Virginia), was payable at the Bank of Hagerstown.

60.6.3 R-7

25c Printed date July 4, 1837. Letterpress, imprint: Murphy & Spalding, printers, 1 Light St., Baltimore. (Va.#PB2004)

60.6.5 R-7

$1.00 Printed date July 4, 1837. Letterpress, imprint: Murphy & Spalding, printers, 1 Light St., Baltimore. (Va.#PB20-08)

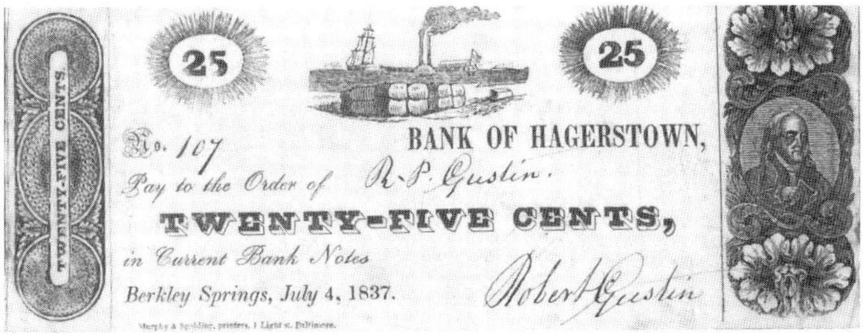

60.6.3

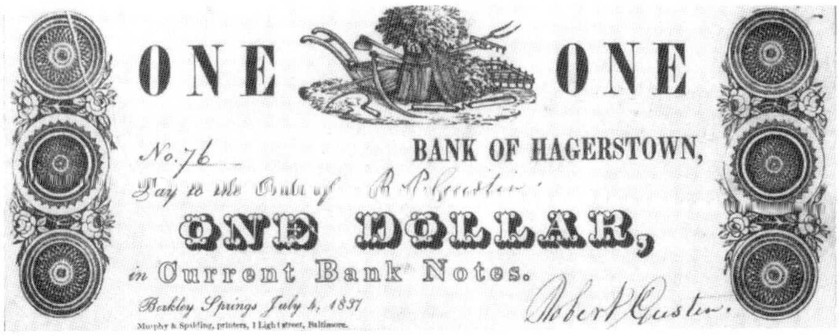

60.6.5

60.7 The Hagerstown Bank

Operated as an unchartered association until 1808. Charter approved January 15, 1808; merged with the Hagerstown Bank & Trust Co. in 1928. The bank published a historical booklet in 1910, "History of the Hagerstown Bank" which, on page 55, contains the following interesting sentence: "In common with other banks of the day, the Hagerstown Bank sought to supplement the scarcity of change by issuing notes and, in June 1814, printed two thousand notes of the denominations of fifty cents and six and one-quarter cents, the latter being the value of the Spanish half real and known as the fip or fipenny." The authors have not seen examples of these fractional notes.

60.7.1 SENC

6 1/4c Printed date June 1814. Reported by the bank as having been issued. Design and format unknown, surviving examples not confirmed.

60.7.3 R-7

25c Printed date November 16, 1815. Letterpress, no imprint.

60.7.4 SENC

50c Printed date June 1814. Reported by the bank as having been issued. Design and format unknown, surviving examples not confirmed.

60.7.5 SENC

$1.00 Ca. before 1808. Association issue. No information available. (MD240G2)

60.7.7 SENC

$1.00 Ca. 1808–10s. No information available. (MD240G20)

60.7.7 C SENC

$1.00 Ca. 1808–10s. Engraving, no imprint. Assumed to be a counterfeit of No. 60.7.7, for which no information is available.

60.7.8 A SENC

$1.00 Ca. 1840s. Engraving, imprint: Underwood, Bald, Spencer & Hufty; Danforth, Underwood. *Center:* 1; Justice facing left and Liberty facing right, both seated and resting arms on shield surmounted by large eagle; 1. *Left:* 1 / medallion head / 1, all on scrollwork. *Right:* 1 / 3/4-length figure of woman with rake and grain, in square / 1. *Between signatures:* Hay wagon. Altered from $1.00 Farmers & Millers Bank of Hagerstown, No. 60.3.1. (MD240A5)

60.7.9 S R-6

$1.00 Ca. 1843. Partially printed date 181_ with "4" written over "1." Engraving, imprint: Murray, Draper, Fairman & Co. Spurious. (MD240S5)

60.7.3

60.7.9 S

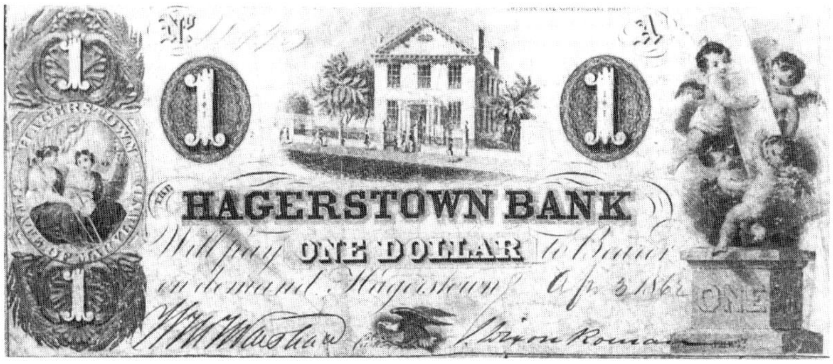

60.7.11

60.7.14 C

60.7.10 SENC

$1.00 Ca. 1856–61. Engraving, imprint: Toppan, Carpenter & Co. Same as No. 60.7.11, except for imprint. (MD240G26)

60.7.11 R-7

$1.00 Ca. 1862. Engraving, imprint: American Bank Note Company, Phila. (MD240G26b)

60.7.12 SENC

$2.00 Ca. Before 1808. Association issue. No information available. (MD240G4)

60.7.14 SENC

$2.00 Ca. 1808–10s. Engraving, imprint: Unknown. Similar to counterfeit, No. 60.7.14 C. (MD240G28)

60.7.14 C R-6

$2.00 Ca. 1810s. Engraving, no imprint. Counterfeit of No. 60.7.14. (MD240C28)

60.7.16 S R-7

$3.00 Ca. 1840s. Engraving, imprint: Murray, Draper, Fairman. Spurious. (MD240S10)

60.7.18 SENC

$5.00 Ca. before 1808. Association issue. No information available. (MD240G8)

60.7.19 SENC

$5.00 Ca. 1808–10s. No information available. (MD240G36)

60.7.20 SENC

$5.00 Ca. 1810s. Engraving, imprint: Murray, Draper, Fairman. Probably similar to $10.00, No. 60.7.29. (MD240G30)

60.7.21 SENC

$5.00 Ca. 1810s–30s. Engraving, imprint: Murray, Draper, Fairman. Same as No. 60.7.20, except printed on pink paper. (MD240G38a)

60.7.22 SENC

$5.00 Ca. late 1836–50s. Engraving, imprint: Danforth, Underwood & Co. N.Y.; Underwood, Bald, Spencer & Hufty, Philada. Same as No. 60.7.25, except without tint and monogram. (MD240G40)

60.7.22 P R-7

$5.00 Ca. late 1836–50s. Engraving, imprint: Danforth, Underwood & Co., N.Y.; Underwood, Bald, Spencer & Hufty, Philada. Same as No. 60.7.25, except without tint and monogram. Proof.

60.7.23 S R-6

$5.00 Ca. 1840s. Engraving, imprint: Murry, Draper, Fairman & Co. Spurious. (MD240S15)

60.7.16 S

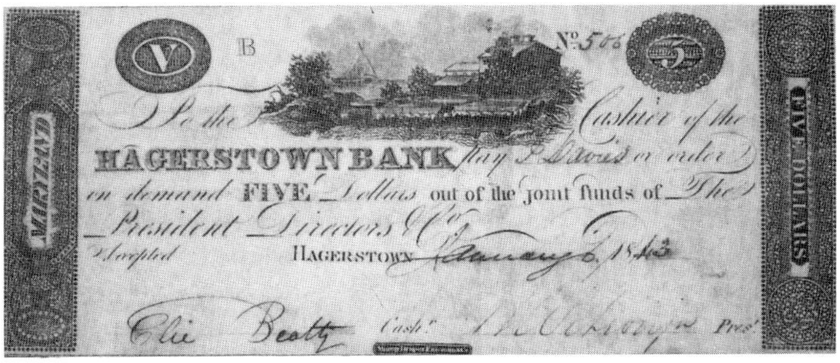

60.7.23 S

60.7.25

60.7.24 A SENC

$5.00 Ca. 1840s. Engraving, imprint: Underwood, Bald, Spencer & Hufty, Philada.; Danforth, Underwood, N.Y. *Center:* 5; Ceres and Commerce reclining on shore, with sheaf, bale and barrel, Commerce pointing to ship in right background. *Left:* 5 / medallion head bearing 5/5, all on scrollwork. *Right:* 5 on U.S. shield / canal scene, in circle / 5, all on scrollwork. *Between signatures:* Wheelbarrow, etc. Altered from $5.00 Farmers & Millers Bank of Hagerstown, No. 60.3.12. (MD240A10)

60.7.25 R-1

$5.00 Ca. 1850s–60s. Engraving, imprint: Underwood, Bald, Spencer & Hufty, Philada. / Danforth, Underwood & Co., New York. ABCo monogram. Large remainders of these notes, unsevered sheets being not uncommon, came to light in the 1930s when the bank moved to new quarters. Imitation sheets of two each of the $5.00 and $10.00 denominations were privately printed in color by photolithography in the 1970s, often being offered as "reprints." Black and red. (MD240G40b)

60.7.25 P R-7

$5.00 Ca. 1850s–60s. Engraving, imprint: Danforth, Underwood & Co., New York / Underwood, Bald, Spencer & Hufty, Philada. Similar to $5.00, No. 60.7.25, but without red security print and with "5" on a medallion head on each end panel. Proof, probably of a rejected design.

60.7.25 P

60.7.26 SENC

$10.00 Ca. before 1808. Association issue. No information available. (MD240G10)

60.7.27 SENC

$10.00 Ca. 1808–10s. No information available. (MD240G42)

60.7.29 SENC

$10.00 Ca. 1810s. Engraving, imprint: Murray, Draper, Fairman. Printed on white paper. Similar to counterfeit No. 60.7.31 C. (MD240G44)

60.7.31 C

60.7.30 SENC

$10.00 Ca. 1810s–30s. Engraving, imprint: Murray, Draper, Fairman & co. Same as No. 60.7.29, except printed on pink paper. (MD240G44a)

60.7.31 C R-7

$10.00 Ca. 1830s. Engraving, imprint: Murray, Draper, Fairman & Co. Counterfeit of No. 60.7.29. (MD240C44)

60.7.32 R-7

$10.00 Ca. 1830s–50s. Engraving, imprint: Danforth, Underwood & Co., Philada / Underwood, Bald, Spencer & Hufty, N.Y. Same as No. 60.7.33, except without tint and monogram. (MD240G46)

60.7.33 R-1

$10.00 Ca. 1850s–60s. Engraving, imprint: Underwood, Bald, Spencer & Hufty, Philada. / Danforth, Underwood & Co., New York. ABCo monogram. Black and red. Large remainders of these notes, unsevered sheets being not uncommon, came to light in the 1930s when the bank moved to new quarters. Imitation sheets of two each of the $5.00 and $10.00 denominations were privately printed in color by photolithography in the 1970s, often being offered as "reprints." (MD240G46b)

60.7.34 R SENC

$10.00 Ca. 1856–61. Engraving, imprint: Toppan, Carpenter & Co. Raised from $1.00, No. 60.7.11. (MD240R5)

60.7.35 SENC

$20.00 Ca. before 1808. Association issue. No information available. (MD240G12)

60.7.36 SENC

$20.00 Ca. 1808–10s. No information available. (MD240G48)

60.7.37 SENC

$20.00 Ca. 1810s. Engraving, imprint: Murray, Draper, Fairman. Printed on white paper. (MD240G50)

60.7.38 SENC

$20.00 Ca. 1810s–30s. Engraving, imprint: Murray, Draper, Fairman. Same as No. 60.7.37 except printed on pink paper. (MD240G50a)

60.7.39 R-1

$20.00 Ca. 1842–63. Engraving, imprint: Underwood, Bald, Spencer & Hufty, Philada. / Danforth, Underwood & Co., New York. (MD240G52)

60.7.39 P R-7

$20.00 Ca. 1842–63. Engraving, imprint: Underwood, Bald, Spencer & Hufty, Philada. / Danforth, Underwood & Co., New York. Proof.

60.7.40 SENC

$50.00 Ca. 1808–10s. No information available. (MD240G54)

60.7.41 SENC

$50.00 Ca. 1810s. Engraving, imprint: Murray, Draper, Fairman. Printed on white paper. (MD240G56)

60.7.42 SENC

$50.00 Ca. 1810s–30s. Engraving, imprint: Murray, Draper, Fairman. Same as No. 60.7.41, except printed on pink paper. (MD240G56a)

60.7.42 C SENC

$50.00 Ca. 1830s. Engraving, imprint: Murray, Draper, Fairman. Counterfeit of No. 60.7.42. (MD240C56)

60.7.44 R-1

$50.00 Ca. 1836–50s. Engraving, imprint: Underwood, Bald, Spencer & Hufty Philada. / Danforth, Underwood & Co., New York. (MD240G58)

60.7.44 P R-7

$50.00 Ca. 1836–50s. Engraving, imprint: Underwood, Bald, Spencer & Hufty, Philada. / Danforth, Underwood & Co., New York. Proof.

60.7.45 SENC

$100.00 Ca. 1810s. Engraving, imprint: Murray, Draper, Fairman. Printed on white paper. (MD240G62)

60.7.46 SENC

$100.00 Ca. 1810s–30s. Engraving, imprint: Murray, Draper, Fairman. Same as No. 60.7.45, except printed on pink paper. (MD240G62a)

60.7.47 R-1

$100.00 Ca. 1836–50s. Engraving, imprint: Underwood, Bald, Spencer & Hufty, Philada. / Danforth, Underwood & Co., New York. (MD240G64)

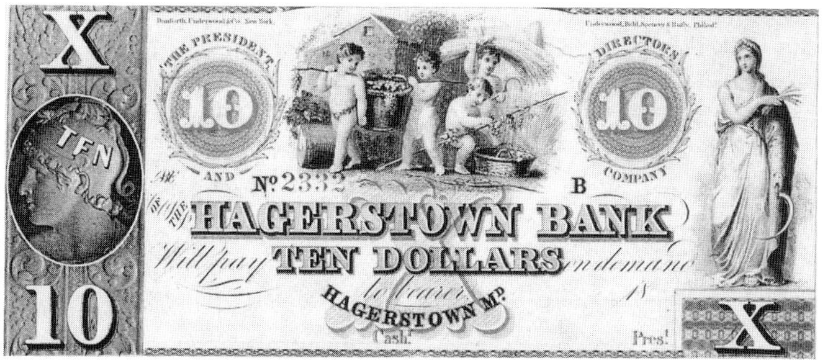

60.7.33

60.7.39

60.7.44

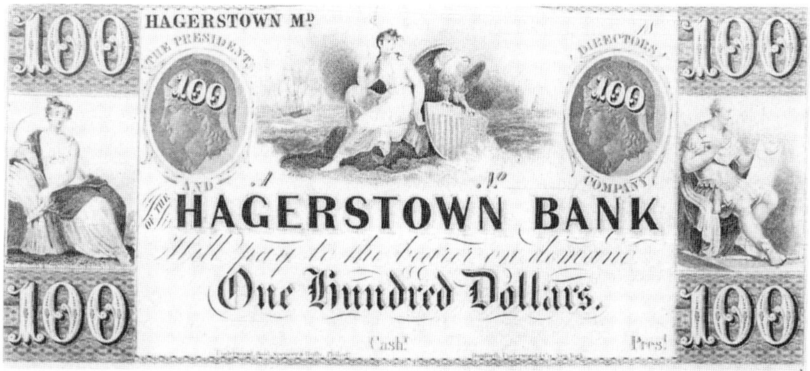

60.7.47

60.8 Hagerstown Savings Bank

Charter amendment approved March 8, 1854, changing name from Hagerstown Savings Institution (1847); converted to and became the First National Bank of Hagerstown in 1865; receivership in 1931.

60.8.1 R-7
$1.00 Ca. 1856–60s. *Center:* Boy under tree, child lying down, cows, sheep, etc. 1 each side. ONE DOLLAR on ONE below. *Right:* Girl seated with flowers and fruit at her feet, 1 above. *Left:* Two children, ONE on 1 above.

60.8.2 R-7
$2.00 May 24, 1861. Engraving, imprint: American Bank Note Co. Security overprint, negative TWO on red engine-turned rectangle with chamfered corners.

60.8.3 R-7
$5.00 Ca. 1856–60s. Engraving, imprint: Danforth, Wright & Co., Philada. & New York. Large V overprint in red.

60.8.3 P R-7
$5.00 Ca. 1856–60s. Engraving, imprint: Danforth, Wright & Co., Philada. & New York. Large V overprint in red. Proof.

60.8.4 R-7
$10.00 Ca. 1856–60s. Engraving, imprint: Danforth, Wright & Co., Philada. & New York. TEN overprint in red.

60.8.4 P R-7
$10.00 Ca. 1856–60s. Engraving, imprint: Danforth, Wright & Co., Philada. & New York. TEN overprint in fancy red letters. Proof.

60.8.5 R-7
$20.00 Ca. 1856–60s. Engraving, imprint: Danforth, Wright & Co., Philada. & New York. Large XX overprint in red.

60.8.5 P R-7
$20.00 Ca. 1856–60s. Engraving, imprint: Danforth, Wright & Co., Philada. & New York. Large XX overprint in fancy red letters. Proof.

60.8.2

60.8.3 P

60.8.4 P

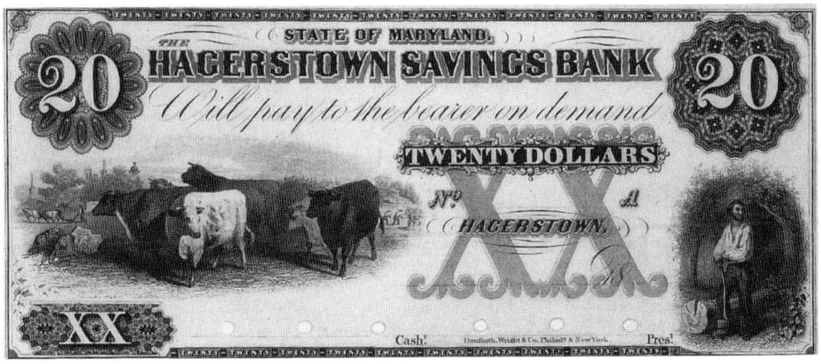

60.8.5 P

60.9 Jno. Smalkin

The name of the signer, Jno. Smalkin, does not appear in census or any other records available to the authors.

60.9.4 R-7

50c Ca. 1838. Lithograph, imprint: Sold by E. P. Whaites 1 1/2 Courtland St. & J. L. Whaites, 549 B.Way. At the SW corner of the huntress figure there appears "Wright. Lith." This note was a "stock note" of the kind sold by stationers for use by those who did not have their own notes printed.

60.9.4

60.10 The Valley Bank of Maryland

Charter approved March 10, 1848; receivership in 1856.

60.10.1 R-1

$5.00 Ca. 1855–56. Engraving, imprint: Rawdon, Wright, Hatch & Edson, New York. Denomination spelled out in large fancy letters at lower center. (MD245G6)

60.10.2 R-1

$5.00 Ca. 1855–56. Engraving, imprint: Rawdon, Wright, Hatch & Edson, New York. Similar to No. 60.10.1, with additional security overprint FIVE in large, red, engine-turned serifed letters. (MD245G6a)

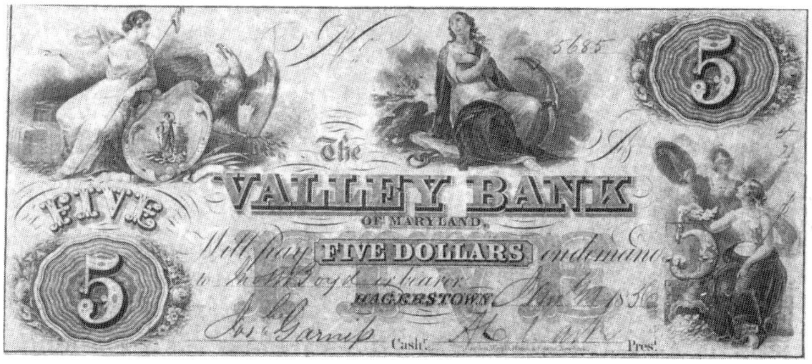

60.10.1

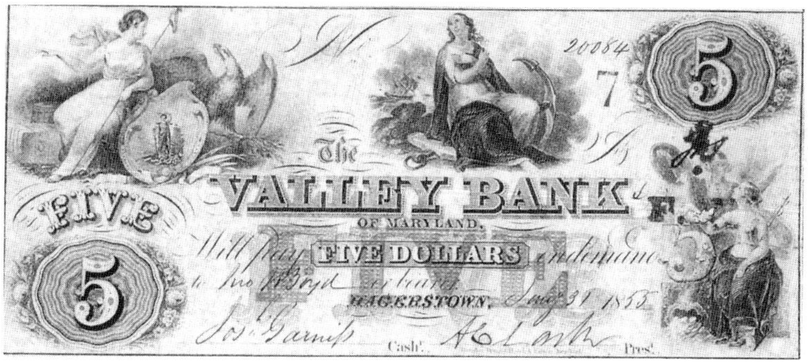

60.10.2

60.10.3 R-1

$10.00 Ca. 1855–56. Engraving, imprint: Rawdon, Wright, Hatch & Edson, New York. Denomination spelled out in large fancy letters at lower center. (MD245G8)

60.10.4 R-1

$10.00 Ca. 1855–56. Engraving, imprint: Rawdon, Wright, Hatch & Edson, New York. Similar to No. 60.10.3 with additional security overprint TEN in large, red, engine-turned block letters. (MD245G8a)

60.10.5 R-1

$20.00 Ca. 1855–56. Engraving, imprint: Rawdon, Wright, Hatch & Edson, New York. Denomination spelled out in large fancy letters at lower center. (MD245G10)

60.10.6 R-1

$20.00 Ca. 1855–56. Engraving, imprint: Rawdon, Wright, Hatch & Edson, New York. Similar to No. 60.10.5, with additional security overprint TWENTY in large, red, engine-turned block letters. (MD245G10a)

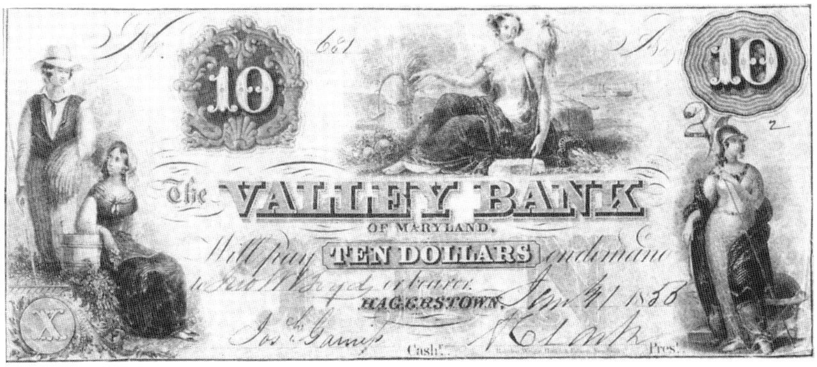

60.10.3

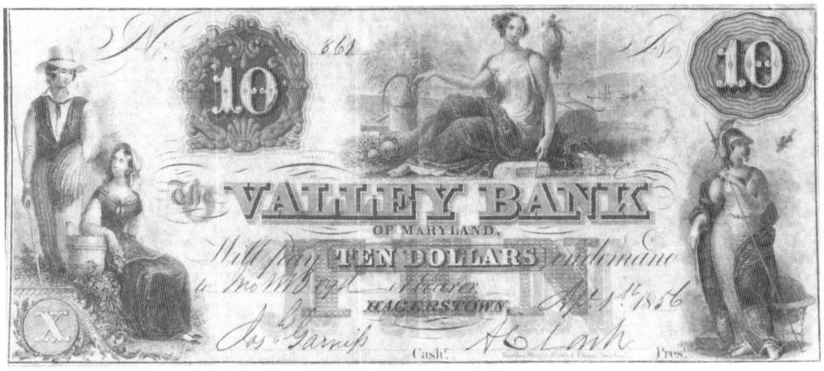

60.10.4

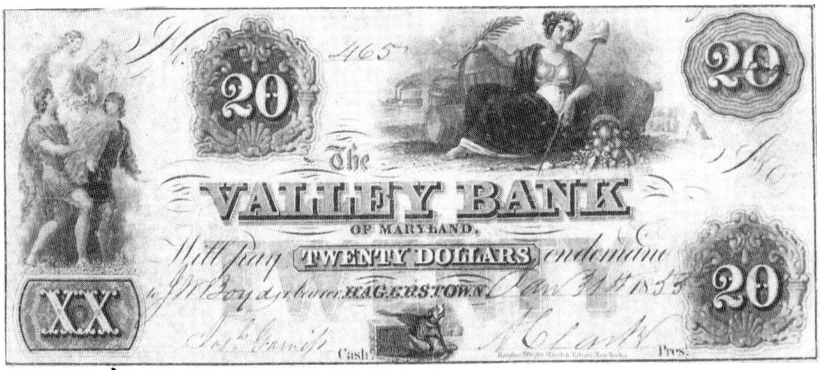

60.10.5

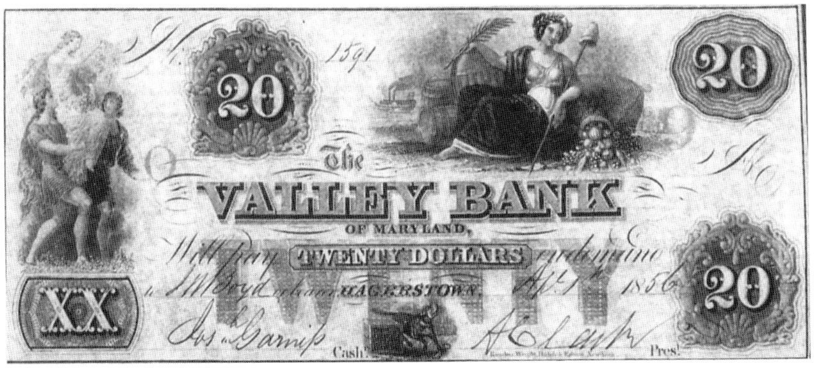

60.10.6

60.11 Washington County Savings Institution

Charter approved March 2, 1837; details of operation not discovered.

60.11.1 R-7

6 1/4c Printed date Oct. 1, 1837. Letterpress, imprint: Robinson, PRINTER, Baltimore.

60.11.3 R-7

12 1/2c Printed partial date July __ 1837. Letterpress, no imprint.

60.11.4 R-7

12 1/2c Printed date Aug. 5, 1837. Letterpress, imprint: Robinson, PRINTER, Baltimore. Similar to 25c, No. 60.11.6.

60.11.5 R-7

25c Printed partial date July __ 1837. Letterpress, no imprint.

60.11.6 R-7

25c Printed date Nov. 1, 1837. Letterpress, imprint: Robinson, PRINTER Baltimore. Similar to 25c, No. 60.11.7.

60.11.7 R-7

25c Printed date June 26, 1840. Letterpress, imprint: Robinson, PRINTER, Baltimore.

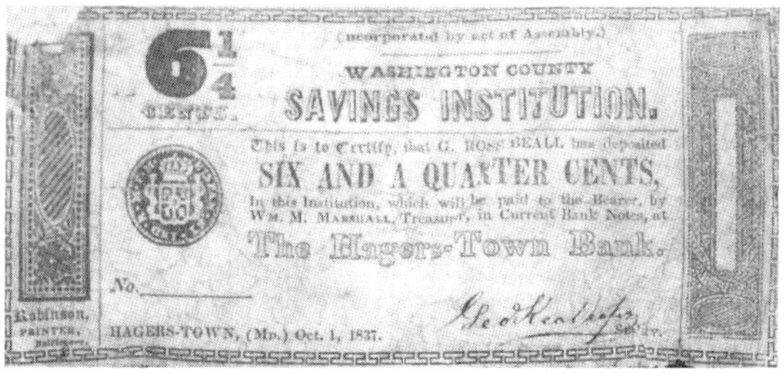

60.11.1

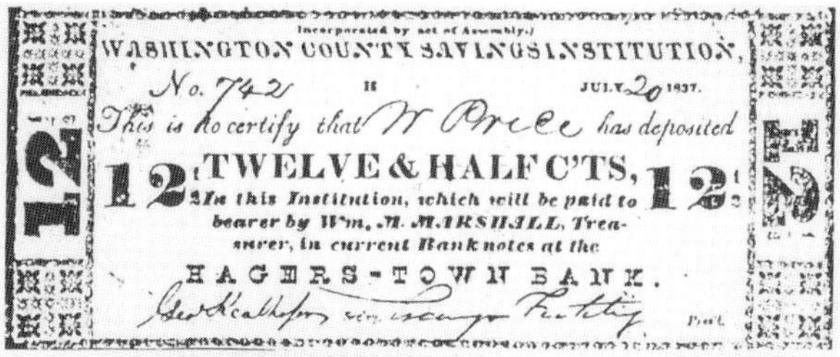

60.11.3

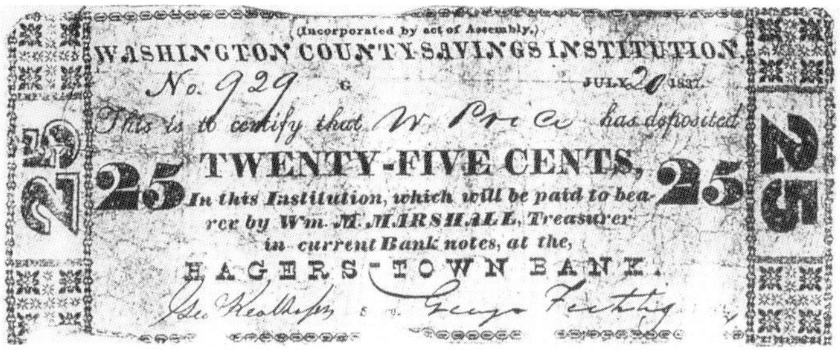

60.11.5

60.11.7

60.11.8 R-7

50c Printed date Aug. 5, 1837. Letterpress, imprint: Robinson, PRINTER, Baltimore.

60.11.9 R-7

$1.00 Printed date July , 1837. Letterpress, no imprint.

60.11.11 R-7

$2.00 Ca. 1837. Letterpress, imprint: Robinson, print., Baltimore. Similar to counterfeit No. 60.11.11 C.

60.11.11 C R-7

$2.00 Ca. 1837. Letterpress, imprint: Robinson, print., Baltimore. (Baltimore and Hagerstown newspapers on June 20, 1840, printed a warning against counterfeit $2.00 notes of this institution.) Counterfeit of No. 60.11.11.

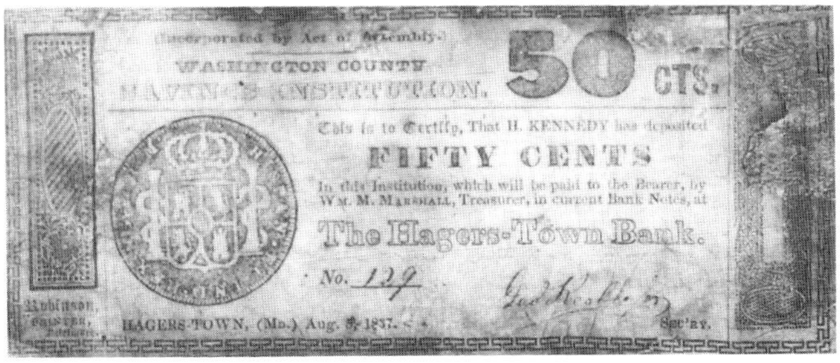

60.11.8

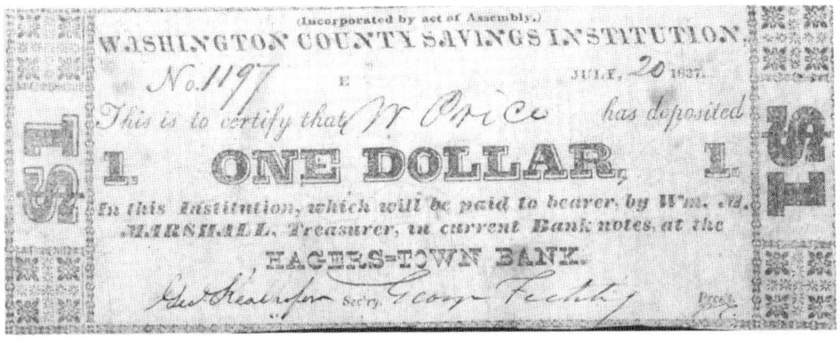

60.11.9

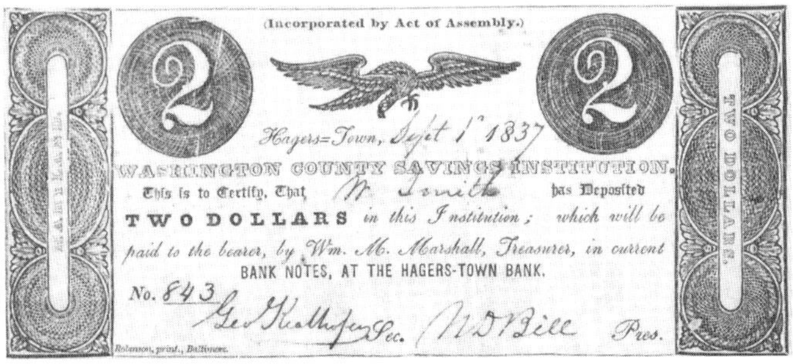

60.11.11 C

62 HANCOCK, WASHINGTON COUNTY

Joseph Hancock, who evidently was in possession of a Crown Grant, settled in the area in 1749 and while the records are vague, it is generally assumed that the town was named for him. The first settlers in the area came in 1732. The town was incorporated in 1853. A post office opened here in 1794.

62.1 Allison Gregory & Co.

The issuers were the proprietors of a general store.

62.1.4 R-7

$1.00 Ca. 1857. A photocopy of the only recorded note seen by the authors is too poor to reproduce acceptably for illustration. The printed portions of the note read "At sight ____ Promise to pay the Bearer One Dollar in Goods at Cash prices." In manuscript were inserted the serial number "q" and "Hancock May 23, 1857"; "at Our Store" and "Allison Gregory & Co."

62.2 C. Robert Taylor

The issuer, C. Robert Taylor, was a merchant in Hancock and appears in the 1840 federal census index.

62.2.4 R-7

50c Partial printed date August __ 1837. Letterpress, no imprint. Reads "On demand, I promise to pay R. Wason or bearer FIFTY CENTS AT MY STORE IN CURRENT BANK NOTES."

62.2.4

63 HAVRE DE GRACE, HARFORD COUNTY

The town was laid out in 1658 for Godfrey Harmer and was called Harmer's Town. In 1659 the property was assigned to Thomas Stockett and renamed Stockett's Town. After 1700, the town became Susquehanna Lower Ferry for the ferry crossing the Susquehanna River.

When the town was incorporated in 1795, the name was Havre de Grace ("Harbour of Grace") inspired by Le Havre, France, whose earlier name commemorated a chapel dedicated to Notre-Dame de Grace.

The reason for the name of the Harford County town appears to be that General Lafayette, when he crossed the Susquehanna at the Lower Ferry in 1782, exclaimed about the resemblance of the place to Le Havre, France. A post office opened here in 1789.

63.1 Lewis Bryant & Co

The issuers were the proprietors of a general store.

63.1.4 R-7

50c Printed partial date May __ 1841. Engraving, imprint: Manly & Orr, Printers, Philadelphia.

63.1.4

63.2 Chesapeake Hotel

Scrip issued by the hotel to facilitate making change when specie was in short supply. These notes can be found bearing the signatures of J. M. Seymour and Wm. Smithers.

63.2.1 R-7

6 1/4c Printed partial date April 1840. Engraving (vignettes and ends) with the inscriptions and denominations printed by letterpress, imprint: Manly & Orr, Printers, Philad.

63.2.2 R-7

12 1/2c Printed partial date April __ 1840. Engraving (vignettes and ends) with the inscriptions and denominations printed by letterpress, imprint: Manly & Orr, Printers, Philad.

63.2.3 R-7

25c Printed partial date April __ 1840. Engraving (vignettes and ends) with the inscriptions and denominations printed by letterpress, imprint: Manly & Orr, Printers, Philad.

63.2.4 R-7

25c Printed partial date June __ 1840. Similar to 25c, No. 63.2.3, except for date.

63.2.1 63.2.2 63.2.3

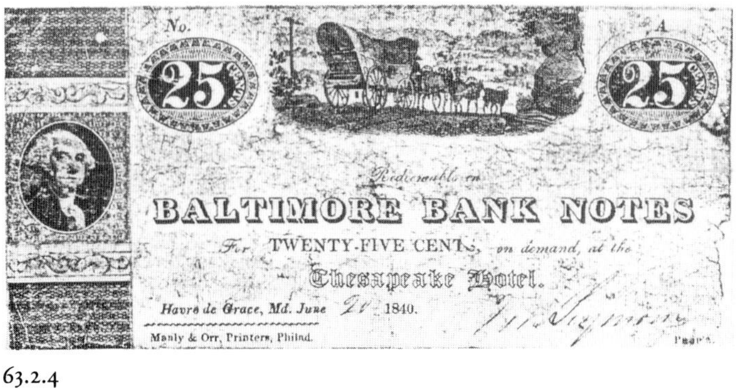

63.2.4

63.3 Dutton & Sullivan

The *Baltimore Sun* of July 11, 1837, contained a humorous report of the refusal of a Baltimore barkeep to accept a "shinplaster" proferred in payment for a bar bill, which included a typeset sketch of the note. The denomination was 50c, the note was dated June 1st, 1837, its serial number was 212, and it bore the signature "Dutton & Sullivan." While there is no proof that an original note of this general appearance was shown to the editor, it seems not unlikely that a genuine note of this type was in circulation. (See Sullivan & Suter, No. 63.9, for notes of a possible successor to this issuer.)

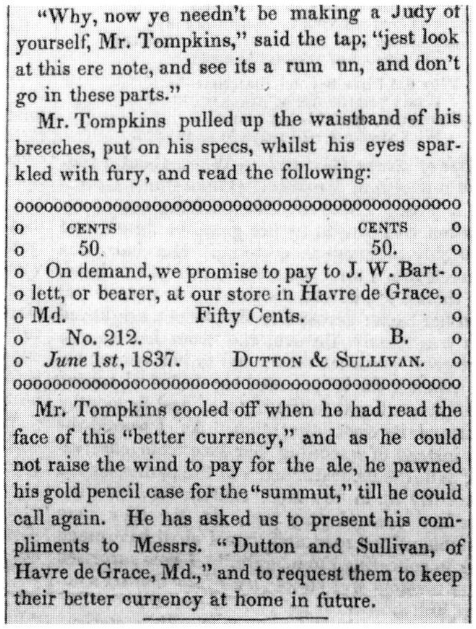

"Why, now ye needn't be making a Judy of yourself, Mr. Tompkins," said the tap; "jest look at this ere note, and see its a rum un, and don't go in these parts."

Mr. Tompkins pulled up the waistband of his breeches, put on his specs, whilst his eyes sparkled with fury, and read the following:

oooooooooooooooooooooooooooooooooooooooooooo
o CENTS CENTS o
o 50. 50. o
o On demand, we promise to pay to J. W. Bart- o
o lett, or bearer, at our store in Havre de Grace, o
o Md. Fifty Cents. o
o No. 212. B. o
o *June 1st*, 1837. Dutton & Sullivan. o
oooooooooooooooooooooooooooooooooooooooooooo

Mr. Tompkins cooled off when he had read the face of this "better currency," and as he could not raise the wind to pay for the ale, he pawned his gold pencil case for the "summut," till he could call again. He has asked us to present his compliments to Messrs. "Dutton and Sullivan, of Havre de Grace, Md.," and to request them to keep their better currency at home in future.

63.4 Havre de Grace Bank

Charter approved January 23, 1815; voluntary liquidation in 1821; reestablished in 1844; failed in August 1850.

63.4.1 R-7

6 1/4c Printed date Sept. 15, 1815. Letterpress, no imprint. Similar to 12 1/2c, No. 63.4.3.

63.4.2 R-7

10c Printed date Sept. 15, 1815. Letterpress, no imprint. Similar to 12 1/2c, No. 63.4.3. (MD250G4)

63.4.3 R-7

12 1/2c Printed date Sept. 15, 1815. Letterpress, no imprint. (MD250G6)

63.4.4 SENC

25c Ca. 1815–17. Engraving, imprint: W. Harrison, fc. Similar to 50c, No. 63.4.5. (MD250G8)

63.4.5 R-7

50c Ca. 1815–17. Engraving, imprint: W. Harrison, fc. (MD250G10)

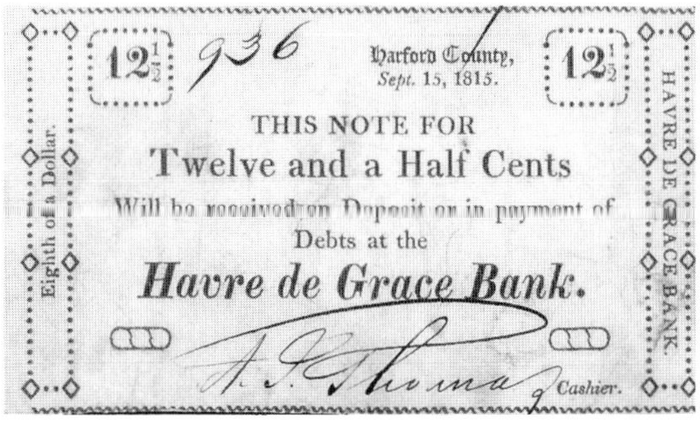

63.4.3

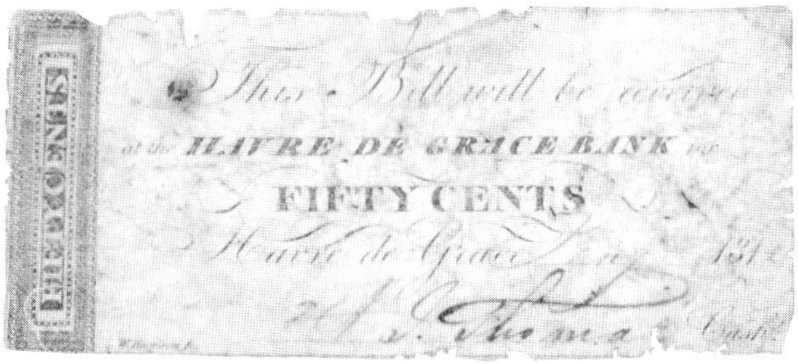

63.4.5

63.4.6 SENC

$1.00 Ca. 1810s. No information available. (MD250G16)

63.4.7 R-7

$1.00 Printed partial year date 181_. Engraving, imprint: Wm. Harrison, Philada. (MD250G14)

63.4.8 R-2

$1.00 Printed date Nov. 18th, 1846. Engraving, imprint: Rawdon, Wright & Hatch, New York. (MD250G30)

63.4.9 SENC

$2.00 Ca. 1810s. Engraving, imprint: W. Harrison. Similar to $1.00, No. 63.4.7. (MD250G18)

63.4.10 R-7

$2.00 Ca. 1815–20. Engraving, no imprint. (MD250G20)

63.4.11 R-2

$2.00 Printed date Nov. 18th, 1846. Engraving, imprint: Rawdon, Wright & Hatch, New York. (MD250G32)

63.4.7

63.4.8

63.4.10

63.4.11

63.4.12 SENC

$3.00 Ca. 1810s. Engraving, imprint: W. Harrison. Similar to $1.00, No. 63.4.7. (MD250G22)

63.4.12 C SENC

$3.00 Ca. 1810s. Engraving, imprint: W. Harrison. Counterfeit of No. 63.4.12. (MD250C22)

63.4.13 SENC

$5.00 Ca. 1810s. Engraving, imprint: W. Harrison. No information available. (MD250G24)

63.4.13 C SENC

$5.00 Ca. 1820s. Engraving, imprint: W. Harrison. Counterfeit of No. 63.4.13. (MD250C24)

63.4.14 R-2

$5.00 Printed date Nov. 18th 1846. Engraving, imprint: Rawdon, Wright & Hatch, New York. (MD250G34)

63.4.15 SENC

$10.00 Ca. 1810s. Engraving, imprint: W. Harrison. No information available. (MD250G26)

63.4.15 C SENC

$10.00 Ca. 1810s. Engraving, imprint: W. Harrison. Counterfeit of No. 63.4.15. (MD250C26)

63.4.16 P R-7

$10.00 Ca. 1810s–10s. Engraving, no imprint. Payable at the Mechanics Bank of Baltimore. Proof.

63.4.17 SENC

$20.00 Ca. 1810s. Engraving, imprint: W. Harrison. No information available. (MD250G27)

63.4.18 P R-7

$20.00 Ca. 1810s. Engraving, no imprint. Payable at the Mechanics Bank of Baltimore. Proof.

63.4.19 SENC

$50.00 Ca. 1810s. Engraving, imprint: W. Harrison. No information available. (MD250G28)

63.4.14

63.4.16 P

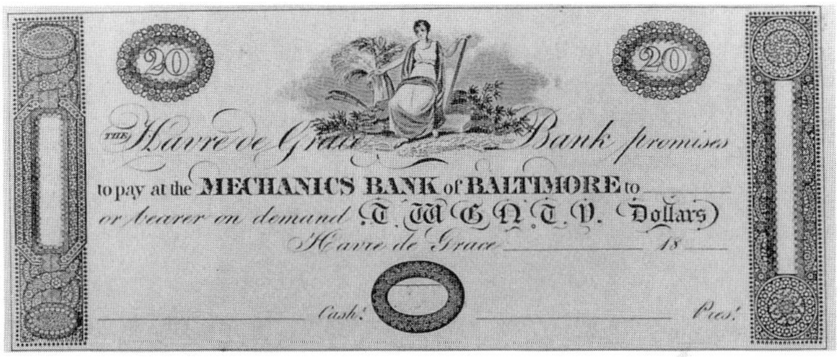

63.4.18 P

63.5 Lyon, Bayard & Co.

Based on genealogical records, it is assumed that the issuers were George Lyon and Samuel Bayard, proprietors of a general store.

Left half of a proof sheet, manuscript notation in left margin, "Lyon, Bayard & Co. OK 1841."

63.5.1 R-7
6 1/4c Printed partial date May __ 1840. Engraving, imprint: Manly & Orr, Printers, Philadelphia.

63.5.2 R-7
10c Printed partial date May __ 1840. Engraving, imprint: Manly & Orr, Printers, Philadelphia.

63.5.4 R-7
25c Printed partial date May __ 1840. Engraving, imprint: Manly & Orr, Printers, Philadelphia.

63.5.5 R-7
50c Printed partial date May __ 1840. Engraving, imprint: Manly & Orr, Printers, Philadelphia.

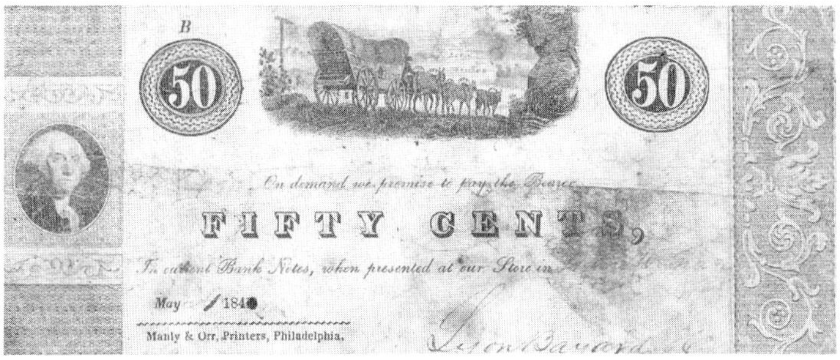

63.5.5

63.6 O'Neal & Brother

The issuers were private bankers and currency brokers.

63.6.1 R-6
$1.00 Printed year date 1840. Engraving, imprint: Draper, Toppan & Co., Phila. & New York.

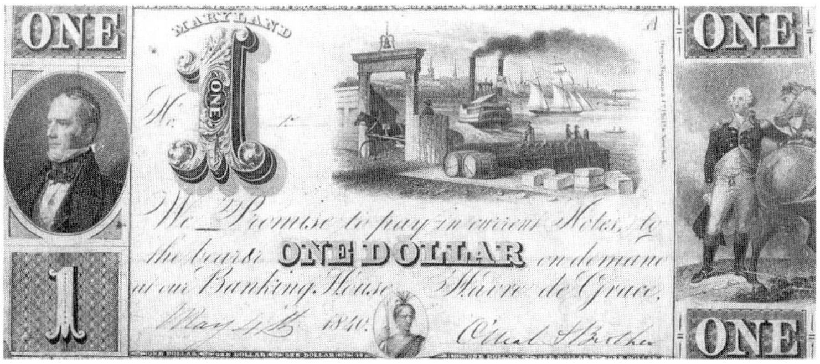

63.6.1

63.6.2 P R-7

$2.00 Printed year date 1840. Engraving, imprint: Draper, Toppan & Co., Phila. & New York. Proof.

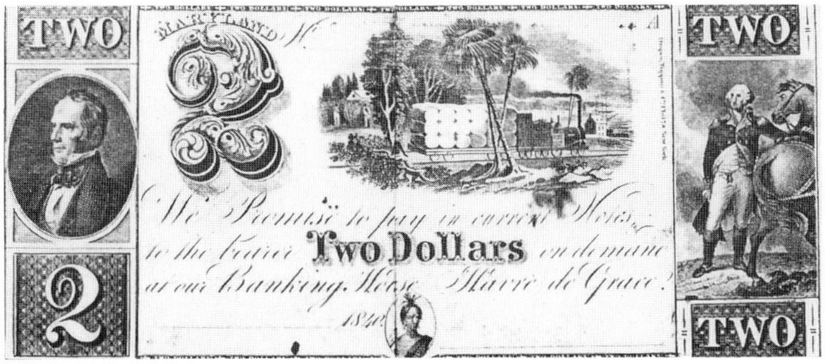

63.6.2 P

63.7 James Padian

The issuer is not positively identified as yet, even the surname in the signature being unclear. It is quite possible that this was the issue of H. A. Zollinger, with Padian being an approved signer. See H. A. Zollinger, No. 63.11.

63.7.3 R-7

25c Printed year date 1841. Letterpress, no imprint.

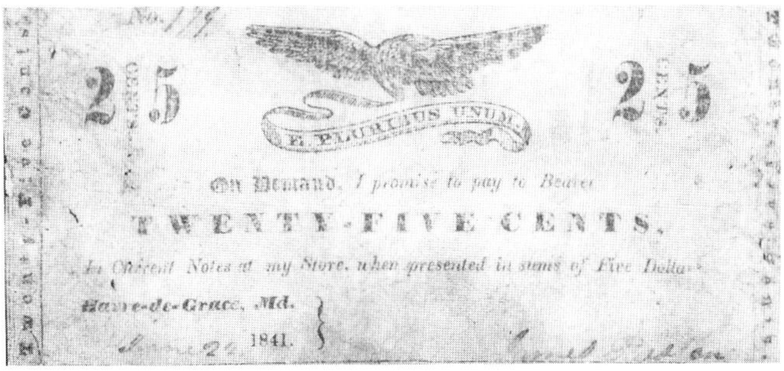

63.7.3

63.8 Potomac Savings Fund

No evidence has as yet been found about the operation or actual existence of this institution. The appearance of the signatures and dates on the two recorded notes create the suspicion that the notes were remainders that were signed at a later date.

63.8.3 R-6

25c Printed partial date 184 . Engraving, no imprint.

63.8.3

63.8.4 R-6

50c Printed partial date 184 . Engraving, no imprint.

63.8.5 R-5

$1.00 Ca. 1840s. Engraving, imprint: Underwood, Bald, Spencer & Hufty, Philada., Danforth, Underwood & Co., New York.

63.8.4

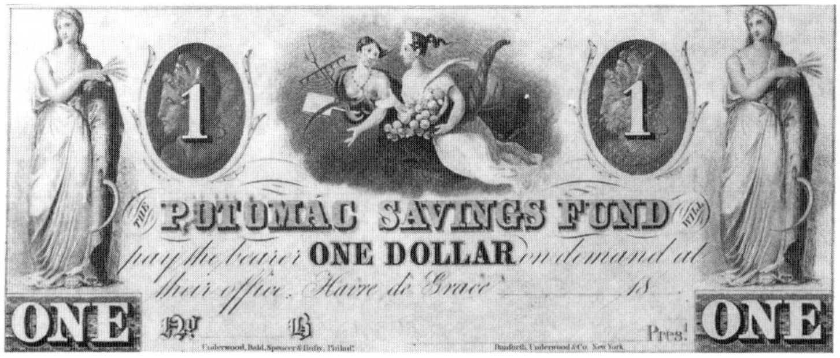

63.8.5

63.9 Sullivan & Suter

While no firm information on these issuers has been developed, it is not improbable that this partnership succeeded Dutton & Sullivan, whose names appear on the newspaper article shown with the illustrated note for 50c (see No. 63.3).

63.9.1 R-7

6 1/4c Printed date Oct. 25, 1839. Letterpress, imprint: MURPHY, PRINT. BALT. Vignette, upper center: Steamboat under full head of steam, flags fore and aft. 6 1/4 in square die to right.

63.9.3 R-7

25c Printed date Oct. 25, 1839. Letterpress, imprint: MURPHY, PRINT. BALT. Brown ink.

63.9.4 R-7

50c Printed date Oct. 25, 1839. Letterpress, imprint: MURPHY, PRINT. BALT. Brown ink.

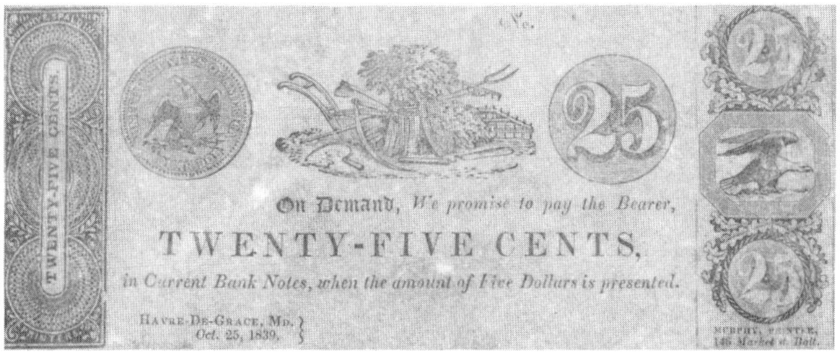

63.9.3

63.9.4

63.9.5 R-7

$1.00 Printed date Oct. 25, 1839. Letterpress, imprint: MURPHY, PRINT. BALT. Brown ink.

63.9.5

63.10 Tide Water Hotel

According to the signature on the one circulated note seen by the authors, the proprietor of this hotel was John Johanis.

Right half of an unissued sheet showing the 25c (63.10.3), 12 1/2c (63.10.2), and 6 1/4c (63.10.1) notes.

63.10.1 R-7
6 1/4c Printed partial date May 1841. Vignette and end designs engraved; legend by letterpress. Imprint: Manly & Orr, Printers, Philadelphia.

63.10.2 R-7
12 1/2c Printed partial date May 1841. Vignette and end designs engraved, legend by letterpress. Imprint: Manly & Orr, Printers, Philadelphia.

63.10.3 R-7
25c Printed partial date May 1841. Vignette and end designs engraved, legend by letterpress. Imprint: Manly & Orr, Printers, Philadelphia.

63.10.1

63.11 H. A. Zollinger

The issuer was the proprietor of a general store.

63.11.1 R-7
6 1/4c Printed year date 1841. Letterpress, no imprint.

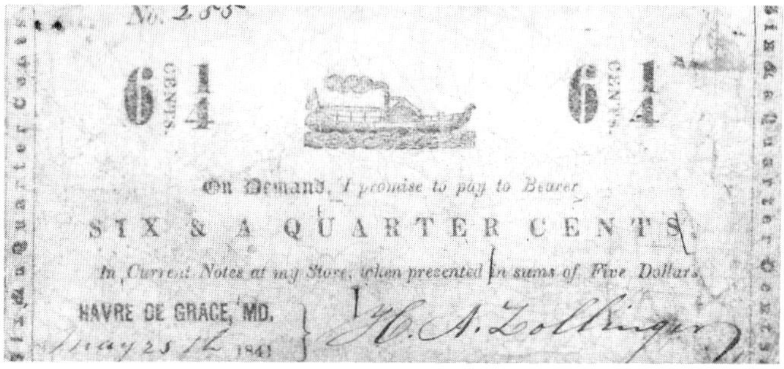

63.11.1

63.12 Unidentified Issuer

63.12.2 R-7
12 1/2c Printed date May 1, 1840. Engraving, imprint: Manly & Orr, Printers, Philad.

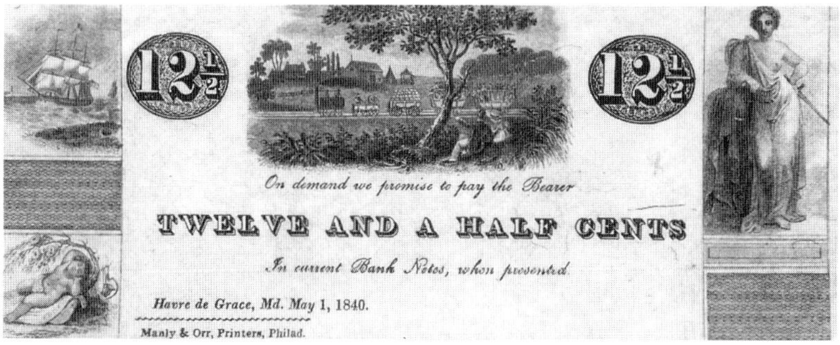

63.12.2

63.12.3 R-7

12 1/2c Printed date May 1, 1840. Engraving, imprint: Manly & Orr, Printers, Philad.

63.12.5 R-7

50c Printed date May 1, 1840. Engraving, imprint: Manly & Orr, Printers, Philad.

63.12.6 R-7

50c Printed date May 1, 1840. Engraving, imprint: Manly & Orr, Printers, Philad.

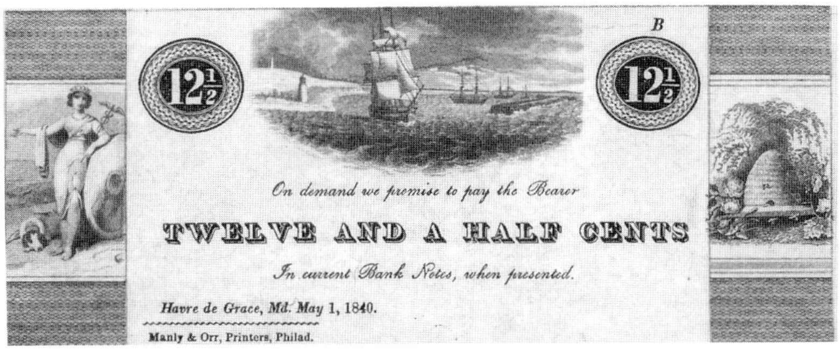

63.12.3

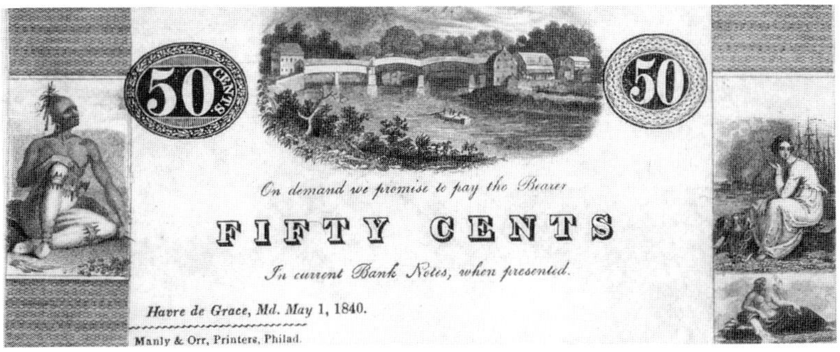

63.12.5

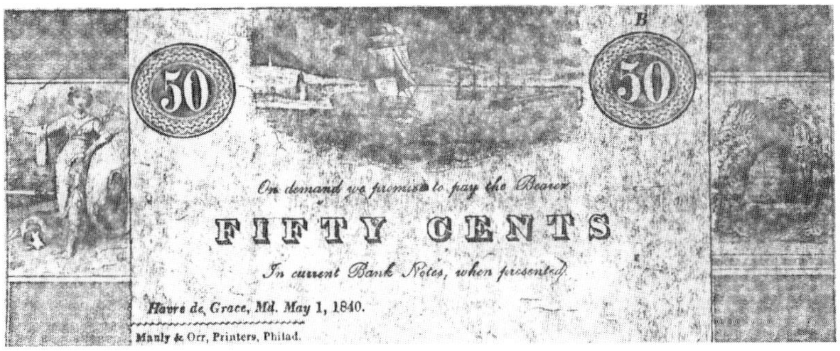

63.12.6

64 HIGH BRIDGE

Although two small villages of this name have at one time or another been located in Maryland (one in Prince George's County near Bowie, and the other in Howard County), neither was of sufficient size to warrant banking activity.

64.1 The High Bridge Bank

64.1.1 S R-7

$1.00 Printed date Nov. 13th, 1854. Engraving, imprint: W. L. Ormsby, New York. Reverse. Spurious. (MD255S2)

64.1.3 S R-7

$3.00 Printed date Nov. 13th, 1854. Engraving, imprint: W. L. Ormsby, New York. Reverse. Spurious. (MD255S4)

This nonexistent bank is represented only by fraudulent notes.

64.1.1 S

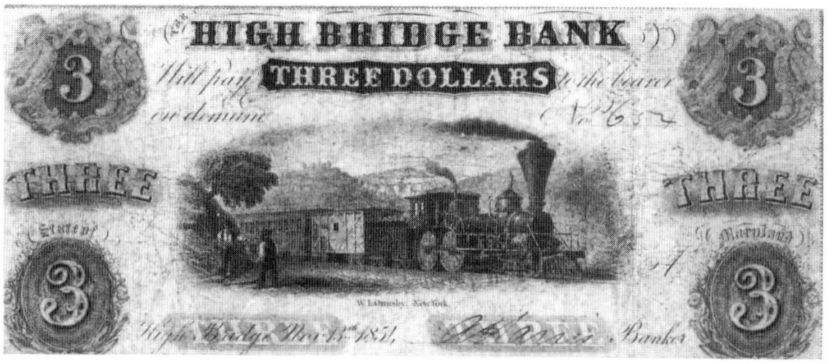

64.1.3 S

65 JOHNSVILLE, FREDERICK COUNTY

This village near Libertytown had a post office from 1811 through 1815, which reopened in 1832. The name probably commemorates a member of the Johns family who left Calvert County in the late eighteenth century and resettled in Frederick County.

65.1 John Kinzer Jr.

65.1.5 R-7

$1.00 Printed date June 1, 1840. Letterpress, imprint: MURPHY, PRINTER, BALTIMORE.

The issuer was the proprietor of a general store.

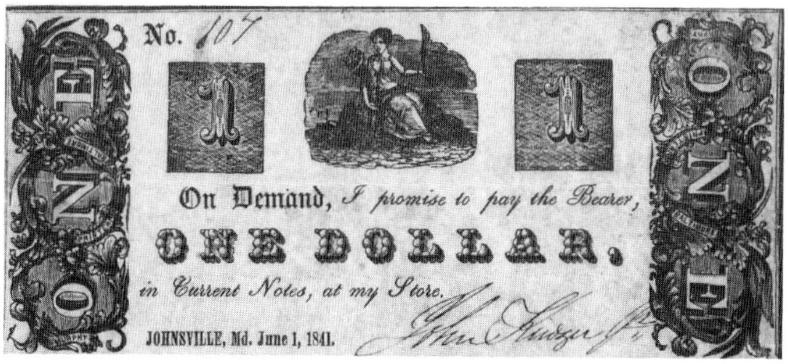

65.1.5

66 KENT ISLAND, QUEEN ANNE'S COUNTY

Capt. William Claiborne settled the island and gave it its present name in honor of his former homeland, the English county of Kent, in 1638. A post office was open here from 1801 through 1807.

66.1 Samuel White

The issuer was the proprietor of a general store.

66.1.2 R-7

12 1/2c Printed date Jan. 1, 1842. Letterpress, imprint: MURPHY / PRINTER / BALTIMORE.

66.1.2

70 LEONARDTOWN, ST. MARY'S COUNTY

Originally known as Seymourtown for Provincial Governor John Seymour. Leonardtown, commemorating Benedict Leonard Calvert, fourth Lord Baltimore, became the name in 1783. A post office opened in 1792.

70.1 Farmers Bank of Leonardtown

Charter approved January 6, 1818, but did not open for business. It is not known if notes were printed in anticipation of opening.

70.2 Wm. Mitchell

The issuer remains unidentified, but was probably a storekeeper, if he actually issued scrip. His use of "Treas." in the signature is suspicious, although a specific date on each seems to indicate an actual issue.

Unissued sheet of six, 6 1/4c (2), 12 1/2c (2) and 25c (2).

70.2.1 R-7

6 1/4c Printed date April 10, 1840. Letterpress, imprints: MURPHY, PRINT. BALT. at right; MURPHY & SPALDING, PRINTER at left. This 6 1/4c note was recorded many years ago with the penciled signature, "Treas. W. Mitchell." The status of this signature is as yet undetermined. No W. Mitchell appears in the 1830, 1840, or 1850 census indexes with a St. Mary's County domicile.

70.2.2 R-7

12 1/2c Printed date April 10, 1840. Letterpress, imprint: MURPHY, PRINT, BALT. at right.

70.2.3 R-7

25c Similar to 12 1/2c, No. 70.2.2, but with MURPHY, PRINTER, BALTIMORE at left and right.

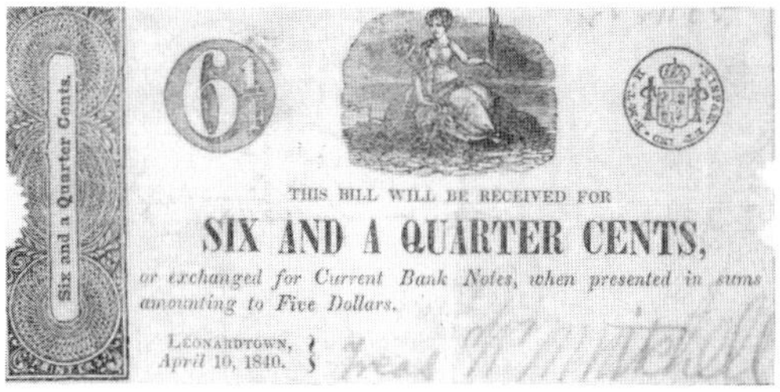

70.2.1

72 LIBERTYTOWN, FREDERICK COUNTY

The town was laid out in 1782 on a 6,000-acre tract and was probably named for patriotic reasons. A post office opened here in 1800.

72.1 Libertytown Savings Institution

Charter approved March 2, 1832; charter expired in 1845 and was not renewed.

72.1.2 R-7
10c Printed year date 1837. Letterpress, imprint: Printed at the Herald Office, Frederick.

72.1.3 R-7
25c Printed year date 1837. Letterpress, imprint: Printed at the Herald Officc, Frederick.

72.1.4 R-7
25c Printed year date 1837. Letterpress, imprint: Printed at the Herald Office, Frederick, Md.

72.1.5 R-7
25c Printed year date 1837. Letterpress, imprint: Printed at the Herald Office, Frederick. Similar to No. 72.1.4, with "Md." omitted from imprint.

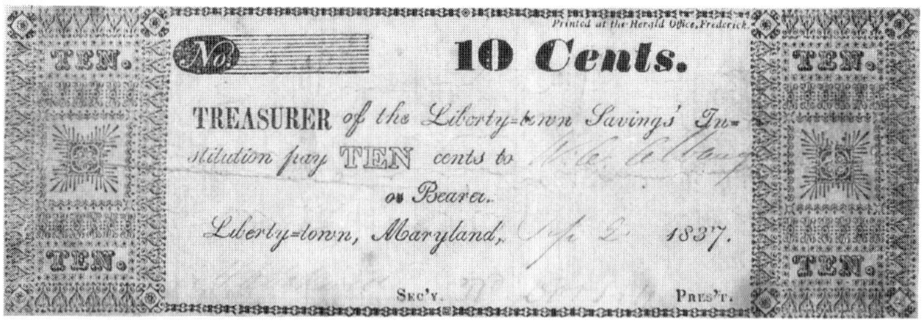

72.1.2

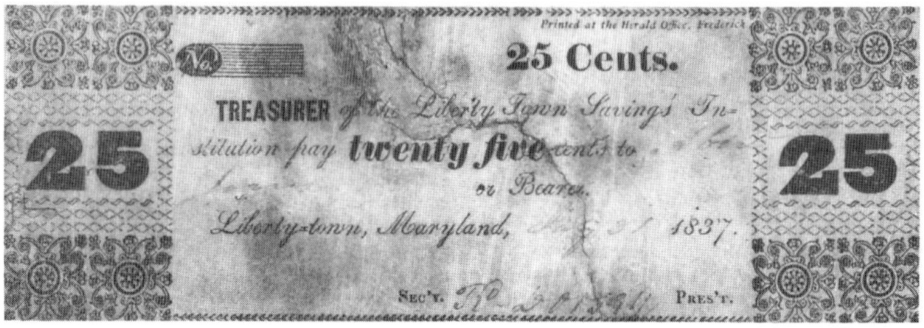

72.1.3

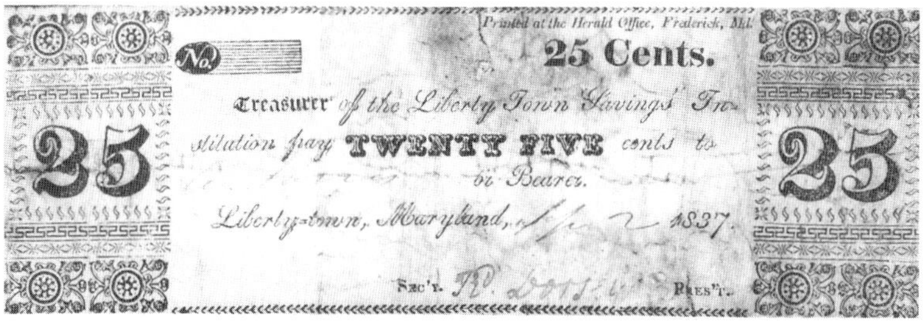

72.1.4

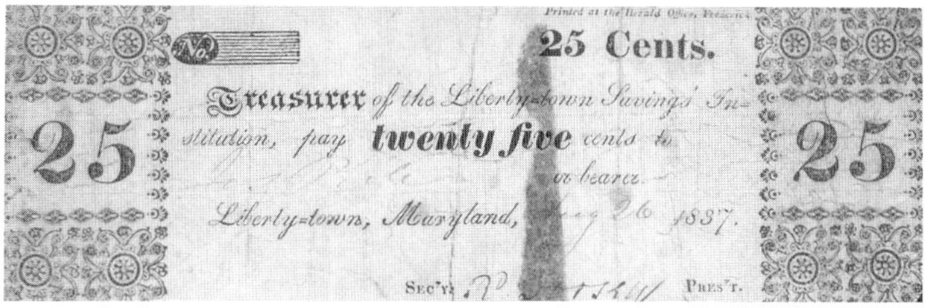

72.1.5

72.1.6 R-7

50c Printed year date 1837. Letterpress, imprint: Printed at the Herald Office, Frederick, Md.

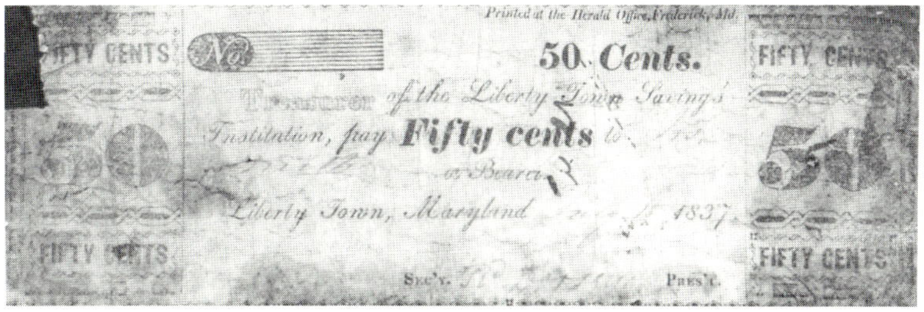

72.1.6

73 LONACONING, ALLEGANY COUNTY

Because Seldom Seen Creek and four other streams meet at this place, many townspeople believe that Lonaconing means "where many waters meet" in one of the Indian languages. This is not substantiated by students of such languages, however, although the word is undoubtedly Indian in origin. The town name is derived from its location on George's Creek, which prior to about 1795 had been known as Lonaconing Creek. A post office opened here in 1837.

73.1 William Alexander

The issuer was the proprietor of a general store.

73.1.2 R-7

10c Ca. 1837. Letterpress, imprint: Toy, Printer. Center vignette is 10c coin.

73.1.3 R-7

25c Ca. 1837. Letterpress, imprint: Toy, Printer. Similar to 10c, No. 73.1.2. Center vignette is 25c coin.

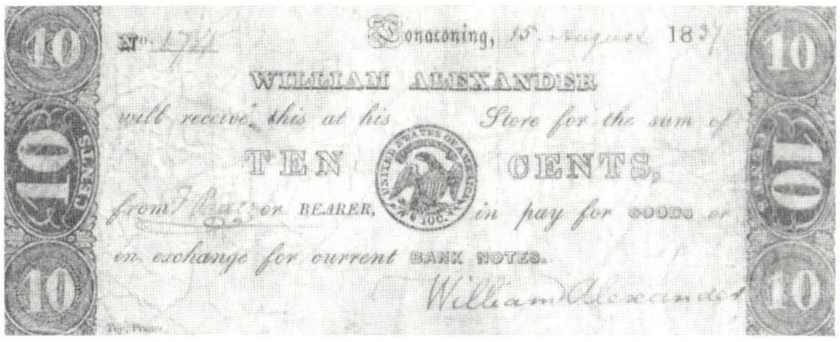

73.1.2

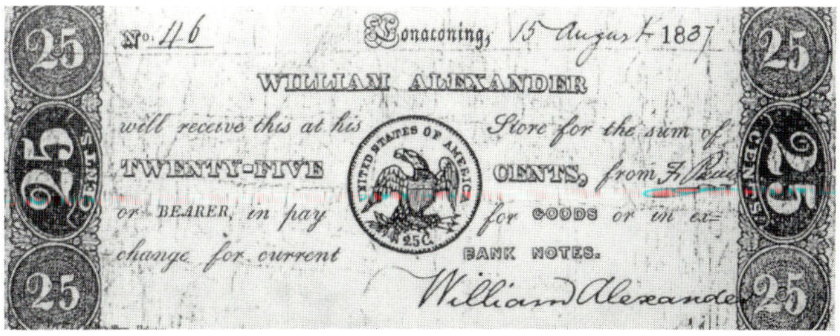

73.1.3

74 LONG POINT, SOMERSET COUNTY

Of the three locations in Somerset County with this place name, the most likely for the place of issue of the single note on record is the point of land on the south shore of the Wicomico River two miles northeast of Dames Quarter, approximately twelve miles from Princess Anne. A William Jones appears in the 1840 census index as living in the middle district of the county, and in the 1850 index a William H. Jones appears in the Princess Anne area.

74.1 W. H. Jones

The issuer was the proprietor of a general country store, evidenced by the redemption statement on the note.

74.1.1 R-7

6 1/4c Printed partial date Jan. __ 1838. Letterpress, imprint: Robinson, PRINTER, BALTIMORE.

74.1.1

76 MANCHESTER, CARROLL COUNTY

Capt. Richard Richards laid out Manchester in 1790 and named it for his native English city. The post office opened here in 1805.

76.1 Manchester Savings Institution

Charter approved March 6, 1850; deed of trust for benefit of creditors executed May 12, 1877. The treasurer, Jacob Shower, was a doctor of medicine with a general practice in Manchester.

76.1.1 R-7

$1.00 Printed date July __, 1861. Letterpress, imprint: Murphy & Co., Printers, Baltimore. Light green wavy-lined security underprint. Large lavender ONE in fancy box on reverse.

76.1.1

76.1.2 R-7

$2.00 Printed date July __, 1861. Letterpress, imprint: Murphy & Co., Printers, Baltimore. Light-green wavy-lined security underprint. Large lavender TWO in fancy box on reverse.

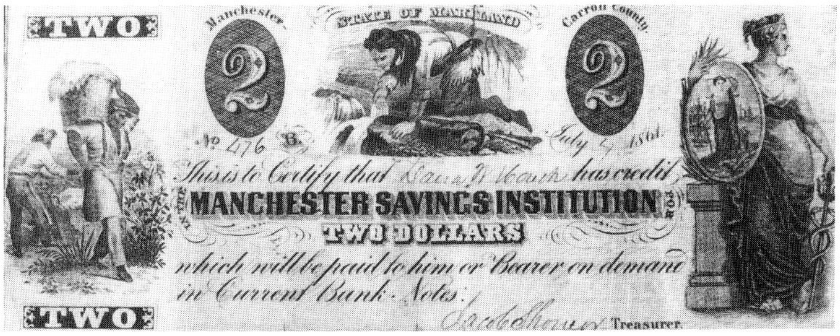

76.1.2

78 MAUS' MILL, CARROLL COUNTY

Although there was never a town of this name, this flour and chop mill was located at the confluence of Pipe Creek and Silver Run just east of the Littlestown (Pa.) Pike. The original proprietor of the mill was George Maus; at the time of issuance of the notes, the owner was Jacob Maus.

78.1.1 R-7

6 1/4c Printed date July 28, 1841. Letterpress, imprint: Murphy, print. Baltimore. Dark sepia.

78.1.2 R-7

12 1/2c Printed date July 28, 1841. Letterpress, imprint: MURPHY PRINTER BALTIMORE. Dark sepia.

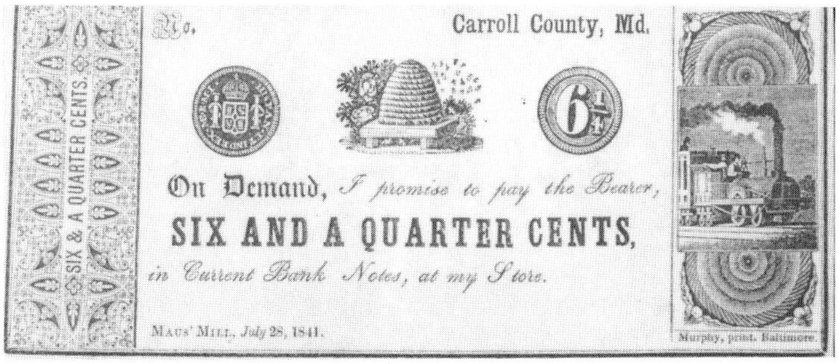

78.1.1

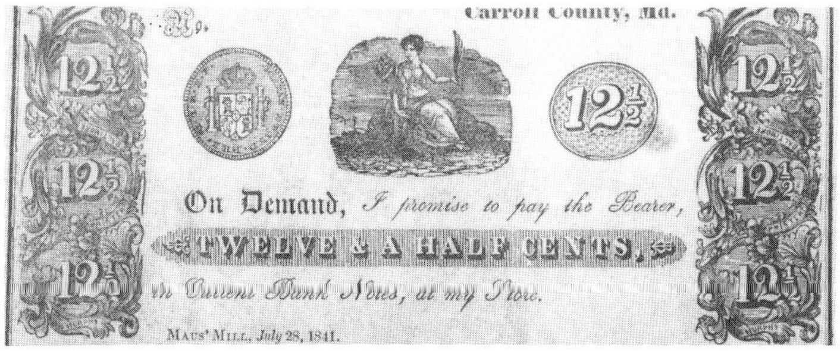

78.1.2

79 MECHANICS-TOWN, FREDERICK COUNTY

A post office opened in 1815 in this small town at the base of the Catoctin and Blue Ridge mountains, 15 miles from Frederick, on the Western Maryland Railroad.

79.1 Wm. Creeger

The issuer was the proprietor of a general store.

79.1.1 R-7
6 1/4c Printed partial date 183_. Letterpress, imprint: Printed at the Citizen Office, Fred'k.

79.1.2 R-7
12 1/2c Printed partial date 183_. Letterpress, imprint: Printed at the Citizen Office, Fred'k.

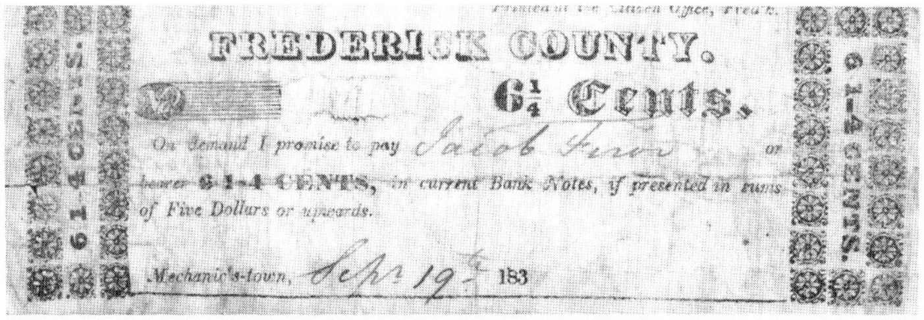

79.1.1

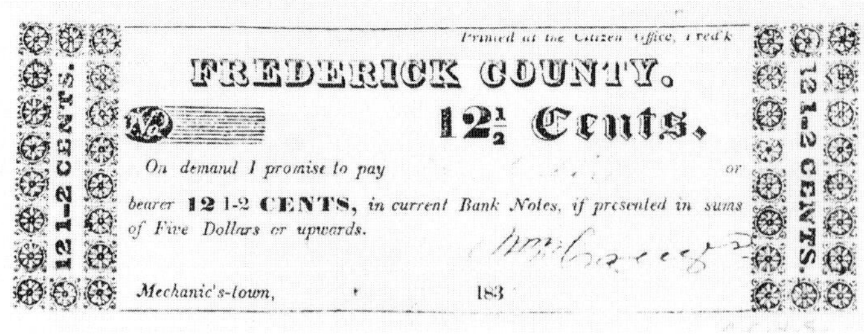

79.1.2

---

81 MICHAELSVILLE, HARFORD COUNTY

Originally Michael's Store, with a post office from 1821 to 1823, the town name became Michaelsville in 1823. No longer in existence, it was located about six miles south of the town of Aberdeen, almost in the center of what is now the Aberdeen Proving Ground.

81.1 Unidentified Issuer

81.1.1 R-7
6 1/4c Printed date November 6, 1839. Letterpress, imprint: MURPHY, PRINT. BALT.

81.1.2 R-7
12 1/2c Printed date November 6, 1839. Letterpress, imprint: MURPHY, PRINT. BALT.

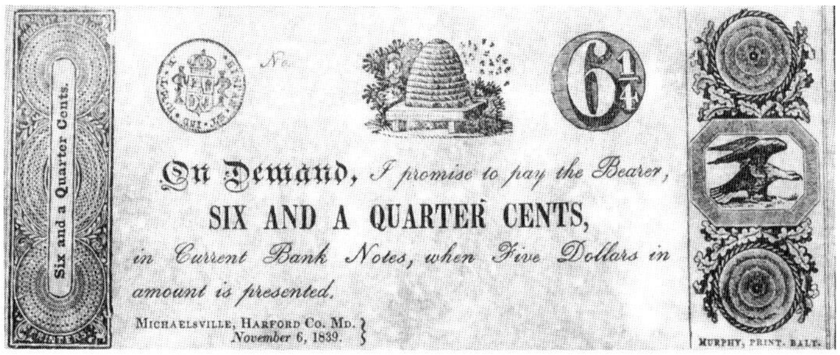

81.1.1

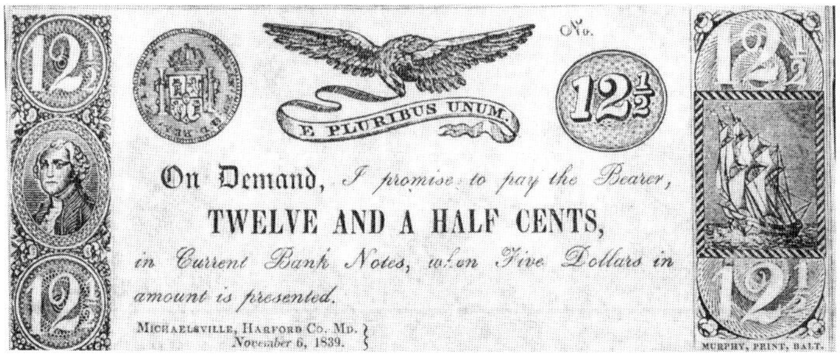

81.1.2

81.1.3 R-7

25c Printed date November 6, 1839. Letterpress, imprint: MURPHY, PRINT. BALT.

81.1.4 R-7

50c Printed date November 6, 1839. Letterpress, imprint: MURPHY, PRINT. BALT.

81.1.5 R-7

$1.00 Printed date November 6, 1839. Letterpress, imprint: Murphy, print. Balt.

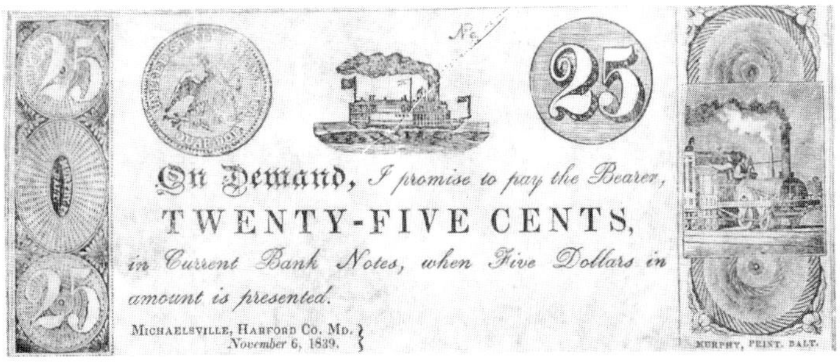

81.1.3

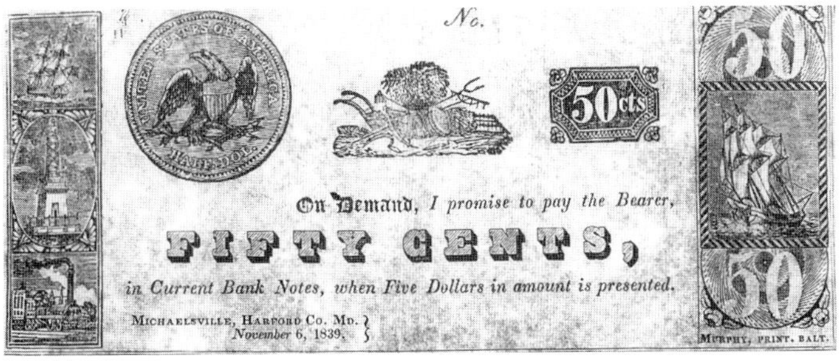

81.1.4

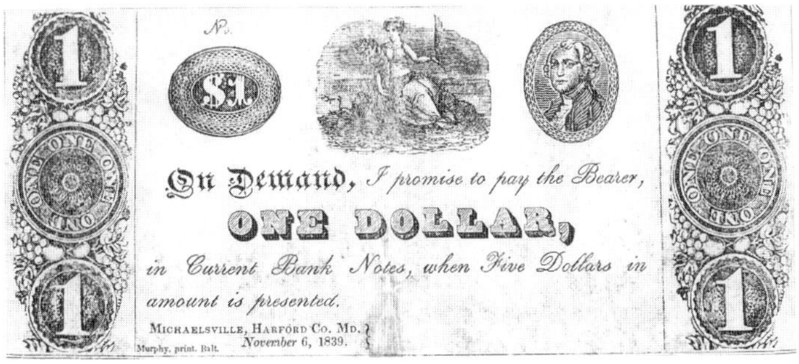

81.1.5

83 MILLINGTON, KENT COUNTY

Originally called Head of Chester because of its location at the head of the Chester River, its name was changed to Millington in 1819. The town grew around six or more waterwheel mills implying that the name arose because of the milling industry.

83.1 The Commercial Bank of Millington

Charter approved March 12, 1832; suspended payments in 1834, voluntary liquidation in 1837. Swindlers gained control of the remaining equipment, stationery, and the plates used to print the bank's notes and in 1839–40 produced numerous notes that flooded many communities in the eastern half of the country. Such spurious notes bear the signatures of W. Adams, cashier, J. C. H. Ellis, F. A. Weed, or W. Webb, President. Notes issued during the 1832–34 period are very difficult to find; they bear the signatures of G. Garrettson as cashier and Wm. M. Kaffon as president. On October 14, 1840, the "bank" closed and most of the management decamped, only the "president," Ellis, being apprehended. Weed was ultimately apprehended in New Orleans in December 1840. The plates were altered several times to produce notes of the Commercial Bank of Columbia, S.C.; the Traders Bank of

Boston; the Commercial Bank of Pennsylvania (Philadelphia); the Commercial Bank of New York; "The New York Safety Fund"; the Commercial Bank of Portsmouth, N.H.; the Merchant's Bank of Baltimore; the Commercial Bank of Cincinnati; Commercial Bank of Bristol, R.I.; Tazwell County Commercial & Fire Insurance Company, Pekin, Ill.

83.1.1 R-7

$5.00 Ca. 1832–34. Engraving, imprint: Draper, Underwood, Bald & Spencer. Same as No. 83.1.2, except for manuscript date prior to ca. 1838, and signatures of the original officers, G. Garrettson, cashier, and Wm. M. Kaffon, president. (MD265G2)

83.1.1 P R-7

$5.00 Ca. 1832–34. Engraving, imprint: Draper, Underwood, Bald & Spencer. Same as No. 83.1.2, except for date. Proof.

83.1.2 R-2

$5.00 Ca. 1839–40. Engraving, imprint: Draper, Underwood, Bald & Spencer. (MD265G14)

83.1.3 R-1

$5.00 Ca. 1839–40. Engraving, imprint: Rawdon, Wright & Hatch, New York. Altered notes of this design have been recorded bearing inscriptions of the Merchant's Bank, Baltimore; Commercial Bank of Cincinnati; Commercial Bank of Pennsylvania, Philadelphia. (MD265G16)

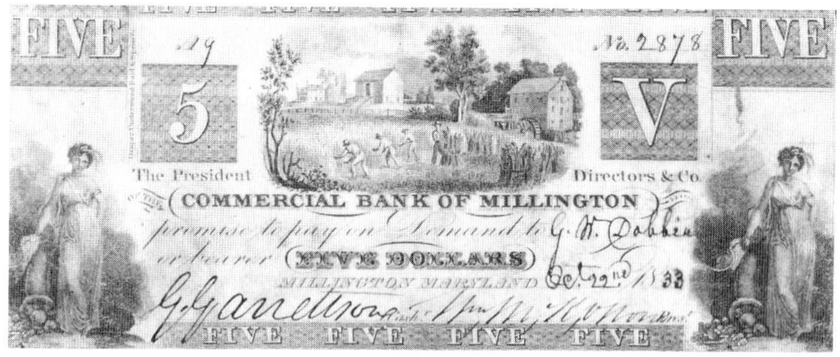

83.1.1

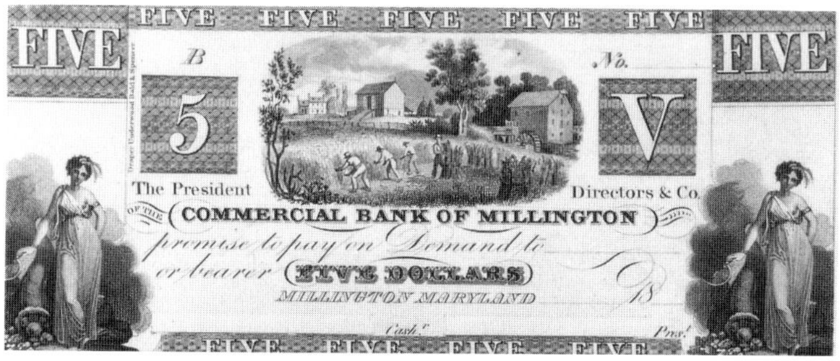

83.1.1 P

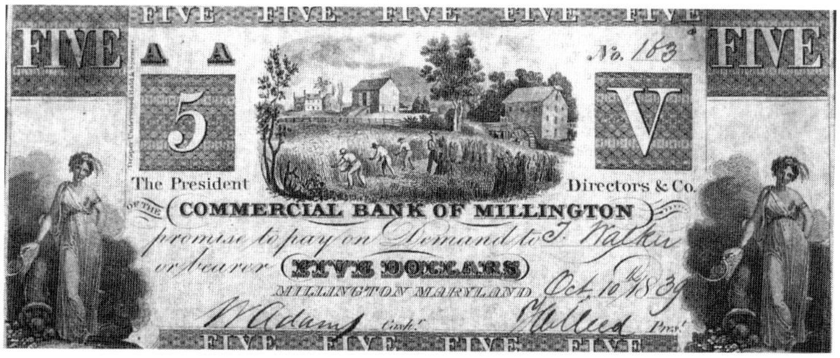

83.1.2

83.1.3

83.1.4 R-5

$5.00 Printed date January 1st, 1840. Engraving, imprint: Rawdon, Wright & Hatch, New York. Payable at the Tazwell County Commercial & Fire Insurance Company, Pekin, Ill. Brown reverse with "5 FIVE 5" in fancy layout.

83.1.5 R-7

$10.00 Ca. 1832–34. Engraving, imprint: Draper, Underwood, Bald & Spencer. Same as No. 83.1.6, except for date and signatures of the original officers. G. Garrettson, cashier, and Wm. M. Kaffon, president. (MD265G4)

83.1.5 P R-7

$10.00 Ca. 1832–34. Engraving, imprint: Draper, Underwood, Bald & Spencer. Same as No. 83.1.6, except for date. Proof.

83.1.6 R-3

$10.00 Ca. 1839–40. Engraving, imprint: Draper, Underwood, Bald & Spencer. Altered notes of this design have been recorded bearing inscriptions of the Merchants Bank, Baltimore; Commercial Bank of Cincinnati; Commercial Bank of Pennsylvania, Philadelphia. (MD265G18)

83.1.7 R-1

$10.00 Ca. 1839–40. Engraving, imprint: Rawdon, Wright & Hatch, New York. Altered notes of this design have been recorded bearing inscriptions of the Mechanics Bank of Baltimore and the Commercial Bank of Bristol, R.I. (MD265G20)

83.1.8 R-7

$20.00 Ca. 1832–34. Engraving, imprint: Draper, Underwood, Bald & Spencer. Same as No. 83.1.9, except for date and signatures of the original officers, G. Garrettson, cashier, and Wm. M. Kaffon, president. (MD265G6)

83.1.4

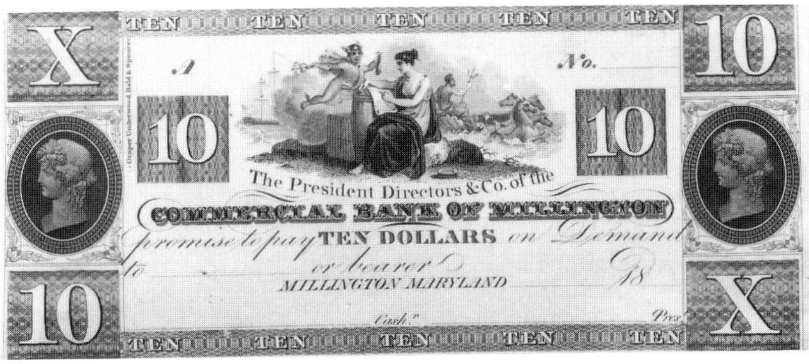

83.1.5 P

83.1.6

83.1.7

83.1.8 P R-7

$20.00 Ca. 1832–34. Engraving, imprint: Draper, Underwood, Bald & Spencer. Same as No. 83.1.8, except for date. Proof.

83.1.9 R-4

$20.00 Ca. 1839–40. Engraving, imprint: Draper, Underwood, Bald & Spencer. (MD265G22)

83.1.10 R-5

$50.00 Ca. 1839–40. Engraving, imprint: Rawdon, Wright & Hatch, New York. (MD265G24)

83.1.11 R-6

$100.00 Ca. 1839–40. Engraving, imprint: Rawdon, Wright & Hatch, New York. (MD265G26)

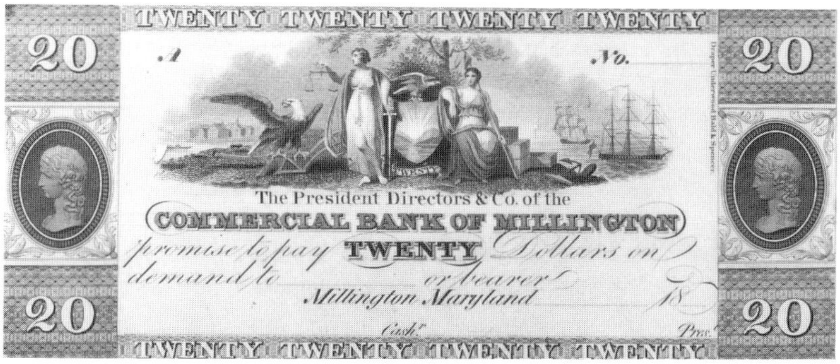

83.1.8 P

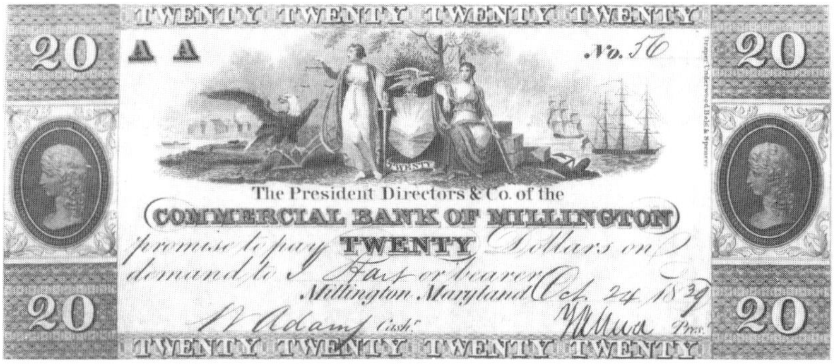

83.1.9

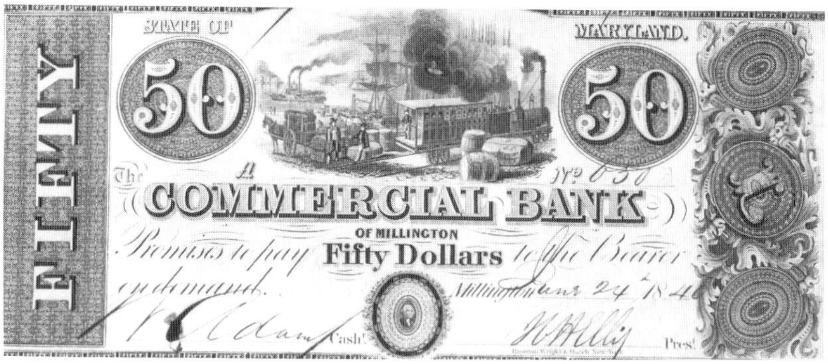

83.1.10

83.1.11

83.1.12 R-7

$500.00 Ca. 1839–40 Engraving, imprint: Underwood, Bald, Spencer & Hufty, Philada / Danforth, Underwood & Co., New York. (MD265G28)

83.1.12 P R-7

$500.00 Ca. 1839–40. Engraving, imprint: Underwood, Bald, Spencer & Hufty, Philada / Danforth, Underwood & Co., New York. Proof of central vignette, with denomination and text lightly penciled in.

83.1.12

83.1.12 P

Watkins & Walker See No. 26.1.

---

85 MONOCACY MILLS, FREDERICK COUNTY

This village on the Monocacy River, about one mile east of Buckeystown, was the site of a gristmill as early as 1812. It was named for the river, which is a tributary of the Potomac, and is derived from the Delaware Indian language.

85.1 Monocacy Mills

Originally owned by Dr. Ignatius Davis and D. Richardson. By 1841–42, when the scrip was issued, the mill was jointly owned by Daniel Buckey, Thomas J. Myers, David Bready, and Ezekiel Wysham. Signed examples bear the signatures of Myers and Bready although one example exists with signatures of Wyand and Keedy, which were possibly forgeries on an unsigned note.

85.1.2 R-7

12 1/2c Printed date July 27, 1841. Letterpress, imprint: MURPHY, Pr. Balto.

85.1.3 R-7

12 1/2c Printed date July 27, 1841. Letterpress, imprint: MURPHY, Pr.Balto. Similar to No. 85.1.2, but Spanish coin inverted.

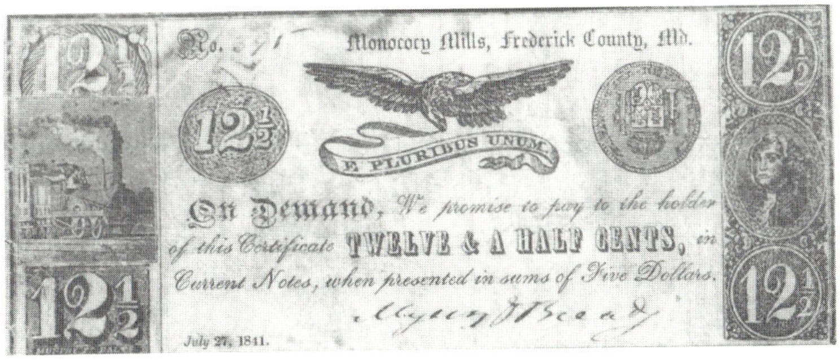

85.1.3

85.1.4 R-7

25c Printed date July 27, 1841. Letterpress, imprint: Murphy, printer, Balt.

85.1.5 R-7

50c Printed date July 27, 1841. Letterpress, imprint: MURPHY, PRINTER, 146 Market st. Baltimore. Vignette is a woodcut of Baltimore harbor from Federal Hill.

85.1.6 R-7

$1.00 Printed date July 27, 1841. Letterpress, imprint: MURPHY, PRINTER, 146 Market st. Baltimore.

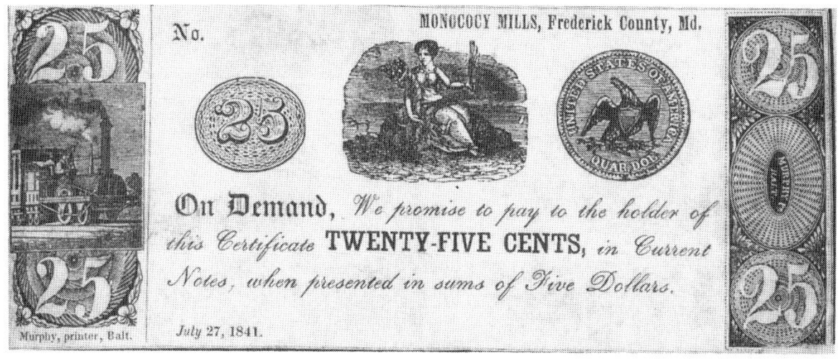

85.1.4

85.1.5

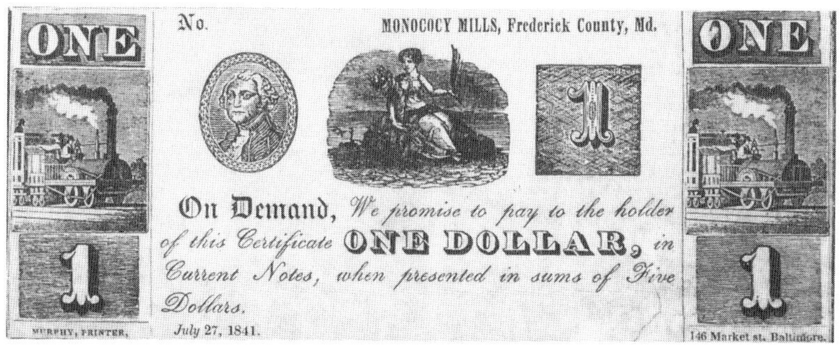

85.1.6

86 MOUNT SAVAGE, ALLEGANY COUNTY

Originally called Jennons Run, the name was changed to Mount Savage in 1847, for the Mount Savage Iron Works, which opened there in 1839, and for the local Great Savage Mountain.

86.1 Mount Savage Iron Works Store

The Mount Savage Iron Works was established in 1839, the first president being Col. William Young. It ceased operations in 1847. The "Rail Mill" was established in 1843 at Mount Savage to roll the first solid track rail in the U.S.

86.1.4 R-7

50c Undated. Lithography, no imprint. Large green double-lined "50," overprint. "Receivable for merchandise at Mount Savage Furnace" on reverse in green.

86.1.5 R-7

75c Printed partial year date 184_. Letterpress, imprint: Murphy print, Balt. Denomination inserted in manuscript.

86.1.4

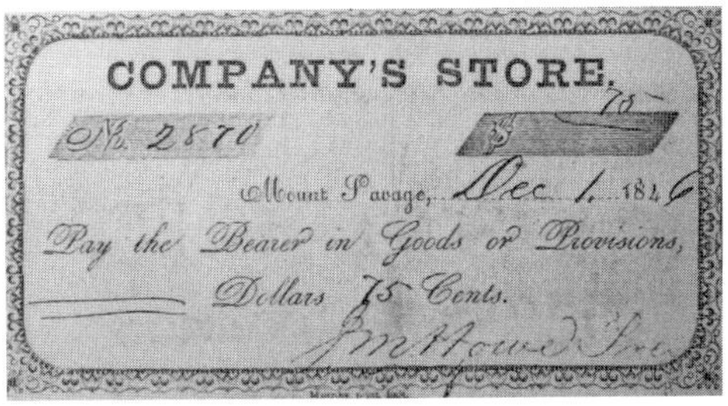

86.1.5

88 NANTICOKE POINT, SOMERSET COUNTY

Named for the Nanticoke River, which is derived from the Delaware Indian word meaning "tidewater people," this locality is on a point of land at the mouth of the Nanticoke River, now known as Roaring Point. In 1867 this area became a part of Wicomico County, which was created from portions of Somerset and Worcester counties.

88.1 William J. L. Willing

The issuer was the proprietor of a general store.

88.1.1 R-5

5c Ca. 1862–63. Printed partial year date 186_. Letterpress, no imprint.

88.1.2 R-5

10c Ca. 1862–63. Printed partial year date 186_. Letterpress, no imprint.

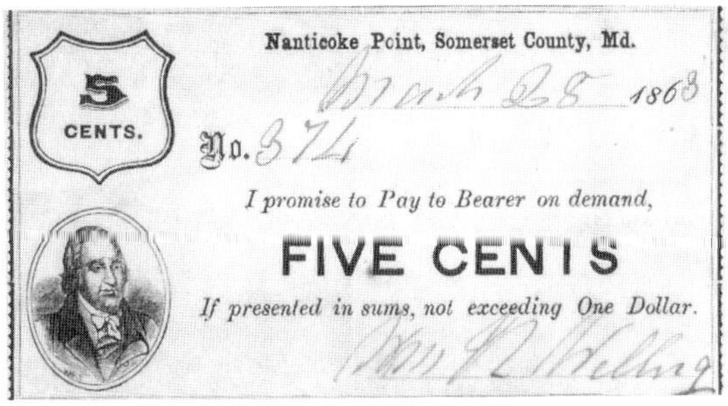

88.1.1

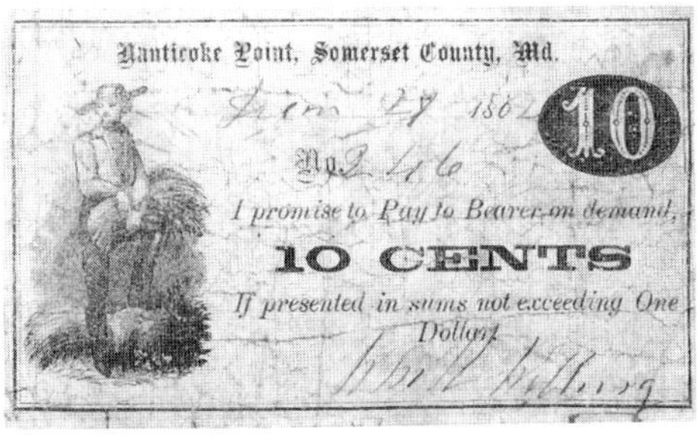

88.1.2

88.1.3 R-5

25c Ca. 1862–63. Printed partial year date 186_. Letterpress, no imprint.

88.1.4 R-5

50c Ca. 1862–63. Printed partial year date 186_. Letterpress, no imprint.

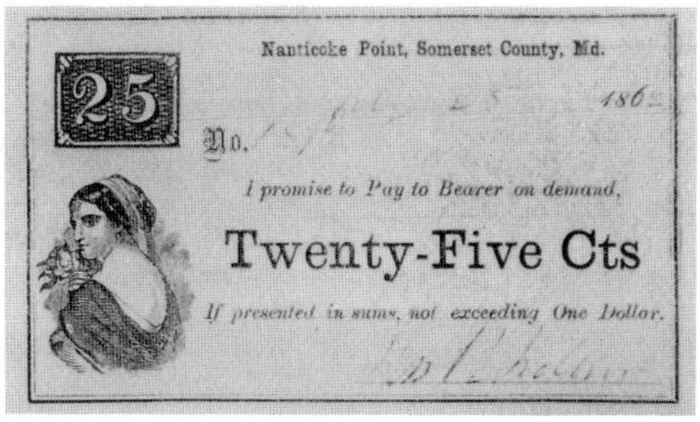

88.1.3

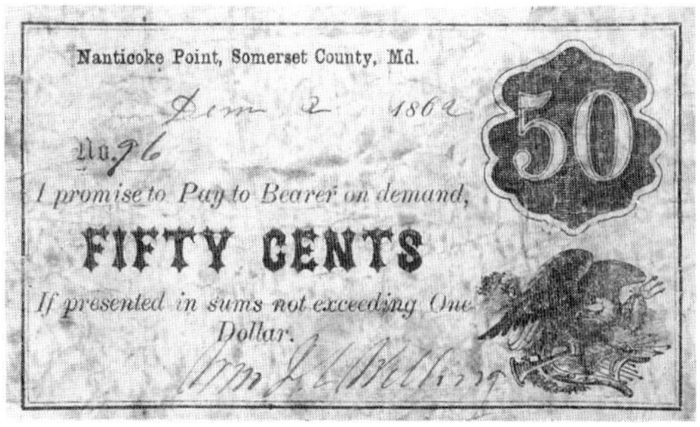

88.1.4

92 NEWARK, WORCESTER COUNTY

Named for Newark-Upon-Trent, Nottinghamshire, England, this village is midway between Berlin and Snow Hill.

92.1 Wm. J. Scott

The issuer was the proprietor of a country store. His principal business was a general store in Berlin, where he issued notes that he also utilized for the Newark store by crossing out "Berlin" in the inscription and inserting "New Ark" [sic] in manuscript.

92.1.4 R-7

50c Ca. 1841. Engraving and letterpress, imprint: Manly & Orr, Printers, Philad.

93 NEW HAVEN, SOMERSET COUNTY

This small hamlet was located near Dames Quarter in the Middle District, approximately 13 miles west of Princess Anne.

93.1 Littleton Harris

The issuer was an oysterman and the proprietor of a general store.

93.1.1 R-7

6 1/4c Printed date April 1840. Letterpress, no imprint, although probably printed by Bull & Tuttle, Baltimore. (*See* 12 1/2c, No. 93.1.3, for imprint.)

93.1.2 R-7

6 1/4c Printed date September 1841. Letter, imprint: Toy, pr. Balt.

93.1.3 R-7

12 1/2c Printed date April, 1840. Letterpress, imprint: Printed by Bull & Tuttle, Balt.

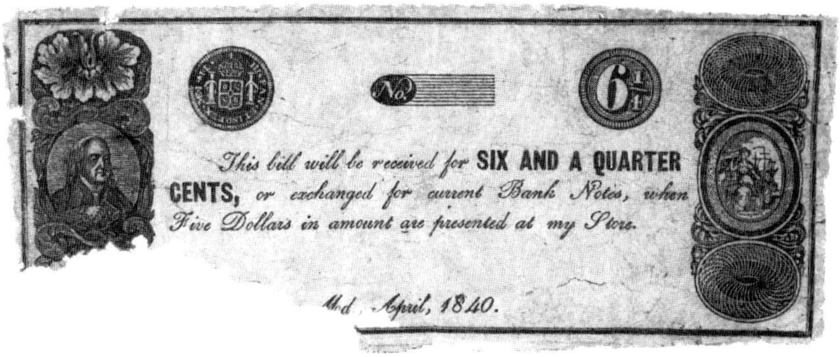

93.1.1

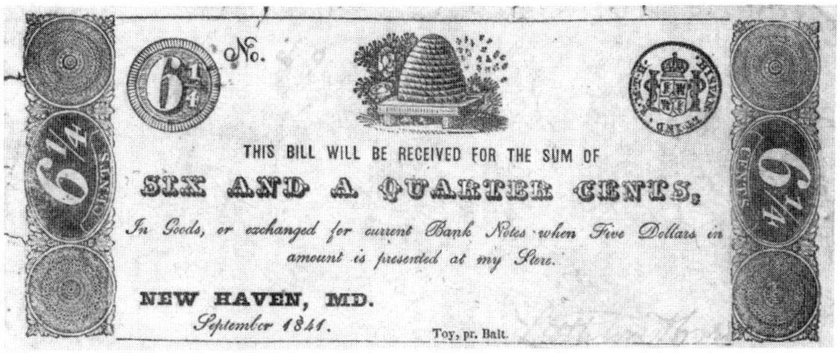

93.1.2

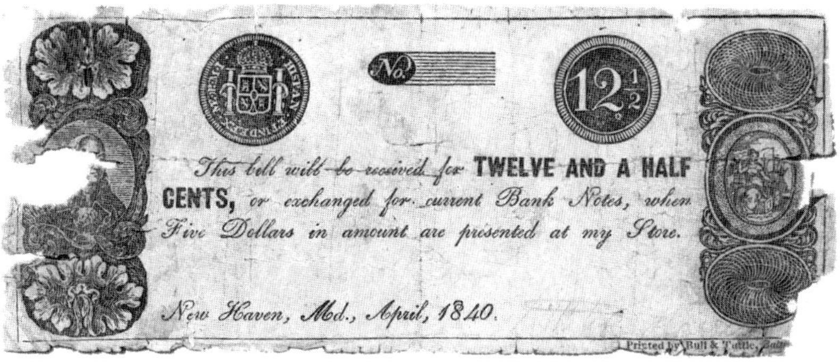

93.1.3

94 NEWTOWN, WORCESTER COUNTY

This town is located on the Pocomoke River about 14 miles southwest of Snow Hill. Name changed to Pocomoke City in 1878.

94.1 W. J. S. Clarke

The issuer conducted a general store, marine railway, and steam sawmill in the 1860–75 period.

94.1.1 R-7

5c Printed date December 1, 1862. Letterpress, no imprint. Similar to 20c, No. 94.1.3.

94.1.3 R-7
20c Printed date December 1, 1962. Letterpress, no imprint.

94.1.4 R-7
25c Partially written date January 1, 1863. Letterpress, no imprint. Similar to 20c, No. 94.1.3.

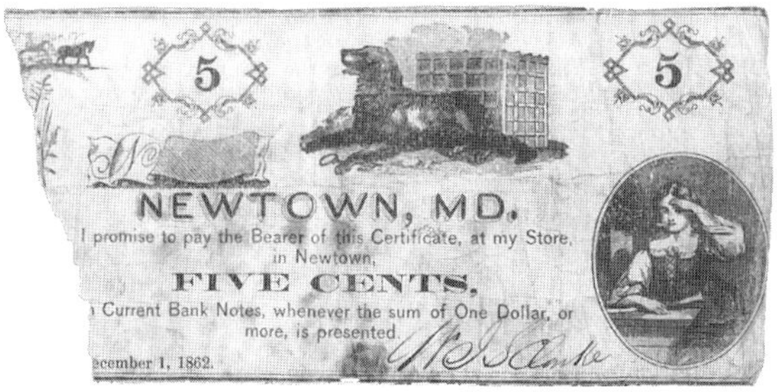

94.1.1

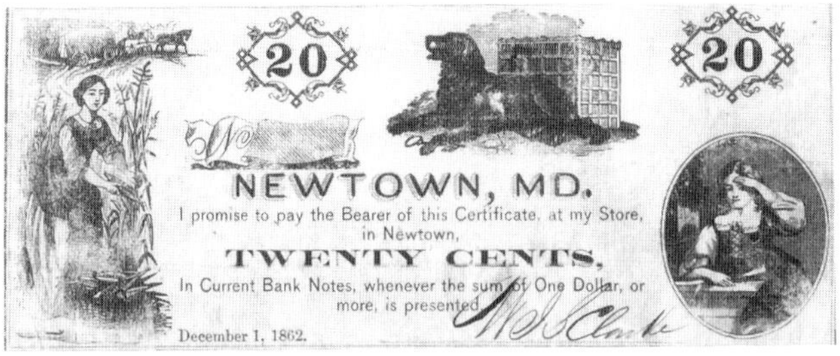

94.1.3

94.1.4

94.2 Hall & Bro.

The issuers were proprietors of a general store and steam sawmill.

94.2.1 R-7
3c Ca. 1863. Lithography, no imprint. Type A (as illustrated on page 444), blue.

94.2.2 R-7
5c Ca. 1863. Lithography, no imprint. Type B (as illustrated on page 445), blue.

94.2.1

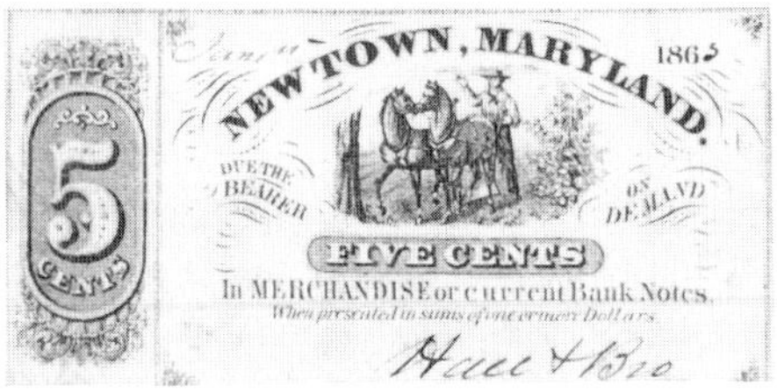

94.2.2

94.2.4 R-7
25c Ca. 1863. Lithography, no imprint. Type D (as illustrated on page 445), blue.

94.2.4

94.3 Hargis & Dickinson

John P. Hargis and William S. Dickinson (1833–91) operated a store, selling dry goods and groceries, at the corner of Market and Commerce streets, from 1855 until 1865 when, by mutual consent, the partnership was dissolved. Hargis continued the business for about six years and then retired.

Dickinson formed a partnership in 1867 with I. N. Merrill and E. H. Dryden, selling groceries, hardware, footware, and gentlemen's furnishings until the partnership ceased in 1878.

94.3.1 R-7
3c Ca. 1863. Lithography, no imprint. Type A (as illustrated on page 444), dull purple.

94.3.2 R-7
5c Ca. 1863. Lithography, no imprint. Type B (as illustrated on page 445), dull purple.

94.3.1

94.4 H. B. Henderson

The issuer was the proprietor of a general store.

94.4.3 R-7
10c Ca. 1863. Letterpress, no imprint.

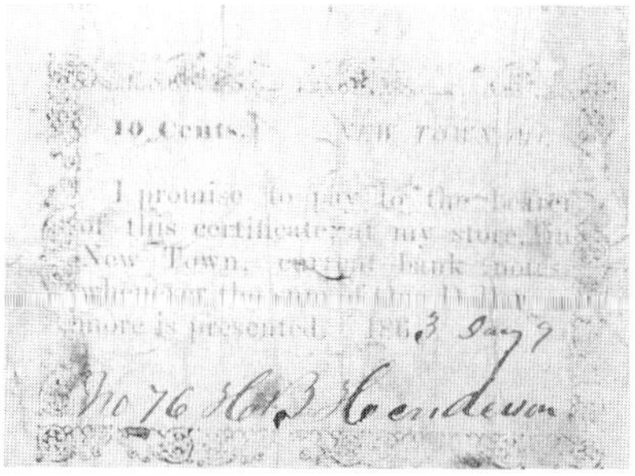

94.4.3

94.5 A. Smith

The status of this signature is as yet undetermined, examples on at least two different colored notes being on record.

94.5.1 R-7
3c Ca. 1863. Lithography, no imprint. Type A, red.

94.5.1

94.5.2 R-7
5c Ca. 1863. Lithography, no imprint. Type B, green.

94.5.3 R-7
5c Ca. 1863. Lithography, no imprint. Type B, red.

94.5.4 R-7
10c Ca. 1863. Lithography, no imprint. Type C, red.

94.5.5 R-7
25c Ca. 1863. Lithography, no imprint. Type D (as illustrated on page 445), red.

94.5.2

94.5.4

94.6 David J. O. Smith

The occupation of this issuer has not as yet been determined.

94.6.3 R-7
10c Printed partial year date 186_. Letterpress, no imprint.

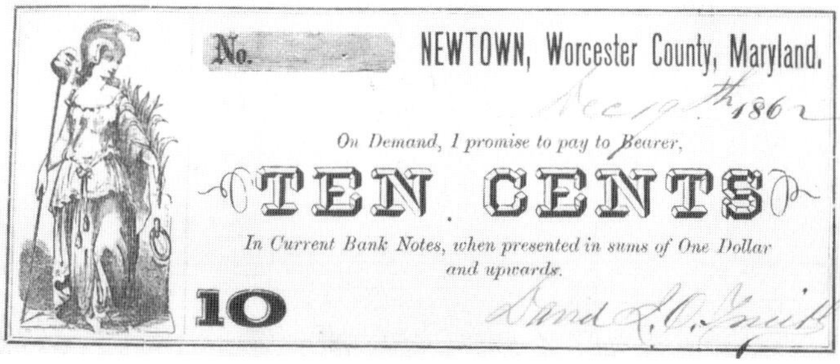

94.6.3

In addition to individually designed notes, sets of notes in the denominations illustrated below are to be found lithographed in blue, dull purple, red, and green. Possibly, the colors were to have been used to distinguish the issuers for ready identification in the town, all notes in the same color apparently to have been issued by only one merchant. Those that have been positively identified appear in the following alphabetic listing, with illustrations of one denomination showing the recorded signatures. The notes were printed by lithography, there being no imprint to identify the printer. A printed partial date, 186_, appears on each note.

Notes bearing satisfactorily identifiable signatures have been recorded for Hall & Bro., Hargis & Dickinson, and perhaps A. Smith.

TYPE A

TYPE B

TYPE C

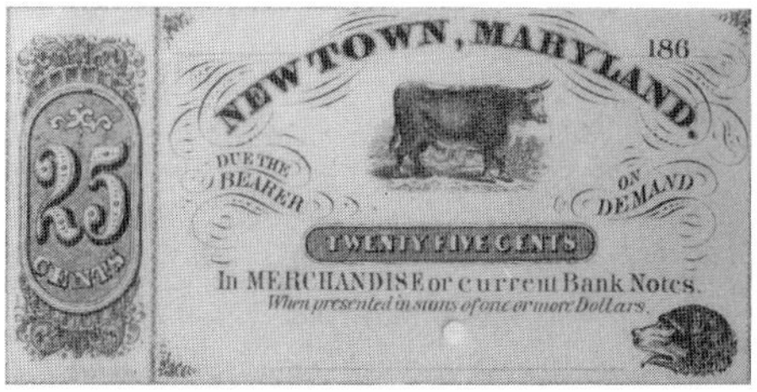

TYPE D

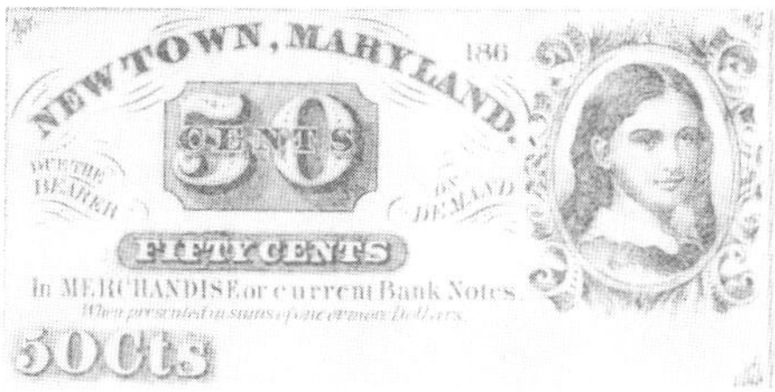

TYPE E

95 **NEW WINDSOR, CARROLL COUNTY**

A tavern opened here in 1788, lots were recorded in 1797, and until 1816 the village was named Sulphur Springs because of a nearby sulphur spring. The present name came about when a Mr. Atlee, the original settler, suggested that it be named for a friend visiting from Windsor, England.

95.1 Samuel and Jonas Euker

The issuers were the proprietors of a general store that opened for business on April 14, 1837.

95.1.1 R-7
5c Printed date October 1, 1840. Letterpress, imprint: Murphy, pr. Balt.

95.1.2 R-7
6 1/4c Printed date October 1, 1840. Letterpress, imprint: Murphy, printer, Baltimore.

95.1.5 R-7
25c Printed date October 1, 1840. Letterpress, imprint: Murphy, printer, Baltimore.

95.1.7 R-7
$1.00 Ca. 1840. Letterpress, imprint: Murphy, print. Balt.

95.1.9 R-7
$3.00 Ca. 1840. Letterpress, imprint: Murphy, print. Balt.

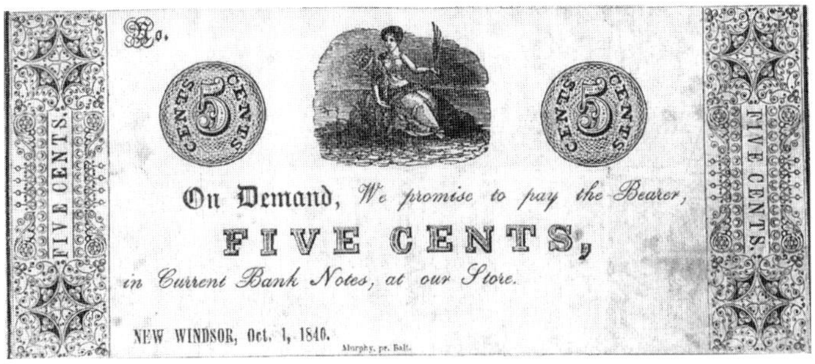

95.1.1

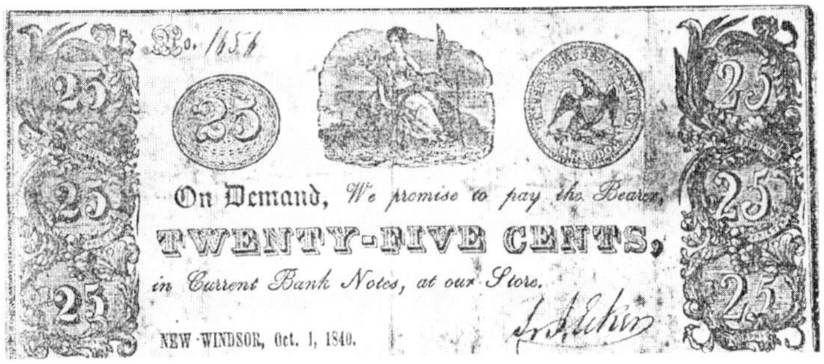

95.1.5

95.1.7

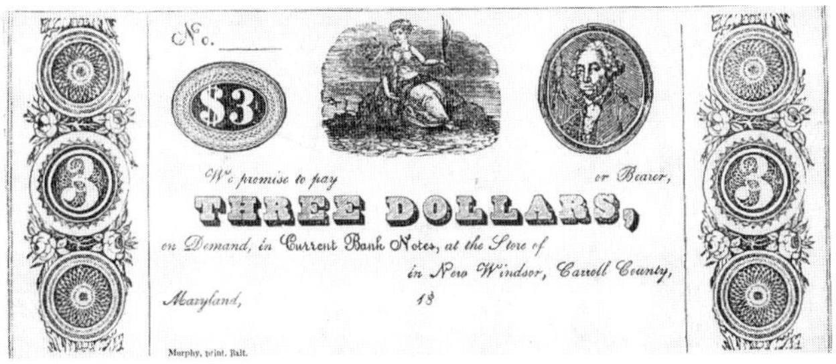

95.1.9

97 NORTH EAST, CECIL COUNTY

The town owes its name to being at the head of the Northeast River about seven miles west of Elkton. The first settlement here was in 1716 when iron works and a flour mill were built.

97.1 North East Manufacturing Co.

Incorporated on March 8, 1847, by act of the General Assembly with capital stock not to exceed $100,000, this company was engaged in the "manufacture of fire bricks and all other articles or wares of which clay is a component part." At the time of incorporation, the named stockholders were John Griffin, J. M. Nichols, and A. E. Lain. The act also included the proviso that "nothing herein contained, shall be so construed as to authorize this company to issue any note, token, scripdevice, or other evidence of debt to be used as currency."

While the authors have not recorded any examples of circulated notes of the company, proofs from which the following listings were made were in the archives of the American Bank Note Company.

97.1.1 P R-7
$1.00 Ca. 1851. Engraving, imprint: Draper, Welsh & Co., Philada. Proof.

97.1.2 P R-7
$2.00 Ca. 1851. Engraving, imprint: Draper, Welsh & Co., Philada. Proof.

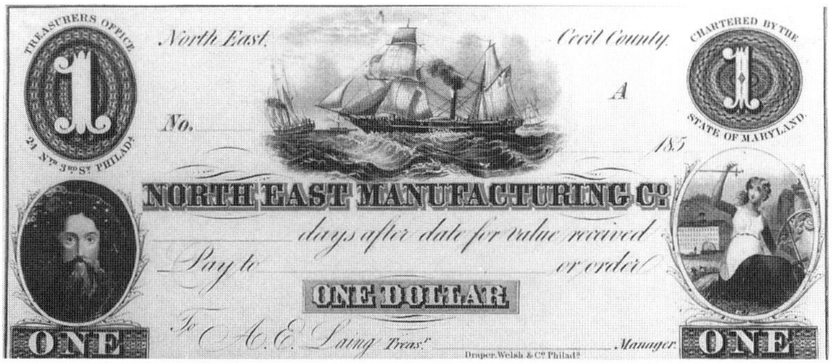

97.1.1 P

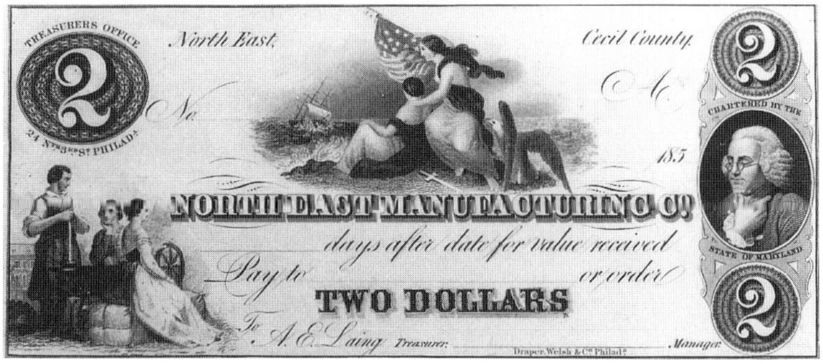

97.1.2 P

99 OLD TOWN, ALLEGANY COUNTY

This village is about 12 miles southeast of Cumberland on the North Branch of the Potomac River. Supposedly the oldest village in the county, it was settled in 1741, originally being known as Skipton.

99.1 North & South Bank of Potomac

Bank chartered in 1817, but did not go into operation. It is not clear whether notes were prepared in anticipation of its opening.

100 OWENSVILLE, WEST RIVER, ANNE ARUNDEL COUNTY

This small village is three miles northwest of Galesville, and 15 miles southwest of Annapolis.

100.1 J. E. Bird

The issuer, J. E. Bird, and the payee, Stephen L. Bird, were prominent millers in the area for many years.

100.1.2 R-7

12 1/2c Printed year date 1841. Letterpress, no imprint: Vignette in center of right end panel is the Battle Monument, Baltimore.

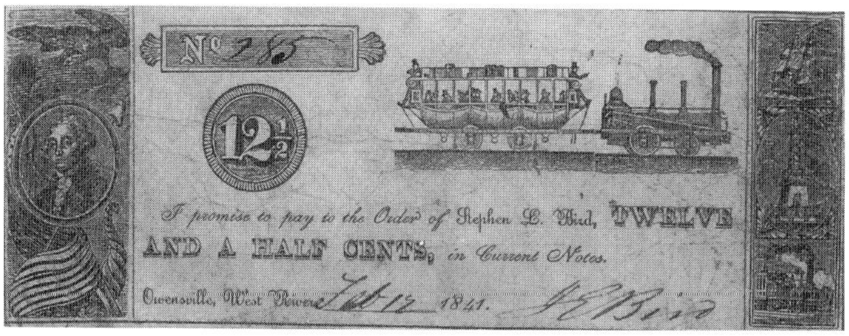

100.1.2

102 PORT DEPOSIT, CECIL COUNTY

This town is located on the Susquehanna River approximately 3 1/2 miles north of Perryville. In 1729, a ferry began operation and the area became known as Smith's Ferry, later changed to Creswell's Ferry, and officially in 1812 to Port Deposit. This name was derived from the fact that the town was a port of deposit for produce and lumber brought down the river and stored prior to transshipment.

102.1 Town of Port Deposit

Scrip issued by the commissioners of Port Deposit to alleviate the shortage of small change, depending on the date of issue, may refer to the town as "the village," "the borough," the "corporation," or simply identify the circumstances of issue as the "Port Deposit Loan."

102.1.1 R-7

5c Printed partial date July __, 1837. Letterpress, imprint: Robinson, Printer, Baltimore. Interest-bearing note, redeemable on February 1st, 1839.

102.1.2 R-3

5c Printed date Nov. 3rd, 1862. Engraving, imprint: American Bank Note Co. Philada. With brick red security underprint: CENTS above and "5" below.

102.1.3 R-4

5c Printed date Nov. 3rd, 1862. Engraving, imprint: American Bank Note Co. Philada. Same as No. 102.1.2, without CENTS and "5" security underprint.

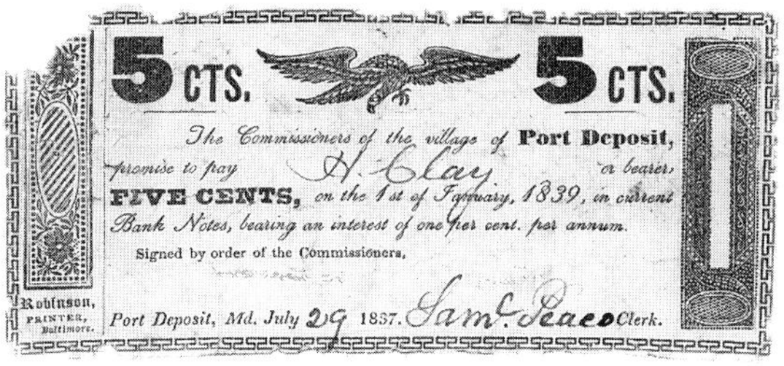

102.1.1

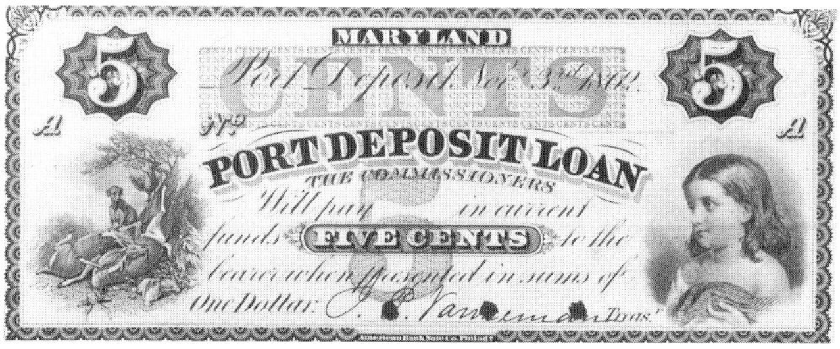

102.1.2

102.1.6 R-7

6 1/4c Printed partial date April __, 1840. Engraved vignettes, counters, and end plates with text in letterpress, imprint: Manly & Orr Printers, Philadelphia.

102.1.7 R-7

10c Printed partial date July __, 1837. Letterpress, imprint: Robinson, PRINTER, Baltimore. Interest-bearing note, redeemable on Jan. 1st, 1839.

102.1.8 R-7

10c Printed date Nov. 3rd, 1862. Engraving, imprint: American Bank Note Co., Philada. With brick red underprint CENTS.

102.1.9 R-7

12 1/2c Printed partial date October 1839. Letterpress, imprint: Robinson, PRINTER, Baltimore.

102.1.11 R-7

25c Printed partial date April __, 1840. Engraved vignettes, counters, and end plates, with text in letterpress, imprint: Manly & Orr, Printers, Philadelphia.

102.1.6

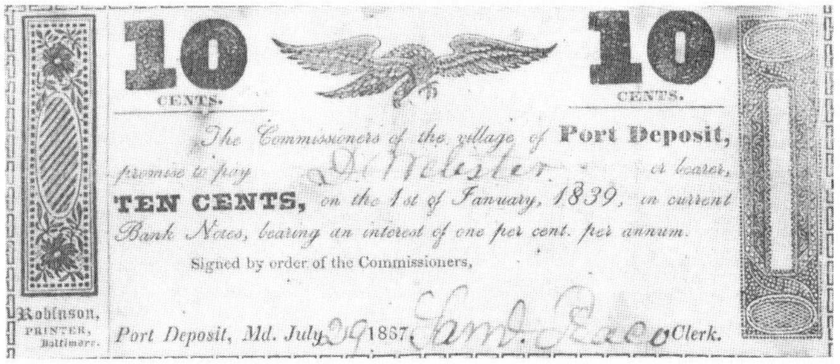

102.1.7

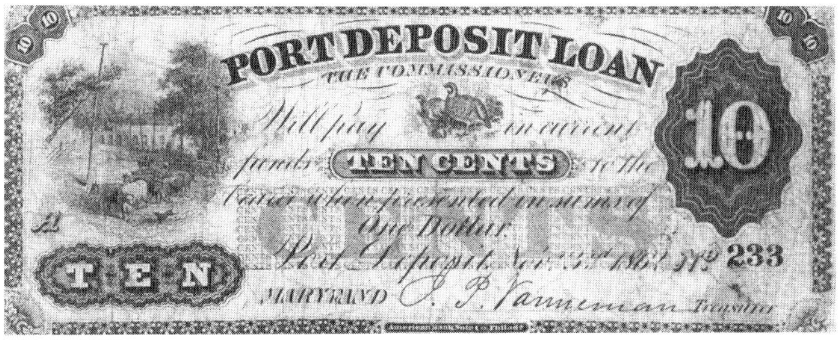

102.1.8

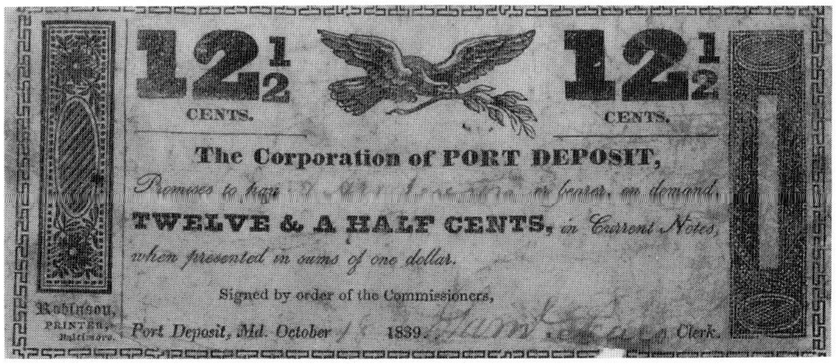

102.1.9

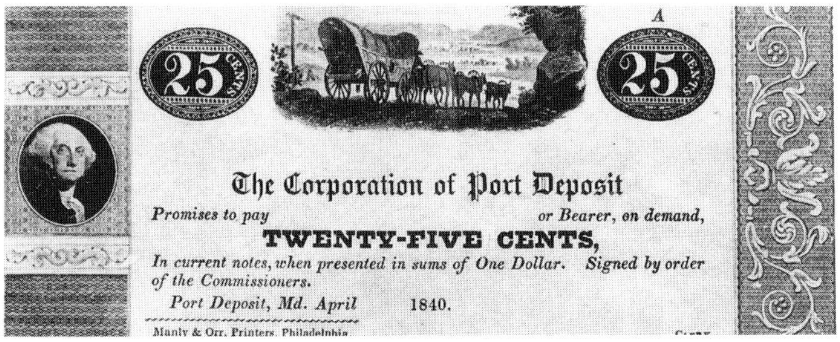

102.1.11

102.1.12 R-7

25c Printed partial date April __, 1840. Engraved vignettes, counters, and end plates, with text in letterpress, imprint: Manly & Orr, Printers, Philadelphia.

102.1.13 R-4

25c Printed date Oct. 25th, 1857. Engraving, imprint: Draper, Welsh & Co., Phila.

102.1.14 R-3

25c Printed date Nov. 3rd, 1862. Engraving, imprint: American Bank Note Co., Philada. Brick red security underprint CENTS.

102.1.15 R-7

50c Printed partial date July __, 1837. Letterpress, imprint: Robinson, PRINTER, Baltimore.

102.1.16 R-7

50c Printed partial date October __, 1839. Letterpress, imprint: Robinson, PRINTER, Baltimore.

102.1.17 R-5

50c Printed partial date April __, 1840. Engraved vignettes, counters, and end plates, with text in letterpress, imprint: Manly & Orr, Printers, Philadelphia.

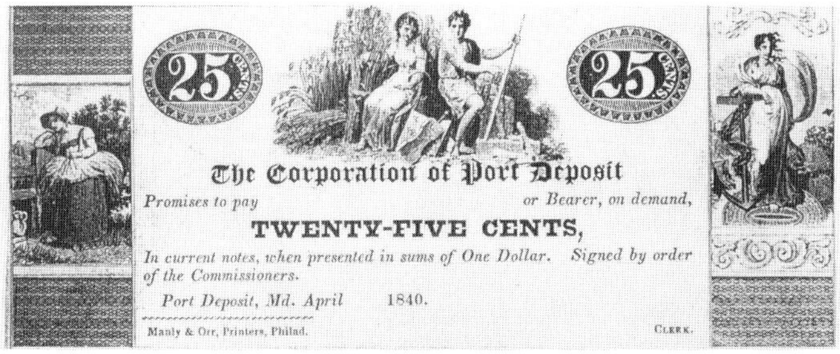

102.1.12

102.1.13

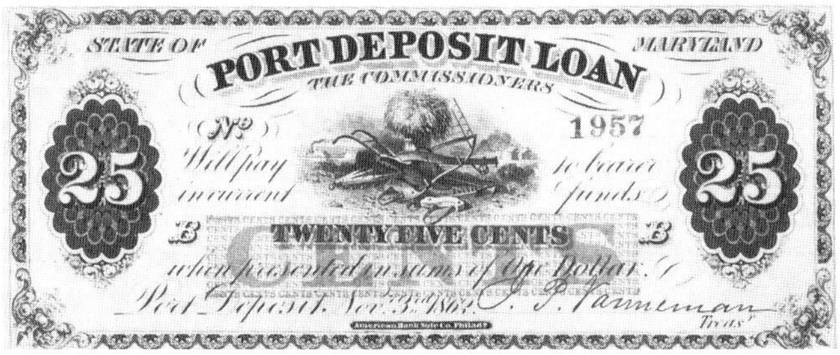

102.1.14

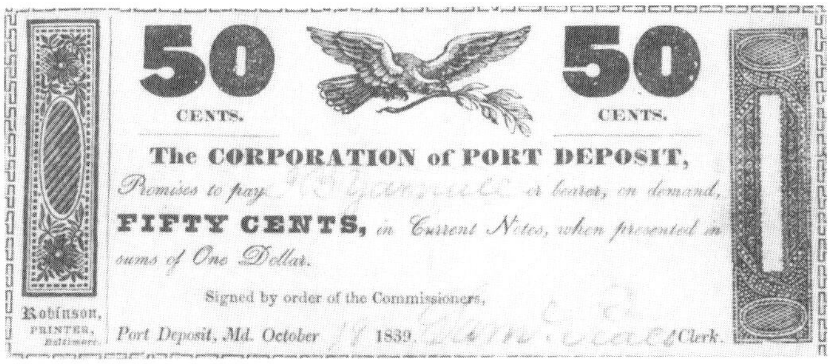

102.1.16

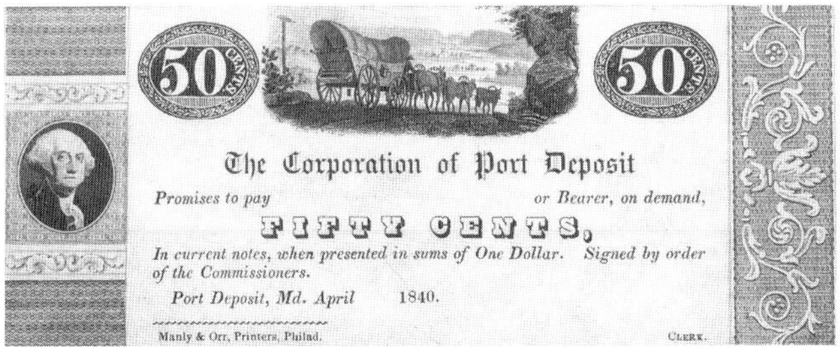

102.1.17

102.1.18 R-4

50c Printed date Oct. 25th, 1857. Engraving, imprint: Draper, Welsh & Co., Phila.

102.1.19 R-3

50c Printed date Nov. 3rd, 1862. Engraving, imprint: American Bank Note Co., Philada. With brick red security underprint CENTS.

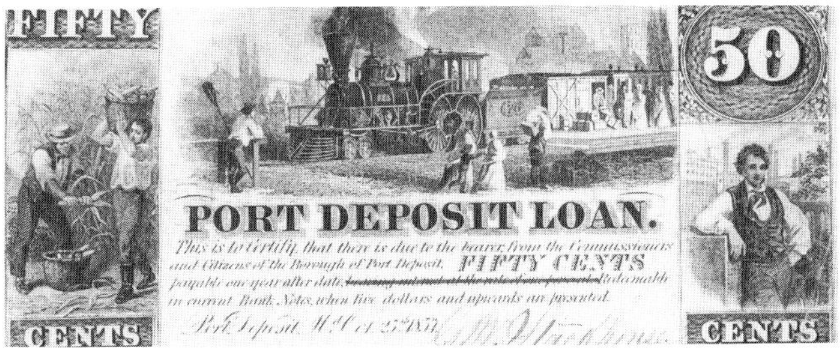

102.1.18

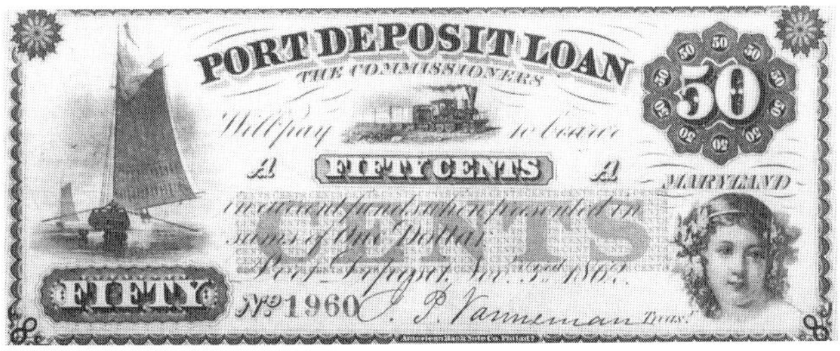

102.1.19

Uncirculated right half sheet comprised of $1.00 (102.1.22), $1.00 (102.1.23), and 25c (102.1.12).

102.1.22 R-7

$1.00 Printed partial date April __ 1840. Engraved vignettes, counters, and end plates, with text in letterpress, imprint: Manly & Orr, Printers, Philadelphia.

102.1.23 R-5

$1.00 Printed partial date April __ 1840. Engraved vignettes, counters, and end plates, with text in letterpress, imprint: Manly & Orr, Printers, Philadelphia.

102.1.24 SENC

$1.00 Printed date Oct. 25, 1857. Engraving, imprint: Draper, Welsh & Co., Phila.

102.1.24 P R-7

$1.00 Printed date Oct. 25, 1857. Engraving, imprint: Draper, Welsh & Co., Phila. Proof of $1.00, No. 102.1.24.

102.1.22

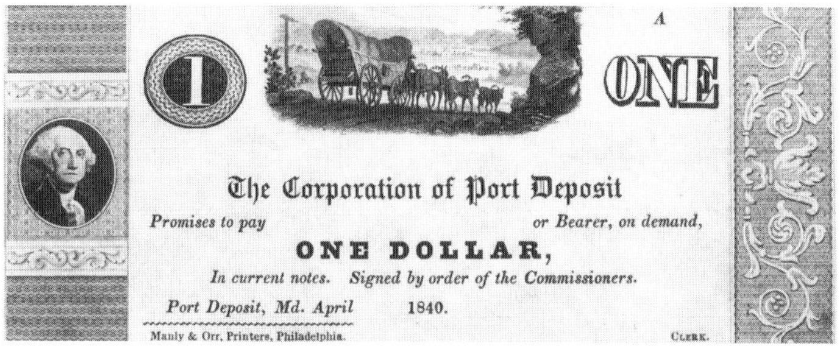

102.1.23

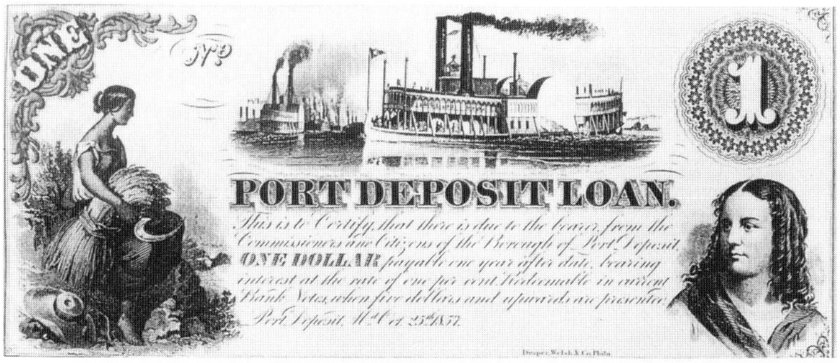

102.1.24 P

102.2 J. W. Abrahams

The precise status of the "note" listed and illustrated below has not as yet been determined. The surname "Abrahams," or occasionally "Abrams," has been familiar to residents of the area for many years. The 1860 federal census index lists four Abrahams (Henry, James C., Mary, and Thomas Jr.), all in the Fifth District of Cecil County; and thirteen Abrams (including J. W., James, and two Johns), all again in the Port Deposit area. In a list of marriage licenses issued in Cecil County, 1840–63, John W. Abrams and Lucy J. Egan were licensed October 25, 1859. The note, dated in the latter part of the Civil War, may have been simply a receipt for a small expenditure or, just as possibly, a piece of privately issued scrip. In any case, it is listed for the record.

102.2.1 R-7

2c Printed partial year date 186_. Letterpress, no imprint.

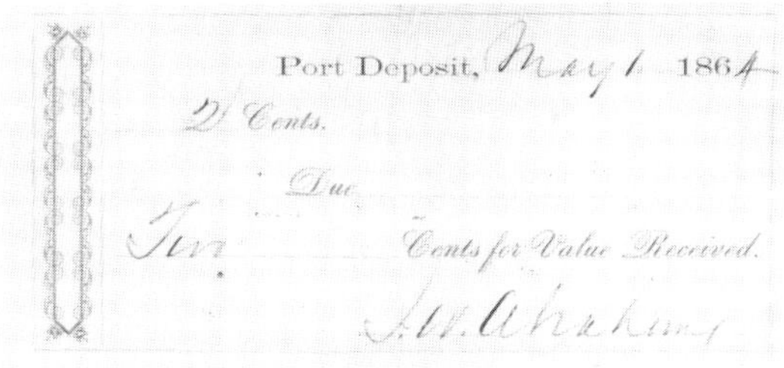

102.2.1

102.3 Barnes & Rowland

The issuers were proprietors of a general store.

102.3.1 R-7

6 1/4c Printed date May 20th, 1840. Engraving, imprint: Manly & Orr, Printers, Philad. This heavily circulated note identifies the issuers of this scrip.

102.3.2 R-7

12 1/2c Printed date May 20th, 1840. Engraving, imprint: Manly & Orr, Printers, Philad.

102.3.3 R-7

25c Printed date May 20th, 1840. Engraving, imprint: Manly & Orr, Printers, Philad. Similar to 12 1/2c, No. 102.3.2.

102.3.5 R-7

$1.00 Printed date May 20th, 1840. Engraving, imprint: Manly & Orr, Printers, Philad. Center vignette depicts Admiral Perry's victory on Lake Erie.

102.3.1

102.3.2

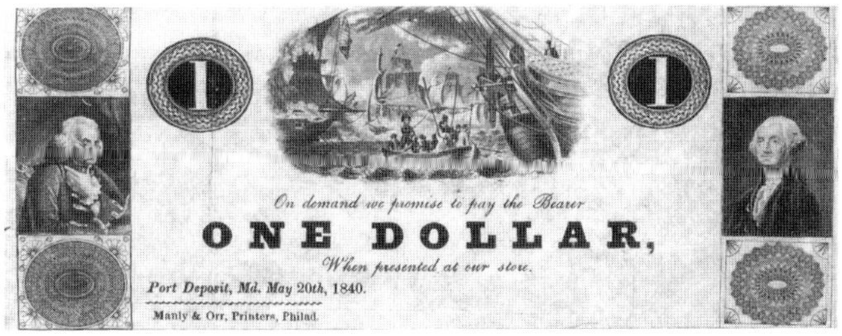

102.3.5

102.4 The Cecil Bank

Charter approved March 7, 1850; converted to and became the Cecil National Bank of Port Deposit in 1865.

102.4.1 R-7

$1.00 Ca. 1851. Engraving, imprint: Toppan, Carpenter, Casilear & Co., Phila.

102.4.2 R-6

$1.00 Printed date May 2nd, 1861. Engraving, imprint: American Bank Note Company, Phila. Red security underprint outlining white ONE. Similar to No. 102.4.1, except for printed date, security underprint, and different printer. (MD275G2b)

102.4.2 P R-7

$1.00 Printed date May 2nd, 1861. Engraving, imprint: American Bank Note Company, Phila. Red security underprint outlining white ONE. Proof.

102.4.3 R-7

$2.00 Printed date May 2nd, 1861. Engraving, imprint: American Bank Note Company, Phila. Red security underprint outlining white TWO. (MD275G4b)

102.4.3 P R-7

$2.00 Printed date May 2nd, 1861. Engraving, imprint: American Bank Note Company, Phila. Red security underprint outlining white TWO. Proof.

102.4.4 P R-7

$5.00 Ca. 1850s. Engraving, imprint: Draper, Welsh & Co., Philada. Similar to No. 102.4.6, except without red overprint. Proof. (MD275G6)

102.4.5 R-7

$5.00 Ca. 1850s. Engraving, imprint: unknown. Train at center and female portrait at lower right. (MD275N5)

102.4.1

102.4.2

102.4.3

102.4.4 P

102.4.6 R-7

$5.00 Ca. late 1858–60s. Engraving, imprint: Draper, Welsh & Co., Philada., and with American Bank Note Co. monogram. Red security overprint "5-5." (MD275G6b)

102.4.8 R-7

$10.00 Ca. 1850s. Engraving, imprint: Draper, Welsh & Co., Philada.

102.4.8 P R-7

$10.00 Ca. 1850s. Engraving, imprint: Draper, Welsh & Co., Philada. Proof. (MD275G8)

102.4.10 R-7

$10.00 Ca. 1858–65. Engraving, imprint: Draper, Welsh & Co., Philada., and American Bank Note Co. monogram. Red security overprint. Similar to No. 102.4.8. (MD275G8b)

102.4.11 R SENC

$10.00 Printed date May 2nd, 1861. Engraving, imprint: American Bank Note Co. Raised from $1.00, No. 102.4.2. (MD275R5)

102.4.12 P R-7

$20.00 Ca. 1850s. Engraving, imprint: Draper, Welsh & Co. Philada. Proof. (MD275G10)

102.4.13 SENC

$20.00 Ca. 1858–65. Engraving, imprint: Draper, Welsh & Co. Philada., and American Bank Note Co. monogram. Red security overprint. Similar to No. 102.4.12 P. (MD275G10b)

102.4.6

102.4.8

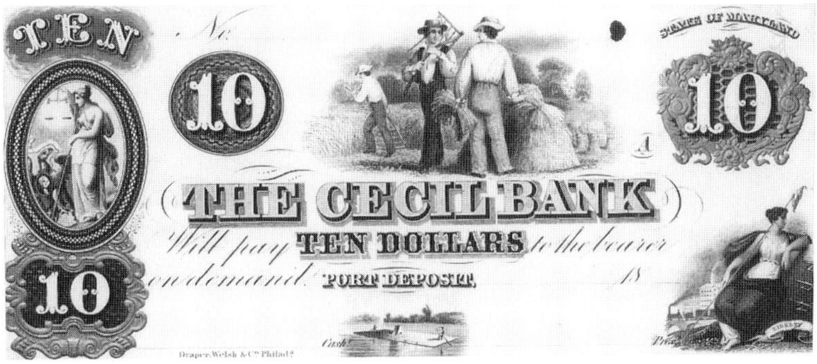

102.4.8 P

102.4.12 P

102.4.15 P R-7

$50.00 Ca. 1850s–60s. Engraving, imprint: Draper, Welsh & Co., Philada. Proof. (MD275G12)

102.4.17 P R-7

$100.00 Ca. 1850s–60s. Engraving, imprint: Draper, Welsh & Co., Philada. Proof. (MD275G14)

102.4.15 P

102.4.17 P

102.6 J. A. Davis & Co.

Included in the index card records of a collector active prior to the mid-1950s was a description of a note he had seen, the amount and name of the payee written in ink. The recorded note is illustrated below, having been included in a 1993 auction sale. No information on the identity of the issuer has as yet been found, although the company obviously operated a store.

102.6.1 R-7

___ cents, printed partial date 186_. Letterpress, no imprint.

102.6.1

102.7 Andrew Kidd

The issuer was the proprietor of a general store. Remainder notes are known bearing a penciled signature, M. Morris; and others with "York, Pa." in manuscript.

102.7.1 R-7

5c Printed date April 22, 1841. Engraving, imprint: Manly & Orr, Printers, Philadelphia.

102.7.2 R-7

6 1/4c Printed date April 22, 1841. Engraving, imprint: Manly & Orr, Philadelphia. Similar to 25c note, No. 102.7.5.

102.7.3 R-7

12 1/2c Printed date April 22, 1841. Engraving, imprint: Manly and Orr, Philadelphia.

102.7.4 R-7

25c Printed date April 22, 1841. Engraving, imprint: Manly & Orr, Philadelphia.

102.7.5 R-7

25c Printed date April 22, 1841. Engraving, imprint: Manly & Orr, Philadelphia.

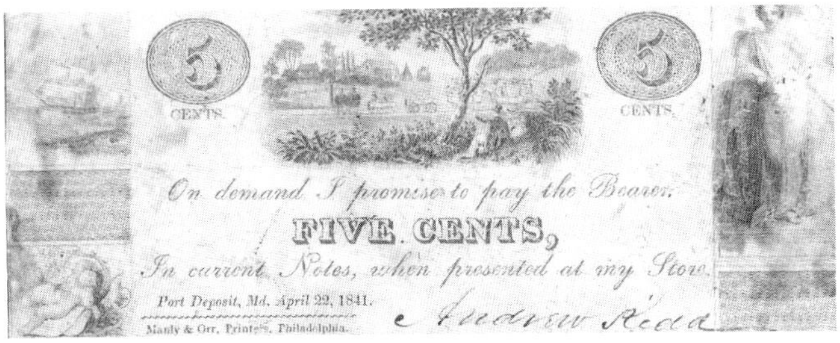

102.7.1

102.7.2 102.7.4 102.7.3

102.8 Kidd's Purchase

The issuer was the proprietor of a general store near Port Deposit.

102.8.1 R-7

5c Printed date April 26, 1838. Lithography, no imprint.

102.8.2 R-7

10c Printed date April 26, 1838. Lithography, no imprint. Similar to 5c, No. 102.8.1, except with TEN CENTS across each end.

102.8.3 R-7

25c Printed date April 26, 1838. Lithography, no imprint.

102.8.1

102.8.4 R-7

50c Printed date April 26, 1838. Lithography, no imprint.

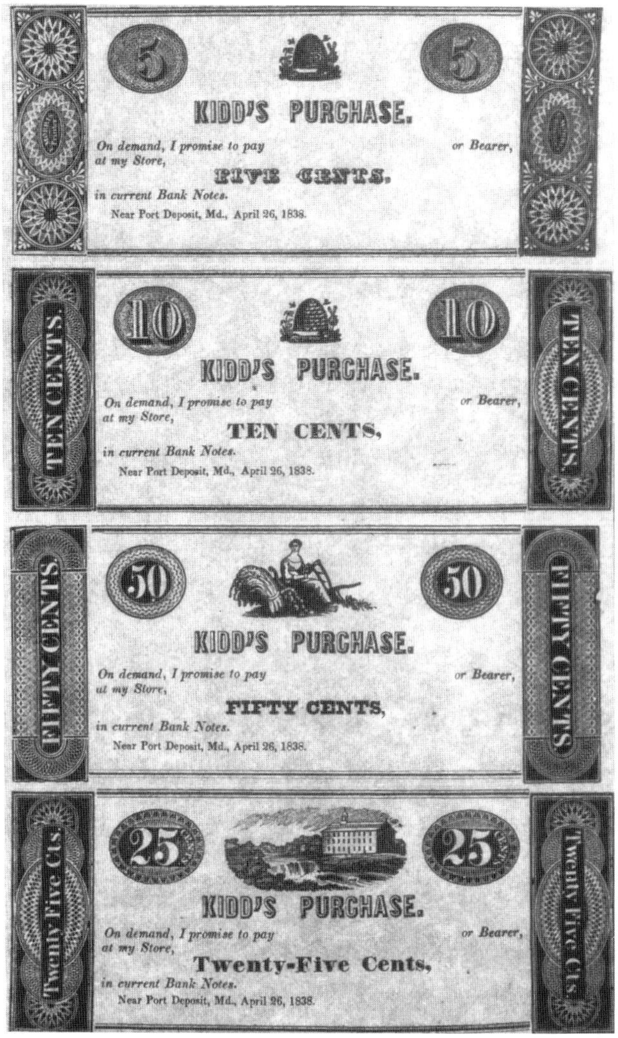

102.8.1 102.8.2 102.8.4 102.8.3

102.9 Lyon & Lumsden

Based on available genealogical records, it seems probable that the issuers were George F. Lyon and John Lumsden, proprietors of a general store.

102.9.2 R-7

10c Printed date July __ 1837. Letterpress, imprint: Printed by J. Robinson, Baltimore.

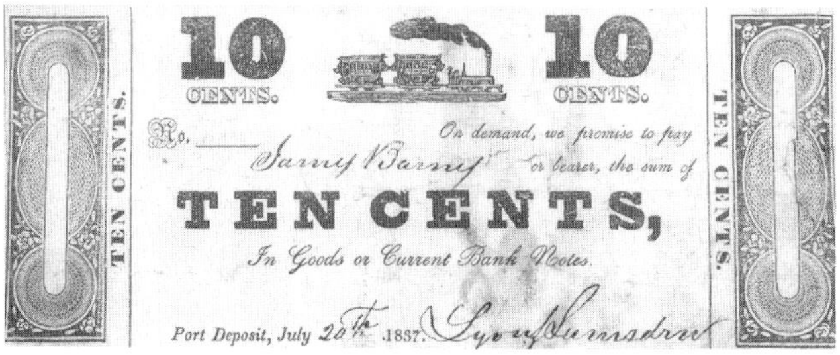

102.9.2

102.9.4 R-6

50c Printed date May __ 1841. Engraving, imprint: Manly & Orr, Printers, Philadelphia.

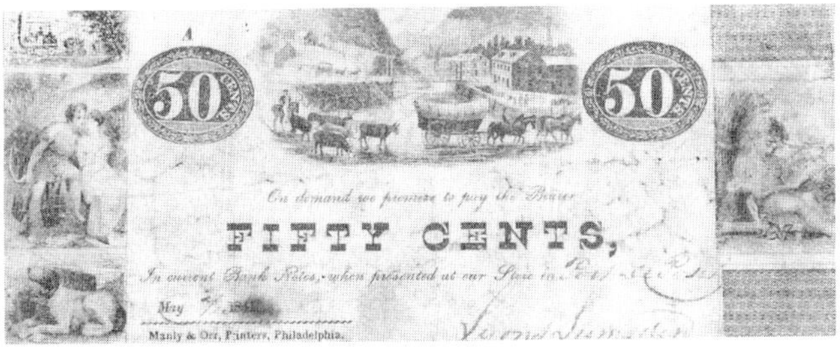

102.9.4

102.11 The Susquehanna Bank

Charter amendment approved January 18, 1834; formerly Susquehanna Bridge & Bank Co. (1815); payment of notes refused in 1834; reorganized and reopened in 1836; failed in 1838. Apparently the bank made arrangements with the Missouri Life Insurance and Trust Co. in St. Louis to redeem their notes when presented for payment as evidenced by $5.00 and $10.00 proof notes as listed below.

102.11.1 R-2

$1.00 Ca. 1837. Engraving, imprint: Chas. Toppan & Co., Phila. (MD280G2)

102.11.1 P R-7

$1.00 Ca. 1837. Engraving, imprint: Chas. Toppan & Co., Phila. Proof.

102.11.2 R-3

$2.00 Ca. 1837. Engraving, imprint: Chas. Toppan & Co., Phila. (MD280G4)

102.11.2 P R-7

$2.00 Ca. 1837. Engraving, imprint: Chas. Toppan & Co., Phila. Proof.

102.11.1

102.11.1 P

102.11.2 P

102.11.3 R-3

$3.00 Ca. 1837. Engraving, imprint: Chas. Toppan & Co., Phila. (MD280G6)

102.11.3 P R-7

$3.00 Ca. 1837. Engraving, imprint: Chas. Toppan & Co., Phila. Proof.

102.11.4 R-2

$5.00 Ca. 1837. Engraving, imprint: Chas. Toppan & Co., Phila. (MD280G8)

102.11.5 P R-7

$5.00 Ca. 1836–38. Engraving, imprint: Draper, Toppan, Longacre & Co., Phila. & N.Y. Payable at the office of the Missouri Life Insurance & Trust Co. in the City of St. Louis. Proof.

102.11.6 R-2

$10.00 Ca. 1837. Engraving, imprint: Chas. Toppan & Co., Phila. (MD280G10)

102.11.3

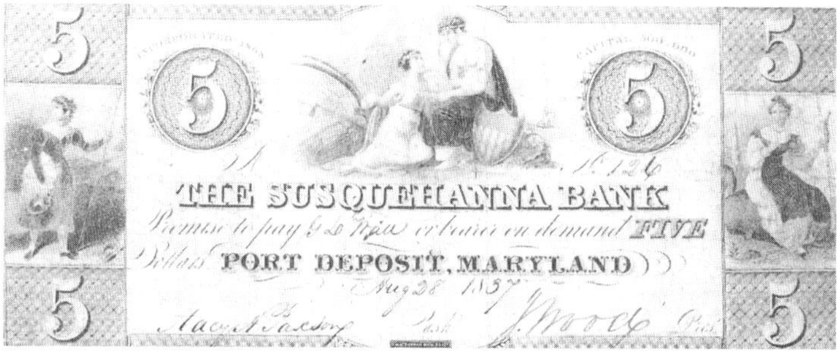

102.11.4

102.11.5 P

102.11.6

102.11.7 P R-7

$10.00 Ca. 1836–38. Engraving, imprint: Draper, Toppan, Longacre & Co., Phila. & N.Y. Payable at the office of the Missouri Life Insurance & Trust Co. in the City of St. Louis. Proof.

102.11.8 R-2

$20.00 Ca. 1837. Engraving, imprint: Chas. Toppan & Co., Phila. Remainder. (MD280G12)

102.11.9 P R-7

$20.00 Ca. 1836–38. Engraving, imprint: Draper, Toppan, Longacre & Co., Phila. & N.Y. Payable at the office of the Missouri Life Insurance & Trust Co. in the City of St. Louis. Proof.

102.11.10 R-3

$50.00 Ca. 1837. Engraving, imprint: Chas. Toppan & Co., Phila. Remainder. (MD280G14)

102.11.11 R-3

$100.00 Ca. 1837. Engraving, imprint: Chas. Toppan & Co., Phila. Remainder. (MD280G16)

102.11.7 P

102.11.8

102.11.10

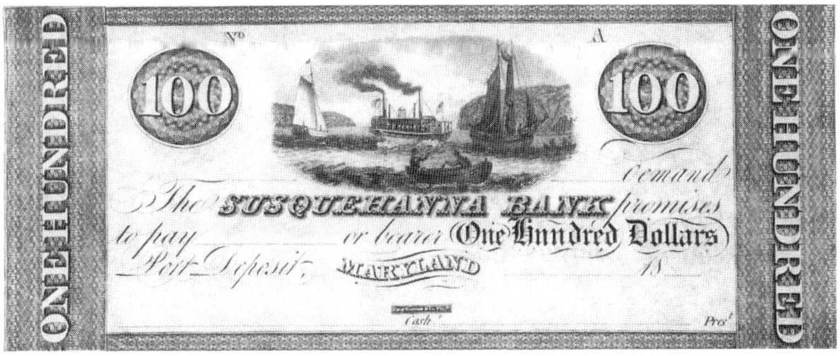

102.11.11

102.12 The Susquehanna Bridge & Bank Company

Originally chartered December 25, 1808, as the Susquehanna Bridge Company, a charter amendment approved January 19, 1815, changed the name of the institution to the Susquehanna Bridge & Bank Company. Beginning in 1816, the bank apparently operated an office in Baltimore, which existed until 1833 or 1834. In addition, the bank issued notes payable at the Maryland Savings Institution in Baltimore, which operated from approximately 1831 to 1833 and operated an office in Louisville, Ky., during the same period. A further amendment approved January 18, 1834, to comply with Maryland and Delaware law, changed the name to the Susquehanna Bank.

102.12.1 R-6

6 1/4c Printed date March 20th, 1816. Engraving, imprint: Rd. Hn. St. (Richard Harrison). Similar to 12 1/2c, No. 102.12.3.

102.12.2 R-7

10c Printed date March 20th, 1816. Engraving, imprint: Rd. Hn. St. (Richard Harrison). Similar to 12 1/2c, No. 102.12.3. (MD281G50)

102.12.3 R-6

12 1/2c Printed date March 20th, 1816. Engraving, imprint: Rd. Hn. St. (Richard Harrison). (MD281G52)

102.12.4 R-7

20c Printed date March 20th, 1816. Engraving, imprint: Rd. Hn. St. (Richard Harrison). (MD281G54)

102.12.5 R-7

25c Printed date March 20th, 1816. Engraving, imprint: Rd. Hn. St. (Richard Harrison). (MD281G56)

102.12.6 R-7

50c Printed date March 20th, 1816. Engraving, imprint: Rd. Hn. St. (Richard Harrison). Similar to 20c, No. 102.12.4. (MD281G58)

102.12.7 R-6

$1.00 Ca. 1818. Engraving, imprint: Richard Harrison, St., Printed by C. P. Har. Redeemable at the Office, Baltimore. (MD281G66)

102.12.9 SENC

$3.00 Surviving example not confirmed but recorded by D. C. Wismer in the *Coin Collectors Journal,* December 1940. No other information known.

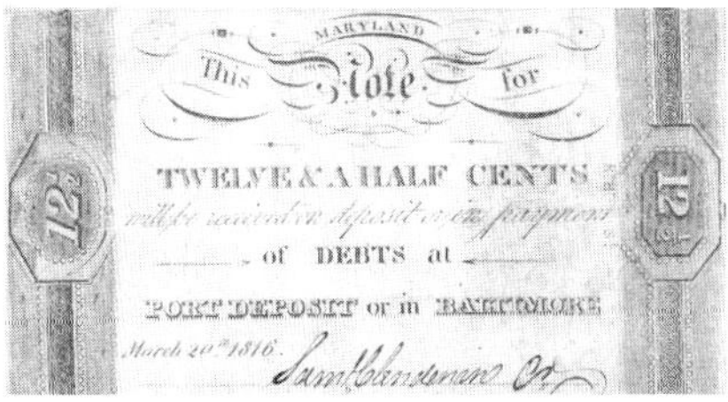

102.12.3

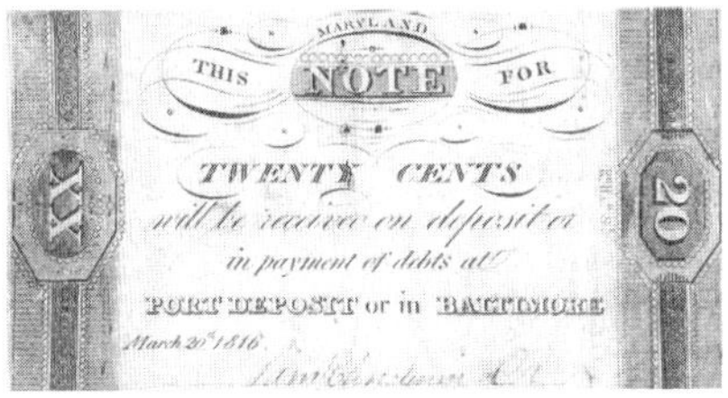

102.12.4

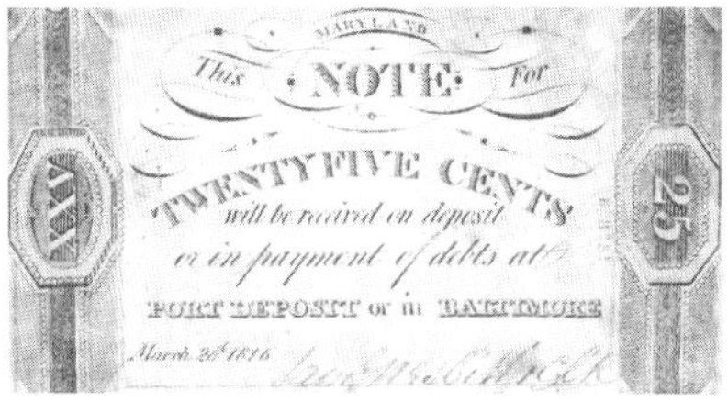

102.12.5

102.12.7

102.12.11 R-7

$5.00 Ca. 1818. Engraving, imprint: Richard Harrison, St., Printed by C. P. Har. Redeemable at the Office, Baltimore. (MD281G74)

102.12.12 R-4

$5.00 Ca. 1831. Engraving, imprint: Fairman, Draper, Underwood & Co. (MD281G10)

102.12.12 P R-6

$5.00 Ca. 1831. Engraving, imprint: Fairman, Draper, Underwood & Co. Proof.

102.12.13 R-1

$5.00 Ca. 1831. Engraving, imprint: CHAS. TOPPAN & CO., Phila. Payable at the Maryland Savings Institution, Baltimore. (MD281G120)

102.12.13 P R-6

$5.00 Ca. 1831. Engraving, imprint: CHAS. TOPPAN & CO., Phila. Payable at the Maryland Savings Institution, Baltimore. Proof.

102.12.14 R-1

$5.00 Ca. 1831–33. Engraving, imprint: CHAS. TOPPAN & CO., PHILA. Payable at Baltimore office. (MD281G80)

102.12.11

102.12.12

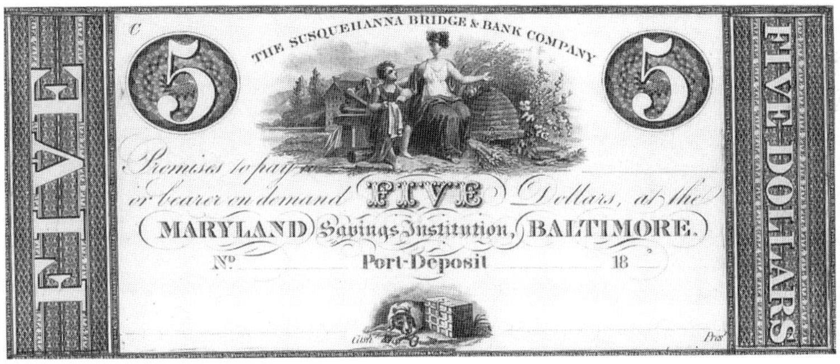

102.12.13 P

102.12.14

102.12.14 P R-5

$5.00 Ca. 1831–33. Engraving, imprint: CHAS. TOPPAN & CO., PHILA. Payable at Baltimore Office. Proof.

102.12.15 R-1

$5.00 Ca. 1833. Engraving, imprint: CHAS. TOPPAN & CO., Phila. Payment location not specified. (MD281G12)

102.12.15 P R-6

$5.00 Ca. 1833. Engraving, imprint: CHAS. TOPPAN & CO., Phila. Payment location not specified. Proof.

102.12.16 R-7

$5.00 Ca. 1833. Engraving, imprint: Chas. Toppan & Co., Phila. Payable at the office, Louisville, Ky. (MD281G106)

102.12.16 P R-6

$5.00 Ca. 1833. Engraving, imprint: Chas. Toppan & Co., Phila. Payable at the office, Louisville, Ky. Proof.

102.12.18 SENC

$10.00 Ca. 1810s. Engraving, imprint: Richard Harrison, St., Printed by C. P. Har. No other information available. (MD281G82)

102.12.19 R-4

$10.00 Ca. 1829–31. Engraving, imprint: Fairman, Draper, Underwood & Co. Payable in gold or silver or in scrip notes of the Bank of the United States, location not specified. (MD281G16)

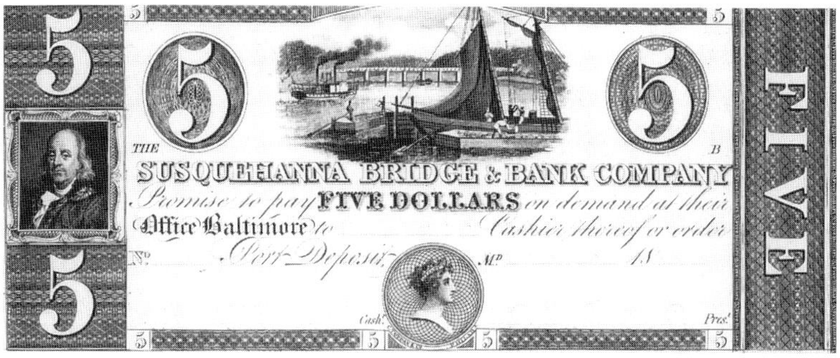

102.12.14 P

102.12.15

102.12.16 P

102.12.19

102.12.19 P R-7

$10.00 Ca. 1829–31. Engraving, imprint: Fairman, Draper, Underwood & Co. Payable in gold or silver or in scrip notes of the Bank of the United States, location not specified. Proof.

102.12.20 R-1

$10.00 Ca. 1831. Engraving, imprint: CHAS. TOPPAN & CO., Phila. Payable at the Maryland Savings Institution, Baltimore. (MD281G124)

102.12.20 P R-6

$10.00 Ca. 1831. Engraving, imprint: CHAS. TOPPAN & CO., Phila. Payable at the Maryland Savings Institution, Baltimore. Proof.

102.12.21 R-1

$10.00 Ca. 1832. Engraving, imprint: CHAS. TOPPAN & CO., Phila. Payable at the Baltimore Office. (MD281G84)

102.12.21 P R-6

$10.00 Ca. 1832. Engraving, imprint: CHAS. TOPPAN & CO., Phila. Payable at the Baltimore Office. Proof.

102.12.19 P

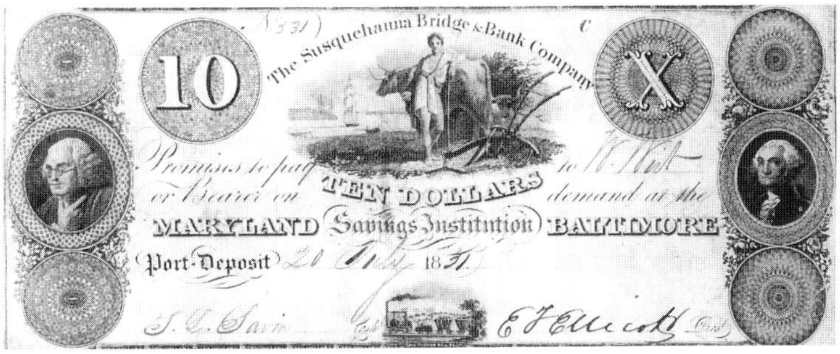

102.12.20

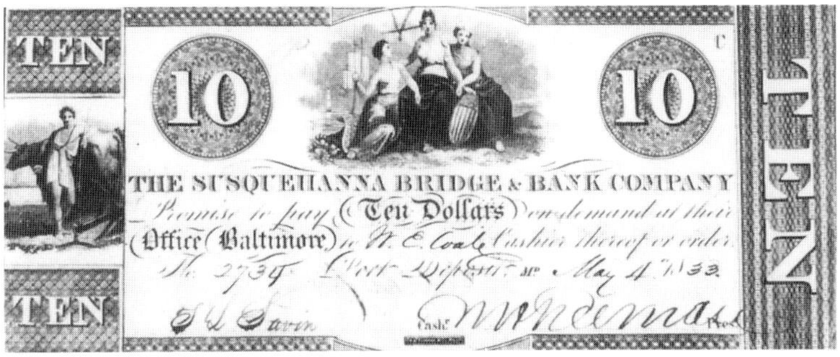

102.12.21

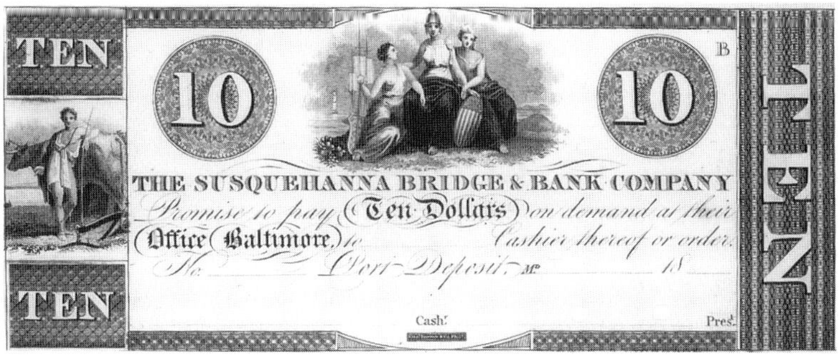

102.12.21 P

102.12.22 R-1

$10.00 Ca. 1833. Engraving, imprint: Chas. Toppan & Co., Phila. (MD281G18)

102.12.22 P R-6

$10.00 Ca. 1833. Engraving, imprint: Chas. Toppan & Co., Phila. Proof.

102.12.23 R-7

$10.00 Ca. 1833. Engraving, imprint: Chas. Toppan & Co., Phila. Payable at the office, Louisville, Ky. (MD281G110)

102.12.23 P R-7

$10.00 Ca. 1833. Engraving, imprint: Chas. Toppan & Co., Phila. Payable at the office, Louisville, Ky. Proof.

102.12.25 R-6

$20.00 Ca. 1818. Engraving, imprint: Rich Harrison, fc. Prin'd by C. P. Harrison. Redeemable at the Office, Baltimore. (MD281G86)

102.12.26 R-4

$20.00 Ca. 1831. Engraving, imprint: CHAS. TOPPAN & CO., Phila. Payable at the Maryland Savings Institution, Baltimore. (MD281G128)

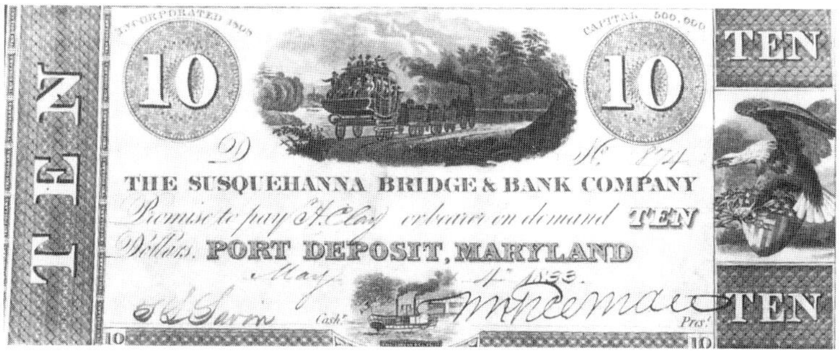

102.12.22

102.12.23

102.12.25

102.12.26

102.12.26 P R-7

$20.00 Ca. 1831. Engraving, imprint: CHAS. TOPPAN & CO., Phila. Payable at the Maryland Savings Institution, Baltimore. Proof.

102.12.27 R-3

$20.00 Ca. 1832. Engraving, imprint: CHAS. TOPPAN & CO., Phila. Payable at the Baltimore Office. (MD281G88)

102.12.27 P R-7

$20.00 Ca. 1832. Engraving, imprint: CHAS. TOPPAN & CO., Phila. Payable at the Baltimore Office. Proof.

102.12.28 R-4

$20.00 Ca. 1833. Engraving, imprint: CHAS. TOPPAN & CO., Phila. Place of payment not specified. (MD281G22)

102.12.26 P

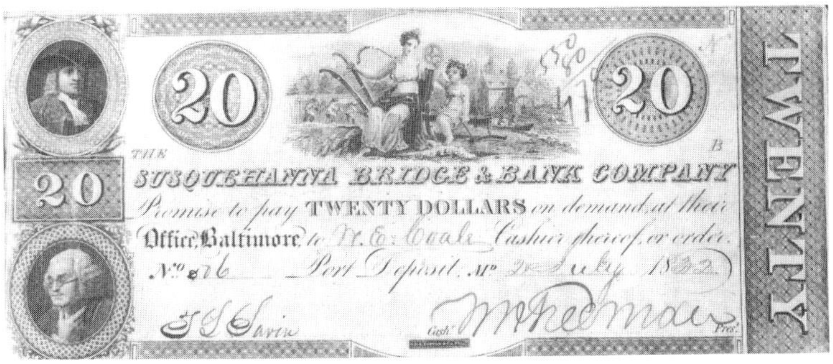

102.12.27

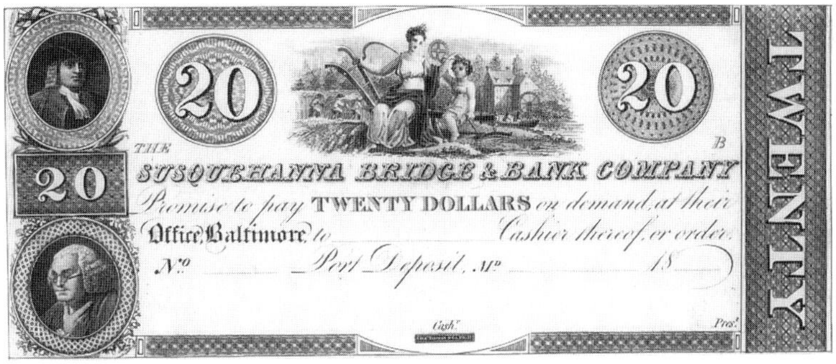

102.12.27 P

102.12.28

102.12.28 P R-7

$20.00 Ca. 1833. Engraving, imprint: CHAS. TOPPAN & CO., Phila. Place of payment not specified. Proof.

102.12.29 SENC

$20.00 Ca. 1833. Engraving, imprint: Chas. Toppan & Co., Phila. Payable at the office, Louisville, Ky.

102.12.29 P R-6

$20.00 Ca. 1833. Engraving, imprint: Chas. Toppan & Co., Phila. Payable at the office, Louisville, Ky. Proof.

102.12.31 P R-7

$50.00 Ca. 1810s. Engraving, imprint: Rich Harrison, fc. Printed by C. P. Harrison. REDEEMABLE AT THE OFFICE, BALTIMORE. Proof. (MD281G90)

102.12.32 R-5

$50.00 Ca. 1831. Engraving, imprint: Chas. Toppan & Co., Phila. Payable at the Maryland Savings Institution, Baltimore.

102.12.32 P R-7

$50.00 Ca. 1831. Engraving, imprint: Chas. Toppan & Co., Phila. Payable at the Maryland Savings Institution, Baltimore. Proof.

102.12.33 R-5

$50.00 Ca. 1832. Engraving, imprint: Chas. Toppan & Co., Phila. Payable at their OFFICE BALTIMORE. (MD281G94)

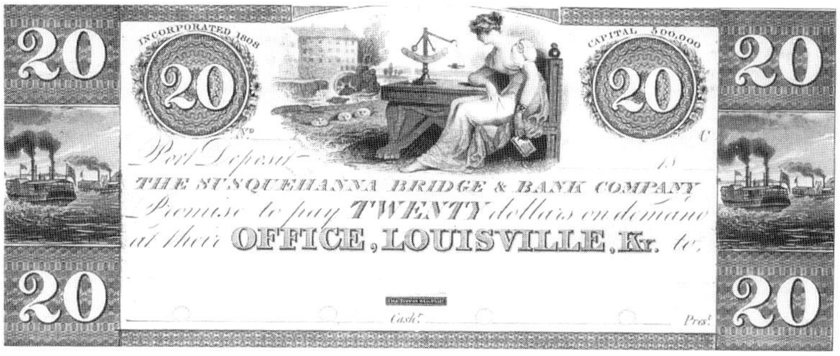

102.12.29 P

102.12.31 P

102.12.32 P

102.12.33

102.12.33 P R-7

$50.00 Ca. 1832. Engraving, imprint: Chas. Toppan & Co., Phila. Payable at their OFFICE BALTIMORE. Proof.

102.12.34 R-4

$50.00 Ca. 1833. Engraving, imprint: Chas. Toppan & Co., Phila. (MD281G26)

102.12.34 P R-7

$50.00 Ca. 1833. Engraving, imprint: Chas. Toppan & Co., Phila. Proof.

102.12.35 SENC

$50.00 Ca. 1833. Engraving, imprint: Chas. Toppan & Co., Phila. Payable at the office, Louisville, Ky.

102.12.35 P R-7

$50.00 Ca. 1833. Engraving, imprint: Chas. Toppan & Co., Phila. Payable at the office, Louisville, Ky. Proof.

102.12.37 R-4

$100.00 Ca. 1832. Engraving, imprint: CHAS. TOPPAN & CO., Phila. Payable at their office, Baltimore. (MD281G100)

102.12.33 P

102.12.34

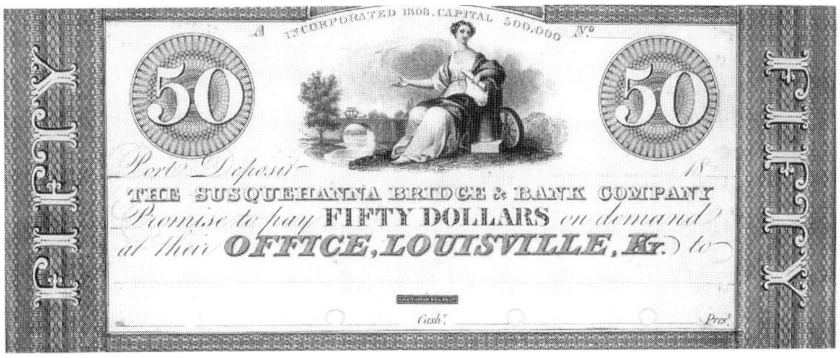

102.12.35 P

102.12.37

102.12.37 P R-7

$100.00 Ca. 1832. Engraving, imprint: CHAS. TOPPAN & CO., Phila. Payable at their office, Baltimore. Proof.

102.12.38 R-5

$100.00 Ca. 1832. Engraving, imprint: CHAS. TOPPAN & CO., Phila. Post note payable six months after date. (MD281G36)

102.12.38 P R-7

$100.00 Ca. 1832. Engraving, imprint: CHAS. TOPPAN & CO., Phila. Post note payable six months after date. Proof.

102.12.39 R-5

$100.00 Ca. 1832. Engraving, imprint: Chas. Toppan & Co., Phila. (MD281G30)

102.12.39 P R-7

$100.00 Ca. 1832. Engraving, imprint: Chas. Toppan & Co., Phila. Proof.

102.12.41 R-6

$500.00 Ca. 1832. Engraving, imprint: CHAS. TOPPAN & CO., Phila. Post note payable four months after date. (MD281G38)

102.12.41 P R-7

$500.00 Ca. 1832. Engraving, imprint: CHAS. TOPPAN & CO., Phila. Post note payable four months after date. Proof.

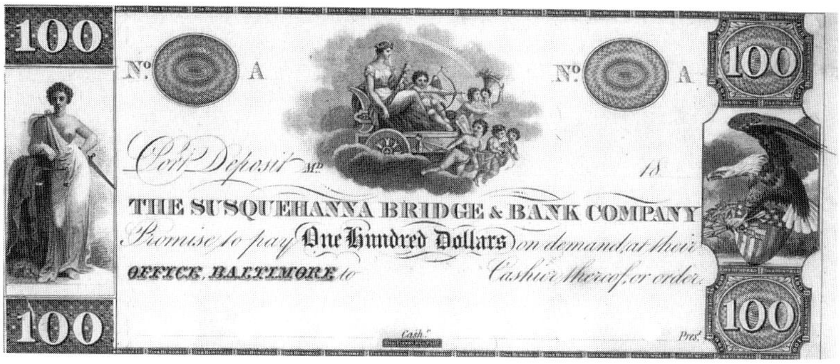

102.12.37 P

102.12.38

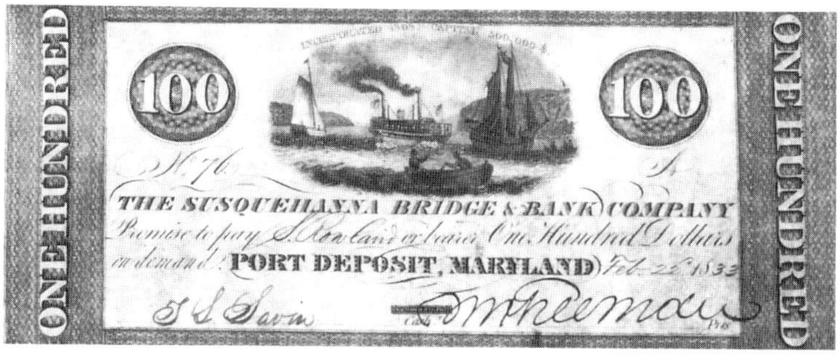

102.12.39

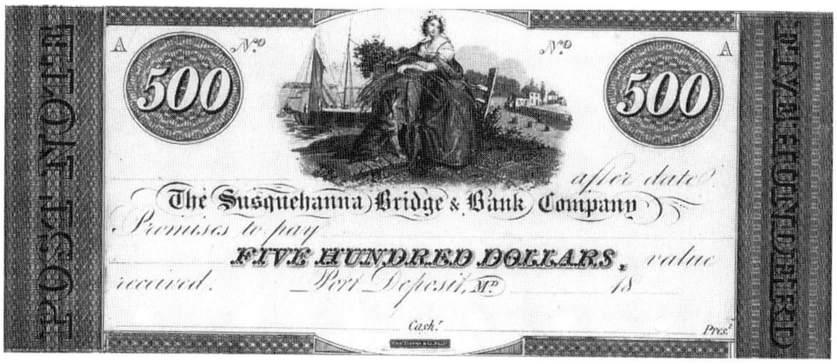

102.12.41 P

102.12.43 R-6

$1,000.00 Ca. 1832. Engraving, imprint: CHAS. TOPPAN & CO., Phila. Post note payable four months after date, labeled POST NOTE. (MD281G40)

102.12.43 P R-7

$1,000.00 Ca. 1832. Engraving, imprint: CHAS. TOPPAN & CO., Phila. Post note payable four months after date, labeled POST NOTE. Proof.

102.12.43

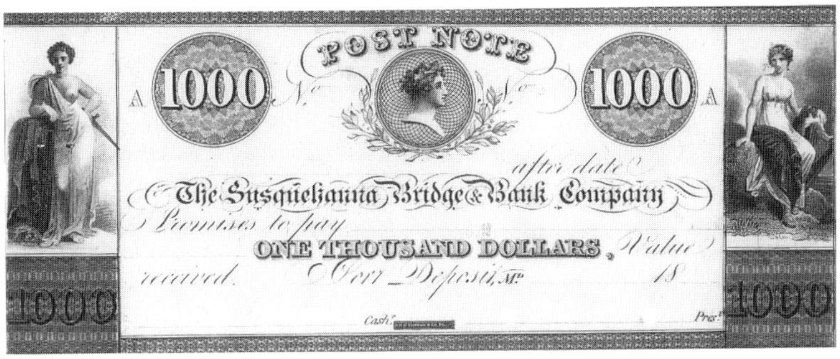

102.12.43 P

104 PORT TOBACCO, CHARLES COUNTY

In 1728 this town was officially named Charlestown. Its name was changed in 1820 to Port Tobacco, which was derived from the Algonquin Indian term "Potapaco," meaning a jutting of the water inland, and the Port Tobacco Creek on which it is located.

104.1 Beall Hodges

According to a resident of the area in 1976, the issuer was a storekeeper, one of whose ledgers was still in existence. A search of the federal census records has revealed no Beall Hodges, although there are a number of listings with that surname in the 1820–50 period.

104.1.1 R-7

6 1/4c Printed date May 1, 1838. Letterpress, imprint: Murphy & Spalding, printers, 1 Light st. Balt.

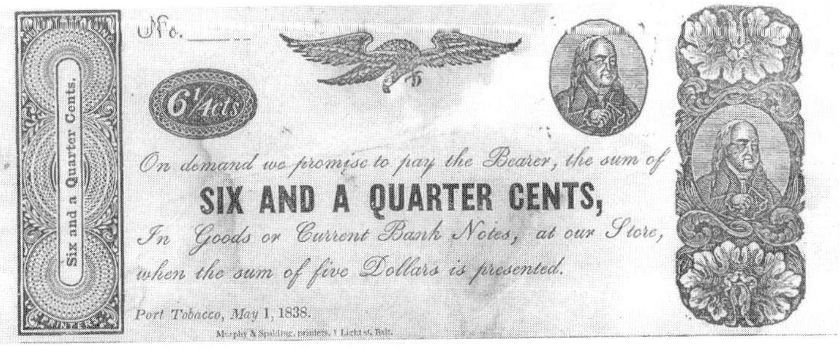

104.1.1

104.1.2 R-7

12 1/2c Printed date May 1, 1838. Letterpress, imprint: Murphy & Spalding, printers, 1 Light st. Balt.

104.1.3 R-7

25c Printed date May 1, 1838. Letterpress, imprint: Murphy & Spalding, printers No. 1 Light st. Balt.

104.1.4 R-7

50c Printed date May 1, 1838. Letterpress, imprint: Murphy & Spalding, printers, 1 Light street Baltimore.

104.1.5 R-7

$1.00 Printed date May 1, 1838. Letterpress, imprint: Murphy & Spalding, printers, 1 Light street Baltimore.

104.1.6 R-7

$2.00 Printed date May 1, 1838. Letterpress, imprint: Murphy & Spalding, printers, 1 Light street Baltimore.

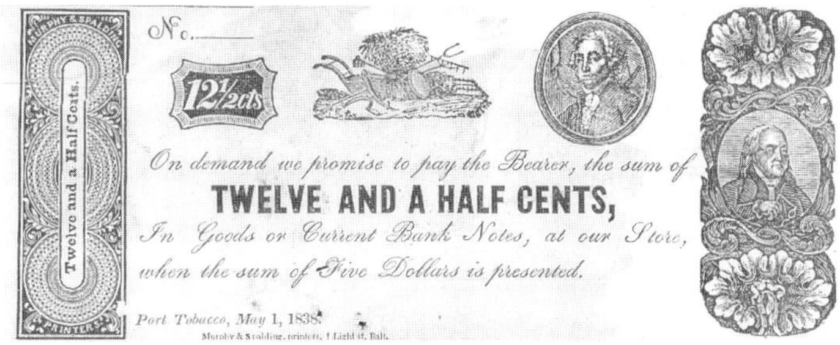

104.1.2

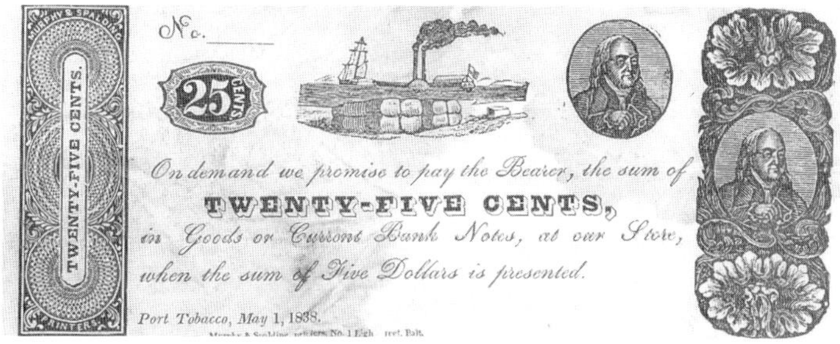

104.1.3

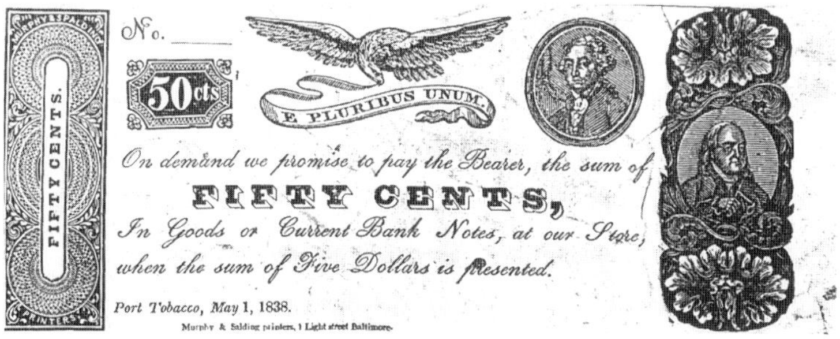

104.1.4

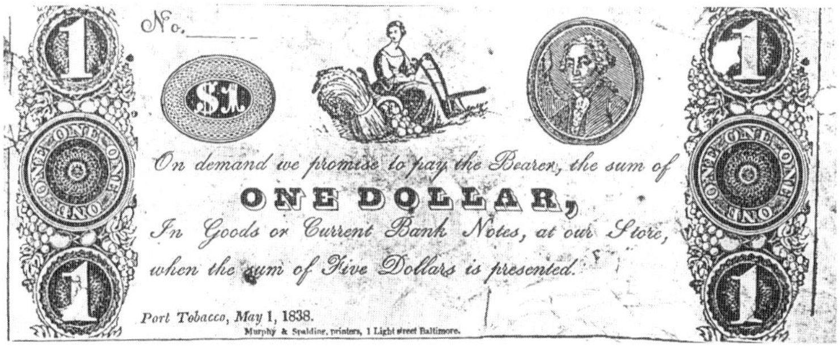

104.1.5

104.1.6

106 PRINCESS ANNE, SOMERSET COUNTY

Laid out and established in 1733 as Princess Anne Town in honor of Anne (1709–59), the daughter of King George II, this town is 13 miles from Salisbury, near the head of the Manokin River, and is the county seat.

106.1 Commissioners for Somerset County

Small-change scrip was issued by the county commissioners to fill the void caused by the disappearance of specie during the Civil War.

106.1.2 R-7

10c Printed date Jan. 20, 1863. Letterpress, no imprint.

106.1.2

106.2 The Eastern Shore Railroad Company

The company was incorporated March 29, 1836, operation being contingent upon raising capital of $2,000,000 from stock subscriptions. According to a "Report of the Commissioners of the Eastern Shore Railroad to the Governor of Maryland" (Annapolis, 1837), the line would run "118 miles, 377 yards long, from a point in the Wilmington and Susquehanna Railroad near Elkton, to Tangier Sound where a line of steamers would then connect with Portsmouth, Virginia, 85 miles." The first annual report to stockholders, December 6, 1838, showed little progress, principally as the result of a series of legal battles "with Mr. Teackle of Princess Anne and his daughter." No changes were planned in the proposed line between Little Annamessex on the Nanticoke River and Greensborough, but there were to be some deviations between Greensborough and the head of the Bohemia River, according to the president, Thomas Emory. The second annual report by Emory, in Millington, January 14, 1840, again showed relatively little progress. In his annual "Governor's Message to the Legislature" (December 30, 1840), the governor of Maryland reported that "the affairs of the Company wound up in 1840 and the road was abandoned." The "Panic of 1837" had done its work; the railroad failed to open. The project was resurrected in 1860 and ultimately the railroad reached Somer's Cove (now Crisfield). Failure came in 1879 and the New York, Philadelphia and Norfolk Railroad took over the Eastern Shore Railroad tracks.

106.2.1 SENC

$1.00 Dated March 4, 1848. *Center:* Two females holding pole and cap and fasces, bust of female between signatures. *Right:* Bust of female, 1 on U.S. shield above. *Left:* Head of female, 1 on U.S. shield above. Surviving example not confirmed but recorded by D. C. Wismer in *The Numismatist,* September 1925. No other information available.

106.2.2 SENC

$1.00 Date unknown. *Center:* U.S. shield, female, and 3 children on right, Indian squaw and child on left. *Right:* Female seated, 1 on die above. *Left:* Justice with scales, 1 on ONE above, ONE below. *Between signatures:* Locomotive. Surviving example not confirmed but recorded by D. C. Wismer in *The Numismatist,* September 1925. No other information available.

106.2.3 R-7

$5.00 Ca. 1837–40. Engraving, imprint: Rd. G. Harrison, Sct, Philada.

106.2.3 P R-7

$5.00 Ca. 1837–40. Engraving, imprint: Rd. G. Harrison, Sct, Philada. Similar to $10.00, No. 106.2.4. Proof.

106.2.4 R-7

$10.00 Ca. 1837–40. Engraving, imprint: Rd. G. Harrison, Sct, Philada.

106.2.4 P R-7

$10.00 Ca. 1837–40. Engraving, imprint: Rd. G. Harrison, Sct, Philada. Proof.

106.2.5 R-7

$20.00 Ca. 1837–40. Engraving, imprint: Rd. G. Harrison, Sct, Philada. Similar to $10.00, No. 106.2.4.

106.2.5 P R-7

$20.00 Ca. 1837–40. Engraving, imprint: Rd. G. Harrison, Sct, Philada. Similar to $10.00, No. 106.2.4. Proof.

106.2.6 SENC

$50.00 Date unknown. Surviving example not confirmed but recorded by D. C. Wismer in the *Coin Collectors Journal,* December 1940. No other information available.

106.2.3

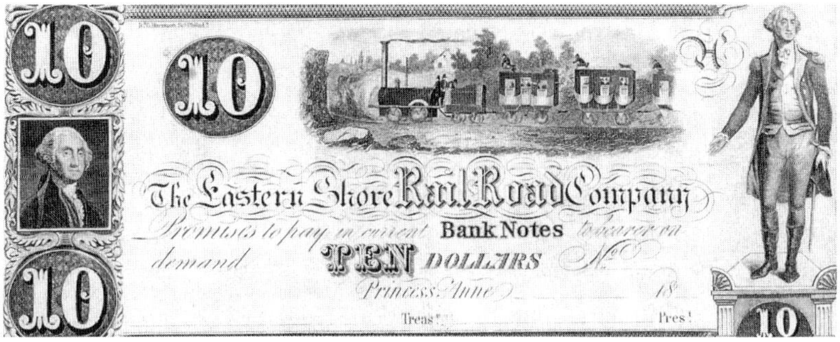

106.2.4

106.2.5

106.3 Bank of Somerset

Charter approved January 3, 1814; voluntary liquidation in 1821.

106.3.3 R-7

25c Printed date Feb. 12, 1816. Engraving, imprint; Murray, Draper, Fairman & Co.

106.3.4 R-7

50c Printed date August 23, 1815. Engraving, imprint: Murray, Draper, Fairman & Co. Similar to 25c, No. 106.3.3.

106.3.5 R-6

$1.00 Ca. 1814–18. Engraving, imprint: Murray, Draper, Fairman & Co. (MD285G18)

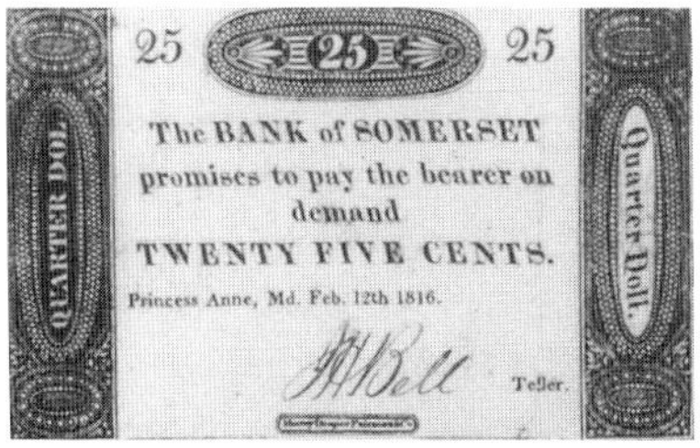

106.3.3

106.3.6 R-5

$2.00 Ca. 1814–18. Engraving, imprint: Murray, Draper, Fairman & Co. (MD285G20)

106.3.7 R-6

$3.00 Ca. 1814–18. Engraving, imprint: Murray, Draper, Fairman & Co.

106.3.8 R-7

$4.00 Ca. 1814–18. Engraving, imprint: Murray, Draper, Fairman & Co.

106.3.9 R-5

$5.00 Ca. 1814–18. Engraving, imprint: Murray, Draper, Fairman & Co. (MD285G24)

106.3.5

106.3.6

106.3.7

106.3.9

106.3.9 P R-7

$5.00 Ca. 1814–18. Engraving, imprint: Murray, Draper, Fairman & Co. Proof.

106.3.10 R-5

$10.00 Ca. 1814–18. Engraving, imprint: Murray, Draper, Fairman & Co. Similar to $5.00, No. 106.3.9. (MD285G26)

106.3.10 P R-7

$10.00 Ca. 1814–18. Engraving, imprint: Murray, Draper, Fairman & Co. Similar to $5.00, No. 106.3.9. Proof.

106.3.11 R-5

$20.00 Ca. 1814–18. Engraving, imprint: Murray, Draper, Fairman & Co. Similar to $5.00, No. 106.3.9. (MD285G28)

106.3.11 P R-7

$20.00 Ca. 1814–18. Engraving, imprint: Murray, Drpaer, Fairman & Co. Similar to $5.00, No. 106.3.9. Proof.

106.3.12 R-7

$50.00 Ca. 1814–18. Engraving, imprint: Murray, Draper Fairman & Co. (MD285G30)

106.3.13 R-7

$100.00 Ca. 1814–18. Engraving, imprint: Murray, Draper Fairman & Co. Similar to $50.00, No. 106.3.12.

106.3.9 P

106.3.10

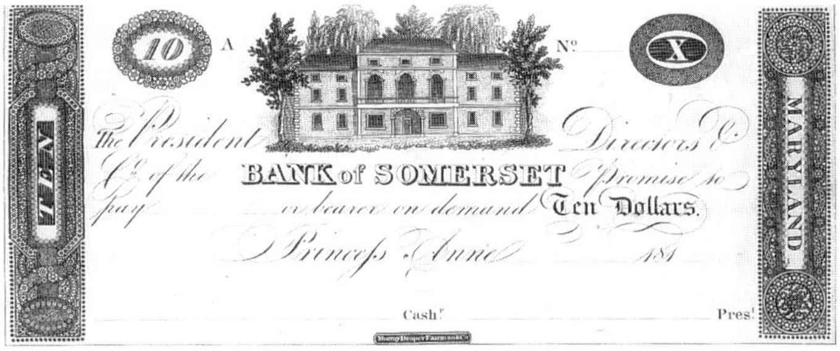

106.3.10 P

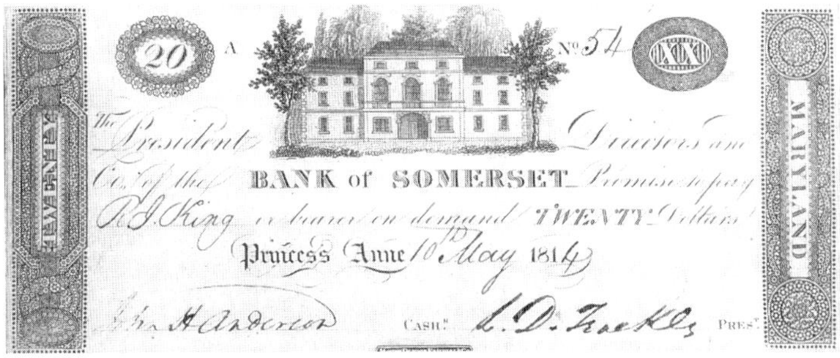

106.3.11

106.3.12

106.4 Steam Company of Princess Anne

This company was chartered by an act passed by the General Assembly of Maryland on January 5, 1816, for the purpose of "erecting a steam mill and manufacturing company."

106.4.1 P R-7
$1.00 Ca. 1816. Engraving, no imprint. Progressive die proof.

106.4.2 P R-7
$2.00 Ca. 1816. Engraving, no imprint. Progressive die proof.

106.4.3 R-7
$3.00 Ca. 1816. Engraving, imprint: Murray, Draper, Fairman & Co.

106.4.3 P R-7
$3.00 Ca. 1816. Engraving, imprint: Murray, Draper, Fairman & Co. Proof.

106.4.1 P

106.4.2 P

106.4.3

106.4.3 P

106.4.4 R-7

$5.00 Ca. 1816. Engraving, imprint: Murray, Draper, Fairman & Co.

106.4.4 P R-7

$5.00 Ca. 1816. Engraving, imprint: Murrary, Draper, Fairman & Co. Proof.

106.4.4

106.4.4 P

108 PROVIDENCE MILLS, DORCHESTER COUNTY

Despite its appearance on the illustrated notes, no such placename has appeared in the various gazetteers and similar publications available to the authors. A search of contemporary census records for anyone with the surname "Urie" (the signature on both notes is James Urie) yields the fact that the only listed Uries in Maryland in the 1830–60 records were residents of the First and/or Second Election Districts in Kent County. There was a small village or hamlet, called Urieville, about 2 1/2 miles from Kennedyville, which was a post office from 1846 to about 1855. Due to the availability of good water power in much of Kent County, there were a number of flouring and grist mills in the general area, one of which may have borne the name Providence.

108.1 James Urie

According to the redemption legend on his notes, James Urie was a storekeeper. Whether he was a miller as well is not known. He appears in the 1830 and 1850 censuses, but not in that for 1840. Perhaps he opened his store in Dorchester County in the mid- to late 1830s and then moved to Kent County at about the time the 1840 census was being conducted, thus missing listings in both census years. He appears in 1850 as a farmer with six children and two slaves, and with a $15,000 property valuation, not a small holding in those times.

108.1.3 R-7

10c Printed date December 20, 1839. Letterpress, imprint: Murphy, Print, Balt. (*right*); Murphy & Spalding, Printers (*left*). "Dorchester" lined out and "Kent" written at lower left.

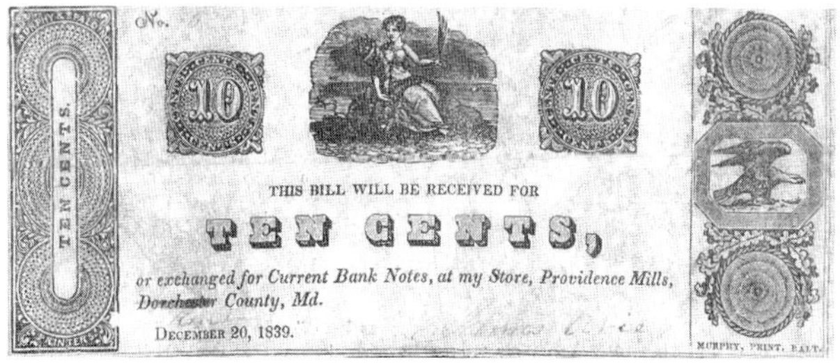

108.1.3

108.1.4 R-7

12 1/2c Printed date December 20, 1839. Letterpress, imprint: Murphy, Print., Balt.

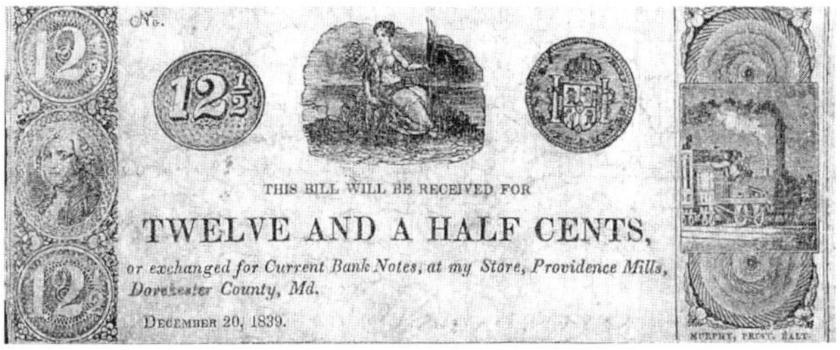

108.1.4

110 QUEEN ANN'S COUNTY

The county was established in 1706 in honor of Queen Anne of England.

110.1 Issuer Unidentified

110.1.1 R-7

5c Ca. 1862–63. Letterpress, imprint: LUCAS & SON, PRINTERS, BALT. Woodcut vignette at left has negative imprint: JOCELYN.

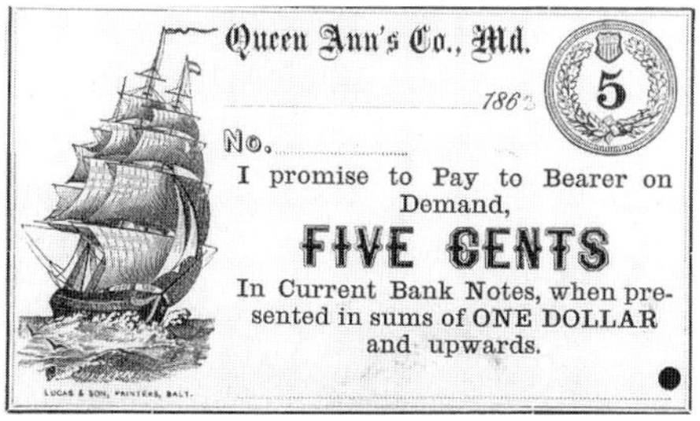

110.1.1

112 REISTERSTOWN, BALTIMORE COUNTY

Originally known as Reister's Desire, this town was settled in 1758 by John Reister, a German immigrant, on a 20-acre grant by the Calvert family.

112.1 Reisterstown Savings Institution

This institution was probably formed in 1840 or 1841 by the president, John Sumwalt, a leading citizen of the town.

112.1.1 R-7

6 1/4c Printed partial date ____ 1841. Lithograph, imprint: Lith. by Ed. Weber & Co., Balt. Similar to 12 1/2c, No. 112.1.2, with farm scene vignette.

112.1.2 R-7

12 1/2c Printed partial date ___1841. Lithograph, imprint: Lith. by Ed. Weber & Co., Balt.

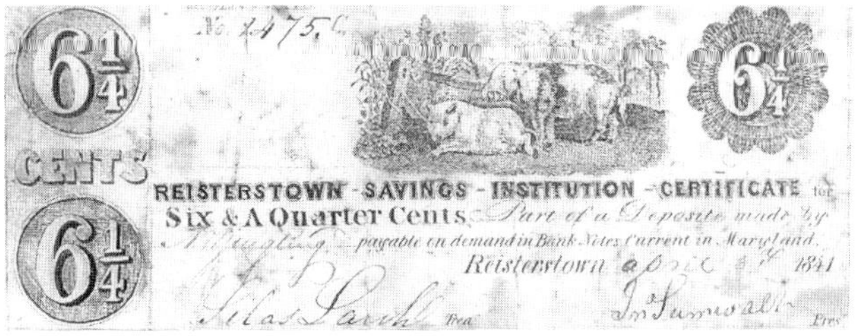

112.1.1

112.1.2

114	**ST. MARTIN'S, WORCESTER COUNTY**	This village is located on the present-day Route 346 about four miles north-northwest of Berlin.

114.1 Unidentified Issuer

The status of the signature, Thomas Warner, on these notes is undetermined. From the use of the word "We" in the redemption statement, it would seem that a merchants' partnership was the intended issuer.

114.1.1 R-7
6 1/4c Printed partial date September __ 1837. Letterpress and engraving, no imprint.

114.1.4 R-7
50c Printed partial date September __ 1837. Letterpress and engraving, no imprint.

114.1.5 R-7
$1.00 Printed partial date September __ 1837. Letterpress and engraving, no imprint.

114.1.1 114.1.4 114.1.5

116	**SALISBURY, WICOMICO COUNTY**	In 1732, by authorization of the Provincial Assembly, 20 lots to be called Salisbury-Town were surveyed and laid out. The name came from Salisbury, Wiltshire, in England. Wicomico County was formed in 1867 from portions of Somerset and Worcester counties; prior to 1867, the town was partially located in each of the two counties.

Farmers Bank of Somerset & Worcester, Salisbury Branch

See No. 128.2.

116.1 Dr. John Huston

In 1816, the issuer to whom these scrip notes are attributed operated a "banking house" from his office at Bank Alley and Bridge Street, which in 1932 became 316 Main Street when the original structure was razed. The later building was destroyed by fire in 1960.

116.1.1 R-7
2c Printed date Jan. 2, 1816. Letterpress, no imprint.

116.1.2 R-7
3c Printed date Jan. 2, 1816. Letterpress, no imprint.

116.1.3 R-7
6 1/4c Printed date Jan. 2, 1816. Letterpress, no imprint.

116.1.4 R-7
12 1/2c Printed date Jan. 2, 1816. Letterpress, no imprint.

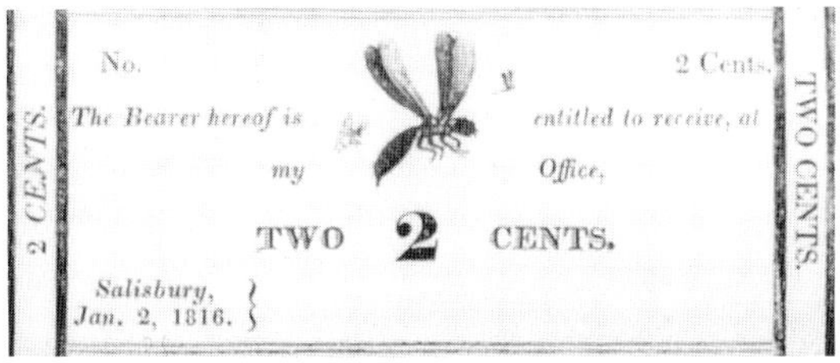

116.1.1

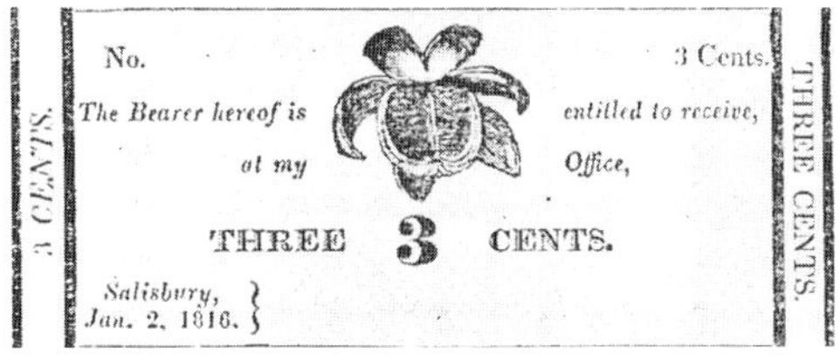

116.1.2

116.1.3

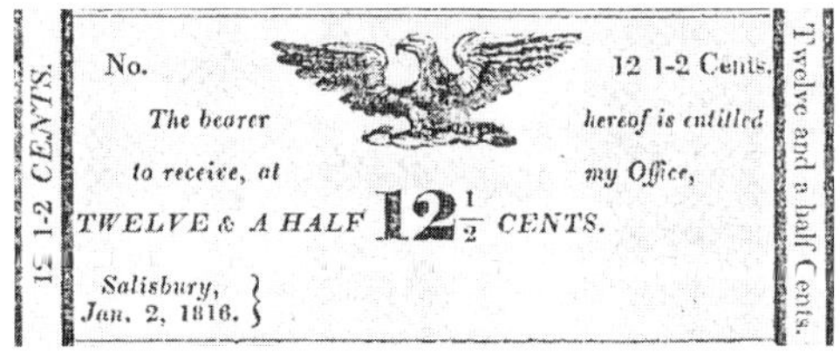

116.1.4

116.2 Benjamin Parsons (1789–1873)

The issuer was listed in a directory as a tailor from 1825 to 1830 and then "progressed into other endeavors."

116.2.3 R-7
10c Ca. 1839. Letterpress, no imprint.

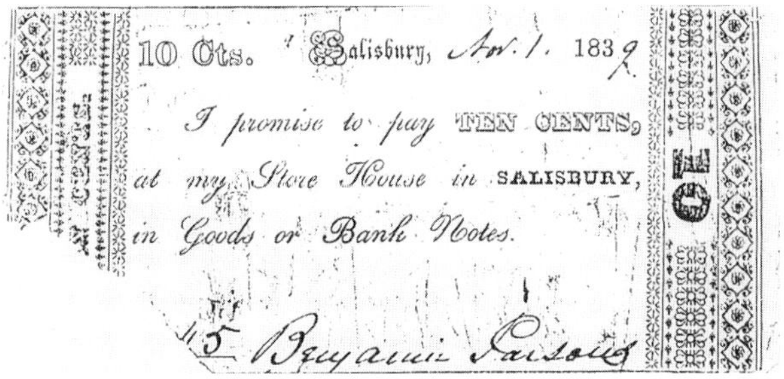

116.2.3

116.3 J. F. Parsons

The issuer was the proprietor of a general store.

116.3.1 R-7

5c Ca. 1862–64. Letterpress, no imprint.

116.3.1

116.4 The Bank of Salisbury

Charter approved February 15, 1830; failed in September 1851.

116.4.1 R-4

$1.00 Ca. 1846. Engraving, imprint: Danforth, Underwood & Co., New York / Underwood, Bald, Spencer & Hufty, Philada. Listed by Haxby as an altered note; however, a genuine proof note was discovered in the American Bank Note archives. (MD290S5)

116.4.1 P R-7

$1.00 Ca. 1846. Engraving, imprint: Danforth, Underwood & Co., New York / Underwood, Bald, Spencer & Hufty, Philada. Proof.

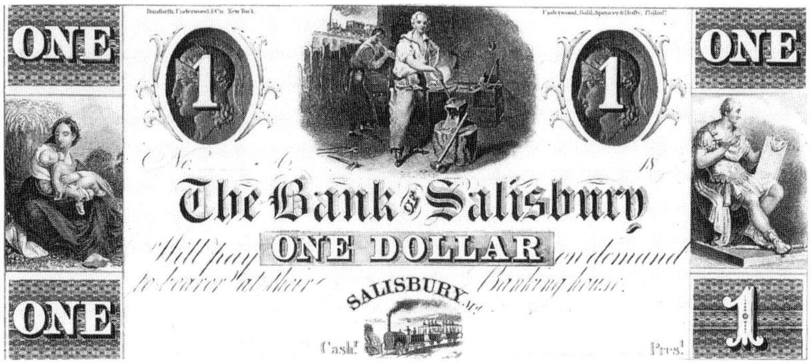

116.4.1 P

116.4.2 R-3

$1.00 Printed date March 4, 1848. Engraving, imprint: Danforth & Hufty, New York & Philada. Mrs. Andrew Jackson at lower left. (MD290G26)

116.4.2 P R-7

$1.00 Printed date March 4, 1848. Engraving, imprint: Danforth & Hufty, New York & Philada. Mrs. Andrew Jackson at lower left. Proof.

116.4.2

116.4.3 R-7

$1.00 Printed date March 4, 1848. Engraving, imprint: Danforth & Hufty, New York & Philada. With large orange-red fancy "1-1" security imprint. Mrs. Andrew Jackson at lower left. (MD290G26a)

116.4.3 P R-7

$1.00 Printed date March 4, 1848. Engraving, imprint: Danforth & Hufty, New York & Philada. Proof of No. 116.4.3.

116.4.3 P

116.4.4 R-3

$1.00 Printed date March 4, 1851. Engraving, imprint: Danforth, Bald & Co., New York & Philada. (MD290G28)

116.4.4 P R-7

$1.00 Printed date March 4, 1851. Engraving, imprint: Danforth, Bald & Co., New York & Philada. Proof.

116.4.5 R-5

$2.00 Ca. 1846. Engraving, imprint: Danforth, Underwood & Co., New York / Underwood, Bald, Spencer & Hufty, Philada. Listed by Haxby as an altered note; however, a genuine proof note was discovered in the American Bank Note Co. archives. (MD290S10)

116.4.5 P R-7

$2.00 Ca. 1846. Engraving, imprint: Danforth, Underwood & Co., New York / Underwood, Bald, Spencer & Hufty, Philada. Proof.

116.4.6 R-4

$2.00 Printed date March 4, 1848. Engraving, imprint: Danforth & Hufty, New York & Philada. Mrs. Andrew Jackson at lower left. (MD290G30)

116.4.7 R-7

$2.00 Printed date March 4, 1848. Engraving, imprint: Danforth & Hufty, New York & Philada. Same as No. 116.4.6, except large fancy "2 2" overprint in orange. (MD290G30a)

116.4.4

116.4.4 P

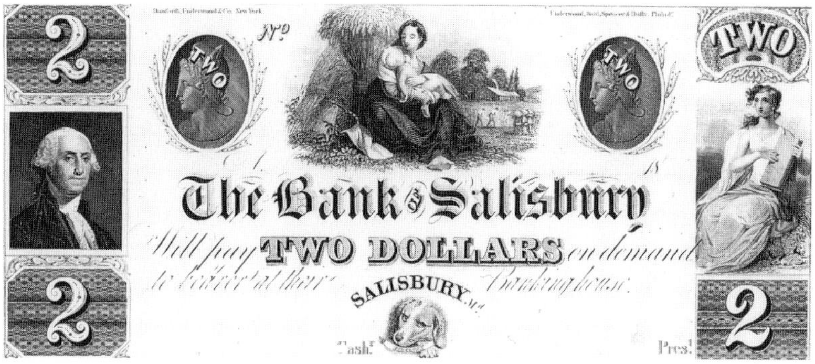

116.4.5 P

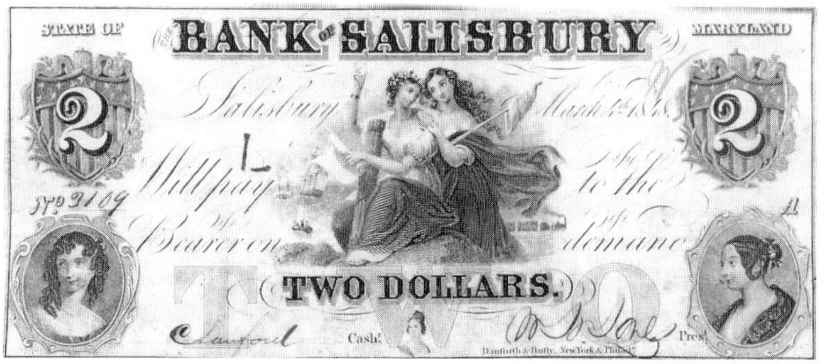

116.4.6

116.4.7 P R-7

$2.00 Printed date March 4, 1848. Engraving, imprint: Danforth & Hufty, New York & Philada. Same as No. 116.4.6, except large fancy "2 2" overprint in orange. Proof.

116.4.8 R-4

$2.00 Printed date March 4, 1851. Engraving, imprint: Danforth, Bald & Co., New York & Philada. (MD290G32)

116.4.8 P R-7

$2.00 Printed date March 4, 1851. Engraving, imprint: Danforth, Bald & Co., New York & Philada. Proof.

116.4.9 R-7

$3.00 Ca. 1845–56. Engraving, imprint: Danforth, Underwood & Co., New York / Underwood, Bald, Spencer & Hufty, Philada. Listed by Haxby as an altered note; however, a genuine proof note was discovered in the American Bank Note Co. archives. (MD290S15)

116.4.9 P R-7

$3.00 Ca. 1845–56. Engraving, imprint: Danforth, Underwood & Co., New York / Underwood, Bald, Spencer & Hufty, Philada. Proof.

116.4.10 P R-7

$5.00 Ca. 1830s. Engraving, imprint: Fairman, Draper, Underwood & Co. Proof.

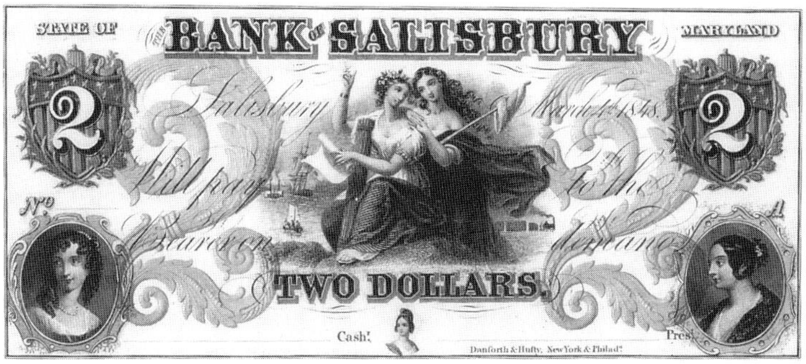

116.4.7 P

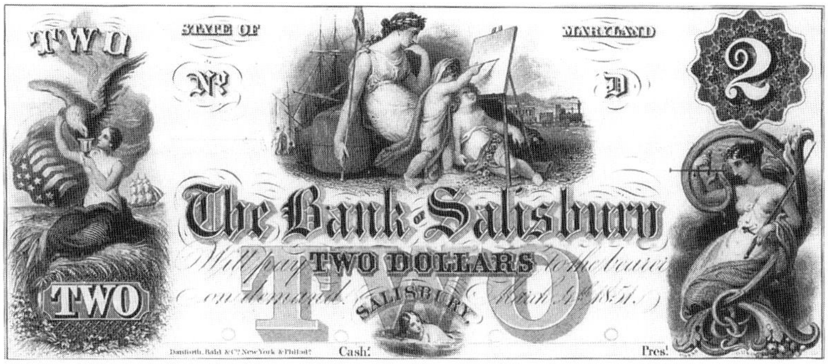

116.4.8 P

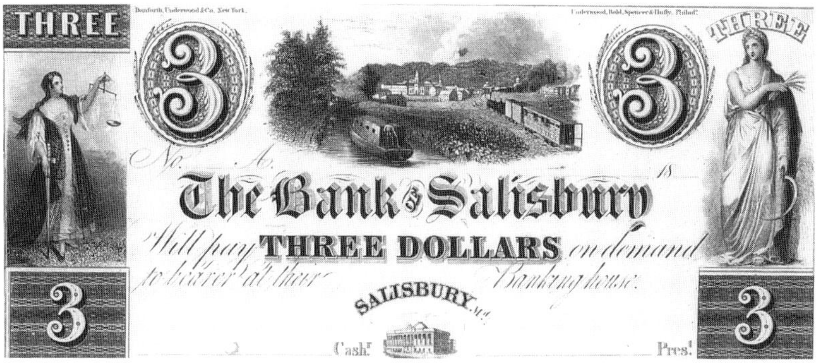

116.4.9 P

116.4.10 P

116.4.11 P R-6

$5.00 Ca. 1830s. Engraving, imprint: Chas. Toppan & Co. Phila. Proof. (MD290G10)

116.4.12 R-7

$5.00 Ca. 1846–53. Engraving, imprint: Underwood, Bald, Spencer & Hufty, Philada / Danforth, Underwood & Co., New York. *Center:* Child reclining with five on medallion head each side. *Left:* FIVE. *Right:* 5; 5 on medallion head; 5.

116.4.13 R-4

$5.00 Printed date March 4, 1848. Engraving, imprint: Danforth & Hufty, New York & Philada. Zachary Taylor at lower right. (MD290G34)

116.4.13 P R-7

$5.00 Printed date March 4, 1848. Engraving, imprint: Danforth & Hufty, New York & Philada. Zachary Taylor at lower right. Proof.

116.4.14 SENC

$5.00 Printed date March 4, 1848. Engraving, imprint: Danforth & Hufty, New York & Philada. Zachary Taylor at lower right. Same as No. 116.4.13, except for addition of large lazy "5" and orange tint.

116.4.14 P R-7

$5.00 Printed date March 4, 1848. Engraving, imprint: Danforth & Hufty, New York & Philada. Zachary Taylor at lower right. Same as No. 116.4.13, except for addition of large lazy "5" and orange tint. Proof. (MD290G34a)

116.4.15 R SENC

$5.00 Printed date March 4, 1848. Engraving, imprint: Danforth & Hufty, New York & Philada. Raised from $1.00, No. 116.4.2. (MD290R5)

116.4.16 P R-7

$10.00 Ca. 1830s. Engraving, imprint: Fairman, Draper, Underwood & Co. Proof.

116.4.17 P R-7

$10.00 Ca. 1830s. Engraving, imprint: Chas. Toppan & Co., Phila. Proof.

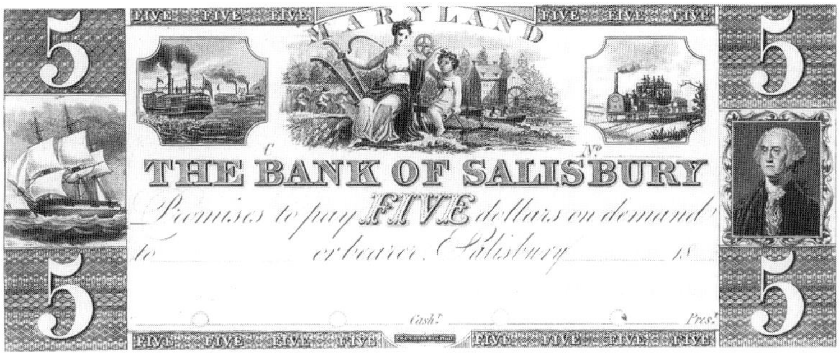

116.4.11 P

116.4.14 P

116.4.16 P

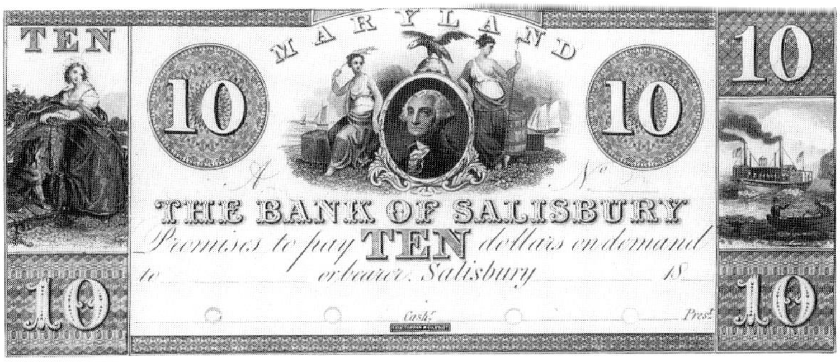

116.4.17 P

116.4.18 R-7

$10.00 Ca. 1846–53. Engraving, imprint: Underwood, Bald, Spencer & Hufty, Philada. / Danforth, Underwood & Co., New York. *Center:* Signing of the Declaration. *Left and right:* X TEN on medallion head, 10.

116.4.19 R-7

$10.00 Printed date March 4, 1848. Engraving, imprint: Danforth & Hufty, New York & Philada. (MD290G38)

116.4.19 P R-7

$10.00 Printed date March 4, 1848. Engraving, imprint: Danforth & Hufty, New York & Philada. Proof.

116.4.20 SENC

$10.00 Printed date March 4, 1848. Engraving, imprint: Danforth & Hufty, New York & Philada. Same as No. 116.4.19, except for large fancy "10" in orange.

116.4.20 P R-7

$10.00 Printed date March 4, 1848. Engraving, imprint: Danforth & Hufty, New York & Philada. Same as No. 116.4.19, except for large fancy "10" in orange. Proof. (MD290G38a)

116.4.21 R SENC

$10.00 Printed date March 4, 1848. Engraving, imprint: Danforth & Hufty, New York & Philada. Raised from $1.00, No. 116.4.2. (MD290R10)

116.4.22 P R-7

$20.00 Printed date 183_. Engraving, imprint: Fairman, Draper, Underwood & Co. Proof.

116.4.23 P R-7

$20.00 Ca. 1836–43. Engraving, imprint: Underwood, Bald, Spencer & Hufty. Charles Carroll of Carrollton at left. Proof. (MD290G16)

116.4.24 P R-7

$50.00 Ca. 183_. Engraving, no imprint. (Fairman, Draper, Underwood & Co.) Proof.

116.4.20 P

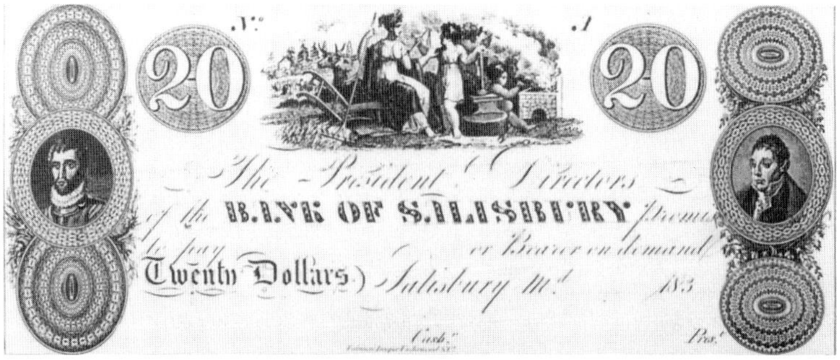

116.4.22 P

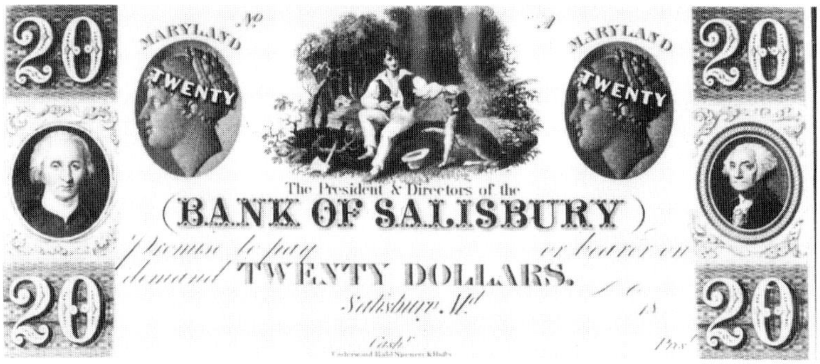

116.4.23 P

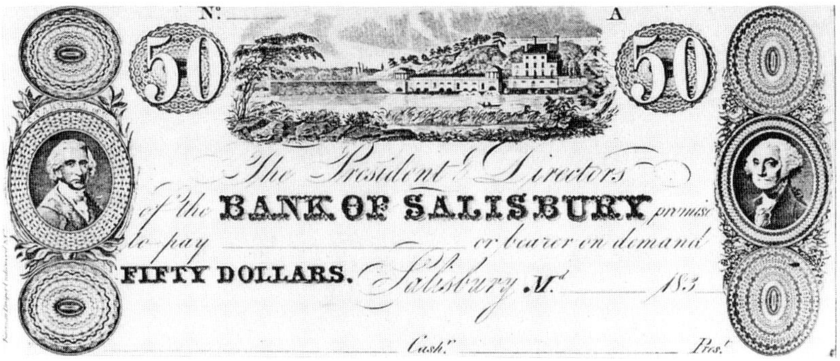

116.4.24 P

116.4.25 P R-7

$50.00 Ca. 1836–43. Engraving, imprint: Underwood, Bald, Spencer & Hufty. Proof. (MD290G20)

116.4.26 P R-6

$50.00 Ca. 183_. Engraving, imprint: Fairman, Draper, Underwood & Co. Similar to 116.4.24 P except no underline where payee to be written in. Proof.

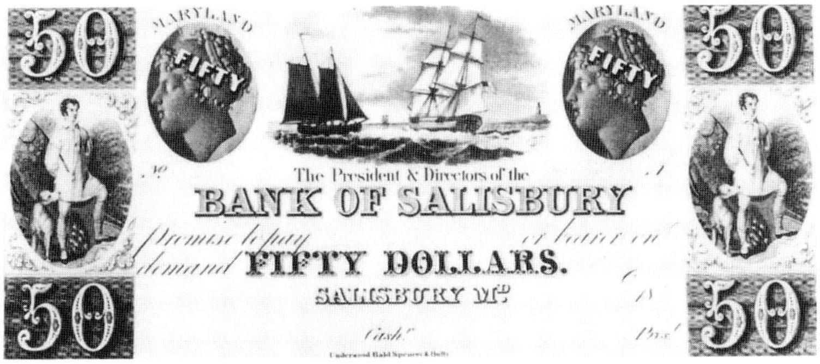

116.4.25 P

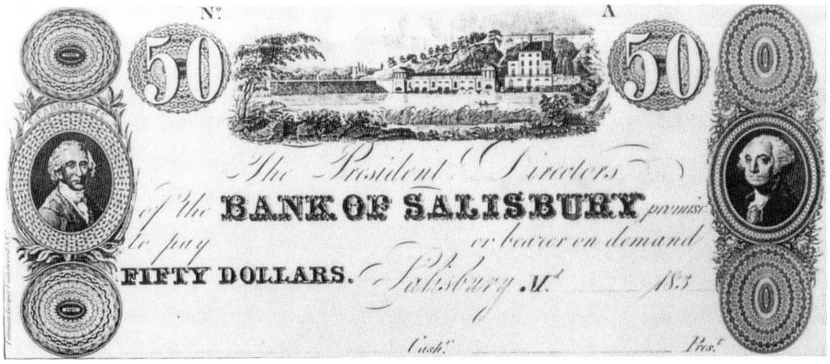

116.4.26 P

116.5 The Somerset and Worcester Savings Bank

Charter approved February 27, 1856; ceased operations about 1863–64. Black uniface notes were probably the first to have been issued, all recorded copies showing evidence of relatively heavy circulation. Well-circulated examples of both the red and black and the green and black notes are to be found, but uncirculated copies are much more frequently encountered. An opinion has been expressed to the authors that the black uniface notes were the last to be issued as the bank officers wished to spend less on the cost of printing by eliminating the colored security prints. It seems more likely that the reverse is the case, the bank officers attempting to increase public confidence in an institution that was in financial difficulty by improving the appearance and security of their notes by using color.

Sets of all four denominations of the red and black notes can be formed in which the final digit of the printed 1862 year date has been changed in manuscript, in red ink, to "3," "4," or "5." All four denominations of the red and black notes are occasionally found printed on very thin, almost transparent paper, often with an almost oily appearance.

116.5.1 R-2

$1.00 Printed date Nov. 1, 1862. Engraving, imprint; American Bank Note Co., New York. Same as No. 116.5.2, except without overprint, plain back.

116.5.2 R-1

$1.00 Printed date Nov. 1, 1862. Engraving, imprint: American Bank Note Co., New York. Green security overprint, negative ONE in serifed block letters on engine-turned green background. Back of $1.00 note in green.

116.5.3 R-1

$1.00 Printed date Nov. 1, 1862. Engraving, imprint: American Bank Note Co., New York. Same as No. 116.5.2, except red security overprint, negative ONE in serifed block letters on engine-turned red background, plain back.

116.5.4 R-1

$1.00 Printed date Nov. 1, 1862. Final digit in year date changed in manuscript to "3," "4," or "5." Otherwise, same as No. 116.5.3. Engraving, imprint: American Bank Note Co., New York. Red security overprint, negative ONE in serifed block letters on engine-turned red background, plain back.

116.5.5 R-1

$1.00 Printed date Nov. 1, 1862. Engraving, imprint: American Bank Note Co., New York. Red security overprint, negative ONE in serifed block letters on engine-turned red background. Same as No. 116.5.3, except printed on very thin, almost transparent paper, plain back.

116.5.6 R-2

$2.00 Printed date Nov. 1, 1862. Engraving, imprint: American Bank Note Co., New York. Same as No. 116.5.7, except without overprint, plain back.

116.5.7 R-1

$2.00 Printed date Nov. 1, 1862. Engraving, imprint: American Bank Note Co., New York. Green security overprint, negative TWO in serifed block letters on engine-turned green background. Back of $2.00 note in green.

116.5.8 R-1

$2.00 Printed date Nov. 1, 1862. Engraving, imprint: American Bank Note Co., New York. Same as No. 116.5.7, except red security overprint, negative TWO in serifed block letters on engine-turned red background, plain back.

116.5.9 R-1

$2.00 Printed date Nov. 1, 1862. Final digit in year date changed in manuscript to "3," "4," or "5." Otherwise, same as No. 116.5.8. Red security overprint, negative TWO in serifed block letters on engine-turned red background, plain back.

116.5.10 R-1

$2.00 Printed date Nov. 1, 1862. Engraving, imprint: American Bank Note Co., New York. Red security overprint, negative TWO in serifed block letters on engine-turned red background. Same as No. 116.5.8, except printed on very thin, almost transparent paper, plain back.

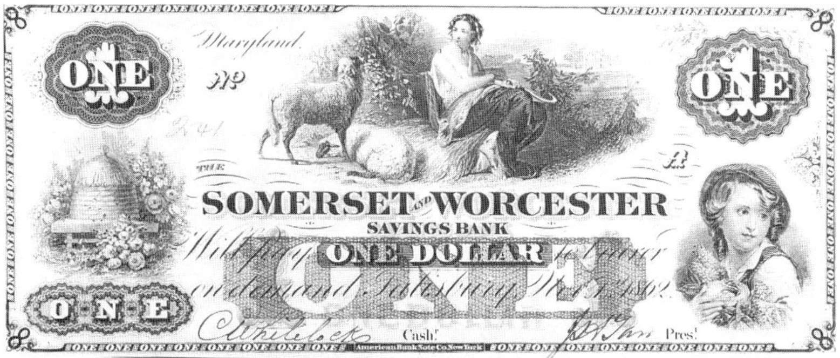

116.5.2

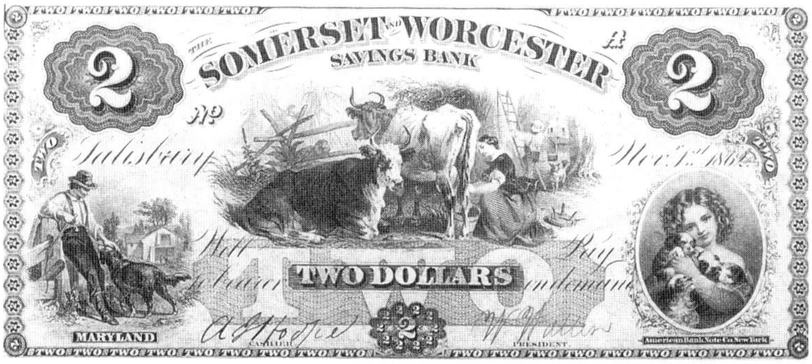

116.5.7

116.5.11 R-2

$3.00 Printed date Nov. 1, 1862. Engraving, imprint: American Bank Note Co., New York. Same as No. 116.5.12, except without overprint, plain back.

116.5.12 R-1

$3.00 Printed date Nov. 1, 1862. Engraving, imprint: American Bank Note Co., New York. Green security overprint, negative THREE in serifed block letters on engine-turned green background. Back of $3.00 note.

116.5.13 R-1

$3.00 Printed date Nov. 1, 1862. Engraving, imprint: American Bank Note Co., New York. Same as No. 116.5.12, except red security overprint, negative THREE in serifed block letters on engine-turned red background, plain back.

116.5.14 R-1

$3.00 Printed date Nov. 1, 1862. Final digit in year date changed in manuscript to "3," "4," or "5." Otherwise, same as No. 116.5.13. Engraving, imprint: American Bank Note Co., New York. Red security overprint, negative THREE in serifed block letters on engine-turned red background, plain back.

116.5.15 R-1

$3.00 Printed date Nov. 1, 1862. Engraving, imprint: American Bank Note Co., New York. Red security overprint, negative THREE in serifed block letters on engine-turned green background. Same as No. 116.5.13, except printed on very thin, almost transparent paper, plain back.

116.5.16 R-2

$5.00 Printed date Nov. 1, 1862. Engraving, imprint: American Bank Note Co., New York. Same as No. 116.5.17, except without overprint, plain back.

116.5.17 R-1

$5.00 Printed date Nov. 1, 1862. Engraving, imprint: American Bank Note Co., New York. Green security overprint, negative FIVE in serifed block letters on engine-turned green background. Back of $5.00 note.

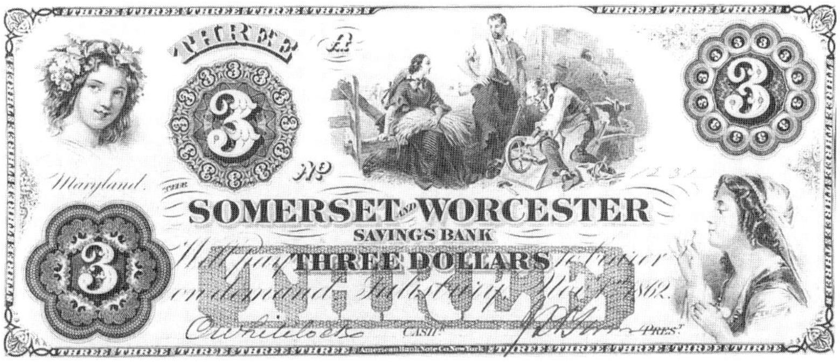

116.5.12

116.5.17

116.5.18 R-1

$5.00 Printed date Nov. 1, 1862. Engraving, imprint: American Bank Note Co., New York. Same as No. 116.5.17, except red security overprint, negative FIVE in serifed block letters on engine-turned red background, plain back.

116.5.19 R-1

$5.00 Printed date Nov. 1, 1862. Final digit in year date changed in manuscript to "3," "4," or "5." Otherwise, same as No. 116.5.18. Engraving, imprint: American Bank Note Co., New York. Red security overprint, negative FIVE in serifed block letters on engine-turned red background, plain back.

116.5.20 R-1

$5.00 Printed date Nov. 1, 1862. Engraving, imprint: American Bank Note Co., New York. Red security overprint, negative FIVE in serifed block letters on engine-turned red background. Same as No. 116.5.18, except printed on very thin, almost transparent paper, plain back.

116.6 Jos. H. Tarr

The issuer, Joseph Hopkins Tarr, was a young lawyer who represented the "eastside" of Salisbury at the Maryland constitutional convention of 1867. Along with Thomas J. F. Rider, a Quantico lawyer, and Purnell Toadvine, a retired Salisbury merchant, he was instrumental in securing passage of the necessary constitutional amendment to create the new county of Wicomico with Salisbury as its county seat.

116.6.2 R-7

10c Ca. 1860s. Lithography, imprint: Ferd. Mayer & Co., 96 Fulton St., New York.

116.6.3 R-7

25c Ca. 1860s. Lithography, imprint: Ferd. Mayer & Co., 96 Fulton St., New York.

116.6.4 R-7

50c Ca. 1860s. Lithography, imprint: Ferd. Mayer & Co., 96 Fulton St., New York.

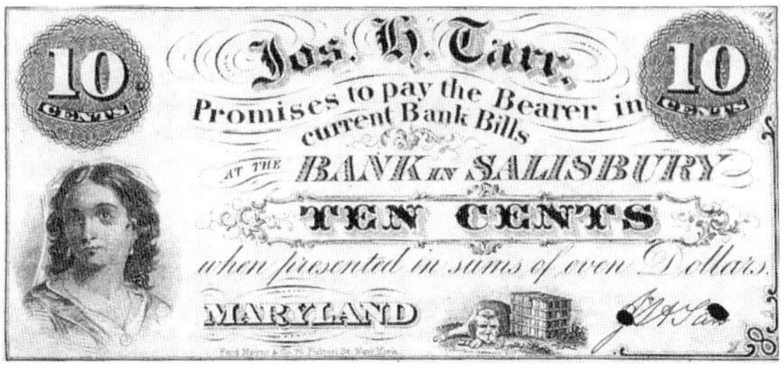

116.6.2

116.6.3

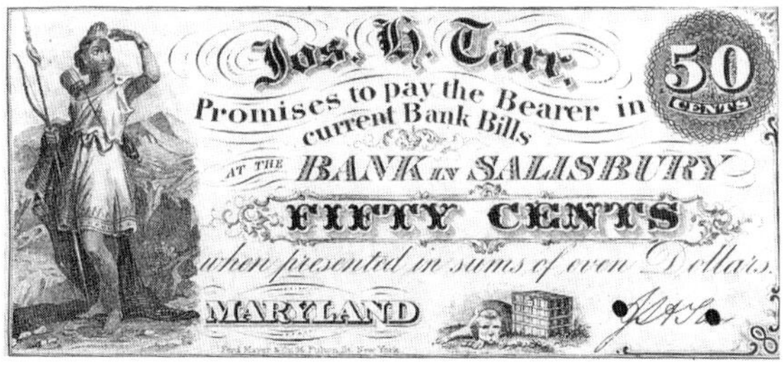

116.6.4

116.7 Toadvine & Vincent

The issuers, Alexander Toadvine and Thomas Vincent, were proprietors of a general store.

116.7.1 R-7

5c Printed partial year date 186_. Letterpress, no imprint.

116.7.3 R-7

10c Printed partial year date 186_. Letterpress, no imprint.

116.7.4 R-7

10c Printed partial year date Nov. __, 1862. Letterpress, no imprint.

116.7.5 R-7

15c Printed partial year date Nov. __, 1862. Letterpress, no imprint.

116.7.6 R-7

15c Printed partial year date 186_. Letterpress, no imprint.

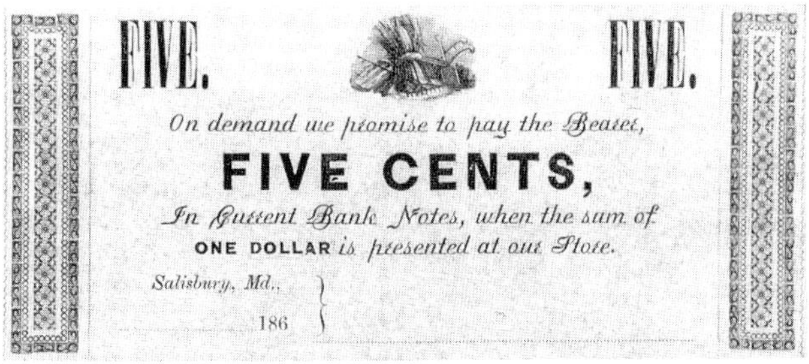

116.7.1

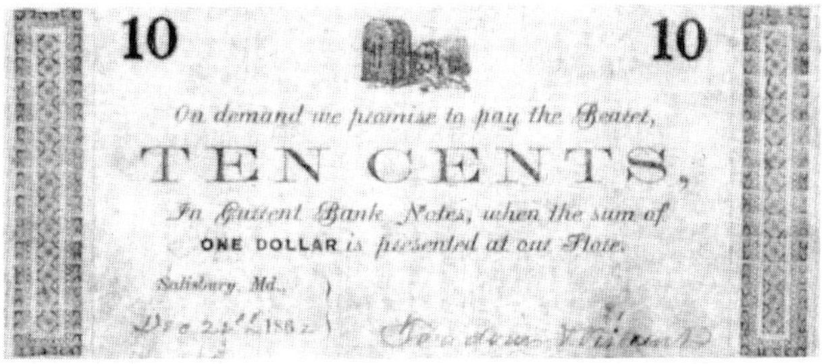

116.7.3

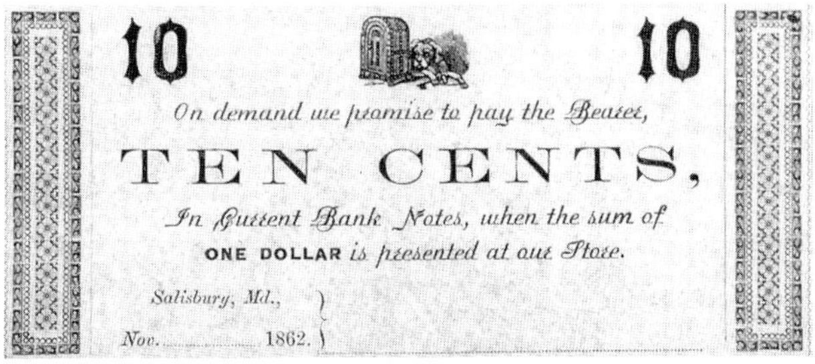

116.7.4

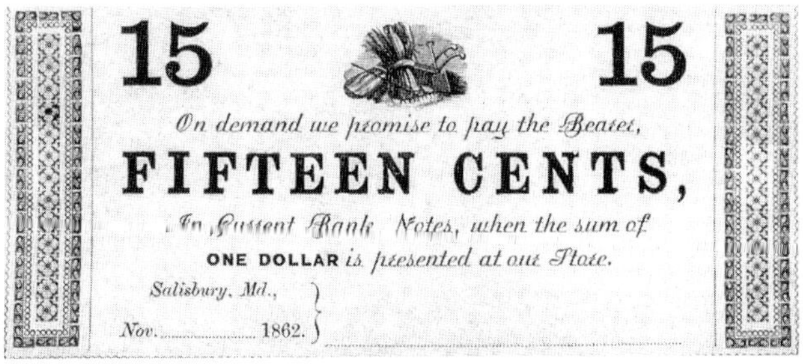

116.7.5

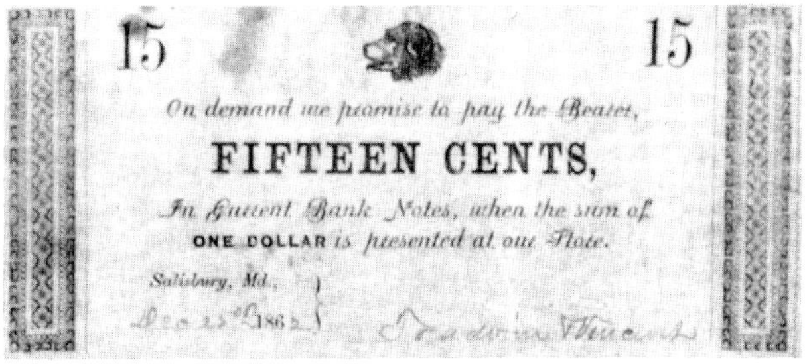

116.7.6

116.7.8 R-7

20c Printed partial date Nov. __, 1862. Letterpress, no imprint.

116.7.12 R-7

50c Printed date Nov. 1862. Letterpress, no imprint.

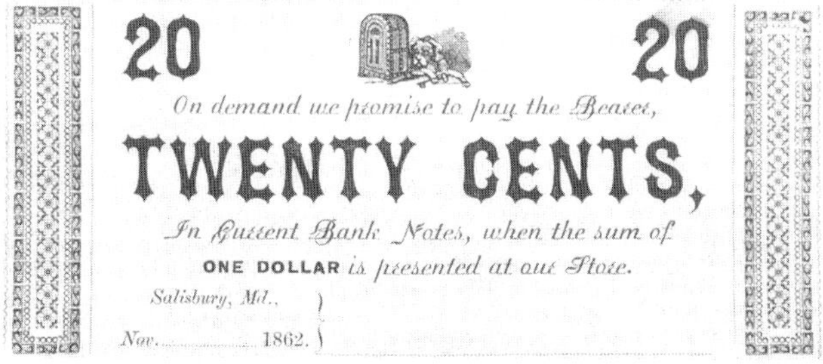

116.7.8

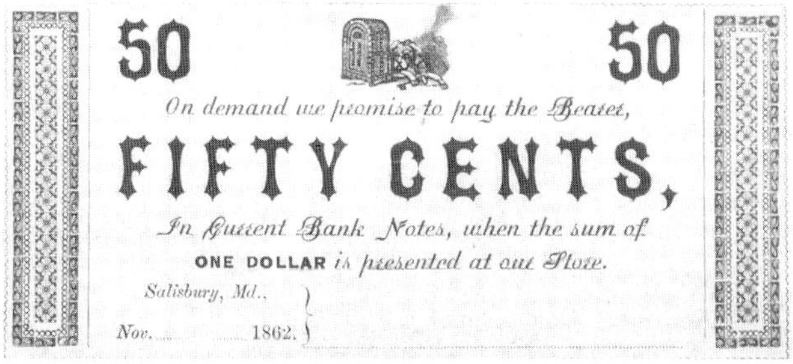

116.7.12

118 SAM'S CREEK, CARROLL COUNTY

This small village was, and is, located on the Carroll-Frederick county boundary line about 3 1/2 miles from New Windsor, near Sam's Creek, a small stream from which it takes its name. The creek's name probably derives from a family surname, Sams (variants: Sames, Samms, Sammes).

118.1 D. & D. Engel

The issuers were proprietors of a general store. Daniel Engel was also postmaster at Sam's Creek in 1841, a county commissioner in 1842, and agent for the sale of Stainburn's Vegetable Extract Anti-bilious pills.

118.1.2 R-7

12 1/2c Printed date July 20, 1841. Letterpress, imprint: MURPHY, PRINTER, BALTIMORE.

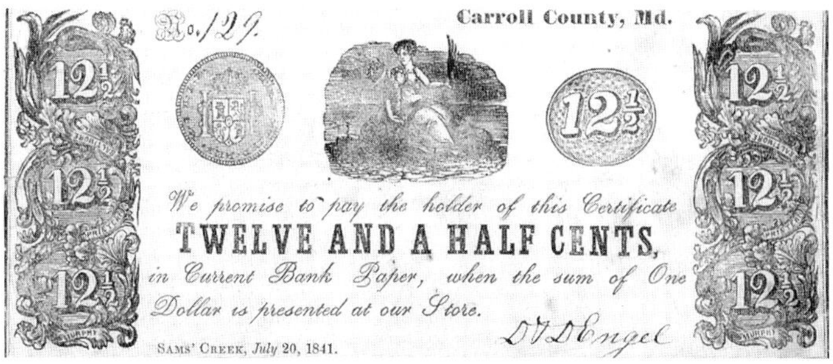

118.1.2

120 SANDY HILL, WORCESTER COUNTY

This small village was located at or near present-day George Island Landing on the western shore of Chincoteague Bay almost due east of Newtown (Pocomoke City).

120.1 Unidentified Issuer

120.1.3 R-7

25c Printed partial year date 186_. Letterpress, no imprint.

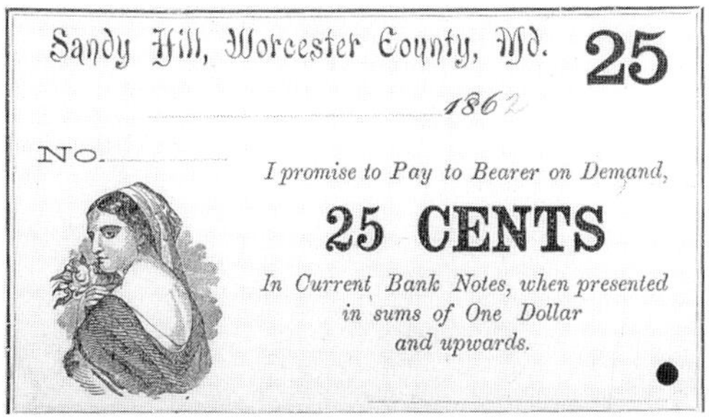

120.1.3

122 SAVAGE, ANNE ARUNDEL COUNTY (NOW HOWARD COUNTY)

In 1823, 500 acres were purchased in 1823 by John Savage, a Philadelphia merchant. Mr. Savage and others developed a cotton mill at the falls of the Little Patuxent River, hence the name Savage.

122.1 Store of the Savage Manufacturing Company

The Savage Mill was erected by Amos Williams and his three brothers in 1822 and was named after their friend John Savage, who had loaned them the money to start their textile-weaving business. Located on the banks of the Little Patuxent River, the mill's machinery was powered by the flow of water over a 30-foot waterwheel. The main original product was canvas used for sails of the Baltimore clipper ships; later, canvas was produced for military use in the Civil War and the two world wars. For many years the mill was owned and operated by the Savage Manufacturing Company, which was engaged in the production of various kinds of cotton goods. The mill ceased operations in 1947.

122.1.3 SENC

25c Ca. 1839–43. Engraving, imprint: Underwood, Bald, Spencer & Hufty, Philada. / Danforth, Underwood & Co., New York.

122.1.3 P R-6

25c Ca. 1839–43. Engraving, imprint: Underwood, Bald, Spencer & Hufty, Philada. / Danforth, Underwood & Co., New York. Proof.

122.1.3

122.1.4 R-7

50c Ca. 1839–43. Engraving, imprint: Underwood, Bald, Spencer & Hufty, Philada. / Danforth, Underwood & Co., New York.

122.1.4 P R-6

50c Ca. 1839–43. Engraving, imprint: Underwood, Bald, Spencer & Hufty, Philada. / Danforth, Underwood & Co., New York. Proof.

122.1.5 SENC

$1.00 Ca. 1839–43. Engraving, imprint: Underwood, Bald, Spencer & Hufty, Philada. / Danforth, Underwood & Co., New York.

122.1.5 P R-7

$1.00 Ca. 1839–43. Engraving, imprint: Underwood, Bald, Spencer & Hufty, Philada. / Danforth, Underwood & Co., New York. Proof.

122.1.6 P R-7

$2.00 Ca. 1839–43. Engraving, imprint: Underwood, Bald, Spencer & Hufty, Philada. / Danforth, Underwood & Co., New York. Proof.

122.1.4

122.1.4 P

122.1.5 P

122.1.6 P

124 SLAUGHTER CREEK, DORCHESTER COUNTY

Slaughter Creek was a small village situated on a branch of the Little Choptank River, 2 1/2 miles northeast of Taylor's Island.

124.1 John Bays

The issuer was the proprietor of a general store.

124.1.3 R-7

25c Printed date March 1, 1841. Letterpress, imprint: Murphy, Printer, Baltimore.

124.1.3

128 SNOW HILL, WORCESTER COUNTY

The town was established by direction of the Maryland Assembly in 1686. Named for a London, England, suburb at the time.

128.1 J. A. Benson

Jesse A. Benson was the proprietor of a confectionary and variety store on Green Street.

128.1.1 R-7

5c Printed partial year date 186_. Letterpress with vignette and end plates engraved, no imprint.

128.1.2 R-7

10c Printed partial year date 186_. Letterpress with vignette and end plates engraved, no imprint. (*See* Dr. L. Flemming, No. 128.3, for similar note.)

128.1.1

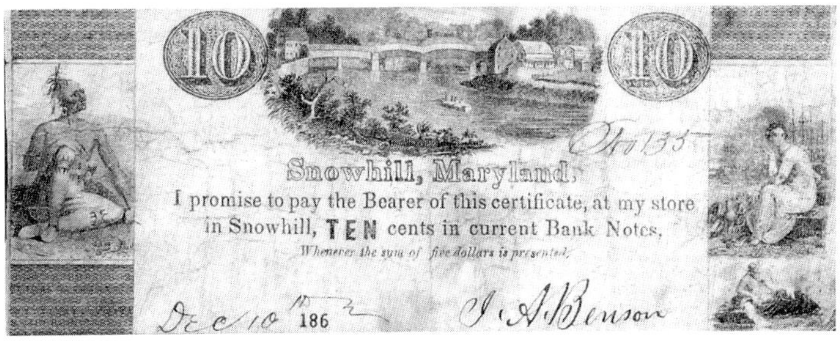

128.1.2

128.2 The Farmers Bank of Somerset & Worcester

Charter approved January 7, 1812; voluntary liquidation in 1821.

128.2.1 SENC
$1.00 Printed partial year date 181_. Engraving, imprint: Murray, Draper, Fairman & Co. No other information available. (MD295G12)

128.2.2 SENC
$2.00 Printed partial year date 181_. Engraving, imprint: Murray, Draper, Fairman & Co. Similar to $1.00, No. 128.2.15. (MD295G14)

128.2.3 R-7
$5.00 Printed partial date 181_. Engraving, imprint: W. Harrison, fct. Phila. Similar to $20.00, No. 128.2.5. (MD295G18)

128.2.4 SENC
$10.00 Printed partial year date 181_. Engraving, imprint: W. Harrison, fct. Phila. Similar to $20.00, No. 128.2.5. (MD295G22)

128.2.5 R-7
$20.00 Printed partial year date 181_. Engraving, imprint: W. Harrison, fct. Phila. (MD295G26)

128.2.6 SENC
$50.00 Printed partial year date 181_. Engraving, imprint: W. Harrison, fct. Phila. Similar to $20.00, No. 128.2.5. (MD295G30)

128.2.7 R-7
$100.00 Printed partial year date 181_. Engraving, W. Harrison, fct. Phila. (MD295G32)

128.2.15 R-7
$1.00 Printed partial year date 181_. Engraving, imprint: Murray, Draper, Fairman & Co. (MD295G36)

128.2.3

128.2.5

128.2.7

NOTES PAYABLE AT THE BRANCH IN SALISBURY (WHICH OPERATED DURING THE 1810S)

128.2.15

128.2.16 SENC

$2.00 Printed partial year date 181_. Engraving, imprint: Murray, Draper, Fairman & Co. Similar to $1.00, No. 128.2.15. (MD295G38)

128.2.17 SENC

$5.00 Printed partial year date 181_. Engraving, imprint: W. Harrison, fct. Phila. Similar to $20.00, No. 128.2.5. (MD295G42)

128.2.18 SENC

$10.00 Printed partial year date 181_. Engraving, imprint: W. Harrison, fct. Phila. Similar to $20.00, No. 128.2.5. (MD295G46)

128.2.21 P

128.2.19 SENC

$20.00 Printed partial year date 181_. Engraving, imprint: W. Harrison, fct Phila. Similar to $20.00, No. 128.2.5. (MD295G50)

128.2.20 SENC

$50.00 Printed partial year date 181_. Engraving, imprint: W. Harrison, fct. Phila. Similar to $20.00, No. 128.2.5. (MD295G54)

128.2.21 P R-7

Post Note. Printed partial year date 181_. Engraving, no imprint. Proof.

128.3 Dr. L. Flemming

The issuer was the proprietor of a drugstore for many years.

128.3.1 R-7

1c Printed date December 15, 1863. Lithography, imprint: Lith. by A. Hoen & Co. Balto.

128.3.2 R-7

2c Printed date December 15, 1863. Lithography, imprint: Lith by A. Hoen & Co. Balto.

128.3.5 R-7

10c Printed partial year date 186_. Letterpress, with vignette and end plates engraved, no imprint. (*See* J. A. Benson, No. 128.1, for similar note.)

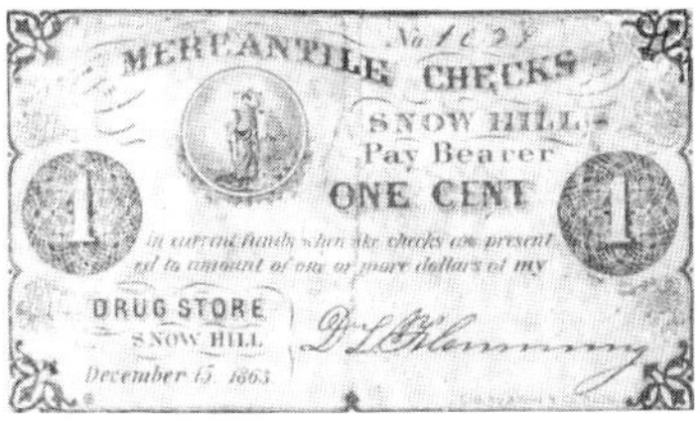

128.3.1

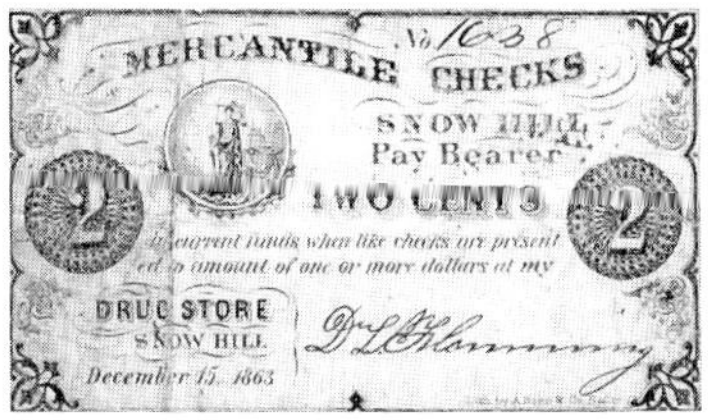

128.3.2

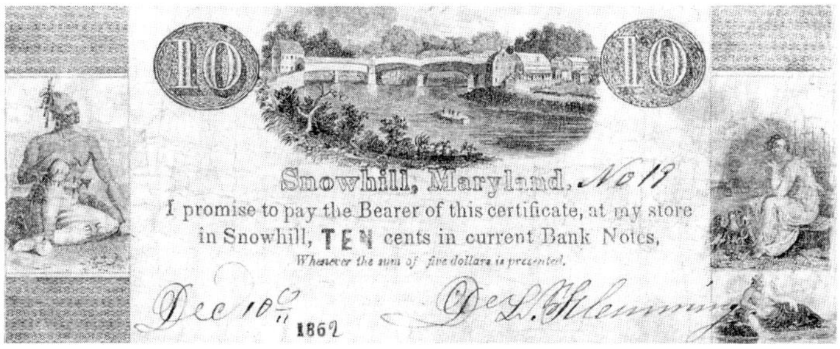

128.3.5

128.3.6 R-7

25c Printed partial year date 186_. Letterpress, with vignette and end plates engraved, no imprint.

128.3.7 R-7

50c Printed partial year date 186_. Letterpress, with vignette and end plates engraved, inscription letterpress, no imprint.

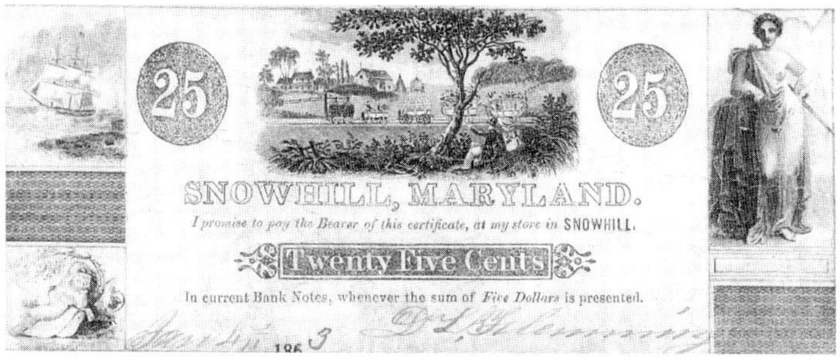

128.3.6

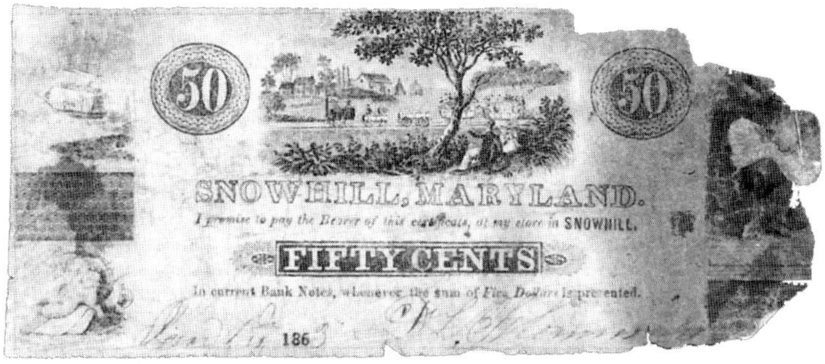

128.3.7

128.4 M. Manard

The status and identity of the signer, M. Manard, are undetermined. See comments and listings, nos. 128.8.1–12.

128.4.4 R-7

25c Printed partial year date 186_. Lithography, no imprint. Purple.

128.4.4

128.5 J. P. Norris

The issuer was apparently the proprietor of a general store.

128.5.2 R-7

12 1/2c Printed date January 22, 1840. Lithography, imprint: Murphy, Printer Baltimore. Note reads "I promise to pay the bearer TWELVE AND A HALF CENTS, when the BANK OF SALISBURY shall resume specie payments or to receive it as cash for goods."

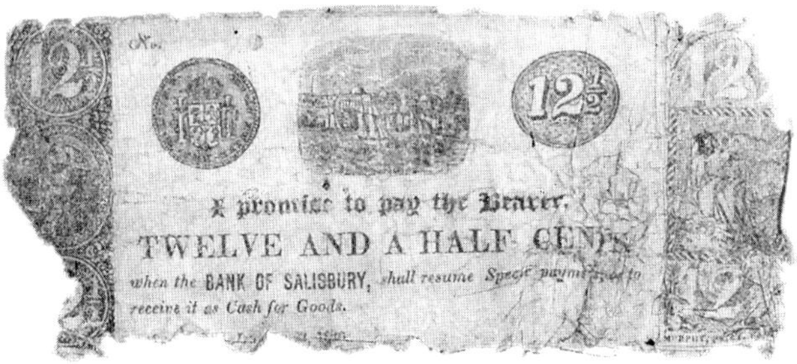

128.5.2

128.5.3 R-7

25c Printed date January 22, 1840. Lithograph, imprint: Murphy, Printer, Baltimore. Note reads "I promise to pay the Bearer TWENTY FIVE CENTS, when the BANK OF SALISBURY shall resume specie payments or to receive it as cash for goods."

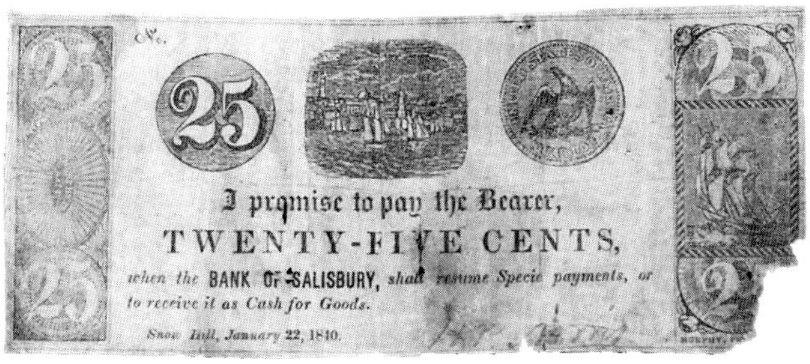

128.5.3

128.6 Thos. D. Purnell

The issuer was the proprietor of a general store.

128.6.4 R-7

25c Printed date January 1st, 1863. Letterpress, no imprint. Blue.

128.6.5 R-7

50c Printed date January 1st, 1863. Letterpress, no imprint. Blue.

128.6.4

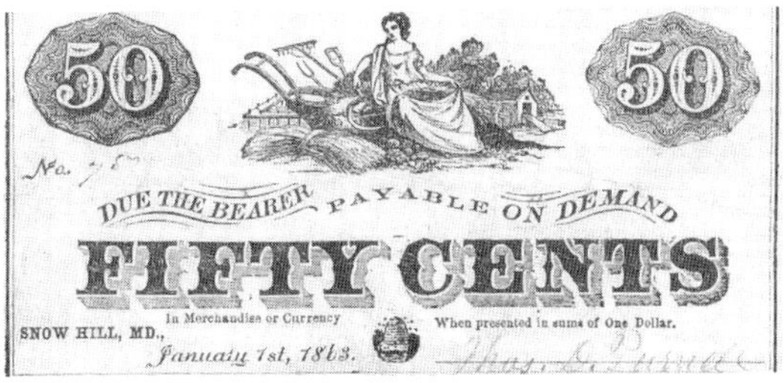

128.6.5

128.7 The Union Company

By an act of the General Assembly passed on January 18, 1815, the Union Company of Snow Hill was incorporated for the purpose of erecting a steam mill and manufacturing establishment. The initial financing was raised by the subscription to stock by local investors in the amount of $30,000. The company issued scrip to alleviate the chronic shortage of small-denomination coins caused by the War of 1812.

128.7.1 R-7

6 1/4c Printed date Sept. 30th, 1815. Engraving, imprint: Murray, Draper, Fairman & Co.

128.7.3 R-7

25c Printed date Sept. 30th, 1815. Engraving, imprint: Murray, Draper, Fairman & Co. Similar to 6 1/4c, No. 128.7.1.

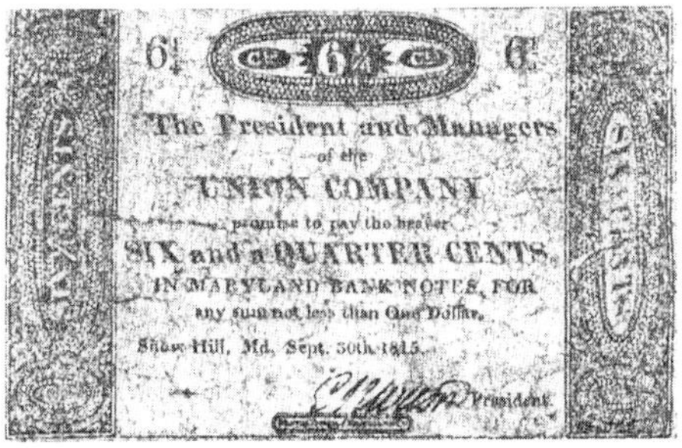

128.7.1

128.7.7 R-7

$3.00 Printed partial year date 181_. Engraving, imprint: Murray, Draper, Fairman & Co.

128.7.7

128.8 Unidentified Issuers

Small-change notes of the types illustrated can be found in three colors: red, green, and purple. With one exception, all of those on record are unsigned and most have one or more punched holes in the signature space.

128.8.1 R-6

5c Printed partial year date 186_. Lithography, no imprint. Red.

128.8.1

128.8.2 R-6

5c Printed partial year date 186_. Lithography, no imprint. Green.

128.8.3 R-6

5c Printed partial year date 186_. Lithography, no imprint. Purple.

128.8.4 R-6

10c Printed partial year date 186_. Lithography, no imprint. Red.

128.8.4

128.8.5 R-6

10c Printed partial year date 186_. Lithography, no imprint. Green.

128.8.6 R-6

10c Printed partial year date 186_. Lithography, no imprint. Purple.

128.8.7 R-6

25c Printed partial year date 186_. Lithography, no imprint. Red.

128.8.7

128.8.8 R-6

25c Printed partial year date 186_. Lithography, no imprint. Green.

128.8.9 R-6

25c Printed partial year date 186_. Lithography, no imprint. Purple.

128.8.10 R-6

50c Printed partial year date 186_. Lithography, no imprint. Red.

128.8.10

128.8.11 R-6

50c Printed partial year date 186_. Lithography, no imprint. Green.

128.8.12 R-6

50c Printed partial year date 186_. Lithography, no imprint. Purple. (*See* No. 128.4.4 for an example bearing a doubtful signature.)

128.9 Unidentified Issuer

128.9.4 R-7

25c Printed partial year date 186_. Lithography, no imprint.

128.9.4

130 SWANSBURY MILLS, HARFORD COUNTY

The town of Swansbury, no longer in existence, was located on Swan Creek about 1 1/2 miles northeast of the town of Aberdeen.

130.1 F. D. Anderson and Co.

The Swansbury Mill, apparently operated by F. D. Anderson and Co., was a "tide mill" on Swan Creek, powered by water accumulated upstream at high tide which ran the undershot mill wheel. Swan Creek empties into the upper Chesapeake Bay about five miles south of Havre de Grace.

130.1.3 R-7

25c Ca. 1837–39. Letterpress, imprint: MURPHY & SPALDING PRINTERS.

130.1.4 R-7

50c Ca. 1837–39. Letterpress, imprint: MURPHY & SPALDING PRINTERS.

130.1.5 R-7

$1.00 Ca. 1837–39. Letterpress, imprint: Murphy, print. Balt. Vignettes of seated female and Washington.

130.1.3

130.1.4

130.1.5

132	SYKESVILLE, CARROLL COUNTY	Named for James Sykes, an Englishman who lived and operated a mill there, first a flour mill and then a cotton mill. The town was a stop on the old Baltimore & Ohio Railroad, just below Eldersburg.

132.1 William N. Dorsey & Bros.

The issuers were proprietors of a general store.

132.1.1 R-7
5c Printed date July 20th, 1840. Letterpress, imprint: Printed at the "Herald" Office.

132.1.5 R-7
25c Printed date July 20th, 1840. Letterpress, imprint: Printed at the "Herald" Office.

132.1.6 R-7
50c Printed date July 20th, 1840. Letterpress, imprint: Printed at the "Herald" Office.

132.1.1

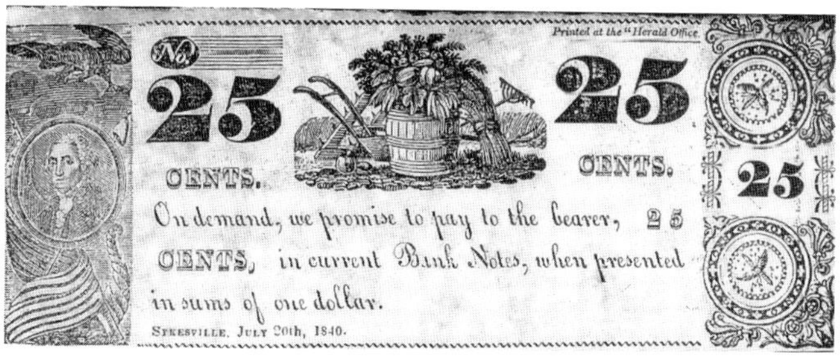

132.1.5

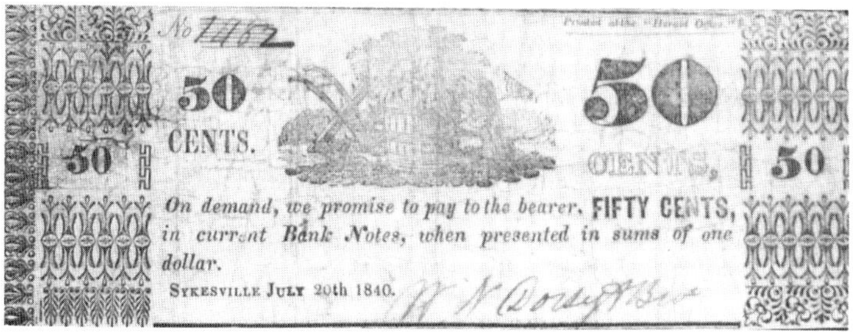

132.1.6

134 TURKEY POINT, CECIL COUNTY

See Fisherman's Bank of Charlestown, No. 22.1.

138 UPPER MARLBORO, PRINCE GEORGE'S COUNTY

Named for John Churchill Marlborough (1650–1722), hero of Blenheim and Ramillies (1706). The town was settled in 1704 by Scottish merchants and they gave the name because it was at the time of the great victory at Blenheim.

138.1 Planters Bank of Prince George's County

Charter approved January 5, 1818. Operations were suspended in 1829. The charter was revived and extended in 1832, but the bank failed and the charter was forfeited in 1843. The following list of notes was obtained from contemporary counterfeit detectors. However, no surviving examples are known to exist.

138.1.1 SENC
$5.00 Ca. 1818–20s. No additional information is available. (MD300G8)

138.1.2 SENC
$5.00 Ca. 1830s. No additional information is available. (MD300G30)

138.1.3 SENC
$10.00 Ca. 1818–20s. No additional information is available. (MD300G12)

138.1.4 SENC
$10.00 Ca. 1830s. No additional information is available. (MD300G32)

138.1.5 SENC
$20.00 Ca. 1818–20s. No additional information is available. (MD300G16)

138.1.6 SENC
$20.00 Ca. 1830s. No additional information is available. (MD300G34)

138.1.7 SENC
$50.00 Ca. 1818–20s. No additional information is available. (MD300G20)

138.1.8 SENC
$50.00 Ca. 1830s. No additional information is available. (MD300G36)

138.1.9 SENC
$100.00 Ca. 1818–20s. No additional information is available. (MD300G24)

138.1.10 SENC
$100.00 Ca. 1830s. No additional information is available. (MD300G38)

140 VIENNA, DORCHESTER COUNTY

Laid out in 1706 on the Nanticoke River as Emperor's Landing for the emperor or chief of the Nanticoke Indians. The actual name, Vienna, was from a derivative of an Indian word.

140.1 J. R. Turner

The issuer was the proprietor of a general store.

140.1.4 R-7
25c Printed partial year date 186_. Letterpress, no imprint.

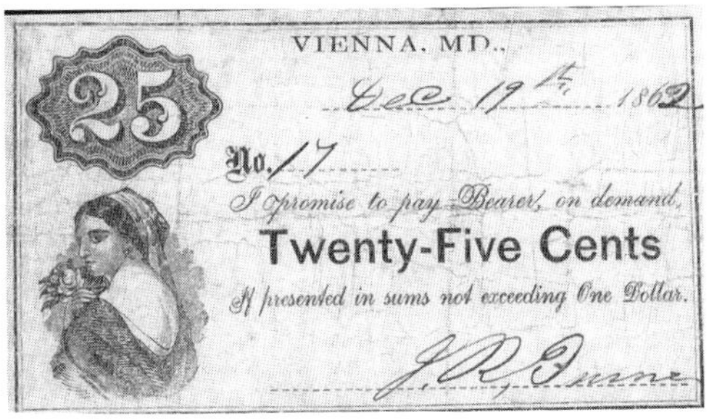

140.1.4

142 WARFIELDSBURG, CARROLL COUNTY

Originally Warfield's Store, until name changed to Warfieldsburg in 1837.

142.1 R. Nelson

The issuer was the proprietor of a general store and agent for Stainburn's Vegetable Extract Anti-Bilious Pills.

142.1.1 R-7
6 1/4c Printed date July 20, 1841. Letterpress, imprint: MURPHY, PRINTER, 146 Market St., Balt.

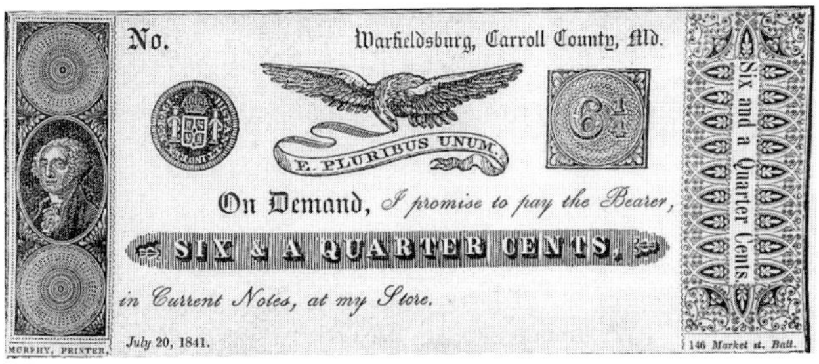

142.1.1

142.1.2 R-7

12 1/2c Ca. 1840–41. Letterpress, imprint: Murphy Printer Baltimore.

142.1.3 R-7

12 1/2c Printed date July 20, 1841. Letterpress, imprint: MURPHY, PRINTER, BALTIMORE.

142.1.4 R-7

25c Printed date July 20, 1841. Letterpress, imprint: MURPHY, PRINTER, BALTIMORE. Vignette is a woodcut view of Baltimore Basin (inner harbor).

142.1.5 R-7

50c Printed date July 20, 1841. Letterpress, imprint: MURPHY PRINTER BALTIMORE.

142.1.6 R-7

$1.00 Printed date July 20, 1841. Letterpress, imprint: MURPHY PRINTER BALTIMORE.

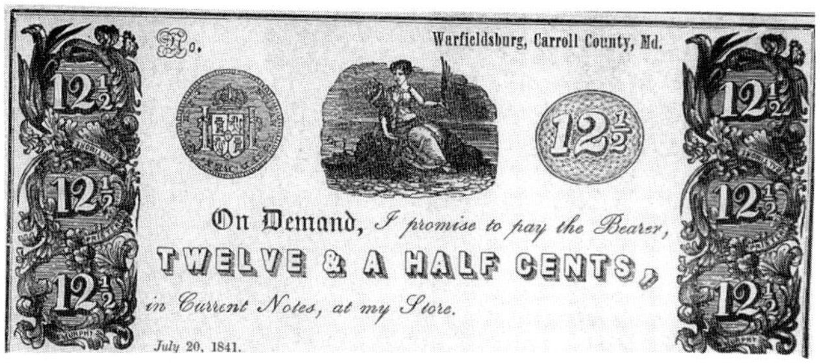

142.1.3

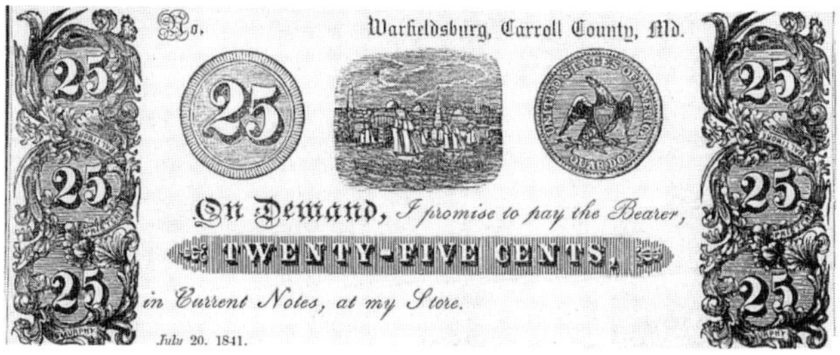

142.1.4

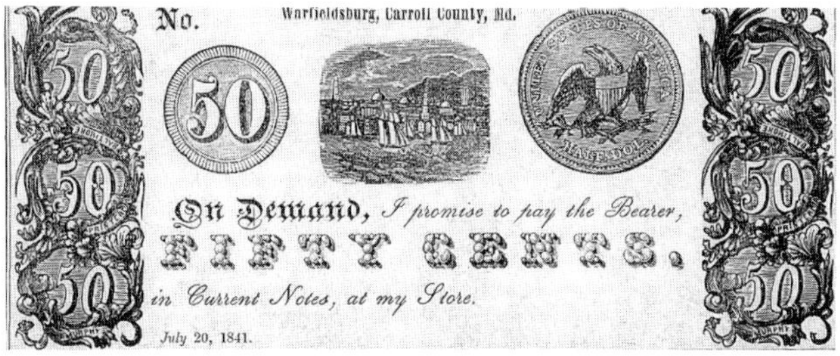

142.1.5

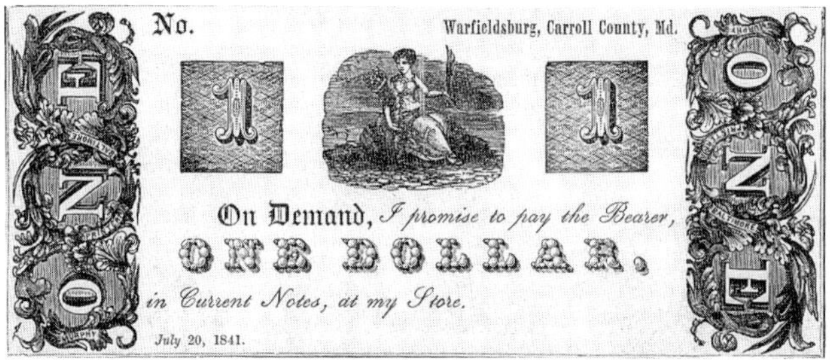

142.1.6

142.2 John Nicodemus of H.

The issuer was the proprietor of a general store beginning in January of 1841 with a partner, Hezekiah Crout.

142.2.1 R-7

6 1/4c Printed date July 30, 1841. Letterpress, no imprint.

142.2.1

144 WASHINGTON COUNTY

144.1 J. C. Stone

The identity of the issuer and his precise location in Washington County have not as yet been determined.

144.1.5 R-7

75c Printed partial year date 183_. Letterpress, imprint: Murphy & Spalding, printers, 1 Light street, Baltimore.

144.1.5

146 WESTERNPORT, ALLEGANY COUNTY

Located at the junction of George's Creek and the North Branch of the Potomac River. Originally known as Hardscrabble, the name was changed to reflect the fact that the town was the westernmost navigable port on the North Branch of the Potomac River.

146.1 The Clinton Bank

Charter approved March 10, 1858. No reports on operations filed. Failed about 1860–61.

146.1.1 R-2

$5.00 Ca. 1858–60. Engraving, imprint: American Bank Note Company. Security underprint, red lacy background with upper left "5" and fancy negative FIVE at lower center, both in bright red. Portrait at left of Philip E. Thomas, first president of the Baltimore & Ohio Railroad. (MD305G8)

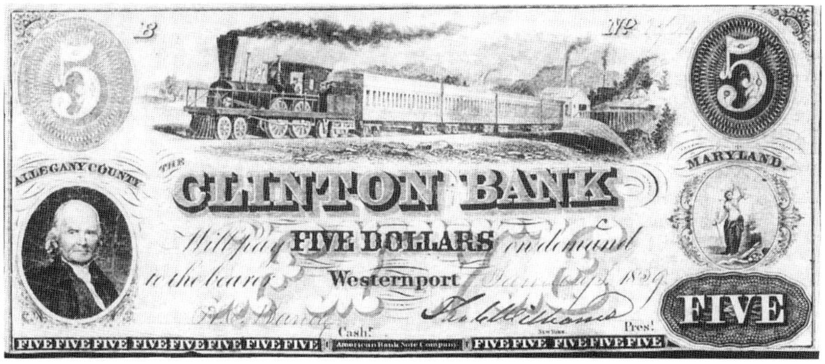

146.1.1

146.1.2 R-4

$5.00 Ca. 1860. Engraving, imprint: American Bank Note Company. Same as No. 146.1.1, except die at upper left is black and not part of tint. (MD305G8a)

146.1.3 R-2

$5.00 Ca. 1860. Engraving, imprint: American Bank Note Company. Similar to No. 146.1.1, except security overprint, negative FIVE in serifed block letters on red, lacy engine-turned background, in lower center. (MD305G8b)

Altered notes of this design have been recorded bearing the inscriptions of the Merchants Bank, Norwalk, Conn.; the Monson Bank, Monson, Mass.; the Merchants Bank of Albany, N.Y.; Perrin Bank of Rochester, N.Y.; Miner's Bank of Pottsville, Pa.

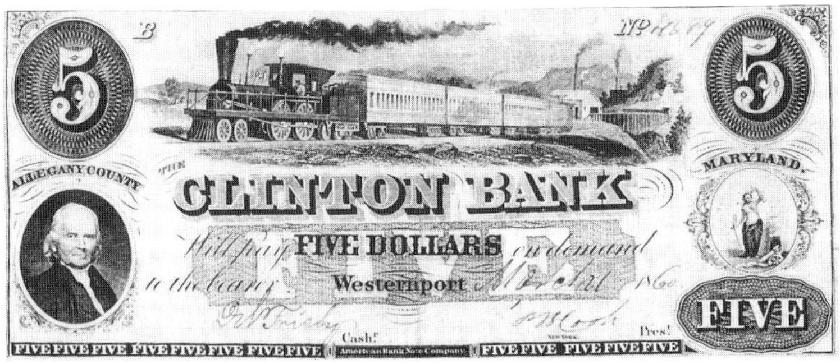

146.1.2

150 WESTMINSTER, CARROLL COUNTY

In 1764, Winchester was the name of the village, given for its founder, William Winchester, who came to Maryland in 1729. Soon after the beginning of the Revolutionary War the town was renamed due to the confusion with Winchester, Virginia. It was incorporated in 1837. The reason for choosing Westminster is unknown.

150.1 Samuel A. Blintzinger

The specific business of the issuer has not been verified. However, beginning in 1843, Samuel Blintzinger commenced a tinning business at a brick house "opposite Henry Saltgiver's Hatting Establishment."

150.1.1 R-7

6 1/4c Printed date June 10, 1841. Letterpress, imprint: MURPHY, PRINTER, 146 Market street, Balt.

150.1.2 R-7

12 1/2c Ca. 1842. Letterpress, imprint: Murphy, print. Balt.

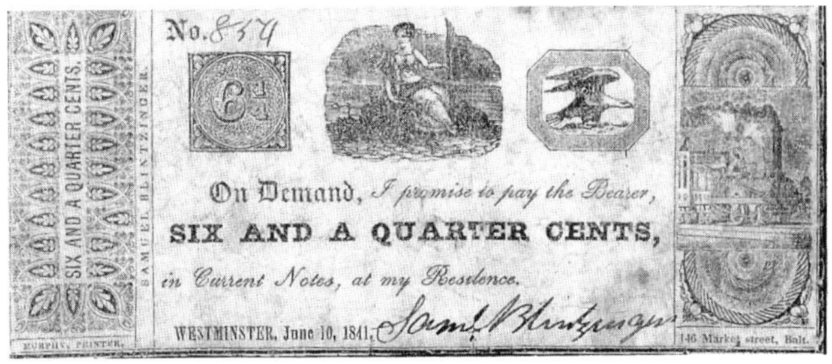

150.1.1

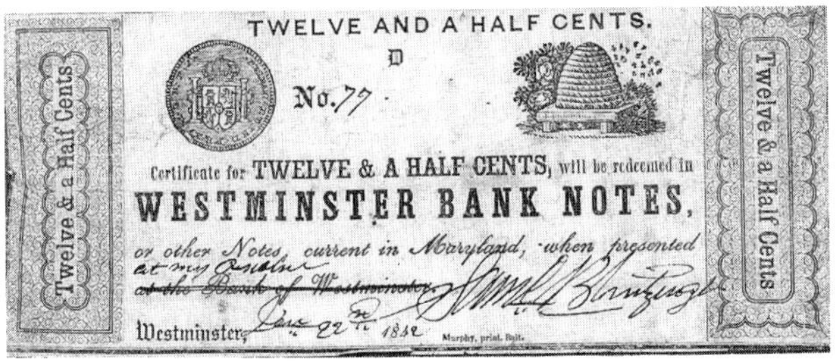

150.1.2

50.2 The Farmers & Mechanics Bank of Carroll County

Charter approved February 27, 1850. Converted to and became the Farmers & Mechanics Bank of Westminster in 1865.

150.2.1 SENC

$1.00 Ca. 1850–52. Engraving, imprint: Danforth, Bald & Co., Philada & New York. (MD310G2)

150.2.1 P R-6

$1.00 Ca. 1850–52. Engraving, imprint: Danforth, Bald & Co., Philada & New York. Proof.

150.2.1 P

150.2.2 SENC

$1.00 Ca. early 1850s. Engraving, imprint: Toppan, Carpenter, Casilear & Co. Similar to No. 150.2.3, except for imprint. May lack overprint. (MD310G4)

150.2.2 P R-7

$1.00 Ca. early 1850s. Engraving, imprint: Toppan, Carpenter, Casilear & Co. Similar to No. 150.2.3, except for imprint. May lack overprint. Proof.

150.2.3

150.2.3 R-7

$1.00 Ca. 1862. Engraving, imprint: American Bank Note Company, Phila. Brick red security overprint ONE. (MD310G4b)

150.2.4 R-7

$5.00 Ca. 1850s. Engraving, imprint: Danforth, Bald & Co. (MD310G6)

150.2.4

150.2.4 P R-6

$5.00 Ca. 1850s. Engraving, imprint: Danforth, Bald & Co. Proof.

150.2.5 SENC

$5.00 Ca. 1850s. Engraving, imprint: Rawdon, Wright & Co., Philada & New York. Charles Carroll at lower right. Similar to No. 150.2.6 P, except without red FIVE overprint. (MD310G8)

150.2.4 P

150.2.5 P R-7

$5.00 Ca. 1850s. Engraving, imprint: Rawdon, Wright & Co., Philada & New York. Charles Carroll at lower right. Similar to No. 150.2.6 P, except without red FIVE overprint. Proof.

150.2.6 P R-7

$5.00 Ca. 1850s. Engraving, imprint: Rawdon, Wright & Co., Philada & New York. Charles Carroll at lower right. With red FIVE overprint. Proof.

150.2.7 A R-6

$5.00 Ca. 1850s. Engraving, imprint: Rawdon, Wright & Hatch, New York. Altered from $5.00 Farmers & Mechanics Bank, Pontiac, Mich., MI335G8. (MD310A5)

150.2.8 R SENC

$5.00 Ca. 1850s. Engraving, imprint: Danforth, Bald & Co. Raised from $1.00, No. 150.2.1. (MD310R5)

150.2.9 SENC

$10.00 Ca. 1850s. Engraving, imprint: Danforth, Bald & Co. (MD310G10)

150.2.9 P R-6

$10.00 Ca. 1850s. Engraving, imprint: Danforth, Bald & Co. Proof.

150.2.10 SENC

$10.00 Ca. 1850s. Engraving, imprint: Danforth, Bald & Co. Same as No. 150.2.9 with large TEN overprint in red.

150.2.10 P R-7

$10.00 Ca. 1850s. Engraving, imprint: Danforth, Bald & Co. Same as No. 150.2.9 with large TEN overprint in red. Proof.

150.2.11 A R-7

$10.00 Ca. 1850s. Engraving, imprint: Rawdon, Wright & Hatch, New York. Altered from $10.00 Farmers & Mechanics Bank at Pontiac, Mich., MI335G10. (MD310A10)

150.2.12 R SENC

$10.00 Ca. 1850s. Engraving, imprint: Danforth, Bald & Co. Raised from $1.00, No. 150.2.1. (MD310R10)

150.2.13 R SENC

$10.00 Ca. 1850s. Engraving, imprint: Toppan, Carpenter, Casilear & Co. Raised from $1.00, No. 150.2.2. (MD310R15)

150.2.6 P

150.2.7 A

150.2.10 P

150.2.11 A

150.2.14 SENC

$20.00 Ca. 1850s. Engraving, imprint: Danforth, Bald & Co. (MD310G14)

150.2.14 P R-7

$20.00 Ca. 1850s. Engraving, imprint: Danforth, Bald & Co. Proof.

150.2.15 SENC

$20.00 Ca. 1850s. Engraving, imprint: Danforth, Bald & Co., Philada. & New York. Same as No. 150.2.14 with large TWENTY overprint in red.

150.2.15 P R-7

$20.00 Ca. 1850s. Engraving, imprint: Danforth, Bald & Co., Philada. & New York. Same as No. 150.2.14 with large TWENTY overprint in red. Proof.

150.2.16 R SENC

$20.00 Ca. 1850s. Engraving, imprint: Danforth, Bald & Co. Raised from $1.00, No. 150.2.1. (MD310R20)

150.2.17 SENC

$50.00 Ca. 1850s. Engraving, imprint: Danforth, Bald & Co., Philada. & New York. (MD310G18)

150.2.17 P R-7

$50.00 Ca. 1850s. Engraving, imprint: Danforth, Bald & Co., Philada. & New York. Proof.

150.2.18 SENC

$50.00 Ca. 1850s. Engraving, imprint: Danforth, Bald & Co., Philada. & New York. Same as No. 150.2.17 with large FIFTY overprint in red.

150.2.18 P R-7

$50.00 Ca. 1850s. Engraving, imprint: Danforth, Bald & Co., Philada. & New York. Same as No. 150.2.17 with large FIFTY overprint in red. Proof.

150.2.19 SENC

$100.00 Ca. 1860s. Engraving, imprint: Danforth, Wright & Co., Philada. & New York. (MD310G22)

150.2.19 P R-7

$100.00 Ca. 1860s. Engraving, imprint: Danforth, Wright & Co., Philada. & New York. Proof.

150.2.20 SENC

$100.00 Ca. 1860s. Engraving, imprint: Danforth, Bald & Co., Philada. & New York. Same as No. 150.2.19 with large "C" at center in red.

150.2.20 P R-7

$100.00 Ca. 1860s. Engraving, imprint: Danforth, Wright & Co., Philada. & New York. Same as No. 150.2.19 with large "C" at center in red. Proof.

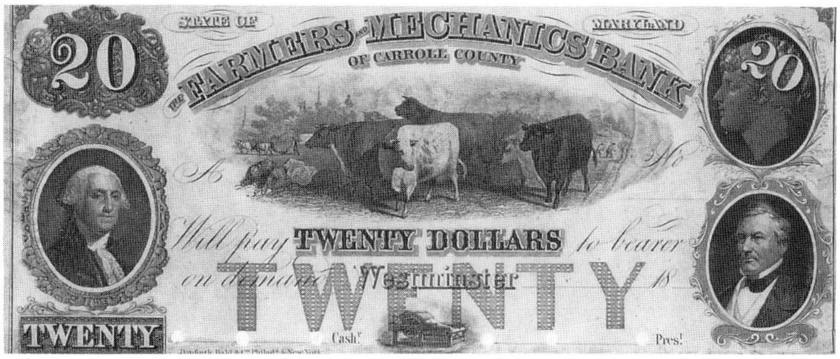

150.2.15 P

150.2.17 P

150.2.19 P

150.2.20 P

150.3 Jesse J. Manning

The issuer was the proprietor of a general store.

150.3.3 R-7

25c Printed date June 2, 1841. Letterpress, imprint: MURPHY, PRINTER, BALTIMORE.

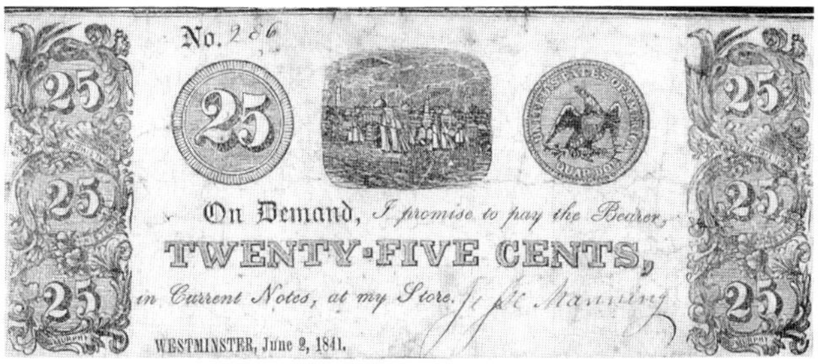

150.3.3

150.4 The Bank of Westminster (First)

Charter approved January 10, 1816, a branch known as the "Office of Pay and Receipt" being established in Frederick in 1817. The name was changed to Farmers & Mechanics Bank of Frederick County and the corporate office moved to Frederick in 1827, a branch being kept at Westminster until 1830. See the Bank of Westminster (Second), No. 150.5.

150.4.3 R-7

25c Ca. 1816. Letterpress, no imprint.

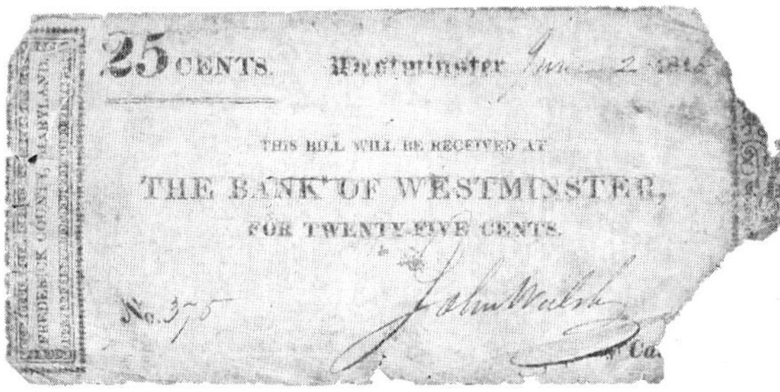

150.4.3

150.4.5 R-4

$1.00 Ca. 1810s–20s. Engraving, imprint: Murray, Draper, Fairman & Co. At top center: "Capital 100,000 Dollars" in double-lined typeface, "Cashr." and "Pres.t" in italics. (MD315G20)

150.4.6 R-4

$1.00 Ca. 1810s–20s. Engraving, imprint: Murray, Draper, Fairman & Co. Similar to No. 150.4.5 except "No." and plate letter "A" smaller in size and "Cafhr." and "Pref.t." in upright script.

Notes of these designs (nos. 150.4.5 and 150.4.6) were used again during the Civil War period. *See* Bank of Westminster (Second), No. 150.5. Uncirculated stocks in the bank's possession were used to offset short supplies of Farmer's & Mechanic's Bank notes.

150.4.7 SENC

$2.00 Ca. 1810–20s. Engraving, imprint: Murray, Draper, Fairman & Co. Similar to $1.00, No. 150.4.5. (MD315G24)

150.4.8 R-7

$5.00 Ca. 1810–20s. Engraving, imprint: Murray, Draper, Fairman & Co.

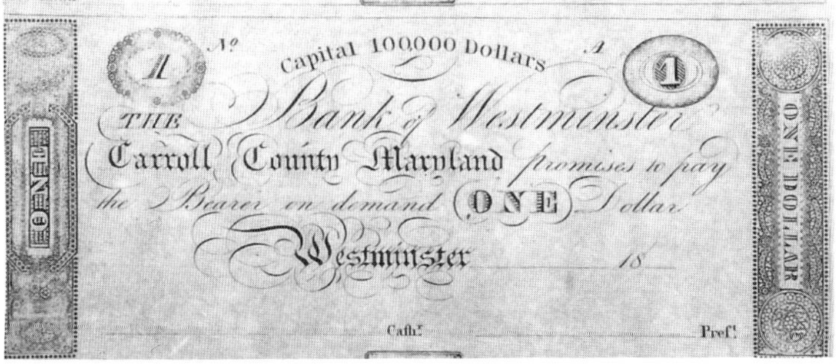

150.4.5 150.4.6

150.4.9 SENC

$10.00 Ca. 1810–20s. Engraving, imprint: Murray, Draper, Fairman & Co. Similar to counterfeit No. 150.4.9 c. (MD315G30)

150.4.9 P R-7

$10.00 Ca. 1810–20s. Engraving, imprint: Murray, Draper, Fairman & Co. Proof.

150.4.9 C R-7

$10.00 Ca. 1810–20s. Engraving, imprint: Murray, Draper, Fairman & Co. Counterfeit of No. 150.4.9. (MD315C30)

150.4.11 SENC

$20.00 Ca. 1810–20s. Engraving, imprint: Murray, Draper, Fairman & Co. Similar to 150.4.9. (MD315G32)

150.4.8

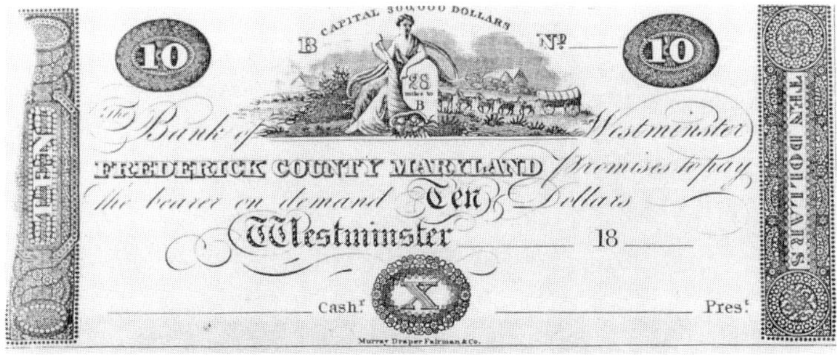

150.4.9 P

150.4.9 C

BANK OF WESTMINSTER (FIRST), FREDERICK BRANCH

Notes payable at the branch in Frederick, which operated from 1817 to 1827, when it became the Farmers & Mechanics Bank of Frederick County.

150.4.20 R-5

$5.00 Ca. 1810s. Engraving, imprint: Cone, Freeman & Co., Baltimore. (MD315G40)

150.4.20

150.4.21 R-5

$10.00 Ca. 1810s. Engraving, imprint: Cone, Freeman & Co., Baltimore. (MD315G42)

150.4.22 R-5

$20.00 Ca. 1810s. Engraving, imprint: Cone, Freeman & Co., Baltimore. (MD315G44)

150.4.23 R-5

$50.00 Ca. 1810s. Engraving, imprint: Cone, Freeman, & Co., Baltimore. (MD315G46)

150.4.21

150.4.22

150.4.23

150.5 The Bank of Westminster (Second)

This institution was established to take over the assets and liabilities of the Westminster branch of the Farmers & Mechanics Bank of Frederick County, formerly the Bank of Westminster, the new charter being approved January 15, 1830. Converted to and became the Union National Bank of Westminster in 1865.

150.5.1 R-6

$1.00 Ca. 1861. Engraving, imprint: Murray, Draper, Fairman & Co. Notes originally produced for use by the Bank of Westminster (First) during 1810s and 1820s. Unused notes from the bank's stock were used to offset the short supply during the Civil War. (MD316G2)

150.5.1

150.5.2 SENC

$2.00 Ca. 1840s. Engraving, no imprint. *Center:* Hebe feeding eagle. *Left:* Ram and dog. *Right:* Drove of cattle. (MD316N5)

150.5.3 R-7

$3.00 Ca. 1835–43. Engraving, imprint: Underwood, Bald, Spencer & Hufty, New York & Philada.

150.5.4 SENC

$3.00 Ca. 1840s. Engraving, no imprint. *Center:* Indian and man with gun, anchor and bales. (MD316N10)

150.5.5 SENC

$5.00 Ca. 1833. Engraving, imprint: Draper, Underwood, Bald & Spencer. (MD316G6)

150.5.5 P R-7

$5.00 Ca. 1833. Engraving, imprint: Draper, Underwood, Bald & Spencer. Proof.

150.5.6 SENC

$5.00 Ca. 1850s. Engraving, imprint: Draper, Welsh & Co., Philada. Similar to counterfeit No. 150.5.6 C. (MD316G8)

150.5.6 P R-7

$5.00 Ca. 1850s. Engraving, imprint: Draper, Welsh & Co., Philada. Similar to counterfeit No. 150.5.6 C. Proof.

150.5.3

150.5.5

150.5.5 P

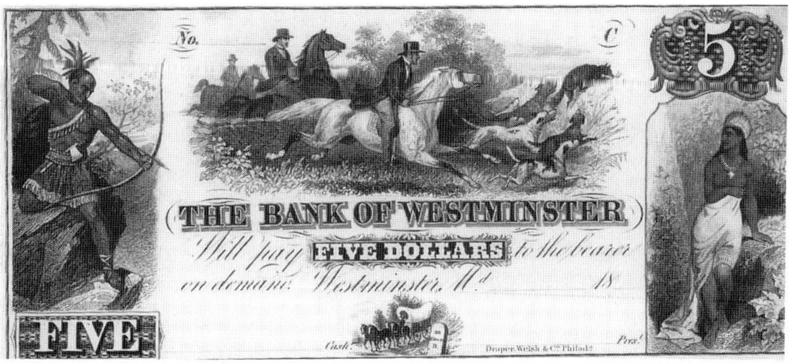

150.5.6 P

150.5.6 c R-7

$5.00 Ca. 1856. Engraving, imprint: Draper, Welsh & Co., Philada. Counterfeit. (MD316C8)

150.5.8 R-7

$10.00 Ca. 1830. Engraving, imprint: Murray, Draper, Fairman & Co. (MD315C30)

150.5.6 c

150.5.8

$5.00–$5.00–$10.00. Progressive plate proof of $5.00 and $10.00, Nos. 150.5.5 and 150.5.9.

150.5.9 SENC

$10.00 Ca. 1830s–40s. Engraving, imprint: Draper, Underwood, Bald & Spencer. (MD316G10)

150.5.9 P R-7

$10.00 Ca. 1830s–40s. Engraving, imprint: Draper, Underwood, Bald & Spencer. Proof.

150.5.10 SENC

$10.00 Ca. 1850s. Engraving, imprint: Draper, Welsh & Co., Philada. Similar to counterfeit No. 150.5.10 C. (MD315G12)

150.5.10 P R-7

$10.00 Ca. 1850s. Engraving, imprint: Draper, Welsh & Co., Philada. Proof.

150.5.10 C SENC

$10.00 Ca. 1850s. Engraving, imprint: Draper, Welsh & Co., Philada. Counterfeit of No. 150.5.10. (MD316C12)

150.5.12 P R-7

$20.00 Ca. 1823–27. Engraving, imprint: Fairman, Draper, Underwood & Co. Proof.

150.5.13 SENC

$20.00 Ca. 1830s–50s. Engraving, imprint: Danforth, Underwood, Bald & Spencer. Similar to proof, No. 150.5.13 P. (MD316G14)

150.5.13 P R-7

$20.00 Ca. 1830s–50s. Engraving, imprint: Danforth, Underwood, Bald & Spencer. Proof.

150.5.14 P R-7

$50.00 Ca. 1825–27. Engraving, imprint: Fairman, Draper, Underwood & Co. Proof.

150.5.15 SENC

$50.00 Ca. 1830–50s. Engraving, imprint: Danforth, Underwood, Bald & Spencer. Similar to proof, No. 150.5.15 P. (MD316G18)

150.5.15 P R-7

$50.00 Ca. 1830–50s. Engraving, imprint: Danforth, Underwood, Bald & Spencer. Proof.

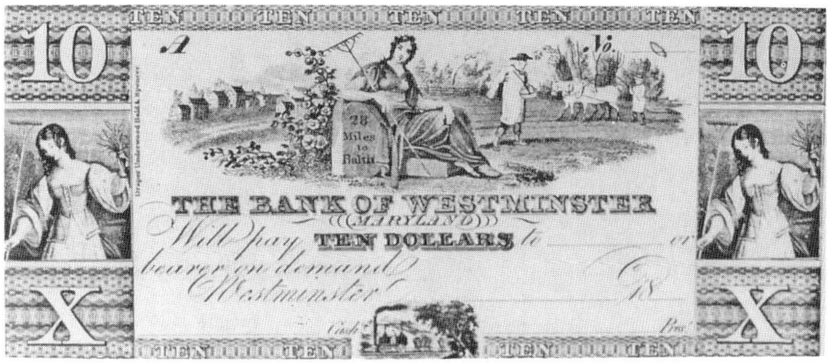

150.5.9 P

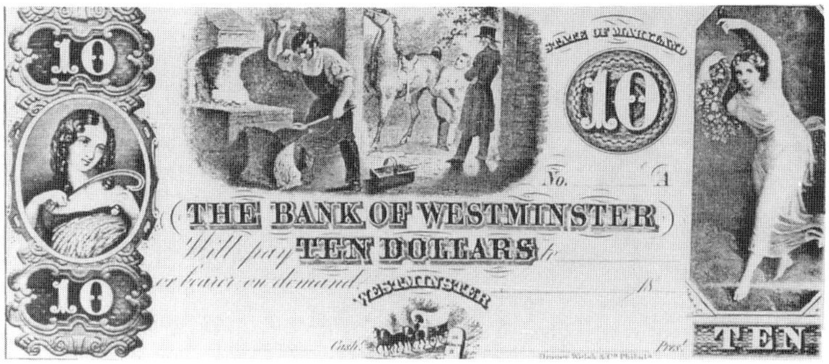

150.5.10 P

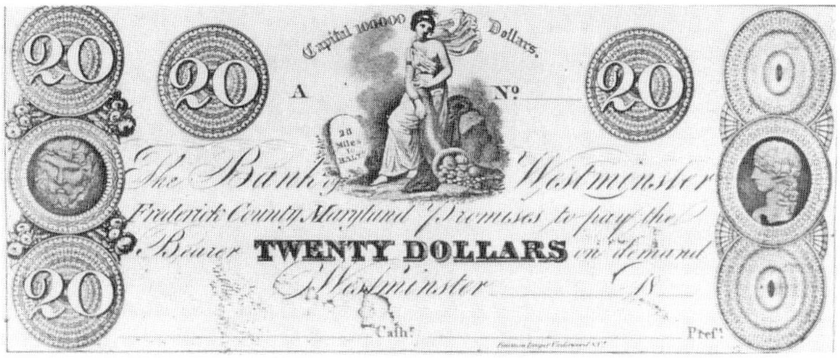

150.5.12 P

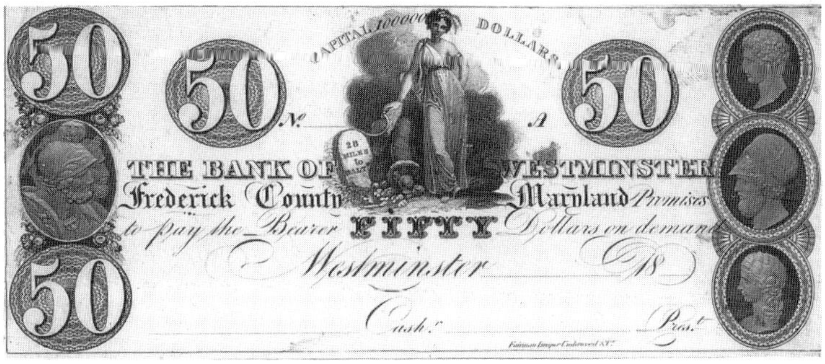

150.5.14 P

150.6 Westminster Savings Institution

Charter approved February 21, 1828; in operation 1837–38; charter expired in 1856 and not renewed. Officers beginning in 1833: Pres.: Dr. William Willis; Treasurer: Jacob Reese. Dr. Willis was clerk of the Carroll County Court until his death in 1842; Jacob Reese was a local merchant and director of the Bank of Westminster.

150.6.1 R-6

6 1/4c Printed year date 1837. Letterpress, imprint: Murphy & Spalding, printers, 1 Light street, Baltimore.

150.6.2 R-7

6 1/4c Printed year date 1837. Letterpress, imprint: Murphy & Spalding, printers, 1 Light street, Baltimore. Same as No. 150.6.1, except "Westminster," "Treas'r," and "1837" in different typeface and "Md" deleted.

150.6.3 R-7

12 1/2c Printed year date 1837. Letterpress, imprint: Murphy & Spalding, printers, 1 Light street, Baltimore.

150.6.4 R-7

12 1/2c Printed year date 1837. Engraving, imprint: Rawdon, Wright & Hatch, New York.

150.6.4 P R-7

12 1/2c Printed year date 1837. Engraving, imprint: Rawdon, Wright & Hatch, New York. Proof.

150.6.1

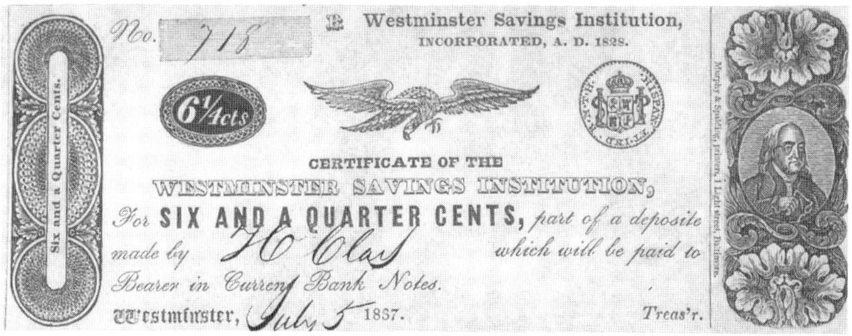

150.6.2

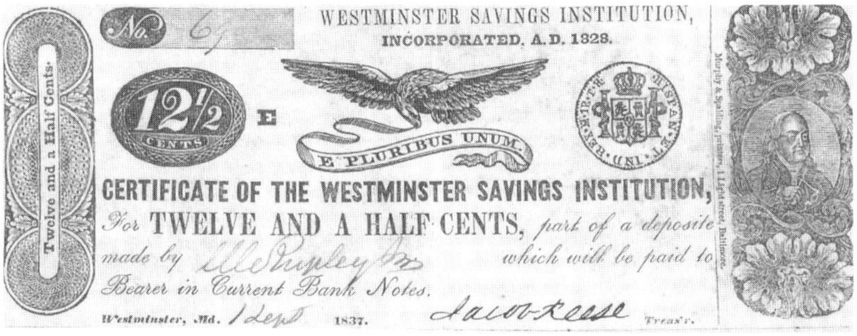

150.6.3

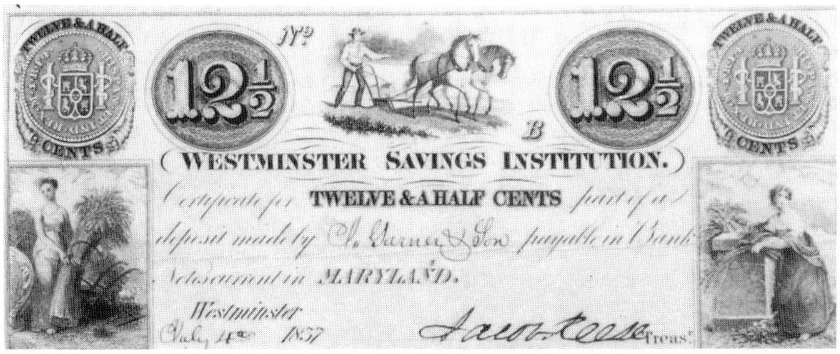

150.6.4

150.6.5 R-7

12 1/2c Printed year date 1839. Engraving, imprint: Rawdon, Wright & Hatch, New York. Same as No. 150.6.4, except for date.

150.6.6 R-7

25c Printed year date 1837. Engraving, imprint: Rawdon, Wright & Hatch, New York. Same as No. 150.6.7, except for year date.

150.6.6 P R-7

25c Printed year date 1837. Engraving, imprint: Rawdon, Wright & Hatch, New York. Same as No. 150.6.7, except for year date. Proof.

150.6.7 R-7

25c Printed year date 1839. Engraving, imprint: Rawdon, Wright & Hatch, New York. Same as No. 150.6.6, except for year date.

150.6.8 R-7

50c Printed year date 1837. Engraving, imprint: Rawdon, Wright & Hatch, New York.

150.6.8 P R-7

50c Printed year date 1837. Engraving, imprint: Rawdon, Wright & Hatch, New York. Proof.

150.6.9 R-7

50c Printed year date 1839. Engraving, imprint: Rawdon, Wright & Hatch, New York. Same as No. 150.6.8, except for year date.

150.6.10 R-7

$1.00 Printed date 1837. Engraving, imprint: Rawdon, Wright & Hatch, New York. Similar to proof, No. 150.6.10 P.

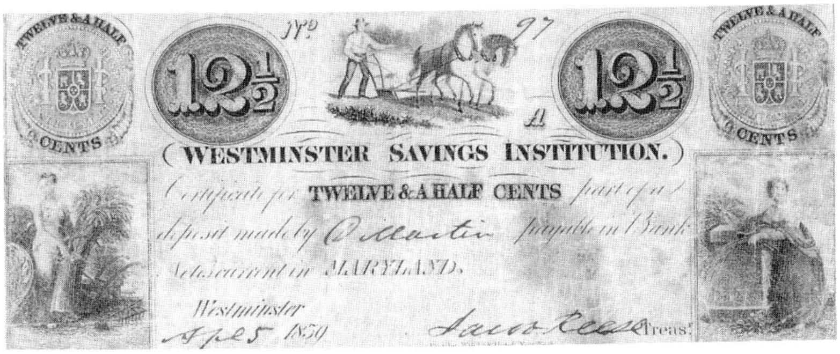

150.6.5

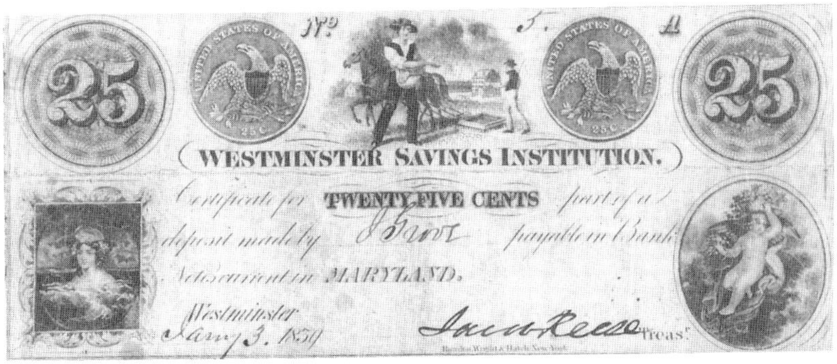

150.6.7

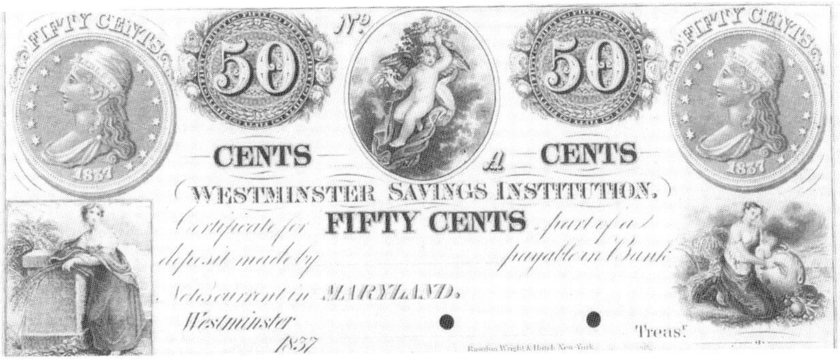

150.6.8 P

150.6.9

150.6.10 P R-7

$1.00 Printed date 1837. Engraving, imprint: Rawdon, Wright & Hatch, New York. Proof.

150.6.11 R-7

$2.00 Printed date 1837. Engraving, imprint: Rawdon, Wright & Hatch, New York. Similar to proof, No. 150.6.11 P.

150.6.11 P R-7

$2.00 Printed date 1837. Engraving, imprint: Rawdon, Wright & Hatch, New York. Proof.

150.6.10 P

150.6.11 P

152 WILLIAMSPORT, WASHINGTON COUNTY

The town was laid out in 1786 by Gen. Otho Holland Willliams (1749–94). The nearby Potomac River was used extensively for the shipment of grain and merchandise.

152.1 Conococheague Bank

Photocopies of vignettes that at one time were either owned or recorded by Charles Affleck, who gave them to Dr. Leonard Rothstein in May 1970. The specific denominations to which the illustrated vignettes pertain is not as yet known.

Charter approved January 7, 1814. Voluntary liquidation in 1820. Liquidation continued with final dividend to stockholders in 1843. The following listing of notes was obtained from contemporary counterfeit detectors. However, no surviving examples are known to exist.

152.1.1 SENC

$5.00 Ca. 1814–20. No additional information is available. (MD320G20)

152.1.2 SENC

$10.00 Ca. 1814–20. No additional information is available. (MD320G24)

152.1.3 SENC

$20.00 Ca. 1814–20. No additional information is available. (MD320G26)

152.1.4 SENC

$50.00 Ca. 1814–20. No additional information is available. (MD320G28)

152.2 John Garrett

Redeemable at one day's sight in current Virginia bank notes at the office of John H. King, George Town, D.C.

152.2.1 R-5

25c Printed partial year date 184_. Engraving, imprint: Underwood, Bald, Spencer & Hufty, Philada. / Danforth, Underwood & Co., New York.

152.2.2 R-5

50c Printed partial year date 184_. Engraving, imprint: Underwood, Bald, Spencer & Hufty, Philada. / Danforth, Underwood & Co., New York.

152.2.3 R-5

$1.00 Printed partial year date 184_. Engraving, imprint: Underwood, Bald, Spencer & Hufty, Philada. / Danforth, Underwood & Co., New York.

152.2.1

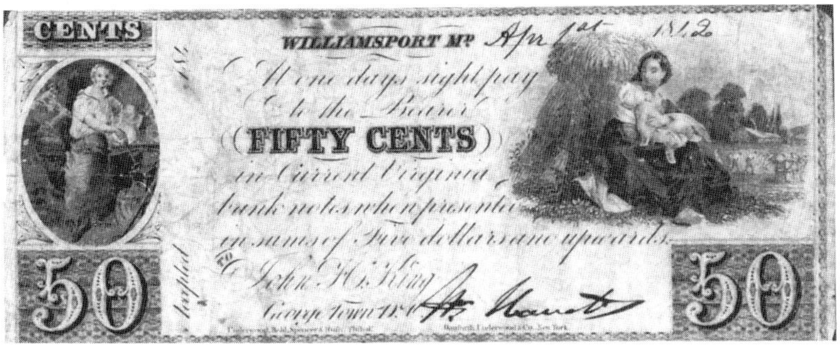

152.2.2

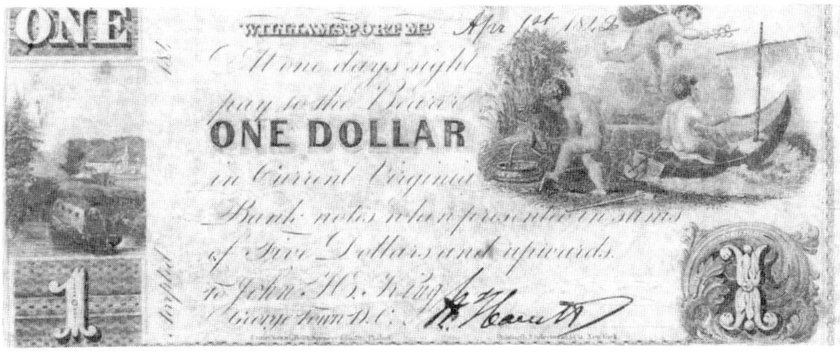

152.2.3

Unsevered sheet of the three denominations (25c, 50c, and $1.00).

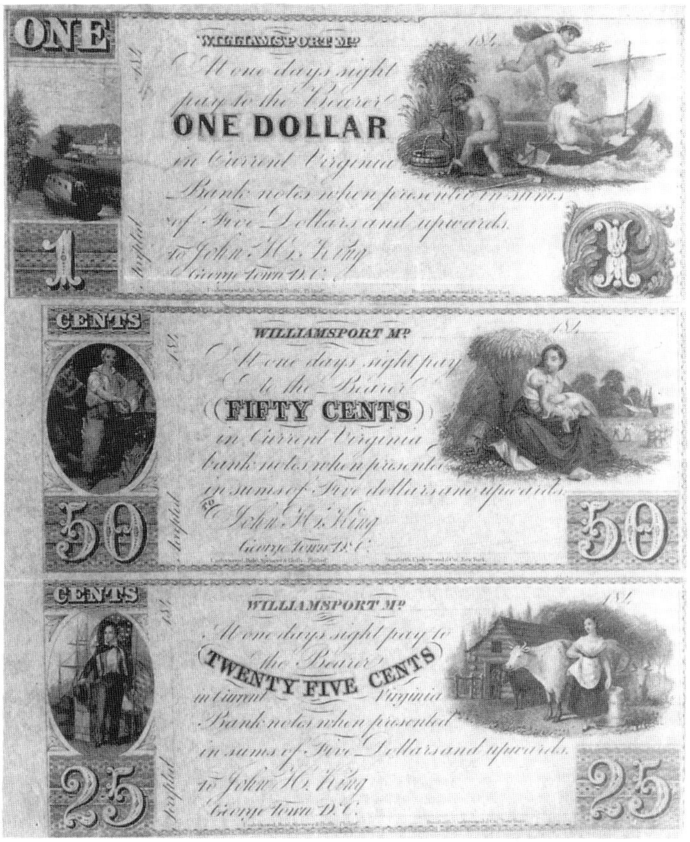

152.3 John T. Miller

The issuer was the owner of a gristmill near Williamsport.

152.3.1 R-7

6 1/4c Printed date May 1, 1838. Letterpress, imprint: Robinson, PRINTER, Baltimore.

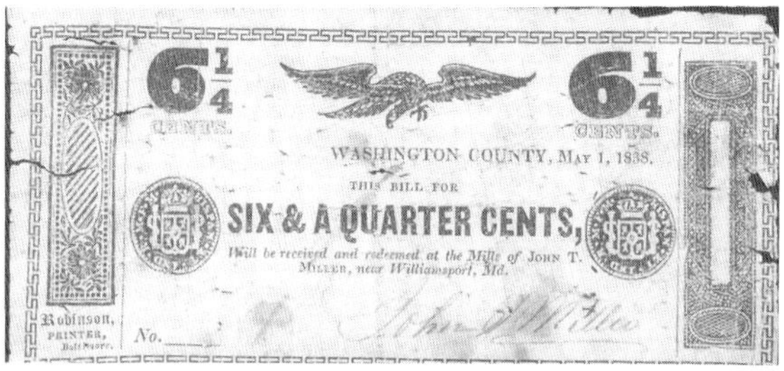

152.3.1

152.4 The Washington County Bank

Charter approved February 27, 1832; converted to and became the Washington County National Bank in 1865.

152.4.1 C SENC

$1.00 Ca. 1840s. Counterfeit note listed in Sibbet's "WESTERN REVIEW AND COUNTERFEIT DETECTOR" of 1845. Promises spelled "Promases." No other information available.

152.4.2 R-7

$1.00 Ca. 1840s and early 1860s. Engraving, imprint: Underwood, Bald, Spencer & Hufty, Philada. / Danforth, Underwood & Co., New York. Same as No. 152.4.3, except for imprint. (MD325G2)

152.4.2 P R-7

$1.00 Ca. 1840s and early 1860s. Engraving, imprint: Underwood, Bald, Spencer & Hufty, Philada. / Danforth, Underwood & Co., New York. Same as No. 152.4.3, except for imprint. Proof.

152.4.2 C SENC

$1.00 Ca. early 1860s. Engraving, imprint: Underwood, Bald, Spencer & Hufty, Philada. / Danforth, Underwood & Co., New York. Counterfeit of No. 152.4.2. (MD325C2)

152.4.3 R-7

$1.00 Ca. 1861. Engraving, imprint: American Bank Note Company, Phila. Same as No. 152.4.2, except imprint. (MD325G2b)

152.4.4 R-7

$1.00 Ca. 1862. Engraving, imprint: American Bank Note Co., Philada. Red security underprint at end panels, ONE in negative, double-lined, serifed uppercase letters. (MD325G4a)

152.4.5 S SENC

$2.00 Ca. 1840s. Engraving, imprint: Charles Ely, Philadelphia or no imprint. *Center:* Medallion head with 2, eagle on shell in ocean, clutching arrows and U.S. shield; medallion head with 2. *Left:* 2 / sailing ship / TWO. *Right:* 2 / Indian man standing on cliff viewing train in left background / TWO. *Between signatures:* Dog and strongbox. From a fraudulently modified plate, originally for a $2.00 (OH355G4) on the Geauga Insurance Co., Painesville, Ohio. Spurious. (MD325S5)

152.4.6 SENC

$5.00 Ca. 1830s–50s. Engraving, imprint: Chas. Toppan & Co., Phila. (MD325G12)

152.4.6 P R-6

$5.00 Ca. 1830s–50s. Engraving, imprint: Chas. Toppan & Co., Phila. Proof.

152.4.7 S SENC

$5.00 Ca. 1840s. Engraving, imprint: Rawdon, Wright & Hatch. *Center:* 5; eagle on shell in ocean facing left; 5. *Left:* 5 / locomotive at wharf / 5. *Right:* 5 / sailing ship / 5. *Between signatures:* Dog and strongbox. From a fraudulently modified plate, originally for a $5.00 (OH355G8) on the Geauga Insurance Co., Painesville, Ohio. Spurious. (MD235S10)

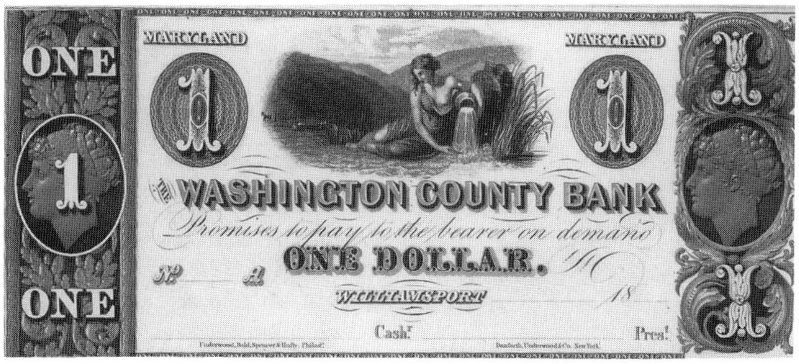

152.4.2 P

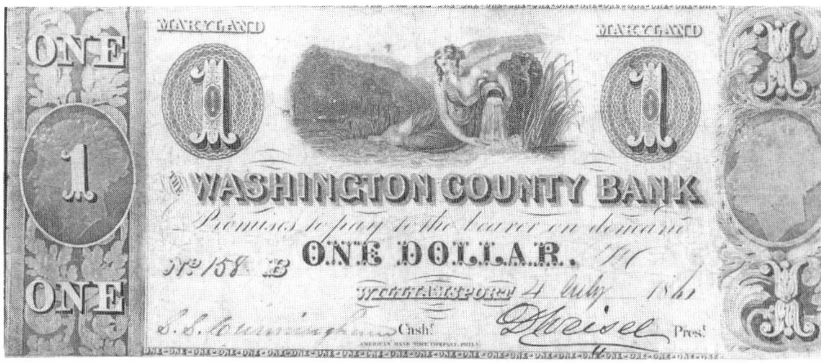

152.4.3

152.4.4

152.4.6 P

152.4.8 R-7

$10.00 Ca. 1830s–50s. Engraving, imprint: Chas. Toppan & Co., Phila. (MD325G16)

152.4.8 P R-7

$10.00 Ca. 1830s–50s. Engraving, imprint: Chas. Toppan & Co., Phila. Proof.

152.4.9 A R-7

$10.00 Ca. late 1830s. Engraving, imprint: Terry, Pelton & Co. *Center:* X / spread eagle with shield and arrows, motto E PLURIBUS UNUM above / X. *Left:* 10 / oval portrait of Washington, held by cherub at left / 10. *Right:* 10 / standing Indian male / 10. *Between signatures:* Ship. Altered from $10.00 Citizens Bank, Augusta, Maine, ME20G24 or from notes of other failed banks using the same plate. (MD325A5)

152.4.10 S SENC

$10.00 Ca. late 1840s. Engraving, imprint: Rawdon, Wright & Hatch. *Center:* X / Indian man with arm raised watching train at lower right / X. *Left:* X / Indian man standing facing left / X. *Right:* X / sailing ship / X. *Between signatures:* Dog and strongbox. From a fraudulently modified plate, originally for a $10.00 (OH355G10) on the Geauga Insurance Co., Painesville, Ohio. Spurious. (MD325S15)

152.4.11 SENC

$20.00 Ca. 1830s–50s. Engraving, imprint: Chas Toppan & Co. *Center:* Washington, after crossing the Delaware River during the battle of Trenton, 1775. Similar to proof, No. 152.4.11 P. (MD325G20)

152.4.11 P R-7

$20.00 Ca. 1830s–50s. Engraving, imprint: Chas. Toppan & Co. *Center:* Washington, after crossing the Delaware River during the battle of Trenton, 1775. Proof.

152.4.12 SENC

$50.00 Ca. 1830s–50s. Engraving, imprint: Chas. Toppan & Co. (MD325G24)

152.4.12 P R-7

$50.00 Ca. 1830s–50s. Engraving, imprint: Chas. Toppan & Co. Proof.

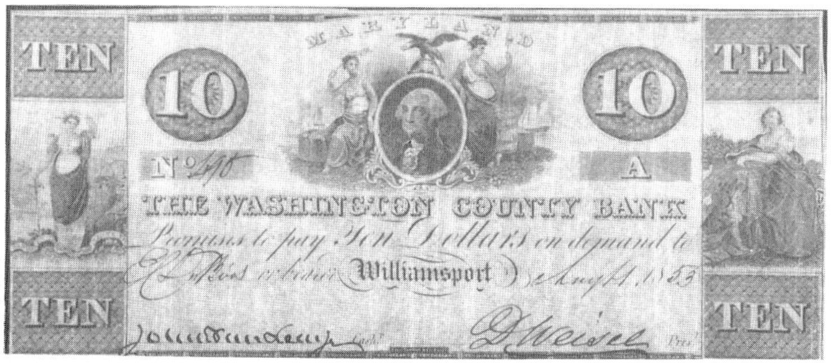

152.4.8

152.4.8 P

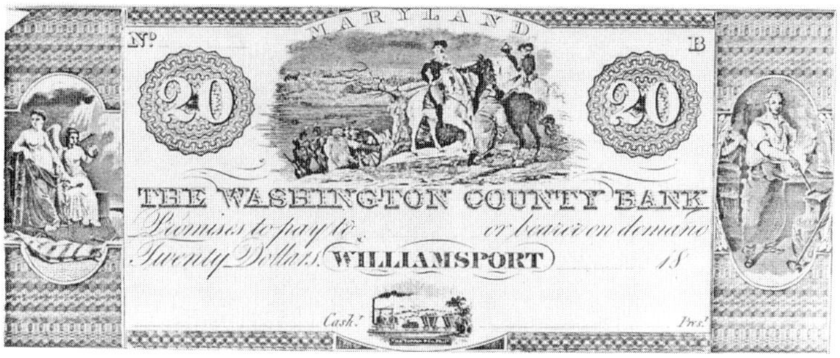

152.4.11 P

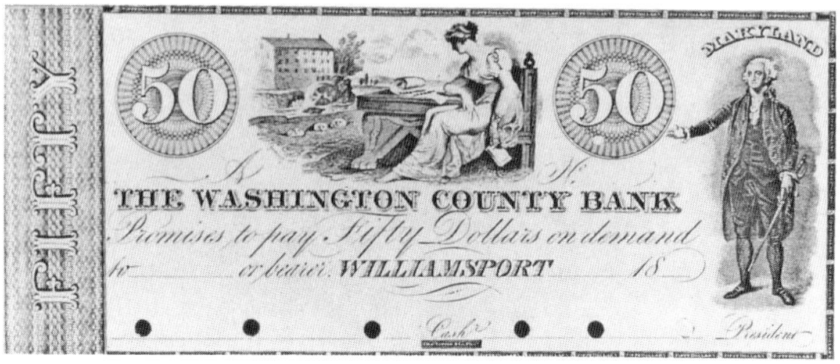

152.4.12 P

156 WYE LANDING, TALBOT COUNTY

This landing on the Wye East river, 3 1/2 miles southwest of Wye Mills and approximately 14 miles from Easton, apparently took the name Wye from a Welsh river of the same name.

156.1 John H. Holt

The issuer was a merchant and farmer who maintained an office at Wye Landing.

156.1.1 R-7
5c Printed date October 28, 1839. Letterpress, imprint: MURPHY, PRINT. BALT. Vignette of the Battle Monument, Baltimore, in oval at left.

156.1.3 R-7
10c Printed date October 28, 1839. Letterpress, imprint: MURPHY, PRINTER, 146 Market st. Balt.

156.1.4 R-7
12 1/2c Printed date October 28, 1839. Letterpress, imprint: MURPHY, PRINT. BALT.

156.1.5 R-7
25c Printed date October 28, 1839. Letterpress, imprint: MURPHY, PRINT. BALT.

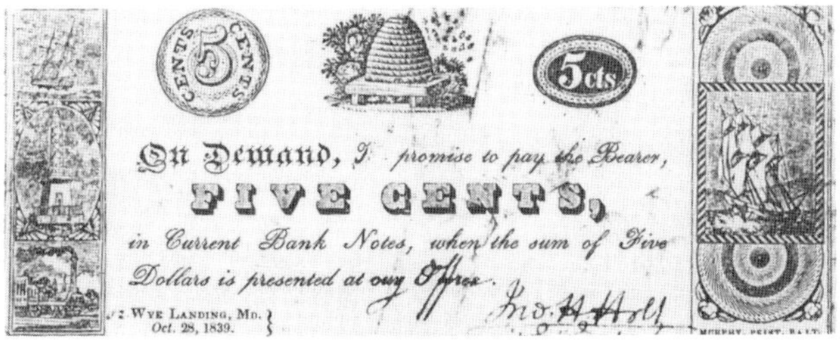

156.1.1

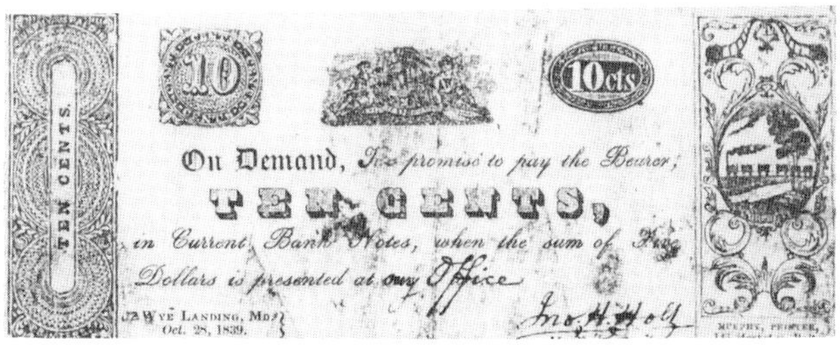

156.1.3

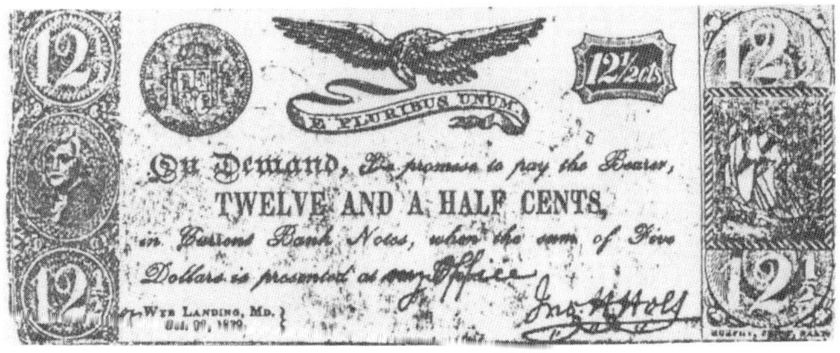

156.1.4

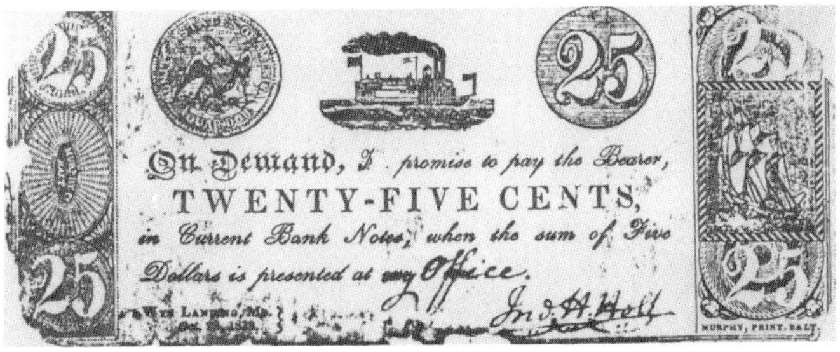

156.1.5

156.1.6 R-7

50c Printed date October 28, 1839. Letterpress, imprint: MURPHY, PRINT. BALT.

156.1.7 R-7

$1.00 Printed date October 28, 1839. Letterpress, imprint: MURPHY, PRINTER 146 Market st. Balt.

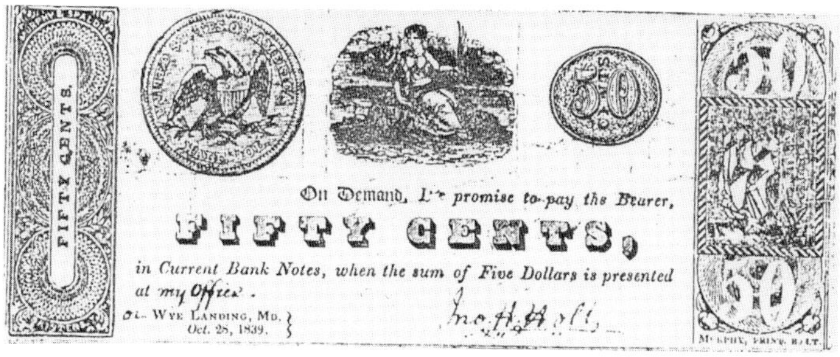

156.1.6

156.1.7

160 UNIDENTIFIED PLACE OF ISSUE

160.1 Unidentified Issuer

Proof sheet showing six denominations, three with manuscript deletions of the word, "Bank," in redemption legend.

Printed partial date, April __, 1840. End panels, redemption legends, and central vignettes printed from engraved plates; denominations by letterpress. Imprint: Manly & Orr, Printers, Philad.

160.1.1 R-7

6 1/4c Printed partial date April __, 1840.

160.1.2 R-7

12 1/2c Printed partial date April __, 1840. "Bank" deleted by penstroke.

160.1.3 R-7

25c Printed partial date April __, 1840.

160.1.4 R-7

50c Printed partial date April __, 1840. "Bank" deleted by penstroke.

160.1.5 R-7

75c Printed partial date April __, 1840. "Bank" deleted by penstroke.

160.1.6 R-7

$1.00 Printed partial date April __, 1840.

160.2 Unidentified Issuer

This essay or proof of an unfinished design is similar in format to nos. 128.8.1–12 of Snow Hill, and the ship vignette matches that used on the 50c, No. 128.8.11. Rather than assigning it definitely to Snow Hill, it has been placed in an unidentified category, at least temporarily.

160.2.3 R-7

25c Ca. 1864. Lithography, no imprint. Grayish green.

160.2.3

Bibliography

Bates, Marlene, and Martha Reamy. *Abstracts of Carroll County Newspapers, 1831–1846.* Westminster, Md.: Family Line Publishers, 1988.

A Brief History of a Bank. Baltimore: Western National Bank, 1938.

Bryan, Alfred Cookman. *History of State Banking in Maryland.* Baltimore: Johns Hopkins University, 1899.

Buse, Elliott. *150 Years of Banking on the Eastern Shore.* Easton, Md.: Easton National Bank, 1955.

Business Guide to the Baltimore & Ohio Railway. Baltimore: Sherwood and White, 1871.

"Canals in Maryland." Wheeler Leaflet on Maryland History. Baltimore: Maryland Historical Society, n.d.

Clain-Stefanelli, Elvira, and Vladimir Clain-Stefanelli. *Two Centuries of American Banking.* Washington, D.C.: Acropolis Books, 1975.

Cohn, Louis F. *Sesquicentennial History.* Frederick, Md.: Farmers and Mechanics National Bank, 1967.

Criswell, Grover C., Jr. *North American Currency.* 2d ed. Citra, Fla.: Criswell's Publications, 1969.

Dillistin, William H. *Bank Note Reporters and Counterfeit Detectors, 1826–1866.* New York: American Numismatic Society, 1949.

Durand, Roger H. *Interesting Notes about Denominations.* Published by the author, 1988.

———. *Interesting Notes about History.* Published by the author, 1990.

Durrenberger, Joseph Austin. *Turnpikes: A Study of the Toll Road Movement in the Middle Atlantic States and Maryland.* Cos Cob, Conn.: John E. Edwards, 1931. Reprint 1968.

Earle, Alice Morse. *Stagecoach and Tavern Days.* New York: Macmillan, 1900.

Fielding, Mantle. *American Engravers upon Copper and Steel. Biographical Sketches and Check Lists of Engravings.* New York: Burt Franklin, 1917.

Fisher, Richard Swainson. *Gazetteer of the State of Maryland, 1852.*

Gazetteer of Maryland, 1941. Maryland State Planning Commission and Department of Geology, Mines, and Water Resources, 1941.

Groce, George C., and David H. Wallace. *The New York Historical Society's Dictionary of Artists in America, 1564–1860.* New Haven: Yale University Press, 1957.

Haxby, James A. *Standard Catalog of United States Obsolete Bank Notes, 1782–1866.* Iola, Wis.: Krause Publications, 1988.

Hepburn, A. Barton. *A History of Currency in the United States.* New York: Macmillan, 1915.

Hollifield, William. *Difficulties Made Easy: History of the Turnpikes of Baltimore City and County.* Cockeysville, Md.: Baltimore County Historical Society, 1978.

Howard, George W. *The Monumental City.* Baltimore: M. Curlander, 1889.

Jones, Richard, and Keith Littlefield. *Virginia Obsolete Paper Money.* Annandale, Va.: Virginia Numismatic Association, 1992.

Kendall, Rev. D. Homer. *Maryland Postal History and Handstamped Markings of the Stampless Period.* North Miami, Fla.: David G. Phillips Co., n.d.

Kenny, Hamill. *The Placenames of Maryland, Their Origin and Meaning.* Baltimore: Museum and Library of Maryland History, Maryland Historical Society, 1984.

Lewis, J. Frank. *The Maryland Directory.* Baltimore: J. Frank Lewis & Co., 1878.

McCauley, Lois B. *A Hoen on Stone.* Baltimore: Maryland Historical Society, 1969.

———. *Maryland Historical Prints, 1752–1889: A Selections from the Robert G. Merrick Collection, Maryland Historical Society, and Other Maryland Collections.* Baltimore: Maryland Historical Society, 1975.

McGrain, John W., Jr. "The Molinography of Maryland. A Tabulation of Mills, Furnaces, and Primitive Industries." Typescript. Towson, Md., 1968; Microfilm c. 1976, Maryland Historical Society Library, Baltimore.

Maryland Directory and State Gazetteer, 1887. Rev. and ed. John R. Bland, Secretary for the Merchants and Manufacturers Association of Baltimore. Baltimore: Baltimore Publishing Co., 1887.

Meeks, Harvey Eugene (former chief bank examiner, Maryland State Banking Department). *Maryland Bank Register, 1790–1979.* Baltimore: Maryland State Banking Department, 1982.

Muscalus, John A. *An Index of State Bank Notes that Illustrate Presidents.* Bridgeport, Pa.: Author, 1939.

———. *Paper Money of the 6 1/4 Cent and 12 1/2 Cent Denominations.* Bridgeport, Pa.: Author, n.d.

———. *Paper Money Pertaining to Druggists, Medicines, and Medical Practitioners.* Bridgeport, Pa.: Historical Paper Money Research Institute, 1969.

———. *Shakespeare on Paper Money.* Bridgeport, Pa.: Historical Paper Money Research Institute, 1969.

———. *State Bank Notes.* New York: Wayte Raymond, Inc., 1942.

———. *State Owned Banks, the Pet Banks, and Their Bank Notes.* Bridgeport, Pa.: Author, 1940.

———. *Transportation Currency: Bank Notes and Scrip Representative of Forty-five Varieties of Transportation Companies, 1777–1900s.* Bridgeport, Pa.: Historical Paper Money Research Institute, 1974.

"The National Road." Wheeler Leaflet on Maryland History. Baltimore: Maryland Historical Society, n.d.

Newman, Eric P. *The Early Paper Money of America.* Racine, Wis.: Western Publishing, 1990.

Powers, Roger T. *Postal Markings of Maryland.* Baltimore: Associated Stamp Clubs of the Chesapeake Area, 1960.

Preston, Dickson J. *Newspapers of Maryland's Eastern Shore.* Centreville, Md.: Queen Anne Press and Tidewater Publishers, 1986.

Randall, John Wirt. *The Farmers National Bank of Annapolis.* Annapolis, Md.: Published by the Directors, 1905.

Scharf, J. Thomas. *History of Baltimore City and County.* Philadelphia: Louis H. Everts, 1881.

Searight, Thomas B. *The Old Pike: A History of the National Road.* Uniontown, Pa.: Author, 1894.

Sprinkle, Frank F. *Master List of Uncut Sheets of Obsolete Bills and Old Bank Checks.* Privately printed, 1964.

The State Gazette and Mechanics and Farmers Directory for Maryland and the District of Columbia. Baltimore: Sadler, Drysdale & Purnell, 1871.

Stauffer, David McNeely. *American Engravers upon Copper and Steel:* Part 1, *Biographical Sketches Illustrated;* Part 2, *Check-List of the Works of the Earlier Engravers.* New York: Burt Franklin, 1907.

Tovart, Paul Baker. *Somerset: An Architectural History.* Princess Anne, Md.: Maryland Historical Trust and Somerset County Historical Trust, 1990.

Truitt, Charles J. *Historic Salisbury, Maryland.* Garden City, N.Y.: Country Life Press, 1932.

In addition to the volumes listed above, the authors have made extensive use of newspapers and other periodicals in the libraries of the Maryland Historical Society and the Maryland Room of the Enoch Pratt Free Library. Of particular value in researching the numerous notes issued during the "hard times" of 1837–41 have been the files of the *Baltimore Sun* 1, no. 1 (May 17, 1837–1865) and the *Baltimore Clipper* 1, no. 35 (October 18, 1839) to 24, no. 152 (June 27, 1851).

Index of Names, Places, and Financial Institutions

(*References to figures or tables appear italicized.*)

ELKTON BANK OF MARYLAND
Directors
demand TEN
3
5
No.
439
FIVE DO
ALLEGANY COUN
CUMBERLAND
American Bank Note Company
Cash
5
MARYLAND
BANK
Denton, January 31st 1863.
FIVE CENTS
The Commissioners of Denton, will pay to Bearer, Five Cents, in current Bank, or U. S. Treasury Notes, when presented in sums of One Dollar
SECURED BY DEPOSIT.
Redeemable only within twelve months after date.
Sec'y Board of Commissioners.
President Board of Com
FIVECENT
BANK
Bearer
18
5
ALLEGANY COUNTY
TWENTY
CLINTON